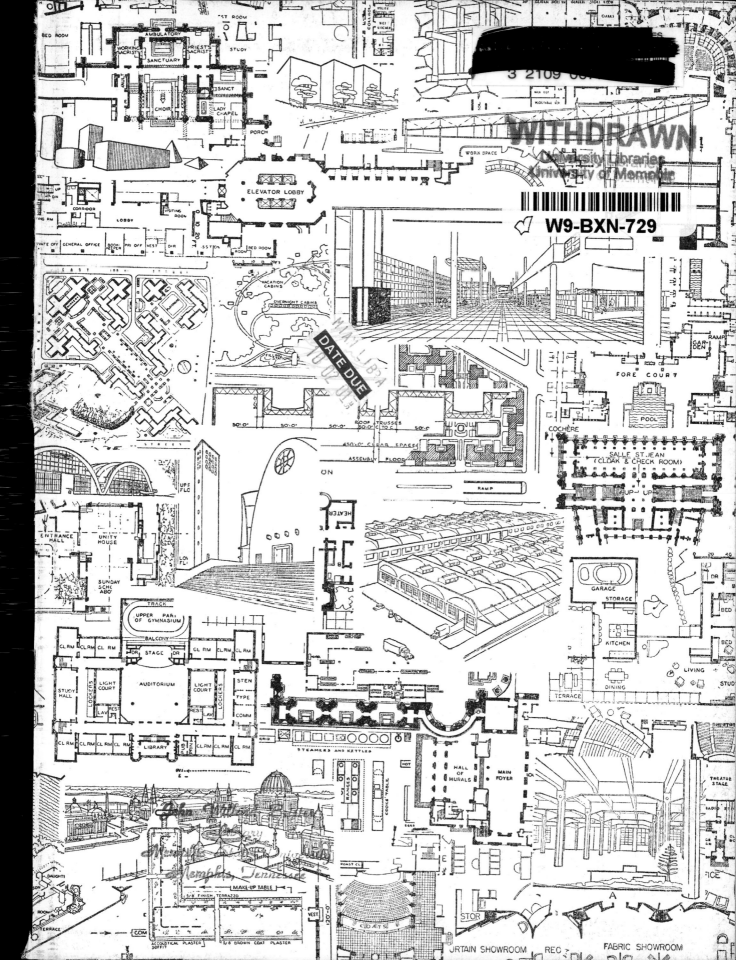

FORMS and FUNCTIONS
of TWENTIETH-CENTURY
ARCHITECTURE

IN FOUR VOLUMES

VOLUME IV

Building Types

BUILDINGS FOR COMMERCE AND INDUSTRY, FOR PUBLIC HEALTH,
FOR TRANSPORTATION, FOR SOCIAL WELFARE AND RECREATION
THE COMMUNITY AS ARCHITECTURE

FORMS and FUNCTIONS
of TWENTIETH-CENTURY
ARCHITECTURE

Edited by TALBOT HAMLIN, *F.A.I.A.*

With an Introduction by Leopold Arnaud, F.A.I.A.

VOLUME IV

Building Types

BUILDINGS FOR COMMERCE AND INDUSTRY, FOR PUBLIC HEALTH,
FOR TRANSPORTATION, FOR SOCIAL WELFARE AND RECREATION
THE COMMUNITY AS ARCHITECTURE
BY A SELECTED LIST OF CONTRIBUTORS

Prepared under the auspices of the
School of Architecture of Columbia University

New York COLUMBIA UNIVERSITY PRESS *1952*

Acknowledgments

F OR AID in the illustration of this volume the editor wishes to make grateful acknowledgment to:

The United States Air Force Base at Dayton, Ohio, the United States Army Signal Corps, the National Park Service, the Graphic Materials Section of the Tennessee Valley Authority, and the National Harbor Board of Canada;

The British Information Services, the Netherlands Information Bureau, and the Swiss State Railways;

The Connecticut Department of Highways, the Oregon Highway Commission, the New York Housing Authority, the New York City Park Department, the Triborough Bridge and Tunnel Authority, and the Port of New York Authority;

The Fort Lauderdale Publicity Bureau, the Los Angeles Harbor Department, the Port Authority of New Orleans, the Port of Long Beach (California), and the Public Relations Department of the Port of Seattle;

Boys' Town in Nebraska, the Hudson Guild of New York, the Museum of Modern Art in New York, and Ripley House in Houston, Texas;

The *Architect and Building News* and the *Architectural Review*, both of London, and the *Daily News* of New York, for permission to reproduce illustrations;

Many corporations, architects, and photographers who have furnished illustrations or permitted them to be used, the detailed credits for which will be found in the List of Illustrations;

And, especially, the contributors, whose co-operative spirit and technical knowledge have made this volume what it is.

Contents

PART VIII: BUILDINGS FOR SOCIAL WELFARE AND RECREATION

PART IX: THE COMMUNITY AS ARCHITECTURE

INDEXES

Planned and prepared by Jessica Hamlin

Illustrations

PART V

Buildings for Commerce and Industry

BANKS

BY JOHN A. WALQUIST

DEPARTMENT STORES

BY KENNETH C. WELCH

SMALL SHOPS

BY MORRIS KETCHUM, JR.

SHOPPING CENTERS

BY PIETRO BELLUSCHI

OFFICE BUILDINGS

BY WALLACE K. HARRISON

RADIO STATIONS

BY WILLIAM LESCAZE

FACTORIES

BY ALBERT HALSE

POWERHOUSES

BY ROLAND WANK

IT IS A TRUISM that the mid-twentieth century is an age that is dominated to a large degree by industrial production and the business activity which accompanies it. The industrial production of goods is one cause of the vast population increase that has marked the Western world; it has produced the rapid urbanization of the population; it has created new building problems of all sorts. Among these new problems, those concerned with store buildings (to help the distribution of goods), with office buildings (to house the administrative and professional sections of industry), and with factories (to house the production itself) are outstanding. Into such structures pours an increasing proportion of the total building appropriation of the country.

The United States, among all capitalist countries, has been the one in which the distribution of goods has been most highly developed. It is the premier home of advertising; it is the country where the pressures to buy, buy, buy are greatest. Naturally this has meant the development of precise and calculated selling techniques, and these in turn have created new kinds of store and shop structures. No longer are bazaars an adequate solution; no longer is a standardized counter sufficient. Today special types of counters are required for different types of goods, they have to be arranged in the proper order, and their lighting and aesthetic effects are directed toward the specific job of making purchasing attractive. Outside and in, the modern competitive store must offer an invitation to the passerby to enter and to spend. The store must glamorize this process.

But other problems have also arisen. The development of large and new suburban areas or of new residential neighborhoods, together with the vast increase in the use of private automobiles, has necessitated a fresh attack on the problem of store location; out of it has come the idea of decentralizing the stores in big cities and, in the suburbs and smaller towns, of building shopping centers in which automobile parking space is ample and the stores are so grouped that daily local shopping is easy for the purchaser and hence profitable to the dealer. The specialty shop, the department store, the branch store, the supermarket, and the shopping center are the results of this new approach. They are all types either comparatively novel or with new standards and requirements, and the chapters in the present section will attempt to clarify the elements that condition them.

In factory design, both the increasing rationalization of the production process (culminating in the system of assembly-line mass production) and the growing realization of the importance of labor relations have vastly transformed the simple rectangular mill of a century ago. Types have been specialized; one-story and multi-story schemes have developed; systems of interior lighting, both natural and artificial, have been carefully studied. The different requirements of powerhouses, of factories for light and for heavy industry, of mills for metals and for textiles, and of printing plants and chemical plants have given rise to factory structures of differing types, planned specifically for their special purposes. It has come to be realized that the visual qualities of color and form are factors which condition a plant's efficiency. The earlier factories of the mass-production era were designed primarily around a *process*, but today this is not the controlling factor. The good modern industrial plant is also designed around the *worker*, for only interested and happy workers can have an efficiency that corresponds with the efficiency of the machines they direct or operate. Thus an entirely new emphasis has been brought into the field of factory design; the chapters on industrial buildings in this section point out some of the ways in which these new concepts will affect the architect's task.

JOHN A. WALQUIST, F.A.I.A., author of the chapter "Banks," a member of the architectural firm of Reinhard, Hofmeister & Walquist, in New York, served for three years as Assistant Professor of Architecture at the University of Oregon. For many years his firm was intimately concerned with the Rockefeller Center project and was architect for a number of banks located there as well as elsewhere.

KENNETH C. WELCH, A.I.A., author of the chapter "Department Stores," is Vice-President in Charge of Design for the Grand Rapids Store Equipment Company. He has served as consulting architect and interior designer for many large stores throughout the country and is the author of numerous articles on stores and store design. He is also a consulting expert for a number of large community and regional shopping centers and has pioneered in analyzing community shopping needs and the techniques for satisfying them.

MORRIS KETCHUM, JR., A.I.A., author of the chapter "Small Shops," is a member of the firm of Ketchum, Giná & Sharp, New York architects. He and his firm have designed more than two hundred specialty shops and chain stores, as well as several department stores, and have been the architects for a number of regional shopping centers. He is the author of *Shops and Stores* (New York: Reinhold, 1948), a reference book on store design.

PIETRO BELLUSCHI, F.A.I.A., author of the chapter "Shopping Centers," was the designing partner of the architectural firm of A. E. Doyle & Associate until it was dissolved in 1943; later, practicing under his own name in Portland, Oregon, he designed many important projects, including housing, private houses, and commercial buildings; since 1950 he has been Dean of the School of Architecture and Planning at the Massachusetts Institute of Technology. He was an American delegate to the League of Nations Institute of Intellectual Cooperation in 1934 and is a past president of the Oregon Chapter of the American Institute of Architects and of the Trustees of the Portland (Oregon) Art Museum. He has lectured at many universities and for a period was resident critic at the School of Architecture of Yale University.

WALLACE K. HARRISON, F.A.I.A., author of the chapter "Office Buildings" (in part), is the senior member in the New York architectural firm of Harrison & Abramovitz. He was one of the collaborating architects in the creation of Rockefeller Center, and his firm has designed a large number of important commercial and other projects, including office buildings and large apartment houses. He is Director of Planning for the United Nations buildings in New York and was formerly a director of the Office of Inter-American Affairs.

WILLIAM LESCAZE, F.A.I.A., author of the chapter "Radio Stations," was from 1929 to 1934 a member of the architectural firm of Howe & Lescaze; since then he has been practicing in New York under his own name. He is the designer of a large number of important and revolutionary architectural works, including office buildings, schools, radio stations, and housing projects, and has been instrumental in introducing into the United States many modern architectural ideas. He has been the recipient of numerous awards, both national and international, and is the author of *On Being an Architect* (New York: Putnam's, 1942). He is a member of the State Building Code Commission of New York.

ALBERT HALSE, A.I.A., author of the chapter "Factories," is an Assistant Professor in the School of Architecture of Columbia University. For a number of years he was intimately connected with the field of industrial architecture and has designed important plants of several kinds, including many erected for the war effort during the Second World War.

ROLAND WANK, F.A.I.A., A.I.P., author of the chapter "Powerhouses," is associated with the New York architectural firm of Fellheimer & Wagner. From 1933 to 1944 he was head architect of the Tennessee Valley Authority, and he has served also as architectural consultant to the Rural Electrification Administration as well as to the United Nations Headquarters Commission. He has lectured at many universities and contributed numerous articles to various magazines.

27

Banks

By JOHN A. WALQUIST

IN PLANNING AND ARCHITECTURAL EXPRESSION the bank program in the middle of the twentieth century is experiencing a complete reversal in emphasis; safety and security are taken for granted and service to the customer is the pre-eminent consideration. Security is still important, but, with the general increase in credit transactions, the guarantee by government of small deposits, and the stability afforded by the Federal Reserve system, danger from robbery or mob violence has been minimized. New business and promotional activities have now been placed first on the banker's agenda; getting new business and keeping the old have become the preoccupation of every officer and employee of modern banking institutions.

How has this change in the point of view affected the planning and the appearance of banks? It has introduced the "drive-in" bank, where a customer may make deposits without leaving his car. It has put tellers' booths into suburban railway stations so that the commuter rushing to his train may cash a check. In almost every city bank it has put a depository on the outside of the building for the customer's convenience. Bank exteriors have been altered so that great windows now replace solid wall masses and glowing electric signs supersede Roman letters incised in stone. Similarly, the interior arrangements have been pulled inside out. The tellers' counters today are placed for the convenience of the customer rather than in accordance with a preconceived ideal working arrangement. Officers have been brought out of private rooms in the rear to an open platform at the front. The teller's cage with its window is fast disappearing, and the barrier between him and the customer is down.

Modern banking is a product of the nineteenth century. In the eighteenth century the operation of such institutions as the Bank of England, the Royal Bank of Berlin, the Municipal Bank of Vienna, and the Bank of France was a function of government. Prior to that time, money lending and exchange were the private enterprise of wealthy individuals or public authorities. At first,

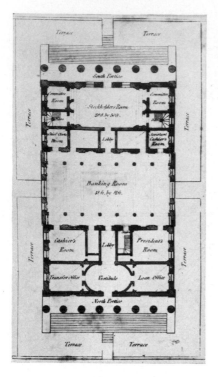

FIGURE I. BRANCH BANK
OF THE UNITED STATES,
PHILADELPHIA, PENNSYLVANIA. PLAN

William Strickland, architect

One of the first monumental bank buildings in the
United States; masonry-vaulted throughout.

From Haviland and Bridport,
The Builders' Assistant

banking was practiced in a private residence or in the treasury of an order or a
monastery, and only later the merchants' offices. By the end of the eighteenth
century, private banks with a clearing house were in operation in England, the
Bank of England acting as a bankers' bank. In the nineteenth century, credit
banks were established in England, France, and Germany.

In the United States, the establishment of the first bank—the Bank of North
America, in Philadelphia, in 1781—marked the beginning of commercial banking in this country. One of the earliest and best examples of domestic banks is
William Strickland's building for the Second Bank of the United States—the
Branch Bank in Philadelphia (Fig. 1). It is significant that this building was in
the classic style, for it set a precedent that was scarcely challenged for a hundred and fifty years (see Figs. 2, 3).

The architectural solution of the modern bank problem is to be found, as
always, in the requirements of the program, the conditions of the site, and the
imagination of the architect. Controlling the result will be the economics of
site, cost, and maintenance. The day of building architectural monuments to
banking institutions has passed; now the banker surveys the architect's plans
with one compelling thought in the back of his mind: "Will the proposed ex-

FIGURE 2. TWO EARLY CLASSIC BANKS IN THE UNITED STATES

ABOVE: Branch Bank of the United States, Philadelphia, Pennsylvania; William Strickland, architect. From a drawing by A. J. Davis, courtesy Avery Library. LEFT: Bank of Louisville, Louisville, Kentucky; Gideon Shryock, architect. Photograph Caufield & Shook.

The classic tradition in bank design was strongly established by many early important bank structures.

penditure justify itself as an investment by bringing new business and keeping old business?" In general a high standard of architectural design and construction has been established in the banking field, but any extravagant inclusion of non-utilitarian features will always be carefully scrutinized by the building committee.

In this chapter it is proposed to consider banks as a general building type and to point out the details that distinguish the various groups within the class as a

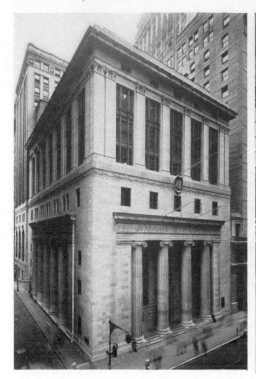

FIGURE 3. GUARANTY TRUST COMPANY, NEW YORK. EXTERIOR AND INTERIOR
York & Sawyer, architects
The heyday of the eclectic period: the bank as a temple of financial power.

Courtesy Guaranty Trust Co.

whole. The Federal Reserve Bank building represents a special category that is exempt from the usual factors controlling bank planning and is therefore hardly within the scope of such a discussion. This newest type of bank building has been cast in the oldest architectural mold; the outstanding example is the New York structure, by York & Sawyer, with its heavy Italianate architecture and tremendous scale.

Commercial banks of all kinds and savings banks represent the more common problem. Here the greatest differences between individual buildings will be found to lie in the questions of whether the location is in a commercial or a suburban area and whether the structure is to house the head office or a branch office. Often, however, in reaching out to serve more customers a bank finds its branch offices of greater importance than the head office so far as contact with the public is concerned.

SITE

Usually the site for a proposed structure has been selected before the architect is called in. Whether it is a corner lot, an interior lot, or a location that permits a free-standing building, each site will suggest the appropriate architectural development. A plot surrounded on all four sides by streets—a site which leaves the bank in grand isolation—is ideal for developing an architectural monument but is less desirable for close contact with business, unless in the case of a suburban site it permits the convenience of parking for customers. A lot less than 50 by 100 feet presents special problems.

In consideration of the public's convenience a bank or a branch office is often located on a lower floor of an office building; the bank may own the building or merely rent and alter the necessary space to fit its needs. For a tenant alteration, columns and utilities passing through the space proposed for the bank must be accepted and, if worked into the scheme with imagination, may even help rather than hinder the final solution. Where the bank owns and erects the building, the space to be used for bank purposes can be controlled and consequently the structural and mechanical features may be arranged for a more ideal solution of the bank's special problems. In this instance it is desirable to consider either putting the banking room under a court area or carrying the columns of the superstructure on girders above the bank space to secure a column-free room that will allow more flexible planning.

Certain restricted sites will dictate a development on several levels—almost always on both the ground and basement floors and, if there is extensive need for storage-vault facilities, possibly running into several sub-basements. In all such cases it is desirable to knit the several elements as closely together as the building laws and available funds permit. Broad, easy stairs, with open wells inviting exploration, as well as escalators and elevators are all desirable adjuncts for multi-level schemes and are requisites in any *parti* where the principal banking room is not on the street level.

PLAN TYPES

Since planning of the public areas will influence all the other architectural factors, the design process must begin with a solution of this problem. Whether the institution is large or small, the more functions that can be enclosed in one space—and the larger that space can be made—the simpler and the grander in scale the final result will be. To achieve this, as many areas as possible should be treated as divisions of floor space rather than as partitioned enclosures.

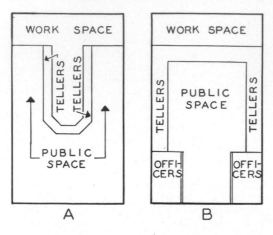

FIGURE 4. DIAGRAMS OF TWO
BASIC TYPES OF BANK PLAN

A: The "island type" used in many savings
banks; B: The type more frequent in
commercial banks. Type A permits tellers
to have free access to large numbers of
records with a minimum of travel from
windows or stations.

There are many ways of expressing the division of banking activities: through
the use of built-in furniture, such as tellers' desks, railings, grilles, and screens;
through changes in level or in flooring materials and in wall color or covering;
through lighting intensity, and so on.

In the past there have been three principal types of plan: (1) that in which
the tellers' cages have been placed at one side or at one end of the room, or
both; (2) that in which the tellers' cages have been arranged in a U shape,
the working space occupying the interior; and (3), the reverse of the second,
that in which the tellers occupy spaces on the exterior of the U shape. (See
Fig. 4.)

Modern communication and reproduction devices have freed the fixed-plan
arrangement of tellers' desks so that now almost any arrangement is feasible.
The counters may even be placed in divided groups, where such divisions seem
desirable, without any sacrifice of business convenience; or they may be laid
out in a continuous line which follows a circular, elliptical, or free form; or
they may cut across the room in a bold diagonal, where such treatment is
logical. The number of tellers' windows and the number of officers to be provided for must be determined in conjunction with the bank's building committee and in accordance with considerations of space limitation. In general it
is desirable to keep the areas for both groups as flexible as possible, because the
amount of business transacted with the public varies from day to day and the
nature of the transactions changes from year to year.

MAIN BANKING ROOM

Viewing the problem from the customer's standpoint, access from the street
should be easy and, if feasible, at more than one point. On entering, he should

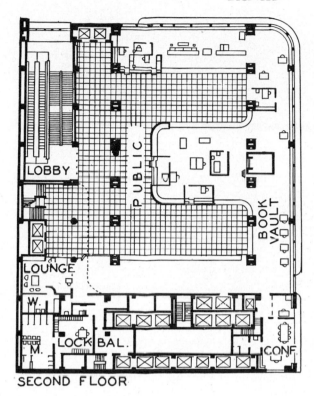

FIGURE 5. PHILADELPHIA
SAVING FUND BUILDING,
PHILADELPHIA,
PENNSYLVANIA.
BANKING-FLOOR PLAN

Howe & Lescaze, architects

A modern variant of the savings-
bank plan; the large floor area permits an attractive freedom in plan.

SECOND FLOOR

receive a favorable impression of an open, well-lighted room, with the officers'
and tellers' locations clearly displayed and with check desks conveniently located. There should be sufficient floor area to permit the customers to form
lines in front of tellers' windows even on busy days without interfering
with one another or with people entering or leaving. For this reason, adjoining
tellers' desks should not be arranged so that they create an internal angle on the
public side or are too close to a column or any other obstruction. Check desks
are better placed across the room from the tellers' desks rather than in the
center of the floor, unless the room is exceptionally wide and has much free
floor space for customer lines. Distribution of activities among the tellers'
windows is helpful so that such special services as "Statements" and "Loans
and Discounts" can be assigned to points where there is the least traffic. It is
also well, in the larger banks, to consider whether or not a special area should
be set aside on a mezzanine or a lower level for pay-roll windows or for
"special" checking accounts, the least profitable though still a desirable business and one which attracts the greatest number of customers.

FIGURE 6.
PHILADELPHIA
SAVING FUND
BUILDING,
PHILADELPHIA,
PENNSYLVANIA.
EXTERIOR

Howe & Lescaze, architect

The exterior follows the tone of both the plan and the interior.

Photograph
Ben Schnall

SAFE DEPOSIT

Another principal public space is that assigned to the safety deposit section. In a small institution all the bank's safekeeping facilities are usually combined in one vault, often placed on the first floor, and its impressive door is made a feature of the interior design. In larger banks there may be several vaults for public and private security; these are often assigned to a lower level or, when bulk storage is involved, to several lower levels. Details of vault enclosures are readily available; usually the walls, roof, and floors are constructed of concrete 18 to 24 inches thick, reinforced with heavy steel bars or rails, and surrounded by a gallery 18 to 24 inches wide, which is lighted and has mirrors set at the angles so that a complete view around the outside is possible at all times. The vault door is an elaborate circular one of steel, about 7 feet in diameter, with an accompanying frame equipped with time locks and electrical protection.

FIGURE 7. PHILADELPHIA SAVING FUND BUILDING, PHILADELPHIA,
PENNSYLVANIA. BANKING ROOM AND ENTRANCE HALL

Howe & Lescaze, architects

An interior eloquently expressive of our time through its brilliant use of modern materials.

Courtesy Philadelphia Saving Fund

In planning for the door, enough height must be maintained to permit entrance through the opening by means of a ramp over the edge of the frame, and there must be enough space at the side to permit the door to turn 180 degrees on offset hinges.

The interior of the vault is lined from floor to ceiling with a system of drawers and compartments, each faced with a stainless-steel door bearing the typical double-keyed lock or a combination knob. The spaces to be rented are of various sizes. Bulk storage for silver and valuable rugs is usually offered in suburban areas and preferably should be provided in another vault. Storage of furs is under consideration as a profitable source of income, but this type is complicated by the necessity of including refrigeration within the bank and of making provisions for the servicing that always accompanies the storage of such goods.

Immediately outside the vault (and in connection with the public space), tables, booths, and rooms must be available where customers may examine the contents of boxes, clip coupons, hold conferences, and so on. Some of these facilities may well be located within the vault itself and may consist of a single table partitioned off by low divisions, for minimum privacy, to give individual spaces of about 30 by 24 inches in size. Coupon booths are desirable for maximum privacy and are designed in two sizes—30 by 36 inches for a single individual and 36 by 36 inches to accommodate two. Each should be entirely enclosed and should have a shelf or small table to hold box and contents and a door

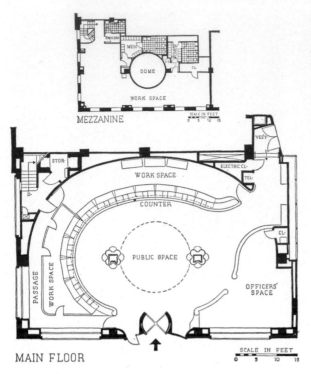

MEZZANINE

MAIN FLOOR

FIGURE 8. CHASE
NATIONAL BANK,
9 ROCKEFELLER
PLAZA, NEW YORK.
PLANS

Reinhard & Hofmeister, architects

The new freedom in plan and counter arrangement.

From *Architectural Forum*

that can be closed and locked from inside. The shelf is often of glass to expose any papers which might have dropped to the floor. Adequate light and ventilation are essential. For larger groups that may gather at the opening of a deposit box in connection with the settlement of an estate or for certain other family or business conferences, at least one room large enough for ten or twelve people should be provided.

Ordinarily the whole safety deposit area is screened off from the public or circulation space by a grilled barrier equipped with a key-locked gate to be opened from the inside by an attendant. In a small institution one person may attend the gate, check signatures from records kept at a desk, and unlock and later lock the boxes; but in a large bank there must be space for several desks, chairs, and counters, as well as file space to hold signatures and records.

CUSTOMERS' SERVICES

Economic pressure is reducing to a minimum any lounge space assigned to public use outside of the circulation areas. The women customers' waiting room, formerly of some importance, is now only an anteroom to the women's

FIGURE 9. CHASE
NATIONAL BANK,
45 ROCKEFELLER
PLAZA, NEW YORK.
INTERIOR

Reinhard & Hofmeister,
architects

New plan forms generate
new visual space types.

Photograph
Gottscho-Schleisner

toilet. The fewest possible public toilet accommodations are allowed, since it is not within the province of the bank to provide public comfort-station facilities to its customers.

OFFICERS' SPACE

Between the public space and the private or working space lies the officers' space—the contact area or meeting ground between the bank and its customers. Although primarily intended for business conferences, it also takes on a semi-social aspect and sales significance. For this reason it should be placed near the entrance door, where officers may observe entering customers and be in a position to give a friendly greeting or step out for a few moments of conversation. A minimum barrier should be established here—such as a slight change of level, a change in flooring materials, a low rail, or a combination of these. Some seats outside the area are necessary for persons waiting to see the officers. Within the space a comfortable atmosphere should be established, with at least 6 feet between desks in all directions for privacy. Flexibility is essential in the officers' area, as elsewhere in the bank, so that adjustment to an increase or decrease in the number of officers assigned to the platform may readily be made. Near the officers' space, a conference room is desirable. (See Figs. 8, 11, 19.)

The secretaries and "new accounts" personnel in a savings bank are located forward of the officers so that they may intercept the customers and discharge

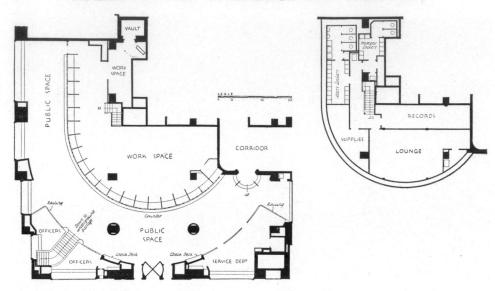

FIGURE 10. EAST RIVER SAVINGS BANK, ROCKEFELLER CENTER, NEW YORK. PLANS

Reinhard & Hofmeister, architects

Free planning concepts adjusted to the needs of a savings bank.

the routine part of new business. A separate space or room for introducing new business or for special seasonal use is an asset to either the savings or the commercial bank. Here personal or real-estate loans are promoted, special savings accounts advertised, and life insurance or government bonds sold, and in suburban or smaller communities this area may be turned over to local committees for recognized community or charity drives. Such a business extension space is a direct-sales area and should be located with that purpose in mind. In the small bank it may be only an assigned teller's window, but in the large institution a room is set aside for the purpose.

After the public space and the officers' space have been considered, we come to the bank's own working area, definitely shut off by the tellers' counter and by locked doors and gates from the public entrance or from intrusion. These barriers must be maintained intact for security reasons; more feared than the great hold-up is small pilfering or the exposure of one customer's business to another. The wire cage enclosure and the grille surmounting the counter in most banks today are ample evidence that the omission of such devices will be the last concession to be granted in establishing a more personal relationship between the bank's side of the counter and the customers'.

FIGURE 11. EAST RIVER SAVINGS BANK,
ROCKEFELLER CENTER, NEW YORK.
EXTERIOR AND INTERIOR

Reinhard & Hofmeister, architects

The bank as an open, shoplike space; the interior,
plainly visible from the outside, is its own best advertisement, and visibility in itself is a protection.

Photographs Robert Damora

TELLERS' WORK SPACE

Leaving for a moment the investigation of the counter itself, let us consider
the entire area behind it. Here we find a marked difference between the
practice in commercial and in savings banks. In the savings bank considerably
more work space is required than in the commercial bank in order to allow

FIGURE 12. BANKERS TRUST COMPANY, ROCKEFELLER CENTER, NEW YORK. CUTAWAY VIEW

Reinhard & Hofmeister, architects

A bank developed on several levels, with each level designed for a specific type of service.

Courtesy Bankers Trust Co.

room for the wheeled trucks holding depositors' record cards, for in a small bank all these cards must be available to every teller and in a bank with tellers' windows assigned to depositors alphabetically certain files must be accessible to each group of tellers. In either case, a large area for records and some desks must be reserved back of the tellers.

On the other hand, the commercial teller can operate in a space about 5 feet square if he has access to an intercommunicating phone and duplicate signature cards, and behind him he needs nothing more than a communicating aisle 4 to 5 feet wide. In this case the work area, with its cluttered appearance and noisy processes, may be more advantageously located in less valuable space. There still remains a miscellaneous amount of less bulky paraphernalia which does not fit into or belong in the teller's own compartment; unless considered and provided for, it will produce a messy appearance as seen from the front, even though the architect has taken pains to clean up everything in connection with the teller's counter and the public space. A useful device for concealing such materials is to plan a breast-high partition back of the teller's compartment, thus creating an aisle through which the teller enters. On the back of this barrier, hidden from view, is a small counter or table with compartments for the miscellany, such as forms, rubber stamps, small business machines, pads, loose blotters, and so forth, the appearance of which, if not considered beforehand, can destroy the architectural effect. Some such partition could also be used for a savings bank; but here, since the teller must consult his records for practically every transaction, the circulation must be free.

TELLERS' COUNTERS OR STATIONS

The alterations to the conventional working arrangements as outlined above have necessarily produced certain changes in nomenclature. With the grille enclosure removed, the familiar term "teller's cage" no longer applies. It is his office or "compartment"—a term used here for want of anything more standardized. The portion of the counter occupied by each teller, whether or not it is separated from that of his neighbor by a partition, becomes his desk for transacting business and is often marked from the public side only by a deal plate or a small sign. Since there is no longer a barrier through which to make an opening, there is no "window" and this position is now called a "station." It is the line-up of such adjoining stations which makes the tellers' counter. In physical arrangements one compartment does not differ greatly from another, and from the standpoint of flexibility it is desirable to keep them all alike so that stations may be assigned to different tellers in accordance with changing needs. The combined teller's station and teller's compartment, in reality the most important unit in the bank's working arrangements, deserves considerable detailed study. Great improvement in design has resulted from stripping it of non-essentials.

Formerly each teller was entirely surrounded by a grilled enclosure, which sometimes was even carried overhead to form a ceiling; he had an alarm at his foot to sound a gong and a pistol in a pocket near his hand to use in resisting a hold-up. The wire or grille between the public and the teller was often backed up with obscure glass to cut off the outsider's view of the papers and checks on the teller's side of the counter. But today tellers are not expected to shoot it out with hold-up men; only the guards are armed. When the alarm pedal is pushed by a teller's foot the alarm sounds at the headquarters either of the police or of a private protective service. In some recently executed work the

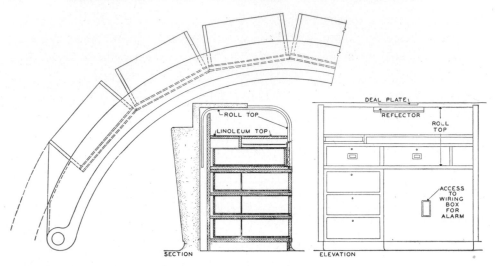

FIGURE 13. CHASE NATIONAL BANK, 9 ROCKEFELLER PLAZA, NEW YORK.
DETAILS OF COUNTER

Reinhard & Hofmeister, architects

A modern bank counter designed for convenience, efficiency, and privacy.

grillework topping the counter has been replaced by a low glass screen, which forms less of a barrier but still seems only a halfway acceptance of the new ideal.

Yet a certain amount of privacy for protection against minor pilfering is necessary. The best solution so far offered is the device of dividing the counter into two parts longitudinally; the public side is raised to a height which creates a natural barrier and on the teller's side a pocket is formed which gives privacy for his papers. In addition a lower shelf is provided on the public side for the customer's convenience when the endorsement of a check or other writing is required at the counter, and on it he may rest gloves, handbag, parcels, and the like while his hands are occupied with passing checks or making deposits. On the tellers' side of the counter the usual cash and paper drawers are provided, plus a rolling shutter top—like that of the old-fashioned roll-top desk—which can be closed partially for additional protection when the teller steps away from his station for a moment or closed and locked when he leaves for a longer period.

On the public side there is nothing to mark the individual stations except the teller himself or the deal plate. Often small movable signs are furnished which read on one side "Paying–Receiving"—or whatever the assignment of the station may be when open for business—and on the other "Next Window" or "Closed." Another simple device is to place these signs flush with the outer counter face, just below the deal plate, with arrangements to illuminate the alternate messages by means of separate switches. The entire counter detail is well illustrated by an example from a branch office of the Chase National Bank in Rockefeller Center, New York, designed by Reinhard & Hofmeister (Fig. 13) In this example the public side of the counter is of terrazzo, which readily adapts itself to the curving form used; the deal plate is of nickel bronze, and the teller's desks behind are of wood.

The top left drawer at a teller's station is a currency drawer from which bills are dealt out. Coin for small change is usually taken in the teller's hand from a machine set at the right side on the lower level of his desk. It would be an advantage to have this machine discharge directly to the customer; at present, however, since the coins fall by gravity, the machine would have to be placed rather awkwardly on the higher level to enable both customer and teller to have a clear view of the transaction. Additional drawers or pockets in the teller's desk are for a reserve of coin in rolls and of bills in bundles. These drawers are customarily partitioned to fit the size of the various coins or the bills; sometimes they contain removable currency boxes for the teller's convenience in transferring his cash. All the drawers should have locks keyed alike.

It is obvious that the teller's desk should be well lighted. This is best accomplished by an incandescent tube or fluorescent fixture mounted under the high part of the counter so that the source is screened from the view of both customer and teller. General room lighting is usually sufficient for the customer's side. The deal plate should be of a plain material so that silver and pennies are easily distinguishable on its surface. Plain or colored glass, unfigured marble, or metal if backed by a sound-absorptive material are all satisfactory. If of glass, the deal plate should be at least an inch thick; if the glass is clear, color may be obtained from backing material. A depression of the surface, placed for the convenience of the customer's right hand, is useful for coin. The best material for the teller's desk top is a special type of linoleum. The teller's desk should be 3'-4" high. The customer's side of the counter should be 4'-3" to the higher level and about 1'-6" wide, with a height of 3'-7" for the secondary front shelf, which should be 6 or 8 inches wide. The total depth of the desk from front to back should be 3'-3" to 3'-6". Four and one-half feet is the minimum width for a teller's compartment.

Savings banks do not adapt themselves so readily as commercial banks to such simplification. Here, because the teller is constantly leaving his station to pick up deposit cards, the roll-top device is not practical for security reasons. Some form of screen may be used, however; this may be kept down to a height of 6 or 8 inches, and as a rule it is obscure or translucent glass. The teller maintains privacy for customer transactions by spindling the records face down. Usually the counter itself is all of one height, 3′–4″, and not over 2′–3″ from front to back. In savings banks the installation of bulky bookkeeping machines in tellers' desks must also be kept in mind. From the practical if not from the architectural point of view, it seems desirable in most banks to maintain some kind of compartment division behind the counter between adjoining tellers in order to avoid the mixing of papers or the clash of personalities; but such divisions may be kept to a minimum.

WORK SPACE

Behind the line of tellers is the work space. Although formerly this was immediately back of the cages, it may now be located elsewhere in the building and in commercial banks it is better so located. In the case of savings banks the present-day method of handling transactions does not permit such a separation, although it is foreseeable that this may sometime be arranged. Pending the working out of new methods, it is still necessary to provide a large area for the card trucks when they are wheeled out of the vaults. In order to maintain a minimum work space on the first floor, communication facilities must be provided with a lavish hand. Depending on the activity of the various stations, there should be a telephone for each teller, or at least one telephone shared between two, connected directly to the workroom. Signature cards must be provided in duplicate files to enable a teller to identify signatures without having to move too far from the counter.

The general work space in a small bank may well be located on a mezzanine to the rear if the first-floor story height permits, or else on the second or any one of the upper floors where the noise of the business machines can be suppressed and the activity kept away from the public. If necessary, the location may be in a separate building near by. For psychological reasons, placing the work space in a basement is undesirable, even though the area may be made physically comfortable by mechanical means.

OFFICERS' AND EMPLOYEES' FACILITIES

The board room, for the officers and members of the board, is usually the most elaborately developed private space in the building. In addition, there must be a president's office, as well as private rooms for certain other officers, with adjoining coat and toilet rooms; also, in a large bank, luncheon facilities are often furnished. As the size of the institution grows, the president's office and the board room are placed farther and farther away from close contact with the public. In the smaller banks the two rooms are often combined. The size of the board room can best be determined by laying out the table (or tables) and spacing the chairs around it until the required number of directors can be accommodated. In a small office a separate table which can be placed like the stem of a "T" against the president's desk is usually adequate. A number of tables which may be put together in various combinations creates a flexible arrangement, but often this is not so desirable as the single conventional board table.

How many additional private offices will be required for officials not on the platform will depend to a large extent on the size of the bank and the nature of its business. Officers' coatroom and toilet facilities may be tucked into odd spaces near the platform, or they may be placed near the board room where they can serve the directors too. Failure to provide coatrooms or closets for officers usually results in a forest of unsightly coat trees on the platform.

An officers' dining room, if one is desired, may be merely a space set aside to be served from outside by caterers. If full kitchen services are to be furnished within the building, adequate refrigerator space for bulk storage of both food and garbage must be provided to permit trucking in and out at times when there will be no possible interference with business.

Employees' restrooms, locker rooms, and toilets should be convenient to the working space and away from the public. There is a growing tendency to make these areas more spacious and more comfortable and thereby contribute to more agreeable working conditions. In the larger institutions a room which serves soft drinks, tea, milk, and coffee to round out a lunch brought from home is an economy appreciated by the employee.

AESTHETIC EXPRESSION—EXTERIOR

In no type of building, except ecclesiastical structures, is there less inclination on the part of the client to consider a non-traditional external architectural expression than in banks. Although the average banker may be intelligently receptive to innovations within the bank, when it comes to the exterior he is baffled, and even the most daring will generally retreat behind the statement: "It has to look like a bank." Generally he means that the bank must look like

FIGURE 14. NATIONAL
FARMERS' BANK (NOW
SECURITY BANK AND
TRUST), OWATONNA,
MINNESOTA.
EXTERIOR AND INTERIOR

Louis H. Sullivan, architect

An important early example of
radically fresh and inventive bank
design.

Photographs Chicago Architectural Photographing Co.

earlier banks, not that the building must have "bank character" as an architect
would conceive it. This is the point at which the architect, if he is to achieve a
modern solution, must exert all his skill in design and in sales persuasion to carry
his point. There is very little in the way of precedent to guide him as to what
constitutes bank character in the modern sense, and all the old values must be
re-examined. If the business character of banking is undergoing a change toward a more open and cordial relation between the bank on the inside and the
customer on the outside, it is reasonable to suppose that this change should find
expression in the architecture of the building. Neither the Egyptian, Greek,
or Roman temple set in a business street nor the Colonial town hall, library, or

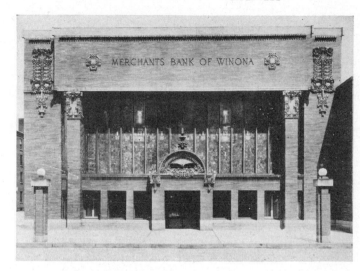

FIGURE 15.
MERCHANTS BANK
OF WINONA,
WINONA,
MINNESOTA.
EXTERIOR

Purcell, Feick & Elmslie, architects

Other architects of the Midwest sought creative solutions for the expressive design of banks.

Courtesy William Gray Purcell

club set in a suburban community may seem incongruous when called a bank because the precedent is so firmly established, but there is no point at which traditional architecture is more vulnerable to attack than in this use of traditional forms in banks.

Deviations from the classical pattern in which bank buildings have been cast since the Columbian Exposition at Chicago in 1893 have been few. An attempt to free the bank from this pattern was made by Louis Sullivan in the early 1900's—notably in a small bank at Owatonna, Minnesota, now the Security Bank and Trust Company (Fig. 14); in the People's Savings and Loan Association, now the People's Federal Savings and Loan Association, at Sidney, Ohio; and in the Farmers' and Merchants' Union Bank of Columbus, Wisconsin (see also Fig. 15). These structures, the highly personal expressions of a great artist, are still—in their organization, design, and use of material—worthy of study. Today they are interesting chiefly as early efforts to break with tradition; we are still struggling with that same problem.

Having reached the decision to cast off the old, we must determine what new form the building should assume to give it bank character. The structure should have dignity, and, though actual physical security is not so important as formerly, it should give an impression of strength and durability. The entrance should be well marked architecturally, and a view of the interior from the street is desirable provided that no business papers are exposed to the public. Materials which suggest permanence and can be kept clean and in good condition at a minimum of expense should be used. If the building can be set back

FIGURE 16. IRVING TRUST COMPANY, 48TH STREET BRANCH, NEW YORK.
INTERIOR

Voorhees, Walker, Foley & Smith, architects

The importance of artificial light in creating the correct atmosphere in bank public spaces; here the lighted coffers furnish efficient light distribution and also give just the right feeling of formality.   Courtesy Voorhees, Walker, Foley & Smith

from the property lines, landscaping is a valuable adjunct to external design. Signs must be carefully considered, because if the architect omits or suppresses them to the point where they have no commercial value they may be supplanted by some horror over which he has no control. Bank architecture offers an opportunity for the exercise of the greatest talent and ingenuity in developing forms which not only shall be adequate to their purpose but also shall take their proper place in the entire architectural picture. Aside from these generalizations it is difficult to point the way.

AESTHETIC EXPRESSION—INTERIOR

There is more modern precedent for interiors than for exteriors, since greater latitude in experiment has been allowed in bank alterations within existing buildings than in new construction. Although it may be argued that organically such interiors are not true examples of bank architecture in the sense that a Gothic church interior is one with its external expression, yet so much of our architecture today consists in clothing basically unrelated structural forms with a certain type of finish that even these attempts at creating

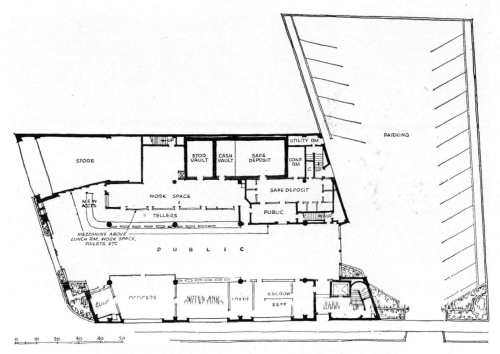

FIGURE 17. CITIZENS NATIONAL BANK, LOS ANGELES, CALIFORNIA. PLAN
Stiles Clements, architect
A plan of simple and convenient directness.   From *Architectural Record*

an up-to-date expression for banks cannot be dismissed. Besides, in them a trend is indicated which will have its influence when opportunities for integrated design are plentiful.

When we stand inside a room we experience a feeling that is produced by the volume, form, lighting, color, and texture of its enclosing surfaces and furnishings. All these elements in a design must be so controlled through the skill of the architect that an agreeable and appropriate response will be produced. Such generalizations must ultimately be translated by him into choices of form and material. Whereas in eclectic architecture the problem was considerably simplified by the selection and faithful following of a certain historical style, the modern architect must rely on his own inventiveness. Considerations of plan and the determination of the volume of the building will have developed the general shape and size of the main banking room and the disposition of its working parts, and in this preliminary study it should be borne in mind (as noted above) that the larger the unobstructed space the better.

FIGURE 18. CITIZENS NATIONAL BANK, LOS ANGELES, CALIFORNIA. EXTERIOR AND INTERIOR

Stiles Clements, architect

A welcoming and attractive service facility rather than a monument.

Photographs Julius Shulman

In the assortment of materials for floors, walls, ceilings, and furniture there is a wide range of choice. For practical reasons floors in public spaces are generally of a hard-surfaced material. Marble, travertine, marble mosaic, terrazzo, and, especially for the smaller banks, wood and rubber tile offer a great variety of colors and textures for areas where there is heavy traffic. Carpet, cork, or rubber tile for the officers' area and linoleum or asphalt tile for the work spaces are almost universally accepted. Proper selection of materials for covering the walls and free-standing columns presents the best opportunity for establishing the architectural character of the room. Stone, marble, terrazzo, brick, wood, and painted plaster, or combinations of these, allow great freedom of choice. The question of cost always influences the selection; when the budget is small, the use of an expensive material may be limited to one wall—or to the free-standing columns, in combination with the counters—and played against a contrasting color and texture in a cheaper material applied to the larger surfaces.

Wood is especially worthy of consideration, for the variety offered in both veneer and solid stock is greater than in any other material. Walnut and teak, with pine in the directors' room, for some reason seem to have found favor with building committees; but many kinds of domestic and imported woods, entirely appropriate and even more interesting, are also available. In the form of veneer, wood has the further advantage that it may be shaped to fit curves. It is worth while to visit a wood-veneer warehouse and to select in advance flitches of a favored wood so that its qualities and limitations may be observed in the design. Counters and furniture may be of the same or of contrasting woods. Cores and solid stock should be fireproofed.

For walls and counters, terrazzo is practical. As a plastic material it is adaptable for use on curved surfaces and in a variety of colors. The execution of terrazzo work should be by expert contractors, and troweled-in-place material should always be applied on metal lath even where there is masonry backing. Plaster walls are economical and can be made interesting if painted an attractive color.

Ceilings, on the decoration of which much money and ingenuity have often been expended in the past, tend today to be as simple as possible and to be considered merely as surfaces to receive the lighting, the acoustic treatment, or the air-conditioning outlets—all of which must be kept in mind as factors in the design. Acoustic treatment is worthy of consideration as an easy and inexpensive way of producing a restful atmosphere.

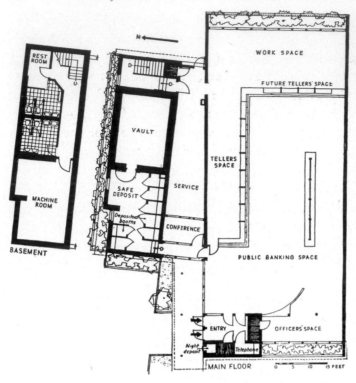

FIGURE 19.
NATIONAL CITY BANK OF CLEVELAND, UNIVERSITY BRANCH, CLEVELAND, OHIO. PLAN

Garfield, Harris, Robinson & Schafer, architects

An inviting small branch bank for a residential area.

From *Architectural Forum*

Counters, check desks, benches, and officers' and secretaries' desks and chairs should all be selected under the architect's supervision. If possible they should be custom-made; the color and finish of the wood or metal, as well as the upholstering material, can then be considered in relation to the entire scheme. The architect's control should be complete over the choice of all the other furnishings and accessories necessary to the bank's operation—including floor coverings, draperies, lighting fixtures, Venetian blinds, clocks, waste baskets, bulletin boards, and calendar frames—because if the selection of any of these details is left to the bank's purchasing agent the result will probably clash with the architectural effect intended.

The subject of decoration as such is a difficult one to introduce into a discussion of twentieth-century architecture, for decorative effects today are sought by means of the color or form of the necessary utilitarian elements. Nevertheless the question of using a wall painting, a photo mural, a mosaic panel, or sculptural treatment will invariably arise, and such a detail can be of value as a focus in an interior. The desire for some such treatment will often originate with the bank's officers, who, accustomed by years of experience to

FIGURE 20.
NATIONAL
CITY BANK OF
CLEVELAND,
UNIVERSITY BRANCH,
CLEVELAND, OHIO.
EXTERIOR AND
INTERIOR

Garfield, Harris, Robinson & Schafer, architects

Even the simplest and least expensive construction if creatively used will produce a bank that is true to its age and harmonious with its environment.

Photographs R. Marvin Wilson, courtesy Garfield, Harris, Robinson & Schafer

the decorative theme as the apex of the design, will feel something missing without it. The architect, too, may want something of the sort. Here is one point where quality is vastly more important than quantity; and the artist should be selected with care. A small bit, well done, well located, and well related to the scheme as a whole, is of vastly greater benefit than a large mural with subject matter that is only remotely connected with the bank's character or individuality.

MECHANICAL EQUIPMENT

Since mechanical services have increasingly become an essential part of our life, they must be taken into account by the architect at an early stage. Elaborate installations will take a big slice out of the budget, and it is well to determine at once how much money is to be allocated to mechanical work. Adequate plumbing and heating are taken for granted, but summer air conditioning is a controversial subject. In the South it must be included, and in the North it is coming to be considered more and more necessary. Heat loads imposed on the system by lighting, supply outlets, and return grilles, the source of the fresh-air supply and the exhaust, and the quantities of available water or space required for an evaporative condenser to effect cooling will all have to be considered at the beginning, and the location of heavy compressors or circulating fans will have to be taken into account because of the noise or vibration from their operation.

In recent years the clients' and the public's standards of lighting have undergone drastic revision. The dim cathedral lighting for the interior of a bank, with accents of light at check desks and tellers' cages, is no longer acceptable. Although even such high levels as fifty foot-candles for working spaces are recommended, thirty to thirty-five seem more reasonable; the lower degree of intensity, moreover, is more easily accomplished with economy of operation than is the higher degree. The foregoing applies particularly to light in public spaces, such as on the tellers' counter, where the lighting source may be in the ceiling at a considerable height above the working plane. Concealed spotlights over the deal plates to illuminate the point at which the transaction takes place may be considered, for this point should be well lighted for the detection of counterfeit money. Architectural lighting to model the planes of walls or to highlight objects used as decoration is one of the designer's opportunities. To accomplish this varied illumination, incandescent, fluorescent, and concealed or focus lighting in different forms or combinations can be put to use.

Flexibility is of the highest importance in the installation of the communications system. Interior telephone connections are essential. An underfloor duct is desirable. The switchboard location should be thoroughly studied, and in a small bank its location on a mezzanine from which everyone may be seen is a distinct advantage. Pneumatic tubes or dumbwaiters for the transfer of papers from floor to floor or from point to point should be investigated early; the tendency now is to replace messengers with such mechanical means.

Protection devices, with connection to a central patrol station, should be worked out with the company representatives as a safeguard against fire, burglary, or theft. Foot treadles for installation under the counter are available; the universal preference seems to be for a silent type of alarm, with a light and annunciator at the guards' station which rouse the protective forces without informing the intruder that signals have been given. Gassing devices and bullet-proof glass are not generally accepted, since the technique of capture is no longer based on shooting it out at the teller's window.

Hope for a distinguished future in bank architecture seems bright. Much of the preliminary work has been done. The barriers limiting bank design to the classic style have been broken down, but the tradition of quality building still remains. That bankers are in a more receptive mood toward a contemporary bank expression, a number of modern interiors and a few modern buildings testify. The mechanics of change are active; the new form will soon follow.

SUGGESTED ADDITIONAL READING FOR CHAPTER 27

Alexander, Aaron G., "How to Choose a Bank Lot," *Banking*, Vol. 33, No. 2 (March, 1941), pp. 74–75.

Architectural Forum, Vol. 38, No. 6 (June, 1923), entire issue, pp. [253]–310; Vol. 48, No. 6 (June, 1928), entire issue, pp. [786]–952.

"Bank Buildings," a critique, *Progressive Architecture*, Vol. 30, No. 3 (March, 1949), pp. 51–64.

Gothold, David J., "Banking Quarters of the Future," *Southern Banker*, Vol. 84, No. 5 (May, 1945), pp. 34–36.

Hamlin, Talbot [Faulkner], *Greek Revival Architecture in America* (New York: Oxford University Press, 1944).

Hopkins, Alfred, *The Fundamentals of Good Bank Building* (Cambridge, Mass.: Bankers Pub. Co., 1929).

LaPierre, Lester S., "How to Plan for a New Bank Building," *Bankers Monthly*, Vol. 62, No. 4 (April, 1945), pp. 159, 178–80.

Odle, Harry V., "New Developments in Bank Quarters," *Burroughs Clearing House*, Vol. 31, No. 1 (October, 1946), pp. 24–27, 56, 59–62.

Seligman, Edwin R. A., and Alvin Johnson (editors), *Encyclopaedia of the Social Sciences*, Vol. I (New York: Macmillan, 1930), article "Commercial Banking."

Smith, Perry Coke, "The Bank of the Future," *Banking*, Vol. 37, No. 9 (March, 1945), pp. 33–35, 84.

—— "What Bankers Want of Their Buildings," *Architectural Record*, Vol. 97, No. 3 (March, 1945), pp. 88–90.

Wilkinson, J. C., "Planning a Bank to Make Friends," *Banking*, Vol. 37, No. 10 (April, 1945), pp. 33–35, 116.

28

Department Stores

By KENNETH C. WELCH

THE BUREAU OF THE CENSUS defines department stores as "general merchandise stores with sales in excess of $100,000, usually of the full-service type, carrying men's, women's, and children's apparel and shoes, furnishings and accessories, dry goods, homewares, and many other lines. Furniture and hardware are often but not necessarily represented, although home furnishings, draperies, curtains, and linens are almost invariably carried." There are many large departmentalized stores, however, which do not carry this full range but nevertheless rank as department stores from the architectural viewpoint.

In 1939 there were only 4,074 department stores in the United States.[1] These represented less than a quarter of one per cent of the total number of stores, but they accounted for 9½ per cent of all sales, and among them 304, or 7½ per cent, produced over 40 per cent of all department store sales.

The exact origin of the department store is uncertain, and the name itself was probably not used until the "gay nineties." Many department stores started as dry-goods stores. Lord and Taylor (New York, 1826), A. T. Stewart (New York, opened in 1825; absorbed in 1896 by John Wanamaker[2]), Bon Marché (Paris, 1838), Rowland H. Macy (1844 in Boston, 1858 in New York[3]), Eben Jordan (jobbing house in Boston, 1851), and Field, Leiter & Company (Chicago, 1870; later Marshall Field) were all in this classification.

Many retail principles have been originated and proved by department stores. Summarized briefly they include: (1) one price, plainly marked; (2) the permitting of returns and adjustments; (3) quantity buying; (4) city-wide publicity; (5) the added convenience of having many lines under one

---

[1] United States Retail Census.

[2] *Golden Book of the Year, 1861–1911, Wanamaker Stores . . . Jubilee* [Philadelphia: c 1911–19].

[3] Ralph M. Hower, *History of Macy's of New York, 1858–1919* (Cambridge, Mass.: Harvard University Press, 1943).

FIGURE 21. A. T. STEWART STORE (LATER JOHN WANAMAKER'S), NEW YORK. EXTERIOR

John Kellum, architect

One of the largest of early American department stores, with an exterior of cast iron. At the time of its erection in the 1860's its eight-foot-wide show windows were deemed almost impractical because of their size. Courtesy John Wanamaker

roof; (6) the ability to reflect fashion changes; (7) new capital structures with larger investments; and (8) the addition of many supplementary services. These principles had such a rapid growth in the United States that the modern department store may be considered largely an American product, and it is unfortunate that we have borrowed, as an environment for this comparatively recent retail process, the academic architectural styles of the past.

Most early department stores started in a small way and expanded from one building to another. Soon, however, large specially built structures with open plans were discovered to be more efficient both in handling crowds and in creating possibilities for display. The growing use of structural iron and glass and the invention and improvement of the elevator were essential contributions to the development of department store architecture. One important problem was that of introducing daylight into the center of the building. Although single-story buildings of considerable size could be lighted by clerestories or glass roofs, the big multiple-level department store required other methods— usually interior skylighted courts.

One of the first large structures built specifically to house a store, the A. T. Stewart building in New York (1863), by John Kellum, had one central sky-

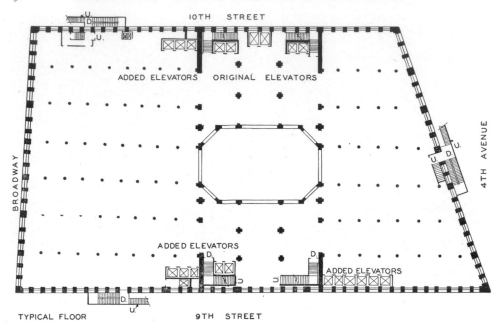

FIGURE 22. A. T. STEWART STORE (LATER JOHN WANAMAKER'S), NEW YORK. PLAN

John Kellum, architect

A plan with the typical central rotunda or court; the present grand stairs were an addition of the 1890's.

lighted court, which, though not too successful in furnishing daylight except on the first floor directly under it and then only for a relatively short distance from its perimeter, created a grandiose effect (Figs. 21, 22). The Magasin au Bon Marché in Paris (1876), by Eiffel & Boileau, was better; it had a number of large skylighted courts. The upper-floor areas were connected across the courts by iron bridges, which materially improved the circulation and formed excellent vantage points (Figs. 23, 24). Although these courts wasted a greater amount of floor area than those of the Stewart building did, they distributed the daylight much better.

The display of merchandise in these early stores was primitive, but lighting was vitally important then as it is today. Around 1878 electric arc lamps were coming into use, but department stores always kept gas lighting as a stand-by. By 1880 Edison's incandescent lamps had arrived on the scene. This new lighting permitted the construction of the "warehouse" type of multiple-level department store, which though less impressive was more efficient. Many stores, however, still retained the skylighted court as an architectural feature.

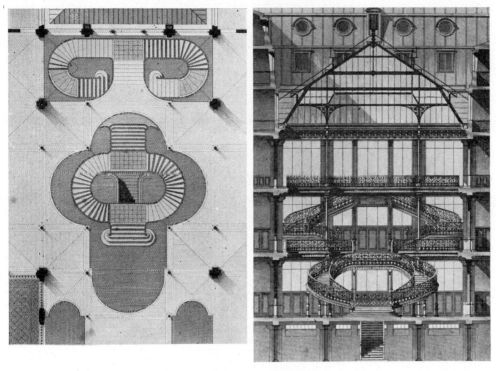

FIGURE 23 (LEFT). BON MARCHÉ, PARIS. PLAN OF STAIRS

Eiffel & Boileau, architects

The largest of the early department stores in Paris, the Bon Marché was famous for its revolutionary use of iron and its light and airy interior.   From *Encyclopédie d'architecture* . . .

FIGURE 24 (RIGHT). BON MARCHÉ, PARIS. SECTION

Eiffel & Boileau, architects

Light from skylights flooded into the building through the courts.

From *Encyclopédie d'architecture* . . .

(See Figs. 25, 26.) The Wanamaker store in Philadelphia (begun in 1902 and completed in 1910), by D. H. Burnham, with its famous pipe organ, endowed to remain the "largest in the world," has a "grand court" 150 feet high and 62 by 109 feet in plan. Marshall Field in Chicago had an open court, but Louis Sullivan did not include one in the Carson-Pirie-Scott building there and this omission was expressive of the general trend in the United States. Yet the use of a large central court or rotunda still remains standard practice in Continental countries; for example, one of the most beautiful and carefully planned of modern department stores—the Bijenkorf in Rotterdam, by Dudok—has a handsome open area (Figs. 27, 28).

FIGURE 25. LE PRINTEMPS, PARIS. INTERIOR

René Binet, architect

The tradition of light ironwork persisted in French stores.

From *Architecte*

ORGANIZATION

A specialty store can be successful without too complex an organization. The large department store, on the other hand, must be efficiently organized. In addition to the more obvious sales instrumentalities there must be facilities for the employment services, for training, and for customer service, as well as for the equally important behind-the-scenes service. When these facilities are all combined in a pleasing environment, the best possible instrument has been provided for department store operation. The success of the design can go a long way toward making management successful.

Table I is a typical organization chart for a large department store and also includes the type of space or facility required. Table II classifies department store merchandise into six groups and supplies certain pertinent information.

PROGRAM

In discussing the department store program we shall follow the merchandise from the receiving point to the point of sale and then, when it is not a "take

FIGURE 26. WERTHEIM DEPARTMENT STORE, BERLIN. EXTERIOR AND INTERIOR

Alfred Messel, architect

This great store—one of the important pioneer works of modern architecture—is distinguished by its fresh exterior design and its large central court; note the lighting by means of small bulbs arranged in long garlands.

From Platz, *Die Baukunst der neuesten Zeit*

with," to the delivery department. In determining the areas and facilities required, the services of a consulting specialist are valuable; in addition, the existing conditions should be studied and the buyers or department managers consulted, for a thorough understanding of the function involved is essential. Management, it should be noted, is usually more interested in selling than in service. The designer is fortunate—and he will doubtless produce a better design—when the service executives have equal authority with those primarily interested in selling.

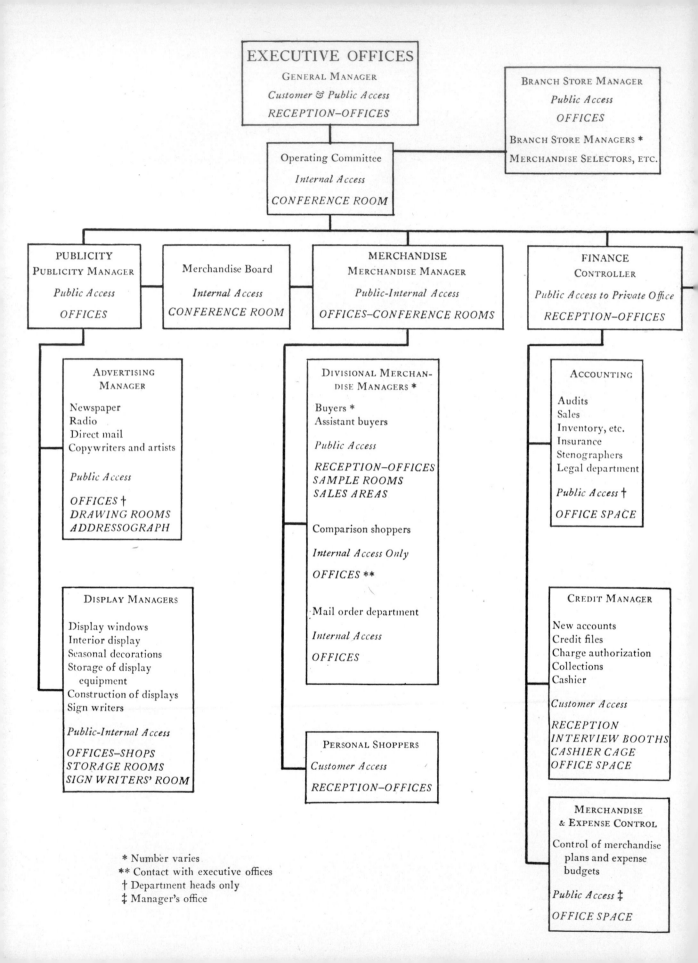

EXECUTIVE OFFICES
GENERAL MANAGER
Customer & Public Access
RECEPTION–OFFICES

BRANCH STORE MANAGER
Public Access
OFFICES
BRANCH STORE MANAGERS *
MERCHANDISE SELECTORS, ETC.

Operating Committee
Internal Access
CONFERENCE ROOM

PUBLICITY
PUBLICITY MANAGER
Public Access
OFFICES

Merchandise Board
Internal Access
CONFERENCE ROOM

MERCHANDISE
MERCHANDISE MANAGER
Public-Internal Access
OFFICES–CONFERENCE ROOMS

FINANCE
CONTROLLER
Public Access to Private Office
RECEPTION–OFFICES

ADVERTISING
MANAGER

Newspaper
Radio
Direct mail
Copywriters and artists

Public Access

OFFICES †
DRAWING ROOMS
ADDRESSOGRAPH

DIVISIONAL MERCHAN-
DISE MANAGERS *

Buyers *
Assistant buyers

Public Access

RECEPTION–OFFICES
SAMPLE ROOMS
SALES AREAS

Comparison shoppers

Internal Access Only

OFFICES **

Mail order department

Internal Access

OFFICES

ACCOUNTING

Audits
Sales
Inventory, etc.
Insurance
Stenographers
Legal department

Public Access †

OFFICE SPACE

DISPLAY MANAGERS

Display windows
Interior display
Seasonal decorations
Storage of display
    equipment
Construction of displays
Sign writers

Public-Internal Access

OFFICES–SHOPS
STORAGE ROOMS
SIGN WRITERS' ROOM

CREDIT MANAGER

New accounts
Credit files
Charge authorization
Collections
Cashier

Customer Access

RECEPTION
INTERVIEW BOOTHS
CASHIER CAGE
OFFICE SPACE

PERSONAL SHOPPERS

Customer Access

RECEPTION–OFFICES

MERCHANDISE
& EXPENSE CONTROL

Control of merchandise
    plans and expense
    budgets

Public Access ‡

OFFICE SPACE

* Number varies
** Contact with executive offices
† Department heads only
‡ Manager's office

TABLE I. TYPICAL ORGANIZATION CHART FOR A LARGE DEPARTMENT STORE Indicating Department Heads, Functions of Departments, Type of Access (Customer, Public, Internal), and Type of Space Used or Controlled.

There will obviously be variations in organization, depending on operating policies; for example, the Mail Order Department can be separate or under the supervision of the Merchandise or Store Manager. Accordingly, as a help in programming, it is well for the designer, whether totally new plans are being made or major alterations are contemplated, to become familiar with the store organization.

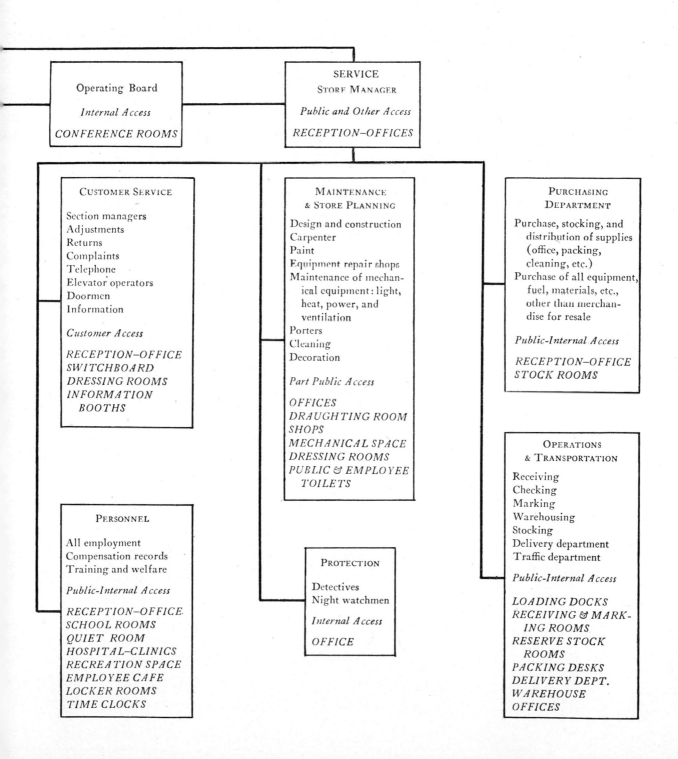

Operating Board

Internal Access

CONFERENCE ROOMS

SERVICE
STORE MANAGER

Public and Other Access

RECEPTION—OFFICES

CUSTOMER SERVICE

Section managers
Adjustments
Returns
Complaints
Telephone
Elevator operators
Doormen
Information

Customer Access

RECEPTION—OFFICE
SWITCHBOARD
DRESSING ROOMS
INFORMATION
  BOOTHS

MAINTENANCE & STORE PLANNING

Design and construction
Carpenter
Paint
Equipment repair shops
Maintenance of mechanical equipment: light, heat, power, and ventilation
Porters
Cleaning
Decoration

Part Public Access

OFFICES
DRAUGHTING ROOM
SHOPS
MECHANICAL SPACE
DRESSING ROOMS
PUBLIC & EMPLOYEE
  TOILETS

PURCHASING DEPARTMENT

Purchase, stocking, and distribution of supplies (office, packing, cleaning, etc.)
Purchase of all equipment, fuel, materials, etc., other than merchandise for resale

Public-Internal Access

RECEPTION—OFFICE
STOCK ROOMS

OPERATIONS & TRANSPORTATION

Receiving
Checking
Marking
Warehousing
Stocking
Delivery department
Traffic department

Public-Internal Access

LOADING DOCKS
RECEIVING & MARKING ROOMS
RESERVE STOCK
  ROOMS
PACKING DESKS
DELIVERY DEPT.
WAREHOUSE
OFFICES

PERSONNEL

All employment
Compensation records
Training and welfare

Public-Internal Access

RECEPTION—OFFICE
SCHOOL ROOMS
QUIET ROOM
HOSPITAL—CLINICS
RECREATION SPACE
EMPLOYEE CAFE
LOCKER ROOMS
TIME CLOCKS

PROTECTION

Detectives
Night watchmen

Internal Access

OFFICE

TABLE II

Basic Category	Time-Need	General Characteristics	Price Level	Other Competing Neighborhood Stores
1. Convenience Goods	Daily— Weekly	Often staple and increasingly being packaged. Standardized to a certain degree as to product and price. Little "shopping" required. Includes apparel with lesser fashion appeal, children's play clothes, work clothes, everyday apparel.	Low	Food, drug, family apparel stores
2. Shopping Goods (a) Fashion [a]	Monthly— Seasonal	Generally women like access to a large and varied selection, preferably in close proximity (high-volume department stores plus specialty shops). Many items are in luxury class. Values increasingly important. Comparatively little standardization. Exclusiveness adds to prestige. Bulk of merchandise must have demand value rather than price appeal. Individual rather than family appeal.	Medium to high	Women's, men's, and children's apparel and accessory stores
(b) Requiring Service	Yearly— Sometimes Lifetime	Standardized items but with certain style appeal, such as appliances, radios, automobiles, etc. A high degree of shopping value and service rendered in normal times important. Often more of a family appeal. National publicity.	Medium but generally high	Appliance, radio, and automotive stores
3. Specialty Goods	Monthly— Seasonal— Lifetime	Often repeat customers, hence not too much shopping. Service and natural accessibility important. Often nationally advertised. Brand names; fashion not too important.		Men's clothing, small electrical appliances, fancy groceries, better furniture, and home furnishings

[a] There is a difference between fashion and style. The former is a contemporary vogue, which may or may not have style; style may be an attribute of items not necessarily fashionable. Only in comparatively recent times have the great majority of people become fashion-minded, particularly in the low- and medium-income groups. This is due to numerous factors but especially to the power of fashion publicity, improved transportation, communications, motion pictures, and broadcasting.

In addition to the above basic categories, merchandise has other classifications and further subdivisions as follows:

4. Impulse Items
(sometimes called "pick up" items)

Though generally in the low- to medium-price field, impulse items can be important adjuncts to convenience, fashion, shopping, and even specialty goods. They can have a definite fashion appeal in the accessory field or a novelty appeal in convenience and specialty goods. They are items which have a certain consumer demand [b] but are not often sought or shopped for by themselves. They are generally semi-luxuries, even though in the lower-price brackets. Men's neckwear is the best example of this classification; but women's neckwear, handkerchiefs, handbags, millinery, etc., are also to a high degree impulse goods. Often a display acts as a reminder. Obviously this classification needs complete and effective display and the maximum amount of natural traffic that is possible, which means good main-floor locations, or, if on upper floors because of their relation with other upper groups, they should be placed in spots adjacent to the highest traffic flow.

5. Necessities or "Pullers"

A large part of convenience goods and even of shopping goods falls in this classification. Pullers can have a high degree of fashion and style appeal and be high in price; therefore they require a maximum amount of shopping. It is obvious that they also require a high degree of consumer demand. Children's wear, women's and men's outer apparel, shoes, notions, baked goods, etc., fall in this classification. Staple goods can also be included, but these are relatively less important in department stores. Puller merchandise can have a less preferred location from a traffic standpoint and can be used to pull customers through the impulse-goods sections.

6. Emergency Items

With certain items—often needed in a hurry—convenience of location and accessibility are the important considerations. Sometimes they are needed not immediately but merely within definite time limits. Drugs, prescriptions, certain groceries, film developing, certain repair services, etc., are in this classification.

[b] Low price alone does not account for the fact that a given article will sell. Merchandise must be in demand; either it must be needed or a demand must be created for it by persistent publicity.

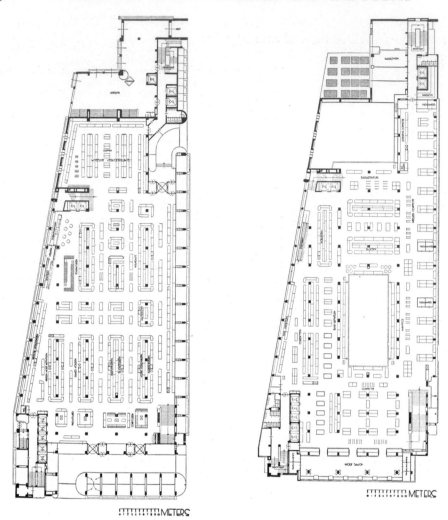

FIGURE 27. BIJENKORF STORE, ROTTERDAM, THE NETHERLANDS. PLANS

W. M. Dudok, architect

One of the most carefully planned of modern European department stores; half destroyed
during the Second World War.   From *Die Bijenkorf Rotterdam, Gedenkboek*

Generally great savings can be made by avoiding the unnecessary moving
of goods. Waste is usually due to bad planning and the allocation of an inadequate area to service. The large central department store, even with outside
warehouse space and remote delivery, can seldom retain over 50 per cent
of its gross area for selling; branches can retain up to 75 per cent.

FIGURE 28. BIJENKORF STORE, ROTTERDAM, THE NETHERLANDS. EXTERIOR AND INTERIOR

W. M. Dudok, architect

Distinguished by a superb and unconventional handling of modern techniques and materials.

From *Die Bijenkorf Rotterdam, Gedenkboek*

RECEIVING POINT

Merchandise is received at a receiving station, which may be located away from the store at a warehouse or, in the case of deliveries by mail and express and in the event that the warehouse is joined to the store, in the store itself. There should be a loading platform at least 3'-0" above grade, with space enough to handle the peak receiving load. As a rule, deliveries can be staggered so that no more trucks will be present at one time than can be accommodated. It is wise to provide complete off-street loading space for trucks, even if city ordinances do not require it, as is increasingly the case.[4]

A receiving station can be at street level or, with a ramp or van lift, in the

[4] The Regional Plan Association proposes for New York (*Highway Research Board Proceedings, 25th Annual Meeting*, 1945) the following number of off-street truck berths in relation to the gross building area of department stores:

Square Feet	No. of Berths	Square Feet	No. of Berths
40,000	1	320,000	5
100,000	2	400,000	6
160,000	3	Each Additional	1 Additional
240,000	4	90,000	

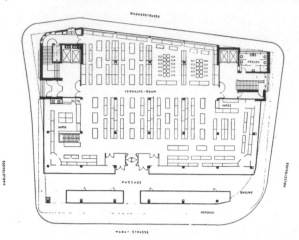

FIGURE 29.
BREUNINGER STORE,
STUTTGART, GERMANY.
PLAN

Eisenlohr & Pfennig, architects

Note the concentration of the vertical circulation and the services to create the largest possible unbroken selling areas.

From Parnes, *Bauten des Einzelhandels . . .*

FIGURE 30.
BREUNINGER STORE,
STUTTGART,
GERMANY.
EXTERIOR

Eisenlohr & Pfennig, architects

Designed entirely in the then current type of modern architecture, with structural rhythms dominant.

From Parnes, *Bauten des Einzelhandels . . .*

basement or sub-basement or on an upper floor; the expense involved in the last case is justifiable only when the land values are high. If it is on the street level, roll-up doors and a booth for the receiving clerk's office should be provided, since all merchandise should be delivered at this one point.

Sometimes mechanical conveyors move the goods from the receiving station to the marking rooms. Often, however, such equipment involves an unwarranted expense, since in addition to a high initial cost it actually increases labor costs by necessitating additional checking. Another solution is to use modern moving and lifting trucks and regular freight elevators, a scheme that enables one person, after the initial check, to take the packages direct from the receiving point to the proper marking room. In any event, every possible method should be studied to determine the most efficient system for a given condition.

MARKING ROOMS

At the designated marking room the merchandise is opened and checked.[5] Efficient machines are commonly used for marking. Portable marking tables will save labor costs in moving merchandise, especially when it is in small packages. The paper work entailed in marking requires intelligent planning. To arrive at the most economical solution, the architect-engineer must be familiar with the procedures and the mechanical equipment—possibly pneumatic tubes—required. As a rule, the managers of the various departments can give him this information, but he must be sure that such details are all incorporated in the plan.

The various marking rooms are best located on the same level with the reserve-stock rooms they serve.

RESERVE-STOCK AREAS

When reserve-stock rooms for different departments can be separated and locked, the merchandise, once it is checked and marked, often becomes the responsibility of the department which handles it. There is a trend toward keeping a larger reserve stock on the same floor with the department, or on a mezzanine close by. Narrow mezzanines over small areas on the periphery, with low head room underneath, seldom harm the total space effect and normally take up no sales space. Under this system the sales force becomes better acquainted with the stock and finds it easily accessible when needed; furthermore, by having the sales force do the re-marking, stock-keeping, and so on in dull hours, indirect costs can be reduced.

In the case of a city-wide chain or an older parent unit with a system of branches, such decentralization is especially advantageous. Branch stores can be better serviced from a warehouse than from a central store which lies in a congested business district, and the delivery department also can then be more closely co-ordinated with regional and national transportation.

[5] This is true unless, as is sometimes the case with standardized merchandize, it is kept packaged in the warehouse, sold to the customer from a displayed sample, and delivered to him from the warehouse.

FIGURE 31.
SCHOCKEN STORE,
CHEMNITZ,
GERMANY.
EXTERIOR

Eric Mendelsohn, architect

The most brilliant of modern German shops; cantilevered selling floors with continuous windows framed by the vertical notes of the vertical circulations required.

Courtesy Museum of Modern Art, New York

Much less reserve-stock space is required in any one selling unit if an efficient distributing system is carefully engineered. In fact, with efficient concealed stock rooms located adjacent to the selling departments there is actually no reserve stock because all the stock is easily accessible at the time of sale. Where reserve stock for small wares and accessories is centrally located, one good scheme is to have it on two levels, with 8-foot (or lower) sprinklered ceilings. The marking rooms can be either on the lower level, along with the more active stock, or on both levels. The layout should be made so that inventory taking can be easily systematized.

SELLING DEPARTMENTS

Most departmentalized stores have adopted the National Retail Dry Goods Association's departmental nomenclature and numbering system. The Controllers' Congress of the Association issues annually its *Merchandising and Operating Results of Department Stores and Specialty Stores* (*M.O.R.*), with which the department store architect should become thoroughly familiar.[6] It gives figures—under various classifications—for the main store, the basement store, and the total store by departments. Of special interest to the designer are figures on the average number of transactions, average gross sales, sales per square foot, transactions per square foot and per salesperson, salespeople's salaries, and so forth.

The Controllers' Congress, however, in its list of basic selling groups as

[6] It can be purchased from the National Retail Dry Goods Association, 100 West 31st Street, New York 1, New York.

shown in Table III, does not include all the sections that a full department store will have, especially those of a service nature. The sections have been added in the table as group XII.

TABLE III

I. *Main-Floor Accessories*
  1. Neckwear
  2. Handkerchiefs
  3. Gloves
  4. Hosiery—women's and children's
  5. Handbags and small leather goods
  6. Umbrellas

II. *Small Wares*
  1. Notions [a]
  2. Toilet articles
  3. Drugs
  4. Costume jewelry
  5. Better jewelry (watches and diamonds)
  6. Books
  7. Stationery
  8. Silverware [b]
  9. Candy

III. *Accessories—Miscellaneous*
  1. Millinery
  2. Shoes—women's and children's

IV. *Piece Goods—Apparel*
  1. Silks and synthetics
  2. Woolens
  3. Wash goods
  4. Patterns [c]
  5. Laces, trimmings, ribbons

V. *Piece Goods—Home Furnishings*
  1. Domestics
  2. Linens
  3. Blankets

VI. *Intimate Wear* (*Women's*)
  1. Muslin and silk underwear
  2. Knit underwear
  3. Corsets and brassières
  4. Negligees
  5. House dresses [d]

VII. *Women's Apparel*
  1. Dresses
  2. Coats and suits
  3. Furs
  4. Junior apparel
  5. Sportswear
     (a) Blouses
     (b) Skirts and other sportswear

[a] Often broken down in large stores, i.e., sewing notions with Piece Goods—Apparel, sanitary goods with Main-Floor Accessories, etc.

[b] Sometimes placed with china, glassware, and related home furnishings, but with main-floor seasonal representation.

[c] Not listed by the National Dry Goods Association, but always located with this group.

[d] Sometimes located with regular dresses.

VIII. *Children's Group*
    1. Infants'
      (a) Layette
      (b) Coats and dresses
      (c) Accessories
      (d) Furniture

    2. Girls' [e]

IX. *Men's and Boys'* [f]
    1. Men's furnishings and robes
    2. Hats
    3. Sportswear
    4. Clothing

    5. Men's and boys' shoes
    6. Boys'
      (a) Furnishings
      (b) Clothing

X. *Miscellaneous*
    1. Art needlework
    2. Gift department
    3. Toys and games

    4. (a) Sporting goods
      (b) Cameras
    5. Luggage

XI. *Home Furnishings*
    1. (a) Furniture
      (b) Beds and bedding
    2. Floor coverings
      (a) Rugs and carpets
      (b) Linoleums
      (c) Oriental rugs
    3. (a) Curtains
      (b) Draperies
      (c) Upholstery
    4. Lamps and shades

    5. (a) China
      (b) Glassware
    6. Pictures—Mirrors
    7. Housewares
      (a) Small electrical appliances
      (b) Kitchenware—Crockery
      (c) Wooden wares
      (d) Cleaning materials
    8. Major appliances
    9. Radios and records

XII. *Sections Not Listed by the Controllers' Congress*
    1. Beauty parlor
    2. Tea room, restaurant, lunch-room, etc.
    3. Baked goods
    4. Groceries—specialties (some stores have complete food sections)
    5. Photographic studio

    6. Optical department
    7. Sewing machines
    8. Patterns (included above with *Piece Goods—Apparel*)
    9. Garden supplies
    10. Hardware
    11. Paints and wallpaper
    12. Building supplies

[e] There can be a number of special subdivisions, for instance, by age—i.e., 2–6, 6–14, and special shops such as Teen Age, High School, etc.

[f] It is a matter of store policy, often determined by the space available, whether the boys' sections are located (1) on the same floor and allied with the men's sections or (2) with the infants' and girls', thus creating a complete children's group. There are good arguments for both policies.

XIII. *Specials*

Often special booths and counter islands, sometimes occupying as much as 10 per cent of the selling area, are located on the main floor. These are used (1) for expansion of regular main-floor gift-type sections in December, (2) for seasonal advertised or non-advertised promotions, or (3) to give upper-floor departments promotional space or additional area in the periods between holiday seasons. Often they are operated together as a special section, with its own manager.

BASEMENT STORES

Basement stores, having fewer departments, are less complicated. They specialize mostly in apparel and include simple sections for accessories, millinery, and shoes. House furnishings as a rule contribute only a small part of the basement volume today. Originally basements were often used as outlets for job lots and obsolete merchandise. In any case, as the automobile became the preferred means of transportation for the medium- as well as the higher-income group, many department stores moved their home furnishings from the basement to the upper floors or to abandoned wholesale areas in order to make room below for merchandise for the lower-income group, the users of mass transportation. In this manner the modern "basement store" was created.

Usually the basement is operated as a separate store and has its own organization, but it is co-ordinated with the upstairs store; it sells not cheaper merchandise than the main store but lower-priced lines. It should generally be provided with its own main entrances, so placed as not to interfere with the main-store first-floor traffic. These entrances should be located close to mass transportation facilities; in fact, the entrance to a large basement store often determines the location of a bus stop.

Basement sales volumes vary (1946) from an average high of 20 per cent of total sales in the largest store down to 8.7 per cent in the smaller department stores. Potential sales for any basement store are dependent upon (1) the basement area available, (2) accessibility, and (3) lower-priced lines. Basement stores thrive in large old midtown department stores; obviously they are unsuited for suburban main streets or "recentralized" shopping centers.

If a basement store is contemplated, all the possible space should be used, because basement selling space is highly productive. Accordingly all mechanical equipment and all service facilities pertaining to main-store sections should be placed elsewhere—in sub-basements, mezzanines, and the more inaccessible areas on upper floors.

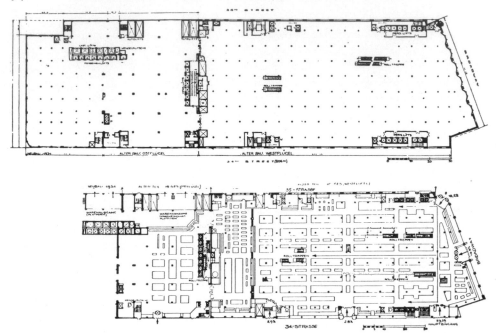

FIGURE 32. MACY'S, NEW YORK. PLANS

A typical plan of the late 1920's, showing a careful massing and spacing of vertical circulations, planned distribution of departments, and counter placing based on column arrangements.

From Parnes, *Bauten des Einzelhandels . . .*

PLANNING PROCEDURE

In planning a department store or a major modernization or expansion, an architect as one of his first steps should estimate the size of the selling and the service areas. Such estimates must of course be tentative; the sizes can be exactly determined only after a detailed planning of the various facilities. The best way to determine preliminary selling areas is on the basis of general standards of productivity. The Controllers' Congress *M.O.R.* gives *typical* sales per square foot and *goal* sales per square foot for various classifications. So many factors affect productivity, however, that it seems wise to determine the projected sales which a given space should produce and then use the "goal productivity" figures in determining its area. The proof for the advisability of this procedure is that the goal figures are consistently exceeded when departments are properly designed and operated. High productivity depends on minimum walking distances for salespeople. Moreover, since the operating costs are often distributed according to the area occupied, it is apparent that optimum productivity, with flexibility for expansion, is essential.

PRODUCTIVITY FACTORS

Three major types of factor affect space productivity: unavoidable factors, management-variable factors, and designer-variable factors.

Unavoidable factors include: (1) size or bulk of the merchandise (for example, furniture takes up more space than hosiery); (2) changing demands for merchandise, or increased sales; (3) change in the per capita purchasing power; (4) additional services required in the sale of goods, as, for instance, additional fitting spaces, fitting rooms, and so on; and (5) inflation or deflation.

Management-variable factors include: (1) miscalculations in the figuring of selling space; (2) unrecorded selling activities; (3) forward stock turnover as compared with total stock turnover; and (4) relative amount of volume of sales.

Another management variable is the fact that the first floor in any multiple-story store receives the heaviest traffic and accordingly is charged with the highest rental. Thus it is obvious that management devotes greater thought to the utilization of space on the ground floor than elsewhere; this naturally increases the typical productivity of the sections there, which include all small accessories and a majority of the small wares. Modern recentralized units offer great advantages in that respect because by having all activities on only two levels the entering or highest-traffic level can house all "impulse" items.[7]

Designer-variable factors are those over which the designer has control. The first is the location of a given department in reference to traffic. The modern designer carefully plans the traffic and thus can place impulse merchandise and potential high-productivity sections adjacent to the best traffic lanes. He can further plan the traffic lanes not only to create a pleasing effect but also to expose the maximum lineal amount of display. These three considerations are all essential to high productivity.

The second designer-variable factor is efficient equipment design. Good equipment displays the merchandise to advantage and in addition houses the stock so that it can be shown with a minimum of effort and in the shortest possible time.

Closely linked to this factor is the third, accessibility of the reserve stock. For example, every day in certain sections all of the stock estimated for the day's sales might be placed each morning in the department, perhaps on display, to save time in replenishing it during active hours. The planning of space for this is important.

[7] For a definition of impulse goods, see Table II.

The fourth designer-variable factor—a vitally important one—concerns the provision of maximum expansion and contraction in area and facilities for seasonal sales fluctuations. Instead of attacking this problem from the angle of adding space to a department during its seasonal peak, it is better to think of it in terms of providing a sufficient amount of space (even if crowded) to take care of its normal peak and then reducing the area during periods of minimum sales; the space thus gained can be utilized either by other departments then at a peak or to promote important seasonal sales of merchandise usually placed in other less accessible locations.

December is the peak month in department stores. The December sales will be double those of the average month and about two and a half times those of the poorest month, generally July. Moreover, certain departments, particularly those with a high gift appeal, will produce a high proportion of their annual sales in December. The departments which should decrease their space

TABLE IV

DEPARTMENTS MOST SUBJECT TO SEASONAL VARIATION
Percentage of Total Annual Sales

	December	July
Toys	33% to 40%	3% to 5%
Handkerchiefs	24% to 34%	4% to 5%
Men's furnishings	23% to 30%	5% to 6%
Negligees and robes	22% to 32%	4½% to 6%
Jewelry	21% to 26½%	4% to 6%
Books and stationery	21% to 24%	4% to 6%
Toilet articles	21% to 25%	6% to 7%

for the rest of the year are listed in Table IV. On the other hand, some departments have a higher peak in the spring and fall. For example, millinery will produce only from 6 to 8 per cent of its total sales in December but will run from 13 to 17 per cent in March, prior to Easter.

It is obvious that if there can be an interchange of space so that there is uniform activity throughout, instead of excessive activity in some areas and little or no activity in others, the highest total productivity will result. This problem affects the relating of departments to each other as well as their design and equipment.

Fifth among the designer-variable factors is lighting. If there is proper light to attract the customers' attention and ample light of proper quality so that

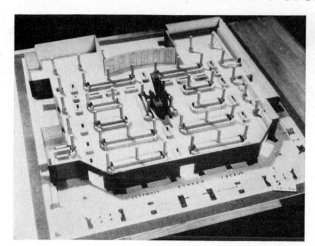

FIGURE 33.
WILLIAM H. BLOCK STORE,
INDIANAPOLIS, INDIANA.
MODEL

A characteristic arrangement of
the conventional rectangular type.

Courtesy Kenneth C. Welch

merchandise can be speedily appraised, productivity can be materially increased.

The sixth and last designer variable factor, possibly the most important of all, is the use of space in all the selling departments. In each case the space can be broken down into five functional areas, as follows: customer circulation; salesperson circulation; selling or selling-and-display facilities; stock or stock-and-display facilities, and sales-area servicing facilities.

FIVE SPACE-USE FUNCTIONS OF SELLING AREAS

It is important that each of the foregoing functions be carefully analyzed to handle a given amount of traffic and a given number of sales.

Customer Circulation. Customer circulation should be designed to channel natural traffic over as great an area as possible between entrances and known pulling points, such as interfloor transportation centers and some of the merchandise and service sections known as pullers (see Table II). Such a plan not only will expose most customers to the display of impulse goods but also, by more evenly distributing the traffic, will achieve a higher total space productivity.

The circulation arteries should be laid out in much the same way as modern highways are planned; a carefully considered number of lanes should be placed where the traffic is heaviest and then reduced proportionally at dead ends and cul-de-sacs. It is impossible to achieve this maximum utilization of the space and the elimination of bottlenecks by using the conventional grid pattern based on column spacing. (See Figs. 33, 37.)

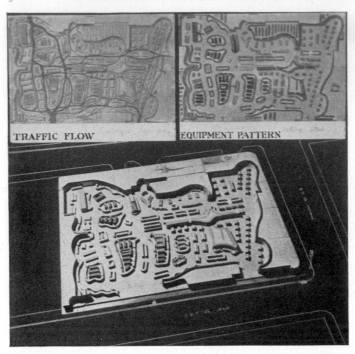

TRAFFIC FLOW   EQUIPMENT PATTERN

FIGURE 34. MACY'S, JAMAICA, NEW YORK. MODEL

Robert D. Kohn, architect; Richard G. Belcher, consultant; Daniel Schwartzman, interior architect; Kenneth C. Welch, interior consultant

A study model to show the newer type of free-flow circulation. Aisle width is determined by the amount of traffic.

Courtesy Kenneth C. Welch

A simple method for determining aisle width is to figure 18 inches for a person standing at a counter or show case and 22 inches per lane for customers in motion. For example, near an important entrance where the traffic might be initially channeled in one aisle, with selling counters on each side, six lanes might be required; this would call for an aisle 14'–0" in width. Or, a rather important aisle—with selling on either side requiring a total of 3'–0", plus 3'–8" for two lanes of traffic—would need to be 6'–8" wide. When an aisle is narrowed down to 4 or 5 feet the space will be relatively non-productive, for obviously in a 3½- or 4-foot aisle there is room for only one person to stop to examine merchandise and for one person to pass.

If customer circulation is properly designed, it flows freely from one point to another and does not follow the zigzag pattern of the old grid type. It is often possible to create rotary traffic, thus eliminating the usual bottlenecks at congested aisle intersections. In a carefully planned traffic circulation the total area necessary may show a decrease of as much as 10 to 15 per cent under that of the traditional plan, and better flow of traffic with a minimum of congestion will result.

Salesperson Circulation. Although this is combined with the customers' circulation in such sections as outer garments and furniture, it should be

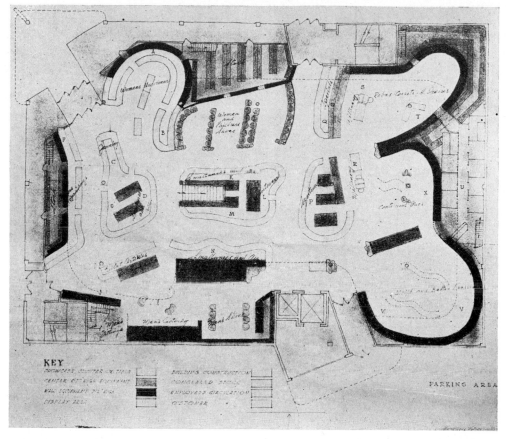

FIGURE 35. SMITH, BRIDGMAN COMPANY, MIDLAND, MICHIGAN. PART PLAN
Grand Rapids Store Equipment Company, interior designers
Selling areas arranged to give easy circulation and maximum storage and display.

Courtesy Kenneth C. Welch

separated in accessory and small-wares departments. Selling tables can be properly serviced only in inactive areas. Heretofore not enough salesperson movability has been provided. In modern layouts a greater area is allotted to this function in order to eliminate unnecessary steps between the selling display point and the forward stock and service stations. Proper planning will also improve flexibility. For example, in some of the free-shape islands (see the Macy plan, Fig. 37), with ample salesperson cross aisles, all the stock is easily accessible from any point on the peripheral selling counters. These islands are large enough to house several departments, so that any part of the stock is usable by any of the departments concerned.

FIGURE 36. LASALLE & KOCH, TIFFIN, OHIO. TWO PLANS AND VERTICAL SECTION

Bellman, Gillett & Richards, architects and engineers; Lynn Troxel, associate architect; J. G. R. Porter, consultant

A rationalized distribution of selling and service areas in a two-story store.

Courtesy Kenneth C. Welch

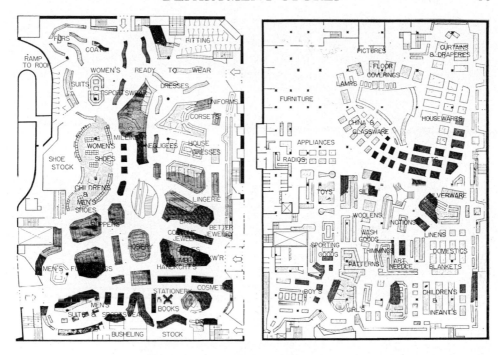

50-75% IMPULSE   25-50% IMPULSE
25-50% DEMAND   50-75% DEMAND   OVER 75% DEMAND

FIGURE 37. MACY'S, JAMAICA, NEW YORK. PLANS

Robert D. Kohn, architect; Richard G. Belcher, consultant; Daniel Schwartzman, interior architect; Kenneth C. Welch, interior consultant

The final plan arrangements of a large branch department store; note the careful attention to circulation and the relation of service and storage areas to selling facilities.

Courtesy Kenneth C. Welch

Selling or Selling-and-Display Facilities. Various criteria are used in determining the size of selling facilities. In small wares and accessories sold over the counter, the lineal feet of counter and show case can be the measurement. In the case of impulse goods, where display is necessary, and also in any section where an opportunity for "pre-sale selection" by the customer is desirable, as with handbags, a greater amount of lineal footage is allotted per salesperson than in the type of section where total display in relation to stock is unimportant, as with gloves. In shoe departments it is the number of shoe chairs required to handle a peak that controls, in the dress department it is the open

FIGURE 38. MACY'S,
JAMAICA, NEW YORK.
TWO EXTERIORS

Robert D. Kohn, architect; Richard G. Belcher, consultant; Daniel Schwartzman, interior architect; Kenneth C. Welch, interior consultant

Branch department stores need less show-window space than the parent urban shops; in-broken wall spaces and dramatized entrances are therefore possible.

Courtesy R. H. Macy Co.

floor area and number of fitting rooms, and so on. The selling equipment in some departments is also the entire stock-carrying medium, and in most small-wares sections it is part of the stock-carrying equipment.

Stock or Stock-and-Display Facilities. The amount of stock-carrying equipment and its disposition depend on the necessity for and the importance of display. It is vitally important, however, that there be ample stock capacity and that it be properly proportioned to the selling facilities. With the traditional patterns of the past, the selling facilities were often too great in relation to the stock space. For example, the typical men's furnishings department in July often had as much as 80 or 100 feet of counter per economic salesperson. Ade-

FIGURE 39. MACY'S, WHITE PLAINS, NEW YORK. INTERIOR AT ENTRANCE

Voorhees, Walker, Foley & Smith, architects; Ketchum, Giná & Sharp, interior architects

A welcoming informality. Photograph Rudolph Edward Leppert, Jr.

quate coverage of this area was impossible, and a loss of potential profits resulted, not only because of waste in area but also because of the excessive number of salespeople required.[8]

Merchandise should be as plainly visible as possible not only to display it to the customers but also to assist the salespeople in learning their stock. With free planning methods and a careful consideration of important vistas, more high equipment than is customary can be used without destroying visibility. The criterion of the stock facilities required is based on an analysis of merchandising policy, and this information can come only from the merchandise division direct. In branch department stores with ample parking, greater provision should be made for certain forward stock because of the increased "take with" purchases.

Sales-Area Servicing Facilities. Sales-servicing facilities are those necessary for completing the sale—making change, wrapping, authorizing charges, and kindred matters. Cash was formerly handled from central desks; uniformed cash girls or boys summoned by the salesperson's cry of "Cash!" carried the payments and change. Gradually this process was mechanized, first with cable conveyors and later with tube systems, cash registers, and charge telephones. The cash register is becoming an increasingly efficient business machine which, with the many records it keeps, saves auditing, time, and effort.

Sales transactions are of several kinds:

[8] "Adequate coverage" as used here means that there are enough salespersons to wait on customers properly and to prevent pilfering by kleptomaniacs and professional shoplifters.

1. Cash   (a) Take with
            (b) Send
2. Charge   (a) Take with
            (b) Send
                (1) To same address as charge account
                (2) To another address
3. C.O.D.

The servicing of an active sales section can best take place at strategically located desks; an analysis of transactions by departments in relation to traffic and other facilities determines the locations. There are two basic systems. The first, called "clerk wrap," is often used in an active low-average-sale department; here the salesperson makes the change (in a cash sale), places the merchandise in a paper bag or otherwise wraps it, and delivers it direct to the customer. The second provides maximum protection and is called the "inspection wrap–cashier" system. This system is well adapted for use in individual shops or certain departments, such as men's furnishings. It requires a large desk, where as many as three wrappers may work during peak hours, and often a space for a separate cashier. Sometimes supplementary desks are established during December. Various combinations of these two systems are possible; the store, however, will have a definite policy of which the designer must be aware if he is to plan intelligently.

Cash sales can be handled by a cash register, by a cashier with either a cash drawer or a cash register, or by pneumatic tube to a central desk.

Charge authorizations for "charge takes" are handled in one of three ways: (1) by the floor or section manager, (2) through identification cards or plates, or (3) by telephone or pneumatic tube to the credit department. If the sale is a "charge send" the customer need not wait for authorization [9] and the merchandise is either wrapped immediately at a selling service desk and sent to delivery or put in a canvas bag unwrapped and sent to a central packing desk and then to delivery; in both cases the merchandise may be put in hampers, which are regularly collected, or be placed on a mechanical conveyor, which delivers it to a central desk or to the primary delivery station. The conveyor, generally attached to the basement ceiling, is economically justifiable only in the most active stores. Spiral chutes that feed the delivery station from the upper floors are standard in all multiple-level department stores. Refuse and paper chutes are often located close to the package chutes.

---

[9] Since unfortunately this scheme often tends to increase the expense of delivery service, it is well to provide all possible facilities and service to speed up charge authorization.

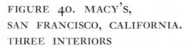

FIGURE 40. MACY'S,
SAN FRANCISCO, CALIFORNIA.
THREE INTERIORS

W. P. Day, store architect; Curt
Helmstaedter, interior architect

Modern store fixtures combine
storage, service, and selling portions with a maximum opportunity
for display.

Courtesy R. H. Macy Co.

Selling-service facilities should provide space for the wrapping supplies and
the necessary equipment, and their location in relation to the four sales facilities already mentioned is vitally important. When there is a high percentage
of "take with" sales and a desk with a wrapping clerk is in order, it is often
best to place this desk so that the customers can wait for the wrapper to hand
them their wrapped packages direct. In the past, as a rule, insufficient space
has been devoted to service desks.

Gift wrapping is becoming increasingly important. Sometimes supplies for
this special service are kept in a department desk; frequently, however, gift
wrapping is a separate and featured department, especially in December, in
which case the customer generally takes the merchandise there to be wrapped.

ADDITIONAL SALES SERVICES

Service sections such as the delivery department or the returned goods department can be broken down into two categories: those not requiring cus-

FIGURE 41.

LASALLE & KOCH,

TIFFIN, OHIO.

TWO INTERIORS

Bellman, Gillett & Richards, architects and engineers; Lynn Troxel, associate architect; J. G. R. Porter, consultant

Greater informality designed to increase the sales appeal.

Photographs Photo Service, courtesy Kenneth C. Welch

tomer contact, and those requiring it. Departments of this kind which require direct contact with the customer must be placed on floors serviced by the main interfloor transportation system; frequently they can be placed on selling floors which are comparatively inactive.

Delivery. Delivery service has often represented 2 per cent on the total net sales. It is still an expensive service for the large store located in a congested center, but in some recentralized branches—especially those with adequate and convenient parking—delivery costs have been reduced by as much as 60 per cent or more. As cities spread, the delivery problem becomes more difficult. There are two common-sense solutions of this problem: first, a greater use of

FIGURE 42. HERPOLSHEIMER'S,
GRAND RAPIDS, MICHIGAN.
TWO EXTERIORS

Perry, Shaw & Hepburn, architects

Large blank walls, impressive entrances, and small but well-designed show windows distinguish many department stores.   Photographs Kenneth C. Welch

a co-operative delivery system, which serves many stores; and, second, a greater use of parcel post. Despite the prestige value to the individual store of having its name on hundreds of vehicles, these expense-saving practices are being competitively forced on most large stores. The management will generally have a preferred delivery system, for which the architect has only to make the most efficient plan. In branch stores, pick-up stations (accessible to the parking area) for wrapped packages can save delivery costs.

   Returned Goods and Adjustments. This service involves a heavy expense which stores are trying to reduce; in some cases the value of the returned goods exceeds 10 per cent of the gross sales. The adjustment department nevertheless is important in creating and maintaining good will. Often salespersons as well as section managers can make adjustments. Sometimes, however, all complaints are sent to a bureau of adjustment, which usually is located adjacent to the public-contact offices; it should be easily accessible, have a restful environment, and be well furnished and well lighted. In the larger stores most complaints are handled by such a bureau at special counters which are often divided by acoustical baffles into sections each accommodating only one customer.

   Telephone Orders. Telephone orders are a form of department store selling. Large stores have extensive and complicated special switchboards with trained saleswomen as operators. The orders received are generally for staple merchandise; but the operators are also trained to sell advertised style merchandise, samples of which are displayed in the telephone order room for the operators to inspect.

Mail Orders. The importance of this department varies. Some stores issue mail-order catalogues, which are sent out seasonally to customers on the mailing list. If such is the case, the department maintains its own list, and space for an addressograph and similar equipment is necessary.

Will-Call or Lay-Away Orders. This department provides counter space, accessible to the storage stock room, for "will call" packages. Often customers pay for part of a more expensive style item and have it "laid away" for a certain period until they can make full payment; in popular-priced stores such storage requires a considerable area. It should be convenient to the point of final payment, which generally is at the cashier's desk but may be in a space specifically allotted to the purpose.

Final Fittings. Many stores provide a separate department, convenient to the will-call and the alteration department, where customers may return later and try on altered garments. It consists of a waiting room, a receptionist's desk, and the required number of fitting rooms.

Fur Storage, Alteration, and Cleaning. A receiving and delivery desk for fur service must be provided. Generally special desks are set up in the spring, sometimes on the main floor, for taking storage orders for fur garments, but for such business at other times there should also be a regular place close to the workrooms for fur cleaning and alterations if these are on the premises. Cold-storage space, with its expensive equipment and comparative inflexibility, is being superseded by gas vaults, which are claimed to give even better protection.

Rest Rooms and Toilets. A combined lounging and writing room, with lavatories and toilets, is usually provided for women's use, at a central point not too accessible from the street; sometimes as many as 8 per cent of the women entering a store will take advantage of the facilities. They can be located to act as a semi-puller, but these women are not always in a buying mood, and consequently care must be taken that the traffic passes on the periphery of a selling area and not through it. In large stores, in addition to a main rest room, several customers' toilets for both sexes should be furnished, dispersed according to traffic activity in order to save interfloor transportation.

Public Telephones. Public pay stations should be conveniently placed on upper floors, especially in connection with the rest rooms but in areas least valuable for selling.

Auditorium. An auditorium, so located that it can be used for sales-space expansion, is desirable. In December this area can be utilized for the expansion of the toy department, but at other times it provides a place for fashion and home-furnishing demonstrations, exhibitions, and employees' social affairs and meetings; on occasion, to foster good will, it can be lent to women's groups for certain activities. The best location for it is one convenient to the public restaurant, if there is one.

Information desks and facilities, centrally located or convenient to the main entrance, are necessary. Modern combined public-address systems and customer information service can be provided at conveniently located stations throughout the store.

Post-office substations, check rooms, supervised children's playrooms or nurseries, theater-ticket sales booths, and travel bureaus (the last often located near the luggage department) are some of the free facilities and services many large stores offer.

PERSONNEL DEPARTMENT

Happy, satisfied workers are one of the department store's greatest assets—especially the 50 to 70 per cent of the employees who comprise the sales force, because this group constitutes the store's all-important human contact with the public. Areas that contribute to their physical well-being—the rest rooms, recreational areas, eating places, locker rooms, and health and hospital sections—must therefore be carefully considered. Such facilities provide the large store with one of its marked advantages over the smaller store.

Employees' Toilets. In addition to the employees' central rest rooms, toilets for employees should be easily accessible from every selling floor. One scheme is to place toilets for men and for women on alternate stair landings between floors. This scheme assures a minimum of stair climbing from any sales floor, keeps the toilets in one stack, and simplifies maintenance.

Locker Rooms. Lockers also must be supplied for employees. Policies vary as to whether the location of time clocks and lockers should be centralized or dispersed. In the latter case it is wise to place them in a well-traveled passage, either between sales floors and toilets or in other much frequented service areas. In large stores checking rooms for employees' packages are usually provided; often in addition there are check rooms for extra peak-time employees.

Detectives' Space. Space must be provided where store detectives may interview shoplifters, keep their records, and so forth. It should be close to an

FIGURE 43. MACY'S, WHITE PLAINS, NEW YORK. EXTERIOR
Voorhees, Walker, Foley & Smith, architects; Ketchum, Giná & Sharp, interior architects
A suburban store depending largely on automobile patronage.   Courtesy R. H. Macy Co.

elevator bank and preferably on a mezzanine or upper floor or in the basement.

OFFICES

Most department stores sell on credit. The *credit department* is important architecturally because this is often the customer's first contact with the store office and a suitable atmosphere is desirable. A saving of space, as well as of time, has been effected in this department through the cycle method of billing, by which statements are staggered alphabetically throughout the entire month. Installment buying, prevalent in furniture and home-furnishings sections or stores, sometimes requires special office facilities.

The *accounts-receivable department*, which often employs half of the labor force in the accounting department, should be accessible or close to the reception space for new accounts and to the credit-authorization department. It is not necessarily, however, under the authority of the credit manager.

The *bookkeeping* or *accounting department*, not being a customer-contact section, can be separated from the credit and accounts-receivable departments if necessary.

A *cashier's desk* or *counter*, where customers can pay accounts, cash checks, and so on, may be under the supervision of the general accounting department, but if that is on a non-customer-contact floor it may be contiguous to the accounts-receivable department.

The *sales-auditing department* handles all sales accounting except accounts receivable, and it analyzes all sales. The *accounts-payable department* deals with vendors' invoices and the like. The *statistical department* compiles and issues reports on operating data, sales, stocks, and so forth. The *paymaster* keeps all pay-roll records and dispenses checks or cash to employees. Most large stores which handle large sums of cash in this section take special protective precautions.

The *advertising department* in a large store will consist of a publicity manager and under him an advertising manager and a display manager. Copywriters and artists work under the advertising manager; their offices should be convenient both to the executive offices and, because of frequent contact with the sales departments, to the interfloor transportation system. The display manager, who has sign writers, workshops, and display-fixture storage under his supervision, may be more remotely located; straight-line access with large doors is desirable between these facilities and the display windows.

DESIGN DETAILS

OFFICES

Office standards vary. Before designing a related group of offices, the architect should get detailed individual space and equipment requirements from each department head. In his plan he should make allowances for some future expansion, and flexibility in the design of any section of a department is essential to attain and maintain the maximum efficiency and productivity of both space and personnel. The location of the various offices depends on the type of contact for which each is required—customer, public, or internal. Table I indicates these contacts in detail. Equally important is the relation of the offices to one another, and on this relationship the management will have definite ideas. For example, some large stores prefer to have the buyers' offices grouped together, off the sales floor and in close contact with the divisional merchandise manager, the sample rooms, and their own stenographic and clerical staff. The policy of other stores is to have the buyers' offices on the sales floors so that contact between buyers and customers can be more fre-

quent. Carefully planned relationships between the various offices and between them and other parts of the structure are vital in creating easy communication between personnel, in eliminating waste motion, and in facilitating the movement of goods.

SELLING DEPARTMENTS

Sometimes it is desirable for the architect to work directly with the buyers. Since merchandise managers and buyers have a complete statistical picture of their departments—including expense ratios, number of transactions, and sales per square foot—and usually have an intelligent understanding of these figures, they will be sympathetic to an approach to planning which is based on such factual data. And good store buyers today know and appreciate good design.

It is vitally important that the environment—the "selling climate," so to speak—be in keeping with the taste displayed in the merchandise. Occasionally a chain store, catering largely on a price basis, must have flashy merchandise to cover up mediocre values. In this event a flashy environment may be justified, but it is also possible that an environment in better taste might compensate somewhat for the garishness of the merchandise. When the merchandise is in good taste, naturally the environment must harmonize. A simple contemporary environment is best for the display and sale of contemporary merchandise.

In the large store, when any section or department—for example, one devoted to women's and misses' dresses—reaches an area in excess of 10,000 to

15,000 square feet, it should be broken down into separate divisions, generally according to price lines. Separate shop effects can be created for these divisions, and each shop can be given an identifying name—"Little Shop," "Forecast," and the like. Care must be taken, however, not to create too many small cul-de-sacs with poor visibility from one to another, because this makes supervision and adequate coverage difficult and thus increases operating costs. There is a marked trend today toward providing space for so-called *ensemble selling*, especially in home furnishings. Model rooms which display correlated furniture, draperies, floor coverings, linens, lamps, pictures, and even china and glassware are increasingly successful from a sales standpoint.

Location. A number of important elements determine the location of departments. If a store sells on many floors instead of a few, numerous impulse lines must be placed on upper floors, and locations near demand sections and other pullers must be relied on to create the traffic which will aid their success. It is manifestly a disadvantage to have to sell on many floors: the cost involved in transporting people vertically is great; there is the lack of flexibility, with consequent reduction in total productivity; supervision becomes more complicated; the fact that naturally related departments cannot be assembled on one level limits related selling; and costly services are of necessity split up and spread over several floors.

Flexibility. It is obvious that certain related merchandise should be placed together. Thus it is desirable to have all intimate wear together—underwear, negligees, and corsets. It must be noted, however, that negligees and, to a great extent, silk and muslin underwear are December peak sections; if ample space is provided for them at that time, it is possible to contract it at other times to allow for an expansion in house dresses or other apparel sections.

Another example of interchange of space to increase productivity is in the men's furnishings and clothing departments; in the spring and fall it is possible to contract men's furnishings in order to provide additional selling and display space for men's clothing during its two peak seasons. To do this, however, they must be on the same floor or on adjacent levels, with complete visibility between them.

Related Selling. So-called related selling may increase productivity. If, for example, the hat department is easily visible from the men's clothing section, the sale of a hat may be suggested after the purchase of a coat. The same principle applies to breakable goods, such as chinaware, gifts, and lamps; moreover, if these can be located on the same level with their stock and packing areas, breakage and other expenses can be reduced. Many similar relationships exist, and

FIGURE 45. OHRBACH'S,
LOS ANGELES, CALIFORNIA.
EXTERIOR

Wurdeman & Becket, architects

A characteristic example of a modern clothing shop.

Courtesy Kenneth C. Welch

FIGURE 46. MACY'S,
KANSAS CITY, MISSOURI.
EXTERIOR

Kivett & Meyers, store architects; Kivett & Meyers, Gruen & Krummeck, and Daniel Schwartzman, interior architects; Charles F. Orean, consulting architect for interiors of first and basement floors.

A large unbroken upper wall dramatized.   Courtesy R. H. Macy Co.

the merchandise department can help the designer anticipate and plan for them.

The logical relation of some of the miscellaneous departments is fluid. For example, art needlework can be placed near the fabrics, a section which today generally includes the dressmaking part of the notion department; or it can be adjacent to the gift shop, which is another department in this miscellaneous group.

Toys, games, sporting goods, and cameras are sometimes placed next to men's and boys' sections for the atmosphere they lend and because of obvious selling connections. In this case the toys would have to be moved in December, when they need greatly increased space. Luggage can also have varying locations. Sometimes it is placed with home furnishings because of administrative requirements, but it also might well be related to apparel, since traveling and new clothing are more closely associated than are baggage and home furnishings. Some typical groupings are shown in Table II.

INTERFLOOR CIRCULATION

Although the area [10] required by interfloor transportation in multiple-level stores may not consume over 5 per cent of the total gross area, the location of both passenger and freight facilities is extremely important. One reason for this is that such transportation is permanently fixed, whereas entrances and the selling areas can be flexible.

Freight and Service Circulation. The circulation of goods from the time of their delivery to the marking and stock rooms has already been traced. The location of the freight elevators, the dumb-waiters, and even the spiral chutes should be as close to the selling area as possible so that heavy merchandise, such as floor coverings, need not be moved great distances or through other sales areas. It is also important to see that this traffic does not cross or unduly interfere with customer traffic; often in very large stores employees' interfloor transportation should be segregated from customer traffic.

Customer Circulation. Customers' transportation is a major consideration, especially in stores selling to the mass market; it must make for seeming convenience to the customer and at the same time evenly and thoroughly distribute the traffic throughout the entire selling space. The type of interfloor transportation selected and its location in relation to entrances, stairways, and selling areas play the same part in the effective distribution of store-wide traffic as the customers' aisles previously discussed. Both elevators and escalators are essential in department stores today. Even with modern signal-control equipment the capacities of elevators, although they remain fairly constant (elevator manufacturers can furnish detailed figures), are limited; escalators, on the other hand, allow a continuous flow of traffic, eliminate waiting, and, when properly located, permit interesting views of the store. Escalators are the most efficient way to transport great numbers of people. The wider ones carry 8,000 persons per hour and require no attendants; when a store reaches such a size that it needs to take people off the main floor at anything approaching this rate, the expense of installing escalators is justified. They should be supplemented with elevators, however, especially if the store is over five stories in height, not only because with both types of transportation available the elevators can act efficiently as expresses to the upper floors and in addition can serve service areas above the top selling floor, but also because certain custom-

---

[10] This should include the contiguous circulation space necessary to serve the transportation; for example, 6 feet in front of elevators should be included.

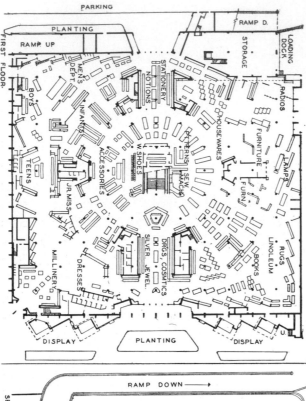

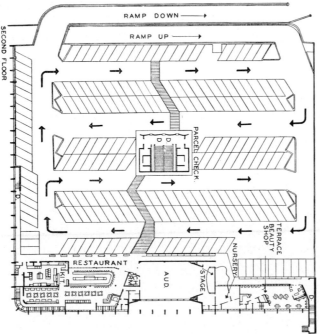

FIGURE 47. MILLIRON'S
DEPARTMENT STORE,
LOS ANGELES, CALIFORNIA.
TWO PLANS

Gruen & Krummeck, architects

Parking areas on the site as well
as on the roof of the building
show the basic importance of
the automobile trade to the
success of shops in many parts
of the United States. Here the
necessity of providing parking
space served as an important
generating idea in the entire
concept.

ers will not or cannot use escalators. In suburban stores catering to the "baby carriage trade," elevators become relatively more important than escalators. The best location for escalators is in the center of the store and convenient to the more important entrances; to promote their maximum use they should be more conveniently placed than the elevators. It is vitally important to consider the interfloor transportation from the standpoint of the upper floors and the main floor as well as in relation to the entrances; people must be brought as close to the center of all the large selling areas as possible.

SHOW WINDOWS

Show windows are not only an important architectural motif but also an important publicity medium. Their publicity value varies with the quantity of the traffic and with the ratio of the entering to the passing-by traffic. Since several traffic counts have shown that as many as 90 per cent of the women who pass a store enter it, it is evident that, if the traffic is heavy, interior displays at the point of sale can be more useful than a display window on the street. To prestige stores in locations with heavy pedestrian traffic, however, display windows are valuable in attracting doubtful shoppers and their cost can be justified on this score.

In suburban branches where adequate parking is provided and a majority of the customers use private automobiles for transportation, a well-designed and convenient circulation scheme will make display windows less important. Here, therefore, initial as well as maintenance cost can be reduced by including only a few exterior display areas and locating these with care. Blank wall spaces enhanced by skillful planting can lend an interesting suburban atmosphere. This is a place, too, where the "open front" that permits a view into the store can be of value.

It must be remembered, however, that in all stores reflections on the window glass can be so bad in the daytime that the value of the display is almost lost. Most shallow display windows with backgrounds are actually daylighted, but the open-front store with its interior as the window background presents a more difficult problem. To find the answer the architect must analyze the surrounding exterior brightnesses and so dispose the glass that it reflects, from normal viewpoints, areas that are in shade, including areas that can be controlled because they are a part of the structure.[11]

[11] For a more detailed discussion of this problem and its possible solution, see the *Architectural Record*, July, 1946, p. 107.

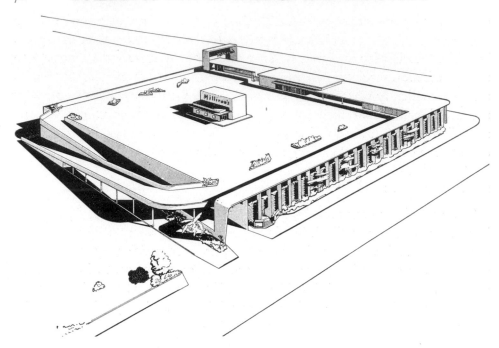

FIGURE 48. MILLIRON'S DEPARTMENT STORE, LOS ANGELES, CALIFORNIA. PERSPECTIVE

Gruen & Krummeck, architects

EXTERIOR DESIGN

Much latitude in exterior design is allowed the architect today since to a great degree it is possible to eliminate the necessity for daylighting the upper-floor areas. As a result, emphasis can be placed on the display windows, the entrances, and the store name and other exterior publicity. The large department store—which may occupy an entire block—creates at an important scale a simple total effect which has an advantage over the typical confusion produced by a row of small independently designed shops.

If a store has great pulling power, it is sometimes advisable to devote some space within the building lines to additional exterior pedestrian ways, a scheme which helps eliminate the window reflections previously discussed. In any event a covered sidewalk, either within the building line or outside it with a projecting canopy, has a number of advantages. It encourages shopping in inclement weather by protecting the pedestrian, it often eliminates the nuisance of a canvas awning, and from the design viewpoint it produces the desirable effect of bringing the store interior out into the street. Moreover, it tends to focus the passers' attention on the window display by screening the upper part of the store façade as well as adjacent hanging signs and other distractions. Of course both initial expenditure and the minimum maintenance cost must be considered, but if a covered walk is well proportioned and is designed with discrimination in the choice of materials and their appropriate use, the true smartness thus attained will justify the expense and eliminate any visual conflict with advertising signs above.

INTERIOR DESIGN

In any store, and especially in one with smart-looking merchandise, it is basic that the merchandise itself be the main decorative interest and that the interior be designed primarily as a background for it. All the ingenuity of the designer must be called into play, not only in the use of related materials and colors but also in the planning of the most effective illumination. It is seldom that an over-decorated interior can be justified, because even in departments with concealed stock—such as higher-priced apparel—when the merchandise is brought out to be shown it is more effectively displayed against a simple background.

INTERIOR LIGHTING

Modern illuminating-and-brightness engineering is playing an increasingly important role in interior store design. Good store design stresses quality in lighting, taking an ample quantity of illumination for granted. The designer cannot control the reflection factor of the merchandise, but he can regulate that of its immediate surroundings and the total environment.

There are three main factors in interior lighting: the brightness of the merchandise itself, which is the most important; that of its immediate surroundings; and that of the other architectural surfaces, including floors, walls, and ceilings. The first function of store lighting is to attract attention to the merchandise by giving it or its immediate surroundings the highest relative brightness; this theory of attracting attention through brightness has been completely accepted. Second, it should supply a sufficient quantity and quality of brightness for the customer to appraise the merchandise quickly and correctly. Since the location factors and surface characteristics vary considerably, the lighting must be flexible and susceptible of variation.

FIGURE 49.
MILLIRON'S
DEPARTMENT STORE,
LOS ANGELES,
CALIFORNIA.
THREE EXTERIORS

Gruen & Krummeck, architects

The exterior dramatizes the construction; the roof entrance from the parking area is made as interesting and inviting as the street-floor entrances.

Photographs Julius Shulman, courtesy Gruen & Krummeck

Quality in lighting has two important aspects. The first is the directional quality of the lighting. Most merchandise has form, texture, and color. To display it to advantage both directional and diffused light are desirable—the directional to create highlights and shadows in order to bring out the form and texture, the diffused to illuminate the detail in the shadows and prevent too great a brightness contrast. Diffused lighting can well come from the brightnesses that are created on the architectural surfaces, which, as already stated, are intended primarily for the enhancement of the merchandise.[12]

The second aspect is the color quality of the lighting. Two important light sources are available—incandescent and fluorescent—and both should be used. The warm, directional, more easily controlled light from the incandescent lamp combines naturally with the cooler, diffused light from the fluorescent lamp; when properly distributed, together they produce the best possible effect on most merchandise.

TRENDS

With increasing urbanization, a continuing decrease of population in the metropolitan centers, and an increase of population in the suburbs, the large city department store must of necessity have branches to serve the changing population. Because in many suburban residential areas the automobile is practically the only means of transportation, such branches should be so located that they are served by ample traffic arteries and that they have ample parking space for handling normal seasonal peaks. Further, since department stores are premised on the idea of ample stocks and wide selections under one roof they must produce enough sales to warrant carrying such reserves. This means that branches designed today must be larger than most branches were before the Second World War; they should produce not less than $5,000,000 annually in volume, as based on 1946 economic conditions. It is desirable, too, that there be neighboring constructive competition, because such competition is fundamental in the selling of fashion apparel and home furnishings; the consumer insists on making a comparison of style and values. Also, through this combined pulling power it is possible to create a concentration of consumers in a buying mood. To achieve both these conditions, the location should not be on existing main streets, which can never be satisfactorily reconstructed.[13]

---

[12] For a more detailed discussion of store lighting, see the author's "New Concepts in Store Lighting," *Architectural Record*, Aug., 1946.

[13] These points are illustrated in "Shopping Center for Suburban Boston, The North Shore Center," *Architectural Forum*, June, 1947. See also *Architectural Forum*, August, 1950; *Architectural Record*, March, 1951.

FIGURE 50. MILLIRON'S DEPARTMENT STORE, LOS ANGELES, CALIFORNIA. INTERIOR

Gruen & Krummeck, architects

Openness of feeling controls the interior design.

Photograph Julius Shulman, courtesy Gruen & Krummeck

In the smaller city the department store has similar problems, complicated by transportation difficulties. Here it behooves the store owner to lend aggressive support to his local city planning agency, for this agency can best co-ordinate the thoroughfares and parking terminals so necessary to relieve the current congestion. It is certain, however, that in the future the large city will have few big department stores. Instead, to care for expansion, branches will be built in the outlying areas, near the suburbs and easily reached from the small villages within a trading radius of thirty to forty-five minutes' travel. If that is done constructively, it will help make this kind of shopping infinitely more convenient and at the same time it will lower the distribution costs.

SUGGESTED ADDITIONAL READING FOR CHAPTER 28

Brisco, Norris A., *Retailing*, 2d ed. (New York: Prentice Hall, 1947).
Golden Book of the Year, 1861–1911, Wanamaker Stores . . . Jubilee [Philadelphia: c1911–19].

Hower, Ralph M., *History of Macy's of New York, 1858–1919* (Cambridge, Mass.: Harvard University Press, 1943).

Ketchum, Morris, Jr., *Shops and Stores* (New York: Reinhold, 1948).

National Retail Dry Goods Association, Controllers' Congress, *Departmental Merchandise and Operating Results of Department Stores and Specialty Stores, 1943–1946* (New York: the Association, 1944–47).

Operating Results of Department and Specialty Stores in 1944–1945 (Cambridge, Mass.: Harvard University, Graduate School of Business, Division of Research [1946]).

PERIODICALS

"Department Store, Garage, and Warehouse, Houston, Texas," Raymond Loewy, architect, *Architectural Forum*, Vol. 86 (1947), April, pp. 106–9; *Progressive Architecture*, Vol. 29 (1948), July, pp. 49–59.

"Department Stores," Building Types Study No. 95, *Architectural Record*, Vol. 96 (1944), November, pp. 90–110.

Desmond, H., "Schlesinger & Mayer Building," Louis H. Sullivan, architect, *Architectural Record*, Vol. 16 (1904), July, pp. 53–60.

"Five Stores for Sears-Roebuck," Nimmons, Carr & Wright, architects, *Architectural Record*, Vol. 88 (1940), September, pp. 32–42.

"40 Stores," *Architectural Forum*, Vol. 88 (1948), May, pp. 93–144.

Owings, N. A., "Economics of Department Store Planning," *Architectural Record*, Vol. 101 (1947), February, pp. 87–91.

Parnes, Louis, "Intermediate Floors for Greater Efficiency . . ." *Architectural Record*, Vol. 101 (1947), February, pp. 95–97.

Welch, Kenneth C., "Lighting and Brightness for Selling," *Illuminating Engineering*, Vol. 41 (1946), May, pp. 386–418.

—— "New Concepts in Store Lighting," *Architectural Record*, Vol. 100 (1946), August, pp. 117–20.

—— "Reflection Factors in Store Windows," *Architectural Record*, Vol. 100 (1946), July, pp. 107–10.

"World's New 32-Acre Apparel City," *Architect and Engineer*, Vol. 163 (1945), December, pp. 18–23, 38, 42.

29

Small Shops

By MORRIS KETCHUM, JR.

THE SOLE FUNCTION of a small shop is to sell either merchandise or service (in a few types both). Of the bewildering variety of small shops on Main Street, the majority are basically organized as specialty shops. Their sales methods, planning and equipment, and adaptation to the shopping environment around them are the factors which set their final form and character.

A *specialty shop* is one that sells a single type of merchandise or provides a specialized type of service. Sometimes the merchandise is low-priced and marketed to a volume trade; sometimes it is more expensive and sold to an exclusive clientele. In either case, specialty shops depend on concentrated sales appeal and individual attention to each customer.

There were specialty shops in ancient Greece and Rome, along the narrow twisted streets of medieval cities, and on the public squares of Renaissance England and the Continent. (See, for Roman examples, Figs. 51, 52.) These city shops were generally near the market places which they supplemented but never completely supplanted. For the merchant-craftsman it was better to have an enclosed and protected shelter in which to live, to work, and to sell than to depend upon casual rights to a few square feet under an open sky, in a tent, or even in a booth.

Today's customers would find themselves at home in almost any of those Old World shops. During the Renaissance and later, store fronts and sales floors were much the same as those of the twentieth century. Sometimes the fronts were completely open to the weather during business hours; sometimes they were closed, with a sign, a door, and perhaps a small show window. The choice depended on whether the purpose was a mass display of popularly priced goods or a small display of high-priced luxury merchandise.

The sales spaces as well as the counters and the storage cabinets were also similar to those of a modern shop. Sales methods and equipment varied with

FIGURE 51. RESTORATION OF A ROMAN SHOP FROM POMPEII, ITALY

From a drawing by Friedrich in von Falke, *Hellas und Rom . . .*

FIGURE 52. ROMAN DRINK STAND, OSTIA, ITALY

A Roman "soda fountain"; hot and cold drinks were sold over a counter gay with colored marbles. Photograph Leopold Arnaud

the trade involved. Superficially the differences between the shops today and those built before the early nineteenth century lie in the different structural methods, materials, and equipment which each century and each civilization developed. The fundamental differences in character are found behind the scenes.

Yesterday's handicraft shops were combined factories, homes, and salesrooms. Each merchant manufactured on the premises the goods he later sold,

and he usually lived behind or above his shop. In our time the individual retailer, whether he owns his business or acts as store manager for a chain organization, is first and last a salesman—not a craftsman. The goods he sells may be
produced in a factory a thousand miles away, and the merchant himself may
live far from his shop. The sales floor in his store is not basically different from
that of an eighteenth-century shop, but concealed from view there are storage
spaces and packing rooms where incoming stock and outgoing merchandise
are handled.

The modern specialty shop is a product of the Industrial Revolution. The
same tremendous forces that changed our ways of living and working also
revolutionized our methods of buying and selling. The shops and stores on
our Main Streets and highways have been reshaped during the last hundred
years to fit new ways of buying and distributing mass-produced merchandise.
The small shop has been standardized, but even so it still relies for its commercial existence on the advantages inherent in personal service, intimate
shopping conditions, and an air of exclusiveness or individuality. It remains
a powerful rival to the variety stores, the department stores, and the mail-order
houses, all of which owe their existence to the new trading conditions produced
by the Industrial Revolution.

The Industrial Revolution also has provided the tools of contemporary store
design. The small-paned show windows of the handicraft age are now supplanted by single sheets of glass. The ancient open fronts, which had long
since disappeared because of the need for permanent protection, have been
revived through the use of glazed entrance walls, which eliminate the visual
barrier between store front and interior. Closed show-window backs, once
required for both insulation and fire protection, are now—thanks to efficient
heating systems and the invention of sprinklers—no longer needed except as
display props. Artificial illumination has revolutionized the art of display as
well as the lighting of both store front and interior and at the same time has
eliminated the need for outside windows as a light source. Finally a score of
new building materials—steel, aluminum, plywood, porcelain enamel, asbestos,
plastics—and new structural systems based on steel or reinforced concrete
have all helped to establish a fresh basis for store design.

These new building tools did not change store planning overnight; in fact,
it took a major economic catastrophe to overcome building habits that had
remained fixed for centuries. The depression that engulfed continental Europe
after 1918 and reached the United States in 1929 swept away the pompous

emporiums of the lush years. Till then, architects everywhere had disguised their shops as Italian palaces, Tudor cottages, or Georgian town halls. They were ashamed to admit that stores were sales machines or even that shops could exist as a valid type of architecture; to do so would have been almost as bad as "going into trade" themselves. Hence they stuffed the shops into low-ceilinged cubbyholes in some monumental eclectic building and left the detailed design and equipment to a building contractor. The day arrived, however, when merchants had not a penny to spare on ornamentation that would not help to keep merchandise moving. Then a new generation of architects—in the United States and abroad—began to design and build shops that really interpreted the functional needs of retailing. Today we have just begun to adapt ourselves to the requirements of and the opportunities in realistic store design.

The problem of the contemporary specialty shop is basically simple. Like any store, the specialty shop consists of an interior space where merchandise is displayed and sold, an area behind the scenes where store operations are conducted, and a store front that may be used for sidewalk advertising. The way in which these three elements are planned and interrelated will determine the success or failure of the shop.

GENERAL DESIGN FACTORS

SALES SPACE

The designer must start with the sales space—the point of contact between clerk and customer. The sales space is an arena where streams of moving traffic —customers, clerks, and merchandise—meet. The contact should be as well regulated as auto traffic along a parkway.

Merchandise locations must be carefully co-ordinated. All merchandise falls into one of three classifications—demand, convenience, or impulse.[1] *Demand* goods are best located farthest from the entrance, *convenience* goods midway, and *impulse* goods nearest to the entrance. Customer traffic will then move automatically from the entrance door to the shop's most remote sales department and be exposed to the maximum amount of merchandise on display. The various sales departments within each of the three basic sales groups should be located in friendly fashion. Ties and shirts, shoes and hosiery, hats and gloves should stand cheek by jowl along the shopping aisles. There is no better way

---

[1] For a more detailed treatment of this point see Chap. 28, "Department Stores."

to promote impulse sales, and without impulse sales every shop would soon be in bankruptcy.

If a small shop has more than one selling floor, the same fundamental planning principles should control merchandise locations and the flow of customer traffic. Impulse departments will take their natural place at the entrance level, convenience goods and services will be concentrated midway between the entrance level and the more distant sales floors, and demand departments will be placed on the most remote sales level. This arrangement promotes maximum customer traffic up or down through the store and assures each sales department its fair share of trade. A two-floor women's apparel shop, for example, will usually place its impulse merchandise—jewelry, cosmetics, handbags, and scarfs—near the shop entrance, its convenience departments such as hosiery, underwear, and negligees farther back, and its demand departments—sports wear, dresses, and coats and suits—on an upper or lower level.

By breaking down the merchandise in each sales department into impulse, convenience, and demand groups, each group can be properly located within the department. Such classification within sales departments enables customers to find with ease what they seek and at the same time keeps them aware of the impulse items carried in the department. It also helps merchants maintain a close check on profits or losses and simplifies the labor of stocking and displaying all merchandise.

TRAFFIC SPACE

Space for traffic should be as carefully organized as space for merchandise. Customer traffic must have room to move through the store; service traffic demands space for sales personnel and for moving merchandise in and out of the shop.[2] A blind attempt to squeeze the greatest amount of merchandise on the sales floor regardless of good shopping conditions is a sure way to kill trade. Employees should have enough room for selling operations and for servicing a sale. A clerk's aisle between fixtures should never be less than 1'–10" wide, and often in active departments as much as 2'–6". Every transaction on the sales floor must be serviced—if a cash sale, change must be made; if a charge, the charge must be approved. Merchandise must be wrapped and, unless taken by the customer, sent to the delivery department; therefore cash and wrap stands must be carefully located for maximum efficiency. Short, convenient routes from sales counter to cash and wrap stands and also from

[2] For a detailed discussion of aisle width, see Chap. 28, "Department Stores."

sales counters to reserve-stock areas help cut down the time spent on each sale.

SALES AND DISPLAY EQUIPMENT

Each sales department requires appropriate sales and display fixtures. *Sales fixtures* have three purposes: (1) they must store merchandise; (2) they must display all or part of that merchandise; and (3) they must protect merchandise from dust, excessive customer handling, accidental breakage, and spoilage. The size, shape, and character of the merchandise involved will logically determine the form and function of each sales fixture. The physical requirements imposed by the human figure will also influence their design. Sales personnel should not be expected to reach too high or stoop too low; this will limit the total height and depth of all sales fixtures.

Sales fixtures are a means to an end. If treated as fussy decorative pieces they defeat their own purpose and if adorned with too many surface moldings, cornices, or trims they become dust-catching nuisances. Instead, fixtures should be designed simply as functional sales equipment. They should be built of *appropriate materials* and be *durable* in withstanding wear and tear, *flexible* in use, and *economical* in initial and maintenance cost.

Displays are an important stimulus to impulse sales. From a distance they serve to identify the various sales divisions; close at hand they add glamour and interest to the goods. A woman's dress is far more effective on a display mannequin than it is hanging on a rack. Furniture pieces when shown in a model room have more sales appeal than when arranged in endless rows on the sales floor. Displays also add to the drama of shopping. A good show at the store front should always be supplemented by a series of strategically located displays on the sales floor, so that the buying impulse does not die at the entrance door.

Some shops and sales departments need sales furniture, fitting rooms, and other conveniences. *Furniture* for sales use has different requirements from that for household use. First of all, it must be far more durable; the construction should therefore be extra strong and the upholstery tough and easy to clean. Second, sales furniture should not be too comfortable; it is intended to ease a customer's waiting time, not for lounging. *Fitting rooms* are a necessary adjunct to any clothing department, except small children's clothing departments; they vary from small, one-person cubicles to luxurious private salesrooms large enough for four people, depending on the sales methods used and the merchandise sold.

LIGHTING

Lighting, colors, textures, and equipment on the sales floor should set off the merchandise but never compete with it. All should be subordinated to the requirements of good salesmanship—in other words, to the decorative interest of the goods on sale. Lighting is one of the most important elements in store design; light sets the stage for shopping, both indoors and out. With the right lighting, store designers can create the entire atmosphere of a shop and then vary it from week to week or from day to day. Soft, over-all illumination on walls, ceilings, and sales backgrounds can be used to create the right mood; more intense accent lighting on displays will capture attention and aid customers in appraising the goods.[3]

SERVICES

Concealed space and equipment are needed by all store employees in varying amounts. The majority of a shop's personnel are busy on the sales floor during shopping hours and will require only off-stage lockers and washrooms. Those who check, handle, repair, or store merchandise, however, will need specialized workrooms and service spaces, conveniently planned and equipped. Still others, busy with the preparation of displays, price tags, and signs, must have room to work and space for storage of their materials. There should also be porters' closets and mechanical-equipment service areas. In small shops and stores, the mechanical equipment is usually located in the basement or at the rear of the shop, behind the sales area; a shop located in its own store building can often utilize the roof for elevator machinery penthouses, air-conditioning equipment, and the like.

Management needs for space and equipment must similarly be satisfied. Such facilities for the administrative staff will range from a manager's desk (in the smallest shops) to elaborate offices for credit, accounting, advertising, and administrative departments.

STORE FRONTS

Show windows, entrances, and signs should be designed for the attraction of moving window-shopping traffic, for maximum display value, and for effective outdoor advertising. Store fronts are essentially three-dimensional posters, as wide and high as the store itself and as deep as the limits set either by show windows with closed backgrounds or by the rear walls of the sales space of an

[3] For a further discussion of the principles of store lighting see Chap. 28, "Department Stores."

"open" front. Each shop front must have a distinctive character, good balance and composition, timely illustrations in the form of displays, and a brief, easily read message expressed in sign lettering.

The depth of the display frontage is particularly important. Sidewalk-traffic counts prove that window shoppers often avoid building-line show windows because of the jostling crowds. Economy of space should never compel store designers to squeeze store-front show windows against the sidewalk. Instead, entrance fronts should be planned just as definitely for pedestrian traffic as are the customer aisles on the sales floor. Sidewalk traffic, which is always in motion, should be pulled past the store-front displays and through the entrance door, with elbow room for all. One of the best ways of accomplishing this is to pull the sidewalk itself into the store as a store-front lobby. Such lobbies, sometimes called arcades, make the transition between store front and sales floor easy and thus help in turning window shoppers into store shoppers. Even where available space does not permit a full-fledged store-front lobby, it is still advisable to allow room for window shoppers along the shop front. This can be done by recessing all or part of the store front about two to three feet back from the sidewalk line.

There are other real reasons why small shops can use a store-front lobby to advantage, especially in crowded shopping districts where both sidewalk space and display frontage are at a premium. Such lobbies multiply the display possibilities of a narrow frontage; within a given shop width a recessed front can provide three times the show-window space of a front on the building line. Again, with a store-front lobby a variety of display treatments is possible—large and small show windows, shadow boxes, and table-top displays. Finally, such lobbies provide the clearest way to extend a hospitable welcome to window shoppers. They afford freedom from the sidewalk's heavy traffic, shelter from the weather, and leisure to study the merchandise on display. On an inside lot, store-front lobbies will not only give added dignity and importance but also attract window-shopping traffic. And even on a street corner these advantages will be strengthened by the fact that here an open lobby can pull pedestrian traffic from both streets.

Shop fronts, whether set on the building line or recessed, can be designed either as open or closed fronts. The closed front is the more familiar type. It is flat, as wide and high as the store front itself, and as deep as the shallow depth of its own show windows and their closed backgrounds. This type of store front will always have its uses, chiefly where privacy or exclusiveness is essential, but its general popularity is waning. The open front is one in which the sales interior may be seen from the sidewalk, framed by the store front. An architectural treatment of this type may turn the whole shop into a display window. Thus only merchandise from those sales departments which are more remote need be featured in the show windows. The open front is also a flexible store front. If the necessary equipment is provided, it is an easy matter to put up solid backgrounds whenever a closed front is desired.

Show windows should always be designed with the average human eye level in mind. The size and type of merchandise to be displayed will then determine the height and depth. In show windows intended for small-size merchandise, such as jewelry, cosmetics, perfumes, and other feminine accessories, displays should be as near eye level and as close to the observer as possible; that requires a high bulkhead and a small, shallow window. Large merchandise, such as clothing displayed on a mannequin, should be seen in larger and deeper show windows with low bulkheads; this type of merchandise can be placed farther back in the show window, since it looks well at a distance. The fact that most small shops sell more than one kind of goods affords an opportunity to create an interesting store front from a pattern of different-sized display units.

The signs and sign backgrounds above the shop-front displays should be treated as an integral part of the store front. They are one of the designer's best opportunities to create interest. Every store needs two types of signs— one or more large-sized signs placed above street traffic for distant identification; others, smaller in size, placed at eye level or below for window shoppers to read at close range. Contrast is important; sign lettering in value, color, and texture should differ from its background yet harmonize with it.

The entrance is the store's final invitation to step in and buy. It should never present an apparent barrier to incoming customers. Entrance doors should be light in weight, easy to operate, and as a rule visually open. Only the smallest shops can get along with a single entrance door; larger shops need at least a pair of doors to avoid traffic jams at the entrance. The shop entrance should be logically located in relation to customer traffic in the interior sales space. If possible, however, a central entrance is to be avoided unless symmetry and formality are important. Central entrances invariably create symmetrical display line-ups at either side which are usually limited in scope and flexibility. If the shop entrance can be placed off center, it will be easier to create a large show window that is capable of subdivision into several different display units from time to time. It is also wise to avoid corner entrances, since although a street-corner location is ideal for display purposes it is drafty and inconvenient for customer traffic.

SITE

At the same time that a shop is being planned as an independent sales unit, it must also be related to the shopping environment around it. City and suburban shopping districts create crowded sidewalks jammed with a multitude of window shoppers drawn from every income level. Such districts as a rule fail to give motorized customers a chance to park and shop, and because of high land values and rentals it is difficult to find enough space for generous sales and operational facilities. It is only in planned shopping centers and along our main highways that store design really comes into its own. There, on less expensive land, a shop or store can afford to have its own building, freely located to permit the best use of interior space for sales and service and of exterior space for advertising, customer parking, and deliveries.

In planning a shop or store in any location, however, existing street patterns, climate, and regional characteristics should be respected. If a shop as an alteration project must be located in some existing commercial building, its design should harmonize in materials and scale with the rest of the building, even though the shop itself is entirely different in character. If built as an independent unit within a shopping center, the shop must make some visual concessions to its neighbors—such as conformity with them in sign lettering, store-front heights, materials, and colors. With some measure of control, whether imposed by a landlord or intelligently self-inflicted by the merchants, a group of shops will draw more customers as a shopping unit and also benefit more individually than they would in isolated locations. Merchants and store designers should also give more care and consideration to the demands of climate. A store-front formula that may be ideal in a northern city will seldom function as well under a southern sun. It is equally absurd to import building materials when local stone, brick, or wood may be just as suitable and more appropriate.

Today the quality level of merchandise offered for sale in retail shops throughout the country is almost uniform; sales methods also are thoroughly standardized, whether they are based on personal service or on self-service. The day is past when the best merchandise at the lowest price is enough to capture trade. Interpreted in terms of the cash register this means that the design of the shop itself will offer each merchant his best chance for survival. Its atmos-

FIGURE 53.
HENRY WYLE CANDY STORE,
NEW YORK. EXTERIOR

Gruen, Krummeck & Auer, architects
Little space is required for reserve stock.

Courtesy Gruen &
Krummeck Associates

phere and character, indoors and out, are of vital importance. Primarily the public is attracted to small shops because of their friendly personal contact, their comfortable shopping conditions, and their intimate scale and size. Shoppers know that once inside they will not be compelled to walk through a vast warehouse of sales floors. All this must be visibly expressed in the physical organization of each shop, whether it sells candy, jewelry, shoes, women's apparel, or men's wear.

SPECIAL TYPES OF SHOP

CANDY SHOPS

The average candy shop is neither large nor complex; it needs only space enough to house the customers and the necessary sales fixtures for bulk candy, hard candy, chocolates, nuts, and novelties, together with a cash and wrapping desk. Since the sales turnover in such perishable merchandise is rapid, only a small reserve-stock space is necessary. Often the candy sold is made on the premises; if so, space is required for a workroom. Yet from these simple beginnings many more complex types have evolved. Soda fountains were added, then bakery departments, then groceries and meats, until the result now is often a supermarket. Or the trend may have gone in another direction—from candies to sodas to a restaurant—as was the case with several candy-store chains like Loft's and Schrafft's.

FIGURE 54. HENRY WYLE CANDY STORE, NEW YORK. INTERIOR AND DETAIL

Gruen, Krummeck & Auer, architects

Atmosphere and character—"styling"—are of the first importance in candy-store design.

Photographs Robert Damora, courtesy Gruen & Krummeck Associates

Location, equipment, and size are not so important to the average candy store as is character. That is vital. The shop can be small, the counters few and simple, and the location an average one in the middle of the block. It is the atmosphere and character—in short, the styling—that will make or break a candy store (Figs. 53, 54). The reason for this lies in the character of the merchandise.

Directly or indirectly, most candy is sold to women. The appearance of most candy boxes and candy stores reflects this fact. Candy displays can be fascinating in themselves, and candy packaging is an art that has been brought to a high peak of perfection. In the candy kitchen, candy may be dull; in an attractive package it can capture your fancy. Box shapes, colors, and lettering can be as tempting as the taste of the candy inside. The same techniques used for beautifying the package will be equally successful if applied to the shop itself. Store-front and interior sales space should be styled as far as possible with the same kind of lettering, colors, and textures as the candy boxes they display. White and soft pastel colors such as pink, chocolate-brown, gray-green, or gray-blue are best—with silver or gold occasionally in letters or insignia. Paint, wallpaper, fabrics, and mirrors can be used with a light touch. Trade-marks run to crowns, hearts, or flowers. Signs and lettering should be in the same spirit as the candy boxes; here delicate script is a favorite choice.

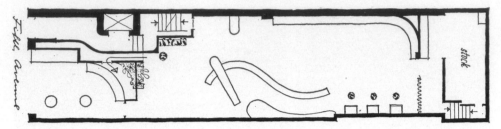

FIGURE 55. REBAJES JEWELRY SHOP, NEW YORK. PLAN

José A. Fernandez, architect

Created for the sale of many small and precious items.   From *New Pencil Points*

Not every kind of stock illuminating equipment will serve well in a candy shop. Under the wrong kind of light the sales atmosphere will melt away just as quickly as will the goods themselves under too hot a lamp. For general illumination, salesroom walls and ceilings should be bathed in soft light from concealed or shielded lighting fixtures; harsh, glaring globes or tubes should be eliminated. The lighting fixtures, if visible, should reflect and enhance the character of the store. As always, higher-intensity illumination is preferable for store-front and salesroom displays, whether these be in show windows, display cases, or sales fixtures, but cold cathode or fluorescent light should be used rather than incandescent, to avoid melting the merchandise.

Sometimes a simple closed store front with a good sign, the right colors and materials, and one or two show windows will be all that a candy store needs to attract window shoppers. More often, a visually open shop front will be better. If the salesroom is opened up and the show-window bulkheads are lowered so that window shoppers can see over them, an easy traffic pattern from sidewalk to entrance to sales counter is established. Many successful shops are of this type.

JEWELRY SHOPS

Jewelry-store design is controlled by the following principles:

1. Luxury merchandise must be sold in surroundings that emphasize its value and its glamour.

2. Individual attention must be given to each customer.

3. Since jewelry is impulse merchandise, buying should be stimulated by means of well-studied visual-appeal techniques.

FIGURE 56. REBAJES JEWELRY SHOP, NEW YORK, EXTERIOR AND THREE
INTERIORS

José A. Fernandez, architect

Distinction, glitter, glamour, all are required in jewelry stores.

Photographs Voss, courtesy José A. Fernandez

4. An atmosphere of dignity, reliability, and style leadership must be created as a psychological basis for trust. No one but an expert knows the worth
of the merchandise at a glance.

These merchandising principles should be interpreted by the designer in
terms of a well-organized sales floor and shop front (Figs. 55, 56). A closed,
building-line store front, once the rule for jewelry shops, is on the way out.
Modern jewelry stores dealing with a mass clientele rely on varied displays,

lobby entrances, and open fronts to turn pedestrians into window shoppers and window shoppers into customers. Overhead and eye-level signs are brief and simple for the refined, exclusive shop; for costume or commercial-credit jewelers they are likely to be bold and strident.

The typical jewelry shop is a highly departmentalized gift shop combined with a workshop—since the repair of jewelry and watches is a major income factor. Its departments may include silver, china and glass, wooden salad bowls, fountain pens, pottery, and engraved stationery. The present trend is toward locating the repair department in the rear of the sales floor in order to expose repair customers to merchandise displays. Other service units include credit, private salesrooms, offices, vaults, lockers, and toilets. Reserve stocks, being small in bulk and easy to handle, are usually kept in the sales fixtures themselves—protected by electric signal systems which are also wired to the storefront windows and the doors.

The general decorative scheme should be quiet and unobtrusive, with simple backgrounds and rich textures, for small objects cannot compete with "busy" wall surfaces. Display backgrounds in contact with the merchandise are traditionally of velvet—dark blue or green for silver and diamonds, deep crimson for gold, brass, and copper. As a compromise color, suitable for all types of merchandise, most jewelers pick a light French gray. Other formulas are dangerous without careful experimentation. Correct lighting is vital. Incandescent lighting throws a sharp beam and makes precious stones sparkle—but, except for the best daylight bulbs, it gives a yellowish light that is "poison" for silver, pewter, or platinum. Hence fluorescent lighting with its soft, diffused glow and its even color and tone is often used in addition.

The sales fixtures, furniture, walls, and ceilings are best kept in pastel shades and quiet textures, to contrast with the richly colored jewelry displays. Light woodwork is especially appropriate; it provides contrast, makes the shop look larger, and shows dirt, dust, and scratches less than a dark finish. A white ceiling is the conventional favorite—often in acoustic tile or acoustic plaster for quietness. Because women customers in particular like to see how their jewelry selections set off their costumes, a few full-length mirrors (or a mirrored wall) have become a necessity. Small retail jewelry shops sell about 90 per cent of the jewelry and related accessories purchased in this country. Since most of the sales are to women—directly or indirectly—these shops are intimate, elegant, efficient, and planned for a leisurely personal selection of merchandise.

Neither a great deal of sales space nor a corner location is necessary. The

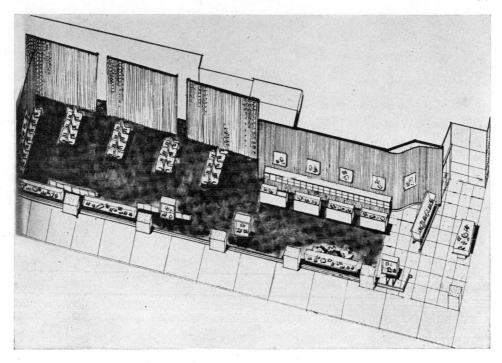

FIGURE 57. FLORSHEIM SHOE SHOP, NEW YORK. ISOMETRIC
Ketchum, Giná & Sharp, architects
An open-faced store is the most logical arrangement.　　　　　From *Architectural Forum*

store fronts should be dignified, simple, and straightforward in treatment. Individual show windows are preferable to ribbon windows; store-front lobbies
and open fronts should be used with discretion. Indoors the jewelry, silverware, gift, and repair departments are the most important elements. Jewelry,
watches, and silver flatware are sold over desklike counters, with two customer
chairs on one side and a clerk's chair on the other. A glass-enclosed display on
top, with the knee-hole space below it, is supported by stock pedestals at
either side. For silver hollow-ware, china, pottery, and the like the gift-shop
technique of display on open shelving is used.

Costume jewelry has climbed from the status of a cheap imitation to that of
a respectable accessory. Costume-jewelry stores should be located on busy
shopping streets where they can draw on a volume trade attracted by quantity
displays. Since corner locations are expensive, deep store lobbies and transparent store fronts are commonly used to obtain greater display value in narrow, mid-block frontages. Repair, service, and credit departments are usually

FIGURE 58. FLORSHEIM SHOE SHOP, NEW YORK. EXTERIOR

Ketchum, Giná & Sharp, architects

Inviting comfort for shoppers, alluring indoor displays, and soft but dramatic lighting.

Photograph Gottscho-Schleisner, courtesy Morris Ketchum, Jr.

FIGURE 59. FLORSHEIM SHOE SHOP, NEW YORK. INTERIOR

Ketchum, Giná & Sharp, architects

Photograph Gottscho-Schleisner, courtesy Morris Ketchum, Jr.

omitted here, and chairs for customers are eliminated as a hindrance to volume sales. The merchandise is displayed and sold at long ribbonlike counters with back fixtures.

All jewelry shops house an ancient retail trade, bound by tradition but alive to the need for clean-cut contemporary store planning.

SHOE SHOPS

Marked differences in the customer demands of the two sexes have resulted in shoe-store specialization, and most shops carry either men's or women's shoes exclusively. Both sexes need shoes for business, for the country, for evening wear, and for the bedroom and bath. Women, however, because they are style conscious, demand greater variety in their shoe wardrobe and tolerate a shorter life for each pair. Since the great majority of shoe shops cater to a volume trade, their merchandise is styled and priced on a competitive basis and they should be organized for speedy, comfortable, and efficient service, with eye-catching displays and effective identification up and down the street. (See Figs. 57–59.)

The most fundamental problem here is how to obtain the maximum number of chairs in the salesroom without crowding traffic lanes for customers, infringing on the necessary fitting space in front of the customers' chairs, and obstructing the salesmen's own traffic routes from customers' chairs to shoe boxes. Unless the salesroom is effectively planned for maximum efficiency, the shop will fail to sell enough shoes to justify its existence.

In open-faced stores the most logical layout for the rows of shoe chairs is one parallel to the store front. Then the aisles between chairs, where customers wander about in their stockinged feet, are not exposed to the street and to the window shopper's eye. In well-planned shoe shops the public is carefully routed from entrance door to customer's chair and out again. The show-window displays that originally drew them into the store should be repeated in the salesroom so as to remind them that the store sells a wider range of merchandise than the shoes which they came in to buy. Such indoor displays are effective silent salesmen.

Customers' chairs should be carefully chosen for comfort, appearance, and durability, all within the smallest practical size to seat the customers properly. These chairs should have arms so that each customer will be separated from his neighbor. The upholstery should be durable and easy to maintain; for this reason leather is a favorite finish. The salesroom floors are usually carpeted for comfort to stockinged feet. Plenty of shoe-level mirrors and an occasional full-length mirror will enable customers to see their new shoes in relation to their entire costume. The right lighting and decoration as well as air conditioning are vital factors in creating a steady clientele.

The average shoe box is uninteresting, and even when the boxes are properly styled in an attractive color scheme it is still hard to make endless rows of them take on a pleasing pattern; since the majority of shoe shops still keep their stock on view in order to conserve floor space and to have the shoes within easy reach, this is frequently a problem that must be solved. The boxes should be arranged in orderly vertical and horizontal rows along the walls of the sales space. The rows should not, however, be higher than a clerk can reach. Ladders for climbing to upper-level stock slow up sales and are now obsolete except in reserve-stock areas. The monotony of endless rows of boxes may be varied with a series of recessed shadow-box displays of shoes and related merchandise. If these displays are kept at the eye level of the customer when seated he will have something to study while he is being waited on.

The interior of a shoe store needs high-intensity over-all lighting in order to show all the detail of its small-scale merchandise. Whatever general system of illumination is used, it should not come from prominent fixtures which compete for attention with the goods on display. Special requirements include enough incandescent down lighting to make polished shoes shine and enough general illumination to allow the reading of numbers on the shoe boxes. Sales-room and show-window displays need a good blend of incandescent and fluorescent light to set them off and to supplement the general illumination of the salesroom.

It is important to provide ideal working conditions for the shoe salesman. There should be short clear traffic lanes between the customers' chairs and the shoe-box reserve stock; hence it is customary to keep most of the reserve stock either in or immediately adjacent to the salesroom. Basement space in shoe stores is commonly used merely for additional reserve stock and for shipping and employee facilities. The cashier's desk, sometimes combined with a storage unit for "will call" shoes that have been altered or repaired, is best placed in a centralized location which affords visual control of the sales space. Hosiery, slippers, evening shoes, and other special items can best be displayed and sold at or near the cashier's counter—or near the entrance—in order to promote impulse sales.

The trend in shoe stores today is to combine store front and interior into one by using an open-face front. Volume sales to a volume trade require a maximum amount of display opportunities; the open store meets this demand. Only a "salon" type of shoe shop, selling a few expensive shoes to the carriage trade, can afford to use a closed front with one or two shoe windows.

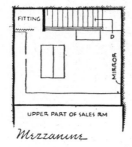

FITTING

MIRROR

UPPER PART OF SALES RM

Mezzanine

Scale 0   5

DISPLAY   WRAP

Cloves

SCREEN

Underwear

MEZZANINE

Bags

Jewelry

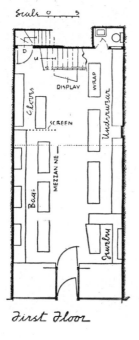

First Floor

FIGURE 60 (LEFT). PLYMOUTH SHOP,
187 BROADWAY, NEW YORK. PLANS

Ketchum, Giná & Sharp, architects

Excellent provision for demand, convenience, and impulse
goods.   From *Progressive Architecture*

FIGURE 61 (ABOVE). PLYMOUTH SHOP,
187 BROADWAY, NEW YORK. EXTERIOR

Ketchum, Giná & Sharp, architects

Women's shops require a "stylish" yet inviting exterior.

Photograph Lionel Freedman, courtesy Morris Ketchum, Jr.

Shoe stores, like candy shops, are comparatively simple planning problems
because only one staple type of merchandise is featured.

WOMEN'S APPAREL SHOPS

Women's-wear merchants make their living out of one of the hardest jobs
in the world—pleasing women. They must be able to keep ahead of seasonal
and style demands—all the whims, fads, and fancies of the season—while
satisfying the shrewdest shoppers in the world. Women's shopping habits are
very different from those of the average man. Women are inveterate window

shoppers who keep going from shop to shop making comparisons. To survive keen competition and the high mortality rate common among women's shops, the proprietors must be expert merchandisers equipped with a better-than-average store plant. (See Figs. 60–63.) Goods with a short-lived, seasonal sales appeal require exciting store-front stage settings and equally dramatic backgrounds on the sales floor, both properly interpreted in terms of color, texture, and lighting. A "free show" of shop-front displays, an inviting entrance, and a well-planned trip through the store all help to make shopping a pleasure. Women—even more than men—take their shopping seriously, but they also insist that shopping be fun.

Women's wear generally falls into three classifications: impulse or luxury

FIGURE 63.
PLYMOUTH SHOP,
187 BROADWAY, NEW YORK.
DETAIL

Ketchum, Giná & Sharp, architects
Details are important in creating
the atmosphere desired.

Photograph Lionel Freedman,
courtesy Morris Ketchum, Jr.

accessories, convenience or standard accessories, and demand goods that are necessities. With so much emphasis on style, however, it is hard to draw clear-cut divisions between the three groups. Shoes, hosiery, and lingerie—necessities—often fall into the impulse or convenience class. For simplicity, we can divide women's apparel as follows:

Impulse accessories: jewelry, cosmetics, bags and pocketbooks, and many small luxury items
Convenience accessories: gloves, millinery, hosiery, shoes, blouses, sweaters, lingerie, and underwear
Demand clothing: dresses, coats and suits, furs, evening apparel, and such specialized items as bridal gowns

These merchandise groups must be organized into separate, well-related departments—each with a different selling job, with its own type of equipment, displays, and services, and with its appointed location, properly related to customer traffic aisles, service facilities, and other sales departments.

The fundamental planning will be the same whether the shop is small, medium-sized, or large, in the middle of the block or on a corner location, on one or several sales floors. In essence, each shop's sales space should be treated as an indoor shopping street, each sales department as a separate specialty shop. Following the usual rules, demand merchandise should be farthest from the shop entrance, convenience goods midway, and impulse merchandise nearest to the start of the shopping tour. At the same time, each sales division must be tied in with the service traffic that links it to hidden stock rooms, work spaces, and the receiving and shipping departments. Although personal service predominates in most women's shops, some sales departments or even the entire store may be run on a self-service basis. The policy in this respect will depend largely on the type, quality, and price of the merchandise on sale. There are as many different kinds of women's-wear shops as there are of women shoppers.

The type of store front is determined by the kind of shop it serves. A closed shop front with a sign, one or two show windows, and an entrance door—all set on the sidewalk building line—is best for an exclusive shop. A deep store-front lobby, many show windows, a varied display, and a visually open entrance wall will best satisfy those shops which sell average-priced goods to a volume trade. In any case, large show windows with low bulkheads are needed to display clothing mannequins; small, eye-level show cases are desirable for accessories.

Inside or out, the individual requirements of each shop must be studied. Exterior displays and advertising, interior sales and service must all be fitted into or wrapped around the available selling space in a working pattern that will also have individual character.

MEN'S-WEAR SHOPS

Most men are conservative shoppers, the greater part of the merchandise they buy is almost static in quality and style, and shopping conditions in the men's-wear field are usually quiet, personal, unhurried. The average man hates to shop. He does not like crowded stores. Hence he appreciates expert, courteous, soothing salesmanship and a serene atmosphere. Because most men are in a hurry to get their shopping done, the store location is important. Men's shops are likely to cluster together, depending on better displays, better merchandise, and better store plants to beat near-by competition.

As a result of all these factors, men's clothing shops have been the most conservative of retail trade outlets (Figs. 64–66). Until recent years this attitude expressed itself not only in an imitation of English sales methods but also in the building of pseudo-English stores with dark woodwork and a heavy "roast beef and plum pudding" atmosphere. As the novelty of such stage sets wore off, their discomforts and inconveniences began to appear, and the depression of the early 1930's swept them out of existence. Today men's-clothing

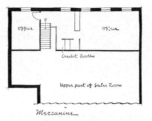

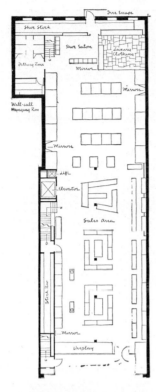

FIGURE 64. HORSFALLS, HARTFORD, CONNECTICUT.
TWO PLANS

Ketchum, Giná & Sharp, architects

Accessories are on the ground floor; clothing is on the floor
above.   From *Progressive Architecture*

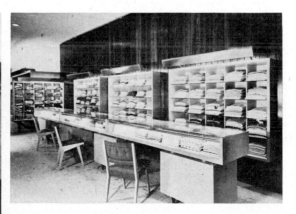

FIGURE 65. HORSFALLS,
HARTFORD, CONNECTICUT. EXTERIOR AND
INTERIOR

Ketchum, Giná & Sharp, architects

The tone must be restful.

Photographs Ben Schnall,
courtesy Morris Ketchum, Jr.

FIGURE 66. THE CUSTOM SHOP, 50TH STREET AND LEXINGTON AVENUE, NEW YORK. EXTERIOR AND INTERIOR

Paul Bry, designer

The pleasant shopping conditions created by intelligent contemporary designing.

Photographs Ben Schnall, courtesy Paul Bry and the Custom Shop

merchants are eager to employ all the latest methods of store planning. Experience has shown them that their customers appreciate the comfortable, pleasant shopping conditions created by intelligent contemporary design.

Men buy their clothing as a long-term investment. Style changes are infrequent; durability, suitability, and correct tailoring are the most important sales factors. With this minimum of style turnover, it is easy to make a clear-cut classification of the merchandise into two main divisions: men's furnishings and men's clothing.

Men's furnishings include both impulse and convenience goods. Jewelry, leather goods, toiletries, suspenders, belts, garters, and ties may be classed as impulse furnishings. Shirts, underwear, hosiery, pajamas, robes, hats, and shoes fall into the class of convenience furnishings. With the exception of shoes—often sold separately in men's shoe stores—all these items taken together represent a complete list of goods for a small haberdashery shop.

Men's clothing is demand merchandise in character. It includes sports wear, suits, overcoats, evening wear—items that are staple or seasonal necessities in a man's wardrobe. Sold by themselves, these items might represent the complete inventory of a custom tailor shop, but combined with men's furnishings they add up together to form the merchandising program of a complete men's-wear shop.

The fundamental planning for a men's-wear shop will be basically the same as that for any other type of retail store, whatever its size, merchandising program, number of sales floors, or location. As always, impulse, convenience, and demand divisions must be logically disposed on the sales floor. Because a man who needs a suit will get one regardless of what is in the way, clothing departments should be relegated to the more remote locations—at the rear of a one-floor shop or on the second floor of a two-story store. Furnishings departments along the way thus have a better chance to promote impulse and convenience sales. Jewelry, toiletries, leather goods, hats, suspenders, belts, garters, hosiery, and shoes usually follow one another back from the entrance door; then come ties and shirts, underwear, pajamas, and robes; finally, sports wear makes a good connecting link between the furnishings and clothing divisions. Service routes must be provided to bring goods in and out from the receiving and shipping rooms to the reserve stock spaces and sales fixtures of each department. Specialized equipment for men's shops includes mirrors for the hat, shoe, and clothing departments; shoe chairs and shoe salesmen's stools; fitting spaces and dressing rooms for clothing.

A good display pattern, dramatized by good lighting, should run through the entire shop. Vivid, carefully composed window displays are necessary. The store-front show should be continued through the entire sales space—not in concentrated show-window form but in small doses taken one by one. Clothing merchants have long been aware of the value of this technique. In addition to having feature displays in each department, they have also displayed furnishings in the clothing department and clothing dummies in the furnishings departments, to remind their customers constantly of the things they did not come in to buy.

The type of store front best suited to a men's shop depends on the shop's location, its neighbors, and the kind of sales and service it offers. Whether the store front be open or closed, with few or many displays, it should be simple, clean-cut, and inviting—rather than bizarre—in order to capture and hold the interest of male shoppers. The entire shop, indoors and out, should be modern

FIGURE 67.
OFFICES OF
ALBERT MCGANN,
SOUTH BEND,
INDIANA. EXTERIOR

Ketchum, Giná & Sharp,
architects

Photograph Hedrich-
Blessing, courtesy
Morris Ketchum, Jr.

in a conservative way—a sort of gentlemen's club, radiating friendliness, dignity, and the promise of comfortable shopping.

SERVICE SHOPS

Stores that have only service to sell are specialty shops just as much as those which feature a single type of merchandise. The service field is wide and varied. It includes: *personal service* (barbers, beauticians, tailors, shoe repair, rental libraries); *household service* (laundries and dry cleaners, clock and watch repair, radio and appliance repair); *business service* (advertising, personal-finance investments and loans, sign painting); *transportation service* (auto repair shops, service stations, and many other examples too numerous to catalogue). In 1939, according to the United States Census Bureau, 645,966 service establishments in such fields did nearly $3,500,000,000 worth of business, a not inconsiderable portion of the nation's total retail trade. (See Figs. 67, 68.)

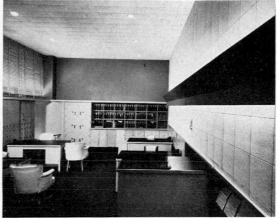

FIGURE 68. OFFICES OF ALBERT MCGANN, SOUTH BEND, INDIANA. TWO INTERIORS

Ketchum, Giná & Sharp, architects

The atmosphere created in a "service shop" does much to inspire confidence in the clientele.

Photographs Hedrich-Blessing, courtesy Morris Ketchum, Jr.

Almost all service shops are small in size and have the same basic plan. This plan consists of a sales and work space—kept visible to the passer-by if human craftsmanship or merchandise processing is the chief product of the shop or closed by a billboard front if neither is to be featured and a maximum of advertising or privacy is desired. In this sales space, workroom, or business office the customers are received and the working activities are carried on. Whatever private offices are required and the necessary storage, supply, receiving, and shipping rooms adjoin this public space.

When service shops feature craftsmanship as their chief product, they can put on an exciting show. Unlike the average retailer, whose displays are limited to inanimate merchandise, the service shop proprietor can dramatize a living product—human labor. This opportunity to display human activity can be translated into powerful store-front advertising when allied with good design. There is an equal opportunity for effective design where service shops supply business advice or personal loans, instead of merchandise, or else are simply pick-up stations for some remote central plant. In such cases the most striking effects can be obtained by closing off the store front with an eye-level sign panel, useful as a background for advertising and always in eye-catching contrast to neighboring store windows stocked with merchandise.

Service is still sold in small doses to small groups of people. The old-fashioned tailor, cobbler, or blacksmith operated a small shop for near-by customers; the modern beauty parlor, shoe-repair shop, or barber shop still operates on the same basis. Even today, though cities have grown and distances have been annihilated by swift transportation, small service units remain highly profitable, whether individually owned or operated by some large chain.

In planning for the enjoyment of the customer and the profit of the shop-keeper, store architects should always remember that their efforts must add up to a sound building investment. There is little or no sentiment involved in store design; results are measured by the cash register. A shop must be well built at an economical cost; it has to be tailor-made for the business it shelters; above all, it must be designed to advertise, display, and sell merchandise successfully. Whatever the nature of a specialty shop may happen to be, its final character will be set by its designer's own freshness of invention. His imagination and inherent creative ability will determine whether it is just another average shop or a step forward in commercial architecture. Native ability, however, must be sharpened and sobered by knowledge and experience. Store design is no field for a prima donna.

SUGGESTED ADDITIONAL READING FOR CHAPTER 29

Fernandez, José Antonio, *The Specialty Shop, a Guide*, with a foreword by Leopold Arnaud (New York: Architectural Book Pub. Co. [1950]).

Ketchum, Morris, Jr., *Shops and Stores* (New York: Reinhold, 1948).

Labò, Mario, *Architettura e Arredamento del Negozio* (Milan: Hoepli, 1936).

Nicholson, Emrich, *Contemporary Shops in the United States* (New York: Architectural Book Pub. Co. [1945]).

Schumacher, Adolf, *Ladenbau* . . . (Stuttgart: Hoffmann [c1939]).

Westwood, Bryan, and Norman Westwood, *Smaller Retail Shops* (London: Architectural Press, 1937).

PERIODICALS

"The Art of Display," *Interiors*, Vol. 105 (1946), April, pp. 89–[113].

"Buildings for Selling Services Offer Unique Design Opportunities," *Architectural Record*, Vol. 90 (1941), July, pp. 84–[89].

"Design of Retail Stores," *Progressive Architecture*, Vol. 29 (1948), September, pp. 50–69.

"40 Stores," *Architectural Forum*, Vol. 88 (1948), May, pp. 93–144.

Ketchum, Morris, Jr., "Current Trends in Store Design," *Architectural Record*, Vol. 103 (1948), April, pp. 109–44.

"The Lighting of Shops and Stores," *Architectural Forum*, Vol. 58 (1933), May, pp. 353–56; this is part of complete "Shops" issue, pp. 343–428.

Pawley, Frederic Arden, "The Shop Check List," *Architectural Forum*, Vol. 58 (1933), May, pp. 381–88.

"Retail Stores . . . ," *Pencil Points*, Vol. 28 (1947), May, pp. 53–83.

"Store Design," Morris Lapidus and the editors, *Architectural Record*, Vol. 89 (1941), February, pp. [113]–36.

"Store Fronts of Tomorrow," premiated designs for new P. P. Kawneer Company store-front competition, and "Store Design Practices," by Joseph Douglas Weiss, *New Pencil Points*, Vol. 24 (1943), February, pp. [29]–47.

"Stores," Building Types Study No. 110, *Architectural Record*, Vol. 99 (1946), February, pp. 99–128.

"Stores," Building Types Study No. 122, *Architectural Record*, Vol. 101 (1947), February, pp. 86–104.

Trade Section of "Design Decade Number" of *Architectural Forum*, Vol. 73 (1940), October, pp. 286–99.

30

Shopping Centers

By PIETRO BELLUSCHI

THE MARKET PLACE as an institution for the exchange of goods goes back to the earliest days of history and has remained more or less unchanged through the centuries. It was one of the first manifestations of community life, curiously similar in the most widely separated parts of the globe. It may be said that a majority of the cities in Europe and Asia, as well as in the new continents, owe their existence to the early establishment of centers of trade. Such cities as Palmyra in Asia Minor, where camel caravans trading between the East and West could meet and exchange goods, offer a perfect example. The ample watered courtyard of the market place, surrounded by porticos affording the merchants shelter from rain and sun, was the prototype of what later became the forum, which in Rome was brought to a highly organized form. In the Roman Forum we find specialty shops as well as bazaars, arcades in addition to game areas and meeting halls; here people congregated for their various expressions of community living.

In the East, and in numerous European cities even now, the trading of goods of many types is still carried on in the bazaar or in the piazzas, either under the open skies or protected from sun or rain by porticos. In Spain, France, and Italy the cathedral square of the smaller town is the place where, daily or weekly, merchants still display their goods in the shadow of the old church; here for centuries has been the center of community life, much as the forum was the community center in Roman times. In many of the larger cities some of the narrowest streets near the market place are the busiest trade centers, although vehicular traffic is prohibited. Arcades for pedestrians only, such as the glass-covered *gallerie* in Milan and Naples, have long been successful centers of specialized shopping.

Although this pattern of the market as a meeting place where goods are exchanged is still basically the same, the rise of large towns, the advent of mass factory production, and the need of obtaining supplies from wide national or international areas have tended to create complex problems of distribution, with inevitable waste and paradoxically with increased efficiency. For instance, the growth of rapid transportation created the necessity of bulk handling and led to the large terminal warehouse. This in turn necessitated the development of refrigeration. Efficient and economical marketing became a basic need out of which emerged the chain store.

The rapid urbanization of the last decades and, above all, the advent of the automobile have created extreme traffic congestion around downtown public markets. Decentralization of many types of retail shops has occurred in practically all the larger cities in the United States. The automobile has been responsible for creating conditions which, without guidance, have made merchandising a difficult task but have also made possible a solution. We see, therefore, the rise of a new concept, that of the shopping center, and indirectly that of the "neighborhood" as the cellular organization of the modern city. This concept has shown its maximum development near residential sections in the suburbs of large cities, and especially in the cities of the West, like Los Angeles, where the use of land still is not too highly concentrated.

Shopping centers should not necessarily be thought of as rivals to the main downtown shopping district. The latter still is essential to the stability of most of our cities, although many believe that only radical replanning can save it from disintegration. But we may say that with the increased use of the automobile the shopping center in the United States has been a spontaneous development—a necessary extension, so to speak, of the corner store—the corner grocery in particular. The trouble with the corner grocery, when the automobile took over, was the very fact that it was located on the corner—that is, on a prominent intersection. It took some time to discover the shortcomings of having it situated directly on a busy traffic artery. When corner groceries grew into a ribbon development along main arteries, the traffic dangers and snarls multiplied. Not until then did the idea of shopping centers as self-contained, well-organized units begin to develop. Perhaps the full consummation of the shopping-center idea will come only with the full development of the neighborhood as a solution to this problem that is common to all our cities.

Naturally the West, with more opportunity to expand and generally with more automobiles per capita, made more rapid advances than the East. Although the ideal solution has been realized in only a few places, some valuable knowledge and experience have been gathered. In recent years the large housing projects erected during the Second World War have provided an

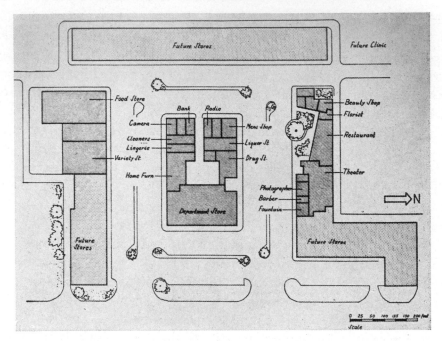

FIGURE 69. SHOPPING CENTER, BELLEVUE, WASHINGTON. PLAN

Bliss Moore, Jr., and Robert Massar, architects

From *Architectural Forum*

opportunity to put into practice and test some of these theories, although in them various abnormal wartime factors came into play.

STORE AREA REQUIRED

Numerous formulas have been used to arrive at the number of square feet of floor space needed in relation to the population, but many variables and many different opinions among operators make it impossible to work out reliable standards. In general it may be said that the amount of commercial space required has been overestimated. The Federal Housing Authority during the Second World War established maximum floor areas to provide a basis for the correlation of commercial facilities throughout the housing program. For instance, it specified a maximum of 40 square feet of commercial area for every family dwelling unit in projects of 100 units or less; in larger projects the area set aside for commercial purposes decreased from 30 square feet per unit to 10 square feet per unit in projects of over 500 units. This of course was a rough wartime estimate, and it was affected by the availability of other facilities within the area but outside the project.

FIGURE 70.
SHOPPING CENTER,
BELLEVUE, WASHINGTON.
TWO VIEWS

Bliss Moore, Jr., and Robert Massar, architects

Photographs Dearborn-Massar

Pre-war surveys of thirteen large cities show an average of 1.47 stores per 100 people. In the New York Regional Plan Study, based on several cities of varied size, it was found that a population of 6,000 people would require 3,000 feet of store frontage; if we assume the average store front to be 25 feet, two stores per 100 persons would therefore be needed. This was a maximum rather than an optimum figure, as discovered by Stein and Bauer. In their study on "Stores and Neighborhoods" [1] they quote the 1929 Census of Distribution; this shows that half the stores of the country had sales of less than $1,000 per month, which seems too low for subsistence and explains the tremendous mortality among business concerns. The result of other studies shows that a population of 10,000 would require a total of 70 stores, distributed among thirty lines of business.

[1] Clarence S. Stein and Catherine Bauer, *Architectural Record*, Feb., 1934.

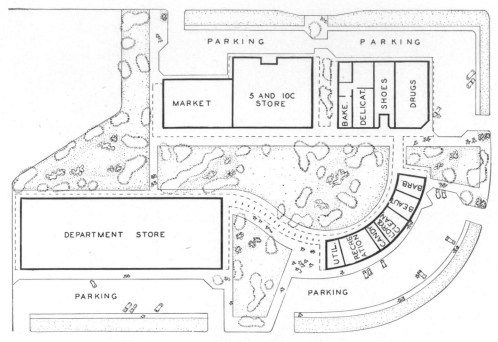

FIGURE 71. SHOPPING CENTER, LINDA VISTA, CALIFORNIA. PLAN

Earl F. Giberson and Whitney R. Smith, architects; H. Dankworth, landscape architect

FIGURE 72.
SHOPPING CENTER,
LINDA VISTA,
CALIFORNIA. VIEW

Earl F. Giberson and Whitney R. Smith, architects; H. Dankworth, landscape architect

Photograph Maynard
Parker,
courtesy Museum of
Modern Art,
New York

Although as noted above the New York Regional Plan Study proposed an average of 2 stores per 100 persons—the average for the country before the war being about 1.3 stores per 1,000 population—nevertheless, in the face of

FIGURE 73. RIVER OAKS SHOPPING CENTER, HOUSTON, TEXAS. BIRD'S-EYE VIEW
Hugh Potter, designer

From *Architectural Forum*

the high record of failures, it would appear that 1 store per 100 of population would be the best available guide for allocating stores in an urban neighborhood. This must be considered only a rough rule-of-thumb method, which becomes unreliable if used without several reservations and a thorough knowledge of local conditions.

NUMBER AND VARIETY OF SHOPS

Obviously the family income of the neighborhood has a direct bearing on the types, numbers, and sizes of shops and other facilities to be included. There will be differences in the consumption habits and merchandising practices of the local families according to whether they live in one-family houses, row houses, or multi-floor apartment houses. If a large proportion of the people are living in apartments, there is a greater demand for ready-made goods and personal services than if most of the people live in separate houses and a more traditional way of life prevails. All studies made on the subject by various experts point out a method by which certain conclusions may be reached with a fair degree of accuracy. Before planning the size of a shopping center the probable purchasing power available in the neighborhood must be determined; from this knowledge it will then be possible to arrive at some assumption as to the variety and sizes of shops, the amount of parking, and so on. Purchasing power in all cases is determined by the population surrounding the proposed site, the distance from which customers may be attracted, the density of the population, the adequacy

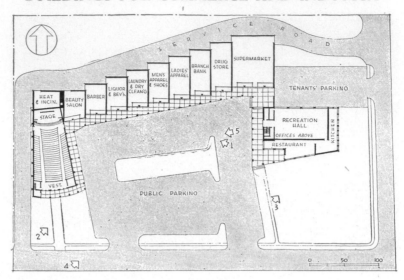

FIGURE 74. AERO ACRES, MIDDLE RIVER, MARYLAND. PLAN

Jan Porel, designer; Skidmore, Owings & Merrill, consulting architects

From *Architectural Record*

of existing centers within the area, and, last but not least, the average income per family. Finally, to arrive at a decision as to the size of the future center, the planner must weigh the following questions: How much local business is there? How much can be gained from other shopping centers? How will the retail dollar be divided? What is the minimum volume of business a store must have in order to survive? How much can it pay in rent?

Despite wide differences between localities, certain constants exist for the local needs of a neighborhood of 5,000 population within an area of a square mile. The needs may vary according to the location of the community— whether in the North or in the South—and according to its density, that is, whether there are single or multiple dwellings. For various types of store the Census of Distribution made available by the Department of Commerce gives the per capita expenditures, net sales, number of stores, number of employees, operating expenses, type of management, and so forth, all classified according to different sizes of community and further broken down with respect to oper- ating expenses as well as rent in percentage of net sales in all classifications. From these data the amount of business a merchant must transact in order to make a profit and pay a fair rent can be estimated. A food store, for example, according to all authorities, must conduct $50,000 worth of business yearly in order to be a permanently paying proposition. Expenditures for food, incidentally, ac-

FIGURE 75. AERO ACRES, MIDDLE RIVER, MARYLAND. TWO VIEWS
Jan Porel, designer; Skidmore, Owings & Merrill, consulting architects

From *Architectural Record*

count for approximately 30 to 40 per cent of the average family income and
make food stores by far the most important ones in any community. Estimates
on their size indicate that grocery stores vary from 20 feet to 40 feet in width
and from 35 feet to 60 feet in depth; the addition of a meat market will necessitate increasing the width to 60 feet and the depth to 100 feet.

The general needs of families grow as the size of the community grows. This
makes possible an increase in the number of kinds of shops. A small community
of 50 families can support a general store. A 500-family population will support
all the primary stores, such as a cash-and-carry grocery store, a drug store
with a sandwich and fountain bar, a cleaning, dyeing, and laundry agency, a
beauty parlor, a bakery, a filling station, a shoe-repair shop, a variety store, and
a barber shop. In some cases, when sales are too small to permit separate units,
two or more of these may be combined; but in other cases, when volume is
high, such facilities may be duplicated so as to give shoppers the important

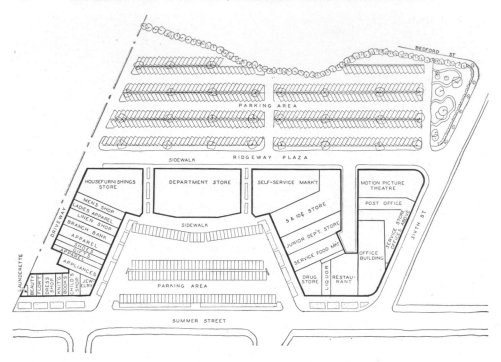

FIGURE 76. RIDGEWAY SHOPPING CENTER, STAMFORD, CONNECTICUT. PLAN
Alfons Bach, designer; Thorn & Jorge, architects

element of competition—which usually stimulates business appreciably. Next
to be added are some of the more specialized shops, usually in approximately
the following order: delivery-service grocery, florist, milliner, radio shop, five-
and-ten-cent store, shoe store, gift shop, candy-and-nut shop, lingerie and
hosiery shop, and liquor store. About 6,000 families, representing a population of 20,000 to 24,000, will support a movie theater of about 1,500 seats as well
as a fixit shop, a dress shop, a frozen-food and refrigerator-business locker, a
café or drive-in restaurant, a book and stationery shop, a baby and toy shop,
a haberdashery, and an athletic goods store, in addition to dentists' and physicians' offices, which should be on the second floor of a commercial building.

Some planners strongly advocate the setting aside of special areas for children's playgrounds for use while the mothers shop. Experienced operators,
however, are skeptical about this because of the possibility of expensive law-
suits arising if any of the children should contract contagious or infectious
diseases or be injured. At all events it seems desirable in shopping centers to
allow space for baby carriages and to have an overseer who watches them but

FIGURE 77. RIDGEWAY SHOPPING CENTER, STAMFORD, CONNECTICUT. THREE VIEWS

Alfons Bach, designer; Thorn & Jorge, architects

Courtesy Thorn & Jorge

renders no service. Inclusion of a bowling alley is sometimes advocated, but it must be remembered that its long blank walls (like those of a theater) may tend to create dead areas which are damaging to the shopping continuity unless small shallow stores are placed in front of them or the building itself is located on the outskirts of the shopping center.

In contrast with the excessive mortality among retail stores in the United States—due to ignorance or disregard of the law of supply and demand as well as to the tendency in cities of zoning for too high a commercial concentration—the well-planned shopping center offers security against cutthroat competition and failure and thus attracts the best and most forward-looking merchants.

CHOICE OF A SITE

In general it may be said that a proper site for a shopping center would be one that is determined by the center of population and also by the area's prox-

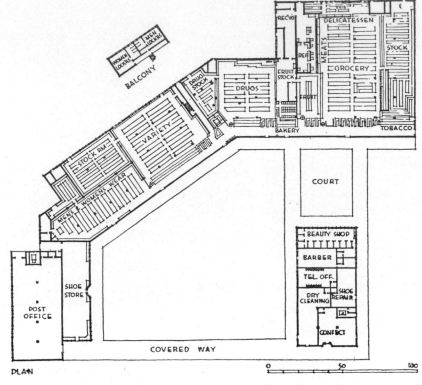

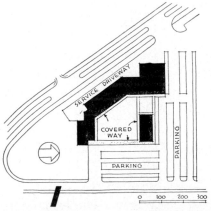

FIGURE 78. SHOPPING CENTER,
VANCOUVER HOUSING AUTHORITY,
VANCOUVER, WASHINGTON.
TWO PLANS
A. E. Doyle and Associate, architects
From *Architectural Record*

imity to main avenues of access to the neighborhood. Most planners agree,
however, that it should not be directly on such thoroughfares, but there is
some difference of opinion on this point. It may be well to remember that,
although the shopping center depends on vehicular traffic, pedestrian patronage
may also be important, especially if a large apartment group is located near by.

A shopping center should be so located that any resident of the community can reach it safely on foot, without walking more than half a mile, or conveniently by car with the assurance that he will find a parking space upon arrival. It should be on as level ground as possible and must be capable of accommodating great variations in store depth, since some shops may need a depth of only 20 feet whereas others require as much as 200 feet. All the access streets from surrounding and contributing areas must be studied carefully; if necessary, land may be given up to access roads in addition to the parking space in order to make it easier for all members of the community to circulate easily through the center (see Fig. 86). Consideration must be given to possible future competitive areas in adjoining districts and to the distances customers have to walk. Small centers should never be less than a mile apart; larger ones with capacious parking facilities should be separated by a much greater distance. Small shopping centers of perhaps four or five units are a risky venture unless definite plans are contemplated for future increase. In general, it takes at least twenty shops of various types to make a successful center.[2]

In order to eliminate the extra traffic of delivery trucks through the residential lanes, as well as to make it convenient for the residents to stop on their way home from work, a center should be located at the periphery rather than in the heart of a neighborhood, and preferably it should be on the going-home side of the street. As mentioned before, through traffic, such as that along main highways, will not bring patronage; on the contrary, it will divide rather than integrate the center and will make parking more difficult. On the other hand, merchants are almost unanimous in their desire for their shops to be seen by as many people as possible and to be close to the flow of population.

PARKING FACILITIES

In a survey made in 1933 in Los Angeles it was found that a far larger percentage of automobiles entering a retail district stopped if the center was off the main traffic road and if the parking space was adequate and easily accessible. A parking area is a dominant requirement in the planning of shopping centers. Automobile traffic, as far as practicable, should be separated from pedestrian traffic, but the best methods for accomplishing this must be left to the designer, who will weigh all the factors of accessibility, cost, organization of space, and the like before attacking this important problem. The majority of the shopping

[2] There are two exceptions to this generalization: (1) the small local shopping center for a comparatively isolated housing group; and (2) small specialized shopping centers at strategic locations in high-income suburbs.

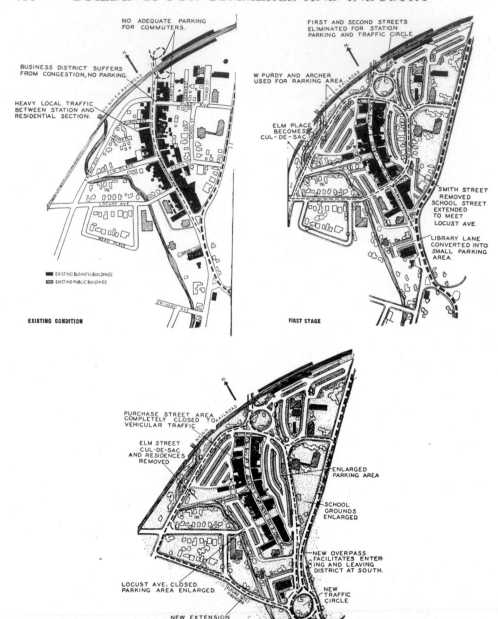

FIGURE 79. PROPOSED SHOPPING CENTER, RYE, NEW YORK. EXISTING, FIRST-STAGE, AND FINAL PLANS

Ketchum, Giná & Sharp, architects

From *Architectural Forum*

FIGURE 80. PROPOSED SHOPPING CENTER, RYE, NEW YORK. VIEW
Ketchum, Giná & Sharp, architects

From *Architectural Forum*

centers built to date have faced the main thoroughfare and have been set back from it just enough to provide various depths of parking. The enclosed or court type of parking space, which usually requires more land, is far more attractive and satisfactory because it allows traffic to be much more efficiently organized and trucks, autos, and pedestrians more easily separated. In this case, although the shops may turn their backs to the main highway, large signs will identify them just as effectively as would the store fronts themselves.

Parking facilities, as determined by the probable amount of drive-in, should always be visible, convenient, and accessible. Except for store operations customer parking is the major factor. The customer parking space should be as close to the shop entrances as possible, so that people need not carry their packages for long distances, especially in regions like the northern part of the United States where there is much adverse weather. Since women do most of the shopping and most of the driving, angle parking is an important consideration. Women want free access and exit from the parking area, aisles wide enough so that their cars will not get bumped by other cars trying to maneuver in and out of parking spaces, and free access to their car doors when other cars are parked alongside. Two square feet of parking for every square foot of store area is a minimum requirement; in California three square feet of total parking for each square foot of floor space is advocated, and the tendency in recent years has been to allow even more. The minimum stall width per car should be 8 feet, but 8 feet 6 inches or 9 feet is better. The minimum width of lot for diagonal parking is 50 feet; for right-angle parking, 65 feet.

In some cities back parking is prevalent, but in many others, especially if the shopping centers are of moderate size, front parking is preferred. In either

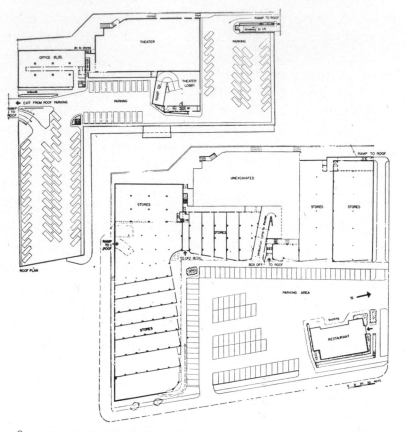

FIGURE 81. SHOPPING CENTER, COLLEGE PARK, MARYLAND. TWO PLANS
Berla & Abel, architects; John and Drew Eberson, architects for the theater

From *Architectural Forum*

case it is important to lay out the parking space with safety for pedestrians in mind. Some large units have provided parking facilities on the roofs of their buildings. In order to prevent center employees from using customers' areas, which usually have a large turnover, it has become necessary to provide and designate separate parking areas for them; these, however, can be less accessibly located. Space for delivery trucks is a necessity, and such traffic should be separated from the customer auto traffic. Customer parking areas should be made attractive by suitable landscaping and well-designed entrances.

PLANNING AND DESIGN

It is impossible to lay down strict recommendations on the planning and design of the shopping center proper, because the variables are too great; these depend on the objectives of the management (quite different in each case), the area available, the climate, local customs, changing conditions, types of buying power, building codes, transportation facilities, labor conditions (as well as union conditions), the feasibility of self-service operations, highway systems, and many other factors, all of which affect the solution of a given problem. It may be said in general, however, that in designing a shopping center, the architect must consider the practical needs first and he must weigh carefully the cost of the investment against the financial returns.

A center designed as a group can be controlled and made attractive. People take pride in a well-designed and well-organized center. Several wartime projects demonstrated the architectural possibilities inherent in the problem; they showed, too, that the manner in which a center is planned and its development is controlled is instrumental in retaining the maximum amount of spending power of the community within the neighborhood. People learn to think of the shopping center as the focus and symbol of their community life, especially if in addition to the bare shopping requirements there are theaters and tearooms and meeting halls where people may use their leisure time in various social and cultural pursuits. It is by speculating on the far-reaching possibilities of these renewed community ties—akin to those existing in the New England towns of old with all their restraining as well as liberating powers—that we begin to see the importance of a fully developed center as a unit of community life in contrast to the cruel, amorphous, and disorganized modern city

In designing a center it is important to strive for a harmonious architectural character. Harmony may be obtained by interestingly relating each building to the whole and also by the intelligent use of color, which in a dynamic way may help to integrate many otherwise unrelated forms, but above all it may be gained by proper landscaping. Good arrangement of planting material and the use of lawn areas dotted with shade trees and sitting spaces may do a great deal to draw people to the center; it will provide an area where children may play while shopping is being done, and for the shoppers themselves it affords a pleasant place to rest and linger or to consort with their neighbors. In order to preserve a pleasing harmony, the exterior signs should be controlled, not only because they may affect any well-studied color scheme but also because cheap posters, such as those currently used by some beverage companies, can spoil the general tone of the whole center. Unfortunately such controls are usually enforced with difficulty. The architectural effect of the center should be ob-

FIGURE 82. SHOPPING CENTER, MCLAUGHLIN HEIGHTS, OREGON. VIEW
Pietro Belluschi, architect

Photograph Leonard Delano, courtesy Pietro Belluschi

tained primarily through an imaginative solution of the problem. As in all convincing architectural solutions, no practical usefulness should be sacrificed for mere architectural effect; but a sensitive use of materials, fixtures, and colors can give great distinction to a project without adding to its cost.

Second-floor space in small shopping centers is of questionable value. It becomes valuable only in the larger centers, those with forty or fifty stores, where doctors' offices, insurance agencies, and lawyers' and auditors' offices are in demand. It must be remembered that, although these professional men may bring desirable customers to the center, space for them is usually divided into small offices with a great deal of equipment and such offices cost more to build and operate. It is important to keep both floor and ceiling levels in adjoining shops the same to allow them to be thrown together should necessity arise. This also means avoiding structural partitions, which cannot be removed without expensive trussing, as well as partitions with piping and ducts. The ceiling height in small stores need not be more than 11 or 12 feet unless a mezzanine is needed, in which case the minimum height will be 16 to 17 feet.

FIGURE 83.
SHOPPING CENTER,
MCLAUGHLIN HEIGHTS,
OREGON. TWO VIEWS
Pietro Belluschi, architect
Photographs Leonard Delano,
courtesy Pietro Belluschi

When the slope of the land is not too great, it has been found desirable in some cases to slant the entire floor of the building in order to avoid steps when several bays are thrown together. This necessitates adjusting the fixtures to the slant; this is not difficult if the slope is slight. Even if all the leases are signed before construction begins, it is desirable to make the floor plan extremely flexible to take care of future changes, both in tenants' occupancy and needs. To accomplish this, among other things it is desirable to space the columns evenly and have them as far apart as possible, with the outer row perhaps set back from the property line from 4 to 6 feet to allow complete freedom of design on the store front proper; this of course necessitates cantilever construction.

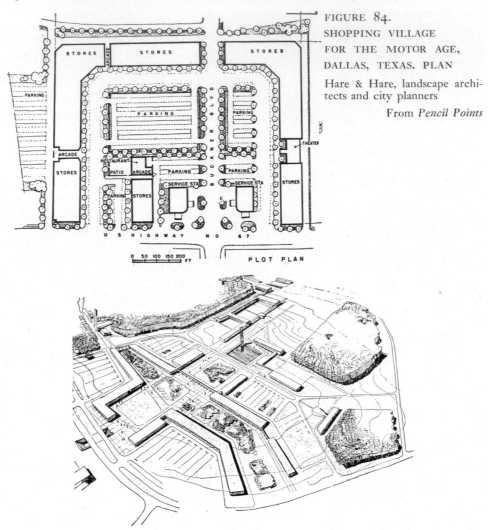

FIGURE 84.
SHOPPING VILLAGE
FOR THE MOTOR AGE,
DALLAS, TEXAS. PLAN

Hare & Hare, landscape architects and city planners

From *Pencil Points*

FIGURE 85. PROPOSED TOWN CENTER, WILLOW RUN, MICHIGAN. BIRD'S-EYE VIEW

Saarinen & Swanson, architects

From *Architectural Forum*

Marquees are not looked upon with equal favor in all parts of the country. They are more desirable perhaps where there is an abundance of sunshine than where there is considerable rain—because sun is more damaging to displayed merchandise and awnings are unsightly and hard to maintain; also because in rainy climates marquees shut out too much natural light. If awnings are used, their color and design as well as the manner and the time in which they can be operated are factors in their selection, which should be under the architect's control.

DISTRIBUTION OF SPACE

The modern food store needs a greater width in proportion to depth than did the old store, since everything that is for sale must be visible and within reach of the purchasers. Open shelves and good circulation facilitate self-service and therefore reduce the cost of clerks and increase the rate of turnover. Easy delivery of stock by auto truck has greatly reduced the necessity of devoting large spaces to storage. The need for a basement varies with different conditions. If the land is cheap and the lots are deep, basements are not so necessary as in high-cost land. Supermarkets with a large turnover and daily deliveries need not have basements, but some variety or specialty stores can use all the storage space they can get. It must be remembered that, although basements may be necessary for heating plants, in many cases they are expensive to construct or to keep dry. Some large chain stores, especially in certain cities, have made it a policy to use basements for bargain merchandising, and at times a larger volume of business is transacted there than on the ground floor.

It is important to group the merchants who have the same type of clientele and whose merchandise is similar in nature; a hardware store, for instance, should not be placed near a women's apparel shop. It may be well to designate the general types of merchandise a merchant is permitted to sell and also to state the hours when a store shall be opened and closed. Uniformity in the latter respect is important in a center; if possible, all the merchants should be required to stay open one or two nights a week. It is good planning in a large shopping center to distribute strong trade pullers so as to avoid serious dead spots. Certain service shops, such as the post office, even though not profitable, are essential and bring customers to a center; sometimes they even help in getting a small center started. A hardware store or a theater, however, should not be given the best or the most central location. Filling stations and drive-in eating places should be placed not between retail shops but at the edge of the center near the main arteries, and they should be properly controlled and required to keep their areas neat and orderly. The same principle in the matter of position applies to banks, which because of their early closing hours should be placed somewhat "off location."

General maintenance shops and supply quarters, as well as administration

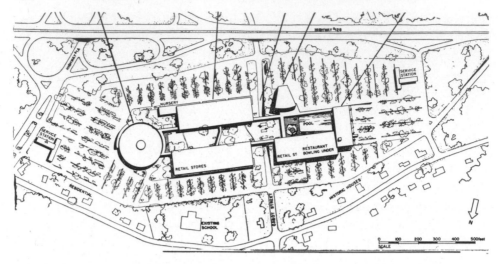

FIGURE 86. NORTH SHORE SHOPPING CENTER, BEVERLY, MASSACHUSETTS. PLAN

Ketchum, Giná & Sharp and Anderson & Beckwith, associated architects; Kenneth Welch, consultant; Frederick J. Adams, site planner; A. & S. Shurcliff and Thomas D. Church, associated landscape architects

offices, must be included in the planning of a shopping center. Merchant associations usually are willing and eager to promote co-operation as well as to keep the center clean and adequately policed.

THE SUPERMARKET

A trend that has been evident for many years—that of joining retail stores of different kinds into one large establishment where efficient methods of merchandising can be put into full effect—has finally blossomed in the retail grocery field into the supermarket. In the United States this type of market is progressively handling more and more (recently as much as 70 per cent) of the nation's total food distribution (see Figs. 88, 89). One of the most successful innovations in this type of business has been the self-service supermarket, which has become an important and typically American institution. Begun as an experiment, it soon proved an enormous success and demonstrated beyond a doubt that people like to look over the stock and make their selections at leisure, changing their minds as they wish. The visibility of all the merchandise displayed greatly increases sales. Both sales methods and sales psychology have been developed to a fine art—for example, sharp corners that obscure merchandise are no longer tolerated and special cash registers take care of

FIGURE 87.
NORTH SHORE
SHOPPING CENTER,
BEVERLY,
MASSACHUSETTS.
AIR VIEW AND
VIEW IN COURT

Ketchum, Giná &
Sharp and Anderson
& Beckwith, associated
architects; Kenneth
Welch, consultant;
Frederick J. Adams,
site planner; A. & S.
Shurcliff and Thomas
D. Church, associated
landscape architects

Courtesy
Ketchum, Giná
& Sharp

customers with small purchases who may be in a hurry. Many other features have been added by enterprising managers; even meat is cut and packaged for self-service. This increase of self-service is changing present packaging methods and making packaging an art: every article on the shelf must draw the buyer's attention to itself and must have the selling power of an advertising poster.

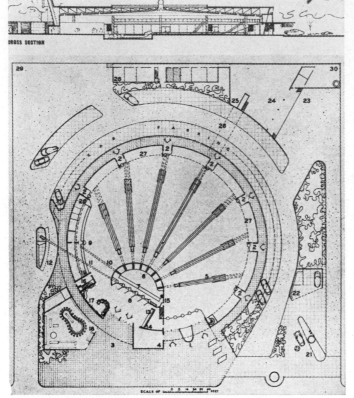

FIGURE 88.
SUPERMARKET
FOR 194X.
PLAN AND SECTION

J. Gordon Carr, architect

From *Architectural
Forum*

Similar features have been introduced in almost all the departments of a shopping center.

Today in the United States there are 10,000 self-service markets, which comprise only 2.6 per cent of the number of retail grocery stores yet sell almost 30 per cent of the groceries. The trend is toward bigger and better but fewer stores. The Atlantic & Pacific has cut the number of its stores from 15,000 to 6,000 and at the same time has increased its volume over the billion-dollar-a-year mark. This it has achieved by continually improving its methods, hiring competent help, and emphasizing the importance of attracting customers by having better merchandise more strikingly displayed.

Some managers have hired hostesses to keep friendly contacts; others have professional dietitians; still others have established nurseries where young children are taken care of by competent nurses while their mothers shop. Free color movies have been scheduled for some neighborhood supermarkets in New York, Chicago, and Los Angeles. Here the purpose, frankly stated, is

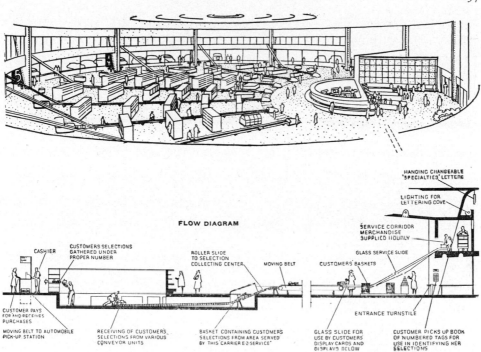

FIGURE 89. SUPERMARKET FOR 194X. INTERIOR AND FLOW DIAGRAM

J. Gordon Carr, architect

From *Architectural Forum*

to sell the housewife right up to the moment she parts with her money. The free movie program is to run for about ten minutes and to include entertainment and educational shorts as well as commercials. The supermarket is a natural outgrowth of the shopping center, and under skillful management its future is bright indeed.

Yet no supermarket can take the place of a well-planned shopping center, although it may occupy a dominant position in one. The major advantage of the shopping center so far as the customer is concerned lies in the fact that in a relatively small space he can find available many different kinds of goods and services for which he has frequent need. With the spreading out of suburban growth around all the great cities of the United States the necessity for strategically located and well-planned shopping centers is increasing.

Two basic classes of shopping center, both founded on natural demands, have arisen. The first is the local center, which may depend as much on pedestrian as on automobile traffic. The second is the much larger recentralized shopping center, which serves a wide area and depends entirely on automobile traffic. The latter may even be in the open country provided it is convenient to important thoroughfares, and it may be large in size and perhaps centered around a branch department store. In both cases the shopping center not only will act as a focus for the distribution of goods but will also furnish a new opportunity for social intercourse. In this respect it may become an important feature in the social life of the future and may supply, at least to some degree, the neighborliness and the dynamic yet personal quality which characterized the market squares of the older towns.

SUGGESTED ADDITIONAL READING FOR CHAPTER 30

Baker, Geoffrey, and Bruno Funaro, *Shopping Centers* . . . (New York: Reinhold, 1951).

"College Park Shopping Center," Berla & Abel, architects, *Architectural Forum*, Vol. 84 (1946), March, pp. 137–38.

"Community of Markets" for the University of Southern California, Rowland H. Crawford, architect, *California Arts and Architecture*, May, 1942, Industrial Supplement No. 1, pp. 39 ff.

"Community Shopping Centers," *Architectural Record*, Vol. 87 (1940), June, pp. [99]–120.

"Desert Shopping Center near Phoenix, Arizona," *Architectural Forum*, Vol. 83 (1945), November, pp. 164–65.

Dowling, Robert, "Neighborhood Shopping Centers," *Architectural Forum*, Vol. 79 (1943), October, pp. 76–78.

"Linda Vista," Whitney Smith, architect, *Architectural Forum*, Vol. 81 (1944), September, pp. 81–93.

"Neighborhood Shopping Center," *Architectural Record*, Vol. 102 (1947), December, pp. 123–25.

"194x Shopping Center," Gruenbaum (Gruen) & Krummeck, architects, *Architectural Forum*, Vol. 78 (1943), May, pp. 101–3.

"Oak Ridge, Tennessee, Town Center," Skidmore, Owings & Merrill, architects, *Architectural Forum*, Vol. 83 (1945), October, pp. 106–7.

"Planning Neighborhood Shopping Centers" (pamphlet by Marcel Villeneuve), reviewed in *Architectural Record*, Vol. 99 (1946), January, p. 122.

"Proposed Shopping Center, Stamford, Connecticut," *Architectural Forum*, Vol. 83 (1945), December, pp. 107–9.

"Remedy for a Common Commercial Ailment—Ridgeway Shopping Center, Stamford, Connecticut," Alfons Bach, designer; Thorn & Jorge, architects, *Architectural Record*, Vol. 102 (1947), December, pp. 112–14.

"Rye Shopping Center," Ketchum, Giná & Sharp, architects, *Architectural Forum*, Vol. 85 (1946), August, pp. 76–79.

"Shopping Center in Bellevue, Washington," *Architectural Forum*, Vol. 86 (1947), April, pp. 76–78.

"Shopping Center for Suburban Boston," Ketchum, Giná & Sharp, architects, *Architectural Forum*, Vol. 86 (1947), June, pp. 84–93.

"Shopping Center for Vancouver" (McLoughlin Heights), A. E. Doyle & Associates (Pietro Belluschi), architects, *Architectural Record*, Vol. 92 (1942), October, pp. 66–67.

"Shopping Facilities in Wartime—Design and Planning," *Architectural Record*, Vol. 92 (1942), October, pp. 62–78.

"Shopping Terminals and Stores," Building Types Study, *Architectural Record*, Vol. 97 (1945), February, pp. 85–109.

"Shopping Village for the Motor Age, Dallas," *Pencil Points*, Vol. 29 (1945), July, p. 78.

Stein, Clarence, and Catherine Bauer, "Store Buildings—and Neighborhood Shopping Centers," *Architectural Record*, Vol. 75 (1934), February, pp. 175–187.

Welch, Kenneth C., "Regional Shopping Centers," *American Institute of Planners Journal*, Vol. 14 (1948), fall number, pp. 4–9.

31
Office Buildings

By WALLACE K. HARRISON

A REMARKABLE FEATURE of twentieth-century life has been the extraordinary development of complex types of business and industry. This development has been marked by the growing importance of the administrative and distributing factors in industry, which have come to the fore through enormous elaborations in business. In both of these—industry and business—the growing complexity resulted largely from the widened scope of credit in the broadest sense of the term and from the huge increase in all types of paper work. The well-designed office building is the perfect reflection of that trend.

Office buildings exist to provide space in which modern business and the executive activities of modern industry can be efficiently carried on. The operations involved are of two major types—those that require the meeting of individual minds through conversation, conferences, committee meetings, seller-buyer meetings, and the like and those concerned with the producing, reproducing, and storing of the multitudinous records which have become indispensable in the successful functioning of the system. The office space necessary is therefore of two basic types—the first represented by individual private offices and conference rooms, the second by file rooms and general offices where typing or accounting takes place.

Since efficiency is gained when representatives of many different businesses can be close enough together to ensure rapid and easy communication between them, it is natural that offices tend to clot together in easily accessible localities, especially in the central or downtown areas of large cities. This centralizing tendency has given rise to the office building as we know it today. Because offices of varying and easily convertible sizes and shapes are required—for even in a single company comparatively small changes in policy may entail major shifts of personnel—the first objective in the designing of office space is flexibility; the older scheme, according to which office buildings were con-

FIGURE 90. OFFICE BUILDING FOR THE SCHUCKL CANNERY COMPANY, SALINAS, CALIFORNIA. TWO VIEWS

Wurster, Bernardi & Emmons, architects

Convenient for work and in harmony with its rural environment.   Photographs Roger Sturtevant

structed with fixed partitions, is obsolete. The efficient office building, then, consists of rentable floor area that is safe, readily accessible, and as well lighted as possible. Since large numbers of people spend their entire working day in office buildings, certain services for their health and comfort are necessary.

On account of this tendency of office buildings to cluster together in centralized areas, their growth has naturally extended preponderantly in a vertical rather than a horizontal direction. This development has given rise to the typical city skyscraper of the United States. In small towns, however, although a considerable amount of office space is frequently needed, high office buildings are usually out of place and the small amount of business centered there would not support them. Nevertheless the same general space requirements obtain in both cases. The small office building of one, two, or three stories, like the large office building, must provide completely flexible, well-lighted, and rentable floor space, as well as the usual services—toilets and so forth—and easy and inviting accessibility. Beyond this the form will be dictated largely by the site conditions and by functional and other needs, all of which must be carefully considered in order to produce an economic and efficient structure and one that in its design reflects something of the vital role which business plays in the community.[1]

PLANNING OFFICE SKYSCRAPERS

The office skyscraper was developed in the metropolitan commercial centers of the United States. It is a multi-storied building whose exterior is hung on a steel or reinforced concrete framework This framework forms a multicellular steel cage built around a core of elevators, stairs, and other services. The various floors are usually subdivided into convenient work areas accessible by corridors leading from the stairs and elevators. The major factor in its plan and construction is functional over-all efficiency.

Historically the sixteen-story Monadnock Block in Chicago, one of the highest of the bearing-wall buildings, affords a convenient yardstick for measuring skyscrapers against other types of tall structures. Since the Monadnock (meaning "hill") rises to about the practical limit of a building supported by masonry walls alone, it may be said to mark the cleavage point between ancient and modern building methods. If a building is to rise above the Monadnock's roof line, it is necessary to utilize a cage of steel or of steel and concrete to support it. Steel gives to skyscrapers their vertical thrust. The builders of the Monadnock, in order to provide a foundation that would sustain the heavy weight, used walls fifteen feet thick at the base. But the mid-twentieth-century skyscraper's envelope is seldom more than two feet thick and need not vary from the ground to the roof level. It will not be long, we hope, before wall thicknesses can be reduced to as little as six inches.

The erection of tall buildings on relatively small plots of ground necessitates the use of the new type of foundation made possible by the concrete pile, the steel tube, the pneumatic caisson, and steel sheet piling. These are the engineer's and the architect's answer to the tremendous loading necessary on single slender columns, and it is these which make skyscrapers practicable under varying soil conditions. The buildings of New York, for example, stand on

---

[1] This introduction is by the editor, as are a few later paragraphs dealing with circulation and services.

FIGURE 91. TWIN OFFICE BUILDINGS, HOUSTON, TEXAS. EXTERIOR

MacKie & Kamrath, architects

One-story office buildings designed for sites near residential neighborhoods in a widely spread city.

Photograph Dorsey and Peters

firm igneous base rock; in Chicago, on the other hand, the base rock underlies a thick covering of sand and hardpan, and Miami's buildings are supported on what was formerly a part of the ocean bottom. Wherever possible, however, the supports of modern skyscrapers are carried on the firm rock core of Mother Earth. In any case the extraordinary safety record of multi-storied buildings on varying substrata attests the stability of the foundations developed for use today.

HISTORICAL PANORAMA

L. S. Buffington, a young Minneapolis architect, as early as 1880 "dreamed" of thirty-, fifty-, and even one-hundred-story buildings and made drawings, sketches, and certain engineering calculations relating to fantastic "cloud-scrapers." He did not file a patent claim until 1887 or 1888, however, and this delay permitted architect William Le Baron Jenney to complete, in 1885, the ten-story Home Insurance Building in Chicago, thus throwing the skyscraper invention into the public domain.

Regardless of the merits of Buffington's cloud-scraper, Jenney deserves credit for having given the metal cage its crucial test. About 1886 the twelve-story Rookery Building, also in Chicago, reproduced Jenney's skeleton. Subsequently the architectural firm of Burnham & Root went one step further by designing steel-grill and concrete footings in lieu of the traditional stone and cement pyramids. The result was a firmer foundation on a smaller base. A one-thousand-ton weight can pulverize natural rock, even granite; a steel and concrete grillage, when laid directly on rock, distributes the load without injuring the contacting surfaces.

Chicago, then, was both the birthplace of and the proving ground for sky-

FIGURE 92. OFFICE BUILDING FOR THE
SEABOARD FINANCE CORPORATION, LOS
ANGELES, CALIFORNIA. TWO VIEWS

Eugene Weston, architect

A small urban office building, direct and simple in treatment.   Photographs Fred R. Dapprich

scraper planning and construction. In 1887 the architectural firm of Holabird & Roche collaborated with Purdy & Henderson, bridge engineers, on the fourteen-story Tacoma Building there, the first skyscraper with outer walls that served only to enclose the structure and protect its tenants against exposure and weather. The exterior brick and terra cotta were carried at each floor by steel spandrel beams attached to cast-iron columns. Chicagoans were the first to witness the strange spectacle of bricklayers commencing walls halfway between the street and the roof.

In rapid succession came the Rand-McNally Building, built around a skeleton of rolled steel beams and columns riveted together, and Jenney's Leiter Building, the first without a single self-supporting wall. Then in 1890, climaxing what was one of the most fruitful ten-year periods in the history of human shelter, Burnham & Root designed the twenty-one-story Masonic Temple, the highest inhabited structure in the world and a leading attraction of its day. In a single decade the skyscraper concept had sprung from a dream to actual competition with a mountain.

ORGANIC STYLE

Grudgingly, in 1889, New York City's Building Department authorized the first steel-skeleton structure, the Tower Building, on lower Broadway. Ap-

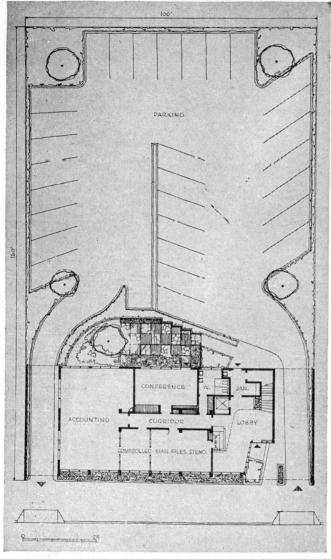

FIGURE 93. OFFICE BUILDING FOR THE SEABOARD FINANCE CORPORATION, LOS ANGELES, CALIFORNIA. PLAN

Eugene Weston, architect

Even in small office buildings both efficiency and flexibility in plan must be considered.

From *Architectural Record*

parently it failed to impress the pundits who wrote on architecture for the New International Encyclopedia of 1904:

. . . In spite of the radical character of these changes in construction and plan, no sign of any architectural result has appeared. This is in part owing to the purely commercial character of such buildings . . . Hitherto in the history of the world, no architecture of any value has been developed out of any such condition.

Although as an expression of "base commercialism" the early skyscrapers

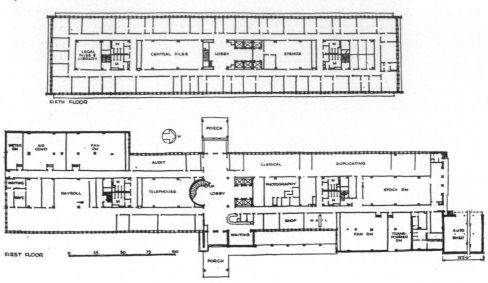

FIGURE 94. ESSO BUILDING, BATON ROUGE, LOUISIANA. PLANS

Lathrop Douglass, architect; Carson & Lundin, associated

An office building of medium height planned with careful regard for simple circulation.

From *Architectural Record*

earned abuse from critics in all parts of the Republic, nevertheless their plain advantages over four- and five-story buildings—both as efficient machines and especially as profit makers—soon attracted more and more promoters, investors, and tenants.

The story of the skyscraper, unlike that of any other manifestation of architecture, is associated primarily with two American cities: born in Chicago, it matured in New York. In both we can identify almost every significant building that contributed to its development. At the outset Louis Sullivan discerned and expressed in his buildings the functional nature of the skyscraper; many of his successors, however, were not content with this and applied historical motifs and designs to the façade. We find church steeples surmounting commercial skyscrapers; a dome crowns the New York World Building on Park Row, and elaborate Gothic relief covers Woolworth's "Cathedral of Commerce" on lower Broadway. Such embellishments often obscured but they never changed the architectural nature of the steel grill. Some of us now regard those and similar anachronistic structures as symbols of groping and confusion; they certainly fail to interpret the life or state of affairs in a present-day Ameri-

FIGURE 95. ESSO BUILDING, BATON ROUGE, LOUISIANA. MODEL

Lathrop Douglass, architect; Carson & Lundin, associated

A pleasant mass results from the imaginative use of necessary elements and the creative expression of structure and materials.   Photograph Louis H. Dreyer, courtesy Carson & Lundin

can city. Conventional styles in architecture disappear slowly, but in this century of flash communication and high-speed travel traditional forms are at last yielding to the demands of efficiency. Out of sheer necessity men are conceiving a functional architecture and letting the simplicity and beauty of the new forms and materials speak for themselves.

OVER-ALL EFFICIENCY THE AIM

Office buildings are places where human beings, in centers where the density is highest, can work and exchange ideas with efficiency and comfort. The skyscraper like the human organism is multicellular, its distinguishing internal feature being the repetition of a unit type of space or module based on human scale and designed to promote over-all efficiency.

The Romans are supposed to have built apartment houses ten or eleven stories high, with a height of less than 6 feet from floor to ceiling on the upper floors. But most cities today have health and building safety standards which demand a minimum of 8 feet of clear space from floor to ceiling. From practical experience in the more recent past it has been found necessary in an average office building to make the height from floor to floor about 11'–6"; this is the prevailing height in the buildings of Rockefeller Center in New York. Modern air conditioning, however, demands such great spaces for duct work that, until new and more efficient means of moving cold fresh air or liquid are devised, the heights from floor to floor must be made about 12'–6" in order to achieve 8'–0" in the clear at the lowest point. With this new factor

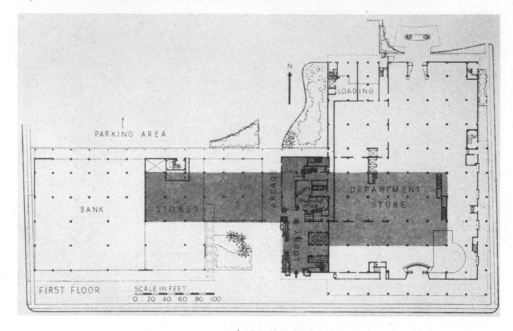

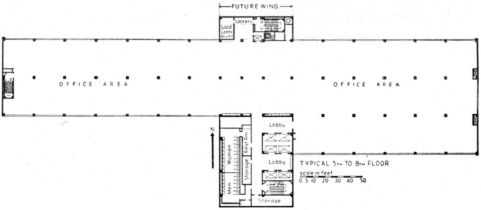

FIGURE 96. PRUDENTIAL INSURANCE COMPANY BUILDING, LOS ANGELES, CALIFORNIA. PLANS

Wurdeman & Becket, architects

An office building combined with a large store; note the careful handling of the entrances and the vertical-circulation core.　　　　　　　From *Architectural Forum*

of air-conditioning ducts to consider, office heights in the clear will seldom for reasons of economy be more than 9'-0".

The dimensions of office units have changed but little in the first half of the twentieth century. We figure that "workable" daylight normally penetrates

FIGURE 97.
PRUDENTIAL
INSURANCE
COMPANY
BUILDING,
LOS ANGELES,
CALIFORNIA.
EXTERIOR

Wurdeman & Becket, architects

The complexities of the program give rise to a mass composition of great interest.

Photograph
Julius Shulman

into a building a distance about one and one-half times the height of the top of the window from the floor. This means that, if the head of the window is between 8 and 9 feet high, workable daylight will penetrate to a depth of about 12'–0"; hence the normal depth of a daylight-lit office is usually set at 12'–0". Generally a man with a 12'–0" office needs an inner space of approximately 12 to 15 feet for a secretary or a reception room. If, on the other hand, a deep office or a large conference room is wanted, the outer and inner offices can be combined into one space between 24 and 27 feet deep from the wall to the corridor. The width of corridors varies from 5 to 8 feet.

The steel frame in an office building performs several functions: (1) it supports all the weights of the building vertically, including its own; (2) it provides enough rigidity against the wind to permit the inhabitants to maintain a satisfactory level of comfort and a feeling of security; and (3) it protects the building from being overturned by hurricanes or earthquakes. A skyscraper is like a vertical pole held firmly on the ground either by its own weight or by being fastened to the ground. To provide enough stiffness so that human beings at the top of this "pole" will not get seasick, wind bracing must be provided in the form of what are known as "bents." These must reach from wall to wall transversely throughout the building; since the beams and columns which make up the bents are large, it is generally better to place them back of the elevators. In a high building the spacing of the columns on the outside walls is ordinarily based on the distance from back to back of two

FIGURE 98. DAILY NEWS
BUILDING, NEW YORK

Howells & Hood, architects

A brilliant vertical accent, emphasizing the four-foot units, combined with a subtle rhythmic mass
design.   Courtesy *Daily News*

elevator banks with a lobby between them; this is usually 27 to 28 feet.[2] The
generally accepted rule is to divide the outside walls into vertical units of
approximately 4'–0" for convenience in laying out average offices from 8 to
12 feet wide and 12 feet deep.

In the high buildings of the past the outside wall was of masonry at least
12 inches thick; of this the middle 4 inches (or more) rested on the spandrel
beams, with waterproofing and insulation on the inside and stone or brick on
the outside. Such walls have three major defects: their weight (except in very
tall buildings where such weight is necessary to withstand the overturning
moment due to wind pressure), their thickness, and the possibility of water
seepage. The new skyscrapers will be constructed with walls of thin metal,
with not over 5 inches of insulation on the inside—a total of 6 inches instead
of 12 to 24 inches in thickness. No window that is as tight and simple for use in
a high building as the double-hung window has been developed. It has, however, only one great drawback—it can only be cleaned from outside. The new
windows will be not only economical to build as well as tight but also reversible
so that they can be cleaned from the inside of the building. Possibly a sprinkler
washing system will be invented which will automatically wash the outside of

[2] Frequently that spacing will apply in one direction only; the spacing of the columns at right
angles to this will be determined by two considerations: one the economical bay width and the
other the typical office module. (See also Vol. II, Chap. 16, page 435).

FIGURE 99.
MCGRAW-HILL BUILDING,
NEW YORK

Raymond Hood, architect

The horizontal expression results
from the emphasis on the floor
planes and the continuity of window bands, into which the column
faces are absorbed by their colored
facings.

Courtesy McGraw-Hill
Building Corp.

skyscraper windows; an adjustable exterior scaffold is already being proposed.

VERTICAL CIRCULATION

Generally the skyscraper is composed of a series of approximately fifteen-story buildings placed one on top of another. At every fifteenth floor are placed the elements ordinarily kept in the basement: tanks, fire-fighting equipment, mechanical grouping rooms, and so on. This height of approximately fifteen stories is determined by the laws governing an efficient elevator system.[3] In a large measure the success of an office skyscraper depends on the efficiency of its vertical transportation system. To promote this efficiency, the elevator shafts are usually located within a 100-foot to 125-foot walking radius of all the office units on a floor. The otherwise rentable floor area taken up by the elevator shafts increases in direct proportion to a building's height. Thus in a typical eight-story building the elevators occupy about 1.90 per cent of

[3] The vertical zoning of tall structures is also necessitated by various plumbing and heating requirements See Vol. I, Chap. 7, on mechanical equipment.

FIGURE 100.
ROCKEFELLER
CENTER, NEW YORK.
AIR VIEW FROM
THE EAST

Reinhard & Hofmeister;
Corbett, Harrison & Mac-
Murray; and Hood &
Fouilhoux, associated ar-
chitects

Sufficient separation of
the towers permits light
and air to penetrate the
group.

Photograph Thomas
Airviews, courtesy
Rockefeller Center,
Inc.

the total theoretical floor area, whereas in a skyscraper of seventy-five stories the shafts take up about 9.78 per cent of that area.

High buildings cannot function with inadequate vertical transportation. The modern multi-voltage, signal-control, micro-leveling passenger elevator contributes much to the premium values of skyscraper offices. It is now commonplace for elevators to travel from 1,000 to 1,200 feet per minute, and the waiting period averages only thirty seconds. In practice this means that one can reach the top office stories of the 1,250-foot Empire State Building in slightly more than a minute after leaving the ground. Similar elevator standards prevail in other modern skyscrapers. To maintain an average thirty-second waiting period, one elevator is required for every 15,000 to 17,000 square feet of rented space. For a height of fifteen stories it has been found through practice that six to eight elevators, carrying between twenty and twenty-five passengers each, form the most efficient grouping of elevators in

FIGURE 101. ROCKEFELLER CENTER, NEW YORK. VIEW FROM THE NORTH, THE RCA BUILDING IN THE MIDDLE

Reinhard & Hofmeister; Corbett, Harrison & MacMurray; and Hood & Fouilhoux, associated architects

The breaks in the side plane of the buildings both parallel and express the heights of the various elevator banks.   Photograph Maurey Garber, courtesy Rockefeller Center, Inc.

a bank. More than eight means that too much time is lost in getting to the farthest elevator; less than eight will not generally provide, with present-day traffic, the interval necessary for efficiency.

Real-estate analysts frequently maintain that skyscrapers divert much pedestrian traffic from the street and thus help reduce congestion in metropolitan areas. In the Equitable Life Building in New York, for instance, the forty-eight passenger elevators carry about 96,000 people per day between the hours of 8 A.M. and 6 P.M.; in the course of a year these elevators travel 275,000 miles, roughly equivalent to eleven globe-girdling trips around the equator. The building's permanent population is about 12,000 people, and 135,000 individuals enter and leave in a normal business day.

Inter-floor circulation is also important, especially in buildings where the

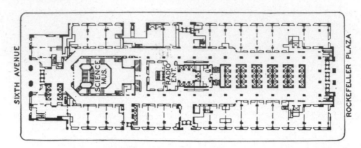

FIGURE 102. RCA BUILDING, ROCKEFELLER CENTER, NEW YORK. MAIN-FLOOR PLAN

Reinhard & Hofmeister; Corbett, Harrison & MacMurray; and Hood & Fouilhoux, associated architects

A typical arrangement of elevator banks as a central core; note the large area necessary for the ground floor of a skyscraper.

tenants all belong to one industry. The volume of this traffic is indicated by more statistics from the Equitable Life Building. In this skyscraper, six of the forty-eight elevators are reserved solely for circulation between the second and thirty-eighth stories. An average of forty people are continually ascending or descending between those two floors all through the working day. In buildings occupied either by a single tenant or by several tenants engaged in interlocking types of business, the inter-floor traffic often equals that on the main floor. In actual practice, elevator service for the lower three floors is generally a more time-consuming operation than that for the upper stories. In some recent buildings elevator efficiency has been aided by one or more escalator installations on the lower two stories. With a capacity of 5,000 to 6,000 passengers per hour (for the 2-foot width), escalators have proved their economy and their efficiency.

Supplementary to the elevator system, adequate fireproof stairs running from the top to the bottom of the building are required by the demands of safety. Local building codes frequently determine the number and type of such stairway exits. In any case, however, the architect must make sure that the building can be easily evacuated in case of power or elevator failure or in the event of sudden catastrophe. This will mean that buildings of average size must have two such continuous vertical stair towers and that these must be enclosed by fireproof walls and entered through fireproof, self-closing doors. In many cases the approach to at least one such tower must be by means of exterior open-air balconies. The lighting of stair exits must be carefully studied, and some means of subsidiary lighting must be furnished in case of power breakdown.

FIGURE 103. ESSO BUILDING, ROCKEFELLER CENTER, NEW YORK. ENTRANCE
Carson & Lundin, architects
The main entrance does much to set the tone of the entire structure.

Photograph Ezra Stoller—Pictorial Services; courtesy Carson & Lundin

HORIZONTAL CIRCULATION

All horizontal circulations from street door to office door must be as direct and as simple as possible. Upper floors will therefore need adequate lobbies where people can wait for elevators out of the main corridor circulation, and the upper corridors must be so planned as to combine the smallest possible area with the most direct approach from elevator to office. Where whole floors or parts of floors are rented to one tenant, much of this corridor space will be omitted, but in such cases the approach from the elevators to these large office areas is all the more important. Naturally on each floor public corridors must give adequate access to the toilet rooms and the exit stairs.

Ground-floor circulation is also an important feature of skyscraper planning. To facilitate access and egress to and from the building, it is desirable to have a main entrance to the lobby and several auxiliary entrances. A spacious lobby has a direct bearing on a building's attractiveness and safety as well as on its efficiency. The elevator banks should be easily accessible from all entrances. Since their position becomes a determining factor in the planning of the ground-floor circulation, it is necessary to study their location and

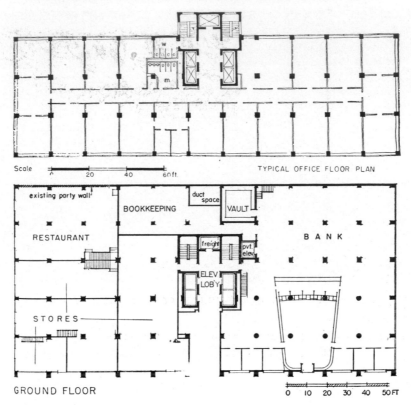

FIGURE 104. EQUITABLE BUILDING, PORTLAND, OREGON. PLANS

Pietro Belluschi, architect

The rectangularity of the urban pattern efficiently used by concentration of the circulation and the services.　　　　　　　　　　　　　From *Architectural Forum*

arrangement integrally with the basic ground-floor circulation plan. Too many turns from entrance to elevator or too great a concealment of the elevator lobbies not only destroys the possibility of effective and straightforward interior treatment but also forms a definite hindrance to easy circulation.[4]

Ample first-floor circulation to rentable concession areas is crucially important, but the first floor of a modern office building in a large city has store values which are so high that it is necessary to cut down to a minimum the circulation areas devoted to corridors, elevators, and stairs. In other words, where the greatest freedom of space is needed the renting agents push the hardest. This battle has been going on for many years. In the International Building in Rockefeller Center only the large and generous point of view of John D. Rockefeller, Jr., and his managers, Todd, Robertson & Todd, made

[4] For a further discussion of this point, see Vol. I, Chap. 6, pages 186 to 190.

FIGURE 105. EQUITABLE BUILDING,
PORTLAND, OREGON. EXTERIOR

Pietro Belluschi, architect

The same rectangularity frankly dominates
the exterior; distinction results from the austere expression of the construction and the
refined use of brilliant modern materials—
sheet metal and glass.

Photograph Roger Sturtevant through
Pictorial Services

the large entrance and halls possible. The success of Rockefeller Center shows
that this generous use of space pays in the end.

As escalators become more efficient and are more generally used in office
buildings—and possibly outdoors—the entrance lobby will probably be moved
to the second floor; then the first floor can be devoted to clear floor spaces
which, if sufficiently good, can be rented for a sum large enough to pay the
annual rental of the land on which the building stands. In such a scheme the
newsstands, drug stores, barber shops, telephone booths, and occasionally
banks and specialty shops would be located on the second, or entrance, floor.
In some skyscrapers the office population alone furnishes a patronage for
such business as large as that of a small city. When these store units are on the
first floor, however, it is well to have them accessible both from the lobby and
from the street.

SERVICES

Toilets should be provided on every floor of a multi-story office building;
in all but small buildings there should be on every floor both a men's and a
women's toilet, the approaches to which should be distant from each other

FIGURE 106. EASTERN
AIR LINES BUILDING,
ROCKEFELLER CENTER,
NEW YORK. EXTERIOR VIEW
AND MAIN-FLOOR PLAN

Reinhard & Hofmeister and Harrison & Fouilhoux, associated architects

The size and the placing of the first-floor circulation areas permit both the feeling of adequate space and large concession or shop areas.

Photograph F. S. Lincoln; plan from *Architectural Forum*

and yet convenient to the entire working area of the floor. Naturally the rigid necessity for obtaining the greatest possible amount of rentable area will affect this requirement. The general tendency will be to produce a central core containing the elevators and their lobbies, the toilets, and the exit stairs; this will bring all the non-revenue-producing parts of the building into the central dark space. The more efficient the design of that core, the more efficient will be the resultant floor plan.

DAYLIGHT AND DARKNESS

Many notions and theories are current regarding the interior illumination of a skyscraper. It is difficult to set hard-and-fast rules, but certain facts and observations deserve consideration. Despite talk about windowless air-conditioned skyscrapers, no promoter or investor has yet found the courage to build one; in fact, all available data tend to minimize the probable success of such an undertaking. A windowless skyscraper would involve no great problem for the architect and engineer, but economic, psychological, legal, and sociological factors tend to weigh against it.

FIGURE 107.
EASTERN AIR
LINES BUILDING,
ROCKEFELLER
CENTER, NEW YORK.
ENTRANCE LOBBY

Reinhard & Hofmeister
and Harrison & Fouil-
houx, associated archi-
tects

An entrance lobby of
moderate size dramatized
by the stair to the important basement areas and
beautified by a discrimi-
nating use of rich materials.

Photograph Edward
Ratcliffe, courtesy
Rockefeller Center,
Inc.

Although there is still some controversy over what constitutes the correct illumination for office work, there is no question but that tenants pay premium rentals for daylight and sunlight. An office with a first-class view and permanent unobstructed daylight nets from 40 to 400 per cent more revenue than a similar office layout dependent on artificial light. In spite of the improvements in lighting fixtures and techniques, access to natural light and a pleasant view continue to be salient factors in the practical economics of skyscrapers.

Medical and health specialists agree that the therapeutic value of daylight in working quarters is so vital that it should be given high priority in architectural planning. It is still difficult, however, to determine quantitative standards for such illumination; hence minimum requirements have not been fixed as yet, though certain conclusions may be drawn from various investigations. First, a southern exposure affords the most light; northern or eastern exposures come next in line of preference; the least desirable is a western exposure. Second, inner courts reduce the amount of natural light and frequently cut it off entirely; consequently, in current practice, courts are avoided unless they can be large, and it is the goal of many planners to separate buildings by a distance equal to their height.

Plainly the quantity of daylight which penetrates a building depends on its area of fenestration. A scientific charting of luminosity reveals a rapid decrease of light with each foot of depth. Thus on a clear day in June light enters a well-exposed window with somewhat the following results: one foot away from the window the luminosity measures 130 foot-candles, as compared with only 5 foot-candles at a distance of twenty feet from the opening. On a clear December day, however, the luminosity at a distance of one foot from the window measures about 60 foot-candles, as against 33 foot-candles twenty feet away. Since light intensity varies as the square of the distance from the source, natural illumination is rarely adequate beyond a depth of twenty-five feet. The physical law of light radiation has now become a potent factor in planning the bulk and form of buildings as well as the design of their windows and the layout of their offices.

Even if natural light were possible in all rentable skyscraper spaces, we could not do without artificial light for the daily dependability that many office operations require. In actual practice, artificial illumination is the main source of light for many thousands of office workers in New York and Chicago. In the unprecedented congestion of lower Manhattan, the vast bulk of skyscrapers and their proximity to others preclude the benefits of daylight for more than half of their occupants. Since the quality of light has a direct bearing on mental, nervous, and physical fatigue, proper illumination is extremely important for health and efficiency. Independent of or in combination with natural light, an over-all illumination of 35 foot-candles is considered desirable for most office operations. Current practice relates lighting to the modular base of an office layout and attempts to achieve over-all luminosity of the ceiling and wall areas. Direct rays of artificial light, specular glare, and sharp contrasts should be avoided.

The absence of exterior windows produces some unfavorable reactions on the part of office personnel. Modern lighting fixtures, in combination with pleasant room colors or glass partitions, help to reduce, but not to overcome, the general dissatisfaction. In a normal era of competition for office tenants, windowless space cannot match the value or attraction of offices affording natural light and view.

AIR CONDITIONING

Coincident with light control, there is some demand for year-round control of temperature, humidity, and the germ content of office air. Some skyscrapers are at mid-century completely air-conditioned, and more such buildings are projected. The immobility and inflexibility of air-conditioning units, however, make this type of equipment a very expensive part of the cost of a skyscraper.

The air-conditioning experts of the future may find a way to provide such comfort at a price that the average man can afford.

ECONOMICS OF HEIGHT, BULK, AND FORM

The common basis for ascertaining the most economical form, bulk, and height of an office skyscraper is the value placed on the site. Therefore *land value* constitutes an index of earning potential and a primary factor in planning the most economical and profitable building. Generally a 10 per cent gross return on equity in office buildings is considered a minimum inducement for capital investment, and this 10 per cent is a second base from which to compute the form, bulk, and height a building should possess. Assuming that rentals increase in the same ratio as land values, it is possible to determine the *true economic height* for an office skyscraper on a given plot. Various studies apply the formula that the higher the land value the higher the economic height of a building may be. Thus it was figured that, on land worth $100 per square foot, the maximum possible return would come from a building with 33 rentable square feet for each square foot of ground—which means approximately a building of sixty-three stories. Similarly, for $300 land the maximum return would come from a building of slightly more than eighty stories. Above a height of about sixty stories, however, it is very difficult to make a skyscraper pay.

Although these figures may not apply to construction after the Second World War, the ratios do. Increased metropolitan land values and higher building costs are reflected in higher rentals. Pre-war skyscraper construction ranged from 55 cents to $1.00 per cubic foot; the 36,000,000 cubic feet of the Empire State Building cost about $35,000,000, or slightly less than $1.00 per cubic foot. A post-war air-conditioned building costs at least $1.75 per cubic foot. Before the war the cost of a building rose in direct ratio to its height:

> One cubic foot in an 8-story building cost 53½ cents
> One cubic foot in a 22-story building cost 55⅙ cents
> One cubic foot in a 50-story building cost 63½ cents
> One cubic foot in a 75-story building cost 70⅓ cents

But, though pre-war building costs as between a structure of eight stories and one of seventy-five registered a cubic-foot differential of about 50 per cent, the differential in rental increases ran between 70 and 140 per cent. That is, for skyscraper towers the *rental differential* varied from as little as 50 per cent to as high as 250 per cent greater than the corresponding differential in cubic-

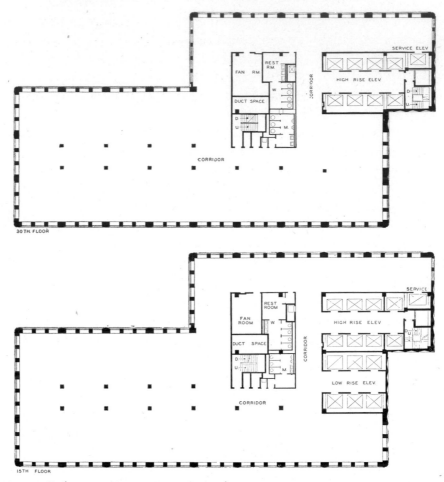

FIGURE 108 (ABOVE AND OPPOSITE, TOP). BUILDING FOR ALUMINUM COMPANY OF AMERICA, PITTSBURGH, PENNSYLVANIA. PLANS

Harrison & Abramovitz, architects; Altenhof & Brown and Mitchell & Ritchey, associate architects

The unconventional entrance arrangement (opposite) gives interest and adds to usable space.

foot building costs. Again it is pertinent to add that, although the figures have changed since pre-war days, the approximate ratios between costs and rentals still apply.

Thus it is evident that the higher construction costs of towering skyscrapers are offset by the rental premiums which the topmost stories command. Permanent daylight, unobstructed view, and privacy are some advantages which skyscraper elevations give a tenant; furthermore, traffic noise, auto-gas concentration, and the dust count decrease rapidly as higher levels are reached.

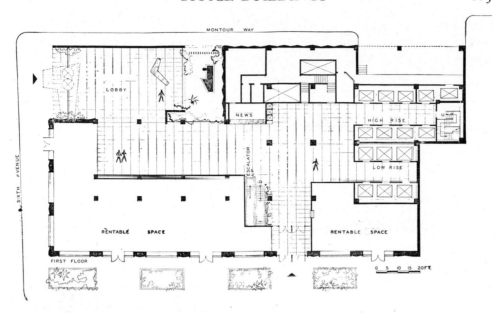

FIGURE 109. BUILDING FOR ALUMINUM COMPANY OF AMERICA, PITTSBURGH, PENNSYLVANIA. MODEL

Harrison & Abramovitz, architects; Altenhof & Brown and Mitchell & Ritchey, associate architects

Photograph James S. Hornbeck, courtesy Harrison & Abramovitz

The therapeutic and psychological value of high-level office space yields commensurate profits to building owners. Post-war skyscraper construction costs may rise to $1.50 or $2.00 per cubic foot, but these climbing prices will be compensated for by equivalent increases in revenue. In effect, a real-estate boom enhances the worth of attractive sites, and, since land value determines the true economic height of a skyscraper, a strong demand for office space means higher rentals and higher buildings. In pre-war days the true economic height on $200 land was figured by one analyst at sixty-three stories; in post-war days, the higher construction and overhead charges have indicated a lower limit to the economic height. High land values actually prohibit the construction and maintenance of low office buildings. For instance, an eight-story building on $200 land would yield only 4.22 per cent in pre-war days, whereas a building of sixty-three stories would yield the maximum 10.25 per cent.

The above figures indicate that the true economic height of a skyscraper still falls short of the maximum engineering height, commonly estimated at between 1,500 and 2,000 feet. In line with changing costs, the true economic height fluctuates from year to year, but the ratios between the components which make up capital investment and net income remain relatively stable. In some skyscrapers, the top-floor rentals per square foot are about twice as high as the second- and third-story rentals. In one New York skyscraper all the office space is rated $3.50 per square foot, plus the value placed on each window. A fifteenth-story window facing north, east, or west commands a rental of $200 per year; the same window exposure on the thirtieth story commands $500 per year. A southern exposure window on the fifteenth floor is rated at $500; on the stories between the sixteenth and the thirty-second floors this same exposure fetches $600 per window.

Another effect of great height is to increase the rentals which apply to the space on the lower four or five stories. The value of such space is generally determined by the number of people frequenting the immediate area. Since many skyscrapers attract upwards of 25,000 people in addition to a permanent tenancy of about 15,000, the near-ground floors provide strategic locations for shops, stores, and services. These areas are also favorite locations for banks.

In metropolitan areas the skyscraper form is steadily adapting itself to economic realities. Though zoning laws often permit a 100 per cent occupancy of the site up to a height of about 125 feet, there is a growing tendency to sacrifice possible bulk and floor space on the lower levels in order to gain the more desirable rental areas obtainable in the tower form. The setback provisions of the law play a large part in the final determination of economical form and bulk. Article III of the New York Building Zone Resolution divides the city into "height districts," and some of Manhattan's most valuable sites fall into the "two times height district," where ". . . no building shall be erected to a height in excess of twice the width of the street, but for each one foot that the building or a portion of it sets back from the street line four feet shall be added to the height limit of such building. . . ." In effect, the law makes setbacks imperative for most office skyscrapers.

In the case of the Empire State Building the foundation covers about two acres. The first major setback begins above the fifth floor, and other setbacks occur at the fourteenth and twenty-sixth stories. The lofty tower covers only about one-fourth of the ground area, thus assuring light and view to most of the office tenants and to the neighboring buildings.

Rockefeller Center points an object lesson. Here for the first time it was possible to plan simultaneously a group of office structures for a three-block site, and it was decided not to provide any more deep space in each than was necessary. The Center's ten buildings are all detached or semi-detached, yet they form a unit. The intervening spaces do not contribute rentals directly, but, by guaranteeing light and view to many offices which would ordinarily be denied such advantages, the outdoor spaces endow the offices with a substantial part of their rental value.

TRENDS

The Second World War, paradoxically enough, bestowed some benefits on mankind. It introduced atomic power, developed new processes and techniques, and gave birth to new wood products, textiles, plastics and other synthetic materials. Moreover, it brought aluminum out of the kitchen, so to speak, and placed unprecedented quantities of it at the disposal of architects. Although skyscraper construction was virtually suspended in the four war years, nevertheless progress was made during that hiatus; for progress in the building arts is concerned with improvements in materials and processes. War-inspired developments afforded architects fresh materials for planning new buildings and revising old concepts.

Careful appraisal for more than fifty years has shown that many of the shortcomings of the office skyscraper can be overcome but that some of its inherent advantages remain to be exploited. Its major faults stem not so much from the skyscraper itself as from its unplanned and chaotic surroundings. The ailments of many American cities can be traced to the piling up of commercial buildings without regard to the social results or the community welfare. The full evidence now points to the fact that to function most perfectly the skyscraper must stand in isolation.

The first skyscrapers were designed to relieve metropolitan space pressures, but the almost universal availability of modern travel, transport, and communication facilities leads us to inquire whether office skyscrapers are exclusively fixtures of the urban scene or whether they cannot fit into the rural pattern equally well. A number of planners contend that a country setting is functionally correct and financially sound. When situated on a main communication artery the country skyscraper can be integrated into the regional plan; its release from urban restraints will serve to magnify the beauty of its perpendicular line, and as a machine for transacting daily business it will function just as efficiently here as in the city. The trend toward industrial decentralization seems to favor such a development. Even though mass production may require horizontal buildings, it is conceivable that office efficiency may require the skyscraper.

The future also portends a dispersal and a more harmonious grouping of metropolitan skyscrapers. Available data point to the economic fallacy of crowding tall structures together into an indiscriminate patchwork. Inevitably economic and social considerations will require that office buildings be detached and also integrated into both a block plan and a regional plan.

After more than half a century of skyscraper planning, the time is ripe for the appearance of designs which will cast off unnecessary restraints and conventions. We need no longer insist on a painstaking revelation of girders and columns; the man on the street is aware that a steel grill supports our tall commercial buildings. This general understanding should invite and inspire variations on the well-known theme.

To state the trends succinctly, then, future planning is likely to veer toward a further detachment and separation of high office buildings and toward their integration with the immediate vicinity. Block planning and group planning are already demanding larger sites, more diversified ratios in plan dimensions, and even new street patterns. Large cities will doubtless experience a further segregation of industries and crafts, such as those which naturally group themselves into a garment center, furniture mart, or textile trades center.

The tall, broad-sided building will probably supersede the familiar skyscraper tower, and only the most valuable sites will justify the carrying of a building above the fiftieth floor. Conditions point to a more intensive commercialization of the lower stories of office buildings—for shops, services, showrooms, restaurants, and the like—and this calls for an extension of escalator service. More metal will be employed for building trim and enclosure purposes—notably stainless steel, aluminum, and various specialized alloys. The high value set on natural light and a view calls for maximum fenestration. Summer-sun penetration and winter heat loss can be reduced substantially by the use either of double-sheet windows, the thermal insulation properties of which promise wide application, or of special forms of Venetian blinds. The coming skyscrapers will make a more generous use of glass for admitting light to their lower stories, as well as for doors, interior partitions, and lobby treatments.

The significance of our new world architecture is seeping gradually into the public consciousness. This awakening of interest and of pride stirs more discussion about the shape of office shelters to come. In brief, the planner's program is to fit the skyscraper's bulk, form, and height to current economic realities; to gear the power of steel, stone, and glass to man's dimensions; and, finally, to provide the human spirit with its most favorable climate for useful work. Contrary to one current notion, the new architecture does not reduce itself to a form of engineering. Engineering helps to translate architecture from imagery to reality, but it does not create architecture. Somewhere between the extreme objectivity of mathematics and an explicit interpretation of today's life and culture lies the meeting ground for the creation of a living architecture. All the modern arts and techniques can contribute something toward this promise and its fulfillment.

SUGGESTED ADDITIONAL READING FOR CHAPTER 31

Birkmire, William Harvey, *The Planning and Construction of High Office-Buildings* (New York: Wiley, 1898).

Chamberlain, Samuel, *Rockefeller Center, a Photographic Narrative* (New York: Hastings House [c1948]).

Chicago Tribune, *The International Competition for a New Administration Building for the Chicago Tribune, MCMXXII . . .* (Chicago: Chicago Tribune [c1923]).

Clark, William C., and J. L. Kingston, *The Skyscraper; a Study in the Economic Height of Modern Office Buildings* (New York and Cleveland: American Institute of Steel Construction [c1930]).

Mujica, Francisco, *History of the Skyscraper* . . . (Paris: Archaeology and Architecture Press, 1929).

Museum of Modern Art, *Early Modern Architecture, Chicago, 1870–1910* . . . 2d ed. rev. ([New York: the Museum, 1940]).

Rockefeller Center, Inc., *Rockefeller Center* (New York: Rockefeller Center, Inc., 1932).

—— *The Story of Rockefeller Center* . . . ([New York:] Rockefeller Center, Inc., 1939).

Royal Institute of British Architects, Business Buildings Committee, *Business Buildings*, No. 16 in Post-War Building Studies (London: H. M. Stationery Office, 1944).

Tallmage, Thomas E. (editor), *The Origin of the Skyscraper; Report of the Committee Appointed by the . . . Estate of Marshall Field for the Examination of the Structure of the Home Insurance Building* (Chicago: Alderbrink Press, 1939).

PERIODICALS

Caparn, H. A., "The Riddle of the Tall Building," *The Craftsman*, Vol. 10 (1906), pp. 477–88.

"Current Notes on Planning: Office Buildings," by E. and O.E., *Architect and Building News*, Vols. 150 and 151, including:

I (June 18, 1937), pp. 348–49	VI (July 23, 1937), pp. 119–20
II (June 25, 1937), pp. 386–87	VII (July 30, 1937), pp. 140–41
III (July 2, 1937), pp. 19–20	VIII (Aug. 6, 1937), pp. 173–74
IV (July 9, 1937), pp. 49–50	IX (Aug. 13, 1937), pp. 201–2
V (July 16, 1937), pp. 79–80	X (Aug. 20, 1937), pp. 223–24

"Design Reference on Office Buildings," *Architectural Record*, Vol. 84 (1938), December, pp. 86–118.

Fleming, Robert, ". . . For and Against the Skyscraper . . ." *Civil Engineering*, Vol. 6 (1935), June, pp. 347–51.

". . . Immeubles de bureaux . . ." *L'Architecture d'aujourd'hui*, Vol. 10 (1939), June, entire issue.

"Office Building Initiates . . . Aluminum Facing over Reinforced Concrete Frame [Equitable Building, Portland, Oregon]," Pietro Belluschi, architect, *Architectural Forum*, Vol. 86 (1947), April, pp. 98–101.

"Office Buildings," Building Types Study No. 130, *Architectural Record*, Vol. 102 (1947), October, pp. 119–46.

"Office Buildings," Building Types Study No. 145, *Architectural Record*, Vol. 105 (1949), January, pp. 96–116.

Office Buildings Reference Number, *Architectural Forum*, Vol. 52 (1930), June, pp. [771]–920.

Sullivan, Louis H., "The Tall Office Building Artistically Considered," *Western Architect*, Vol. 31 (1922), January, pp. 3–11.

32

Radio Stations

By WILLIAM LESCAZE

BROADCASTING in the United States began about 1920. The growth of radio has been incredible—one of the most rapid in the history of American industry. It is difficult to chart that growth, but several comparisons may help to measure it. For example, in the United States there were 30 broadcasting stations in January, 1922; twenty-five years later, in January, 1947, there were nearly 1,000 AM (amplitude modulation) broadcasting stations actually on the air. In addition to this almost fortyfold increase, there were 134 FM (frequency modulation) stations and 6 television stations. In terms of radio sets, there were 60,000 radio sets in January, 1922, and more than 60,000,000 in 1947, or a thousandfold increase. Moreover, it was estimated in 1948 that 93 per cent of American families had radios and that in some cities the percentage ran as high as 99.7 per cent. About 17,000 programs were broadcast each day, and most of the stations were on the air sixteen or more hours per day.[1]

Obviously this amazing growth has necessitated corresponding increases in the studio buildings, program-origination facilities, offices, and auxiliary services. Thus within twenty-five years—and with no precedent—a new building type [2] has evolved. (See Figs. 118, 129.)

---

[1] The author wishes to thank William Ackerman and C. R. Jacobs, both of the Columbia Broadcasting System, and W. A. Clarke of the National Broadcasting Company for their valuable help in assembling these data.

[2] Despite this use of the term "building type" the author would like to voice, as he has often done before, his personal objection to the label. Labels obviously do not make the ware, yet mere invocation of the label is still making its mystic, and often decisive, hampering contribution to those conventional forces which demand that our architecture conform to building types. No railroad station, these forces claim, can be designed by an architect who has not designed many such stations before, no department store by one who has not specialized in department-store construction. As a consequence of this widespread attitude, most of the railroad stations, most of the department stores, most of the schools, and so on have continued to be true to their respective types. The early-twentieth-century adherence to types has resulted finally in complete stagnation—lack of invention—in architecture. Labels are lazy cultural props, and they can be dangerous. Surely they have their use, but a limited one; a broadcasting building naturally enough is not like a railroad station. But these labels have been abused; we have had too many

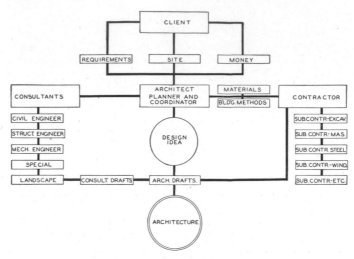

FIGURE 110. THE FUNCTIONAL RELATIONSHIPS OF ARCHITECT, CLIENT, AND CONTRACTOR

A chart illustrative of the thinking, planning, and design processes necessary in the creation of a building; the architect is the center and the leader of the team required to bring a dream into reality.

When, early in the 1930's, a new building need for housing a young and fast-growing industry appeared, suddenly—without either the guidance or the limitations which a precedent would have furnished and imposed—that need had to be met. First came the inevitable makeshifts: space was carved out of existing buildings, where the ceilings were too low and the columns too close, or else out of old garages (Fig. 112).

Of course conditions have improved since then. Yet few of us realize how inadequate some of the broadcasting facilities still remain. Shortly after the end of the Second World War the author and a group of radio engineers were asked to investigate the possibility of improving the broadcasting accommodations in the White House. We were amazed to discover that when the President of the United States wanted to address the nation he had to sit in a sort of lobby or alcove off a main corridor, with hardly enough room for the members of his official family around him. Everything had been improvised,

labels and too little architecture. Good architecture is conceived by a creative mind and talent. It results from an analysis of all the conditions of (1) the site, (2) the budget, and (3) the needs to be housed, and then from the final step—the organization of these findings into a form. How completely that form succeeds in being good architecture is in direct proportion to the ability and the creative talent of the architect.

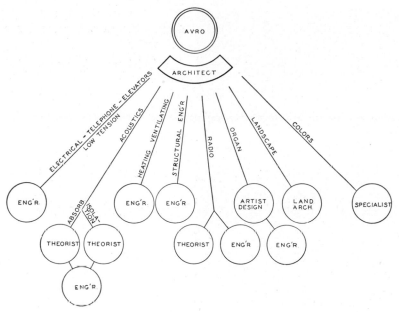

FIGURE 111. THE ARCHITECT'S RESPONSIBILITIES IN THE DESIGN OF A RADIO STATION. DIAGRAM BASED ON AVRO, HILVERSUM, THE NETHERLANDS

The relationships of processes and people established by AVRO in creating the radio station at Hilversum; the circles represent the architect's staff or special consultants as well as the staff of the broadcasting company.

FIGURE 112.
AN EARLY RADIO
STUDIO.
KDKA STUDIO
IN 1922

The crude improvisations of an early studio.

Courtesy National
Broadcasting Co.

and although broadcasting from the White House had begun in the late 1920's the facilities there were still merely makeshift. Curtained-off booths only partly screened the announcers of the various networks; wires dangled and

FIGURE 113. WCBS TRANSMITTER,
LONG ISLAND SOUND, NEW YORK.
AIR VIEW

A graceful transmitter tower designed integrally with its enclosed portion.

Courtesy William Lescaze

lay on the floor. What a curious phenomenon! [3] We make great strides in
technical developments, but even in the most august places we are very slow
in giving them their proper forms. Yet a civilization is usually characterized
by the fusion of its form and its content.

ESSENTIAL ELEMENTS

Radio broadcasting requires four main types of accommodations: the transmitter; the studios with their auxiliary parts; one or more theaters; and service
and administration areas.

THE TRANSMITTER

In practice, the transmitter is usually located several miles outside the city.
Its main feature is its light and high mast—built of open steel sections—which
juts out and up from the landscape. If the mast has been well designed, which
is sometimes the case, it is simple and bold. The WCBS transmitter on tiny
Columbia Island in Long Island Sound is a good example (Fig. 113). Usually,
however, at the base of the mast there is an ugly pillbox building surrounded
by pigmy cedar trees; this structure houses the control room. Unfortunately
only an occasional example has as yet been properly designed as a whole. The

[3] This condition has been remedied in the reconstruction of the White House during 1950-51.

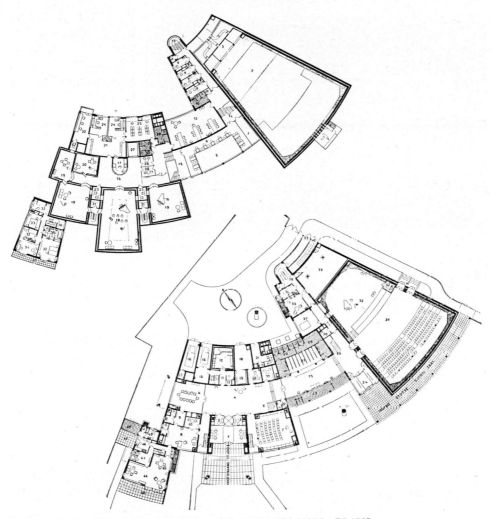

FIGURE 114. AVRO, HILVERSUM, THE NETHERLANDS. PLANS

Merkelbach & Karstens, architects

Large and small studios, offices and reception rooms, and all the other necessary services combined in a plan of imaginative freedom.   From *Hedendaagsche Architektur in Nederland*

problem still seems to have received very little architectural consideration; in spite of the importance of transmitters, they are treated like stepchildren.

THE BROADCASTING STATION

The studios, offices, and theater which comprise the radio broadcasting station as a rule are situated in a city or close to it. For the simple reason that they

FIGURE 115. AVRO, HILVERSUM, THE NETHERLANDS. ENTRANCE

Merkelbach & Karstens, architects

An exterior admirably adjusted to its parklike setting.

Courtesy Netherlands Information Bureau

must be readily available to the thousands who will use them, they are generally grouped together and are often located close to other theater or amusement facilities. (See Figs. 114–119.)

Because of the special type of activities housed in the broadcasting station, city planning commissions might well consider making its location permissible in an area otherwise restricted to residences. Under such an arrangement it is conceivable that the various broadcasting buildings of the future might have a parklike setting where television and other research buildings could be erected as they were needed. In that case, however, rapid communication to other more conventionally situated places of work would have to be provided for the many radio participants whose part-time services are required by two or more stations, by a theater, or by a concert organization.

Circulation Areas. To each of the principal accommodations—studios, offices, services—several distinct types of circulation, both from outside and from within, must be provided in a radio station. These include circulation (1) for the artists, (2) for the control engineers, (3) for the clerical and executive staff, and (4) for the public seeking entertainment. (See Fig. 121.)

This complicated circulation has given rise to many difficult planning problems. The fact that customs vary in different countries has to be considered. For instance, when in 1948 the author was designing the radio broadcasting station for the Iceland State Broadcasting Service (Fig. 117), he found that fairly spacious accommodations had to be provided for the public check rooms, since this station falls within the European tradition, as does the

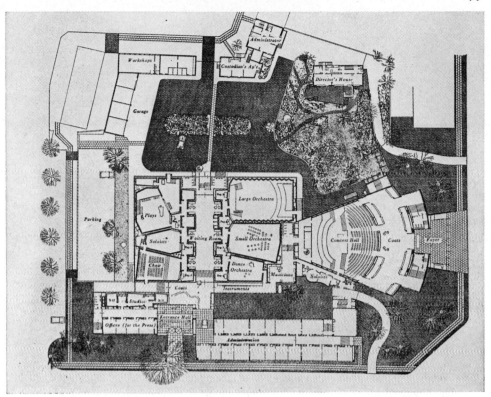

FIGURE 116. RADIO HOUSE, HOME OF THE DANISH STATE BROADCASTING
SYSTEM, COPENHAGEN. PLAN

Vilhelm Lauritzen, architect

A national broadcasting system housed in a structure combining efficiency with the dignity
appropriate to a governmental building. From *Architectural Forum*

new building for Denmark (Fig. 116); in the United States on the other hand
not much more than the equivalent of a good-sized closet is needed for this
purpose. Naturally economic considerations such as the cost of land and the
cost of building space play a part in such differences, but habit also is a strong
influence. Hardly anyone, for example, checks his coat in a legitimate theater
in New York—not because he loves to hold it on his lap but simply because it
would take too long to redeem it from the lonely attendant posted in front of
her cubbyhole cloakroom.[4]

The artists require a separate entrance, a few dressing rooms, and one

---

[4] For a more extended discussion of the coatroom problem see Vol. I, Chap. 2, p. 32.

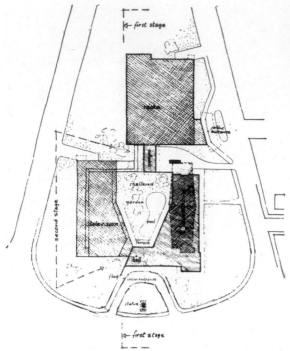

FIGURE 117. GENERAL PLAN
FOR THE ICELAND STATE
BROADCASTING SERVICE

William Lescaze, architect

A comprehensive plan designed in accordance with the local manner of living.

or two small practice rooms; the musicians need locker rooms and a lounge; and there must also be pleasant facilities for guest speakers. Artists should be able to pass from their entrance to the locker rooms, lounges, and studios with little or no interference from the public. Lockers are needed for the ushers. The engineers require locker rooms, a lounge, and in addition offices, a workshop for repairs, and storage space for equipment. Naturally circulation to all these spaces is essential. Similarly, it should be possible for musical instruments, other equipment, and machinery to be brought to the storage rooms and studios in the most direct manner.

Since in the United States the attending of broadcasts is now an accepted part of the recreational program, the public needs direct and unhampered approach to those studios which are designed for their accommodation. Because this circulation may do much to set the tone of the station in the public mind, the design of the public portions of the studios is a matter of primary importance. Adequate waiting spaces close to the medium-sized studios are as necessary as roomy lobbies and foyers in connection with the larger broadcasting theaters.

The most desirable solution of this complex circulation problem (although

FIGURE 118. PANORAMA OVER HOLLYWOOD, CALIFORNIA, SHOWING STATION
KNX, C.B.S., IN THE FOREGROUND

William Lescaze, architect; Earl Heitschmidt, associate

A radio station should be centrally located. At left foreground is the main building, containing
both studios and offices; back of the central court is the principal broadcasting auditorium, and
at the right are shops, a restaurant, and a bank; the whole group is officially termed "Columbia
Square." The view looks northerly toward the Hollywood Bowl.

Courtesy Columbia Broadcasting System

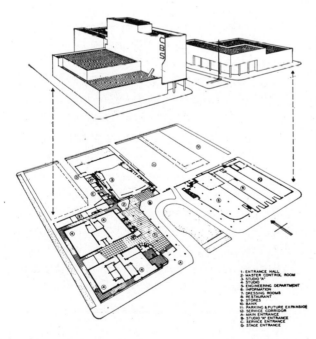

FIGURE 119. STATION KNX,
C.B.S., HOLLYWOOD,
CALIFORNIA. PERSPECTIVE
AND FIRST-FLOOR PLAN

William Lescaze, architect;
Earl Heitschmidt, associate

An ample and welcoming foyer
gives excellent circulation to the
studios.

Courtesy William Lescaze

FIGURE 120. STUDIO IN STATION WBBM, C.B.S., CHICAGO, ILLINOIS

William Lescaze, architect

A studio arranged for spectators; the control room is at the right, and at the rear is a glass-enclosed booth for clients and sponsors.

Photograph Hedrich-Blessing, courtesy William Lescaze

one seldom fully carried out for studios to which the public is admitted) is a double circulation system, with its two parts completely separate—that is, one set of corridors for the engineers, musicians, and broadcasters and another for the spectators. The reasons for the scheme are simple. Props, all kinds of paraphernalia, and instruments have to be moved into the studio, and musicians and engineers must have clear passageways to get to their respective positions easily and quickly. If the entrance is through the same door that the spectators use there is delay and confusion. (See Fig. 121.) On a somewhat reduced and simplified scale the legitimate theater has solved its circulation problem by placing its lobby and public entrance on the street and its stage door and dressing rooms on an alley in the rear.

Service and Administration Areas. Broadcasting requires a number of special service elements. A small reference library, closely related to the lounges or waiting rooms of news reporters or commentators, is one of these essential elements, and a special study should be made of facilities for wire, telephone, or teletype services. A large record library, also conveniently located, will be necessary, since many programs are broadcast from records. In connection with television, special consideration must be given to the placing and storage of large cameras and elaborate electric apparatus. Since television is still in the early stages of its growth, the architect must not only work in close collaboration with the television engineers but also see that the utmost flexibility is pre-

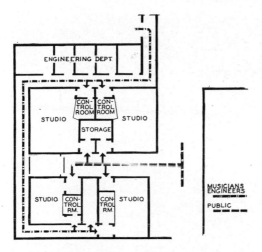

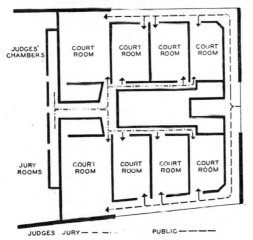

FIGURE 121. DIAGRAM PLANS
SHOWING DOUBLE CIRCULATION FOR
STAFF AND FOR PUBLIC IN A RADIO
STUDIO AND A COURTHOUSE

The dot-and-dash lines show the private circulations for artists and service personnel
(left) and for judges and juries (right); the
plain dashes indicate the public route.

served to take care of future developments. Studios for television require much
more elaborate dressing-room facilities for performers than do those for radio
broadcasting; in addition they need large property rooms and areas for costume
storage.

The amount, number, and arrangement of the necessary administration
offices vary according to the size and importance of the individual station and
according to whether or not it is commercially supported. The commercial
station must have offices for its sales, advertising, and publicity staffs, as well as
ample attractive conference rooms for its sales activities, and in addition some
have luxurious reception rooms and lounges for the special use of program
sponsors. Both commercial and non-commercial stations need adequate space

FIGURE 122. A MEDIUM-SIZED STUDIO, STATION KNX, C.B.S., HOLLYWOOD, CALIFORNIA. INTERIOR

William Lescaze, architect; Earl Heitschmidt, associate

Note the sloping walls to eliminate flutter; the clients' booth is at the rear, and the control room is at the right. Movable curtains permit varying sound absorption, according to the needs.

Courtesy William Lescaze

for directors, assistant directors, and their staffs, and sometimes a special suite for the program director. Treasurers or paymasters require space, and the accounting department may need a large area. If the station is the chief or regional head office of a national or regional chain, the office space must be vastly larger than that necessary for a small local station. Only a careful study of the present and potential organization of the station under consideration will determine the actual amounts of administration space required.

THE STUDIOS

Since the studios themselves are the one requirement of a broadcasting station which is new—that is, not to be found in other buildings—their special characteristics will now be outlined both from the planning and from the design viewpoints.

The design features of a studio should all contribute not only to the good quality of the sounds produced within but also to the elimination of outside noises. Within a given building, the studios should be removed from such sources of noise and vibration as elevators, fans, generators, air-conditioning equipment, plumbing lines, and public corridors. To simplify the electrical wir-

FIGURE 123. A LARGE THEATER STUDIO, STATION KNX, C.B.S., HOLLYWOOD, CALIFORNIA. INTERIOR

William Lescaze, architect; Earl Heitschmidt, associate

Courtesy William Lescaze

ing system the main electric control room should be in a central location.

Number and Size. The number of studios and the size of each depend on the requirements and the type of work which the station does. A formula for the relationship between the size of the studio and the number of artists and spectators which it can accommodate under satisfactory conditions has been established by C. B. Hanson and R. M. Morris of the National Broadcasting Company. This relationship may be expressed as follows: $V = 750\ N$. Here V is the volume of the studio in cubic feet, and N is the number of people most satisfactorily accommodated. The formula is not based on acoustical law but takes into consideration only the amount of air necessary for comfort.

Most broadcasting stations have several studios, and these are of at least three different sizes. First of all there are the small ones—often called speakers' studios—with no space for a public audience; each of these is merely a small room with a table, the microphones, and an adjoining control room. Next there are the medium-sized studios for one or two or more musicians with their instruments—a string quartet, for example, or a small dance orchestra—and

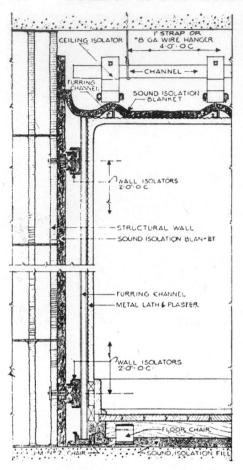

FIGURE 124. CROSS SECTION OF STUDIO WALL, SHOWING METHOD OF ACOUSTIC ISOLATION

This construction prevents the entrance of exterior sounds; the finished surfaces inside the studio are isolated by careful insulation of all connections to the construction.

sometimes for a few spectators. Finally there is the large studio—or theater—with a stage; this will accommodate an orchestra, a chorus, and an audience of 1,000 spectators or more. As a rule all studios, control rooms, and the like, since they must be enclosed, inside spaces, are air-conditioned. The air velocity at the fresh-air grille should be kept below 250 feet per minute; otherwise it is likely to be registered by the microphone. The ducts should be lined with sound-absorbing material, the fans mounted on vibration-absorbing platforms.

Because most broadcast stations are on the air continuously, the same studio can seldom if ever be used for two successive "live" broadcast periods; the program will generally shift from one studio to another at each change point. This will affect both the number and placing of the studios and the arrangement and accessibility of the control rooms and other service areas. Broadcast programs are designed on a strict split-second timing, hence careful planning of the studios and control rooms will contribute to the efficiency of their operation.

Control Rooms. The control room is an essential part of any broadcast studio. It should be so placed that the engineers and directors within it have complete visual command over the players' or performers' area. Usually its floor is raised above the studio floor to make this possible. Control rooms must be rigidly sound-proofed from the studio itself. Often one control room is so designed that it can supervise and serve either of two small studios.

In addition to the control room, many of the larger studios have a somewhat similar glass-front, sound-proofed room—the clients' room—from which the program sponsors can observe and listen to the programs they support.

Acoustics. Figure 124 shows one method of building the walls, ceiling, and floor of a studio—suspended, as it were, so as not to vibrate, as ordinary walls do, with the impact of street noises. Thus the walls, floors, and ceilings are isolated from the building structure. The acoustical treatment of the studio is not shown in the illustration, because it varies according to special requirements and to acoustical taste. Note in the section the complete isolation achieved between building and studio by means of felt and other sound-proofing materials.

Entrance to a studio is usually through a *soundlock*—a small vestibule to trap noises, very much as a maze or vestibule traps light at the door of a photographer's darkroom. Soundlocks are entirely sound-deadened with carpets and other acoustical materials.

Most studios now embody two new applications of the science of sound: (1) the use of a definite room echo to increase the brilliance of music and speech, and (2) the use of carefully designed wooden wall panels to act as sounding boards and thus to enhance the richness of the sounds. Sometimes these wooden panels are movable and so hinged that the brilliance of sound within the room can be either increased or decreased.

One of the important characteristics of all theaters, music rooms, and broadcasting studios is reverberation. When the inner surfaces of a room consist of hard plaster or of any other good reflectors of sound, the sound waves may be reflected back and forth many times between the walls; this is known as *reverberation*.

Reverberation is measured in terms of reverberation time—the number of seconds required for the intensity of a sound reverberating inside a room to die

FIGURE 125. STATION
KNX, C.B.S., HOLLY-
WOOD, CALIFORNIA.
EXTERIOR VIEW AND
INTERIOR OF PUBLIC
LOUNGE

William Lescaze, archi-
tect; Earl Heitschmidt,
associate

An exterior in harmony
with the modern charac-
ter of the building's purpose; an inviting public
lounge with an informa-
tion booth at the right, a
check room and tele-
phones at the rear, and
two doors to medium-
sized studios.

Exterior photograph
W. P. Woodcock;
both courtesy
William Lescaze

away to one-millionth of its original value, corresponding in modern nomenclature to a decrease of 60 decibels. Small rooms lined with felt, loose cloth, or
other effective sound absorbers may have a reverberation time of as little as
three-tenths or four-tenths of a second. Large rooms surfaced in plaster, stone,
or other good sound reflectors may have a reverberation time of as much as
six or eight seconds or even more. A room with great absorption and a very
short reverberation time is called a *dead* room; one with highly reflecting
walls and a long reverberation time is called a *live* room.

The ideal reverberation time is one that is neither too short nor too long:
if too short, speech or music will sound dead or muffled; if too long, speech
or music will sound hollow, blurred, and artificial. New studios are now de-

signed for the reverberation time most suitable for their size and shape. The average reverberation time may vary between four-tenths of a second to a little over one second. Naturally the presence of a studio audience and a group of performers is also a factor that will influence the reverberation time, since clothes and human bodies absorb sound.[5]

A pleasing effect of liveness in a studio may be obtained, without dangerously increasing the reverberation time, by the single-echo effect embodied in some of the new Columbia Broadcasting studios, a modification of the "live end" and "dead end" earlier method of studio design. This means that one end of the studio—the dead end—contains most of the sound-absorbing material and that the other—the live end—has its wall and ceiling finished in reflecting materials. The object of this echo technique is to provide one strong echo for each sound produced in the studio and entering the microphone. Usually the successful use of the effect is possible only in studios of the correct length. If a studio is more than about 70 feet deep, the desirable fused echo from the reflecting rear wall may be heard separately and unpleasantly; this results in what is called a *back-slap*. A direct echo between two opposite and parallel walls and with several successive reflections from each wall in turn is known as a *flutter*. Obviously neither the back-slap nor the flutter is desirable. In some of the Columbia studios in New York these faults have been avoided by arranging all the reflecting areas on the side walls in V shapes so that no sound can be directly reflected back and forth between opposite walls. In some of the Columbia studios in Hollywood the two opposite side walls were built on a vertical slant (Fig. 122). Reflection from the single flat surface installed at the live end of each studio to produce the desirable echo effect cannot produce a flutter, since this echo reflection takes place toward the opposite absorbing wall at the dead end of the studio (Fig. 126).

An essential of good quality in speech or music is the preservation or reproduction of all the necessary frequencies—in musical language, all the necessary pitches. The fundamental tones of lowest pitch ordinarily encountered in music have frequencies of about 30 vibrations or cycles per second. The highest-pitched tones have frequencies of about 5,000 cycles per second. For ultra-modern radio purposes, a frequency range of approximately 60 to 8,000 cycles per second is desirable. Radio receivers capable of reproducing this wider range are already on the market.

The amount of sound absorption achieved by the materials used for studio walls varies with the frequency of the sound absorbed. For example, a studio

[5] For a fuller discussion of acoustics, see Vol. III, Chap. 8.

FIGURE 126. STUDIO B, STATION WLW, CINCINNATI, OHIO

William Lescaze, architect

The successful integration of the required facilities.   Photograph Sarra, courtesy WLW

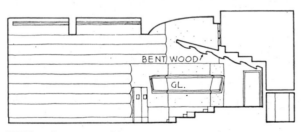

FIGURE 127. STUDIO B,
STATION WLW,
CINCINNATI, OHIO. SECTION

William Lescaze, architect

Walls and ceilings are faced with curved sound-diffusing shapes formed of compressed fiber board. These shapes not only tend to eliminate flutter and reduce reverberation but also serve as baffles for concealed lighting. The greater part of the lighting is by cold cathode units, used to reduce the heating load.   From *Pencil Points*

lined with some kinds of sound-absorbing material may be more reverberant for sounds of low frequency than for those of high frequency. This is undesirable because it causes a hollow or booming effect and an incorrect balance. To avoid such a condition, all the sound-absorbing and other wall and ceiling materials used in the Columbia studios have been chosen to produce as far as possible a uniform reverberation at all frequencies between 60 and 8,000 cycles

FIGURE 128. STATION KNX, C.B.S., HOLLYWOOD, CALIFORNIA. VIEW ACROSS PATIO AT NIGHT

William Lescaze, architect; Earl Heitschmidt, associate

The station should be as attractive by night as it is by day, for in the evenings it will see its most glamorous activity.　　　　Photograph W. P. Woodcock, courtesy William Lescaze

per second. To obtain this desirable but seldom realized flat characteristic several engineering expedients have been resorted to, including the use of a 4-inch thickness of rock wool as the standard sound absorber for walls and ceilings and then covering it with perforated metal of such thickness and character as to aid the uniform absorption of all frequencies. This is especially important in attaining what is called brilliance in music, a quality that is conditioned on an adequate hearing of the higher-frequency tones and overtones. In a too dead studio, these high-frequency tones may be entirely absorbed and lost. If a studio has unbalanced reverberation characteristics, as indicated by a reverberation curve not approximately flat at all frequencies, the high-frequency tones will be obscured by the longer reverberation of the lower tones; consequently brilliance will be lost.

The use of wooden panels on parts of a studio's walls rests on the musical experience gained in concert halls or other music rooms thus finished in wood;

FIGURE 129. STATION KRSC, SEATTLE, WASHINGTON. EXTERIOR

D. D. Williams, architect

A small station aesthetically tuned to its environment.

Photograph Dearborn-Massar

tones obtained in such rooms are considered by musicians to be richer and more sonorous. The Columbia studios in New York, designed in 1936, represented the first attempt to use this effect consciously and purposefully in radio studio design. Just why wood improves the acoustical quality of a music room is a question still somewhat in dispute. Since the wooden panels are not damped or fastened rigidly except at their edges, they are more or less free to vibrate, like the soundbox of a violin or the sounding board of a piano.

The desirable acoustic qualities attained in the studios make it possible to take every advantage of the similarly desirable characteristics of the new velocity microphones, so named because they respond to the velocity of the sound waves instead of to their pressure. These microphones are improvements over earlier types chiefly in two respects: they respond accurately to a wider range of sound frequencies, and they have more marked as well as more uniform directional characteristics.

Ideal acoustics, high-fidelity pickup, and conversion of sound into electrical energy all go for naught, however, unless the entire electrical system is capable of relaying the sounds picked up as they are heard at the point of pickup.

AESTHETIC CONSIDERATIONS

The broadcasting studios as a rule have set a high standard of appearance in their interiors; here their architects have used wall materials that wear well, withstand the crowds, and are easy to maintain. A few of the broadcasting stations which are housed in their own buildings show that intelligent planning and a logical grouping of the diverse activities to be installed result in distinctive and expressive structures—appropriately modern for a modern and growing industry.

The broadcasting companies have already had a phenomenal growth, and they are still growing. Many of them have added FM to their regular AM radio broadcasting; some have added television. Were they to add newspaper publishing (conversely, some newspapers already have their own radio stations), they might well develop into the communications centers of the future—which could become important architectural landmarks in our cities.

SUGGESTED ADDITIONAL READING FOR CHAPTER 32

Knudsen, Vern O., *Architectural Acoustics* (New York: Wiley, 1932).

Radio Corporation of America, *Architects' Manual of Engineered Sound Systems* (Camden, N.J.: the Corporation [1947]).

Sabine, Paul E., *Acoustics and Architecture* (New York: McGraw-Hill, 1932).

Watson, Floyd Rowe, *Acoustics of Buildings* (New York: Wiley, 1923).

33

Factories

By ALBERT HALSE

THE HOUSING of industry has been a matter of concern to the architect since early times. Ancient Egypt had shops connected with residences. Greece had its open-air workshops where hand workers labored, as well as its home industry. In Rome there were fullers, potters, flute blowers, coppersmiths, goldsmiths, carpenters, and shoemakers, all working in houses, but specialized arrangements were already giving promise of true industrial buildings. Some Roman large-scale oil presses in Syria and Africa occupied their own sheds. When the Roman Empire was destroyed, industry reverted to the family unit, which again used the dwelling as a workshop. There followed a transitional period—the twelfth to fifteenth centuries—during which the guild system emerged and produced stained glass, pottery, tapestries, and metalwork in large quantities. Such crafts were usually carried on in small shops.

The forerunner of the present factory system developed during the sixteenth and seventeenth centuries, when individuals distributed raw materials to workers on the outskirts of the towns and later sold the finished product to merchants or consumers in the towns. Often specialized shops were grouped together by trades in growing suburbs. Until the beginning of the eighteenth century, this practice existed along with a system in which the work was accomplished in large city workshops and in shops connected with the monasteries or baronial manors.

The second half of the eighteenth century is considered the beginning of the modern factory system. (See Fig. 130.) The rise of capitalism, together with the invention of the spinning jenny, gave a great boost to manufacturing. Other inventions, such as Samuel Crompton's mule in 1779, Edmund Cartwright's power loom in 1785, and Watt's steam engine in the same year, also helped to develop manufacturing and finally to precipitate the Industrial Revo-

FIGURE 130. DESIGN FOR A CANNON FOUNDRY
C. N. Ledoux, architect
An early attempt (*circa* 1775) to give appropriate architectural form to an industrial building.
From *L'Architecture de C. N. Ledoux*

lution. At this time competition became so keen that owners used barns and old buildings for loom shops.

In the United States, gristmills, sawmills, fulling mills, and metal plants existed as early as the seventeenth century. They were established near small streams whenever the number of settlers warranted production. The buildings were usually of wood and were similar in appearance to the houses or barns of that day.

The textile industry started in the United States in 1790, when Samuel Slater began production with the spinning jenny. By 1810 approximately 250 textile mills were operating in New England. Large mills were usually located on waterways, the small ones generally on traffic lines. The first mills were barn-like structures with many windows and a long monitor. After 1810 the mills became larger, were often built of masonry, and sometimes attained a height of five stories. The typical unit was a long rectangular many-windowed structure with a central cupola, a tower stairway applied on one side, and a large monitor. As space requirements increased, several of these units were joined together, and, although the individual buildings were limited in length by the possible dimensions of single drive shafts, the new mass became an imposing one, with its projecting stairway towers rhythmically spaced, its large window areas, and its inevitable cupola.

FIGURE 131. TWO EARLY
COTTON MILLS IN THE
UNITED STATES

ABOVE: Wooden mill (1847), Davis-
ville, Rhode Island. BELOW: Coventry mill (1873), Washington,
Rhode Island.

Early textile mills in the United
States frequently possessed a distinctive architectural character;
later eclectic and Victorian forms
fogged the clarity of expression.

Photographs by the WPA
Arts Project, courtesy
Avery Library

Romanticism spoiled that earlier simple, expressive clarity—"period" architecture was not suitable for industrial buildings—and eclecticism throttled any
real progress. But as soon as architects began to use steel and concrete and
liberalized the use of glass and sheet metal—and when, finally, efficiency supplanted tradition in machine layout—exterior expression of the building's
function began to appear. The first notable example of a building erected under
these conditions is the Larkin building, erected in 1903 from plans by Frank
Lloyd Wright. This building housed both an administration area and a mail-
order section. It was the first structure to give the feeling of industrial straight-
forwardness and power. (See Fig. 131.)

Progress in the design of industrial buildings since that time has been inter-

national. Before the First World War the greatest advance was made by the Germans. Peter Behrens built for the A.E.G. a group of excellent industrial buildings in Berlin in 1909; particularly revolutionary was the great turbine assembly building with its polygonal roof, large glass area, and walls that were frankly screens (Fig. 132). After the war this progress continued, and other Continental countries followed the German lead. Eric Mendelsohn, Hans Poelzig, Emil Fahrenkamp, Otto Bartning, Hans Hertlein, and both Bruno and Max Taut made distinguished contributions; a building by Emil Fahrenkamp for the Neumann Mills at Zittau is typical. The Van Nelle tobacco factory in Rotterdam, the Netherlands, designed by J. A. Brinkman and L. C. Van der Vlugt in the early 1920's, is an eight-story plant of reinforced concrete characterized by ends which contain the services and stairs and are connected by a cantilevered manufacturing area with continuous walls of glass. The interior of the manufacturing area is marked by the use of octagonal masonry columns which are slotted to receive partitions or machinery (Fig. 133). In the United States the new view of industrial architecture caused a remarkable development. Here, with the nation's customary accent on efficiency, it was not difficult to discard outworn ideas. Although there are still many ugly, disorganized plants throughout the country, a metamorphosis has occurred.

An industrial building's primary purpose is the efficient housing of a manufacturing process. A study of modern manufacturing methods reveals that industry has a pattern, as shown in Figure 134. This pattern necessarily generates form. In this form each person, material, finished product, and even the waste occupies its proper position with relation to the others. The handling of

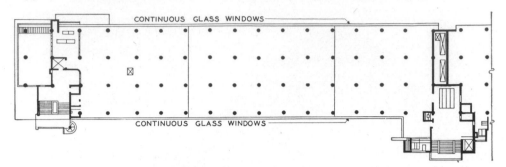

FIGURE 133.
VAN NELLE TOBACCO
FACTORY AND
WAREHOUSE,
ROTTERDAM,
THE NETHERLANDS.
PART PLAN AND
EXTERIOR BY DAY
AND BY NIGHT

Brinkman & Van der Vlugt, architects

The most brilliant of European concrete cantilevered industrial groups prior to the Second World War.

Photographs courtesy Museum of Modern Art, New York

materials is kept to a minimum for the sake of efficiency, but at the same time adequate provision is made for future expansion.

To ensure efficient operation, the architect as the first step in his design after the requirements of the plant are known should make a *flow diagram* which includes all-important movements of both materials and workers. The most important single element of this diagram is the production line, that is,

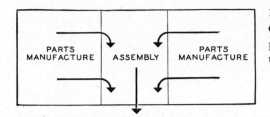

FIGURE 134. BASIC FLOW DIAGRAMS
OF MATERIAL WITHIN A FACTORY

Efficient factory design must be based on
the flow diagram.

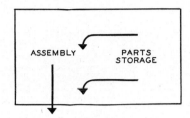

the route to be traveled by the materials from the time they enter the plant as
raw materials to the place where they leave the shipping department as finished products. Dr. Otakar Štěpánek, in "Look to the Flow Analysis for Effective Solutions," [1] indicates the basic production-line arrangements as shown in
Figures 134 and 135.

Freedom of planning is now possible because industry is no longer dependent
on steam-driven power shafts, which formerly determined the location of
lines of machinery. Today electricity permits a separate power element for
each machine and provides a complete fluidity of machine arrangement while
at the same time effecting an economy in power.

Generally speaking, industry may be divided into two classes: light and
heavy. Each presupposes a building with a structure sturdy enough to withstand the loading and the wear and tear of the operations involved.

BUILDINGS FOR LIGHT INDUSTRY

Light industry may be housed in either a single- or a multiple-story structure.

One-Story Buildings. The single-story building has certain advantages.
Among these are the fact that a greater portion of the proposed lot may be
covered because light courts are unnecessary and no space need be given over
to stairs and elevators. Also, since materials may be handled horizontally, the
cost of raising and lowering them is eliminated. Moreover, the one-story build-

[1] *Architectural Record*, Vol. 82 (1937), Aug., pp. 107–11.

FIGURE 135. VARIOUS PRODUCTION-LINE ARRANGEMENTS

The production-flow diagram itself must be carefully studied for directness, economy, and the efficient use of horizontal, inclined, and vertical conveyors.

TOP AND MIDDLE, Upper two at left, from Alford and Bangs, *Production Handbook;* others from Štěpánek, "Look to the Flow Analysis . . ." in *Architectural Record*

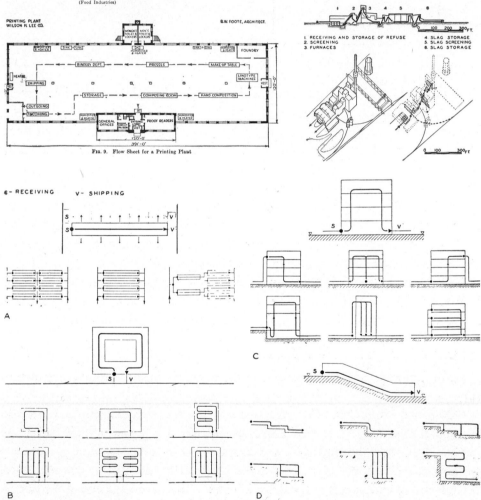

FIG. 10 Flow Diagram of Walnut Shelling Process of California Walnut Growers Assn.
(Food Industries)

FIG. 9. Flow Sheet for a Printing Plant

1. RECEIVING AND STORAGE OF REFUSE
2. SCREENING
3. FURNACES
4. SLAG STORAGE
5. SLAG SCREENING
6. SLAG STORAGE

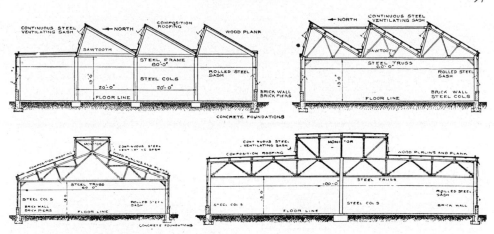

FIGURE 136. SAWTOOTH AND MONITOR LIGHTING

ABOVE, LEFT: Ordinary sawtooth; ABOVE, RIGHT: Super sawtooth; BELOW, LEFT: Monitor; BELOW, RIGHT: Wide-span monitor   From *Architectural Forum*

ing may be provided with natural overhead lighting as well as side lighting; this may take the form of sawtooth roofs or monitors, which distribute the light evenly throughout the plant. With such an arrangement an even north light is easily attained (Fig. 136). The high floor loads demanded by materials or equipment are best solved by the one-story plant. There is greater flexibility for layout changes, and greater efficiency is possible in handling equipment. Also, supervision is simpler and hazardous occupations are more easily isolated. In addition less time is required to erect the one-story building and less area is lost in side walls and column clearance. Structurally, the one-story building permits the use of a relatively small number of light columns and other steel elements. Some typical sections are shown in Figures 144, 145.

Chief among the disadvantages of the one-story building is the large area required. For industrial buildings of equal quality, the one-story structure will cost slightly more per gross square foot than the multi-story because of its large roof area, the complexity of its roof construction, the great number of footings required, and so on. High-priced land will prohibit its use, and the need for additional land for future expansion will add still more to the cost.

Multi-Story Buildings. The choice of a multi-story building for light industry is determined by such factors as the high cost of land, the limited area of a site, a site slope which will allow entrances at different floor levels, a relatively low floor load, a desire for space on upper floors where greater cleanliness and more light is possible, and the lower rate of heat loss because of

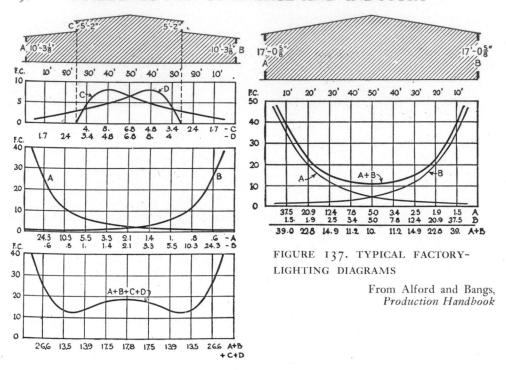

FIGURE 137. TYPICAL FACTORY-
LIGHTING DIAGRAMS

From Alford and Bangs,
Production Handbook

the smaller roof. In addition, the manufacturing process in question may well demand a high building so that materials may be fed vertically.

The principal disadvantage of a multi-story building is the difficulty of securing adequate natural light unless the width can be limited or the ceilings raised above the normal height. The usual width of such buildings, for instance, is 80′–0″ and the normal ceiling height 12′–0″. When this width is exceeded, the center bays become dark and artificial illumination must be used constantly. Occasionally the manufacturing process permits the utilization of these dark areas for storage. Widths up to 120′–0″ with ceiling heights of 15′–0″ have been found to be satisfactory when wide bands of sash rising from bench level to ceiling are used in the outer walls. In many cases such an arrangement has been made possible by cantilevering the floor slabs beyond the outer row of columns, as in the Van Nelle plant in the Netherlands (Fig. 133). Another important consideration in the design of a multi-story building is that the stairs and elevators must be placed so that they will not interfere with the manufacturing process but will meet exit requirements. This is sometimes accomplished by enclosing the stairs in outside towers, as in the early textile mills.

The multi-story building is devoted sometimes to the processes of a single

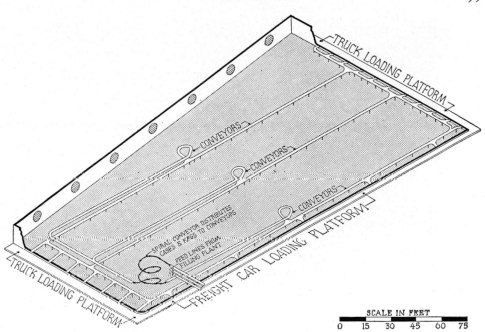

FIGURE 138. BOTTLING PLANT, BALLANTINE & SONS, NEWARK, NEW JERSEY. ISOMETRIC DRAWING

J. S. Shanley, architect

A building designed around a simple flow diagram to provide for an efficient handling of shipments.   From *Architectural Forum*

company, sometimes to those of a number of tenants. Loft buildings and industrial terminals usually are erected in the larger cities and frequently are designed to provide good lighting, elevator service, adequate exits, and as large an unobstructed floor area as possible. The industrial terminal consists of a group of buildings for storage and manufacture and provides numerous small firms with the facilities of a large industrial plant. A central power plant sometimes supplies light, power, and heat at moderate cost, and a pool of service employees is maintained for the benefit of the tenants.

The several types of construction generally used for multiple-story structures include mill construction, steel-frame construction, and concrete. The trend is toward steel or concrete.

Mill or "slow-burning" construction is characterized by exterior walls of masonry, heavy timber interior framing arranged with smooth, flat surfaces and a minimum number of corners, and the avoidance of inaccessible enclosed

FIGURE 139. SPERRY GYROSCOPE PLANT, LAKE SUCCESS, LONG ISLAND, NEW YORK. ADMINISTRATION BUILDING EXTERIOR

Stone & Webster, engineers; N. N. Culin, designer

Windows with lens-type glass in the upper portions to direct the light deep into the interior and, in the lower portions, transparent panes to permit vision to the outside.

Photograph Robert Damora

spaces. The fact that mill construction is rarely used in buildings more than six stories high is due partly to the lack of lateral stability inherent in structures so built and partly to the restrictions imposed by city or state building laws. Usually the building is separated into smaller areas by means of incombustible walls and partitions provided with automatic fire doors. The stairs and elevator shafts are enclosed in fireproof towers, and openings in floors for the passage of belts either are omitted entirely or are protected by automatic hatchways. Generally sprinklers are provided, and the floors are waterproofed to keep water from seeping through to the floors below. Ceilings over combustible material are protected with a fire-retardant material. Mill construction is not fireproof; the heavy timbers employed, however, resist fire and support their load longer than does exposed steel.

Multi-story plants may also be constructed economically with the use of *steel* framework. Wherever a process can be housed in standard bays, the steel sub-assemblies can be fabricated in the shop, making field erection rapid. Sometimes, however, the plant process will not permit a uniform spacing of columns,

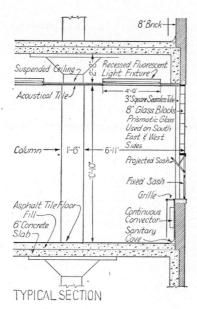

8"Brick

Suspended Ceiling

Recessed Fluorescent
Light Fixture

Acoustical Tile

3"Square Seamless Tile
8" Glass Blocks
Prismatic Glass
Used on South
East & West
Sides

Column   1'-6"   6'-11"

Projected Sash

Fixed Sash
Grille

Asphalt Tile Floor
Fill
6"Concrete
Slab

Continuous
Convector
Sanitary
Cove

TYPICAL SECTION

FIGURE 140. SPERRY GYROSCOPE PLANT,
LAKE SUCCESS, LONG ISLAND, NEW YORK.
SECTION SHOWING CANTILEVER

Stone & Webster, engineers; N. N. Culin, designer

From *Architectural Forum*

and in such a case the design of the structure is fitted to the needs of the process. Occasionally the steel in a single-story building is installed without fireproofing, but in multi-story buildings it is usually fireproofed. If, as is customary, the columns on the lower floors are placed relatively close together, steel trusses are used to provide longer clear floor space on the top floor, which like the single-story building may be lighted by any of the various types of monitors or by a sawtooth roof. One of the greatest advantages of the steel building is the ease with which it can be altered or added to as the process requirements vary. (See Fig. 141.)

The chief virtues of reinforced *concrete* for large plants are its fireproof quality and its adaptability to cantilevered construction, and one of its principal contributions to industrial architecture is the so-called "daylight" factory with its large areas of glass set between flat slab-type floors—a treatment especially effective when the walls are cantilevered (Figs. 133, 140). A reinforced concrete building is practically monolithic and therefore extremely solid and exceptionally resistant to sway. For this reason such construction is well suited for multi-story buildings containing machines which vibrate. Because of the hardness of a concrete floor, however, for employee comfort it is usual to provide a floor of hardwood or some other resilient material.

Reinforced concrete is economical wherever floor loads are extremely heavy (as in warehouses), though in high buildings where the lower columns must

FIGURE 141. NAVAL ORDNANCE BUILDING, SAN FRANCISCO, CALIFORNIA. EXTERIORS

Kump & Falk, architects

A complex building including laboratories and shop areas, magnificently lighted by continuous fenestration and in some portions by carefully designed monitors and skylights; the resulting exterior effect has crystalline beauty.

Photographs Roger Sturtevant

be large the amount of available floor space is cut down markedly. Moreover, the very durability of the building may be a drawback when alterations become necessary or the building is to be demolished, for cutting through floors and other elements is costly as well as deleterious to the structure. Concrete arches and rigid frames are being increasingly used, particularly in roof construction. As in steel-frame factories, the top floor may make use of monitor construction—here in concrete—to let in additional daylight.

The more recent examples of reinforced concrete construction exhibit a fluidity undreamed of in earlier years. Concrete has been combined with new materials, such as glass block and metal, and it has been used more daringly with wide cantilevers. (See also Vol. I, Fig. 572.)

Fire Protection. In all types of industrial buildings it is necessary to provide fire protection. The chief responsibility is to prevent the origin of fire and to provide means for extinguishing any fire that occurs at the point of its origin. Next in importance is the need to prevent fire from spreading either through large areas on one floor or from floor to floor through vertical openings. Also to be prevented is the entrance of fire through exterior openings facing near-by buildings.

In order that rapid spread of a blaze may be checked, limits of areas which may be enclosed within fire walls equipped with fire doors are sometimes established by local building codes and are an important consideration in the design of any industrial building. The building code of the National Board of Fire Underwriters has established the limits of such areas and includes a full description of floor areas permissible under varying conditions and of other required precautions; for instance, it specifies the thickness of bearing walls and calls for the protection of non-fireproof members. This code has contributed greatly to the safety of such buildings. The vertical openings in a factory, such as elevator shafts and emergency exits, must be fireproof, readily available, and protected by fireproof doors. Ordinarily a smoke-proof tower serves not only as a fire escape but also as a means of vertical communication. Vitally important is a stand-pipe system of water supply, usually located in the shaft.

Lighting. Generally speaking, there are three schools of thought on the lighting of industrial buildings. The first advocates the provision of the maximum amount of natural light through side-wall sash, monitors, sawtooth roofs, and so on, together with artificial light for night work. (See Fig. 139.) The second combines the use of a limited number of sash with the provision of ample artificial illumination. The third recommends artificial illumination exclusively and allows slit windows for view only or no windows at all.

An examination of light curves in one-story buildings with side-wall sash shows that the intensity of light diminishes rapidly and the interior floor space is dark. Often the intensity of daylight is raised by the use of monitors. Good daylighting may be obtained by the use of a monitor with vertical sash, designed with the total monitor width equal to half the width of the building. Normally the width of the monitor should not be less than twice the height of its sash; conversely, its height should not be more than half its width. An increase in daylight may be obtained by sloping glass in a wide monitor. The height of sash in sawtooth construction should be at least one-third of the span. Side light for deep rooms may be increased by the use of special directional glass block, which directs the light up to the ceiling and thus into the room interiors. (See Fig. 140.)

Artificial lighting may be classed as either general or supplementary. Experts in this field recommend that general lighting be provided throughout the

FIGURE 142. NAVY ORDNANCE BUILDING, SAN FRANCISCO, CALIFORNIA.
LABORATORY

Kump & Falk, architects

Excellent diffused working light.   Photograph Roger Sturtevant

room, with supplemental lighting at vital areas, as at machines. Types of lighting which have been used in industrial buildings include incandescent, mercury
vapor, and fluorescent. In contrast with daylighting, artificial light can be designed for even distribution and for almost any intensity desired.

The proponents of the windowless plant—in which air, light, heat, humidity,
and sound are controlled—claim that such a building represents the ideal,
since it can be operated at the same level of efficiency on a 24-hour basis.
Nevertheless, because research has proved that employees wish to be able to
look out of a building, the owners of "blackout" plants have sometimes installed
slit windows for this purpose after the building has been completed.

Roofs. In addition to providing weather protection, the roof of an industrial
building usually serves as both the eyes and the lungs of the structure. Roofs
therefore present the architect with a stimulating problem. In the past the
ridge roof with monitor, the sawtooth roof, and various types of flat roof—
with or without skylights, with alternate high and low bays, with longitudinal monitors, with butterfly monitors, and with both longitudinal and transverse monitors—have all been used. Each for its own good points has its proponents. Since no two authorities can agree on a "best section," all types are
found; some examples are shown in Figures 145 and 146.

Not only has the growing use of welded steel construction and of "bent

FIGURE 143. OHIO
STEEL FOUNDRY
COMPANY BUILDING.
EXTERIOR AND
INTERIOR

Albert Kahn, Inc., archi-
tects and engineers

Walls entirely of glass
give maximum daylight;
the section permits effi-
cient ventilation.

Photographs
Hedrich-Blessing

beam" construction for sawtooth and monitor roofs economically simplified
and cleaned up the interiors of industrial plants; it has also aided their artificial
lighting, ventilation, and cleanliness. Moreover, the clear beauty of the new
types of structure is a definite contribution to the architectural scene as well
as to employee eye comfort and efficiency.

BUILDINGS FOR HEAVY INDUSTRY

The housing of heavy industry differs from that of light industry in that
the various processes, because of the different demands of each step in production, often require their own separate buildings. Examples of such differences

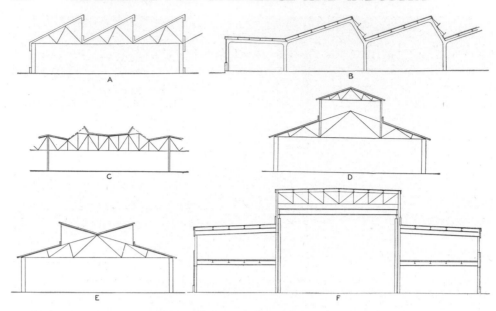

FIGURE 144. TYPICAL INDUSTRIAL BUILDING SECTIONS

A: Ordinary sawtooth; B: Sawtooth with bent and welded sections; C: Long-span trussed butterfly monitor; D: Long-span trussed single monitor; E: So-called butterfly roof; F: Typical
assembly-hall section with traveling crane.

are best seen in foundries, boiler shops, mine heads, and forge buildings, in
pulp and paper mills, and in the chemical industries.

The most common plan type has been that used in the metal-working industries, where the different departments are almost universally housed in
different buildings. For instance, the iron or steel foundry is nearly always in
a one-story building, with one or more aisles of sufficient height to contain
traveling cranes for handling heavy castings, ladles, and flasks. Sufficient clearance is necessary under the crane hook to allow the turning of the largest
flasks to be used. The melting department is commonly situated in a side bay,
with a charging floor at the correct height for the charging of the cupola. The
foundry building is usually of fireproof construction, with adequate provision
for light and ventilation; a typical example is Albert Kahn's Ohio Steel
Foundry Company building, which is light, airy, and clean-looking (Fig. 143).

Forge shops, where ample ventilation is needed, are generally installed in
one-story buildings and the heavy hammers are set on foundations separate
from those of the structure. Roof trusses carry the top bearing of jib cranes
which serve the hammers and forges. A typical section is shown in Figure

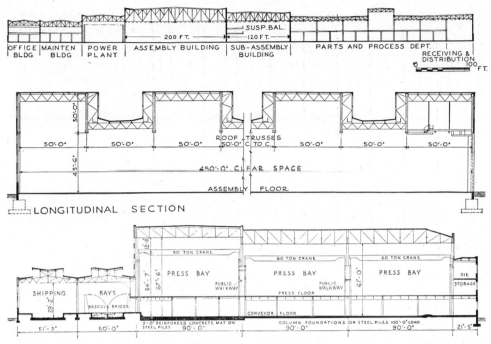

FIGURE 145. INDUSTRIAL BUILDING SECTIONS

TOP: Consolidated Vultee Aircraft Corporation, Fort Worth, Texas; the Austin Company, architects and engineers. MIDDLE: Glenn L. Martin Assembly Plant, Baltimore, Maryland; Albert Kahn, Inc., architects and engineers; from *Architectural Forum*. BELOW: Press shop, Ford Motor Company, Dearborn, Michigan; Albert Kahn, Inc., architects and engineers; from *Architectural Forum*.

144, F. An excellent example of a press shop is that of the Ford Motor Company's River Rouge plant at Dearborn, Michigan, by Albert Kahn, Inc. (Fig. 145). Shops that produce heavy machinery are usually housed in one-story buildings serviced by traveling cranes. Often a railroad spur enters the plant for delivery and shipping. This type of building as a rule is lighted by generous amounts of sash—monitors or glazed sawtooth roofs (Figs. 146, 147).

The large strip rolling mills, such as those built for the Bethlehem Steel Company, turn steel slabs into sheets, strips, or coils. This type of plant must be designed to ensure free and direct movement of the material so that the finishing rolls, for instance, can operate at a speed of 1,500 to 2,000 feet per minute. This generally requires a typical straight-line method of production with no crossing of processes. The cold-roll building of the Ford Motor Company's plant at Bethlehem, Pennsylvania, is lighted by a maximum amount of side-wall sash, together with patented four-way monitors. Here the roof, over

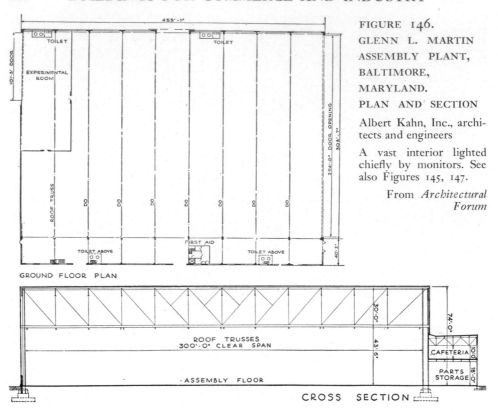

GROUND FLOOR PLAN

CROSS SECTION

FIGURE 146.

GLENN L. MARTIN ASSEMBLY PLANT, BALTIMORE, MARYLAND.

PLAN AND SECTION

Albert Kahn, Inc., architects and engineers

A vast interior lighted chiefly by monitors. See also Figures 145, 147.

From *Architectural Forum*

a building 270′–0″ x 420′–0″, is made up of a longitudinal monitor 24′–0″ high along the building center line, with a series of transverse monitors 12′–0″ high on either side of it, and longitudinal monitors 12′–0″ high at the sides of the building. These side monitors are 19′–0″ wide, the central monitor 26′–0″ wide; the transverse monitors are 20′–0″ wide and 20′–0″ apart. Where prevailing wind currents are at right angles to the length of the monitors, butterfly and A-frame monitors work well. If the air currents blow along the length of these monitors, however, an inward suction is set up which actually pulls bad air back into the building. To guard against this, an increasing number of new plants are being equipped with mechanical ventilators which will remove the bad air and smoke under any conditions.

The chemical industries are varied in character, and each has its peculiar needs and requirements. Generally the buildings are one story in height, except for those plants in which gravity may be used for handling the materials in continuous operation. Occasionally all the processes are carried out under one roof, but for the most part either they are isolated from one another by

FIGURE 147.
GLENN L.
MARTIN
ASSEMBLY
PLANT,
BALTIMORE,
MARYLAND.
EXTERIOR

Albert Kahn,
Inc., architects
and engineers

Photograph
Robert
Damora

fire walls in the same building, as in the Bayer Aspirin plant at Trenton, New Jersey, or they occupy different structures. Large chemical industries, such as those which produce rubber, gasoline, and the like, often house only a small portion of the process and let their impressive-looking tanks, the cracking and cooling towers, the piping, and the framework stand out in the open, like most blast furnaces. (See Fig. 148.)

Buildings for general heavy manufacture, which includes the automobile, airplane, and railroad-car industries, for the most part are centered on an assembly hall and the materials are fed into the assembly area from the parts-making departments. Sometimes the parts are made elsewhere; in this category is the 300'-0" x 450'-0" assembly building for the Glenn L. Martin Company at Baltimore, Maryland, which has a clear span of 300'-0" (Figs. 145–147). Toilets, cafeteria, and parts storage are located on one side of the assembly hall. Construction of the airplane begins at one end of the 450-foot run and, as the plane moves toward the opposite end of the building, parts are added until it is completed. It is then moved outdoors through large hangar-type doors.

The assembly and export plant for Dodge half-ton trucks at Detroit is a two-level structure a quarter of a mile long. On the first floor the frames, motors, wheels, tires, and batteries enter one end of the building where the chassis assembly occurs. Through another entrance at this same end the fenders, sheet-metal parts, and body parts are brought into the building and assembled before they are conveyed to the second floor for painting. When this has been

FIGURE 148. CHEMICAL INDUSTRY FORMS. DOW-CORNING CORPORATION, MIDLAND, MICHIGAN

The dynamic pattern of the chemical industries.   Courtesy Dow-Corning Corp.

completed they are lowered to the first-floor body-trim assembly line, after which the whole truck is assembled on the final assembly line and driven out.

The Fort Worth bomber plant (Fig. 145, top), roughly a mile long, consists of an assembly aisle with a mezzanine on one side from which the materials are fed to the floor below. In some industries exceptionally heavy loads must be moved through assembly aisles, as in those plants where locomotive frames, undercarriages, switch engines, and railroad cars are built. This means that provision must be made for heavy traveling cranes and that due attention must be given to the additional height which they demand. The ventilation is usually mechanical. Some typical heavy building sections are shown in Figures 144 and 145. If power is manufactured on the site, a separate powerhouse is located near the plant itself. For a further discussion, see Chapter 34 on powerhouses.

CONVEYORS AND SIMILAR DEVICES

In any industry raw materials, parts, and finished goods must be moved along the routes indicated by the predetermined flow lines. The flow may

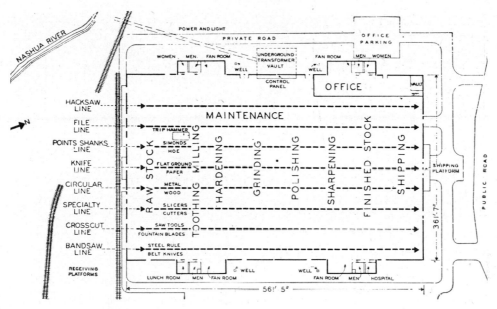

FIGURE 149. SIMONDS SAW AND STEEL COMPANY, FITCHBURG, MASSACHUSETTS.
PLAN, SHOWING STRAIGHT-LINE PRODUCTION

The Austin Company, architects and engineers

Straight-line production methods generated this large rectangular plan.

From *Architectural Forum*

proceed vertically in either or both directions, or it may run horizontally in
a straight line or in a circle. The number of devices used for accomplishing
this is almost limitless and may include overhead conveyors, trucks, or cars;
roller, belt, slat, or chain conveyors; tubes, chutes, elevators, or boosters; or
some combination of these. Each device contributes to the efficiency of the
plant only if it is planned for at the beginning of the design.

The overhead conveyors necessary for heavy work require vertical space
for clearance, and all the heating units, ducts, and piping must be arranged so
as not to interfere with their operation. Trucks or cars may be of either the
hand-operated or the power-driven type; both demand wide aisles clear of
obstruction for direct connection between the various departments. To permit
turning the trucks or cars, the factory machines are sometimes set at an angle
to the aisle. Strong, smooth floor surfaces must be provided to withstand the
hard wear, and storage, maintenance, and charging areas for the trucks are
necessary.

Various flexible systems may be worked out with roller, belt, slat, or chain

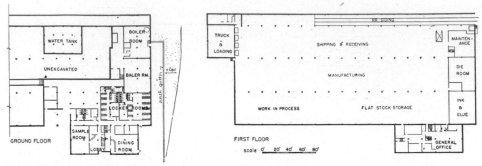

FIGURE 150. CONTAINER CORPORATION OF AMERICA PLANT, GREENSBORO, NORTH CAROLINA. PLAN

Walter Gropius and the Ballinger Company, architects and engineers

Simple production lines, integrating various small processes, are housed in a building where each area is designed specifically for its part in the entire process.   From *Architectural Forum*

conveyors. These are usually developed in a tailor-made fashion for movement between departments and may be located at floor or table level. They may be tilted for multi-floor manufacturing, or they may be connected with boosters for vertical travel. In any case, adequate space as well as clearances and floor openings must be supplied.

When the material to be moved is in a loose or bulk state it is sometimes handled by tubes, either gravity or pneumatic. Correct installation of these must include adequate sizing, pitch, run, length, and curvature. Chutes are employed for the vertical movement of various materials. The speed of travel is controlled by the use of spirals. Sometimes several chutes are included in the same enclosure, and occasionally they serve for storing materials not actually in use. (See Fig. 135.)

EMPLOYEE FACILITIES

Not every plant in existence today is designed with adequate provision for employee welfare. There are still many which lack even the basic essentials, such as inside toilets. Many a workman still eats his lunch at his machine and hangs his clothing on a nail in his shop. Even in the middle of the twentieth century state labor laws and local regulations require only the barest minimum of washing and toilet facilities. Fortunately, however, an increasing interest in employee welfare and comfort has been taken by labor unions, plant owners, and architects. As a result, in most new plants more than the minimum requirements are being installed, partly through a realization that the worker's effi-

FIGURE 151.
CONTAINER
CORPORATION OF
AMERICA PLANT,
GREENSBORO,
NORTH CAROLINA.
EXTERIOR AND
INTERIOR

Walter Gropius and the
Ballinger Company, ar-
chitects and engineers

This exterior beautifully
expresses the clarity of
the entire design.

Photographs Lionel
Freedman: Pictor

ciency is closely connected with his physical well-being and comfort, partly
because of the inclusion of certain maladies under workmen's compensation
laws, and partly through general agreement on the part of all groups that the
worker has rights which must be respected.

Here the basic factor to be considered is employee safety. Occupational
hazards have largely been removed by the use of machine guards and the like.
First-aid departments are now considered standard equipment. The evil effect
of bad odors, vibration, harmful glare, and monotonous wall and ceiling colors

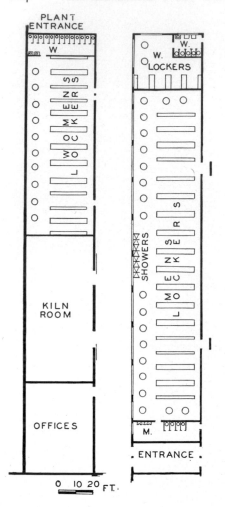

FIGURE 152. EMPLOYEE FACILITIES

LEFT: Singer Manufacturing Company, Finderne, New Jersey. Plans of locker rooms. The Austin Company, architects and engineers. BELOW: DeSoto Plant, Detroit, Michigan. Plan of Welfare Building. Albert Kahn, Inc., architects and engineers.

Locker rooms and welfare services require large, carefully planned areas.

From *Architectural Forum*

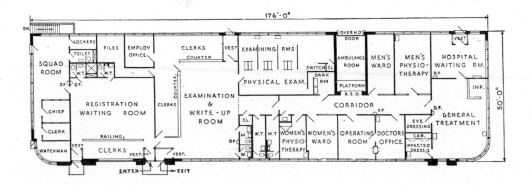

FIGURE 153.

TYPICAL

LOCKER ROOMS

Albert Kahn, Inc., architects and engineers

TOP: Curtiss-Wright Propeller Plant, Caldwell, New Jersey; MIDDLE: United States Naval Ordnance Plant, Amertorp Corporation, Forest Park, Illinois; BOTTOM: Approach to mezzanine locker room, Dodge Half-Ton Truck Plant, Detroit, Michigan.

Courtesy
Albert Kahn, Inc.

FIGURE 154. SHELL OIL COMPANY PLANT, MARTINEZ, CALIFORNIA. CLOTHES-CHANGING AND LOCKER-ROOM BUILDING

Eggers & Kaufmann, architects

Many "dirty" industries need special arrangements for bathing and clothes changing.

Photograph Roger Sturtevant

has been recognized. Proper light, temperature, humidity, air movement, and cool drinking water are provided, as are individual lockers and toilet and rest rooms; the plant interior is pleasantly painted with employee comfort in mind; spacious cafeterias and recreation rooms are sometimes included, and even music is occasionally supplied.

Toilet and locker facilities in both small and medium-sized plants are usually located near the point of entrance so that the employee may change from street to working clothes, lock his possessions in a sanitary steel locker, and take his place in the plant. In this arrangement most of the toilets and wash fountains are installed in the locker rooms and additional toilets are situated at strategic points throughout the plant—usually in the basement, on the main floor, or between the trusses. (See Figs. 152–155.) Although the tendency has been to place the lockers in the same room with the washing facilities, they are sometimes located in adjoining rooms (Fig. 152). The walls and floors of both the locker and the toilet rooms should be of tile or other material which will withstand daily washing.

In large plants, such facilities are widely distributed and their locations are directly related to the distribution of plant personnel. Whether they are on mezzanines, in basements, or adjacent to the working floor, they can usually be so placed that the walking distance is kept to a minimum without impairing the over-all layout of the means of production. Occasionally in a windowless

FIGURE 155.
COLLIERY BUILDINGS,
LANCASHIRE,
ENGLAND. WELFARE
AND RECREATION
FACILITIES

J. H. Forshaw, architect

The British government
has pioneered in devel-
oping bathing, welfare,
and recreational facilities
in close relation to col-
liery pit heads.

Courtesy British
Information Services

plant the employee conveniences are housed in extensions around the perimeter
and opening on the production floor. In long narrow plants where mezzanines
are used for sub-assembly work, these facilities are concentrated directly below
them. Where underground traffic corridors are provided with access stairs
available to all parts of the production area, they are placed in basement areas.
In mines, covered passages are sometimes provided for direct access between
mine-shaft elevator platforms and the change rooms. In certain industries, such
as chemical plants and railroad yards, where there are many small isolated
structures, a separate building commonly houses the employee facilities (Figs.
154, 155). If a department engages in exceptionally grimy operations, showers
should also be provided, preferably in the same building.

Because rest periods are required in some types of work, it is important that
a rest room be provided. Generally this is situated near the dressing room but
is not a part of it. Occasionally in small plants women eat their lunches in the
rest room; this is seldom the case in the larger plants, where separate lunchrooms are more likely to be available.

First-aid and hospital facilities are usually located in conjunction with the
personnel office, so that applicants may be examined by the doctors who stand
by in case of emergency. No layout is satisfactory for all cases; the size and
shape are determined by local conditions, the size of the plant, and the emergency rate in the industry. It is usual to provide easy access from the shop area
as well as to a driveway, where seriously injured patients may be transferred
to an ambulance. The accommodations may approximate in completeness those

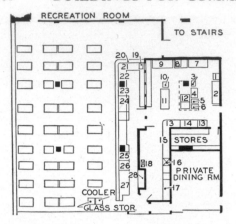

FIGURE 156. HILLS BROTHERS
COFFEE PLANT,
EDGEWATER, NEW JERSEY.
CAFETERIA PLAN

The Austin Company, architects and engineers

Large plants often furnish extensive cafeterias for employees.

1.	SINK	15.	DRAINBOARD AND
2.	BAKERS TABLE, PASTRY		STORAGE
	SHELVES OVER	16.	DISHWASHER
3.	PASTRY COOLING RACK	17.	GARBAGE CANS BELOW
4.	PASTRY OVENS	18.	CART 22 X 38
5.	20 QUART MIXER	19.	TRAYS
6.	PEELER	20.	TRAY SLIDE
7.	REFRIGERATOR	21.	SALADS
8.	SINK	22.	SANDWICHES
9.	SANDWICHES, SALADS	23.	BREAD AND BUTTER
10.	SLICER	24.	STEAM TABLE
11.	TABLE	25.	COLD BOTTLES
12.	GAS RANGES	26.	ICE CREAM
13.	DRAINBOARD	27.	CAKE, CANDY
14.	VEGETABLE SINK	28.	COFFEE URNS

of a small general hospital with regular hospital beds or be limited to a few separate rooms containing only the most necessary equipment. Local first-aid facilities scattered throughout the plant range from a wall cabinet to a small room that will accommodate an injured worker and an attendant. At times a separate employment and welfare building is provided. The one shown in Figure 152, below, designed by Albert Kahn for DeSoto at Detroit, Michigan, includes a watchman's room, employment offices, and fairly complete physical examination rooms.

When industrial plants are located in areas where there are no outside lunchrooms the plant owner generally provides a cafeteria. The recreational value of cafeterias, meeting rooms, and auditoriums has been so emphasized that the cafeterias are often equipped with projection booths, stages, and screens and are used during other than lunch periods. Sometimes a separate room is provided for recreation. The cafeteria should be so located that a quiet and relaxing atmosphere is assured. Where possible, view windows should be provided. Small plants usually have one cafeteria; the larger ones often have several, either in the plant or in separate buildings.

FIGURE 157. SPERRY GYROSCOPE COMPANY, LAKE SUCCESS, LONG ISLAND, NEW YORK. CAFETERIA

Stone & Webster, engineers; N. N. Culin, designer

The factory cafeteria should have the quiet atmosphere of a good restaurant.

Photograph Robert Damora

The layout of both cafeteria and kitchen varies according to their location. In the main, however, the size, number of serving counters, and shape depend on the size of the factory population, the number of eating shifts, and the length of the eating period. Approximately 250 people can be served at one counter per meal. Ordinarily the dining area requires from 10 to 15 square feet per person. Approximately the same area is needed for the serving counters and kitchen. In certain cases private dining rooms are designed for the management. A typical plan incorporating these various features is shown in Figure 156; see also Figure 157.

ADMINISTRATION FACILITIES

Normally administrative offices are housed in a separate building, which is connected with the plant by an enclosed passage. Whenever possible it occupies a position facing the main-highway approaches. In the smaller plant, where a separate administration building is not justified, the offices are sometimes housed in a two-story structure that adjoins the main building on the highway side. If a separate building is used, it is most efficient when long and narrow,

FIGURE 158. TWO PLANT ADMINISTRATION WINGS

The Austin Company, architects and engineers

ABOVE: Penn Electric Switch Company, Goshen, Indiana; BELOW: Illinois Tool Company, Chicago, Illinois.

An inviting atmosphere distinguishes administration areas and not only helps set a healthy atmosphere for an entire plant but also serves to advertise its standards.

Courtesy the Austin Company

with clear spans of 50'–0'' to 60'–0'' which provide an opportunity for flexibility in the office layout. Movable partitions are desirable, and air conditioning and cooling are customary.

The entrance of the office building is designed for speedy handling of traffic, ease of maintenance, and comfort for the visitor. For advertising and publicity

FIGURE 159.
ILLINOIS TOOL COMPANY,
CHICAGO, ILLINOIS.
RECEPTION ROOM AND
GENERAL OFFICE

The Austin Company, architects
and engineers

Courtesy the Austin Company

reasons it is generally made wide and inviting and is sometimes provided with a well-designed sign. Examples are shown in Figures 158 and 159.

Design and research departments, when small, are located within the main plant; if they are large, a separate building with adequate light is required.

SITE

Site selection hinges on a number of factors. Among these are:
  1. Availability of raw materials
  2. A market for finished products
  3. An adequate and stable labor market

4. Cheap fuel and power
5. An adequate and safe means of waste disposal
6. Suitable climatic conditions
7. Receptive topography
8. Size, relative cost, and advertising value of the land
9. Proximity to other industries upon which the process depends
10. Adequate receiving and shipping facilities
11. A helpful community attitude

The site for the plant should be as close as possible to the center of its market. The land must be sufficiently large to receive the roads, walkways, railroad spurs, guardhouses, and parking areas necessary for efficient operation, and when allowance for ultimate expansion has been made there should still be a good deal of space between the building and its neighbors. The parking spaces should be located close to the plant so that employees will not lose time in so-called portal-to-portal travel. Traffic safety is an important factor in planning the site. Care must be taken so that employees who arrive at the plant by bus or trolley may alight and proceed safely to the plant without crossing automobile or truck roads or railroad tracks. Often well-located passenger loading platforms, with provisions for waiting vehicles, are provided. (See Vol. I, Fig. 624.) For the drivers of private cars, one-way traffic movement to and from the parking areas is usually arranged, with separate entrances and exits which open into a service road parallel to and connected with the main highway.

Landscaping of industrial sites is now being carried out on a larger scale than ever before. Not only has the "ugly duckling" in the field of architecture become beautiful architecturally, but the grounds have also become beautiful. Lawns and terraces are as helpful to a factory as to a country house. Through a judicious use of planting a landscape architect can enhance the masses of the structure, point out the paths and roadways, and help the architect to make the most of the site.

Often the main plant of a manufacturing organization is at first located near the owner's home and close to a convenient supply of raw materials. In many cases these factories have developed into giant industries, and all of the products are now mass-produced at the original location. Such an arrangement pays well so long as the market lasts, as in the case of Ford's production of the Model T or that of the Amoskeag plant at Manchester, New Hampshire, which turned out carloads of ginghams. In each of these cases, however, the public became saturated with the product and tastes changed. When demand falls off in mass-production industries, production cannot be readjusted without increasing the cost. The very nature of large-scale mass production makes it impossible to maintain a balance between supply and demand, or at least to bring about a balance quickly enough to prevent a loss. Because of this the Ford organization, like most other large industries, has been decentralizing its production by building smaller plants in several states.

But there are other reasons for the decentralization of industry. If there are several small plants in different locations, a complete shutdown is avoided in case of fire, floods, earthquakes, or other disasters. Labor trouble may hold up production at one but not all of the plants. Usually lower taxes as well as cheaper power and transportation may be found in rural communities. Sometimes branches can be located closer to markets or nearer to the source of supply of raw materials. From the social point of view, also, it is desirable to situate plants in rural areas where living conditions for the employees may be better and where some members of the family may work small farms. Thus decentralization, in the long run, decreases the concentrations of large populations in big cities and at the same time distributes more widely the earnings of industrial workers.

Decentralization is now going on all over the United States and is made increasingly feasible by the wide use of electricity, light metals, air conditioning, and easy transportation. The waste in employees' time which inevitably accompanies employment in large urban industries can no longer be justified socially, nor can the bad housing which the worker usually finds near the large plant. Decentralization combined with advances in plant design is bringing about both an improved quality of manufacture and better employee health.

The industrial building has been the proving ground for new materials, new types of construction, and an unprecedented development in mechanical equipment. It was the first branch of architecture to accept functionalism, and it has led the other branches in its evolution. For that reason it has been one of the most important links between so-called modern architecture and the taste of the lay public. Here the worker first saw the clean lines, the good planning, and the newly developed materials which he later desired in his home; here is the source of his preference for contemporary over traditional structures.

Because of danger from atomic bombs, the United States has been exploring the possibility of locating key industries underground. Whether or not this will ever have to be resorted to, the atomic age in any case will find industrial architecture the most fluid of all, capable of adjusting itself to any conditions, and still acting as the proving ground for new methods and new materials.

A FEW EXAMPLES

The following examples of industrial architecture have been selected for analysis because they represent the main types that have been developed. The number is limited not for want of examples but for lack of space.

COFFEE PLANT

HILLS BROTHERS, INC.

EDGEWATER, NEW JERSEY   *The Austin Company, Engineers and Builders*

The Hills Brothers coffee plant, on the Hudson River at Edgewater, New Jersey (Fig. 160), receives green coffee from South and Central America by boat, and cans as well as other packaging materials by railroad and truck. The green coffee is unloaded from barges to belt conveyors in a long shed and then stored at first-floor level in a warehouse facing the river. Later it is fed by the bag to a conveyor, which takes it to the top of the fourteen-story mixing tower, where it is blended and fed by controlled means to the roasting ovens in the two-story penthouse to the north of the mixing tower. These roasting ovens feed directly to the grinding, packaging, and shipping departments below. The finished product is shipped by railroad (a spur enters a one-story wing on the northern side of the building) and by truck from a dock on the western side of the building. The powerhouse is situated in a separate building to the west of the main structure and joined to it by a bridge. A brick wall encloses the private parking space, which is guarded by a small control building.

For the most part the flow diagram of this plant indicates a vertical direction. With the exception of the raw coffee, which is lifted by conveyor, and of the packaging materials, which are taken up by conveyor and elevator, the main flow is accomplished by gravity. The offices are located on the west and south side on the first, second, and third floors. There is no unnecessary crossing of flow, and the scheme works efficiently. The massing of the main lines of flow is honestly arranged, and the whole presents a pleasant appearance. Most of the plant is of re-enforced concrete with brick facing. In color the brick varies from buff to brown, and the bands between sash, both horizontal and vertical, are made up of selected darker brick. These bands give a general horizontality to the lines of the sash, which might have been more honestly expressed if the outer bay of construction had been cantilevered so that continuous bands of

FIGURE 160.
HILLS BROTHERS COFFEE PLANT,
EDGEWATER, NEW JERSEY.
VIEW FROM THE LAND AND
FROM THE RIVER

The Austin Company, architects and engineers

The exterior reflects the interior usage.

Courtesy the Austin Company

sash could have been used. Also, the main entrance might have been given more importance.

PROPELLER PLANT
CURTISS-WRIGHT CORPORATION
CALDWELL, NEW JERSEY · · · · *Albert Kahn, Inc., Architects and Engineers*

The general layout of this plant (Fig. 161) follows closely the typical Kahn pattern. The symmetrical one-story administration building, 46′–0″ x 260′–0″, featuring an entrance rotunda, contains well-appointed reception

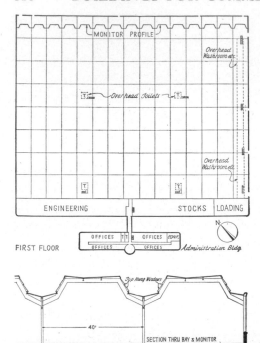

FIRST FLOOR

SECTION THRU BAY & MONITOR

FIGURE 161.
CURTISS-WRIGHT PROPELLOR PLANT,
CALDWELL, NEW JERSEY.
PLAN, SECTION, AND AIR VIEW
Albert Kahn, Inc., architects and engineers

Plan and section from *Architectural Forum;* photograph Robert Yarnell Ritchie, courtesy Albert Kahn, Inc.

and waiting rooms and a large board room, as well as adequate office space. It is connected to the main body of the plant by an enclosed passage. The two-story factory office building, 46'–0" x 602'–0", runs parallel to the administration building at the south end of the shop. The first floor originally housed stock storage, telephone equipment, a first-aid room, a reception and waiting room, a service school, a truck well, loading platforms, and other shop facilities, in addition to the experimental testing and engineering departments. The second floor at first housed a large engineering-department drafting room, a cafeteria, a private dining room, a kitchen, and a number of offices devoted to personnel in charge of plant operation, design, and production. The main shop, 480'–0" x 600'–0", made up of 40'–0" x 60'–0" bays, occupies a position behind this shop office. Future expansion can be made in a northerly and an easterly direction.

Shop toilet facilities are located under monitors on mezzanines, each of which is about 35 feet square and is reached by stairs from the shop floor (see Fig. 153). The single main entrance for shop employees is next to the truck well, near the employees' parking space. Immediately inside this entrance are the mezzanine coatrooms and washroom facilities. The cafeteria, located over the truck dock, is available from this mezzanine as well as from the office area.

In section, the shop is provided with light and ventilation by means of roof monitors of the bent-beam type. A minimum interior height of 18'–6" is maintained. The boiler house is at the side of the plant, where it will not interfere with future expansion. An airport, a test building capable of testing 30'–0" propellers, several hangars, and a trainer building are situated to the north and west of the main plant. A large assembly plant, connected by an under-highway passage, is located across the main highway to the west.

All materials enter the building at the loading platform and proceed, according to use, to their proper destinations. The shop is divided in such a way that about 70 per cent of the floor area is devoted to blade manufacture, on the east side, and the remaining 30 per cent is given over to a general machine shop where such parts as hub, speed-reducer, and blade gears are manufactured. Flat stock is fed directly into the blade-processing section, and material for small parts is moved to the small-parts storage room at the southeast corner of the shop. Among the processes included in blade manufacture are:

1. Milling and grinding
2. Blanking by use of large presses
3. Forming by use of large presses
4. Matching and numbering
5. Welding
6. Heating
7. Forming of blade twist and hub
8. Snagging
9. Removal of scale
10. Shot blasting
11. X-ray examination
12. Brazing
13. Finishing
14. Polishing
15. Checking and balancing
16. Plating
17. Inspection
18. Boxing and shipping

During the Second World War, when this plant manufactured only a few different types of propellers, straight-line production was possible. Since then so many types of propellers have been turned out that for economic reasons straight-line manufacture has been dispensed with and, instead of a single step in the process, each employee handles several not necessarily consecutive operations. In either case, however, the direction of flow is first toward the north wall and then to the east wall for shipment to the assembly plant.

As originally planned for straight-line production, the process was very well housed—adequately but not wastefully. Good general light was obtained through the monitors and the side-wall sash, and very little artificial light was needed for daytime work. The flow of materials and men was carefully designed so that neither interfered with the other, and no crossovers were necessary. Shop circulation was provided for by leaving wide aisles at the perimeter and between production lines. The administration building, efficiently designed, is subdivided by a few permanent partitions around certain offices near the rotunda and by movable ceiling-height steel partitions at the corridor and end offices. De-humidified air is circulated from a small basement area under the rotunda. The structure as a whole, however, may be criticized as too formal for the best expression. The exterior of the entire group of buildings honestly reflects the interior usage. Light buff brick gives a clean, modern, efficient appearance. Generally speaking, the plant is in good scale and good-looking as well as efficient.

LIGATURE BUILDING
JOHNSON & JOHNSON
NEW BRUNSWICK, NEW JERSEY   *R. G. and W. M. Cory, Architects*

This building (Fig. 162), one of several belonging to Johnson & Johnson, is situated on a hill in view of passing motorists on the highway near by. Its function is surgical-gut packaging, and by reason of its prominent position it also serves as an advertisement for the whole group of buildings. Because of the careful study devoted to it, this plant succeeds on both counts.

The process housed is a clean one. Intestines of government-inspected sheep, already split into ribbons, are received via express from a Johnson & Johnson subsidiary plant in Chicago. Women wind the ligatures, or sutures, on small reels which they insert in glass containers; the containers are then sterilized, sealed, and packaged for shipment.

In plan, the 100'–0" x 190'–0" interior is divided by columns into six bays 15'–0" high. The first bay, at the front of the building, contains the reception foyer, with toilets for visitors, an office, a first-aid room, and a laboratory, as well as employees' toilet and locker rooms for men and women and a women's

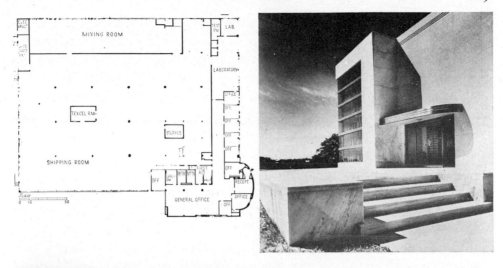

FIGURE 162. LIGATURE BUILDING, JOHNSON & JOHNSON, NEW BRUNSWICK, NEW JERSEY. PLAN AND TWO EXTERIORS

R. & W. Cory, architects

With unusually lavish materials.

Plan from *Architectural Forum;* photographs courtesy Johnson & Johnson

rest room. The reception foyer and the office are paneled in bleached walnut and have marble floors. The second bay houses ten tables at which the sutures are wound on reels. Here for reasons of cleanliness the floor is of terrazzo and the walls are of structural glass. The third bay contains tube-sealing and sterilizing rooms, which are entered through an air-locked dressing room where the employees wash and don sterile work clothes. The interior finish of these rooms is similar to that of the winding room, with the addition of a coved terrazzo base. All wall joints are narrow and flush. The fluorescent fixtures are covered with sealed lenses and are serviced from a crawl space above. The air is conditioned and filtered. A view window between these rooms and the winding rooms enables spectators to watch the operations. The remaining two bays are, for the most part, thrown into one room where the packed ligature tubes are stored in lockers until they can be inspected and tested before being shipped. From a construction standpoint this building is notable for its floor construction—terrazzo laid on structural terra-cotta tile separated by concrete T beams—which permits running the utility lines from a transverse tunnel through ducts formed by the hollow tile to any location in the plant.

The exterior of the building expresses the interior function. The wide windows, 3'–8" high and set about 4'-0" from the floor, are made of 8'-0" sheets of heat-absorbing plate glass, set flush with the face of the building in fixed stainless steel frames. In an attempt to achieve complete horizontality of effect, adjoining planes are butted together with a thin layer of mastic, and the steel columns behind the glass are covered on three sides with a 3'-8" band of black sand-blasted structural glass. A veneer of Vermont marble extends 24 feet up the wall; this is made up of eight courses set with ⅛" flush joints to achieve a monolithic appearance. The entrance doors are of transparent plastic with bronze hardware and are protected by a cantilevered stainless-steel canopy. The lettering atop the coping is well placed and well conceived and may be easily read. As a unit the building mass is in good scale, expresses its use successfully, is suited to the site, and has high advertising and publicity value.

SUGGESTED ADDITIONAL READING FOR CHAPTER 33

Alford, L. P. (editor), *Production Handbook* (New York: Ronald, 1944), p. 794.

American Face Brick Association, *Industrial Buildings and Housing* (New York: Architectural Forum, for the Association [c1926]).

Cheney, Sheldon, *The New World Architecture* (New York: Tudor, 1935).

Dunham, Clarence W., *Planning Industrial Structures* (New York: McGraw-Hill, 1948).

Hiscox, W. J., *Factory Lay-out, Planning and Progress*, 3d ed. by James Stirling (London: Pitman, 1942).

Holme, C. G. (editor), *Industrial Architecture* (London: Studio, 1935).

Jeans, Victorine, *Factory Act Legislation*, Oxford University Cobden Prize Essays (London: Unwin, 1892).

McNamara, Katherine, *Landscape Architecture; a Classified Bibliography* . . . (Cambridge, Mass.: Harvard University, School of Landscape Architecture, 1934)

Metropolitan Life Insurance Company, *Washroom and Locker-Room Facilities; a Discussion of Plant Requirements* ([New York:] the Company, 1942, revised 1948).

Mitchell, Broadus, and George Sinclair Mitchell, *The Industrial Revolution in the South* (Baltimore: Johns Hopkins Press, 1930).

Price, George M., *The Modern Factory* (New York: Wiley, 1914).

Ragatz, Lowell J., *The Industrial Revolution* (London: Thomas [1938]).

Sweetser, Ralph H., *Blast Furnace Practice* (New York: McGraw-Hill, 1938).

PERIODICALS

"An Aircrafts Parts Plant in the Midwest," *Architectural Record*, Vol. 91 (1942), June, pp. 49–52.

"Architecture for War Production; a Military Plant in the Middle East," *Architectural Record*, Vol. 91 (1942), June, pp. 43–48.

"The Automatic Factory," *Fortune*, Vol. 34 (1946), November, pp. 160–64.

"Boeing Aircraft Company, Renton, Washington," *Progressive Architecture*, Vol. 27 (1946), December, pp. 40–49.

"Bottling Plant, Baltimore, Maryland," *Progressive Architecture*, Vol. 26 (1945), November, pp. 72–74.

Brunnier, H. J., "Pacific Coast Shredded Wheat Factory," *Architect and Engineer*, Vol. 47 (1916), November, pp. 81–87.

"Building in One Package," Austin Company, architects, *Architectural Forum*, Vol. 82 (1945), January, pp. 93–112; February, pp. 113–28.

"Building Types; a Reference Study on Factories," *Architectural Forum*, Vol. 85 (1945), February, pp. 113–28.

Burt, Fred M., "Fast Service Industrial Feeding," *Mill and Factory*, Vol. 38 (1946), February, pp. 153–54.

"Coca-Cola Bottling Plant, Asheville, North Carolina," *Architectural Record*, Vol. 90 (1941), July, pp. 55–56.

"Design of Roof for Ford Mill," *Blast Furnace and Steel Plant*, Vol. 24 (1936), February, pp. 161–62.

"Diesel Engine Plant," *Progressive Architecture*, Vol. 26 (1945), March, pp. 79–84.

"Dodge Chicago Plant," Albert Kahn, architect, in association with Airtemp Division, Chrysler Corporation, *Architectural Forum*, Vol. 79 (1943), December, pp. 49–58.

"Drive-in Laundries," *Architectural Record*, Vol. 90 (1941), July, pp. 95–96.

Elsworth, F. C., "Broken Hill Steel Works in Australia," *Blast Furnace and Steel Plant*, Vol. 24 (1936), April, pp. 305–7.

"Enclosed Acreage," *Engineering News-Record*, Vol. 116 (1936), March 5, pp. 337–42.

"Factories," a Building Type Study, *Architectural Record*, Vol. 83 (1938), June, pp. 99–130.

"Factory Administration Building, Bath, Maine," *Progressive Architecture*, Vol. 26 (1945), March, pp. 67–70.

"Factory Design," in "Reference Studies in Design and Planning," *Architectural Record*, Vol. 89 (1941), January, pp. 137–58, including article "Factory Toilets and Locker Rooms," pp. 157–58.

"Factory Design for Low-Cost Production," *Mill and Factory* in collaboration with *Architectural Record*, Vol. 98 (1945), November, pp. 118–40.

Ferguson, H. K., and others, "What Industry Must Know about Building," Part II, *Factory Management*, Vol. 93 (1937), April, pp. 37–76.

Gerner, Egon, Harold Burson, and others, "The Factory of the Future," *Architectural Forum*, Vol. 80 (1944), June, pp. 79–86.

Hamlin, Talbot F., "Factories as Architecture," *Pencil Points*, Vol. 21 (1940), August, pp. 469–80.

"Handling Steel for Modern Mills," *Blast Furnace and Steel Plant*, Vol. 24 (1936), August, pp. 679–84.

"Hardware Warehouse and Retail Store, Atlanta, Georgia," *Progressive Architecture*, Vol. 26 (1945), November, pp. 75–77.

Hyler, John E., "Handling Materials with Tongs, Grips, and Grapples," *Mill and Factory*, Vol. 38 (1946), March, pp. 134–39.

—— "Handling Various Foodstuffs," *Mill and Factory*, Vol. 36 (1945), June, pp. 98–100, 282.

"Industrial Buildings," *Progressive Architecture*, Vol. 29 (1948), August, pp. 47–66.

Industrial Buildings Reference Numbers, *Architectural Forum*, Vol. 39 (1923), September, pp. [83]–152, especially editorial, p. 152; Vol. 51 (1929), September, pp. 265–432.

"Industry on the Move," *Business Week*, No. 391 (Feb. 27, 1937), pp. 44–52.

Jacoby, Hurlbut S., "Chemical Plant Construction," *Industrial and Engineering Chemical News*, Vol. 27 (1935), September, pp. 999–1004.

Leaver, E. W., and J. J. Brown, "Machines without Men," *Fortune*, Vol. 34 (1946), November, pp. 165, 192–204.

"McDonald Mill of the Carnegie-Illinois Steel Corporation," *Blast Furnace and Steel Plant*, Vol. 24 (1936), March, pp. 224–30.

"Machine Shop and Assembly Building," *Pencil Points*, Vol. 25 (1944), March, pp. 36–38.

"A Million Square Feet of Floor," *Architectural Forum*, Vol. 75 (1941), November, pp. 335–37.

"A New Laboratory," *Architectural Forum*, Vol. 85 (1946), September, pp. 81–86.

"A New Station for Milk in Transit," *Architectural Record*, Vol. 87 (1940), February, pp. 51–52.

"Offices for Industry," *Engineering News-Record*, Vol. 46 (1936), March 19, pp. 416–22.

Perry, Ernestine, "Industrial Feeding," *Mill and Factory*, Vol. 37 (1945), August, pp. 119–22, 153–54.

"Portfolio of Industrial Buildings," Albert Kahn, Inc., architects, *Architectural Forum*, Vol. 69 (1938), August, pp. 87–142.

"Printing Plant, Houston, Texas," *Architectural Record*, Vol. 90 (1941), July, pp. 52–53.

"Pulp Mill," *Architectural Forum*, Vol. 66 (1937), March, pp. 171–74.

"Research Laboratory Building, San Francisco," *Architectural Record*, Vol. 90 (1941), July, pp. [48]–50.

"Shipbuilding Yard," *Architectural Forum*, Vol. 77 (1942), October, pp. 81–88.

"Structural System," *Architectural Record*, Vol. 81 (1937), March, pp. BT 36–40.

"Sunrise Dairies, Hillside, New Jersey," Petroff and Clarkson, architects, *Progressive Architecture*, Vol. 26 (1945), November, pp. 78–81.

"A Trio of Modern Plants," *Architectural Forum*, Vol. 75 (1941), November, pp. 331–34.

"Walls, Roofs, and Floors," *Engineering News-Record*, Vol. 116 (1936), March 12, pp. 384–90.

"Warehouse and Bottling Plant," *Architectural Forum*, Vol. 66 (1937), March, pp. 179–81.

"Wartime Developments of Monorail Type Cranes," *Mill and Factory*, Vol. 38 (1946), March, pp. 101–8.

Whitmore, Eugene, "Why Business Is Decentralizing," *American Business*, Vol. 7 (1937), March, pp. 11–13, 59.

"Willow Run Bomber Plant," *Architectural Record*, Vol. 92 (1942), September, pp. 39–46.

"Windowless Offices for Industry," *Engineering News Record*, Vol. 116 (1936), March 26, pp. 456–61.

Wood, Charles P., "Where to Locate the Plant," part of "What Industry Must Know about Building," Part II, *Factory Management*, Vol. 93 (1937), April, pp. 46–49.

Yaglou, C. P., "Abnormal Air Conditions in Industry," *Journal of Industrial Hygiene*, Vol. 19 (1937), January, pp. 12–43.

34

Powerhouses

By ROLAND WANK

THE GRADUAL PROGRESS from the muscle power of the caveman to the atomic power of the twentieth century underlies the evolution of mankind. Each period of civilization is marked and its limits are determined by the per capita amount of power available to society. Any increase in this amount depends mainly on the discovery of new and more efficient types and sources of power.

In our integrated, mechanized age the hum of the powerhouse is truly the heartbeat of civilization. An attacking enemy or a revolution which gained control of the powerhouses of a nation would have victory in its grasp. It would seem fitting, therefore, that such structures should receive the architectural attention and public notice commensurate with their importance. Until recently, though, such recognition has been the exception rather than the rule, perhaps because of the perverted tendency of the Victorian era to regard utility as the antithesis of beauty.

Two or three decades of development and a more technologically minded public focused greater interest on powerhouses, and architects were called in by the designing engineers—more as decorators and festoon-hangers at the start but as genuine working partners later on. Impetus was given to this trend in the United States by the great hydro-electric plants of the Bureau of Reclamation and the Tennessee Valley Authority, by the powerhouses of modern industrial plants, and, in a minor but significant way, by the municipal and co-operatively owned generating stations which are close to the pocketbooks and hearts of their taxpayer or co-operative member owners.

FUNCTIONS

The term "powerhouse" covers buildings devoted to a great variety of functions which necessarily affect the planning and design of the structure. The more common of these functions may be recited briefly. Primarily—and perhaps properly—the word signifies a plant generating and transmitting

FIGURE 163.

WATERSIDE ELECTRIC
GENERATING STATION,
CONSOLIDATED EDISON
COMPANY OF NEW YORK.
TWO EXTERIORS

A characteristic urban powerhouse
that contains generators driven by
steam. The views show an agglom-
eration of construction and illustrate the change from the older
eclectic period to mid-twentieth-
century functionalism.

Courtesy Consolidated Edison
Co. of New York

power. Before the general acceptance of electricity, power as rotary motion
was transmitted by belts and shafts between closely clustered buildings. A
few examples of this method are still in operation. Currently, of course, electricity is the principal form of transmitted power (Fig. 163).

Frequently the boiler or heating plants of large projects are called powerhouses, perhaps for the reason that the heat transmitted in steam or hot water
is also a form of power or because the generation of electric power is often
among their emergency or incidental functions. For example, in projects where
absolutely uninterrupted service is vital, as in hospitals, in broadcasting stations,
and in certain industries, there is often a stand-by battery of generators which
"cut in" automatically in case of failure of the primary supply. In industries
that require large quantities of steam for use in their processing, it is often possible to pass the steam through turbines before or after such use and thus obtain
electric power as a by-product at slight extra cost. Sometimes by-product

power results from conditions peculiar to the process involved: waste heat from incinerators, the heat content of the gases in sewage treatment plants, or the power generated by engines on the test blocks in aircraft or automotive engine works. Many factories which operate on a 24-hour schedule and therefore by continuous use are able to amortize the capital cost of the equipment advantageously find that generating their own current is so close to the border line of economic feasibility that the decision as between doing so or passing up the opportunity becomes simply a matter of policy Last, but not least, it may be mentioned that the installation of generating equipment—or sometimes the mere provision of equipment space—often pays handsome returns as a trump card in bargaining for utility rates.

Besides heat and electric power, an industrial power plant may supply a variety of services. Since several kinds of heavy-service equipment—all requiring control and supervision by operating engineers and the availability of cranes and machine shop for erection and maintenance—are logically placed in the same building, one is likely to find in a single powerhouse compressors for refrigeration, air conditioning, and compressed air; pumps for vacuum systems, water supply, or sprinkler and fire lines; equipment for treating water for drinking, boiler, or process purposes; and incinerators for trash disposal and other similar installations.

POWER SOURCES

Another factor which profoundly affects the layout and appearance of powerhouses is the source from which the power is obtained. For the purposes of this discussion we shall disregard the old friendly windmill, sundry experiments in the direct transformation of the sun's rays into usable energy, atomic power, and reverse-cycle refrigeration, although the last method is used on a large scale in at least one outstanding application—the two large groups of public buildings in Zurich heated by that system from an underground central plant. We shall limit ourselves to a consideration of the four major sources of power today: the energy derived from water, coal, oil, and gas. The source of power affects not only the nature of the building but also its site and surroundings. Since freedom from service interruption is always a primary factor, a stored supply of the source material is characteristic of power plants; moreover, the provision for this storage, together with requirements of access for delivery of the material and, in the case of coal, for the disposal of ashes, often determines the location and the site layout.

FIGURE 164. NORRIS DAM, TENNESSEE. GENERAL EXTERIOR VIEW
Tennessee Valley Authority, architects
The great scale typical of modern flood-control and hydro-electric dams and powerhouses.

Courtesy TVA

Water. For hydro-electric plants, storage of power takes the form of a lake or reservoir—although some day a plant for exploiting the movement of the tides may be built. If it is an artificial reservoir, the water will be held by a dam. Dams usually have spillways, that is, pre-determined channels to carry off flood waters before they can rise high enough in the reservoir to overtop the dam and perhaps wash it out. The spillways of major reservoirs in most cases are equipped with gates which when closed permit maintaining the water at a level above the spillway crest (either for assistance in flood control in the valley or for increased power production); when heavy floods are anticipated, the gates may be opened for lowering the reservoir level. Sluiceways, or openings through the dam close to the bottom, may serve the same purpose after the water level has already dropped below that of the spillway. Inspection and operation of the gates usually require a service deck across the top of the dam; this deck may be made wide enough to accommodate a public highway or even a railroad in order to save the cost of the pier foundations and approach ramps necessary for an independent bridge (Figs. 164, 166).

Normally the water flows mainly through the hydro-electric plant, where it turns the turbines before spilling out into the tailrace; the water reaches the turbines through large-diameter steel pipes called penstocks. When the power-

FIGURE 165.
NORRIS DAM, TENNESSEE.
DETAIL
Tennessee Valley Authority, architects
Concrete expressively used.

Courtesy TVA

FIGURE 166.
PICKWICK DAM,
TENNESSEE.
GENERATOR ROOM
Tennessee Valley Authority, architects
The clean openness of modern generator halls.

Courtesy TVA

house can be located more profitably (that is, lower) at some distance from the dam, the water may reach it through tunnels drilled through rock, open channels or millraces, or wooden troughs serving as channels, often several miles long. All these components of a project, together with their appurtenances—such as valve houses, control stations, approach roads and sidings, power and

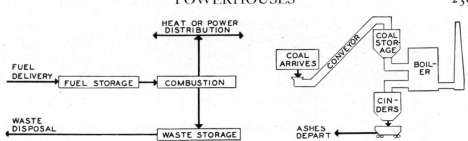

FIGURE 167. FLOW DIAGRAMS OF FUEL USED TO PRODUCE HEAT OR POWER

control lines, pressure relief (surge) tanks, possible navigation locks, and general lighting—should receive architectural attention so that the entire project will be cast in one mold.

Coal. Coal-steam generating plants (except those types, under experiment in the United States and reportedly used in other countries, where coal is burned in the mines without removing it from the ground) require provisions for receiving, handling, and storing coal. (See Fig. 167.) The coal may be hauled in by water, by rail, or—more rarely—by truck. It can conceivably come direct from the mine by conveyor, and there is at least one example abroad where it flows a considerable distance through an underground conduit under hydrostatic pressure. If brought in by barge or steamer, it may be removed by clamshell-bucket cranes or conveyors, or by both in sequence (Fig. 172); if delivered by rail or truck, it will pass first through a weighing station and then on to the coalyard where it is dumped either by the conveyance itself or, in the case of railroad cars, by revolving dumpers which grip the whole car and turn it upside down.

In some older installations the coalyard consists of a system of multiple sidings onto which cars are switched for unloading by crane, and the space between the tracks serves for storage. If such a scheme is used for emergency storage, the tracks may be taken up as the yard is filled and then relaid as the coal pile is reduced. Generally, however, the coal is distributed over the storage area by conveyors, bulldozers, or, in the most efficient installations, by draglines operating between a mast located on a centrally placed control cabin and towers which move on a circular railroad track on the periphery. It is recovered for use by the same means and is then passed through crushers and pulverizers which reduce it to the consistency of flour; finally, it is dumped on a conveyor and carried to the bunkers, which hold about a 24-hour supply and for gravity flow are placed above the boilers. The ashes, which are removed by

FIGURE 168.

WATTS BAR STEAM PLANT, TENNESSEE. MAIN ENTRANCE

Tennessee Valley Authority, architects

The tall portion at the left with hooded ventilating slots is the windowless boiler house; the portion nearer at hand houses a machine shop on the first floor and administrative offices on the second. The glass brick and corrugated asbestos, visible above, is the top of the generator hall.   Courtesy TVA

FIGURE 169. WATTS BAR STEAM PLANT, TENNESSEE. REAR VIEW

Tennessee Valley Authority, architects

The coal conveyor enters the boiler room at a high level. At the left the lower wing is the generator hall, the door of which is large enough to allow the entrance of railroad cars. Forced draft permits the use of relatively short smokestacks.   Courtesy TVA

mechanical means similar to those for handling the coal, are either shipped away from the plant altogether or dumped as fill in low-lying areas in the immediate vicinity, within reach by conveyor.

An ample supply of water for condensing steam is essential to coal-steam generating plants. In some cases the water may require purification or some other special treatment, which may take place in a separate structure at the point of intake.

As has been noted, such generating plants require certain essential facilities—scale house, car dump, control cabin, masts and towers, conveyors and their housing, cranes, and the like—together with approaches, power and control lines, lighting and auxiliary buildings for spare parts, and lockers and showers for the yard crew. The comment previously made with respect to hydroelectric plants applies here also: the site and these appurtenant structures should be so planned that they are harmonious with the powerhouse itself, since any difference in the design approach here will work to the disadvantage of the whole.

Oil. In a plant that uses oil for fuel the storage problem is greatly simplified. The storage tanks may be either aboveground or underground, and the oil can be delivered by tanker, tank car, or truck. If necessary, oil can be pumped for considerable distances through an underground pipeline; in this case heat for immersion heaters may be required at the intake end of the pipeline for the heavy oils which do not flow freely in winter.

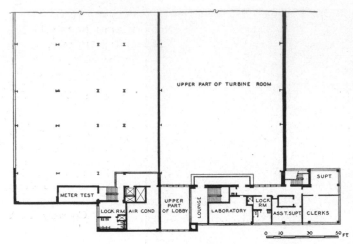

FIGURE 171.
WATTS BAR
STEAM PLANT,
TENNESSEE.
TWO PARTIAL PLANS

Tennessee Valley Authority, architects

The plans show approximately one-half of the total length and include the area necessary for two of the four units. The boiler room is at the left, the generator hall at the right. The front wing contains a lobby with a lounge and an observation balcony for visitors, as well as the machine shop, above which are the administrative offices. Note the observation window from the offices to the generator hall.

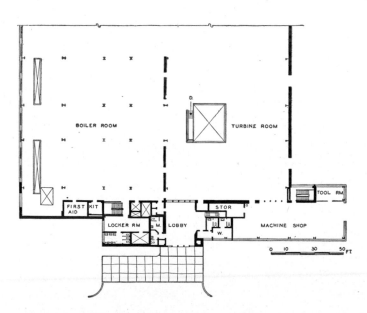

Gas. Plants that burn gas for fuel need little beyond a pipe connection. Because manufactured gas is too expensive except in special applications natural gas is generally used.

FIGURE 172. WATERSIDE ELECTRIC GENERATING STATION, CONSOLIDATED EDISON COMPANY OF NEW YORK. VIEW SHOWING COAL LOADERS AND CONVEYORS

Coal lifts from barges and coal conveyors over a public drive inspired an exciting architectural composition. Courtesy Consolidated Edison Co. of New York

POWER YARDS AND LINES

Powerhouses that produce electric power, whatever the energy source, will have adjoining them transformer yards and switchyards, which together with the connecting power lines and their poles or towers form a vital part of the surroundings—functionally as well as visually. Although the yards and lines must be placed and designed to meet certain technical requirements, often obvious alternatives are available and research will turn up others. It is important, therefore, that the architect include those features in his sphere of interest.

MAJOR ELEMENTS

Turning now to the plant building itself, the main elements may be listed as follows:

Machine Hall. Probably the image most naturally associated with a power plant is a great hall. This is indeed a feature common to practically all plants,

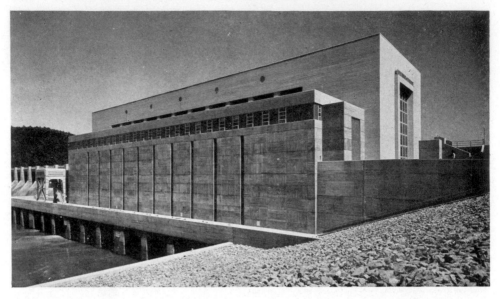

FIGURE 173. GUNTERSVILLE DAM, ALABAMA. EXTERIOR OF POWERHOUSE

Tennessee Valley Authority, architects

This powerhouse shelters four generators. The lower wing contains the electric control equipment; above are the administrative offices. The entire lower section of the building is of heavy reinforced concrete because the flood water, in extreme cases, might back up to a level as high as the parapet at the right; the powerhouse itself would then function as a part of the dam.

Courtesy TVA

although the proportions of the hall and the equipment housed in it may vary greatly, depending on the type and functions of the plant. In a hydro-electric plant it shelters the steel-jacketed generators rotating on their vertical shafts, which are coupled directly to the waterwheels (turbines) underneath. In a steam power plant it houses the steam turbines and electric generators, coupled on horizontal shafts. In Diesel or gas power plants the engines and generators, again laid horizontally, occupy the floor space. In industrial powerhouses the compressors, pumps, and a variety of other machinery may be the primary equipment.

The common feature—and the one which leads to the proportions characteristic of such rooms—lies in the fact that heavy equipment requires some kind of overhead lifting device for its installation, maintenance, and repair. Thus the height of the room must accommodate not only the installed equipment but also the parts as they are lifted and carried over it, the lifting device itself, and in addition the lighting system (usually "high bay" units). To make

FIGURE 174. CHICKAMAUGA DAM,
TENNESSEE. GENERATOR HALL

Tennessee Valley Authority, architects

The clarity of form achieved through the use of steel rigid arched frames. The walls are terra cotta; the floor is ceramic tile.

Courtesy TVA

all parts of the room accessible for the overhead lifting device, subdivision by columns or girders must be avoided; hence the result is likely to be a high, wide, and handsome room of impressive proportions (Fig. 174).

In very small plants a simple monorail running the length of the room over the approximate centers of gravity of the heavier equipment parts may suffice. At a slightly larger scale one is likely to find a beam crane moving on rails bracketed from columns along either side of the hall, with a trolley traveling on the beam in a crosswise direction. Both the crane and the trolley may be operated either by hand or by electric power controlled from the floor. For heavier work a bridge crane with an operator's cabin on it is likely to be needed; this requires enough vertical clearance to account for a considerable height of ceiling above the crane rail.

The hall is usually made long enough to allow clear space for the setting down of dismantled equipment during its erection and repair. When a switch-yard adjoins the power plant, transformers are often brought into the hall for overhaul and repair, and in that case additional space must be provided for them. For bringing in these outside units as well as the stationary equipment a large door is needed, generally at the end of the hall. Sometimes the height of the door is cut to the average dimensions of equipment parts and an operable or removable transom is provided above to permit the passage of especially

FIGURE 175.
CHEROKEE DAM,
TENNESSEE.
EXTERIOR OF
POWERHOUSE

Tennessee Valley Authority, architects

Here the powerhouse is of the semi-outdoor type; the paved area in the foreground is the roof of the generator hall; the removable cylindrical covers are over the turbines and generators. A heavy crane removes the covers or the generator parts for repair or replacement.

Courtesy TVA

high units (such as transformers with insulators attached). Equipment may move through the door on trucks, railroad cars, or railroad-wheeled special carriages; sometimes the main crane tracks extend outward past the building walls and require a special operating transom profiled to the rails.

In hydro-electric plants other means of getting equipment inside may have to be employed, depending on the mode of access through the usually hilly topography. Sometimes heavy parts are lowered into the main hall from upper access levels or are lifted from barges by cranes and passed through large hatches or removable sections of the roof. In some cases an equipment hatch left open through the bulk concrete of the dam leads to a pit adjoining the main hall and connects to it by a large doorway. Heavy equipment will be mounted on blocks of reinforced concrete resting on independent foundations. Vibration joints between foundation blocks and the rest of the floor are closed with overlapping metal plates.

The space underneath the great hall (sometimes left open by wells or by partial omission of the floor) in a hydro-electric plant will contain the turbine shaft couplings and, farther down, the turbines; in a steam generating plant it will contain a maze of Gargantuan piping—for steam, exhaust, condensing water, lubricating oil, carbon dioxide, control wiring, and so forth—comprehensible only to a power-plant engineer.

In some hydro-electric plants the great hall may be lacking altogether or

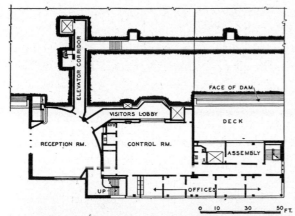

FIGURE 176. CHEROKEE DAM,
TENNESSEE. THREE PLANS

Tennessee Valley Authority,
architects

The inspection gallery along the
sunken generator hall is reached
by stairs from the visitors'
reception room on the upper level.
The entire generator hall may be
submerged in floods up to the level
of its roof without damage.

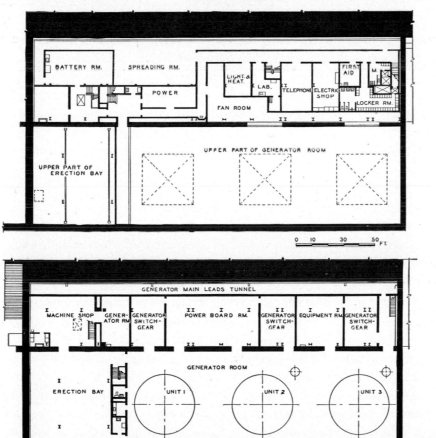

be whittled down so as to allow bare headroom for the generators. In the first case the plant is known as the *open* or *outdoors* type, because the generators in their steel housings protrude over the roof and are handled by a traveling (gantry) crane supported high in the air on its own four legs. The advantage here lies in the fact that instead of numerous building columns, any four of which would have to be capable of supporting the crane carrying the heaviest equipment part, only the four legs of the crane need to be dimensioned accordingly; this constitutes an economy in building costs. The omission of the building envelope provides another saving, which is offset, however, by the greater difficulty of inspection, maintenance, and repair. The "assembly" or "erection" bay is often carried to full height, the crane entering it through an enormous door. A compromise is effected in the *semi-outdoors* type, where the generators in each unit are under a low roof pierced by hatches, through which a gantry crane traveling over the roof can lift up equipment parts and lower them through a similar hatch into the adjacent erection bay.

Boiler Room. This is a characteristic feature of steam plants, whether coal-, oil-, or gas-fired and whether the steam is used for the generation of power or for other purposes. With vertical boilers, the boiler room is likely to be higher than the machine hall, and in coal-fueled plants it will gain even more height because of the bunkers superimposed on the boilers and topped, in turn, by the coal conveyor feeding them. Inside, however, there is no feeling of spaciousness. The great oblong stacks—the boilers—are crowded as close to one another as operating convenience permits, and the height of the room is broken at numerous and irregularly spaced levels by the galleries required for inspection and operation. The remaining space is crammed with other equipment, principally for circulating water, feeding forced draft to the boilers, and maintaining an endurable temperature in the space itself. Thick conduits carry the coal to the crushing mills in the basement and the powdered coal back to the boilers, into which it is blown in an almost explosive intermixture with air. The space remaining in the basement around the boiler foundations is likely to be further crowded by the ash-removal equipment and by the enormous insulated high-pressure piping which carries the steam to the adjoining turbines.

Tall smokestacks, which have long been landmarks and, for the designers and owners, objects of pride, seem to be on the way out. Their economic advantage is dubious in comparison with that of modern forced-draft systems operating with low and inexpensive steel stacks mounted on the plant roof. Furthermore, with the rapid spread of the airways network, few industrial areas escape height restrictions on stacks or at least mandatory requirements as to safety marking and lighting, and these tend to confer an advantage on low chimneys. Steel stacks and breechings (the latter often exposed above the roof) require frequent repainting, because even specially compounded paints deteriorate under high temperatures; but in spite of careful maintenance the life span of such stacks is limited. New inventions and attendant obsolescence, however, have been so rapid in the field of power production that the use of cheaper though shorter-lived construction is in most cases good economics.

Control Room. One of the most interesting—and certainly the most vital—aspects of a power plant is the control center, which may vary from a number of instruments mounted on a wall to a huge aggregation occupying a space with the proportions of a hotel ballroom—though without its unobstructed floor space.

The main contents of the control room are the indicating and recording instruments (usually arranged on vertical panels or cabinet fronts) and the switchboard, which may either be similarly disposed or be arranged on a low pulpit or desklike cabinet, with a diagrammatic representation of all the equipment and lines under control and with colored lights to show the condition of each item. In hydro-electric plants there may be an additional set of instruments to indicate the water level in the reservoir, the positions of the various gates, and the flow of water, and sometimes even to control the gates which regulate the flow. Pipe sleeves and—in major installations—long, open slots under the cabinets admit the wiring from the floor below into the cabinets. Vertical cabinets may have instrument panels along the front or on both the front and the back, with a passage through the center for the mechanics who install, maintain, and make changes to the wiring on the back of the panels. Great pains are taken to enable the operator at the desk to observe the entire layout at a glance, although in the larger installations this goal is seldom attained. (See Fig. 177.)

Traditionally the control room is placed in a central location overlooking as nearly as possible the whole plant; with modern equipment, however, it is scarcely necessary to supplement instrument readings with visual observation —nor would such observation yield much information even if one made use of it. But since the control-room operator is more or less in command of the plant, it seems appropriate to give him the chance to keep an eye on personnel and general goings-on. It is equally desirable to give the operator a view of the switchyard and the transformer yard. The best position is therefore one that

FIGURE 177. FONTANA DAM, NORTH CAROLINA. CONTROL ROOM

Tennessee Valley Authority, architects

The control of enormous power is symbolized in the design.   Courtesy TVA

FIGURE 178. FONTANA DAM, NORTH CAROLINA. EXTERIOR OF POWERHOUSE

Tennessee Valley Authority, architects

Built during the wartime steel shortage, this powerhouse is constructed entirely of reinforced
concrete.   Courtesy TVA

FIGURE 179. FONTANA DAM, NORTH CAROLINA. INTERIOR OF POWERHOUSE
Tennessee Valley Authority, architects
The large concrete rigid frames give great power to the interior.   Courtesy TVA

meets both of the above conditions, but there are many important plants where the control room is not in this location.

Though a view to the outside is desirable, daylight should be almost completely excluded. At the same time, the interior lighting and color schemes should be designed with extreme care to reduce brightness contrasts and to eliminate glare. Even the thin stem of a suspended indirect lighting fixture when reflected in an instrument will make it unreadable. New treatments which reduce the reflectivity of glass are available, but they do not entirely correct this trouble.

Control-room operation is extremely exacting work and demands constant alertness as well as speedy action on occasion. To aid the operator the architect must provide favorable conditions. Acoustic treatment is applied to ceilings to minimize the hum of the machines, and the glass in the opening into the generator hall is sometimes doubled and set into rubber moldings for the same purpose. In at least one example the whole control room—walls, floor, ceiling, and all—has been "floated" on steel springs in anticipation of unusually heavy vibration. There are instances also where the control room and its appurte-

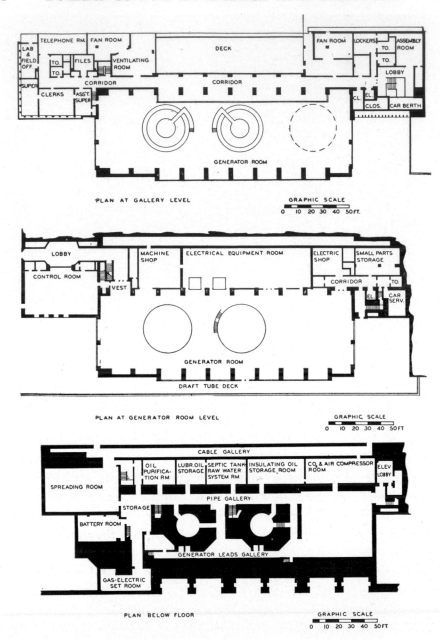

FIGURE 180. FONTANA DAM, NORTH CAROLINA. THREE PLANS

Tennessee Valley Authority, architects

The entrance is at the west end and leads past the control room; shops form a line between the generator hall and the downstream slope of the dam. An inclined, cable railway provides rapid communication to the operating levels at the top of the dam; this is also available for the use of visitors.

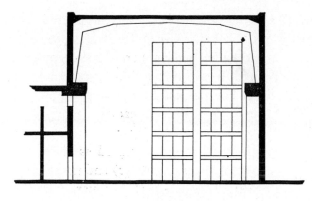

SECTION THRU GENERATOR
ROOM

GRAPHIC SCALE

FIGURE 181.

FONTANA DAM,

NORTH CAROLINA.

PARTIAL SECTION

Tennessee Valley Authority, architects

Note the large concrete crane girders. The visitors' observation balcony looks out over the generators to the river valley; beneath it are cabinets containing recording and controlling devices, floodlighted from the balcony soffit.

nances have been located away from the plant proper in an entirely separate position better suited topographically—since, as mentioned before, technically its location makes no difference provided it is on a more or less direct route between the generators and the transformer yard, so that the main power cables are not forced into detours. When public inspection of power plants is allowed, the control room is invariably a focus of interest. In that case the layout should permit easy access to a sizable glass area through which the room may be observed.

Many of the instruments are of the recording type which automatically note a continuous and detailed history of the operations; aside from this, records are kept by the operators. All graphs and records are carefully preserved, and storage space ranging in character from a few filing cabinets to a large archive must be supplied, usually adjoining the control center. In addition, a washroom and a kitchenette for the storing and warming of food are often provided near the control center—preferably within direct view of the instruments—for the convenience of operators who are on continuous duty during their shifts.

Spaces Accessory to the Control Room. In major installations the switching equipment is of the relay type. Handled by the operator, it activates circuits which in turn set in motion the heavy oil-immersed switches. These may be placed in another room—most handily in one directly under the control room and of the same area though with less headroom, since the switchroom is not occupied by personnel and therefore only so-called utility lighting is required. Cables pass from the equipment to the relay switches above in short vertical runs. The cables coming to the switchroom from the generators and going to the switchyard and the transformer yard, however, require a more complex system of distribution and connections. For this purpose another room—of approximately the same size and known as the cable-spreading room—is allotted in major plants; this normally is located directly below the switchroom. To minimize cable runs, the whole group of rooms is placed as closely as possible between the generators (where the power originates) and the switchyards and transformer yards (from which it is dispatched). Frequently power is generated at a lower voltage than that at which it is transmitted; when this is true, it is particularly important to have the shortest possible run from generators to transformers, since line losses are higher for the low-voltage current. (It may be noted that in addition to the transmission transformers, there are also station transformers which reduce the voltage for use in the power plant itself. These are often housed within or next to the building.)

Network switches and circuit breakers are placed in the switchyards, but they are actuated by relay instruments in the control room. Here proximity, though still desirable, is not so critical; for convenience, the transformers and switches are placed in the same enclosure when topographic conditions permit. Since hydro-electric plants, however, are apt to be located in rough country where ground sufficiently level or suitable for leveling is hard to find in the immediate vicinity, the switchyard in that case may be somewhat farther away and it will probably contain secondary transformers if power is supplied to parts of the network at different voltages. In all major installations the multitudinous cables connecting the control center to the transformer yards and switchyards are normally accommodated in a tunnel originating in the cable-spreading room.

In passing, reference should here be made to the occasional necessity, in switchyards remote from the powerhouse, of including accessory buildings for the storage and purification of the oil used in the equipment as well as for crew toilets and lockers.

Machine Shop. An essential requirement for maintaining the numerous intricate items of equipment is the machine shop. Ideally its location is near the erection bay where equipment is assembled and repaired. In small projects space is sometimes found for it in the machine hall. In major installations, on the other hand, the use of main-hall space would be unwarranted since neither great headroom nor the services of a heavy crane are required; hence the shop is usually placed just outside that space and sometimes is served by a light crane of its own.

The size of the shop and the variety of its equipment depend on the services it is to render. As mentioned earlier, the machine shops of industrial power-houses are often charged with the maintenance, the installation, and even the construction of factory machinery. Utility networks may maintain, in connection with some of their power plants, main repair shops to which equipment may be brought from other generating stations. Aside from mechanical work, repairs may entail electrical, welding, carpentry, and painting operations. Often a separate shop is established for the electrical work, which demands great precision, and in very large projects the other crafts may also be handled independently.

AUXILIARY ELEMENTS

Storage for Spare Parts. Since continuity of powerhouse service is always essential, a stock of replacement parts is kept on hand. In size such items may vary from a bolt to a great generator shaft or even a complete emergency gate for penstocks which weighs scores of tons. The smaller items are most often stored in a special room near the erection bay and the shops. The large pieces may be distributed in and around the power plant in places specifically provided for them in the design; in selecting each spot the architect must consider its proximity to the place where the item stored will be needed, the provision of adequate support for the weight of the piece and of adequate space and facilities for moving it, as well as the general appearance.

Oil Storage. Besides fuel oil (which may or may not be used in individual cases) power plants require a variety of oils for use as lubricants, as cooling agents, and as an insulating bath for switches and circuit breakers. Large tanks are provided for storing these oils in rooms not unlike ancient wine cellars, except for the enormous scale of the larger installations. The tanks are connected both to supply points and to points of use by piping. Some of the oils are kept in constant circulation between storage and equipment, passing through purifying machinery on the way; others are periodically drawn off to be purified for re-use. Equipment for the latter purpose occupies a separate room; this probably will also house the oil pumps, and it must be protected against fire.

Subsidiary Equipment. Electric generating stations as a rule contain battery rooms for direct current, equipped with motor-generator sets, water-distilling apparatus, and separate venting for the removal of fumes. In addition they are likely to have a stand-by source of electricity to furnish light and power in case of a total breakdown of the normal generators. Such equipment, seldom turned over except for periodic testing, is usually based on some source other than that of the normal energy supply; in hydro-electric or coal-steam plants it may be a Diesel or gasoline engine with a generator, in which case of course fuel storage must be included.

Hydro-electric plants usually contain both principal and emergency sets of pumps for keeping the lower reaches of the structure dry of seepage and for draining the turbines for inspection and repair.

On network units, frequent and absolutely dependable communication with other generating stations and possibly with a central power-dispatching room is essential. Therefore, in addition to regular telephone connections, extensive use is made of carrier current (a very-high-frequency communications circuit transmitted over the power lines but with inductive rather than metallic connections at the sending and receiving stations). A separate room is included in such plants to house the communications equipment; although entered only for maintenance, it is supplied with filtered air to protect the delicate installation from air-borne pollution. Under extreme conditions, humidity control is also used.

Heating and Ventilation. Temperature control is important in powerhouse operation, the problems being radically different for the various types. Control of humidity, often a serious operational problem, is particularly necessary in the tunnels and lower-level equipment rooms of hydro-electric plants, where moisture originates not only in an irreducible minimum of seepage but also in condensation caused by the steady cooling of masonry masses by the water passing through penstocks and turbines. Large volumes of air constantly forced through such spaces will carry off the excess moisture, but warm and dry air (such as that of the main hall if the generators are air-cooled) is even more effective.

In steam plants the main difficulty is the heat that emanates from the boilers and steam piping and the turbines; this heat can be reduced—but by no means eliminated—by heavy insulation. For such plants it has been customary to provide ample windows (with much or all of the sash operable) and, in addition, roof vents or turbines. In modern high-pressure, high-temperature plants even this does not guarantee endurable temperatures, especially in the crowded upper-level inspection galleries. Air is therefore circulated in tremendous volume by fans. Windows with over-all patterns of operable sash are not well adapted to a forced circulation of air. Because of this fact and the difficulty of keeping large glass areas clean as well as the continual need of painting the steel sash (though aluminum increasingly displaces steel for sash) some steam plants are being designed with a minimum of windows in the boiler-house section. Here daylight is actually useful only in the very limited section where certain instruments are located, and it is not essential even in those places since artificial lighting is designed for 24-hour operation. In some plants windows have been superseded by screened openings, hooded or louvered to keep out weather and adapted to winter conditions by operable shutters or louvers. Naturally the disposition of such openings must take into account exterior appearance; but it must be based principally on the proposed circulation of air within, resulting from a combination of gravity, the effect of fans, and the very large volumes of air consumed by the boilers. Long, narrow, horizontal slots lend themselves well to the purpose because they supply and exhaust the air evenly around the perimeter of the building and can be disposed vertically to conform with the requirements of the ventilating design.

In Diesel and gas generating plants the problem of dissipating engine heat is similar but, from the quantitative standpoint, much simpler. In both these types the heat of the cooling water is used first for preheating air, water, or fuel; then the residual heat content in some cases is still sufficient to warrant its exploitation for space or water heating. Similarly, steam emerging from the last turbine wheel may be employed for space heating or for process uses. Certain spaces in the power plant itself—such as offices and locker rooms— receive through walls or openings less than enough stray heat for comfort and must depend on conventional heating; any surplus heat can be used in adjacent buildings. In plants where both power and heating are primary functions, the larger proportion of the energy of the steam may purposely be reserved for heating.

In certain installations (such as the stand-by units of power systems based mainly on water power) a complete shutdown is a possibility, and this may take place in winter. Here, incongruous though it may seem, regular space heating must be installed to permit occupancy for stand-by and maintenance during the off period. In Diesel and gas plants, which generate less heat, this condition may even arise during partial operation of a multiple-unit plant.

The reverse problems are likely to occur in hydro-electric plants, depending somewhat on whether the generators are air-cooled or water-jacketed. If air-cooled, summer operation may pose problems similar to but much milder than those heretofore mentioned; if water-jacketed, the main question is how to keep the operating personnel comfortable in winter. Minor rooms can readily be heated, and the availability and low cost of power at the generating station suggest electric heating. The main hall with its great height need not be heated in its entirety; operators perform most of their tasks in a few predeterminable locations which can be taken care of by low-level electric blast heaters or even by portable units, though for comfort the resulting conditions may be somewhat short of perfection.

Ventilating equipment may take up a good deal of space in powerhouses. For ease of operation and maintenance it is consolidated in a few strategic locations or, when practicable, in one room.

Air Conditioning. Air-conditioning installations in powerhouses are relatively new. One of the reasons for their introduction was increasing solicitude for the physical comfort of the personnel; another important reason may be found in public relations. Utility companies in particular look upon air conditioning as a promising new market for power and, since power plants have attracted increasing numbers of visitors in the last two decades, it befits the operating companies to keep in step with their own promotional arguments.

The first space to receive air conditioning is usually the control room, to ease the burden of the exacting work carried on in it. Next comes the management office suite in major plants. Where a reception lobby, an overlook balcony, or similar accommodations are provided for visitors, these are also likely to be air-conditioned. Lockers and other facilities for personnel, especially in extreme climates and when they occupy interior space in the structure, may receive similar treatment.

Employee Facilities. Powerhouse operators, management personnel when separate from the operators, mechanics, and even nominally unskilled help are highly trained, carefully selected persons. Their work entails great responsibility, since the possible consequences of some relatively minor slip are almost incalculable—not to mention the hazards to their own safety. They must be on 24-hour call for emergencies. In the case of many remotely located hydroelectric plants, they must in all kinds of weather travel to work over dangerous mountain roads from their homes in the nearest backwoods towns, where the social, educational, and other community resources available to their families are extremely limited. In order to attract and hold desirable personnel, therefore, the plant facilities are often more complete and luxurious than in other industries. Since it takes but few people to operate a modern power plant, commodious facilities can be provided at a cost that is fairly low in proportion to that of the expensive equipment which goes into such buildings.

The control-room operators, skilled mechanics, and machine-shop and maintenance men rate as aristocracy in the plant and are frequently assigned locker rooms, washrooms, and kitchenettes separate from those for the more strictly manual laborers, in spite of the small numbers in both groups. In the Jim Crow states the colored help will have to depend on still another set of facilities. Also, in large plants there may be a plant manager with a secretary and assistants, and accommodations for them will be necessary. In many of the newer projects a conference room is included for staff meetings, safety education, and the continued training of employees. Elevators may be installed because of the sizable vertical distances; in hydro-electric plants, when the layout permits, elevator access is provided for rapid communication between the powerhouse and the operating and inspection galleries (tunnels) of the dam, as well as for its top deck. If guards are maintained, which is frequently the case in major or outlying projects, a headquarters room for them is incorporated.

Facilities in Automatic Plants. By way of contrast, it may be mentioned that there are plants—some of them of respectable size—which are fully automatic and are never entered by personnel except for periodic maintenance and infrequent emergency repairs. Theoretically plants of any kind and size can be run partly by automatic controls and partly by remote control from a central location, but since the automatic gadgets and the multiple wiring for remote control are expensive, the idea is applied mainly to hydro-electric plants in remote or inaccessible locations where the maintenance of an operating staff would meet unusual difficulties. Personnel facilities, heating, and ventilating, of course, are minimized in such plants.

Visitors' Reception. Visits by technical experts are a common occurrence in every power plant, but admission of the general public is a relatively new concept. This practice is stoutly resisted by many old-line operators and managers as a nuisance and a safety hazard (though it is dubious whether a single visitor has ever been injured by exposure to the supposed risks). Reception of visitors has reached its highest development in publicly owned power plants. Probably the first to welcome the public was the Tacoma, Washington, municipal system, which in addition to inspection of the plant

FIGURE 182. WATTS BAR STEAM PLANT, TENNESSEE. OUTLOOK

Tennessee Valley Authority, architects

In publicly owned power plants, facilities for visitors form an important factor in the design; these include outlooks from which the entire layout can be observed.   Courtesy TVA

itself offered a train ride from the city and a park full of tropical trees and plants (thriving in electrically heated soil) as attractions. Boulder Dam and the projects of the Tennessee Valley Authority (TVA) are operated on the principle that citizens at large are stockholders in the plant and are therefore entitled to all the courtesies and information due to plant owners.

The design features required by such a policy consist, first of all, of adequate parking space, a reception and waiting room—with connecting rest rooms—in which visitors may register and wait until a group is ready to be conducted through the plant, and an inspection route (to be laid out in the first stages of planning) which will include all main points of interest and spectacular views that can be enjoyed without interference with the work.

The TVA makes use of the waiting time in the reception room to give its guests some understanding of what they are about to see, by showing pictorial cross sections, models, and photographic displays and supplying background information on the whole system and its aims and accomplishments; here, too, the guide offers supplementary explanation of the exhibits as the first step of the tour (Fig. 184). At Fontana Dam the visitors have the additional advantage of being permitted to use an inclined railway, built to make the most dramatic parts of the structure accessible to the taxpayers as well as to facilitate the

FIGURE 183.

FONTANA DAM,

NORTH CAROLINA.

TWO VIEWS

OF OUTLOOK

Tennessee Valley Authority, architects

In steep river valleys the outlooks may be dramatic elements.

Courtesy TVA

work of the employees (Fig. 183). Another interesting example is the co-operatively owned Tri-County steam power plant at Genoa, Wisconsin, in which the employee meeting room has been expanded into an auditorium of sufficient size and suitable appointments to function as a general meeting place of the numerous co-op owners and their families.

Since inspection trips may take considerable time, refreshments for visitors are much in demand, especially at outlying projects and in summertime when tourist traffic is at its peak. If the surroundings of the plant lend themselves to recreational attractions (as is usually the case with hydro-electric plants and their reservoir lakes), refreshment stands or even full-fledged restaurants may

FIGURE 184.

CHICKAMAUGA DAM, TENNESSEE.

RECEPTION ROOM

Tennessee Valley Authority, architects

Reception rooms may contain displays of the specific project as well as background information on the entire system.

Courtesy TVA

be combined with boating, swimming, or fishing facilities. The TVA has set a successful precedent in this respect, on the principle that such incidental recreational opportunities as may arise in connection with publicly owned projects are valuable assets of the public domain and should be made accessible and enjoyable.

EXTERIOR TREATMENT

Important as is the exterior design of powerhouses, little can be said about it that is not better conveyed by illustrations. The mere size and conspicuousness of a major plant impose an obligation on the owner and the designer to make it into an object that will enhance its surroundings rather than blight them. The majestic scale of most projects lends itself to the attainment of this result, provided their natural characteristics are not forced into preconceived notions of form but are allowed to express freely the powerful physical forces unleashed within.

Obviously no generally valid instructions on composition can be stated for projects that vary so widely in type. The steam plant in an urban locality, completely enclosed as it is in a masonry structure of monumental proportions, usually with ample windows, comes perhaps nearest to the popular concept of a powerhouse. Some of the Diesel plants of the Rural Electrification Administration (REA) co-operatives have set an interesting new norm in treating the equipment inside as an object of display seen through an entire wall of glass in the manner of a show window (Figs. 185, 186). Toward the other end of the scale are the windowless or "blackout" plants, built chiefly during the Second World War, and hydro-electric plants of the outdoors type where the exposed equipment completely dominates the simple geometric concrete blocks that constitute the building. That many such plants are without windows is due not to war security regulations but to the fact that the building proper lies so low with respect to the tailwater that floods may rise practically to its roof line. Completely underground plants are entirely feasible and have been built under special topographic conditions or—abroad more than in the United States—for war-time concealment or protection.

GENERAL DESIGN PRINCIPLES

Since the principles of good design are generally valid for any kind of project, little need be said here about their specific application to powerhouses. Honesty of design always pays—particularly so when the problem itself has the qualities of monumentality and drama common in power plants. The necessity for a complete integration of the mechanical contents and the visible architecture should be strongly stressed, however, because powerhouses more than many other building types are designed so definitely to suit machine requirements and in them the needs of the few humans who operate and service the machines constitute but a minor problem. It is especially important, therefore, that the designer—before a line is drawn, even before shapes and masses begin to take form in his mind—visualize and understand all the mechanical functions accommodated within and in the vicinity of the building.

Nevertheless, there is such a thing as human scale even for powerhouses, though its principal use may be to step up the dominance of the machinery by contrast. And the surroundings and facilities for employees should be such as befit men who have mastered elemental forces. Visitors—or just passers-by—should also be aided by the space arrangement and by architectural emphasis to grasp the organization and functioning of the works so as to make their comprehension of it part of the mental equipment which citizens of the twentieth century should possess.

Finishes—and especially colors—when skillfully handled are valuable tools for emphasis and clarification. Fresh modern effects increasingly replace the traditional somber treatments, which seem to have prevailed in the past mainly because of the persuasion that they do not show dirt. Dirt, of course, has no place around hundreds of thousands or millions of dollars' worth of super-

FIGURE 185.

REA GENERATING PLANT,
CO-OPERATIVE
POWER ASSOCIATION,
CAMBRIDGE, MINNESOTA.
TWO EXTERIORS

Long & Thorshov and R. G. Cerny,
architects

The equipment inside the building
is the chief object of display.

Photographs Hedrich-Blessing

precise equipment. The bright and almost joyous interiors that are in step
with contemporary aesthetic concepts have proved powerful factors in banish-
ing dirt once and forever. Both the new spirit which pervades the staffs and
the pride and loving care lavished upon the buildings and equipment bear
testimony to the potency of sound architectural planning and treatment.

A choice of permanent, smooth materials and details of the utmost simplicity
benefit almost any building project. In powerhouses particularly, where the
cost of the equipment usually far exceeds that of the structure and where the
investment is planned on a long-time basis, permanence and simplicity are
good economies and will assist the staff in living up to the project.

The trend of future design is difficult to predict for an industry that undergoes revolutionary changes with extraordinary regularity. It is safe to say that
for some time to come, in order to satisfy the insatiable demand of a civiliza-

FIGURE 186.
REA GENERATING PLANT,
CO-OPERATIVE POWER ASSOCIATION,
CAMBRIDGE, MINNESOTA. DETAIL
Long & Thorshov and R. G. Cerny, architects
A detail designed to harmonize with and express the spirit of the installation.

Photograph Hedrich-Blessing

tion in which the manual performance of tasks is becoming more obsolescent day by day, extensions and new plants will be built as fast as the heavy engineering industries can supply the equipment for them. These plants probably will not differ basically from those of the second quarter of the century. Gradually, however, the generation and distribution of atomic energy may make commonplace a type of structure of which even the general characteristics can only be guessed at mid-century. The same chain of events may transform the proudest mechanical marvels of today into quaint relics visited by tourists for their nostalgic thrill, like the windmills of the Dutch or the waterwheels of New England.

SUGGESTED ADDITIONAL READING FOR CHAPTER 34

Boulder Dam Power; a Pictorial History (San Francisco: Electrical West [193–]).

Bucknell, Leonard H., *Industrial Architecture* . . . (London and New York: Studio [1935]).

Das Grosskraftwerk Klingenberg . . . , Klingenberg & Issel, architects (Berlin: Wasmuth [1928]).

Harding, Louis Allen, *Steam Power Plant Engineering* (New York: Wiley; London: Chapman & Hall, 1932).

Hertlein, Hans, *Neue Industriebauten des Siemenskonzerns* . . . (Berlin: Wasmuth [1927]).

Murray, Thomas E., *Electric Power Plants; a Description of a Number of Power Stations* (New York: n.p., 1910).

Reid, Kenneth, and Talbot Hamlin, *Tennessee Valley Authority as Published in the Magazine Pencil Points* [November, 1939] . . . ([Knoxville:] the Authority [1940]).

Tennessee Valley Authority, *A Technical Review of the Chickamauga Project* . . . (St. Louis, Chicago: John S. Swift Co., 1940).

—— *A Technical Review of the Hiwassee Project* . . . ([Knoxville:] the Authority, 1940).

PERIODICALS

Association for Planning and Regional Reconstruction, "Electricity in Its Regional Setting," *Architectural Review*, Vol. 97 (1945), April, pp. 95–128.

Bianculli, M., and others, "Hydro-electric Station Design," *Architectural Forum*, Vol. 82 (1945), August, pp. 151–60.

Bollaert, Émile, "L'Oeuvre de la compagnie nationale du Rhone," *L'Architecture d'aujourd'hui*, Vol. 20 (1949), December, pp. 4–23.

"Cooling Towers at Lincoln . . ." *Royal Institute of British Architects Journal*, Vol. 52 (1944), November, pp. 14–15.

"Four Power Stations," *Architects' Journal*, Vol. 106 (1947), September 11, pp. 229–35.

"The Galloway Hydro-electric Scheme," designed by Sir Alexander Gibb & Partners, *Architect and Building News*, Vol. 154 (1938), April 22, pp. 96–97.

"Generator Building, Cambridge, Minnesota," Long & Thorshov and R. G. Cerny, architects, *Progressive Architecture*, Vol. 29 (1948), January, pp. 65–68.

"Hydro-electric Power Station at Marèges," M. Brachat, architect; Léon Ballot, engineers, *Architects' Journal*, Vol. 84 (1936), September 3, pp. 312–16.

["Munich and Ryburg-Schworstadt and Other Power Stations,"] *Zentralblatt der Bauverwaltung*, Vol. 53, No. 39/40 (September 13, 1933), pp. 461–584.

"Die Murkraftwerke in der Steiermark," *Deutsche Bauzeitung*, Vol. 69 (1935), June 26, pp. 511–16.

"Pacific Gas and Electric Power Station, San Francisco," W. G. Merchant, architect, *Architect and Engineer*, Vol. 175 (1948), October, p. 30 and cover.

Power Magazine, many recent articles.

"Power Plants and River Improvements," *Architectural Record*, Vol. 77 (1935), May, pp. 340–43.

Quigley, H., "Grid and Siting of Power Plants," *Architectural Review*, Vol. 97 (1945), April, pp. 96, 97.

Sharp, Thomas, "Power, People, and Plans," *Architectural Review*, Vol. 97 (1945), April, pp. 116, 117.

["Tennessee Valley Authority,"] *Architectural Forum*, Vol. 71 (1939), August, pp. [73]–114.

"TVA Watts Bar Steam Plant," *Architectural Forum*, Vol. 81 (1944), September, pp. 101–5.

Tournaire, Albert, "La Chute de Donzère-Mondragon en Provence," *Construction moderne*, Vol. 66 (1950), November, pp. 415–24.

"Una Centrale Elettrica in Lombardia," A. E. Aresi, architect, *Rassegna di Architettura*, Vol. 10 (1938), October, pp. 427–29.

PART VI

Buildings for Public Health

HOSPITALS

BY CHARLES BUTLER

DISPENSARIES AND HEALTH CENTERS

BY ISADORE ROSENFIELD

SANATORIUMS AND ASYLUMS

BY WILLIAM L. PEREIRA

AN EXTRAORDINARY development of physiological, psychological, medical, and surgical knowledge has marked the first half of the twentieth century. This has brought thronging problems both to the medical profession and to architects. It has, for instance, given rise to the concept of group practice, so that patients may have the advantage of consulting specialists of many types. It has made the cost of complete medical care an item terrifyingly large under the older systems, and hence it has led to the development of various types of medical insurance and of socialized or government-subsidized medicine.

Accompanying these new factors there have appeared two other important ideals: one derived from a realization that the chief function of the entire medical system must become *preventive* more than merely *therapeutic*, the other prompted by the fact that it is increasingly clear that national and community health depends in large measure on having adequate medical facilities available to all. The first of these has necessitated a changed emphasis on medical buildings and a great proportional increase in clinics of all kinds and in community health centers; it has meant the allotment of greater space to consultation areas and to means for popular education. The second has affected the allocation of medical facilities and has led to careful regional studies to reveal the needs and the best means of supplying them; it has also resulted in a growing understanding that public health is, and must be, in large measure a matter of public responsibility, financial as well as executive. We can no longer afford to let the decision on who is to receive medical care be dictated by such accidents as the location of the patient or his economic status.

The development of all the complicated therapeutic sciences has not been an unmixed blessing. For the doctor it has meant continual re-education and has tended toward an emphasis on the disease—the condition—rather than on the patient. For the patient it has too often resulted in his being considered as a case rather than as a person. Toward the middle of the century, however, a growing realization of the importance of psychological and personality factors on bodily condition and functioning has tended to counteract this unfortunate emphasis. For the builder and designer of clinics and hospitals the complexity of medical and surgical science has led to programs more and more determined by technical details, even to the point where the building has come to be simply a summation of units in the design of which the technical or scientific requirements are paramount.

In this field, therefore, the primary task of the architect is obvious. It is to restore the human balance by stressing the human being for whom the whole system exists. He must see that the patient's whole environment is just as attractive, serene, and refreshing as it can possibly be made. He must think of the clinic visitor or the hospital patient not as a case to be routinized but as a personality. He must see that the shapes and colors, the lighting, and the space allocations are such that they will tend to cheer and soothe and enhearten rather than to frighten or give the sense of a heartless, mechanized system. By so doing the architect can make a priceless contribution to the social welfare of mankind, because only in such a humanized environment can therapies function at their highest level.

CHARLES BUTLER, F.A.I.A., author of the chapter "Hospitals," is a member of the architectural firm of Butler, Kohn & Erdman, in New York. He has been engaged in hospital planning for forty years, and he and his firm have been and are the architects for many important hospitals. He is co-author, with Addison Erdman, of *Hospital Planning* (New York: Dodge, 1946).

ISADORE ROSENFIELD, author of the chapter "Dispensaries and Health Centers," is a New York architect and hospital consultant. For eight years he was Assistant Professor and Special Lecturer in the School of Architecture at New York University, and he was for ten years Senior Architect in Charge of Hospital Planning and Chief Architect in Charge of Hospitals for the Department of Public Works of the City of New York. He has lectured widely on hospitals and has contributed many important articles to the press. He has been the architect of hospitals for the State of New York, the Veterans Administration, the government of Puerto Rico, and other public and private bodies. He is the author of *Hospitals Integrated Design* (New York: Reinhold, 1947).

WILLIAM L. PEREIRA, A.I.A., author of the chapter "Sanatoriums and Asylums," is a member of the architectural firm of William Pereira & Charles Luckman in Los Angeles. His practice has included a number of unusual and successful groups and individual buildings of the types with which his chapter deals. He is Professor of Architecture at the University of Southern California.

35

Hospitals

By CHARLES BUTLER

THE HISTORY of the hospital is a curious and interesting one. Apparently there were no true hospitals in the time of the Greeks and Romans, although centers of the cult of Aesculapius, god of healing, occasionally possessed certain hospital characteristics. That at Epidaurus is an excellent example; it contained curative baths, spaces for pilgrims to sleep, and special treatment and consultation rooms. Piranesi made a view of the Island of Esculapius in the Tiber, but we know little of what the island really was as a hospital. In the earlier period of Christianity, especially in the Near East, provision was often made as a charity for the care of travelers, the aged, and the sick, but the institutions offering such service were not primarily hospitals.

Early in the Middle Ages philanthropic individuals and religious orders began to set up small foundations, usually in existing buildings, for the care of the sick, and by the fifteenth century many hospitals had been built. These were often well planned, with ample light and air and with individual cubicles for patients. The beautiful Hospice de Beaune in Burgundy shows the type. It was designed with an inside balcony around the exterior walls above the open top of the cubicles to enable the Sisters to look down on the patients without entering the cubicles. The whole is covered by a steeply pitched roof with dormers, so that the cube of air is ample and the ventilation excellent. The town of Tonnerre, also in Burgundy, contained two such hospitals in medieval times, and these buildings, too, are still in existence.

During the later Middle Ages the best hospitals were better designed than those which followed them. Larger and very beautiful hospitals were built in Italy during the Renaissance, but their plans showed no advance. Thereafter, as the hospitals cared for more patients, the standards were apparently lowered. We hear of several patients being placed in the same bed in the old

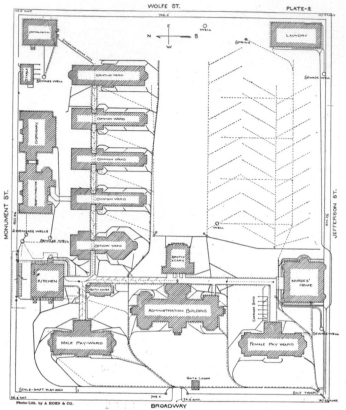

FIGURE 187.
JOHNS HOPKINS
HOSPITAL,
BALTIMORE,
MARYLAND.
GENERAL PLAN

Cabot & Chandler, architects

One of the earliest hospital plans to consider the correct orientation of wards as a controlling factor in design.

From Billings, *Description of the Johns Hopkins Hospital*

Hôtel-Dieu in Paris. Even the new Hôtel-Dieu built in the 1870's was cited at the time of its completion as having a thoroughly bad hospital plan.

The renaissance in hospital design would appear to date roughly from the planning of the Johns Hopkins Hospital in Baltimore, in the 1880's (Fig. 187). The completion of the Pasteur Institute in Paris in 1900 marked a revolution in the planning of hospitals for contagious cases. Since the erection of these, progress has been breath-taking.

From the standard 30-bed ward of fifty years ago we have gone forward to the small wards characteristic of the newer plans. And if this change in the wards has been great, even greater changes have taken place in the hospital services. The accessory spaces connected with the wards have been considerably expanded, so that their area today may amount to as much as 40 per cent of the space occupied by patients; this tends to facilitate efficient nursing service. In like fashion the operating department has been developed with proper

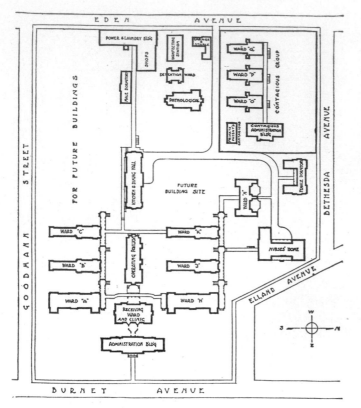

FIGURE 188.

GENERAL HOSPITAL, CINCINNATI, OHIO. GENERAL PLAN

Samuel Hannaford & Sons, architects

The typical hospital of the early twentieth century; a series of oriented ward pavilions are connected by a covered way, beneath which runs a service tunnel.

From Stevens, *The American Hospital of the Twentieth Century*

provision for anesthesia, sterilization, and dressing preparation. The discovery of the X ray has introduced an entirely new element, and the development of laboratories for routine work and research has again increased the space requirements.

Above all, there has been a fundamental change in the purpose of the hospital. In earlier days, the intent was to make the patient as comfortable as possible and also to minister to his soul while waiting for him to die. Instead of remaining the pesthouse of the past, the hospital has become the mecca of those seeking help. With the development of health centers throughout the country, much illness will be prevented and fewer instead of more hospitals in proportion to the population will be needed. In the hospital of today the whole aim is to restore the patient to health and, if this is impossible, at least to arrest the progress of the disease. Yet, despite the new approach, the fundamental purpose of a hospital remains the care of the patient, and everything must be planned primarily for his welfare.

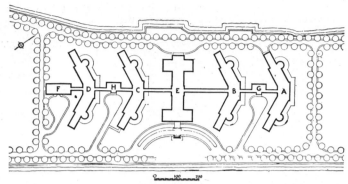

FIGURE 189. GOLDWATER MEMORIAL HOSPITAL, WELFARE ISLAND, NEW YORK. GENERAL PLAN

Butler & Kohn and York & Sawyer, associated architects

A general plan based on small wards and careful orientation.

From Butler and Erdman, *Hospital Planning*

There are many varieties of hospitals. First, there is the general hospital devoted to patients requiring medical or surgical treatment. Then come the maternity and children's hospitals and all the various special hospitals for eye, ear, nose, and throat and for orthopedic surgery, communicable disease, cancer, venereal disease, and mental disease. Hospitals for the treatment of chronic disease and for incurables and convalescents must also be included. Many of these specialties are often incorporated in the large general hospitals of today as departments, but frequently they form separate institutions. There are also teaching hospitals, connected with medical schools, where the students acquire clinical experience while studying the theory of medicine.

An important adjunct to the hospital is the out-patient department, a development of the old charity clinic. In this service are grouped many of the various specialties, so that the patient from outside may secure expert diagnosis and treatment, which may or may not lead to admission to the hospital proper. The great advantage to the patient is that he is examined in one place by a number of specialists working as a group. Another important development in the line of preventive medicine is the health center. Both the out-patient department and the health center are considered in the following chapter. The sanatorium for the care of tuberculous patients is usually a separate institution, although there is a tendency to include a tuberculosis section in some general hospitals, especially since modern thoracic surgery has shortened the hospital stay of patients. The sanatorium is discussed in Chapter 37.

FIGURE 190. GOLDWATER MEMORIAL HOSPITAL, WELFARE ISLAND, NEW YORK. AIR VIEW

Butler & Kohn and York & Sawyer, associated architects

All wards face south and have usable balconies.

Photograph Rodney McCay Morgan—Photolog

GENERAL DESIGN FACTORS

After a survey has shown the need of a hospital in a certain locality the choice of a site is the next step; here the architect, in consultation with the medical board and the administrator, can render valuable service, although the benefits of such collaboration are too rarely recognized. The site should be conveniently located for easy access yet sufficiently isolated from noise, smoke, and other nuisances; the building should be erected on dry, well-drained ground, with room for future expansion; and in northern latitudes it should be protected, if possible, from north winds—at least there should be the possibility of providing protection by tree breaks.

One of the advances in modern planning comes from the realization of the importance of proper orientation. This question was hardly considered in the earlier hospitals; now the principle is fully accepted that a hospital ward building should have sunlight and air on both east and west sides and in the North Temperate Zone on the south side as well. The idea of a symmetrical plan was so firmly implanted in the minds of the architects of the past that ward buildings were often placed around an interior court, with no attempt at orientation;

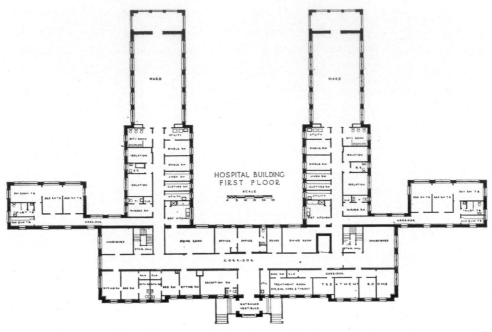

FIGURE 191. LETCHWORTH VILLAGE, THIELLS, NEW YORK. HOSPITAL PLAN
State of New York Department of Architecture and Charles Butler, architects
A low hospital for a country institution.   From Butler and Erdman, *Hospital Planning*

if the wards on one side extended from north to south, those across the court went from south to north, and even where south light and sunshine might have been secured the end of the ward wing was usually blocked up with toilets and baths. In many English hospitals these accessories extended out on either side in such a way as to deprive the ward itself of sunlight. The medical profession is now thoroughly aware of the therapeutic value of sunshine, and architects have come to realize that symmetry is not an essential in hospital design.

The question naturally arises as to whether a hospital should consist of a single building or a number of buildings and particularly whether low or high buildings are preferable. Modern fireproof construction and competent protection against smoke and panic hazards have removed the objection to multi-story hospitals. Although in hospitals for chronic diseases and in convalescent hospitals it is desirable to house the patients in low buildings so that they may easily go from the building to the grounds, in hospitals for acute cases there is no such height limitation. Often in cities the multi-story type will offer more agreeable conditions for patients. Another factor which may influence the height of a hospital is its surroundings; it would probably be quite as unjustifiable to build a twenty-story hospital in a town consisting of two- and three-story buildings as it would be to erect a one-story hospital in a great city. The question of relative costs of construction and operation in high and low buildings is a further consideration. The first cost of elevators in a high building is compensated for by a saving in time and money, because here the horizontal distances between all essential services are markedly less than those in low buildings housing a comparable number of patients.

The planning of a small hospital is especially difficult since it is essential that most of the principal services be included even though the area that can be allotted to them is rigidly limited. The question of how far the services can be reduced and which, if any of them, can be omitted is one that requires earnest consideration.

For a hospital of over 50 beds probably at least a four-story building is desirable; for a smaller hospital a one-story-and-basement building may prove advantageous.

MEDICAL-SCHOOL HOSPITALS

The growing tendency to combine medical school and hospital is to be commended because it enables the student, while making his studies of theory and his laboratory experiments, to acquire practical clinical training at the same time. The medical school may either be directly connected with the hospital or be placed in close proximity to it. Although the plan of the school and its laboratories can hardly be modified as a result of the combination, provision must be made in the hospital for the accommodation of students. Operating rooms must be increased in size, and at least one of them must be planned as an amphitheater to hold a number of observers. Similarly the treatment rooms must be enlarged, and in the nurses' stations space must be provided where students may study the patients' charts. But, even though the hospital is utilized for the training of students, nothing must be allowed to interfere with the care and comfort of the patients. If this is borne in mind the close proximity of the medical school will be of value to the patients, for they will benefit by the services of the teaching staff of the school.

INFIRMARIES FOR SCHOOLS AND COLLEGES

Since most schools and colleges are near large centers, it is usually unneces-

FIGURE 192. HOSPITAL (*circa* 1300), TONNERRE, FRANCE. INTERIOR OF WARD

The airy spaciousness and the privacy achieved in the wards of some medieval hospitals.

From Viollet-le-Duc,
Dictionnaire raisonné . . .

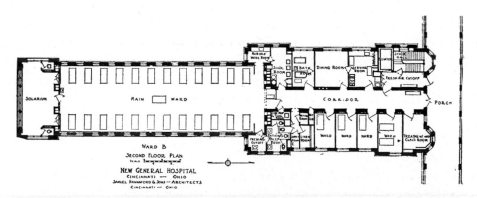

FIGURE 193. GENERAL HOSPITAL, CINCINNATI, OHIO. TYPICAL WARD-UNIT PLAN

Samuel Hannaford & Sons, architects

A large ward of the early twentieth century with a solarium at the south end and service rooms at the north. Patients' beds always face the glare of the windows opposite.

From Stevens, *The American Hospital of the Twentieth Century*

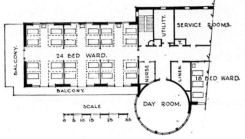

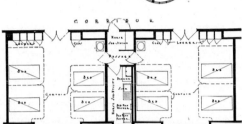

FIGURE 194. SUBDIVIDED AND SMALL WARD PLANS

LEFT: Goldwater Memorial Hospital, Welfare Island, New York; Butler & Kohn and York & Sawyer, associated architects. BELOW: Mount Sinai Hospital, New York; Kohn & Butler, architects.

The typical small or subdivided ward of the mid-twentieth century.

From Butler and Erdman, *Hospital Planning*

sary to provide them with a completely equipped hospital. Nevertheless there should be an infirmary close at hand—a place to house students who are not seriously ill but are ill enough to require special attention. Here they can receive proper care and be kept under observation, first aid can be given to accident cases, and such patients may await removal to a hospital if that should prove advisable. An interesting development of the infirmary has grown out of the physical examination requirement many educational institutions have adopted. As a result the section devoted to examining and treatment rooms, similarly to the out-patient department of some hospitals, has tended to become more important than the infirmary proper.

MAJOR ELEMENTS

HOSPITAL WARD OR NURSING UNIT

In discussing the hospital, we shall consider first the area where the patients are housed. The typical ward plan consists of a building with its main axis running approximately north and south, either with a large ward at the south end or with small wards on each side of a central corridor. At the extreme south end in both cases there is a solarium, enclosed mainly with glass. With this type of plan most of the service rooms are placed at the north end of the building (Fig. 193).

The typical nursing unit consists of approximately 24 beds, together with

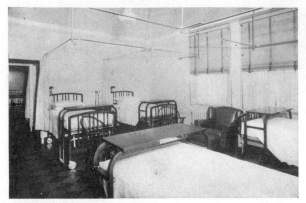

FIGURE 195.
TYPICAL SMALL WARD.
SEMI-PRIVATE PAVILION,
MOUNT SINAI HOSPITAL,
NEW YORK

Kohn & Butler, architects

The new small wards permit a greater privacy and tend to destroy the terrifying institutional impersonality of the older type.

Courtesy Charles Butler

their service rooms. Since this makes for a rather long building, small wards are usually planned, and such service areas as the sub-utility and linen rooms are located in the main stem among the wards so as to reduce the distance the nurses must cover. Preferably, however, the main utility room, the treatment room, and the serving pantry, which are all noise-producing, should not be placed among the patients' wards. The most common arrangement is to distribute the 24 beds in several smaller wards with 4, 6, or 8 beds and to include a few 2-bed rooms and separation rooms (Fig. 194). Yet for reasons of economy and to facilitate ease in nursing, it is sometimes necessary to place as many as 24 beds in one ward. In the past the beds were often set on both sides of a long ward or ranged around the perimeter of a circular or octagonal ward, with the heads against the outer wall. This scheme enabled the patients to see one another but nothing else.

Then early in the century in Denmark a brilliant advance was made—the placing of the beds parallel to the outside wall so that patients might have at least a partial view of the outside world. This idea was carried out in the city hospital in Copenhagen and has received world-wide approval and acceptance. There the beds were separated into groups of four by partitions about 8 feet high which were glazed in the upper section, an innovation that rendered the large ward more human. The addition of curtains, which travel on rods hung from the ceiling and can be drawn completely around each bed when desired, has also done much to make large wards less objectionable (Fig. 195).

If smaller wards are possible they generally contain from 2 to 8 beds each; 4-bed rooms are the most common. Where the site requires that the main axis of a ward building run east and west instead of north and south, the wards are customarily ranged along the south and on the two ends; the north exposure is reserved for service rooms, visitors' waiting rooms, and the like. In connection with the wards there must be a few single separation rooms to which delirious or dying patients may be removed. The tendency today is to include many semi-private 2-bed rooms and private single-bed rooms. These are grouped in smaller nursing units, since obviously it is more difficult to care for patients in this type of plan.

The flooring for the patients' quarters should be clean, long-wearing, and quiet. Terrazzo floors divided into small sections by brass or white-metal strips furnish an excellent wearing surface, but they are noisy. Resilient floors, such as asphalt tile, give good results and are less tiring for the nurses. The bases should be coved; rubber bases 6 inches high in long lengths give excellent results. The most satisfactory wood floors are those of well-seasoned maple.

Of the various ward service rooms the two most important are the serving pantry and the utility room. Since they must be close to the patients they are to serve and the noise necessarily created in both must be reduced to a minimum, acoustical treatment is most desirable.

The serving pantry, or ward diet kitchen, should be adjacent to the service elevator which brings food from the main kitchen, often in bulk containers. Its size will depend on the hospital's method of food distribution. The patients' trays may be set up in the pantry, and the hot food may be served there or brought directly to the bedside. Sometimes the trays are set up in the main kitchen and brought in heated food cars to the patient. No matter how much of the food preparation may be done in the main kitchen, some provision for making tea, coffee, and toast in the serving pantry will always be necessary, and a refrigerator will be required. If china and glass are to be kept in the pantry, a dishwasher must be furnished. One serving technique provides that the completely prepared trays be sent by subveyor from the main kitchen; this will permit a reduction in the size of the serving pantry. Manifestly, therefore, before the architect can plan the ward diet kitchen he must know exactly what method of food distribution is desired.

In the utility room the bedpans and urinals are emptied, washed, and sterilized, basins are washed, poultices prepared, ice-caps filled, and the many other housekeeping duties of the ward carried on. The best practice is to divide the room by a low partition into sections for soiled and for clean equipment. The partition should not extend the full width of the room, for a nurse must be able to pass from one section to the other without going into the hall, but it should establish a definite separation between the different kinds of work carried on in the two sections. In the section for soiled equipment are the bedpan washer and sterilizer, a flushing rim sink, and a soak sink with drainboard; also a bedpan warmer, an airing closet, and, if possible, access to the soiled-clothes chute. On the side for clean equipment is another sink with drainboard, the utensil, instrument, and water sterilizers, blanket and solution warmers, insulated drawers for cracked ice, a gas plate, and a dresser. Usually the sinks and sterilizers are placed back to back against the dwarf partition (Fig. 214).

With the breaking down of the large wards into smaller units, it has become current practice to install small sub-utility rooms in direct contact with the wards. Such rooms are equipped only with sinks, a bedpan washer, a cabinet with drawers for cracked ice, and a gas plate. Thus the carrying of bedpans is reduced to a minimum and the size of the main utility room, which is now more properly described as a ward workroom, is correspondingly reduced. In connection with all wards, toilet rooms for ambulant patients must be provided, as well as a separate patients' bathroom. In surgical wards, since it is increasingly the practice to get patients up and about much sooner after an operation than was the earlier custom, a larger number of patients' toilets is required than was formerly the case.

Another important element in all ward services is the linen closet, which if possible should have outside light and ventilation. Provision must also be made for the usual housemaids' or cleaners' closets with sink and if feasible outside light. In addition a stretcher closet and ample supply closets are essential. In connection with surgical wards a room must be provided to which patients may be removed for the changing of surgical dressings, often a painful process. Other items in a complete ward service are a waiting room for visitors, a small room for the flowers sent to patients, a small consultation room for doctors, and if possible a very small laboratory which may serve two wards. Finally comes the nurse's station, which must be placed in a strategic position not only to enable the nurse in charge to control all access to the ward but also to make her easily accessible. Here all charts are kept, and here the medicine cabinet will be located. Further requirements are a nurses' toilet and lavatory.

From the above enumeration it will be obvious that a great development has taken place in service rooms since the old days—when a sink room and a serving pantry sufficed for all needs—and in the proportion of space devoted to such rooms and to service circulation as compared with that actually occupied by patients in the typical twentieth-century hospital. For example, on a semi-private floor with 26 beds, distributed largely in 4-bed wards, in a hospital erected in New York City in 1930, the proportion is as follows:

Space occupied by patients,

including day room and sun porch	3,295 sq. ft., or 127 sq. ft. per patient
Service rooms	1,576 sq. ft., or 60 sq. ft. per patient
Circulation, stairs, elevators, and corridors	2,030 sq. ft., or 78 sq. ft. per patient

Here the area occupied by the patients is only slightly more than twice that given to the service rooms and only 47.7 per cent of the total floor area (6,901 square feet). Another semi-private floor with 28 beds in a hospital erected in 1942, also in New York City, is apportioned to the following areas:

Space occupied by patients	3,094 sq. ft., or 110 sq. ft. per patient
Service rooms	1,855 sq. ft., or 66 sq. ft. per patient
Circulation	2,048 sq. ft., or 73 sq. ft. per patient

In this case the area occupied by the patients is considerably less than twice that devoted to the service rooms and only 44.2 per cent of the total floor area (6,997 square feet). For private-patient floors, the comparison is equally interesting. Thus, on a floor containing 22 single rooms, in a hospital building for private patients erected prior to the First World War, the areas are allotted as follows:

Space occupied by patients	4,444 sq. ft., or 202 sq. ft. per patient
Service rooms	1,818 sq. ft., or 82 sq. ft. per patient
Circulation	2,722 sq. ft., or 123 sq. ft. per patient

Here the space devoted to patients is much more than twice that occupied by the service rooms and only 49.5 per cent of the total floor area (8,984 square feet). Finally, the figures for the private floor containing 17 rooms in a hospital erected in 1942 are as follows:

Space occupied by patients	3,025 sq. ft., or 177 sq. ft. per patient
Service rooms	2,165 sq. ft., or 127 sq. ft. per patient
Circulation	2,040 sq. ft., or 120 sq. ft. per patient

Thus of the total area of 7,230 square feet, only 41.8 per cent is occupied by patients and 29.9 per cent is devoted to services. In this last plan not only has the space devoted to service rooms been increased, but the size for private rooms has been reduced to a minimum since each private room has a toilet.

As to the number of personnel required to staff a general hospital, it is of interest to note that one such hospital in New York, with a capacity of 542 patients, employs 900 persons, of whom half are nurses—nearly one nurse per patient. Another large hospital in New York reports that the total number on the pay roll, including nurses, orderlies, and maids, as well as clerical and other help, is approximately twice the number of patients. A small hospital of

60 beds, also in New York, has a pay roll of 90. These are so-called voluntary hospitals, supported by private funds, and the figures of course do not include either the medical staff or the volunteer nurses.

OPERATING UNIT

The operating unit also has seen a marked development in recent years. The principal elements are the operating rooms and the sterilizing and scrub-up rooms.

An operating room should be at least 18 feet square, unless it is to be used for teaching, in which case a narrow gallery is generally built at one end—raised 2 or 3 feet above the floor level and having its own entrance from the corridor—so that a few students can see fairly well without being in contact with the field of operation. Modern practice has eliminated all fixed furniture and plumbing equipment from operating rooms. The walls are wainscoted with tile from floor to at least the top of the door trim; to reduce eyestrain, white tile has been abandoned, usually in favor of a dull-finish green, dusty blue, or buff. Every variety of hard-surface flooring is used—tile, rubber, terrazzo. Every effort is made to minimize the explosion hazard inherent in certain types of anesthetic, either by means of grounded metal grids inserted in some types of flooring and powdered copper in others or by maintaining sufficient humidification in the room.

The development of artificial lighting, combined with air conditioning, has greatly affected the natural lighting of operating rooms. No longer is it considered essential to place operating rooms on the top floor of the hospital, and the skylights of the past have disappeared because of the disadvantages of dependence on the varying conditions of this type of lighting. Nevertheless the theory that natural lighting can be neglected is not recommended, and inside operating rooms are considered undesirable. The possibilities of humidification and dehumidification through air conditioning are increasingly exploited for the benefit of both surgeon and patient, but in any case an operating room must be provided with artificial ventilation; the usual practice is to introduce purified and tempered air and to exhaust the air through the adjacent sterilizing room. Such rooms open directly into the operating room and contain instrument, utensil, and water sterilizers, a sink, and cupboards. The scrub-up sinks which formerly encumbered operating rooms have been removed to a position just outside. Since most hospitals need at least two operating rooms, the typical arrangement shown in Figure 196 has developed.

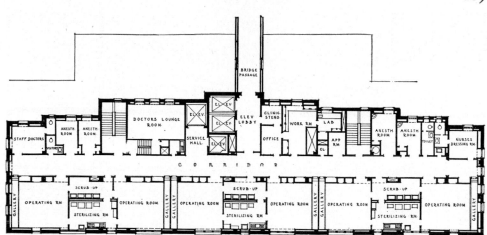

FIGURE 196. MOUNT SINAI HOSPITAL, NEW YORK. OPERATING FLOOR, SEMI-PRIVATE PAVILION. PLAN

Kohn & Butler, architects

An operating floor with well-arranged services.   From Butler and Erdman, *Hospital Planning*

Among other important items in the surgical unit is the bulk sterilizing room for dressings and solutions. On account of the heat generated by the sterilizers, this room should be well cut off from the nurses' workroom where the dressings are prepared. It should be spacious and amply equipped with cupboards, shelves, and sinks with drainboards. A solution room, a room for glove washing, and facilities for the washing and storage of instruments should also be provided. Although some hospitals prefer that anesthesia be administered in the operating room, generally a separate anesthesia room is required; often, too, recovery rooms are provided for ward patients.

In addition, there should be a consultation room and a stenographer's office, a supervisor's office, and a small laboratory for the quick examination of tissues while the patient is being operated on. A surgeons' lounge, locker room, and shower and toilet room will be needed, as well as a nurses' locker room and shower and toilet room. Space will also be required for general storage. Finally, the development of blood transfusion may necessitate not only a blood-bank room but also a room for blood donors.

OUT-PATIENT DEPARTMENT

The out-patient department already referred to is a prime adjunct to the modern hospital. It has been well described by Michael M. Davis, in his book

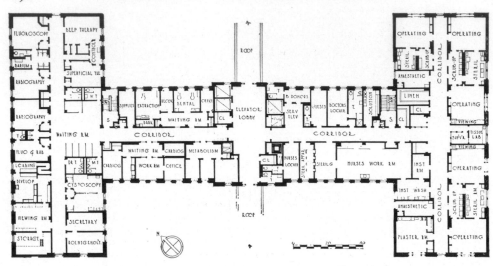

FIGURE 197. GOLDWATER MEMORIAL HOSPITAL, WELFARE ISLAND, NEW YORK.
X-RAY DEPARTMENT PLAN

Butler & Kohn and York & Sawyer, associated architects

From Butler and Erdman, *Hospital Planning*

on dispensaries, as "an institution which organizes the professional equipment
and special skill of physicians for the diagnosis, treatment, and prevention of
disease among ambulatory patients." Since usually the out-patient department
is actually a part of the hospital—though it has its own special entrance, waiting rooms, and examining and treatment rooms—the X-ray, pharmacy, laboratory, administrative, and other services can be used in common. A detailed
consideration of this department is given in the next chapter.

X-RAY AND THERAPY DEPARTMENTS

The X-ray department requires considerable space in the up-to-date hospital.
At a minimum it must include rooms for radiography and fluoroscopy (together with the necessary developing room), a barium room, and probably
rooms for both deep and superficial radiotherapy and for cystoscopy, as well
as a viewing room and office for the roentgenologist and a storage room for
films. Adjacent, in the main corridor, a viewing stack may be installed so that
doctors and surgeons in passing may note interesting and important films on
display. (See Fig. 197.)

The physiotherapy department also needs liberal accommodations. The
amount of space required for general physiotherapy, electrotherapy, and

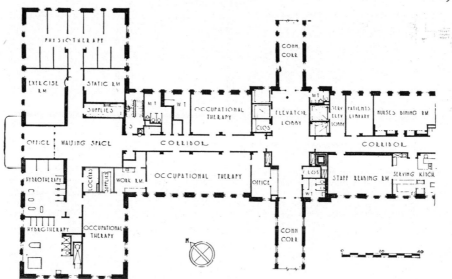

FIGURE 198. GOLDWATER MEMORIAL HOSPITAL, WELFARE ISLAND, NEW YORK. PLAN OF WING DEVOTED TO THERAPIES

Butler & Kohn and York & Sawyer, associated architects

From Butler and Erdman, *Hospital Planning*

hydrotherapy varies with the practice in each hospital and can be determined only by consultation with those in charge of the department. The same holds true for occupational therapy. (See Fig. 198.)

MATERNITY DEPARTMENTS

The maternity department provides not only facilities for the hospitalization of mothers and the delivery of infants but also nurseries for new-born babies. Because of the danger of puerperal infection in maternity cases, the patients must be divided into clean and infected cases, and ample provision must be made for isolation of both mothers and babies. Moreover, the maternity department should be carefully separated from the rest of the hospital in order to lessen the risk of cross-infection, and as far as feasible its nursing personnel should be separate.

Delivery rooms should be similar to operating rooms, and if possible there should be a separate delivery room for infected cases. Good practice calls for labor rooms or wards close to the delivery rooms, with toilets and sinks adjacent; such rooms should be thoroughly isolated for sound. In addition a preparation room for ward patients is desirable, with an adjoining bath or

Plan of Fourth Floor

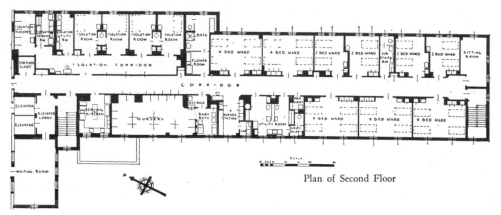

Plan of Second Floor

FIGURE 199. MATERNITY ADDITION TO SALEM HOSPITAL, SALEM,
MASSACHUSETTS. SECOND- AND FOURTH-FLOOR PLANS

Stevens, Curtin, Mason & Riley, architects

The need for nurseries, isolation rooms, and delivery rooms besides bed space for mothers makes
the planning of a maternity hospital a complex task; in addition, maternity departments in a
general hospital should be carefully isolated from the other portions.

From Butler and Erdman, *Hospital Planning*

shower, toilet, and sink. Well separated from the labor room some space should
be reserved where expectant fathers may wait. It is also wise to provide rooms
where obstetricians may rest until their services are required. The usual service
rooms, similar to those already described in connection with the surgical unit,
should be included.

Nurseries should be planned to receive ample sunlight and ventilation and
should have sound-proof doors. Here the babies are isolated from their mothers
except while being nursed; the number in a room is usually limited to eight.
Special provision must be made in any maternity service for the care of pre-
mature infants. It is customary to provide a viewing window, double-glazed,
through which visitors may see the babies without possibility of contact. The

control of visitors is especially essential in maternity wards, since there is always the natural desire to congratulate the mother immediately and admire the baby; yet the period after birth is the one when the greatest danger of infection exists. It is therefore important that the nurses' station be so placed as to provide strict control of visitors as they arrive. There are various techniques for preventing infection among the babies. Sometimes they are kept in individual cubicles, each with its own linen, utensils, and equipment; in some cases even the pediatrician is not allowed to enter the cubicle, the baby being handed to him through a window in the enclosing partition. In some hospitals the individual cubicles are air-conditioned; in others, where the babies are kept in open nurseries, each bassinet is isolated from its neighbor by germicidal rays.

Obviously, in view of the rapid development of varied techniques for baby care, the architect must study the problem thoroughly with the hospital staff before any planning is undertaken. A formula room for the preparation of infants' food must be provided, and sinks with drainboards must always be furnished for bathing the babies. Serving pantries, utility rooms, linen closets, flower rooms, and housemaids' and storage closets, similar to those already described in connection with ward and private services, are essential for maternity services. Solaria should also be provided, for they are even more desirable in maternity units than in the usual medical or surgical wards, since expectant mothers are generally ambulant. (See Fig. 199.)

ELEMENTS IN SPECIAL HOSPITALS

CHILDREN'S HOSPITALS

The infectious character of many of the diseases common among children and the danger of their being introduced into a children's hospital make special precautions necessary in the planning of such institutions. Some space should be provided where incoming patients can be held under observation before they are admitted to the general wards. On the other hand, a child alone in a room will naturally feel lonely and terrified. The usual solution is to place the children in individual cubicles with enclosing partitions that rise only about 8 feet from the floor and are glazed in the upper half; thus a child can see something of what is going on around him and can even call to his neighbors. The wards similarly are divided as a rule into small units by dwarf partitions. The service rooms are like those required for the care of adults except for the low toilets and lavatories and the smaller bath tubs often used here. Day rooms are

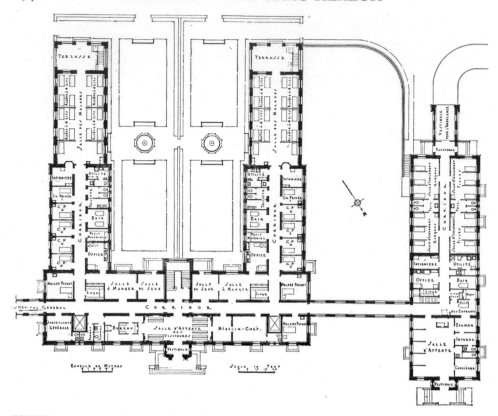

FIGURE 200. AMERICAN HOSPITAL, RHEIMS, FRANCE. FIRST-FLOOR PLAN OF CHILDREN'S PAVILION

Butler & Rodman and Auguste Pellectaer, architects

Children's wards or departments require special planning.

From Butler and Erdman, *Hospital Planning*

a useful adjunct and are commonly decorated with gay murals to cheer and amuse the small patients. It is especially important that the treatment rooms be completely isolated from the wards in children's hospitals so that those awaiting treatment will not be alarmed.

Especially desirable in the case of children are convalescent hospitals where patients making slow recovery from such diseases as infantile paralysis may be retrained and prepared for return to normal life. In these are frequently provided schoolrooms in order that patients may not find themselves left behind when they return to the outside world. Therapies in such hospitals include pools for underwater treatment of infantile paralysis, exercise rooms for

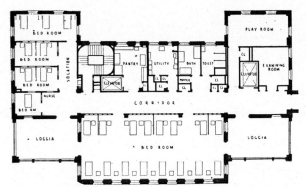

FIGURE 201.

MOUNT SINAI HOSPITAL,
NEW YORK. TYPICAL FLOOR
OF CHILDREN'S BUILDING

Arnold W. Brunner, architect;
Dr. S. S. Goldwater, consultant

Maximum air and light as well as
open space must be sought in hospitals for children.

From Butler and Erdman,
Hospital Planning

the re-education of muscles, and often space for electrical treatments. If at all
possible, convalescent hospitals, whether for children or for adults, should
be located in the country and should consist of low buildings, so that patients
may easily get out into the gardens in wheel chairs. Here the children may even
have pets and help to care for them. Ramps must be provided outdoors to give
access to the gardens, and inside the building they may be used in addition to
staircases; a noteworthy example is the Hospital for Crippled Children, Denver,
Colorado, illustrated in Volume I, Figure 139. (See also Figs. 200, 201.)

HOSPITALS FOR COMMUNICABLE DISEASES

In the past it was felt that hospitals for communicable diseases must be divided into separate wards and services for each type of disease. As a result,
except during epidemics, many of the wards were unoccupied or only a few
were opened for the care of perhaps one or two patients in each ward. This
entailed great expense, and in all but the largest cities contagious-disease hospitals were rare; most patients were cared for in the home, with the result that
the disease was passed on to the entire family.

With the opening of the Pasteur Hospital in Paris, in 1900, a new theory—
that with proper precautions the same nurse and the same doctor could care
for patients suffering from different communicable diseases—revolutionized
current practices in this field. The acutely ill patients were placed in individual
rooms where the upper portion of the partitions between the rooms and between rooms and corridors were glazed so that the patients might not feel
isolated. Balconies were added along the outside walls to permit families and
friends to see the patient. A later development in the Marshal Foch Hospital
outside Paris was the installation of telephones so that patients might not only
see but also talk to their friends. In another hospital, in San Francisco, the

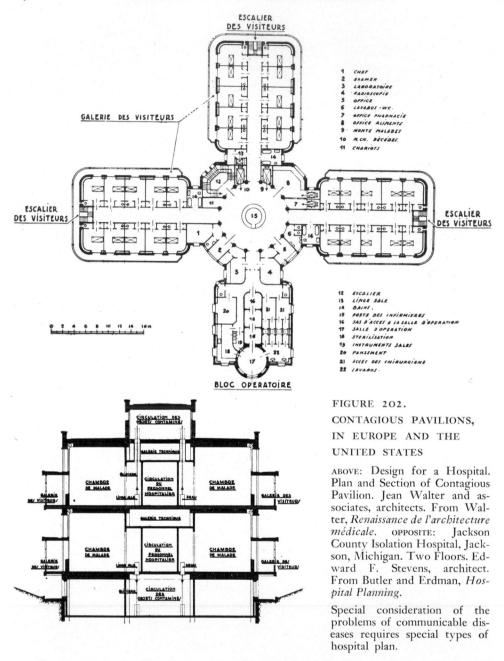

FIGURE 202.

CONTAGIOUS PAVILIONS, IN EUROPE AND THE UNITED STATES

ABOVE: Design for a Hospital. Plan and Section of Contagious Pavilion. Jean Walter and associates, architects. From Walter, *Renaissance de l'architecture médicale.* OPPOSITE: Jackson County Isolation Hospital, Jackson, Michigan. Two Floors. Edward F. Stevens, architect. From Butler and Erdman, *Hospital Planning.*

Special consideration of the problems of communicable diseases requires special types of hospital plan.

corridor partitions do not extend completely to the ceiling and the upper part consists of wire mesh; this arrangement enables friends to call to the patients from the corridor. In the Pasteur Hospital each room contained a lavatory

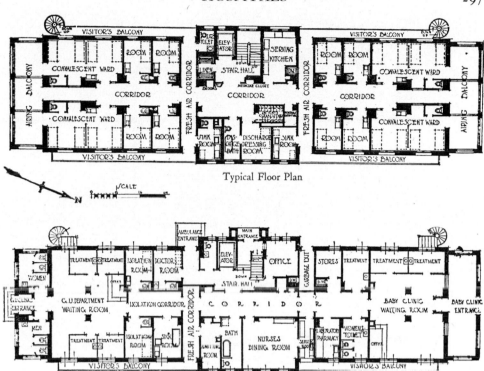

Typical Floor Plan

and wall hooks on which were kept the gowns and masks to be used by the doctor and nurse while caring for the patient. After removing these garments and washing up, the doctor and nurse moved to the next room and proceeded with another set of sterile equipment. A later improvement was the addition in each room of a toilet and a bedpan washer (usually concealed by a dwarf partition), to make it unnecessary to carry bedpans through the corridors.

Small wards for patients convalescing from the same disease may well be provided. These are usually cut off from the single-room section by an open, ventilated cross corridor; each should contain a toilet and lavatory and if possible a sun porch enclosed in glass-and-wire mesh. Generally in this type of hospital there is a separate admitting suite, where patients are bathed and dressed in hospital clothes before being taken to their rooms. A discharge service space is also required; here in a special bathroom the patients are bathed and leave their hospital clothes, then pass into another room where they receive their own clothes, which have been washed and disinfected on their arrival at the hospital. This discharge unit should have a direct exit from the building.

The usual utility room, with ample equipment for the sterilization of utensils, is essential. A special room is needed for soiled linen, with provision for dis-

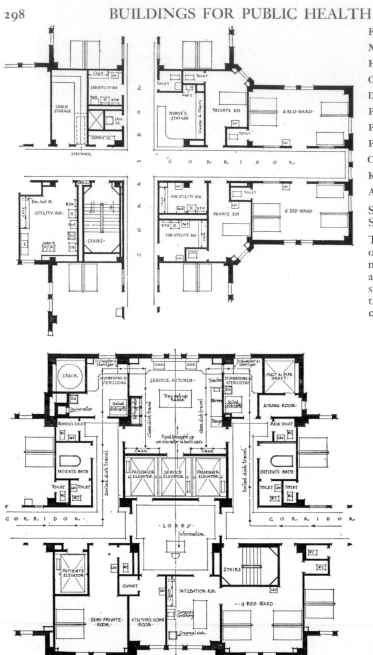

FIGURE 203.
MUNICIPAL HOSPITAL FOR COMMUNICABLE DISEASES, PITTSBURGH, PENNSYLVANIA.
PLANS OF CENTRAL BLOCK, KITCHENS, AND ENTRANCE

Samuel Hannaford & Sons, architects

The careful routing of soiled dishes and materials is necessary, and special attention should be given to the discharge unit for cured patients.

From Butler and Erdman, *Hospital Planning*

infection. In the serving pantry, which must remain uncontaminated, the dish sterilizer is often placed in direct contact with the corridor so that all dishes may be sterilized before they are received in the pantry. (See Figs. 202, 203.)

Quarters for the nurses, although it is unnecessary to segregate them if this contagious-disease service is a section of a general hospital, are customarily provided separately on an upper floor of the building. In this case, however, the nurses should not be deprived of the recreation rooms usual in nurses' homes. Finally, since surgical intervention even in this type of hospital may be necessary it is desirable, at least in a large unit, to provide an operating suite.

A word of warning is necessary as to the possibility of true air-borne cross-infection. If air conditioning is installed, it should never include the recirculation of air; all contaminated air must be evacuated from each room. Although the prevention of true air-borne infection by such methods as dust precipitation and the use of germicidal rays is receiving intensive study, it must be emphasized that in no case can the rigid technique adopted in the Pasteur Hospital be relaxed. The fact that in that hospital less than ten cross-inflections occurred in the care of five thousand patients over a period of years has proved conclusively the efficacy of the method there adopted.

AUXILIARY ELEMENTS

LABORATORIES

Laboratory service has had a notable development as a result of recent scientific progress. It may include research laboratories as well as those for routine diagnostic work; it will probably include the preparation of antitoxins, serums, and vaccines and in many cases provision for teaching. Necessarily the architect who is called on to design a laboratory must work in close co-operation with the pathologist or the director of laboratories.

North light is required for rooms where microscopic work is carried on; south light is acceptable for preparation rooms, offices, and the library. The building should be of fireproof construction, and the centrifuges, motors, and fans should rest on independent or well-insulated foundations to avoid vibration. All windows should extend to the ceilings, which should be fairly high; because laboratory counters will be placed in front of windows, however, the sills should be higher than usual. Throughout the working areas the floors should be finished with asphalt tile or linoleum except in wet spaces, where tile is required along with tile wainscots (see Fig. 204). Alberene is a good material for counters, table tops, and fume hoods, especially in chemical laboratories; in other rooms, wood with an acid-proof or ebonized finish is acceptable.

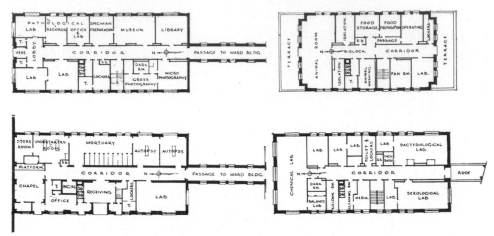

FIGURE 204. GOLDWATER MEMORIAL HOSPITAL, WELFARE ISLAND, NEW YORK. PLANS OF LABORATORY BUILDING

Butler & Kohn and York & Sawyer, associated architects

From Butler and Erdman, *Hospital Planning*

Ventilation is essential in a laboratory building, and exhausts should be carried from the fume hoods in each laboratory. Fresh air may be taken in at the windows, if dust screens are provided. Gas, electric current, vacuum and compressed air, and hot and cold water are usually required under the fume hoods and on counters, as are small sinks and waste lines. It should be possible to control all hood equipment without need of opening the hood door. Where acids are used, the waste lines should be of acid-resisting material. A shower head with a quick-opening valve should be installed in any section of a laboratory where explosions might occur.

If animal experimentation is to be carried on, special attention must be paid to the animal quarters. Usually the larger animals are housed on the ground floor and the smaller ones on the roof. Their quarters must be well lighted and be ventilated by a system independent from that of the rest of the building. Cages (generally of wire mesh) and a cage-washing room must be provided. A small operating room, with a room adjacent to it for bathing the animals, and a small sterilizing room are also required. Other essential spaces include a small isolation unit for animals that have been inoculated and an open roof area where the animals may exercise. In addition there must be space for food storage and preparation.

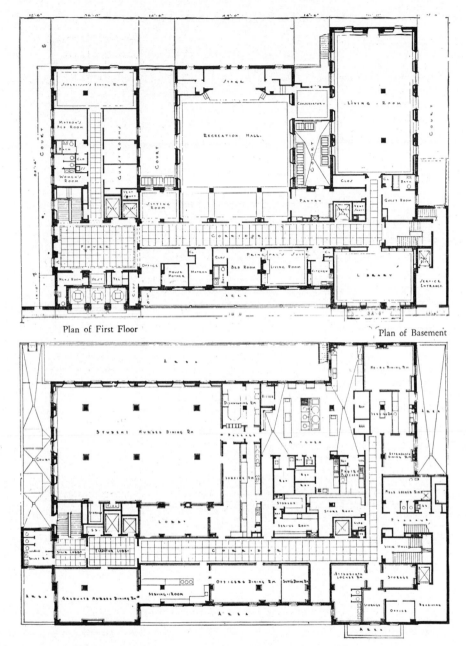

Plan of First Floor   Plan of Basement

FIGURE 205. NURSES' HOME, MOUNT SINAI HOSPITAL, NEW YORK. BASEMENT-
AND FIRST-FLOOR PLANS

Kohn & Butler, architects; Dr. S. S. Goldwater, consultant

Educational and social as well as residential facilities are required.

From Butler and Erdman, *Hospital Planning*

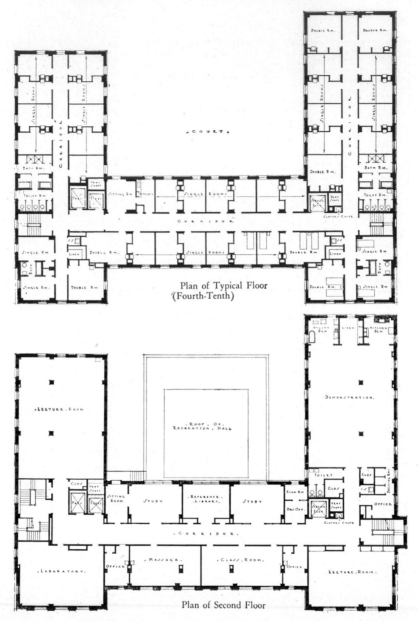

Plan of Typical Floor
(Fourth-Tenth)

Plan of Second Floor

FIGURE 206. NURSES' HOME, MOUNT SINAI HOSPITAL, NEW YORK. SECOND-
AND TYPICAL-FLOOR PLANS

Kohn & Butler, architects; Dr. S. S. Goldwater, consultant

Note the small kitchen and the sitting room on the typical floor.

From Butler and Erdman, *Hospital Planning*

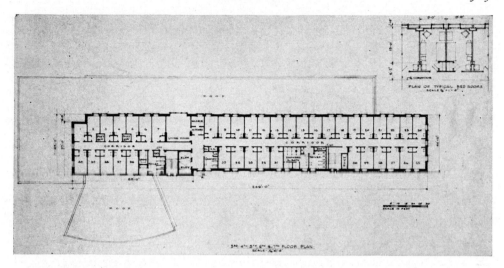

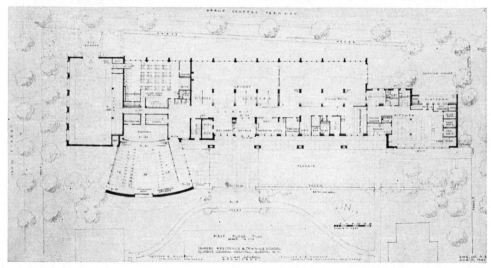

FIGURE 207. NURSES' RESIDENCE AND SCHOOL, QUEENS GENERAL HOSPITAL, NEW YORK. FIRST- AND TYPICAL-FLOOR PLANS

William Gehron, architect; A. Gordon Lorimer and Isadore Rosenfield, associated architects for the Bureau of Architecture and the Department of Hospitals

Large airy social rooms give the student nurses a feeling of relaxation and well being that is essential. Courtesy William Gehron

AUTOPSY ROOM AND MORGUE

As a rule these units are planned in connection with the laboratories. The number of trays in the morgue will depend both on the size of the hospital and

FIGURE 208. NURSES' RESIDENCE AND SCHOOL, QUEENS GENERAL HOSPITAL, NEW YORK. PERSPECTIVE

William Gehron, architect; A. Gordon Lorimer and Isadore Rosenfield, associated architects for the Bureau of Architecture and the Department of Hospitals

Covered and open terraces are a desirable adjunct.   Courtesy William Gehron

on its character. The autopsy room should be adjacent and should be designed along the lines of an operating room, with ample ventilation. An undertakers' room also should be added to this group. Often the inclusion of a small mortuary chapel in proximity to the morgue is desirable; like any hospital chapel it should be suitable for services by any religious sect. If possible the mortuary service should be so placed that the patients in the hospital will not see the arrival and departure of hearses.

PERSONNEL AND SERVICE FACILITIES

NURSES' RESIDENCE

It is essential that hospital nurses, who have onerous duties to perform and grave responsibilities, be in excellent condition both physically and mentally. They must have comfortable quarters, separated from the hospital proper so that when off duty they may be completely withdrawn from the hospital environment. Single bedrooms about 8 by 13 feet—sufficient to provide space for bed and bedside table, dresser, closet, easy chair, and desk and desk chair— are customary. In each room there should be a lavatory; for supervisors and department heads, either private baths or one bathroom between two rooms should be furnished; and the head nurse should have a suite consisting of sitting room, bedroom, and bath. Many of the graduate nurses may prefer to live at home, and this point should be considered in planning the residence. Rooms for nurses on night duty should be placed in such a location as will permit them to sleep undisturbed during the day. The nurses' baths and showers should be placed in one room and the toilets in an adjoining room; both rooms should have ample outside light and ventilation. A small hand laundry should be included. (See Figs. 207, 208.)

A living room and library are essential, and in addition near the entrance there should be small rooms where male visitors may be received. A small sitting room on each bedroom floor is also desirable. Covered and open terraces are a worth-while adjunct to a nurses' residence and may well be placed on the top of the building. Customarily cafeteria service is provided for student nurses and waitress service for graduates, supervisors, and the head nurse. All of the dining areas should be arranged in attractive locations with ample outside light.

In a large hospital an assembly room is a desirable feature, with a kitchen for serving refreshments and, of course, coatrooms and toilets for men and women. If it is feasible a small gymnasium should be included. If a nursing school is connected with the hospital, lecture rooms, a laboratory, and a demonstration suite consisting of a small ward, linen room, utility room, and serving pantry may advantageously be incorporated in the nurses' residence. And if a hospital cares for its nurses in case of illness contracted during service, it will need in the nurses' residence a small infirmary with provision for isolation.

PHYSICIANS' AND INTERNS' QUARTERS

Usually quarters for resident physicians and interns must be included. They should be similar to the nurses' quarters, and since women often serve in these capacities it is necessary to provide accommodations for both sexes.

QUARTERS FOR THE HELP

Quarters for male and female help may also be required, and if feasible they too should have single-room accommodations, even though the rooms may be reduced to minimum size.

SERVICE BUILDINGS

Whether the service areas which provide heat, power, light, laundry, refrigeration, and food are to be grouped in the hospital proper or in a separate building adjacent to it depends on the size of the institution. The boiler plant is often placed in the basement of the building; in any case it should be in close proximity so as to reduce the length of the service mains. Since high-pressure steam is required for sterilizing, cooking, and laundry work, most hospitals find it advantageous to install high-pressure boilers and to heat the building with reduced-pressure steam or with pumped hot water; the latter is

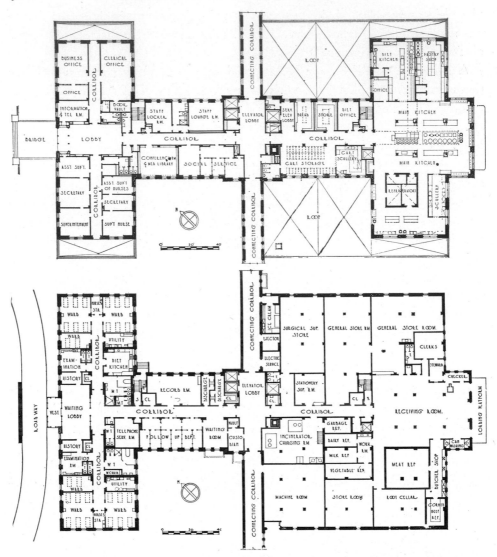

FIGURE 209. GOLDWATER MEMORIAL HOSPITAL, WELFARE ISLAND, NEW YORK.
BASEMENT AND FIRST FLOOR OF ADMINISTRATION BUILDING. PLANS

Butler & Kohn and York & Sawyer, associated architects

Unusually large storage areas often are necessary in addition to the general administration offices
and services.   From Butler and Erdman, *Hospital Planning*

preferable. Panel heating has been rapidly coming into use in hospitals and
will undoubtedly become more common. In a very small hospital, where the
cost of employing a licensed engineer is not justifiable, it is possible to avoid

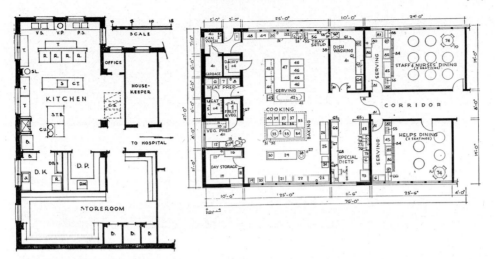

FIGURE 210. TWO KITCHEN PLANS

LEFT: Midtown Hospital, New York; Charles Butler, Clarence Stein, Frank Vitolo, associated architects. From Butler and Erdman, *Hospital Planning*. RIGHT: Plan of kitchen for a 100-bed general hospital; United States Public Health Service, designers. From United States Public Health Service, *Hospitals*.

the use of high-pressure steam by substituting gas or electricity for sterilizing and cooking.

If the boiler plant, kitchen, and laundry are to be located in the hospital building, the designer must make sure that their proximity will cause no annoyance to the patients. Vibration from laundry and kitchen equipment must be controlled, and the chimney of the boiler plant must be so placed in relation to prevailing winds that smoke will not enter the rooms. The delivery area for kitchen and boiler supplies must be so planned that the incidental noise will not be objectionable.

The plan of the kitchen will be dependent on the methods of food distribution. If food is to be sent in bulk to the wards and trays are to be set up in the ward serving pantries, provision must be made for food trucks, either insulated or electrically heated. In this case dishwashers will be provided in the ward pantries and the amount of dishwashing to be done in the kitchen will be decreased proportionately. In general the layout of the hospital kitchen is similar to that of any other kitchen (see Fig. 210). Space must be provided for the reception, checking, and storage of supplies and the refrigeration of perishables. A small kitchen for special diets and an office for the dietician are indispensable. The finish should be designed to resist rough usage; glazed brick or

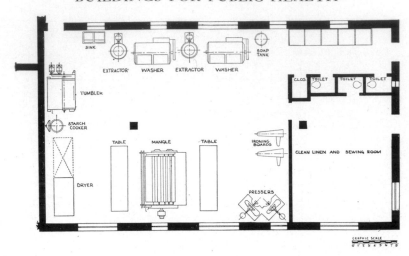

FIGURE 211. MONTEFIORE COUNTRY SANATORIUM, BEDFORD HILLS, NEW YORK. LAUNDRY PLAN

Robert D. Kohn and Charles Butler, associated architects

From Butler and Erdman, *Hospital Planning*

structural tile wainscots are recommended, and the floors should be of a non-slip material such as flint or quarry tile in the "wet" sections and of a resilient material in the remainder. To reduce noise a type of acoustic ceiling which is not affected by steam should be installed. Exhaust ventilation is essential in a hospital kitchen, as are ample outside light and air. A central garbage incinerator in connection with the boiler plant is preferable to the system in which a shaft extends upward through the building with a charging door on each floor.

The laundry layout, if such work is to be performed in the hospital, should accord with typical laundry practice. This in sequence calls for a soiled-linen reception station, next the washers, extractors, and tumblers, then the mangles, pressers, and ironing boards, and finally the carrying of the clean linen to the linen storage and mending room. In large institutions laundries often occupy several floors; the soiled linen is delivered at the top and works its way down, or vice versa. Frequently it is possible to have the soiled-linen chutes discharge directly into the laundry. If infection is to be considered, a disinfector—through which all soiled linen will be passed—may be placed at the laundry entrance. In the laundry, too, the floors should be of non-slip tile and the wainscots of a rugged type. Here also exhaust ventilation and an ample supply of outside light and air are required (see Fig. 211).

If the local supply of electric current is dependable and not excessive in cost, a hospital may prefer to purchase current rather than to install generators. Provision must be made, however, for a breakdown service in case of temporary current failure, especially in operating rooms. Unless a second source of supply is available, a battery system will probably prove the best. Obviously in a hospital an ample wiring layout is necessary, with oversize conduits if possible—in view of the constant increase in electrical equipment of all sorts —in addition to what is needed for lighting.

CONSTRUCTION AND EQUIPMENT

GENERAL CONSTRUCTION

The hospital of the future will be of fireproof or fire-resisting construction. The architect should realize that in the long life of such a building many interior changes will take place, and his plan should therefore be made as flexible as possible.

Protection against fire and smoke is more essential in a hospital than in any other type of building. Stairways should be easy and wide, and continuous handrails on stairs will be of help to the staff, who may have to carry stretcher patients down. The stairs themselves should be cut off from corridors by fireproof doors and should have direct exits to the outdoors. The ordinary type of fire escape is utterly worthless here. The best solution is the provision of additional stairways as near as possible to the ends of all wings. There is a type of metal fire tower containing a spiral chute down which patients may slide to the ground; this has given excellent service where the addition of an inside staircase has proved impossible.

All the various types of fireproof floor construction are used. Sound transmission must be kept to a minimum, and the architect should remember that stone concrete transmits sound more readily than cinder concrete. If short-span concrete arches are used, all ceilings should be furred (unless the expense is prohibitive) in order to produce a flat ceiling and reduce sound transmission. Most types of fireproof partition are acceptable.

The interior finish should be kept free from unnecessary projections and recesses which are apt to form dust pockets. Coved bases are especially desirable, but it is not necessary to round all angles and to have coves at the ceilings. Door bucks of hospital type, without moldings and finished flush with the plaster surfaces, are usually employed; where tile wainscots are used, good practice—by employing thicker structural blocks above the top of the wainscot, so that the plaster will finish flush with the tile—will avoid the dust shelf characteristic of earlier work. The door stop should be cut off a few inches above the floor so as to prevent dust pockets at floor level. If possible, acoustic materials should be employed throughout; for rooms other than those already referred to as requiring acoustic treatment, acoustic plaster, the cheapest of such materials, may well be used.

Hospital windows should be designed to suit the climate of the region. Strip windows are apt to require too much curtaining to be practical. The windows should be so placed in relation to the doors to wards and private rooms that no bed will be in a direct draft. Window heads should be close to the ceiling, and the sills should be low enough so that the patient in bed may be able to look out. Double-hung windows are most commonly used and in temperate climates are the most satisfactory. Projected and casement sash, on the other hand, have the advantage of offering a 100-per cent opening, which is needed in southern climates and in tuberculosis sanatoriums. In planning windows, the architect must often make provision for mosquito screens. For light control, Venetian blinds are preferable to roller shades; if the latter must be used, each window should have two shades with the rollers at the meeting rail so that one shade can be pulled up and the other down, thus eliminating the flapping of shades if the windows are open at both top and bottom.

Door widths in hospitals are a constant subject of discussion. For the doors of minor closets and private toilets a width of 2 feet is ample; 2'–6" is enough in the case of general toilets and baths. The width of room doors is largely determined by the width of beds; a door through which a standard 3-foot bed is to pass should be 3'–8" wide to allow for the space taken by the thickness of the door itself and the throw of the hinges. This width is also satisfactory for doors to operating, labor, and X-ray rooms and the like. Doors wherever used in connection with the care of patients should if possible be of the flush type, but in many other areas one- or two-panel doors with plain beveled moldings may be used.

PLUMBING

Plumbing fixtures in hospitals are subjected to heavy wear and should be of the best quality. To facilitate floor cleaning, the fixtures if possible should be hung on chair carriers, and supply and waste lines should go into walls rather than through floors. Toilets should be of the extended-bowl type with seats cut out in the front. Lavatories should have open drains with strainers so as to induce washing under the faucets, which should be of the combination type

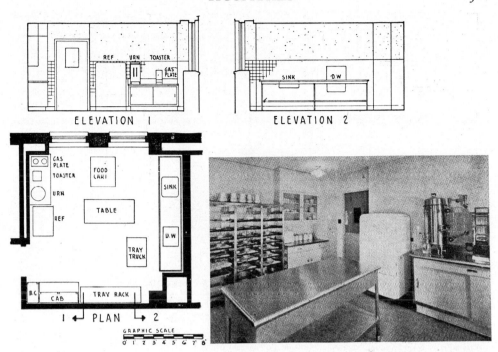

FIGURE 212. METHODIST HOSPITAL, BROOKLYN, NEW YORK. SERVING PANTRY
Charles Butler and Addison Erdman, associated architects

From Butler and Erdman, *Hospital Planning*

with either elbow-control or knee-control mixing valves. In utility rooms it is customary to install a heavy-type, combination spout with a pail hook over the flushing-rim soaking sink. The built-in type of bedpan washer is now generally used: the door opens to receive the bedpan, and when closed the automatic flushing apparatus operates.

Sterile water is usually provided by water sterilizers in the sterilizing room adjacent to the operating room, but in some hospitals water is sterilized at a central point and piped to the various sterilizing rooms.

LIGHTING

The lighting of hospital rooms and wards has been vastly improved as a result of progress in that field. Partially to supplant direct or indirect ceiling lights, more wall lights are being used; if lights are placed in ceilings, various types such as egg-crate ceiling fixtures or recessed lights with diffusing-glass panels are employed. Individual hooded reading lights on the walls above the heads of beds are being introduced into the wards. Night lighting of patients' quarters

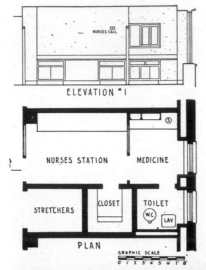

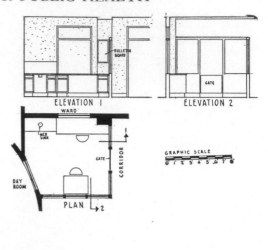

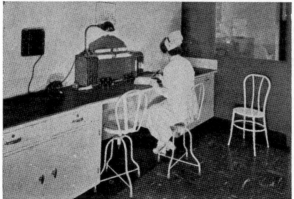

FIGURE 213. TYPICAL
NURSES' STATIONS

LEFT: Methodist Hospital, Brook-
lyn, New York; Charles Butler and
Addison Erdman, associated ar-
chitects. ABOVE, RIGHT: Goldwater
Memorial Hospital, Welfare Island,
New York; Butler & Kohn and
York & Sawyer, associated archi-
tects.

From Butler and Erdman,
Hospital Planning

is generally effected by built-in lights near the floor with diffusing-glass panels;
this scheme permits the nurse to move about the ward without having to turn
on lights that would disturb patients. Mercury switches are often used so that
the patients will not be awakened by the snapping of the ordinary type of
switch.

EXAMPLES OF SERVICE ROOMS

A few illustrations of the various service rooms which play an important
role in the plan of a hospital are included. Figure 212 illustrates a typical serving pantry. Here the food is brought in bulk from the main kitchen. The trays
are set up in the serving pantry and carried to the bedside on a tray truck. A
typical nurses' station, with medicine section, stretcher closet, store closet,
and nurses' toilet. is shown in Figure 213.

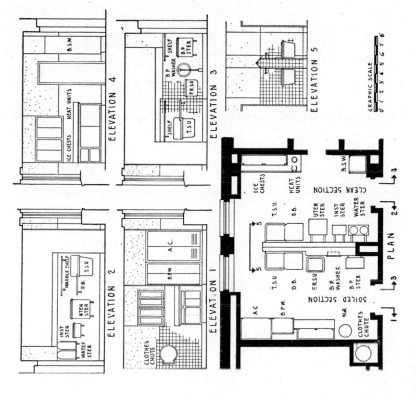

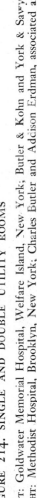

FIGURE 214. SINGLE AND DOUBLE UTILITY ROOMS

LEFT: Goldwater Memorial Hospital, Welfare Island, New York; Butler & Kohn and York & Sawyer, associated architects.
RIGHT: Methodist Hospital, Brooklyn, New York; Charles Butler and Addison Erdman, associated architects.

From Butler and Erdman, *Hospital Planning*

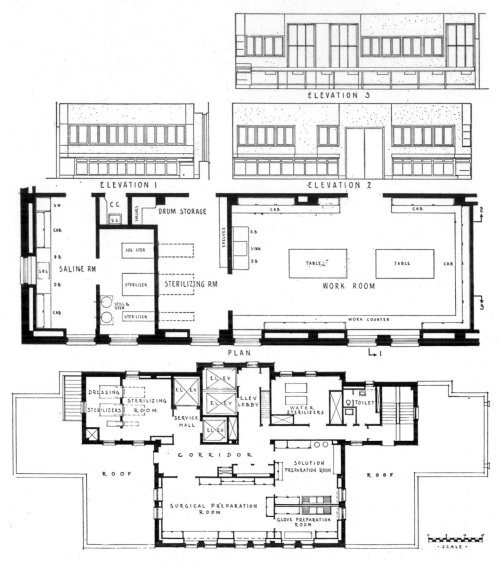

FIGURE 215. SURGICAL WORKROOMS

ABOVE: Methodist Hospital, Brooklyn, New York; Charles Butler and Addison Erdman, associated architects. BELOW: Semi-private pavilion, Mount Sinai Hospital, New York; Kohn & Butler, architects.

From Butler and Erdman, *Hospital Planning*

Two types of utility room are shown—a single room and a double one divided into soiled and clean sections (Fig. 214).

A surgical workroom group, in which bulk-sterilization space is separated from the workroom proper, is presented in Figure 215.

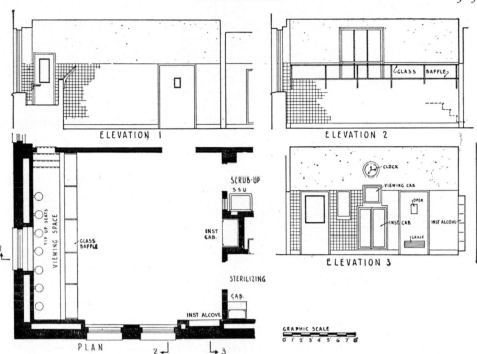

FIGURE 216. METHODIST HOSPITAL, BROOKLYN, NEW YORK. OPERATING-ROOM PLAN AND ELEVATIONS

Charles Butler and Addison Erdman, associated architects

From Butler and Erdman, *Hospital Planning*

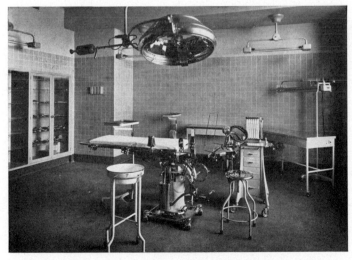

FIGURE 217.

TRIBORO HOSPITAL, NEW YORK.

OPERATING ROOM

Eggers & Higgins, architects; Isadore Rosenfield, chief architect for the Department of Hospitals, New York City

The modern operating room is kept as free as possible from extraneous elements.

Photograph
Gottscho-Schleisner

Figures 216 and 217 illustrate operating rooms, one with a students' gallery.

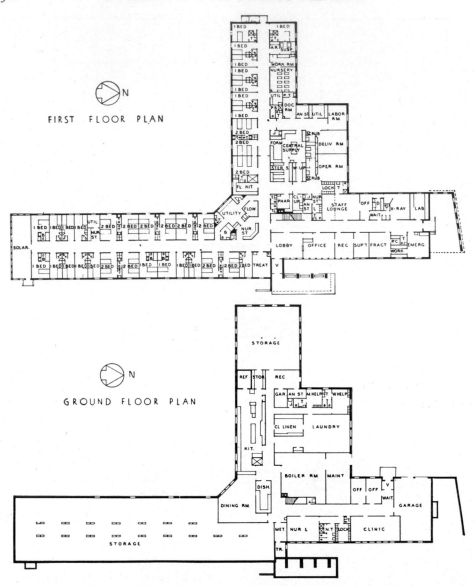

FIGURE 218. A SMALL MID-CENTURY HOSPITAL, LAKE PLACID, NEW YORK.
GROUND-FLOOR AND FIRST-FLOOR PLANS

Cannon, Thiele, Betz & Cannon, architects; Dr. Basil MacLean, consultant

An interesting plan for a 50-bed hospital; the nurses' station controls the entire floor. Note the efficient placing of the operating and delivery rooms close to a central supply room yet completely isolated from each other.   Courtesy Cannon, Thiele, Betz & Cannon

FIGURE 219. A SMALL MID-CENTURY HOSPITAL, LAKE PLACID, NEW YORK.
PERSPECTIVE

Cannon, Thiele, Betz & Cannon, architects; Dr. Basil MacLean, consultant

Drawing by Schell Lewis, courtesy Cannon, Thiele, Betz & Cannon

FIGURE 220. A MID-CENTURY HOSPITAL OF MEDIUM SIZE. ST. FRANCIS
HOSPITAL, COLUMBUS, GEORGIA. TWO EXTERIORS

Schmidt, Garden & Erikson, architects

Photographs Brinson's Studio, courtesy Schmidt, Garden & Erikson

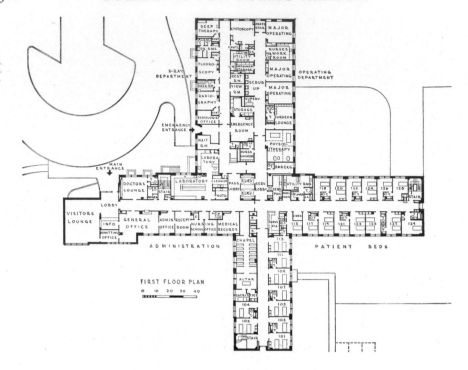

FIRST FLOOR PLAN
0 10 20 30 40

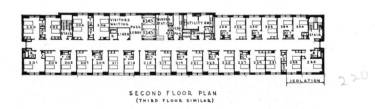

SECOND FLOOR PLAN
(THIRD FLOOR SIMILAR)

FOURTH FLOOR PLAN

FIGURE 221. A MID-CENTURY HOSPITAL OF MEDIUM SIZE. ST. FRANCIS
HOSPITAL, COLUMBUS, GEORGIA. FIRST-, SECOND-, AND FOURTH-FLOOR PLANS

Schmidt, Garden & Erikson, architects

Note the well-placed emergency entrance giving access to the X-ray and operating departments
and also the complete separation of the maternity department.

Courtesy Schmidt, Garden & Erikson

FIGURE 222. UTICA STATE HOSPITAL, UTICA, NEW YORK. EXTERIOR OF
MEDICAL AND SURGICAL BUILDING

William Gehron, architect

The simple directness of modern architecture seems particularly appropriate for hospitals.

Drawing by Schell Lewis, courtesy William Gehron

AESTHETIC CONSIDERATIONS

The design of hospitals has moved with the times; gone are the elaborate
ornamentation, columns, pediments, and domes which were once considered
essential. Because of the great increase in the cost of modern hospital elements,
exterior design has been even more simplified here than in the case of other
building types. Design has become functional; if the hospital faces north, for
example, the architect no longer turns his operating rooms to other exposures
just because operating-room windows would not look well on his front elevation. Nevertheless a hospital should have a pleasing exterior and should not
give the impression that it is merely a machine for curing disease.

In interior appearance radical modifications may also be noted. For generations it was assumed that hospital walls and ceilings must be painted either
dead white or a muddy buff. Now it is realized that color is important and
that attractive hues may be applied to walls and ceilings, that bright chintz
curtains may be used if they are washable and designed not to become dust
catchers, and that even washable wallpapers may be employed. All these
innovations tend to make a hospital a more human and more cheerful place
for those seeking relief from pain and discomfort.

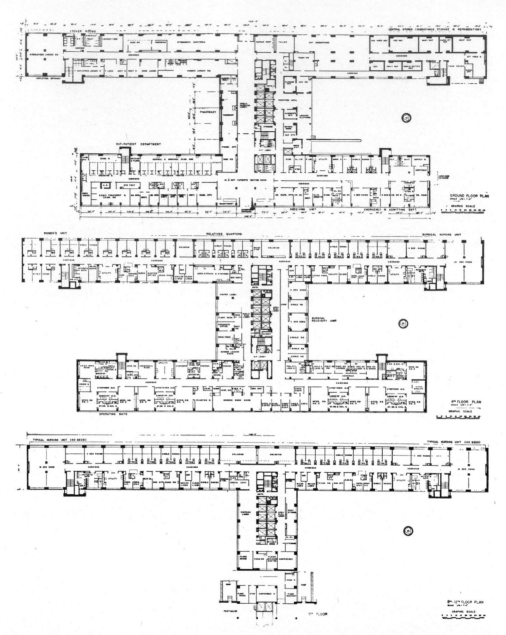

FIGURE 223. A LARGE MID-CENTURY HOSPITAL. VETERANS' HOSPITAL, FORT HAMILTON, BROOKLYN, NEW YORK. GROUND-, FOURTH-, AND FIFTH-FLOOR PLANS

Skidmore, Owings & Merrill, architects

A hospital of great size, efficiently planned on a multi-story basis. The north wing, which includes the treatment rooms for the various therapies, is four stories high; the south wing, containing the patients' rooms, rises to sixteen.   Courtesy Skidmore, Owings & Merrill

FIGURE 224. A LARGE MID-CENTURY HOSPITAL. VETERANS' HOSPITAL, FORT HAMILTON, BROOKLYN, NEW YORK. EXTERIOR

Skidmore, Owings & Merrill, architects

The majority of the patients' rooms are on the south front of the south wing, where they receive the maximum of sun and summer breeze and command a superb view over the Lower Bay and the ocean; this disposition is beautifully expressed in the design

Courtesy Skidmore, Owings & Merrill

SUGGESTED ADDITIONAL READING FOR CHAPTER 35

Birch-Lindgren, Gustaf, *Svenska Lasarettsbyggnader* (Stockholm: Bröderna Lagerströms Förlag, 1934).

Butler, Charles, and Addison Erdman, *Hospital Planning* (New York: Dodge, 1946).

Martin, Louis, "Hygiène Hospitalière," in *Traité Hygiène*, edited by Brouardel and Mosny (Paris: Baillière, 1907).

Moretti, Bruno, *Ospedali* (Milan: Ulrico Hoepli, 1935).

Rosenfield, Isadore, *Hospitals—Integrated Design* (New York: Reinhold, 1947).

Stevens, Edward F., *The American Hospital of the Twentieth Century*, 3d ed. (New York: Dodge, 1928).

United States Public Health Service (Federal Security Agency), Hospital Facilities Section, "Elements of the General Hospital," *Architectural Record*, Vol. 99 (1946), June, pp. 72–90; Vol. 100 (1946), July, pp. 76–90.

—— "Notes on Hospital Planning," *Architectural Record*, Vol. 100 (1946), August, pp. 101–16.

Viollet-le-Duc, E. E., *Dictionnaire raisonné de l'architecture française du XIe au XVIe siècle* (Paris: Morel, 1868), article "Hôtel-Dieu."

Walter, Jean, *Renaissance de l'architecture médicale* (Paris: Desfosses, 1945).

36

Dispensaries and Health Centers

By ISADORE ROSENFIELD

THE DEVELOPMENT of dispensaries and health centers can best be understood as a part of the general evolution of institutional care of the sick. Despite tremendous advances in the construction of hospitals in the last twenty-five years, out-patient departments and health centers are still insufficient in quantity and lacking in quality, and there is as yet in the United States no integration of health institutions into a comprehensive system. In this country today there are no communities whatsoever that have sufficient health facilities regardless of quality. Millions do without medical aid, and where medical facilities are especially inadequate the death rates are unduly high. People of means, to be sure, can obtain necessary medical care either at home, at the doctor's office, or in hospitals. Yet even in the wealthiest communities 80 per cent of the population is still unable to pay for or obtain the medical care it should have, except at heroic sacrifice of family resources.

When hospitals in the United States first emerged as scientific institutions they dealt primarily with surgery; as late as the 1920's the proportion of surgical cases handled was 60 per cent as against 40 per cent for medical cases. By mid-century, however, the proportions were exactly reversed. This trend is a reflection of the fact that early diagnosis and simple preventive treatment can frequently forestall and prevent radical surgical intervention; even serious medical treatment may be markedly reduced by preventive and educational measures. Yet the architectural implications of these self-evident truths are still largely unrealized, and only 2,689 (45 per cent) of 5,982 hospitals [1] have clinics, dispensaries, or out-patient departments to take care of such medical and preventive work for people of small means.

If out-patient departments exist at all, they are largely in improvised spaces —often dark, dingy, and uninviting—and, because physicians usually donate

---

[1] Table V, *American Hospital Directory* (1946). The figure 5,982 represents the hospitals reporting out of the 6,511 registered hospitals.

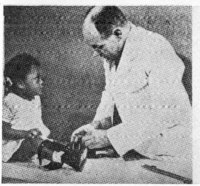 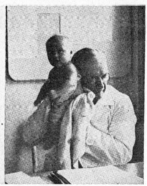

FIGURE 225. CONTRASTING ATMOSPHERES IN OUT-PATIENT DEPARTMENTS. WAITING FOR CHARITY MEDICINE VERSUS THE WHOLESOME SPIRIT

From Rosenfield, *Hospitals—Integrated Design;* all courtesy Isadore Rosenfield

their time in clinic work, the expansion of such departments has been slow; the medical societies, too, have been grudging in their acceptance of the idea. Frequently where such facilities have been planned as part of a hospital building, they have in many cases proved inadequate from the start. For example, in the Kings County Hospital in Brooklyn, opened in 1932, the beautiful ground-floor space assigned to the out-patient department proved inadequate to the demands, and a few years later a five-story building which cost over a million dollars had to be provided.

Parallel with the development of clinics has been the growing recognition of the importance of preventive medicine in public health. It is not enough

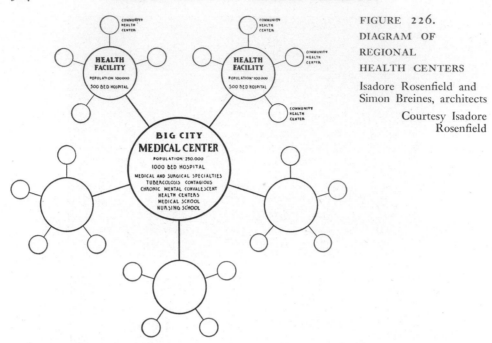

FIGURE 226.

DIAGRAM OF REGIONAL HEALTH CENTERS

Isadore Rosenfield and Simon Breines, architects

Courtesy Isadore Rosenfield

merely to take care of early symptoms; what is necessary is to prevent disease by education, by the safeguarding of water supplies and the like, and by the immunization of individuals. On the local or neighborhood level such preventive work is often handled by institutions known as *health centers* or *health stations*. Today the functions of such units and of dispensaries frequently overlap. Many dispensaries practice immunization as well as pre-natal, educational, and similar preventive work, and many health centers give medical treatment and have dental, eye, tuberculosis, venereal disease, and other clinics.

This confusion is due to the lack of a completely integrated public health system in which hospitals, dispensaries, and preventive activities all find their functional place. It is a fact, however, that hospitals have not always realized their opportunities along preventive lines and that local health departments have been forced to take the initiative in the development of health centers. This specialized activity they justify with the claim that special knowledge is involved in public health work and that a special education for it is necessary. Yet an ideal public health system should combine all public health and curative activities in an integrated program. This concept opens new vistas, and achievement of such a program will mean new types of structure. The consummation of an integrated system requires, in addition, the removal of all the restraints

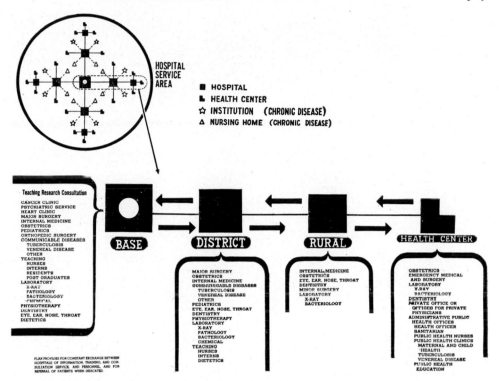

HOSPITAL SERVICE AREA

■ HOSPITAL
▮ HEALTH CENTER
☆ INSTITUTION (CHRONIC DISEASE)
△ NURSING HOME (CHRONIC DISEASE)

Teaching Research Consultation

CANCER CLINIC
PSYCHIATRIC SERVICE
HEART CLINIC
MAJOR SURGERY
INTERNAL MEDICINE
OBSTETRICS
PEDIATRICS
ORTHOPEDIC SURGERY
COMMUNICABLE DISEASES
TUBERCULOSIS
VENEREAL DISEASE
OTHER
TEACHING
NURSES
INTERNS
RESIDENTS
POST GRADUATES
LABORATORY
X-RAY
PATHOLOGY
BACTERIOLOGY
CHEMICAL
PHYSIOTHERAPY
DENTISTRY
EYE, EAR, NOSE, THROAT
DIETETICS

BASE

PLAN PROVIDES FOR CONSTANT EXCHANGE BETWEEN
HOSPITALS OF INFORMATION, TRAINING, AND CON-
SULTATION SERVICE, AND PERSONNEL, AND FOR
REFERRAL OF PATIENTS WHEN INDICATED.

DISTRICT

MAJOR SURGERY
OBSTETRICS
INTERNAL MEDICINE
COMMUNICABLE DISEASES
TUBERCULOSIS
VENEREAL DISEASE
OTHER
PEDIATRICS
EYE, EAR, NOSE, THROAT
DENTISTRY
PHYSIOTHERAPY
LABORATORY
X-RAY
PATHOLOGY
BACTERIOLOGY
CHEMICAL
TEACHING
NURSES
INTERNS
DIETETICS

RURAL

INTERNAL MEDICINE
OBSTETRICS
EYE, EAR, NOSE, THROAT
DENTISTRY
MINOR SURGERY
LABORATORY
X-RAY
BACTERIOLOGY

HEALTH CENTER

OBSTETRICS
EMERGENCY MEDICAL
AND SURGERY
LABORATORY
X-RAY
BACTERIOLOGY
DENTISTRY
PRIVATE OFFICE OR
OFFICES FOR PRIVATE
PHYSICIANS
ADMINISTRATIVE PUBLIC
HEALTH OFFICES
HEALTH OFFICER
SANITARIAN
PUBLIC HEALTH NURSES
PUBLIC HEALTH CLINICS
MATERNAL AND CHILD
HEALTH
TUBERCULOSIS
VENEREAL DISEASE
PUBLIC HEALTH
EDUCATION

FIGURE 227. CO-ORDINATED HOSPITAL SERVICES

From *Public Health Bulletin,* No. 292

which still prevent medicine from becoming available to all people, whatever their racial background or economic situation. This in turn will demand, on the one hand, a marked development of health insurance and, on the other, the development of a true system of democracy.

A diagrammatic visualization of integrated medicine is shown in Figure 226. Graham L. Davis of the Kellogg Foundation and the United States Public Health Service have both proposed somewhat similar systems; [2] the latter in its *Health Service Areas* [3] explains the ideal of integrated medical service in detail and presents maps showing the planned, logical distribution of health and hospital facilities for the entire country (Fig. 227). This concept, further described in *Making Better Health Available to All,* [4] a study by the author of this chapter, was incorporated in every winning design of the Modern Hospi-

[2] "Those Horse-and-Buggy Hospitals Must Go," *Modern Hospital,* Vol. 62 (1944), March, pp. 50–53.
[3] Public Health Bulletin 292 (Washington: U.S. Public Health Service, 1945).
[4] New York: Revere Copper and Brass, Inc., 1944(?).

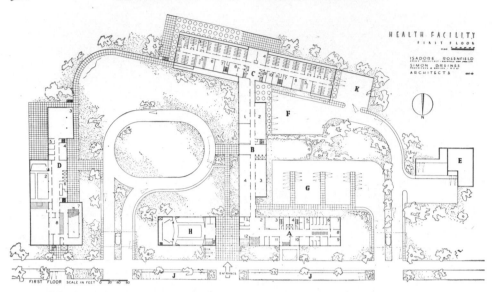

FIGURE 228. A HEALTH FACILITY. FIRST-FLOOR PLAN

Isadore Rosenfield and Simon Breines, architects

A: Out-Patient Department: (1) Sorting and isolation; (2) Main waiting room; (3) Records; (4) Public toilets; (5) Doctors' toilets; (6) Treatment; (7) Baby weighing, etc.; (8) Child guidance; (9) Social service; (10) Pharmacy; (11) Director; (12) Coats. B: Diagnostic and Treatment: (1) General administration; (2) Compensation; (3) Records and information; (4) Social service. C: Hospital: (1) Nurses' station; (2) Six-bed ward; (3) Two-bed ward; (4) Day rooms and dining; (5) Utility room; (6) Treatment; (7) Patients' toilets and bath; (8) Serving kitchen; (9) Linen; (10) Laboratory; (11) Nurses' toilet. D: Nurses' Residence and School: (1) Gymnasium; (2) Assembly hall; (3) Lounge; (4) Administration; (5) Visitors' alcoves; (6) Toilets; (7) Swimming pool; (8) Lockers, showers, and toilets. E: Garage, Laundry, and Power. F: Service and Supplies. G: Staff Parking. H: Public Auditorium. J: Public Parking. K: Ambulance Courtyard. L: Staff Recreation.

A complete health facility requires large areas.

tal competition of 1945.[5] Although these are only hypothetical solutions, the principle of combining health and out-patient activities and placing them in the front areas of hospitals is increasingly recognized in building plans (Fig. 229).

We shall consider first the out-patient department or clinic as developed to date, then the existent health center as detached from regular hospital activities, and finally the proposed health center which embraces preventive and curative activities as a link in the chain of an integrated program of health care.

OUT-PATIENT DEPARTMENTS

The functions of an out-patient department (OPD) should include not only education, prevention, diagnosis, and treatment but also the follow-up of

[5] A. B. Mills (ed.), *The Modern Small Hospital and Community Health Center* (Chicago: Modern Hospital Publishing Co., 1946).

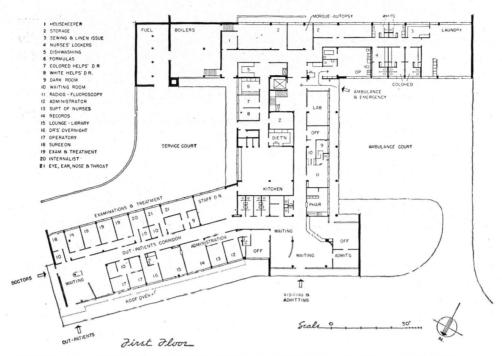

1 HOUSEKEEPER
2 STORAGE
3 SEWING & LINEN ISSUE
4 NURSES' LOCKERS
5 DISHWASHING
6 FORMULAS
7 COLORED HELPS' D R
8 WHITE HELPS' D R.
9 DARK ROOM
10 WAITING ROOM
11 RADIOG - FLUOROSCOPY
12 ADMINISTRATOR
13 SUPT OF NURSES
14 RECORDS
15 LOUNGE - LIBRARY
16 DR'S' OVERNIGHT
17 OPERATORY
18 SURGEON
19 EXAM & TREATMENT
20 INTERNALIST
21 EYE, EAR, NOSE & THROAT

FIGURE 229. NOXUBEE COUNTY GENERAL HOSPITAL, MACON, MISSISSIPPI.
PLAN

Dent & Aydelott, architects

Note the important position given to the out-patient department and its related public health
facilities.   From *Progressive Architecture*

persons who have been discharged from the hospital. Responsibility for the
discharged patient should not terminate at the hospital door. His progress
should be checked through visits to his home or visits by him to the department, or both. If such a follow-up were carried out on a large scale, a reduction
undoubtedly would result in the demand for hospital beds and there would be
a corresponding saving to the community. Among the medically indigent the
amount of sickness due to improper follow-up is enormous.[6]

Provision of ample and properly functioning out-patient departments should
result in a reduction in the amount of major surgery done; when people cannot afford to see a doctor they neglect their symptoms and carry on as best they
can until radical procedures become necessary. The existence of a sufficient
number of suitable OPD's should also result in a reduction of the number of
chronic cases; if a person were able to see a doctor when early symptoms ap-

[6] F. Jensen, H. G. Weiskotten, and M. A. Thomas, *Medical Care of the Discharged Patient*
(New York: Commonwealth Fund, 1944).

peared, his ailment could probably be arrested or cured before it became chronic. The present OPD's are disgracefully crowded, yet the chronically ill clutter up the inadequate wards of general hospitals which are meant for short-term acute cases.[7]

Every out-patient department, if it is not physically a part of a hospital, should have hospital affiliation. Unattached clinics have an extremely limited use, because they can neither readily refer patients to hospitals when necessary nor follow up the cases afterwards. Affiliation with a hospital enables the OPD to assist in the teaching of nurses, interns, and resident physicians.

ESTIMATING THE NEED

The size of an out-patient department depends on the local population's ability to pay even the small fee involved and also on the availability of physicians. Difficulty in estimating the extent of the need for OPD's is due to the absence of data on the number of people who see physicians privately and with what frequency; in New York City, for example, information is available as to the number of people who make use of out-patient facilities, but there is no way of estimating the number who do without such facilities.

In the City of New York in 1941 the out-patient departments of voluntary hospitals gave 2,973,000 treatments. In 1940 the municipal hospitals gave almost the same number—2,933,000. This is close to 6,000,000 treatments per year for a population of 7,400,000, or an average of less than one (0.8) treatment per person per year. The average daily attendance, from the above figures, amounts to about 19,700, or a little better than 2.6 visits per thousand of population per day. Judging by the fact that with few exceptions the OPD's in voluntary and municipal hospitals are generally overcrowded, it may be assumed that there is an unfulfilled demand, though its magnitude cannot be measured.

Necessary Assumptions. There is a relationship, the exact nature of which is not known, between the capacity of the out-patient department and that of the in-patient department of a hospital. If the OPD is over-expanded in relation to the bed capacity of the hospital there is likely to be a waiting list for admission to the hospital, an indication that the hospital is too small for the area served. On the other hand, if the OPD is too small there will be excessive hospital vacancies. What the proper balance should be no one knows. In the absence of conclusive data it is sometimes assumed that the OPD will have a daily attendance equal to three times the bed capacity of the hospital. It is doubtful

[7] Isadore Rosenfield, "Care of the Chronic Sick," *Hospitals*, Nov., 1944.

FIGURE 230.
NOXUBEE COUNTY
GENERAL HOSPITAL,
MACON, MISSISSIPPI.
MODEL

Dent & Aydelott, architects

From *Progressive Architecture*

whether the validity of this assumption has ever been tested. Even when dealing with an existing OPD which needs expansion there is no real way of estimating the need; although the extent of crowding can be measured, the number of people turned away or discouraged from coming is not measurable.

Conditions undoubtedly vary in different communities, but in New York City it would seem reasonable to assume that plans should be based on not less than three visits per day per thousand of population, at least until further data can be obtained. It also seems reasonable to expect that with widespread medical and hospitalization insurance the demand for out-patient facilities will increase considerably.

Whatever the method used to arrive at the total of expected attendance, this figure has to be broken down by clinics (see Table I). A further assumption has to be made on the number of sessions each clinic will hold per week, on which days of the week, and during which portions of the day. Most well-developed out-patient departments are open every week day and for a half day on Saturdays. There are usually both morning and afternoon sessions. Unfortunately very few OPD's are open in the evening, and this causes great hardship and economic loss to people who can least afford it. (The Health Department of the City of New York in its health centers holds evening clinics for venereal diseases and pays its doctors a token fee.) If all OPD's held an evening session in addition to the day sessions their building requirements could be cut down perhaps as much as one-third, or, to put it another way, one-third more people could be accommodated with the same facilities. The duration of the sessions must also be predetermined. Most OPD's are open from 9 to 12 and from 1 to 4. Actually the sessions are much shorter, because

TABLE I [8]

CLINICAL DIVISIONS AND RATIOS, INDIVIDUALS, FIRST VISITS AND REVISITS [a]
(BASED ON 2,973,946 VISITS)

Col. 1 Clinical Divisions	Col. 2 New Patients First Visits Individuals New to O.P.D. — Per Cent of Grand Total	Col. 3 Old Patients Individuals Active in O.P.D. A — Per Cent of Grand Total	Col. 3 B — Ratio of Old to New Individual Patients	Col. 4 Total Individuals New and Old Patients Col. 2 plus Col. 3 — Per Cent of Grand Total	Col. 5 Revisits Only; Old Patients A — Per Cent of Grand Total	Col. 5 B — Ratio of Revisits to First Visits	Col. 5 C — Average No. of Visits per Old Patient	Col. 6 Total All Visits Col. 2 plus Col. 5 A — No. of All Visits	Col. 6 B — Per Cent of Grand Total	Col. 6 C — Average No. of Visits per Patient
SURGICAL SPECIALTIES:										
General Surgery b	22.5	13.7	0.96 to 1	17.2	11.6	5.74 to 1	5.98	372,436	12.5	3.44
Proctology	0.5	0.7	1.95 to 1	0.6	0.8	16.55 to 1	8.47	22,325	0.8	5.95
Urology	2.0	2.6	2.09 to 1	2.4	3.4	18.92 to 1	9.04	97,228	3.2	6.44
Dentistry	6.8	5.8	1.35 to 1	6.2	5.5	9.06 to 1	6.71	157,220	5.3	4.02
Gynecology c	4.1	5.6	2.10 to 1	5.1	4.4	11.73 to 1	5.58	130,582	4.4	4.10
Obstetrics	6.0	3.5	0.24 to 1	4.4	4.8	9.19 to 1	9.94	148,437	5.0	5.30
Orthopedics d	6.5	5.9	1.43 to 1	6.1	5.2	9.05 to 1	6.31	159,294	5.4	4.13
Opthalmology	7.0	6.8	1.53 to 1	6.8	4.6	7.33 to 1	4.78	142,695	4.8	3.29
Otolaryngology	8.2	8.2	1.57 to 1	8.2	5.6	7.55 to 1	4.82	172,783	5.8	3.33
Total Surgical Specialties	63.6	52.8	1.31 to 1	57.0	45.9	8.06 to 1	6.16	1,403,000	47.2	3.90
MEDICAL SPECIALTIES:										
General Medicine e	18.4	25.2	2.15 to 1	22.6	27.2	16.47 to 1	7.65	789,172	26.5	5.54
Neuro Psychology f	1.1	2.6	3.70 to 1	2.0	2.1	21.36 to 1	5.77	60,047	2.0	4.91
Pediatrics	11.4	8.3	1.14 to 1	9.5	6.9	6.79 to 1	5.94	217,010	7.3	3.63
Dermatology and Syphilology	5.3	7.0	2.08 to 1	6.3	9.4	19.82 to 1	9.55	271,443	9.1	6.77
Physical Therapy	0.2	4.1	26.60 to 1	2.6	8.5	32.12 to 1	14.63	233,274	7.9	14.13
Total Medical Specialties	36.4	47.2	2.04 to 1	43.0	54.1	16.58 to 1	8.14	1,570,946	52.8	5.79
Grand Total	100.0	100.0	1.57 to 1	100.0	100.0	11.16 to 1	7.97	2,973,946	100.0	4.71

a Calculations based on figures furnished by the United Hospital Fund, for 54 out-patient departments of as many voluntary general hospitals in New York for the year 1941.

b Includes: Neurosurgery, fracture, hernia, plastic surgery, tumor (cancer) clinics.

c Includes: Sterility and contraceptive clinics.

d Includes: Varicose veins clinics.

e Includes: Allergy, arthritis, cardiac, cardiovascular, chest (TB.), diabetes, endocrine and gastroenterology clinics.

f Includes: Mental hygiene clinics.

8 J. J. Golub, M.D., "Plan Now for That Out-patient Department," *Modern Hospital*, Vol. 61 (1943), Dec., pp. 74–78.

frequently the doctors are late. Under such circumstances it would be safer to plan on sessions of two hours' effective duration.

PROCEDURES AND FACILITIES

Creating the Schedule. Some calculation must be made as to the time required for examining or for treating a patient in each of the several clinical categories. These figures should not be assumed but should be determined pursuant to large-scale time studies. Unfortunately such studies have not been made. When several out-patient departments were being planned by the City of New York, Dr. S. S. Goldwater, then hospital commissioner, wrote out a general or basic duration schedule for "public clinics" (Table II). Using this as a guide and assuming these norms to be reasonably correct, it is possible to compute the number of patients that can be treated per station per session.

TABLE II

NUMBER OF OUT-PATIENTS PER SESSION PER STATION
BASED ON A SESSION OF TWO HOURS

Clinics	Assumed Minutes per Treatment	Treatments per Session of Two Hours per Station	Clinics	Assumed Minutes per Treatment	Treatments per Session of Two Hours per Station
Surgery	8	15	Eye	8	15
Urology	12	10	Orthopedics	8	15
Dental	15	8	Neurology	8	15
Medical	12	10	Pneumothorax	12	10
Cardiac	12	10	Vaginitis	8	15
Ear, Nose, and			Syphilis	5	25
Throat	8	15	Diabetic	12	10
Basal Metabolism	30	4	Gonorrhea	5	25
Physiotherapy	15	8	Dermatology	12	10
Obstetrics	8	15	Allergy	6	20
Pediatrics	12	10	Endocrinology	12	10
Gynecology	8	15	Blood Count	12	10

A "station" is the room, alcove, or place where examinations or treatments [9] are given. The number of patients per station per session multiplied by the number of stations that will be used for each clinic gives an idea of the number of persons that can be treated in each clinic per session. This figure multiplied by the number of sessions the clinic will hold per week gives the number of persons for each clinic per week. With two sessions per day plus a single session on Saturday, the number of sessions that can be held in a 5½-day week

[9] "Examination" and "treatment" are used interchangeably in this discussion.

FIGURE 231. KINGS COUNTY HOSPITAL, OUT-PATIENT BUILDING, BROOKLYN, NEW YORK

Thomas W. Lamb, architect; Isadore Rosenfield, chief architect Department of Hospitals, New York City

In a large hospital the out-patient department often is housed in a separate structure.

Courtesy Isadore Rosenfield

is eleven. Some clinics may be accommodated in a few stations in one session per week. Busy clinics may require many stations at all the sessions during the week.

The clinic schedule of the out-patient building at Kings County Hospital (Figs. 231, 233) as worked out for purposes of planning, is shown in Table III. One must not be too optimistic in deciding on the number of stations and sessions for a specific clinic even where the requirements are reasonably well known, because the number would also depend on the availability of physicians. Frequently, therefore, out-patient departments are planned not to the measure of the people's need but to the availability of physicians who are willing to donate their time.

From the standpoint of economy in building, the ideal scheme naturally would be to arrange the clinical schedule in such a manner as to have as few stations standing idle during the week as possible. To make full use of all

TABLE III

KINGS COUNTY HOSPITAL OUT-PATIENT DEPARTMENT
CLINICAL SCHEDULE

Clinics	No. of Stations	No. of Sessions per Week	No. of Patients per Station per Session	No. of Patients per Week	No. of Patients per Year (50 Weeks)	No. of Patients at Present per Year	% Increase [a]
1st Floor							
Syphilis	10	6	25	1500	75,000	26,304	180
Gonorrhea	10	1	25	250	12,500	6,019	106
Dermatology	10	4	10	400	20,000	10,639	95
2nd Floor							
Obstetrics	8	6	15	720	36,000	14,493	130
Vaginitis	8	1	15	120	6,000	518	1000
Gynecology	8	4	15	480	24,000	11,979	100
Eye	8	10	15	1200	60,000	11,000	400
Ear, Nose, and Throat	6	10	15	900	45,000	16,152	180
Pediatrics	5	10	10	500	25,000	7,477	234
3rd Floor							
Surgery	19	8	15	2280	114,000	52,343	117
Orthopedic	12	3	15	540	27,000	13,000	105
Plastic Surgery	1	3	15	45	2,250	1,000	125
Neuro Surgery	2	3	15	90	4,500	1,500	200
Neurology	4	3	15	180	9,000	3,800	130
X-ray Therapy	5	11	6	330	16,500	10,600	60
TB. and Pneumo-thorax	7	8	10	560	28,000	9,499	200
Urology	7	3	10	210	10,500	4,700	120
4th Floor							
Medical	35	7	10	2450	122,500	64,000	91
Asthma	10	4	15	600	30,000	15,649	91
Endocrine	10	4	10	400	20,000	9,839	103
Blood Count	2	4	10	80	4,000	2,818	41
Diabetic	13	4	10	520	26,000	13,865	87
Cardiac	3	6	10	180	9,000	4,628	94
Metabolism	3	4	3	36	1,800	1,136	56
5th Floor							
Physical Therapy	22	11	8	1936	96,800	48,294	100
Occupational Therapy							
Dental Labora-tory	6	10	8	480	24,000	11,970	100

[a] Indicates increase over previous accommodations.

stations at all sessions would require a large number of physicians and complete control over the physicians' time. It would not be well to plan for 100 per cent occupancy in any case, because clinical requirements, methods of treatment, and the availability of physicians all change. For that reason it would be well to provide at least 25 per cent of blank spaces in the schedule. The important

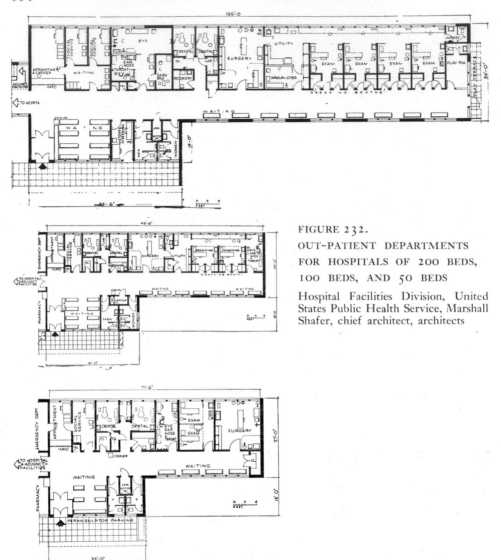

FIGURE 232.

OUT-PATIENT DEPARTMENTS
FOR HOSPITALS OF 200 BEDS,
100 BEDS, AND 50 BEDS

Hospital Facilities Division, United
States Public Health Service, Marshall
Shafer, chief architect, architects

thing to emphasize here is that it is not possible to begin to plan an OPD without first working out the clinical schedule.

Examples. Figure 232 shows hypothetical plans for out-patient departments connected with 50-, 100-, and 200-bed general hospitals as recommended by the Hospital Facilities Division of the United States Public Health Service.

The workings of a large dispensary will be illustrated primarily through the plans of the out-patient building of the Kings County Hospital (see Fig. 233).

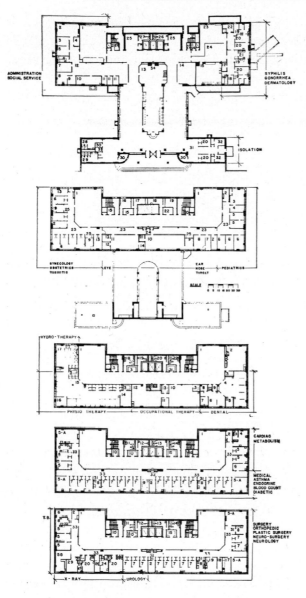

FIGURE 233.

KINGS COUNTY HOSPITAL, OUT-PATIENT BUILDING, BROOKLYN, NEW YORK.

FLOOR PLANS

Thomas W. Lamb, architect; Isadore Rosenfield, chief architect Department of Hospitals, New York City

The simple circulation of patients is a basic planning factor; at the same time adequate control is essential. Outside windows in the waiting rooms do much to prevent that feeling of impersonal herding, or of fear, which characterizes badly planned out-patient departments.

Courtesy Isadore Rosenfield

As a person enters this building he faces an attendant who will tell him where to go. The attendant is trained to discern the confused and those who show dangerous symptoms. These are ushered to the "sorting section," where they are either examined for contagious disease or, if they are inarticulate, questioned in order to determine to which clinic they should be sent. Contagious cases are placed in isolation rooms, where they remain while an ambulance is summoned to take them to a contagious ward or hospital. A special ambulance approach is desirable to minimize the contact of contagious patients with other people.

Minor Facilities. In the smaller neighborhood clinics it is customary to provide a baby-carriage room or shelter. A kindergarten for the care of the children of mothers who have no one with whom to leave their children is sometimes included. The advisability of both these features may be questioned; it would probably be better to supply a neighborhood nursery where mothers could leave their children on other occasions besides attending the clinic.

Public toilets are usually provided but there is seldom a coatroom, the need for which in the United States has been much neglected generally in spite of its obvious hygienic value especially where sick people are gathered.

Registration. Registration facilities are divided into two parts, one for new patients and the other for revisitors. Since each patient averages six visits, the proportion between the two parts should be one to five.[10] New patients should be seated, since they have to register at length and must answer many questions and prove their indigency. Revisitors go through the preliminaries rapidly, since all they have to do is to present their registration or appointment card and obtain another card which admits them to the proper clinic.

Record Room. The size and location of the record room will depend upon whether the hospital maintains a unit record system or the traditional double system. In a unit record system the records are kept at one central place for all patients, regardless of whether they are in- or out-patients. Under the traditional double system not only the out-patient department but the hospital has its own records, but this is unsatisfactory from the standpoint of clinical continuity; with the double system the out-patient records might be located immediately back of the registration counter. With the unit system, or in any case when the record room is located at some distance away from the registration counter, a card file should be kept at the registration desk. In the case of a revisitor the patient's record is sent for and it is then forwarded to the proper clinic on the proper floor.

Record Conveyors. Large out-patient departments require mechanical means to convey the records. Three types of conveyors have from time to time been installed. One is the pneumatic tube, which seems to have been abandoned in

[10] "Outpatient Service Data," *Administrator's Handbook* (New York: United Hospital Fund, Dec. 14, 1944).

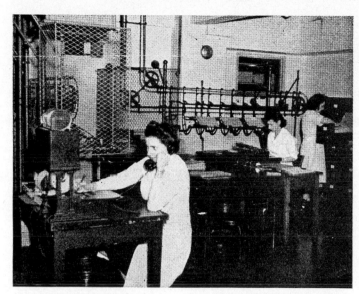

FIGURE 234.
RECORD CONVEYOR,
OUT-PATIENT
DEPARTMENT,
HOSPITAL FOR
JOINT DISEASES,
NEW YORK

Charles B. Meyers, architect

From Golub, "Plan Now for That Out-Patient Department," in *Modern Hospital*

most if not all departments. The installation is costly and a tube at best can carry only one record at a time. A large modern OPD may require up to 2,000 transfers of records a day, and where the unit system of records is maintained the individual record may be voluminous beyond the capacity of a single tube. The second type is the open trolley conveyor (Fig. 234). Here too the capacity is limited and the installation is difficult because of the large clearances required through tortuous turns inevitable in a large building. This system would have virtue in situations where the runs are largely horizontal and basket conveyors can be used. Large municipal out-patient buildings are fairly extensive horizontally; vertically they vary from three to five or more stories, plus a basement where the records are usually kept. In such departments, because of the large volume of records involved, the third type, an electric dumb-waiter, is preferred. This can be seen in the plans of the Kings County Hospital out-patient building.

Administrative Section. The ground floor of an out-patient department also has to have an administrative section. Provisions for social service include administration, interview cubicles, and records. There should be a conference room to be used for lectures as well as for clinical demonstrations. Finally there should be a pharmacy, which should be so located that patients returning from the clinics will have no difficulty in finding it. In the Kings County Hospital example the drug room is opposite the elevators. Patients can leave

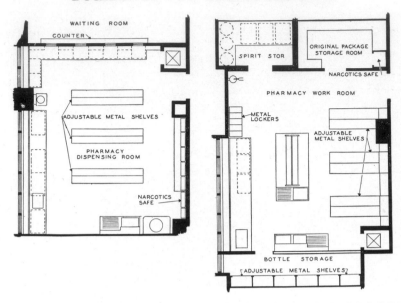

FIGURE 235. WELFARE ISLAND DISPENSARY, NEW YORK. PLANS OF PHARMACY AND PHARMACY WORKROOM

Louis Jallade, architect; Isadore Rosenfield, chief architect Department of Hospitals, New York City

by a side door near the drug room and thus avoid travel counter to incoming patients. (For details of OPD pharmacy see Fig. 235.)

Disposition of Clinics. In multi-story out-patient clinics the question of how to dispose the clinics by floors arises. The general principle is to place venereal, obstetric, orthopedic, and cardiological clinics at the ground level or as near this as possible. The laboratories and the dental, physiotherapy, occupational therapy, and other such clinics—which are not populous but require relatively large spaces—are usually placed on a top floor. By arranging the clinics with the most populous at the bottom and the least populous at the top, elevator traffic can be substantially reduced. (See Fig. 236.)

Record Station. In multi-story buildings it is also necessary to provide a record station on each floor. This consists of a small counter where an attendant can sort the records and man the dumb-waiter. Over the counter there should be shelves for the accommodation of records to be returned to the record room. The dumb-waiter is fitted with shelves corresponding to the stories in the building, so that the records going to clinics on a certain floor are placed in the proper compartment. This system is working with satisfaction in three mid-century large out-patient buildings in New York City.

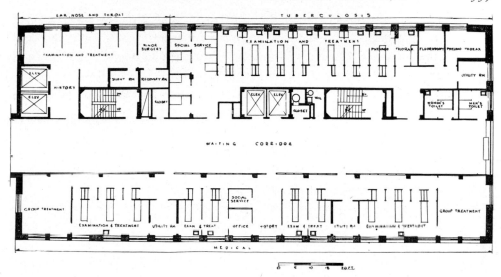

FIGURE 236. HARLEM HOSPITAL, OUT-PATIENT DEPARTMENT, NEW YORK. ONE OF THREE FLOORS. PLAN

William Gehron, architect; Isadore Rosenfield, chief architect Department of Hospitals, New York City

Each department in a clinic must be carefully designed for its specific activities.

Waiting Rooms. The capacity of the waiting rooms should be carefully considered and not merely guessed at. The main waiting room on the ground floor of the Kings County Hospital out-patient building has a capacity of one-third of all of the patients who might come to the maximum session of the week. On the individual floors the capacity should again be one-third of the maximum number of people who would attend on that floor per session. This is based on the assumption that roughly a third of the people would be waiting, another third would be in the history rooms, and the last third would be in treatment rooms.

The traditional out-patient waiting room is a widened corridor extending through from one end of the building to the other; both ends should have as much glass as possible. These corridors are usually made 16 feet wide to accommodate 8-foot benches arranged crosswise in the middle and still leave 4-foot passages on either side. It is obvious that this type would be more suitable in a relatively short building than in a long one, where the correspondingly long corridor would suffer not only from lack of natural light and ventilation but also from noise and confusion. The Kings County Hospital OPD arrangement of a pair of waiting rooms with the clinics wrapped around them is good, because in this manner it is possible to shorten the building. Here the waiting spaces, in addition to being well related to the adjoining clinics, have light and ventilation, remove the crowds from in front of the elevators, do not serve as passageways, and are relatively quiet terminal points.

History Rooms or Corridors. Adjoining the waiting rooms are long elements known as history corridors. The partitions separating them from the waiting room and the main corridor need not be higher than 7 feet. The primary idea behind the history corridor is to save time by having the preliminary data taken down before the patient enters the treatment room. It also serves to reduce the pressure on the treatment room, which without it would open directly into the waiting room. A further purpose is to ensure greater privacy in the examination rooms. Where history corridors are not planned, rooms for that purpose adjoining the waiting room must be provided.

Treatment Rooms. The treatment rooms are cubicles laid out in a row on a module of about 7 to 8 feet. A patient enters through one of two dressing booths; between the inner doors of these there is sufficient wall space to receive the end of the examination table. By virtue of such an arrangement the examination table is accessible from both long sides; on it and facing the window the patient is well illuminated and the physician or nurse will not cast a shadow upon him, and the doctors and nurses have good light yet do not suffer from its glare when examining the patient. The cubicles are made deep enough to allow circulation between them. Every cubicle or treatment room also must have a wall desk or some similar accommodation where the case record can be written up.

One type of grouping is a series of alcoves protected at the open end by curtains. This permits free circulation within the group and allows the doctor and nurses to keep several treatment cubicles in operation simultaneously. In another type the cubicle partitions carry through to the outside wall, and intercommunicating doors are provided between treatment cubicles. Such an arrangement permits optional intercommunication. In a third type each room is completely enclosed, without intercommunication. Where it is necessary to listen to the heart, or where the patient is apt to be noisy as in pediatrics, or where a high degree of privacy is desired as in psychiatry, the rooms should be completely closed off with partitions extending to the ceiling.

Still another arrangement is the group-treatment room. There are certain types of cases which do not require privacy and in which the treatment is simple. In surgery, for instance, where simple dressings on the extremities or

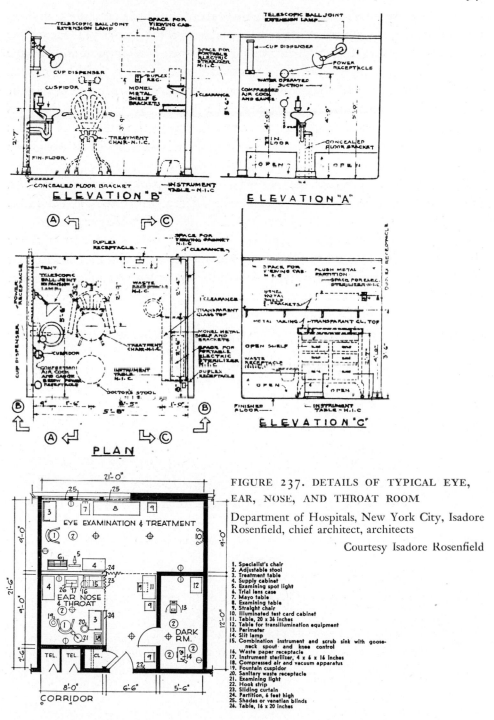

FIGURE 237. DETAILS OF TYPICAL EYE, EAR, NOSE, AND THROAT ROOM

Department of Hospitals, New York City, Isadore Rosenfield, chief architect, architects

Courtesy Isadore Rosenfield

1. Specialist's chair
2. Adjustable stool
3. Treatment table
4. Supply cabinet
5. Examining spot light
6. Trial lens case
7. Mayo table
8. Examining table
9. Straight chair
10. Illuminated test card cabinet
11. Table, 20 x 36 inches
12. Table for transillumination equipment
13. Perimeter
14. Slit lamp
15. Combination instrument and scrub sink with goose-neck spout and knee control
16. Waste paper receptacle
17. Instrument sterilizer, 4 x 6 x 16 inches
18. Compressed air and vacuum apparatus
19. Fountain cuspidor
20. Sanitary waste receptacle
21. Examining light
22. Hook strip
23. Sliding curtain
24. Partition, 6 feet high
25. Shades or venetian blinds
26. Table, 16 x 20 inches

on the head are involved, the question of privacy is not necessarily involved. especially where men and women are not treated simultaneously. Doctors like to use the group-treatment rooms as a sorting or elimination point and to have most patients go through them as a matter of routine. Those with superficial conditions remain, and the patient who requires more serious attention or dressings is sent to a cubicle of his own. The group-treatment room, in terms of treatment stations, is evaluated in accordance with the number of persons who could reasonably be treated simultaneously within it, and that obviously varies with the nature of the treatment involved.

Special treatment rooms are needed for cardiography, metabolism tests, fluoroscopy, minor surgery, eye-ear-nose-and-throat treatments, and the like. A detail of an ear-nose-and-throat cubicle is shown in Figure 237.

Utility and Nurses' Station. For every group of clinics—or at least on every floor—there should be a utility room equipped with a sink, an instrument sterilizer, and a cabinet for supplies. An area equivalent to a typical treatment cubicle is utilized for this purpose. The space that normally would be occupied by the dressing booths is made into a nurses' station consisting of a supply cabinet and a small desk, both of which are generally located at the entrance from the history corridor so that the nurse or attendant can control the flow of patients and give them directions.

DECENTRALIZED DISPENSARIES

Most out-patient departments planned for old hospitals are through necessity located in separate buildings. In new planning they should be made an integral part of the hospital and share with it many of the diagnostic and therapeutic facilities. There is, indeed, a school of thought which would completely decentralize the OPD and make each clinic horizontally contiguous with the corresponding clinical division in the hospital itself. This would be particularly advantageous where medical teaching is involved; also under this arrangement if the patient later became a bed patient he could remain under the care of the same specialist. In such a case it would still be necessary to have a central location for registration and general diagnosis.

DIAGNOSTIC CLINICS

The diagnostic clinic is not new but has long been one of the out-patient functions of many general hospitals. An excellent though improvised example exists in Mount Sinai Hospital, New York. Patients come here for diagnosis

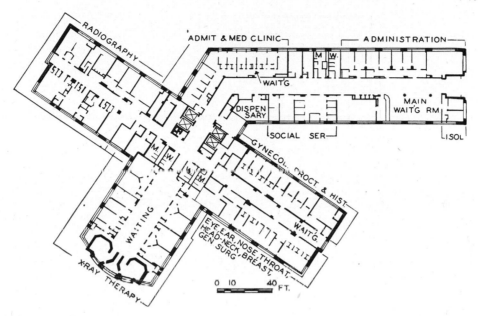

FIGURE 238. FRANCIS DELAFIELD HOSPITAL, NEW YORK. FIRST-FLOOR PLAN

Department of Hospitals, New York City, Isadore Rosenfield, chief architect, architects; James Gamble Rogers, consulting architect

on recommendation of their private physicians. Examinations and determinations are made by specialists, who through the conference method recommend a course of treatment to be followed by the patient's own physician. Such a diagnostic clinic could well serve the decentralized OPD.

SPECIAL CLINICS

All of the above facilities have been discussed as related to the general hospital. There are also special dispensaries which serve special hospitals. Figure 238 shows the out-patient department of a cancer clinic in the Francis Delafield Hospital, New York. Except for the X-ray diagnostic and therapeutic departments, which are used jointly by out-patients and in-patients, almost the entire floor is devoted to out-patient activity. Although in appearance the arrangement is similar to the other clinics shown in this chapter, the names of the clinics have special reference to cancer and related malignancies.

Figure 239 shows the first floor of the Triboro Hospital for Tuberculosis in New York. The right-hand wing of this floor is devoted to a tuberculosis clinic. On the second floor, in a corresponding position, are therapeutic features

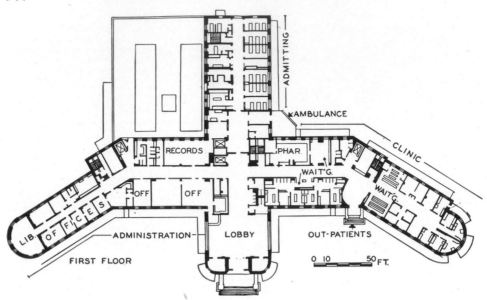

FIGURE 239. TRIBORO HOSPITAL FOR TUBERCULOSIS, NEW YORK. FIRST-FLOOR
PLAN SHOWING OUT-PATIENT DEPARTMENT

Eggers & Higgins, architects; Isadore Rosenfield, chief architect Department of Hospitals, New
York City

which are used in common by in-patients and out-patients. The emphasis here
is on diagnostic X-ray and pneumothorax treatment.

There is an unusual out-patient department in the psychiatric pavilion of the
Kings County Hospital. This type of clinic consists entirely of enclosed rooms.
If possible such rooms should be sound-proofed, because psychiatric patients
are apt to be suspicious of every whisper and in general this work requires a
maximum of privacy. An interesting feature here is the room (at the end of the
wing) where children are observed as they are engaged in play or other activities. The observers occupy small compartments to the right and left of the
corridor, which have windows with one-way-vision glass.

Figure 240 shows the proposed out-patient department for the Philadelphia
Psychiatric Hospital.

GROUP PRACTICE

A progressive movement known as group practice, designed to integrate
medical activity at all levels and to include both out-patient and in-patient departments, is one that will be of increasing interest to the hospital planner. Dr.

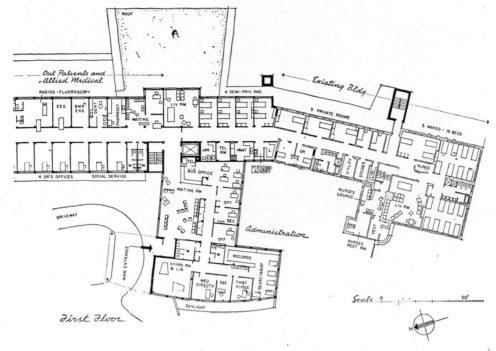

FIGURE 240. PSYCHIATRIC HOSPITAL, PHILADELPHIA, PENNSYLVANIA. FIRST-FLOOR PLAN SHOWING OUT-PATIENT DEPARTMENT

Oscar Stonorov and Louis Kahn, architects; Isadore Rosenfield, hospital consultant

The special requirements of a psychiatric clinic necessitate a special type of plan. Note the interviewing or consultation rooms.   Courtesy Isadore Rosenfield

Alfred Newton Richards, Chairman of the Committee on Medical Research of the Office of Scientific Research and Development, declares it to be an attempt to so reorganize medical practice "as to minimize the ineffectiveness of individual competitive practice." In other words, it is an attempt to integrate medicine so as to make it more useful to society.

Group practice is so called because it recognizes the fact that, though medicine must continue to be practiced by individual physicians, they must group themselves together for greater efficiency and must pool their knowledge and integrate their specialties into a comprehensive instrumentality for the prevention of illness and for the treatment of the sick. The present impetus toward group practice also derives from a higher social consciousness on the part of physicians and a realization of the effectiveness of integrated practices in the armed services. Finally, there is the compulsion of doctors returning from

FIGURE 241.
WEST END HEALTH UNIT,
BOSTON, MASSACHUSETTS.
ORIGINAL UNIT (1916)
AND LATER ADDITION

Courtesy Isadore Rosenfield

military service to band together and associate themselves as teams either in or outside of a hospital, because of their difficulties in finding offices or their inability as individuals to pay high rents and procure the costly technical equipment necessary in modern diagnosis and treatment.

Up to the middle of the twentieth century there has been little experience with civilian group practice, except for a few isolated cases which were aided by the United States Public Health Service. The physical plants of group-practice offices have been and will probably continue for some time to be improvised. Although many such offices are not in a strict sense group-practice units, because they have no basic connection with a hospital and are not subject to the professional discipline which stems from hospital or medical-school as-

FIGURE 242. CHILDREN'S HEALTH CLASS, WEST END HEALTH UNIT, BOSTON, MASSACHUSETTS

The community value of educational activities is great.   Courtesy Isadore Rosenfield

sociation, nevertheless a host of gradations may be noted in their operation and some more or less approach the ideal of group practice. Thus there are "doctors' offices" like those in the Harkness Pavilion at the Columbia Presbyterian Medical Center in New York, where doctors rent offices and make use of the hospital's facilities. This is helpful to the well-paying patient and to the doctor, but in both effort and responsibility it lacks the true collaborative element. Other groups of doctors band themselves together for collaborative practice and establish their offices in a remodeled brownstone house. Here they lack many of the diagnostic and therapeutic facilities to be found in a first-class hospital; also their professional talent, though diversified, is limited to their own small group whereas in a first-class hospital there would be the skill and the stimulation to be gained from a much wider group of experienced specialists. True group medicine can emerge only when there is all-embracing health and hospital insurance.

The reason why group practice is dealt with in this chapter is because its principal activities are concerned with the ambulant patient and also because, to be economical and medically correct, it should be practiced in an environment of medical culture and with the advantage of complete diagnostic and therapeutic facilities such as are available only in a hospital. Under a compre-

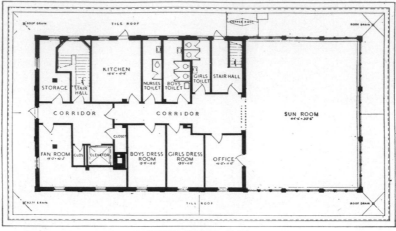

FOURTH FLOOR PLAN
SCALE OF FEET

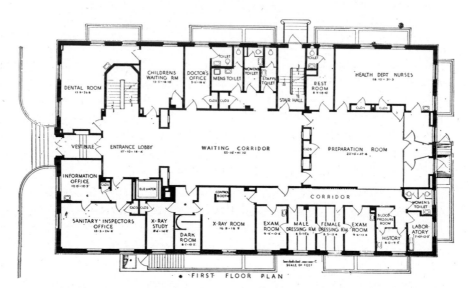

FIRST FLOOR PLAN
SCALE OF FEET

FIGURE 243. GEORGE ROBERT WHITE FUND HEALTH UNIT, BOSTON, MASSACHUSETTS. PLANS

Coolidge, Shepley, Bulfinch & Abbott, architects

hensive health insurance plan most patients who formerly attended out-patient clinics as non-paying or part-pay patients become full-pay patients. The out-patient department completely integrated with the hospital is the logical seat for group practice. Many new hospital projects make provisions for group practice, either as a special division of the OPD or parallel with it; others frankly provide a modern OPD but raise the standards somewhat so that it may be used both for paying patients and for the medically indigent. Inevitably, once the OPD becomes economically self-sustaining, it will come out of the basement and move to the ground floor; instead of being concealed it will be advertised.

HEALTH CENTERS

We shall now briefly examine health centers or health units as they have been developed, from the health or prevention point of view primarily, by health authorities as distinguished from medical authorities.

One of the earliest large-scale efforts in this direction has taken place in Boston, where because of the generosity and farsightedness of George Robert White (1847–1922) the "health units," as they are known in Boston, were made possible. The city appears to have eight such units and eleven sub-units. Figure 241 shows the first health unit (1916) in Boston, which occupied improvised quarters, together with the addition erected in 1930 to serve the same neighborhood.[11] Figure 242 portrays one of the many activities of Boston's health units. Figure 243 shows the floor plans of one of the city's latest health units; clothed in traditional style, it provides its occupants with a minimum of fresh air and light.

Since health-center functions are closely related to general health activities, on the municipal or county level they are usually constituted as a governmental activity. In Boston the buildings are provided by the George Robert White Fund but administered and operated with municipal personnel and tax funds. In New York the projects were first physically implemented at the beginning of the city's progressive administration in 1934. The entire city is divided into health administration districts which average from a quarter to a third of a million persons; although there are thirty-one centers and sub-centers, not many of them are in buildings planned for the purpose and most of the construction program is still in the paper stage. In the beginning the health centers occupied improvised quarters. The early buildings erected for health-center purposes, like their Boston predecessors, were romantic concoctions in the eclectic style of architecture, with small windows, dark and ill-ventilated waiting rooms, and generally unhygienic and uninspiring interiors. Figures 244–247 are designs prepared for execution in New York in the period immediately

[11] Charles Francis Wilinsky, *The Health Units of Boston . . . 1924–1933* (Boston: Printing Department, 1933).

FIGURE 244. RIVERSIDE HEALTH SUBSTATION, NEW YORK. PERSPECTIVE

Magoon & Salo, architects; J. B. Basil, supervising architect Department of Public Works, New York City

The atmosphere of a public health center should be inviting and human.

Courtesy Isadore Rosenfield

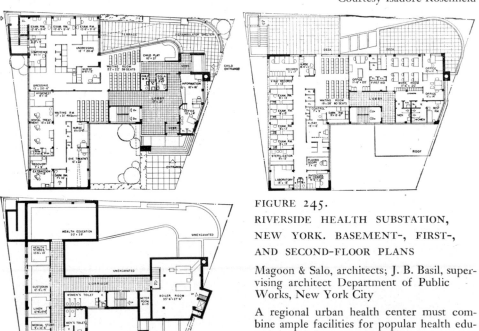

FIGURE 245.

RIVERSIDE HEALTH SUBSTATION, NEW YORK. BASEMENT-, FIRST-, AND SECOND-FLOOR PLANS

Magoon & Salo, architects; J. B. Basil, supervising architect Department of Public Works, New York City

A regional urban health center must combine ample facilities for popular health education with its more usual clinic areas.

Courtesy Isadore Rosenfield

after the Second World War. Here we see release from the iron bands of eclecticism, but future planning will undoubtedly show even greater humanization and more generous assignment of space.

The health-center movement is still in the position of having constantly to justify its existence and ingratiate itself with those who hold the purse strings. Consequently the funds available for capital investment as well as for operation are not ample. One of the reasons why health centers have difficulty in growing freely stems from the fact, on the one hand, that health-center activity seems to duplicate in some respects the activities of the out-patient department and, on the other, that the "man in the street" is not so much interested in advice as in actual therapy. It would seem, therefore, that if health activities could be more closely integrated with hospital activities, and vice versa, it would not be necessary to ask political bodies to make separate provisions for health centers apart from those for OPD's and hospitals.

The Unites States Public Health Service has worked out several types of health center,[12] based apparently on one treatment per day per thousand of population. This seems inadequate compared with the basis used for out-patient departments in general, but perhaps the feeling was that it is better to make a modest beginning than to do nothing at all. Figures 252 and 253 show two of these health-center types. It will be noted here, as in the examples shown earlier, that on the clinical side the activities are devoted largely to tuberculosis work involving pneumothorax treatment, to both dental and eye work, and to the diagnosis and treatment of venereal diseases. Another favorite clinical activity of the health center is the care of mother and child. As a rule, a laboratory is included for testing water, milk, and so on.

Health centers should furnish adequate space for educational activities. This space may be merely a classroom to be used for demonstration and health talks; in some instances the waiting room is taken over for such purposes. Where feasible, however, an auditorium is a very desirable element. The waiting room and corridors should be utilized for visual-education exhibits. Also, to assist in community health administration, there are usually provisions for health statistics, offices for nurses who do home visiting, quarters for sanitarians, and administrative offices for health officers. In Boston, New York, and other large cities the health centers frequently provide quarters for the various voluntary community organizations whose activities bear on health and recreation.

[12] "Public Health Center," Building Types Study No. 67, *Architectural Record*, Vol. 88 (1940), Sept., pp. 83–102.

FIGURE 246. SUNSET PARK HEALTH SUBSTATION, BROOKLYN, NEW YORK.
PERSPECTIVE

John B. Peterkin, architect; J. B. Basil, supervising architect Department of Public Works, New
York City

An exterior that avoids institutional monumentality; it welcomes rather than repels.

Courtesy Isadore Rosenfield

Another type of health center that is gaining in importance is the labor-
management clinic. After the First World War the labor unions made some
minor attempts to build their own health facilities, but on the whole the movement did not make much headway. Much later, after the Second World War,
the unions, realizing the difficulties, began to think increasingly of health
service for the workers as a joint responsibility of the employers and the employees. Although this movement is relatively young, its manifestation in terms
of actual, physical provisions is beginning to emerge.

In general these union-industry clinics have been improvisations and adaptations of existing structures to clinical purposes; under such circumstances the
clinics leave much to be desired from a physical point of view, though they
may be doing first-rate medical work. Recognizing this fact the trustees of
the Men's Apparel Industry Health Center in Philadelphia [13] did not look for
an abandoned building or loft to be remodeled; instead they bought a plot of
land, measuring approximately 172 by 148 feet, in the very heart of the city.

[13] Philadelphia Clothing Manufacturers Association and the Philadelphia Joint Board of the
Amalgamated Clothing Workers of America, Congress of Industrial Organizations.

FIGURE 247 (OPPOSITE). SUNSET PARK HEALTH SUBSTATION, BROOKLYN,
NEW YORK. BASEMENT-, FIRST-, AND SECOND-FLOOR PLANS

John B. Peterkin, architect; J. B. Basil, supervising architect Department of Public Works, New
York City

Courtesy Isadore Rosenfield

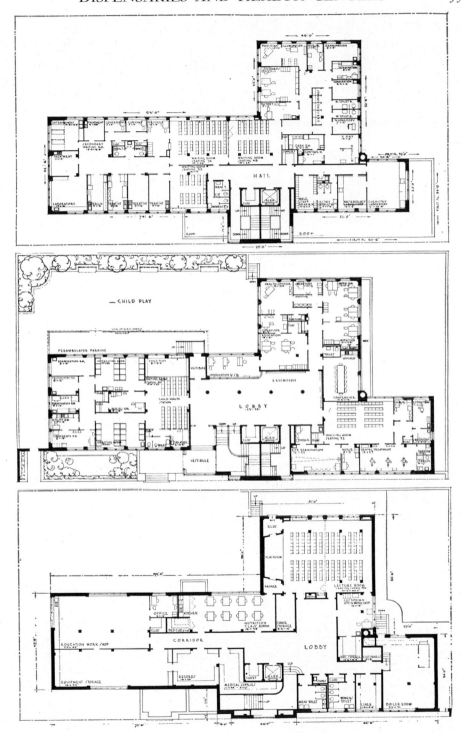

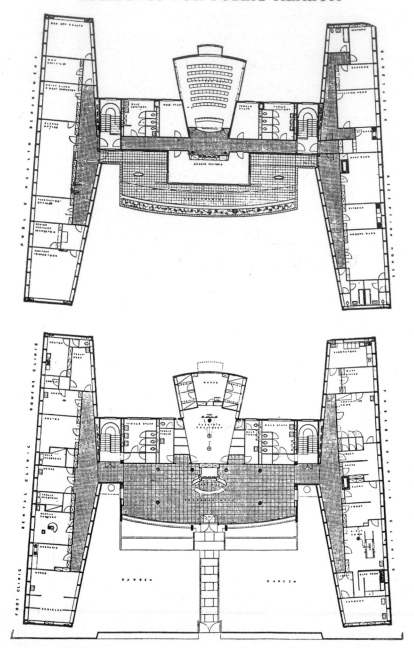

FIGURE 248. FINSBURY HEALTH CENTER, LONDON. TWO PLANS

Lubetkin & Tecton, architects

A complete and well-planned health center for a congested London area.

From *Architectural Review*

FIGURE 249.
FINSBURY HEALTH
CENTER, LONDON.
MAIN ENTRANCE

Lubetkin & Tecton, architects

A dynamic expression of construction and purpose. The walls, largely of glass brick, permit cheerful light to flood the interior.

Courtesy British Information Services

Dr. J. A. Langbord, who had had several years' experience with a similar facility, was retained as medical director and was charged with the preparation of the program of clinics, staff, budget, and so on. The necessary funds were already secure, for the manufacturers not only contributed their share to the building fund but also committed themselves for an indefinite period to bear the cost of maintenance and operation of the building. Architects and a hospital planning consultant were accordingly engaged. Figures 250 and 251 show the result of their co-operative efforts. Here, in addition to medical correctness, the principal desideratum was a clinic without waste or ostentation and, above all, a humanized environment.

REGIONAL INTEGRATION

In the foregoing discussion we have seen the out-patient department as a separate building or as a part of a hospital building. We have also viewed the health center, or health unit, which generally exists independent of either the hospital or its dispensary. The hospitals themselves, in the present scheme of things, are small islands of activity without sinews of integration between them.

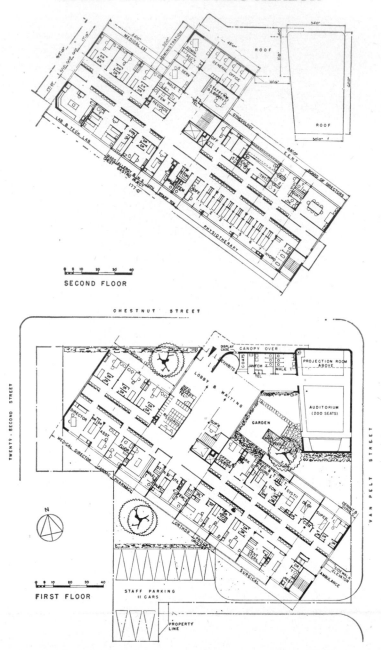

FIGURE 250. MEN'S APPAREL INDUSTRY HEALTH CENTER, PHILADELPHIA, PENNSYLVANIA. FIRST- AND SECOND-FLOOR PLANS

Magaziner & Polss, architects; Isadore Rosenfield, hospital consultant

Courtesy Isadore Rosenfield

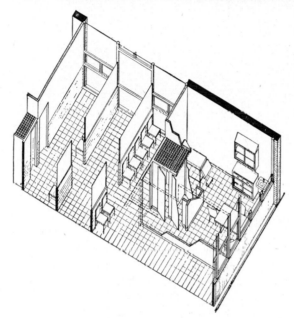

FIGURE 251.
MEN'S APPAREL INDUSTRY
HEALTH CENTER,
PHILADELPHIA, PENNSYLVANIA.
ELEVATION AND ISOMETRIC OF
CONSULTATION ROOM

Magaziner & Polss, architects; Isadore
Rosenfield, hospital consultant

Courtesy Isadore Rosenfield

Under an integrated scheme of health and hospital activity, the country
would be divided into *regions*.[14] Each region would have one or more *primary
districts* in which would be located the base hospital or medical center, where,
in addition to concern for the health and hospital care of the people within the
district, care would also be given to persons coming from secondary and isolated districts for specialized medical care. The medical center or base hospital
would also conduct teaching and research. The medical center would provide
4½ beds per thousand for its own population, plus ½ bed per thousand of
population in all the outlying districts for their specialized needs. (See Fig.
252.) The region would also contain *secondary districts*, each of which would
have 4 beds per thousand for its own population and 1½ beds per thousand of
population for the account of isolated districts. In addition, as explained above,

[14] *Health Service Areas*, Public Health Bulletin 292 (Washington: U.S. Public Health Service,
1945).

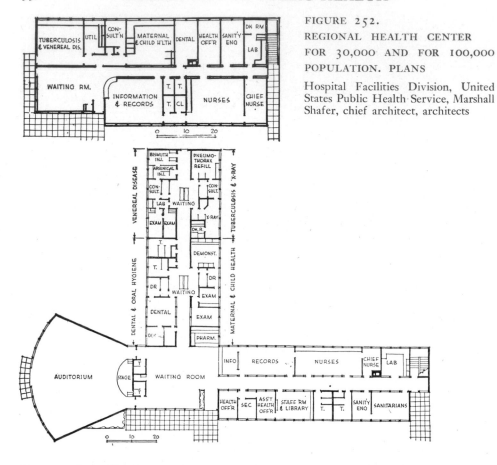

FIGURE 252.

REGIONAL HEALTH CENTER FOR 30,000 AND FOR 100,000 POPULATION. PLANS

Hospital Facilities Division, United States Public Health Service, Marshall Shafer, chief architect, architects

the secondary district would have ½ bed per thousand of its population to its credit at the primary district. The *isolated districts*, besides their credit of 1½ beds per thousand of their population at the secondary district and ½ bed at the primary district, would have rural hospitals with 2½ beds per thousand for their own population.

At each of the three levels there would be a combination health center and dispensary. In isolated and more or less inaccessible rural locations the health center would be the dominant feature and might have attached to it a few beds which could be used for childbirth or for the temporary care of patients pending their transfer to a rural, secondary-district, or base hospital. Figure 253 shows this type of health center.

Many of the recently published examples of proposed rural health centers show relatively extensive operating and obstetric facilities. It would seem after

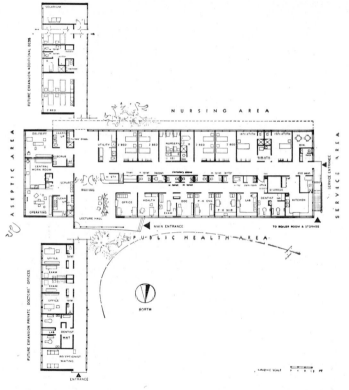

FIGURE 253.
HEALTH CENTER,
WITH BEDS,
FOR ISOLATED
COMMUNITIES.
PLAN AND
PERSPECTIVE

Hospital Facilities Division, United States Public Health Service, Marshall Shafer, chief architect, architects

consultation with competent medical authorities that such provisions are a waste of community resources. In an isolated rural location a desperately sick or injured person would find no competent diagnostician or surgeon to deal with his case. First aid can be given in any clean, simple room; beyond that it would be best in most cases to rush the patient to the nearest hospital center.

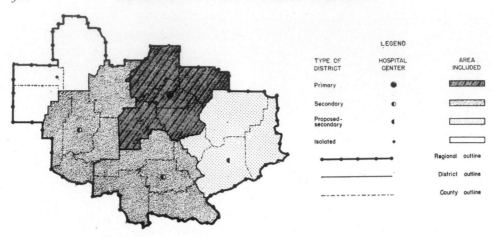

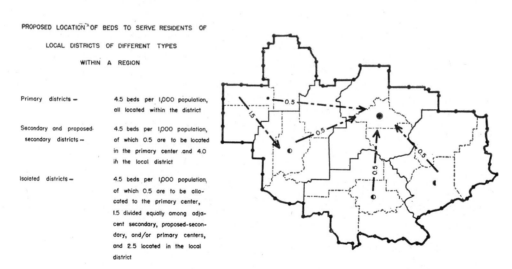

PROPOSED LOCATION OF BEDS TO SERVE RESIDENTS OF

LOCAL DISTRICTS OF DIFFERENT TYPES

WITHIN A REGION

Primary districts —   4.5 beds per 1,000 population, all located within the district

Secondary and proposed-secondary districts —   4.5 beds per 1,000 population, of which 0.5 are to be located in the primary center and 4.0 in the local district

Isolated districts —   4.5 beds per 1,000 population, of which 0.5 are to be allocated to the primary center, 1.5 divided equally among adjacent secondary, proposed-secondary, and/or primary centers, and 2.5 located in the local district

FIGURE 254. REGIONAL HEALTH DIVISIONS AND REGIONAL BED ALLOCATIONS

Courtesy Isadore Rosenfield

In extreme conditions a physician or surgeon should be summoned, by aeroplane if possible.

The entire scheme for the proposed integrated health and hospital organization has been worked out by the United States Public Health Service, as noted earlier, and is shown in Figure 254.

SUGGESTED ADDITIONAL READING FOR CHAPTER 36

Commission on Hospital Care, *Hospital Care in the United States*, A. C. Bachmeyer, M.D., director of study (New York: Commonwealth Fund [1947]).

Emerson, Haven, M.D., *Local Health Units for the Nation* (New York: Commonwealth Fund, 1945).

Hiscock, I. V., *Community Health Organization* (New York: Commonwealth Fund, 1932).

Hospital Association of Pennsylvania, *Better Hospital Care for the Ambulant Patient* (Harrisburg: the Association, 1946).

McGibony, J. R., *Health Center Designed for Rural Needs*, reprinted from *The Modern Hospital* (Washington: Public Health Service, 1946).

Rosenfield, Isadore, *Hospitals   Integrated Design* (New York: Reinhold, 1947).

United States Public Health Service, *A Health Center Unit*, reprinted from *Hospitals* (Washington: Public Health Service, 1945).

—— *Health Service Areas*, Public Health Bulletin 292 (Washington: Public Health Service, 1945).

—— *Outpatient Department for a 50-Bed Hospital*, reprinted from "Elements of the General Hospital," *Architectural Record* (Washington: Public Health Service, 1946).

—— *Outpatient Department for a 100-Bed Hospital*, reprinted from "Elements of the General Hospital," *Architectural Record* (Washington: Public Health Service, 1946).

—— *Outpatient Department for a 200-Bed Hospital*, reprinted from "Elements of the General Hospital," *Architectural Record* (Washington: Public Health Service, 1946).

—— *Public Health Centers*, reprinted from the *Architectural Record*, Building Types Study No. 67 (Washington: Public Health Service, 1942).

—— *A Rural Health Center with 10-Bed Nursing Unit*, reprinted from the *Architectural Record* (Washington: Public Health Service, 1945).

PERIODICALS

"Air Ambulance Has Come to Stay," *Modern Hospital*, Vol. 66 (1946), February, p. 92.

"Health Center for the New York Department of Health [Forest Hills, N.Y.]," Frederick G. Frost and Clay & Corrigill, architects, *Architectural Forum*, Vol. 83 (1945), November, pp. 104, 105.

Hospital issue of *Pencil Points*, Vol. 26 (1945), August, pp. 55–86.

Mountin, Dr. Joseph W., "A Restatement of the General Hospital Situation," *American Journal of Public Health*, Vol. 30 (1940), December, pp. 1406–14.

Neutra, Richard J., "Modern Health Center," *Modern Hospital*, Vol. 66 (1946), February, pp. 46–54.

Rosenfield, Isadore, and Simon Breines, "A Health Facility," *Architectural Forum*, Vol. 78 (1943), May, pp. 150–52.

"Sweden's System of Public Health," *Pencil Points*, Vol. 26 (1945), August, pp. 83–86.

United States Public Health Service, Hospital Facilities Section, "The Small Health Center–Hospital," *Pencil Points*, Vol. 27 (1946), June, pp. 74–76.

"Wayne County Health Center, Michigan," *Pencil Points*, Vol. 28 (1947), November, pp. 74–76.

Wheeler, E. Todd, "Trends in Planning," *Modern Hospital*, Vol. 66 (1946), March, pp. 44–48.

37

Sanatoriums and Asylums

By WILLIAM L. PEREIRA

DESPITE the prevailing usage of the terms "asylum" and "sanatorium" for two separate types of institution, a modern concept of medicine would hardly recognize a distinction between them. Originally the former signified merely a place of refuge, the latter an establishment for the treatment of the sick in a locality offering so-called natural therapeutic agents. Today the sanatorium is an institution designed to diagnose and treat some specific chronic illness of either a physical or a mental nature. It must be regarded as a specialized hospital or institution which—on either a short-term or a custodial basis—is planned, equipped, and staffed to utilize all the scientific forces currently available to prevent, treat, cure, and ultimately eradicate the disease.

The present chapter will deal mainly with psychiatric and tuberculosis sanatoriums and such other specialized units as have not been included in the two preceding chapters.

PSYCHIATRIC INSTITUTIONS

Architecture as both a science and an art demands that its practitioners approach their problems in an analytic spirit. More often than they realize, perhaps, architects are given the privilege of participating in the satisfaction of a fundamental human need. Some realize the responsibility arising from that privilege; others do not. Those who do not are content with secondhand information, superficial research, and, last but not least, the habitual repetition of old techniques. As a result of such an approach, those criteria we roughly call standards accumulate and gain so much influence that automatically they dictate solutions. These automatic solutions become traditional and in consequence create formidable obstacles to an objective program.

That has been the situation in architectural planning for psychiatric care. As though this were not enough to overcome, architects in this branch of practice are faced with the fact that within the medical profession itself there exist broad and basic conflicts of ideas which, when carefully evaluated, have a profound effect on the programming and planning of the psychiatric hospital. When these concepts are unified, standards can be created; until then architects in this field must accept their responsibility in a spirit of pure research and discharge it with humility.

Until about the second quarter of the twentieth century the mental hospital itself made no important contributions to psychiatric care; the main advances had come through individuals outside the hospital field. The custodial care of the mentally ill had degenerated to an almost unbelievably wretched level during the period just preceding the French Revolution. Then, in the wave of humanitarianism which followed the recognition of the social importance of man as an individual, courageous men and women by individual as well as concerted efforts improved the lot of the mentally sick in the so-called insane asylums. That later period is popularly considered to have seen the birth of the modern conception of institutions for the treatment of the mentally ill. The gradual changes witnessed in the mental hospital have had a psychiatric effect of some importance, but it is to be borne in mind that the original impulse was humanitarian rather than scientific.

Obviously the purpose of any building is to enclose its functions. It is not, therefore, the historical development of buildings of any particular type that is important; it is rather the historical origin and the growth of the functions the building is expected to house which are significant. In the case of mental institutions, the aim is to create the means of bringing modern psychiatric diagnosis and therapeutic developments to the point of use—the patients. Historically, then, it is psychiatry and not the insane asylum which is the important factor.

Contemporary psychiatry differs from early psychiatric concepts in that, though still occupied with the custodial care of the insane, it is more concerned with the milder deviations from mental and emotional health. This concern, however, is not a modern invention; it is as old as man. Priests and prophets from the beginning of time have sought to promote the mental and spiritual well-being of man through religion. The writings of Hippocrates, the Father of Medicine, and of his contemporaries reveal not only that many mental and emotional disorders were recognized in those early days but also that effective methods of treatment were practiced. Asclepiades, Caelius Aurelianus, and later Paracelsus—great physicians all—formulated principles for the treatment of the mentally ill that still apply today. Looking back over 2,500 years we find ample proof that psychiatry has always been an important branch of medicine wherever good theory and practice have existed. The fact is mentioned here only because the architect will frequently find a physician in a position of responsibility who disapproves of this "new hocus-pocus" called psychiatry or a psychiatrist who sets himself apart from physical medicine. But these are by no means representative opinions. To quote Edward Weiss, M.D.:

Physicians have always felt intuitively that the emotional life had something to do with illness, but the structural concept of disease introduced by a great German pathologist by the name of Virchow about a hundred years ago led to the separation of illness from the psyche of man and a consideration of disease as only a disorder of organs and cells. . . . Medicine then contented itself with the study of the organism as a physiological mechanism.

The day is near at hand for the final outmoding of the "either or" concept (either functional or organic) in diagnosis, and to place in its stead the idea of how much of one and how much of the other: that is, how much of the problem is emotional and how much is physical, and what is the relation between them. This is truly the psychosomatic concept in medicine.

That recognition of the psychophysical character of disease is also an expression of the new frontier in medicine. In addition it provides the criterion or the formula for a valid approach to the programming and planning of the psychiatric institution, hospital, or sanatorium—by whatever name the establishment may be called.

PROGRAM

To architects of skill and integrity, the solution of a problem comes with reasonable ease; it is the finding and understanding of the problem which is often difficult. To create the program, integrity and perseverance must combine. The program for a psychiatric institution calls upon the creative capacity of the planner as does that of few other building types because today the trends and concepts of psychiatric care are, to put it mildly, in an extremely fluid state. Let the architect talk to any (and hopefully to all) of the various professional people interested in the problem, and he will find that the picture is far from clear. When he undertakes his research he will see or read of many "architectural" solutions, some more imaginative than others, and it may seem that his task is to digest the purpose of each of the elements that appear predominantly in these solutions and then employ his personal skill in adapting them to his specific assignment. But if he proceeds in this way he will have failed to fulfill his responsibilities, because it is impossible to accept solutions arrived at by means of the most popular formulas when the justification for such formulas many not yet exist.

All of this means that programming the psychiatric institution is a tremendous and responsible task. It involves an investigation of the practice of psychosomatic medicine, psychology, and psychiatry, and it challenges the architect to use both his head and his heart to understand the problems before he applies his own professional skill. By this method a diversity of programs will be created, the possible solutions will be varied, and eventually from these—after a period of research and experiment—the architect, hand in hand with the doctor, will be able to make an adequate and successful contribution toward the satisfaction of the enormous human need for perfection in psychiatric care.

Only an approach to such programming can be indicated here. The method will vary with the character of the individual architect. The extent of his findings will be in direct proportion to his interest in the basic problem, and his success will depend in large part on his own emotional growth during the investigation. In the very beginning he will find that in a psychiatric institution nothing exists or happens that does not have a psychological impact; hence, since he is planning for people who are disturbed in varying degrees and for various reasons, the psychological aspect of everything he plans must be considered. This approach is not unfamiliar to many architects, especially to those who possess or achieve the human insight to enclose space in a manner that is psychologically pleasing as well as physically logical.

Quantitative and Qualitative Aspects. The quantitative aspect of the program—the problem of how many patients are to be received as out-patients and how many as in-patients—is not easy to solve. Frequently the architect will find that it is the product of the qualitative aspect—the decision as to what types of mental illnesses will be treated in the institution under consideration. In the complete general voluntary hospital it is presumed that medical science, with all the necessary staff and equipment, is ready to take all problems as they come; thus the hospital is apparently able to cope with its responsibilities, however diverse they may be. But the conception of the service of a psychiatric institution is limited by the prevailing definition or understanding—on the part of well-intentioned people both inside and outside the professional field —of what are the treatable mental illnesses. Thus there exists an area of conflict in the statistics, or in the use of formulas, for determining by percentage

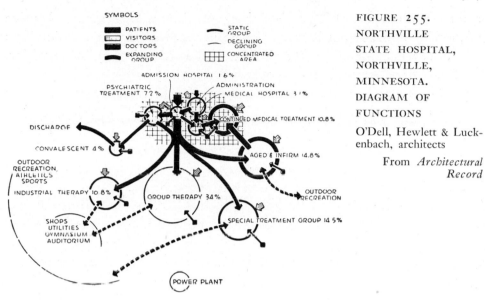

SYMBOLS

■ PATIENTS ▬ STATIC GROUP
□ VISITORS ⌐ DECLINING GROUP
■ DOCTORS
◗ EXPANDING GROUP ⊞ CONCENTRATED AREA

ADMISSION HOSPITAL 1.6%

PSYCHIATRIC TREATMENT 7.2% ADMINISTRATION

MEDICAL HOSPITAL 3.1%

CONTINUED MEDICAL TREATMENT 10.8%

DISCHARGE

CONVALESCENT 4%

AGED & INFIRM 14.8%

OUTDOOR RECREATION, ATHLETICS SPORTS

OUTDOOR RECREATION

INDUSTRIAL THERAPY 10.8% GROUP THERAPY 34%

SHOPS UTILITIES GYMNASIUM AUDITORIUM SPECIAL TREATMENT GROUP 14.5%

POWER PLANT

FIGURE 255.
NORTHVILLE
STATE HOSPITAL,
NORTHVILLE,
MINNESOTA.
DIAGRAM OF
FUNCTIONS

O'Dell, Hewlett & Luck-
enbach, architects

From *Architectural
Record*

methods the relation of psychiatric facilities to the total population served. On this question, even the discerning architect is at the mercy of the concept held by his client.

Methods of Diagnosis and Treatment as Design Criteria. Because the architect, in programming a psychiatric institution, will find it necessary to know what methods of diagnosis and treatment are going to be employed, it may be well to point out categorically and to some extent historically what the various methods are, so that he may refrain from accepting names plus dimensions as his sole criteria and may understand that there are forces of action and reaction constantly at work in this field.

Before the advent of modern scientific medicine, physicians and laymen had initiated a movement to provide humanitarian care in asylums for the mentally sick, and certain crude methods of restraint, purging, vomiting, and bleeding were relinquished by critical medical men. No matter how great the progress in psychiatric care may be in the future, the humanitarian principle established at that time will remain the first tenet in the programming, and it will express itself in preparing for as rational a handling of the patient as his state of mind will allow.

During that early period, medicine separated from psychiatry, and it was not until the last quarter of the nineteenth century that it came to be finally recognized and accepted that no sharp distinction existed between the moral and medical treatment of psychiatric patients. Even so, the therapeutic value of moral treatment alone has never been fully realized; even today, in places where large numbers of the mentally ill are collected and ostensibly cared for, the ideals of well-organized occupational therapy, recreational facilities, and a favorable atmosphere remain unrealized. The fulfillment of these conditions is still a challenge to the architect in his programming. (See Fig. 255.)

The paths of psychiatry and medicine converged again when, on the discovery of microscopic organisms as the cause of many diseases, the practice of medicine changed with dramatic suddenness. The development of specific cures and means of prevention as well as of surgery quickly followed. In applying that discovery to the fields of neuro-anatomy and neuro-pathology, it was found that a great number of mental illnesses had an organic basis. Today, therefore, the psychiatric institution must include in its program this type of mental illness. Facilities for physical diagnosis and treatment become mandatory and are in fact identical with those of the general hospital.

But many mental illnesses or psychiatric disorders, such as the manic-depressive, schizophrenic, and neurotic types, resisted solution from the organic standpoint and remained in the functional category. Here an understanding of the forces in human behavior offered a means of solution, and the work of Dr. Sigmund Freud proved to be the stimulus. His method, known as psychoanalysis, brought insight into the motivation and symptoms of psychiatric disorders. It supplemented descriptive psychiatry with interpretive psychiatry. Psychoanalysis as a specialty and as a specialized technique in psychotherapy demands important consideration in the programming of a mental hospital.

The most recent addition to the therapeutic facilities for treatment of mental illnesses is shock therapy. Insulin shock was introduced in the United States in 1936, metrazol (for the same purpose) in the same year, and electro-shock in 1937. Confronted for so many years with intangibles, the planners of recent institutions have readily accepted the necessity for special shock-therapy units. It should be recorded that, according to many medical men, these methods at mid-century are proving to be an important adjunct to the treatment of mental illnesses. These doctors state that as a result of the shock treatments the course of the illness is frequently shortened and the patients become more quickly responsive to psychotherapy and other therapeutic treatments. But there are many other medical men, whose experience and professional standing are extremely imposing, who feel strongly that the direction which shock therapy is taking is more retrogressive than progressive and is setting back the much-to-

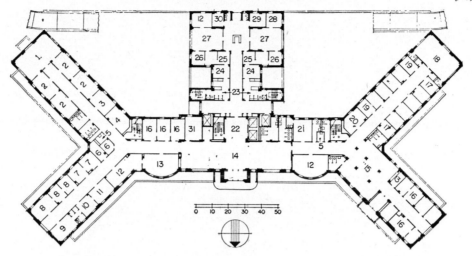

FIGURE 256. PSYCHIATRIC PAVILION, KINGS COUNTY HOSPITAL, BROOKLYN, NEW YORK. FIRST-FLOOR PLAN

Tachau & Vought, architects; Isadore Rosenfield, chief architect Department of Hospitals, New York

Courtesy Isadore Rosenfield

(1) Library	(11) Assistant	(22) Elevator lobby
(2) Conference rooms	(12) Clerks	(23) Preparation
(3) Chief psychologist	(13) Information	(24) Examination
(4) Storage	(14) Visitors' waiting	(25) History
(5) Janitor	(15) Clinic waiting	(26) Quiet room
(6) Coats	(16) Social Service	(27) Patients' waiting
(7) Commitment	(17) Psychol. exam	(28) Investigation
(8) Nursing staff	(18) Children's room	(29) Treatment
(9) Director	(19) Medical exam	(30) Stretcher
(10) Secretary	(20) Records	(31) Property clerk
	(21) Nurses	

be-desired reconciliation of the psychological and somatic points of view. It is true that the shock treatments administered are entirely empirical; they do not conform to any standard of causative orientation. As cases are followed up, there is increasing evidence that appears to lead to the conclusion that the beneficial results in the main are of a temporary nature. In any event it is evident that, in spite of the fact that shock treatments are an established part of practically all current programs of mental therapy, the whole problem is still in a state of confusion. The architect, before programming the building, will have to become fully cognizant of the latest trends and developments in this field. (See Figs. 257, 258.)

Research and Teaching as Determining Factors. From a physical standpoint, research and teaching in any hospital do not necessarily express themselves in demands for additional floor space, extra rooms, or special facilities. They are

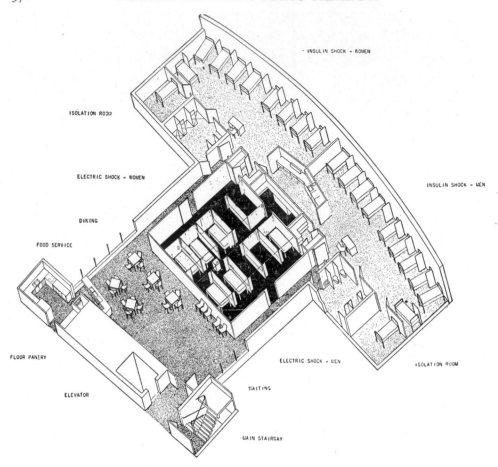

FIGURE 257. PSYCHIATRIC HOSPITAL, PHILADELPHIA, PENNSYLVANIA.
ISOMETRIC DIAGRAM OF SHOCK-TREATMENT FACILITIES
Oscar Stonorov and Louis Kahn, architects; Isadore Rosenfield, hospital consultant

From *Progressive Architecture*

not a tangible thing in the hospital; they are a point of view—a point of view containing the following basic ingredients: the desire and the capacity to investigate and resolve; the talent and the willingness to interpret and disseminate. Where this point of view is an inherent part of any hospital, there are to be found the highest standards of medical practice. And where this concept exists prior to the programming or planning, no single element—irrespective of how mundane it might appear on the surface—will escape attention from the research or teaching point of view. The architect must seek out the implications of this concept before he brings his own skill into play, and ultimately he

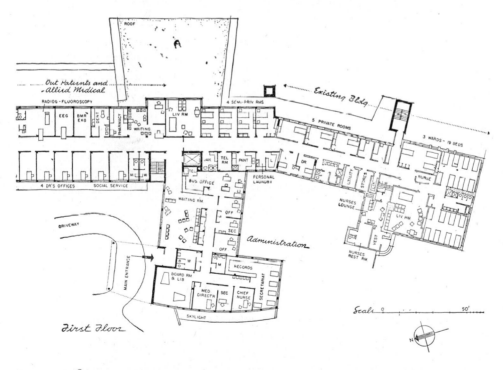

FIGURE 258. PSYCHIATRIC HOSPITAL, PHILADELPHIA, PENNSYLVANIA. GENERAL PLAN AND PERSPECTIVE

Oscar Stonorov and Louis Kahn, architects; Isadore Rosenfield, hospital consultant

Courtesy Oscar Stonorov and Louis Kahn

must fortify his contribution with evidence of the functional aspects of those implications.

Human Effectiveness a Fundamental Objective. Finally, in programming the psychiatric hospital the architect should bear in mind one inescapable conclusion—that no building has ever diagnosed, treated, or cured a patient any more than drafting equipment has ever analyzed and designed a building. In a psychiatric institution it is not the therapies as such that are beneficial; it is the application or the techniques of these therapies which effect the cure. The application is accomplished by *people*—by doctors, nurses, technicians, and attendants—not by things. The planning objective, therefore, must be to create a controlled environment in which continuous and intimate contact can be maintained between the skilled personnel and the sick at all times—and that relationship must be an effortless one.

CLASSIFICATION OF FACILITIES

Some of the professional people concerned with the problem are beginning to create order among the many necessary facilities in the following ways: first, by classifying them according to where the diagnosis and treatment of mental illness can be provided most efficiently and widely; second, by creating limitations on the service in direct proportion to the capacity of the facility to handle the problems; and, third, by disseminating standards for determining in a given institution the minimum ingredients in terms of the personal and therapeutic equipment necessary to provide objective diagnosis and treatment of mentally ill people. A psychiatric institution may be a clinic, a hospital, a portion of either, or the sum of both. It may deal exclusively with out-patients or it may be dedicated to the custodial care of the insane.

It should be borne in mind that a psychiatric disorder is an illness—an illness subject to the widest possible range in degree, from so-called nervousness to so-called insanity. The cause may be completely apparent or completely obscure, and the diagnosis and therapy may be known or not yet incorporated in the body of psychiatric knowledge. Logically, therefore, the classification of facilities is based on the degree of illness, on the sorting of these illnesses into treatable groups, and on locating the facilities where the maximum therapeutic value can be obtained with a minimum of effort.

Today out-patient psychiatry dominates the field. Psychiatric treatment can be administered in the physician's office or in well-organized and well-staffed clinics located wherever the need exists or arises. From there on the problem becomes difficult. Until a comparatively short time ago only two classes of mental illness were recognized. Patients whose illness was of an extreme nature were committed to institutions ostensibly designed and existing for the purpose. Patients with illnesses less severe and therefore not committable under the law were without facilities. This situation for all practical purposes still exists; the only difference lies in today's recognition of the need for facilities in both cases.

It would seem that the first step beyond the physician's office or clinic would take the patient to the large and well-equipped general hospital where a psychiatric department exists. Since the general hospital is not in the province of this chapter, suffice it to say that, from the standpoint of the ultimate in psychiatric care, the staff of a general hospital cannot ignore mental illnesses, nor can the psychiatrist ignore the tremendous advantages of association with the general hospital. From the patient's standpoint, whenever adequate treatment has been available in the general hospital much has been accomplished toward teaching him and his relatives that mental illness carries no more of a stigma than does physical illness; many mental illnesses can be treated there in a matter of a few weeks, thus obviating the necessity for institutionalizing the patient. When the mental illness is accompanied by complicated physical problems, the value of the general hospital is apparent. In the main, the patient to be handled in the psychiatric department of the general hospital is one for whose illness the causative factors have been determined, who is not likely to be (or to remain) chronically ill, and who can respond to the therapies provided in the department. The adding of this feature to the general hospital does not make it a psychiatric hospital—it makes it a complete hospital.

The first class of psychiatric patients for whom a special hospital is really needed consists of those who are not severely or chronically ill enough to be transferred to custodial institutions yet do not or cannot get along well in the general hospital and cannot return to their homes or live in society. They are a group with inadequate, incompetent, and incomplete personalities. They produce a hospital planning problem very different from that of the medical-surgical psychiatric hospital. The kind of institution required is different from both the general and the custodial type of hospital. The location should be on ample acreage not so far removed from population centers as to prohibit a quasi-normal atmosphere. The function of the institution is not to serve as a bridge between the general hospital and the insane asylum but rather to provide for the patient a channel back to normal life.

The second class of psychiatric patients who require a special hospital takes in the groups commonly called the insane and the criminally insane. These too require ample acreage, but in this case the facilities should be located away from population centers in districts that offer a maximum of privacy and quiet. Although the duration of custodial care for these groups may vary from indefinite to permanent, it should be remembered that a fair proportion of the patients may respond to treatment and may recover.

Another class of patients often included in the previous group but in reality requiring a very different type of planning and care comprises the mentally deficient types described as the feeble-minded. They are classified as morons, imbeciles, and idiots. Though hospital care within the walls of the project is essential, the predominant character of institutions for such patients is that of a training school. The location requirements are ample grounds and maximum privacy.

REQUIREMENTS

I. Psychiatric Clinic—*see* Chapter 36, "Dispensaries and Health Centers"

II. Psychiatric Department in the General Hospital—*see* Chapter 35, "Hospitals"

III. Psychiatric Hospital (Non-Custodial)

  A. Basic

    1. Administrative section

    2. Admission—provision for the introduction of patients to the hospital environment and for prompt examination, observation, and classification; employment of the talents of psychiatrists, psychologists, psychiatrically oriented physicians, surgeons, social service workers, technicians, and nurses

    3. Treatment facilities:

      a. Psychiatric: psychotherapy, physical therapy, recreational therapy, educational therapy, music therapy, occupational therapy, bibliotherapy

      b. Medical: general hospital facilities

    4. Nursing service units—generally grouped in three divisions: disturbed, semi-disturbed, and quiet; further divided as to male, female, and children

    5. Discharge service—for convalescents who are about to accomplish a return to normal life

6. Social service department—for investigation and follow-up
7. Visitors' service—means by which relatives and friends can maintain contact with patients
8. Housing for personnel
9. Utility service units

B. Architectural

1. Site free from noise and congestion and containing ample acreage for free planning and the creation of a controlled and peaceful atmosphere
2. Controlled circulation and constant supervision combined so as to give patients the maximum freedom
3. Patients' rooms, dining rooms, and lounges oriented to the best exposures
4. Wards undesirable, except that the disturbed can be housed in alcove arrangements under direct supervision of special staff members in larger rooms providing for three to four such patients; patients' rooms and furnishings designed to prevent self-injury but pleasingly proportioned and varying with the general type of patient involved in that section of the institution
5. Provision for three main groups of therapeutic treatments:
   a. Those *applied* by technicians directly to the patient; these involve the maximum in counsel from the applicators in order to bring about the architectural solution; *examples:* psychoanalysis, hydrotherapy, shock
   b. Those *directed* by technicians and requiring the co-operation and participation of the patient; these involve the architect's contribution in addition to the technician's counsel to obtain the architectural solution; *examples:* occupational therapy, group activities
   c. Those *absorbed* directly or indirectly by the patient himself; in this group the contribution of the architect is at its maximum; *examples:* architectural design, recreational therapy—the grounds, music
6. Total and detailed effect of the atmosphere created by the design, as manifested in scale, materials, colors, and proportions, as well as in units such as rooms, lounges, chapel, etc.

IV. Hospital for Chronic Cases of Mental Illness or Insanity (Custodial)

A. Basic
  1. All or in part the same as for the Psychiatric Hospital (III)
  2. Careful classification of special facilities based on logical cata-
     loguing of patients as to mental deterioration and/or instability
B. Architectural
  1. All or in part the same as for the Psychiatric Hospital (III)
  2. Policing added more emphatically to the circulation problem; less
     freedom
  3. Considerably more thought to construction details
  4. Great opportunity to improve design and planning on existing types
     to establish humane atmosphere in fact as well as in theory

V. Institution for the Feeble-Minded (Custodial)
  A. Basic
    1. Administrative section
    2. Admission—provision for diagnosis and a period of observation for
       classification; employment of the talents of psychiatrically oriented
       physicians, surgeons, social service workers, technicians, and
       nurses
    3. Two general classifications:
       a. Patients completely incapable of doing anything for themselves
       b. Patients capable of doing for themselves
    4. Treatment or training
       a. First type
          (1) For patients incapable of physical accomplishment—mental
              therapy
          (2) For patients incapable of mental accomplishment—physical
              therapy
       b. Second type
          (1) For patients capable mentally and physically to participate
              in recreation and to achieve some living habits
          (2) For patients capable of learning to do something useful
    5. Nursing service units—grouped in accordance with V, A, 4
    6. Visitors' service
    7. Discharge service for final training and preparation for return to
       the family
    8. Medical—general hospital facilities
  B. Architectural

1. Location preferably in the country, with ample acreage for expanding activities for a self-contained, sub-normal society requiring practically all the components of a normal society
2. Controlled circulation
3. Patients' rooms, dayrooms, school classrooms, all oriented to best exposures
4. Entire plant designed for occupational therapy in all trades and departments; schooling and living are one
5. One-story, residential units highly desirable, with a common dining unit
6. This type of institution is a school, not a hospital; the reason for its inclusion here rests primarily on the fact that the problems are the product of mental incompetence, a degree and type of mental illness requiring medical and psychiatric understanding as manifested in a quality of institutional planning

As Dr. Karl Menninger, in "The Future of Psychiatric Care in Hospitals," [1] has said:

Great mistakes have been made in the past by energetic planning boards which felt that it was only necessary to multiply previous experience by some breathtaking mathematical factor in order to make possible enormous colonies, beautifully landscaped and euphemistically labeled psychiatric hospitals. The one thing we are sure of at the moment is that the psychiatric hospital of the future will not be anything like that. . . . The trouble is that all architectural planning and construction have to be done in advance and are already out of date by the time the building is finished. Psychiatry is growing that rapidly. No one knows at the present time just what the structural form of the psychiatric hospital of the future, even of the near future should be.

This will explain the absence of specific illustrations, charts, photographs, and plans in the foregoing discussion.

TUBERCULOSIS SANATORIUMS

It is appropriate here, in view of the material on mental illnesses presented above, to state the connection between psychiatry and the problems attending the care and treatment of tuberculosis. Anyone who has observed patients afflicted with this disease cannot help but realize that other than organic manifestations are involved. In the tuberculosis sanatorium, sensitive doctors and

[1] *Modern Hospital*, Vol. 66 (1946), March, pp. 67–69.

nurses are constantly confronted with the high incidence of neuroses among such patients. Some of this is no doubt caused by the emotional shock of contracting the disease. But it has also been found that the individual constitution has a great deal to do with the development of tuberculosis. Undernourishment and fatigue resulting in emotional strain play an important part in the progress of the disease. And, if prior to its onset neurotic symptoms existed in the personality, these become accentuated by the patient's presence in a sanatorium and frequently increase in degree as the restrictions imposed by the illness are felt by the patient. All of which means that the tuberculosis sanatorium must be a mental therapeutic device as well as a facility for the treatment of the purely organic aspects of tuberculosis.

The history of the tuberculosis sanatorium contributes little toward an understanding of the functions of such an institution today. Changes in the concept of the disease have caused marked changes in the type of plant considered adequate. Architects have probably had more to do with the development of these sanatoriums from a medical point of view than have the doctors themselves, simply because the necessity to meet the modern concept made greater demands on the creative talent of the architect than on that of the medical technician. For sentimental reasons, however, at least one experimental phase should be pointed out.

About sixty years ago Dr. Edward Livingston Trudeau saw his brother die of "consumption," as the disease was then called, and found himself similarly afflicted. In order to die more comfortably and also with the hope of prolonging his days, he removed himself from his warm close room—and from the prevailing idea that the disease was a hereditary, non-infectious, and fatal one—to an Adirondack camp. He responded to the fresh air and outdoor life and lived to found the tuberculosis sanatorium movement in the United States. Here at Saranac Lake and from his own home-made incubator was produced the first artificial culture of the tubercle bacillus—a positive demonstration of the infectious character of the disease. The Trudeau sanatorium became the model for such facilities throughout the country, and all of them exemplified Dr. Trudeau's prescription—outdoor life and exercise in high altitudes. From the gradually evolved Trudeau practice, under which patients who were discharged as "arrested cases" returned to Saranac Lake for periodic check-ups and supplementary "cures," arose the modern concept of the diagnostic clinic.

Although the sanatorium at Trudeau contained the essential features of the modern institution for the treatment and control of tuberculosis, profound changes have occurred since its development and have created radical alterations in the physical plant. In specific cases as well as generally those changes have been as follows:

1. Abandonment of the policy of restricting occupancy to patients in the incipient stage of the disease, since experience has shown that the disease cannot be recognized at that early stage with any certainty

2. Dropping of the Trudeau "Spartan" exercise theory in favor of the modern "rest cure" method, as expressed in the transition from the single-cottage scheme to group planning with central facilities

3. Increase in the number of patients sent to sanatoriums in advanced stages of the disease, necessitating a degree of hospitalization which the cottage type cannot economically provide

4. Realization that the control of tuberculosis hinges on isolating all known cases (from incipient to terminal) from the healthy population, a principle which demands that the tuberculosis sanatorium take on more of the complexion of a general hospital than of the cottage-type sanatorium

5. Addition of a major unit—the clinic for out-patients as well as for in-patients—as a result of the introduction of the X ray as a factor in the diagnosis of tuberculosis and of an increase in the use of the laboratory, thus making the modern tuberculosis sanatorium at last a public health center for the control of the disease as well as for its treatment

The architect must realize that the complete book for the diagnosis, care, and treatment of tuberculosis has not yet been written. When that time comes it will be the signal that the disease is soon due for eradication. Before then, however, even more dynamic changes affecting the physical form of the sanatorium than have appeared in the second quarter of the twentieth century will probably emerge.

PROGRAM

Immunization methods so successfully introduced in connection with typhoid, diphtheria, and smallpox have not as yet materialized in the case of tuberculosis. But an important crusade is now going on in the tuberculosis field. Simply stated, it is an effort to wipe out tuberculosis by the process of going out and looking for it. It is well known that tuberculosis can usually be arrested if discovered early and treated adequately. Although early tuberculosis causes no symptoms and must be searched for, when it is found not only

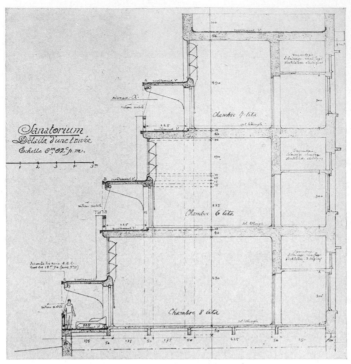

FIGURE 259.
FRANCO–AMERICAN
HOSPITAL,
LYONS, FRANCE.
SECTION THROUGH
SANATORIUM

Tony Garnier, architect

An early example of the terraced section which permits open-air balconies outside all patients' rooms.

From Garnier, *Les Grands Travaux de la ville de Lyon . . .*

can the disease in the individual be arrested but also the danger of its spreading to other persons can be reduced.

The United States Army demonstrated by the use of mass radiography the effectiveness of its case-finding program. In several states the crusade to search out the disease is concentrating on similar surveys of the entire population. This crusade has also manifested itself in the promotion of routine radiological chest examinations of all patients admitted to general hospitals and clinics; where this has been tried, the results have been dramatic. Despite well-meaning obstructionists, there is no doubt that the case-finding crusade will eventually attain its objectives. When it does, either the clinics of general hospitals or the out-patient departments of tuberculosis sanatoriums or hospitals will have to expand and replan for the assumption of the burden. Consequently, in programming the sanatorium it is extremely important to investigate the sponsors' attitude and desires with respect to the public health phase of tuberculosis in the community in question. This will affect the location of the project as well as its internal arrangement.

The considerations that would lead to a complete program for a tuberculosis sanatorium would approximate those for a self-contained community.

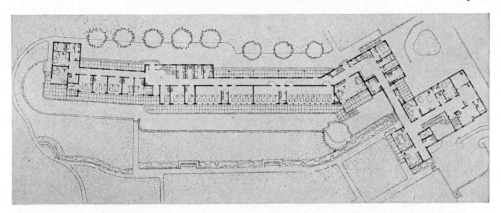

FIGURE 260. WAIBLINGEN SANATORIUM, STUTTGART, GERMANY. PLAN

Richard Döcker, architect

An excellent example of a well-planned sanatorium which has had a profound influence on later buildings. From Döcker, *Terrassentyp* . .

Such a sanatorium is not merely a hospital; it is more than a hospital. The needs of patients will include not only diagnosis and treatment but also provision for work, education, play, and rehabilitation. Every physical, emotional, and spiritual need of every type of patient, irrespective of the stage of the disease, must be met. It is not too difficult to provide the ambulatory patient with facilities for a complete community life. But the chronic or bedridden patient, whom it is comparatively easy to service with hospital facilities, must also be provided with substitutes for community life—a fact that is often overlooked in sanatorium planning.

The patients will generally fall into one of five principal groups:

1. Out-patient group:
   a. Patients who have been treated at the sanatorium and have recovered sufficiently to return to their homes but who return to the clinic for treatment and check-up
   b. Day patients who return to their homes at night
   c. Individuals who may or may not become patients after diagnosis at the clinic

2. Terminal group:
   a. Patients in whom the disease has advanced to such a point that they are about to die
   b. Patients whose general condition may be good and who, though per-

FIGURE 261. WAIBLINGEN SANATORIUM, STUTTGART, GERMANY. VIEW OF TERRACE

Richard Döcker, architect

The terraces are carefully studied to ensure a certain amount of protection and yet permit sunlight to penetrate into the rooms.   From Döcker, *Terrassentyp* . . .

> haps ambulatory, are chronically ill with tuberculosis and will never recover
>
> 3. Acute-stage group—Bed patients who will respond or have responded to treatment and will eventually recover
> 4. Semi-ambulant group—Patients who have progressed from the acute stage and can leave their beds part of the time and thus minister in part to their own needs, such as going to dining rooms for meals, to bathrooms, and to recreation rooms
> 5. Ambulant group—Patients who lead an almost normal life; except for the necessity of treatment from time to time and of regular living habits, these patients have the freedom of the grounds and facilities

There is no argument as to the propriety of grouping patients in the manner described. Tuberculosis is a disease that requires a long period of treatment, and there has been ample opportunity over a period of years to arrive at these classifications. Not every institution, however, has sufficient capacity to provide complete facilities for every group; anything less than 300 beds would make it economically unsound either to plan or to attempt to administer treatment on such a highly developed basis. Smaller sanatoriums have been and will continue to be built, and the ingenuity of the planner will be taxed to create a sufficiently fluid scheme to provide for the various stages of the disease in the best possible manner under the circumstances.

REQUIREMENTS

A. Basic

1. Administration—general offices and admission offices; offices for directors and assistants, supervisor of nurses and assistants, medical records, and social service
2. Clinic—various special and general examining rooms, history room, radiography and fluoroscopy room, pneumothorax room, laboratory, surgery (major and minor), dental room, pharmacy, waiting and dressing rooms, staff room, and library
3. Nursing units—private (preferably), semi-private, and ward rooms; nurses' station, diet kitchen, utility rooms, pneumothorax and "taps" room, interns' quarters, dayrooms, lamp room, laboratory, and sun deck
4. Other medical facilities—central medical supply, morgue and autopsy room, sputum disposal system
5. Dietary—patient, staff, visitor, and help's kitchen or kitchens, dining rooms, and/or cafeterias; day and bulk storage
6. Housekeeping—laundry, sewing room, repair shop, general storage and supply
7. Special storage—for X-ray films, anesthetics
8. Occupational therapy—classrooms for arts and crafts, hobby shop
9. Recreational therapy—auditorium with stage and motion-picture facilities, lounge, game rooms, library, exterior walks and gardens
10. Mechanical units—heating and air conditioning
11. Staff living facilities—for director, resident physicians, interns, nurses, technicians; to include lounges, libraries, game rooms, tennis courts
12. Help's living facilities—to include recreational facilities

B. Architectural

1. The planning objective must be primarily to create ideal living conditions for the patients and to support these conditions with an accessible and efficient arrangement of the common medical and utility facilities. This objective can be achieved only by obtaining a site sufficiently large and attractive to stimulate the planner and ultimately inspire the patients

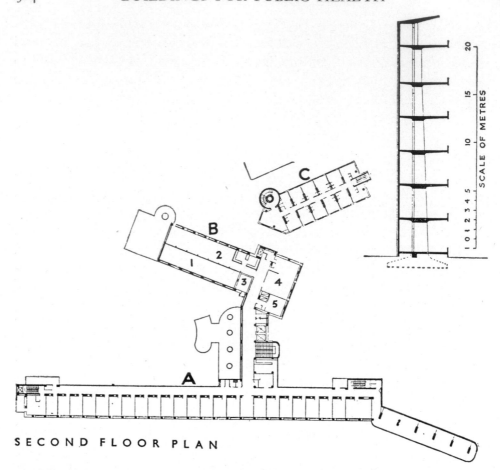

SECOND FLOOR PLAN

FIGURE 262. SANATORIUM, PAIMONI, FINLAND. GENERAL PLAN, FLOOR PLAN AND SECTION

Alvar & Aino Aalto, architects

A: Patients' Wing; B: Administration, Therapies, and Social Wing; C: Service.

The use of reinforced concrete and extensive cantilevering permits a building of considerable height to be furnished with balconies on every floor. The entire plan is well studied for the grouping of related facilities and for efficiency of service.   From *Architectural Record*

with a sense of beauty and of privacy. Orientation of the patients' rooms to the most ideal exposure is mandatory and cannot be compromised. The modern method of treatment prescribes emotional tranquillity, physical rest, wholesome food, fresh air, and regular living habits. It is these conditions which, added to the medical and surgical care, make the tuberculosis sanatorium more than a hospital. (See Figs. 262–268.)

2. Nursing units: The proportion of private rooms to multi-bed wards is

FIGURE 263.
SANATO-
RIUM,
PAIMONI,
FINLAND.
EXTERIOR

Alvar & Aino
Aalto, architects

The dramatic
brilliance of the
structure rising
daringly from
the surrounding
evergreens.

Courtesy
Museum of
Modern Art,
New York

a matter of opinion. The ideal arrangement would be 100 per cent private rooms; if this is not feasible, semi-private and ward rooms may be included as circumstances demand. The planning of each patient's room must be imaginative as to fenestration, storage space, furnishings, and color, and opportunity should be given to the patients (most of whom stay for at least five months) to "personalize" the room with their own possessions. The room itself is incomplete without a balcony at least large enough to accommodate the patient's bed.

The nursing unit for terminal cases should be isolated for psychological reasons. Acute-disease units should invariably contain a lavatory in each room and a toilet if economically possible. Units for semi-ambulant patients should have common dining facilities, dayrooms, and a lounge, with recreational facilities near by. The ambulant-group unit can be comparatively detached. Here the patients have reached a stage where they can practically care for themselves and, except for occasional medical and surgical treatment, are free to live normally on the grounds. This unit forms the link between the sanatorium and a return to normal life.

In all these units provision must be made for a sputum disposal system.

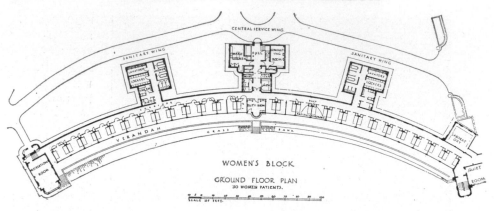

WOMEN'S BLOCK

GROUND FLOOR PLAN

30 WOMEN PATIENTS.

SCALE OF FEET

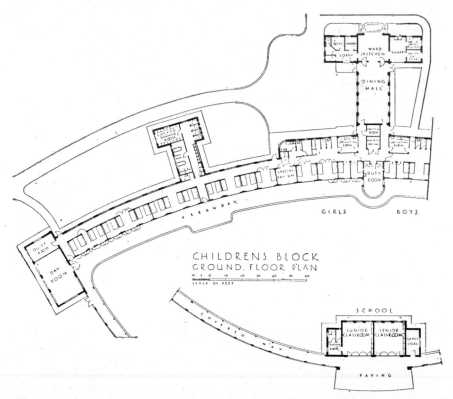

CHILDRENS BLOCK
GROUND. FLOOR PLAN

SCALE OF FEET

SCHOOL

FIGURE 264. TUBERCULOSIS HOSPITAL, HAREFIELD, ENGLAND. PLANS OF WOMEN'S AND CHILDREN'S PAVILIONS

W. T. Curtis, architect

A low and spreading scheme befitting a quiet rural site.   From *Architect and Building News*

FIGURE 265.
TUBERCULOSIS
HOSPITAL,
HAREFIELD,
ENGLAND.
EXTERIORS OF
WOMEN'S AND
CHILDREN'S BLOCKS

W. T. Curtis, architect

Quiet simplicity and the serenity of long horizontal lines.

Photographs Herbert Felton, courtesy *Architect and Building News*

There are several types in existence, and the selection of one of these will be made by the medical director.

3. Occupational therapy: Occupational therapy facilities should not be merely glorified storage rooms or left-over spaces. They are an essential part of the treatment, may assist in producing the emotional tranquillity which the occupation itself is designed to give, and frequently are a means of the patient's learning a new and more suitable pursuit for the time when he leaves the sanatorium. Such units should be taken on as a design and planning problem, and the result should be as substantial as that which prevails in the best trade schools.

4. Recreational therapy: Recreational therapy units are psychologically of tremendous importance. An effort should be made to create the idea that the patient is really "going somewhere" when he enters and utilizes

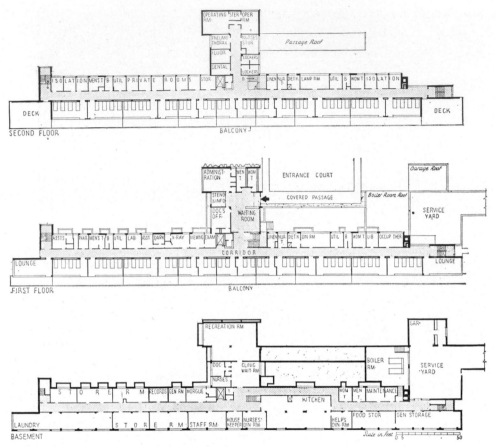

FIGURE 266. SANATORIUM, WAUKEGAN, ILLINOIS. PLANS

William A. Ganster and Offices of W. L. Pereira, associated architects

Careful planning to provide efficient service and adequate privacy for patients' rooms as well
as ample social areas.   From *Architectural Forum*

the lounges, game room, and auditorium. Variations in color and type of
furnishings and a fresh orientation are extremely helpful. The landscaping should be planned to produce interesting walks, covered stopping
points, and areas for mild outdoor games.

5. Special medical facilities: It should be understood that the tuberculosis
sanatorium must to a large extent be equivalent to a general hospital,
since the patients will frequently have to be treated for other illnesses.
Notwithstanding the fact that it is a custodial institution, practically all
of the general hospital facilities will be required. In addition the following are mandatory requirements:

FIGURE 267.

SANATORIUM,

WAUKEGAN,

ILLINOIS.

TWO EXTERIORS

William A. Ganster and Offices of W. L. Pereira, associated architects

Human scale, serenity, and attractive details were the ends desired.

Photographs
Hedrich-Blessing

a. In the surgery section—suction apparatus as well as at least one 36-inch instrument sterilizer for a bronchoscope and its accessories; provision for oxygen tents and a "Drinker" (iron lung) apparatus; a blood bank and plasma storage, pneumothorax and tap treatment rooms; a fluoroscopy room

b. In the nursing units—pneumothorax and tap treatment rooms in each unit if the hospital is sufficiently large; sputum disposal

6. Visitors: Since the patient is likely to be in the hospital for a long period of time, visitors—contrary to the practice in acute-disease general hospitals—are encouraged to come at regular intervals. Much can be done architecturally with plan forms, furnishings, and color to keep the visitors' spirits at a high level and thus produce a corresponding effect on the patients' morale.

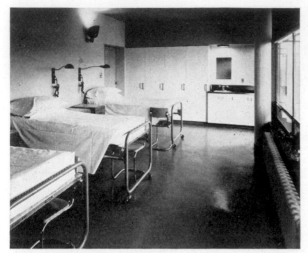

FIGURE 268. SANATORIUM,
WAUKEGAN, ILLINOIS.
WAITING ROOM AND
TYPICAL WARD

William A. Ganster and Offices of
W. L. Pereira, associated architects

Interiors that not only are pleasant
to be in, but in addition stimulate
the desire for recovery and normal
life.   Photographs
           Hedrich-Blessing

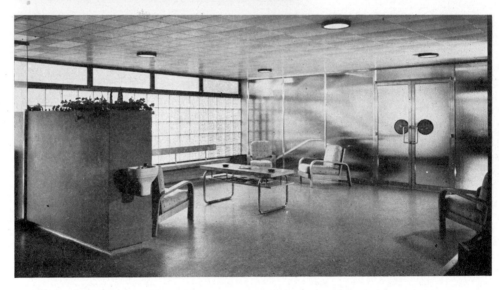

SUMMARY

The tuberculosis sanatorium should serve three purposes:
1. Centralize the tuberculosis control program in the community
2. Fulfill the requirements for a modern chest-disease hospital as well as those of a tuberculosis hospital
3. Effectively promote rehabilitation among its discharged patients

REST HOMES

Probably the most neglected institution in the whole range of medical facili-

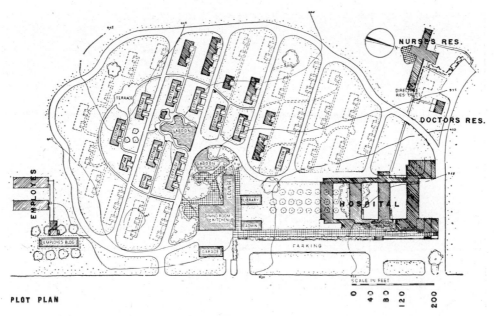

PLOT PLAN

FIGURE 269. MOTION PICTURE COUNTRY HOUSE, SAN FERNANDO VALLEY, CALIFORNIA. GENERAL PLAN

Offices of W. L. Pereira, architects; Frank Gruy, associate

A planned country village for the elderly, designed to furnish health facilities as well as social and residential areas, pleasant and varied.   Courtesy W. L. Pereira

ties is the so-called rest home. Shocking conditions are commonly found here. Although some states have required such institutions to conform to their respective hospital regulation acts, the situation in general remains deplorable. There are reasons for the existence of this kind of medical facility, but until the various types are defined and the organizations graduate from the ancient residences where most of them exist the rest home will remain in ill repute.

Institutions are required for the care of the long-term patient who can or wants to pay for his care. He is sound in mind, not old enough for a so-called old people's home. Either he has no home or the situation at home is not conducive to his happiness. His condition may be the result of paralysis, from which he will never recover, or he may have some other chronic disease which so limits his activity that his home cannot accommodate him. Institutions are necessary also for the indigent patient or for the pensioner who in reaching old age needs to live without responsibilities and yet requires care. One successful experiment along these lines is the industry-maintained Motion Picture Relief Fund Country House at Woodland Hills, in the San Fernando Valley, California (Figs. 269–272). It consists of a small hospital and infirmary, a convales-

FIGURE 270. MOTION PICTURE COUNTRY HOUSE, SAN FERNANDO VALLEY, CALIFORNIA. HOSPITAL EXTERIOR AND COLONNADE OF LOUNGE AND DINING HALL BUILDING

Offices of W. L. Pereira, architects; Frank Gruy, associate

Photographs Shirley C. Burden

cent unit, bungalow residences, and central dining, library, occupational therapy, and recreation units. Its "guests" must have attained the age of sixty-five and have served the profession honorably for a period of years. The hospital and the convalescent unit also serve thousands of other medical indigents in the industry who later return to useful work.

CONVALESCENT HOMES OR HOSPITALS

Fifty per cent of the acute-disease beds in general hospitals are occupied by chronically ill or convalescent patients. No one will deny that in the chain of

FIGURE 271.
MOTION PICTURE
COUNTRY HOUSE,
SAN FERNANDO
VALLEY, CALIFORNIA.
EXTERIOR OF LOUNGE
AND DINING HALL
BUILDING AND
INTERIOR OF LOUNGE

Offices of W. L. Pereira,
architects; Frank Gruy,
associate

Photographs
Maynard L. Parker

medical facilities to be provided a staggering number of convalescent units are needed. These should be institutions that can deliver care at a much lower rate than can the acute-disease general hospital with its vast equipment and large staff. Such a convalescent unit should be neither a hospital in the accepted sense of the word nor a hotel, but a happy combination of both.

SUGGESTED ADDITIONAL READING FOR CHAPTER 37

Alexander, Franz, M.D., and Thomas Morton French, M.D., *Psychoanalytic Therapy* (New York: Ronald Press [1946]).

Bachmeyer, Arthur C., M.D., and Gerhard Hartman (editors), *The Hospital in Modern Society* (New York: Commonwealth Fund, 1943).

FIGURE 272.
MOTION PICTURE
COUNTRY HOUSE,
SAN FERNANDO
VALLEY, CALIFORNIA.
TWO VIEWS OF THE
COTTAGES AND THE
LAGOON

Offices of W. L. Pereira,
architects; Frank Gruy,
associate

Photographs (above)
Shirley C. Burden;
(below) Maynard L.
Parker

Goldwater, S. S., M.D., *On Hospitals* (New York: Macmillan, 1947).
Modern Attitudes in Psychiatry, No. X in "New York Academy of Medicine Lectures to the Laity" (New York: Columbia University Press [1946]).
Rosenfield, Isadore, *Hospitals—Integrated Design* (New York: Reinhold, 1947).

PERIODICALS

"ABC's of Standardization," in special issue "For Better Psychiatric Care," *Modern Hospital*, Vol. 64 (1945), May, pp. 56–57.
Ebaugh, Franklin G., M.D., and Charles A. Rymer, M.D., "Psychiatric Facilities within General Hospitals," *Modern Hospital*, Vol. 55 (1940), August, pp. 71–74.
Felix, Robert H., M.D., "The Psychiatric Hospital Plays a Part in Public Health," *Modern Hospital*, Vol. 66 (1946), February, pp. 67–70.
Haigh, Gerard Victor, "A Plan for Improving Hospital Treatment of Psychiatric Patients," *Modern Hospital*, Vol. 65 (1945), December, pp. 65–69.
Hasenbush, Lester Lee, and Grace G. Hasenbush, "A Plan for Improving Hospital Treatment of Psychiatric Patients" and bibliography, *Modern Hospital*, Vol. 65 (1945), November, pp. 65–71.

"Hospitals Are for Humans," Building Types Study No. 126, *Architectural Record*, Vol. 101 (1947), June, pp. 104–36.

Lozoff, Milton, M.D., and Marjorie Morse Lozoff, "Mediocrity Is the Charge against Psychiatric Hospitals," *Modern Hospital*, Vol. 66 (1946), April, pp. 59–62.

Menninger, Karl, M.D., "The Future of Psychiatric Care," *Modern Hospital*, Vol. 64 (1945), May, pp. 43–45.

"Mental Hospitals," Building Types Study No. 166, *Architectural Record*, Vol. 108 (1950), October, pp. 123–57; especially Paul Haun, M.D., "A Program for a Psychiatric Hospital," pp. 136–42.

"Psychiatric Hospitals," *Architectural Record*, Vol. 84 (1938), August, pp. 105–10.

"Ten Steps toward Better Care for Psychiatric Patients," *Modern Hospital*, Vol. 66 (1946), March, pp. 67–69.

Wendell, Lulu, "If I Am Ever Mentally Ill Again, Perhaps the Hospital Will Be Different," *Modern Hospital*, Vol. 66 (1946), May, pp. 49–53.

NOWHERE has applied science made more changes in the last century than in the field of transportation. In 1850 the building of railroads had hardly more than begun; now almost the entire civilized world is woven together by their trackage. Power-driven vessels have improved markedly in size, speed, and efficiency, and their numbers have vastly increased. Two entirely new methods of transportation—by automobile and by airplane—have made over and, in the middle of the twentieth century, continue to make over the face of the world and the habits of its people.

The result for architects is, of course, a host of new building types. Even the railroad station, although it had taken dignified and efficient architectural form in England in the 1830's, today in serving new and vastly multiplied purposes is a far different building from what it was then. Similarly, different kinds of piers and ports are necessary for the crowded commerce of steam and Diesel-driven vessels from those that sufficed a century ago; the great size of modern ships and the multifarious applications of power to problems of unloading and loading have revolutionized the problem. Moreover, the new demands for efficient city planning have forced a reconsideration of the plans of harbors and harbor districts and of the best relationship of piers to railroads and trucking thoroughfares.

The automobile has created an even more radical change in transportation problems. Garages and service stations are only the beginning; for the continual increase in motor traffic, by truck and bus and private car, has made obsolete the road systems of half the world and has forced the planning of parkways and through ways, the relocation and redesign of existing roads and streets, and the building of bridges and tunnels to accommodate the whizzing, crowded traffic.

But the most novel problems have derived from the growth of aviation. This development is as yet in its infancy; the increasing speed and size of planes seem to demand continual changes in airport areas and layouts. Major airports have grown to such enormous size that space for them can be found only in sections relatively far from town and city centers, and as a result the time spent in reaching the airport by train or bus or motorcar adds so much to the total travel time that the advantages of airplane speed are often lost except for comparatively long hauls. Perhaps this is a temporary stage; it is quite possible that some revolutionary invention or discovery may reverse the trend. So fluid is this problem that any treatise concerning it is necessarily time-bound by the date of its composition.

In a sense this is true of all modern structures, but it is specially so in connection with those dealing with transportation. If new types of midget automobile become popular, the whole problem of parking and of garage design will change. If foolproof private planes become common, country-house plans will have to include a shelter for them, as they do for cars today. If swifter, more efficient helicopters come into general use, landing places for them may have to be contrived where airports for the conventional airplane are impossible. And, if the ear-shattering noise from large planes is reduced, one great objection to the close-in landing area will be overcome.

The chapters in this section cannot, therefore, be final. But they do indicate many of the technical problems and point toward their solution. It is the architect's task to solve these problems in ways that will make the solutions—often necessarily monumental in scale—as beautiful and as significant as is their importance in the world today.

AYMAR EMBURY II, author of the chapter "Bridges and Highway Architecture," is a New York architect of long and wide experience in many types of structure. He graduated as a civil engineer and is deeply interested in the design of engineering structures. He has been associated with several engineers in the design of numerous distinguished bridges, including the Triborough, Bronx-Whitestone, and Henry Hudson bridges in New York, the Rainbow Bridge at Niagara Falls, and bridges over the Chesapeake and Delaware Canal. He has also designed the architectural elements in connection with many highways.

ALFRED FELLHEIMER, F.A.I.A., A.S.C.E., author of the chapter "Railroad Stations," is a member of the New York firm of Fellheimer & Wagner, architects and engineers. He has been intimately connected with the design of many large railroad stations, including the Grand Central Station in New York, and his firm was the architect of the Union Station at Buffalo and that at Cincinnati as well as of many smaller railway structures. He is the author of the article "Railway Passenger Terminals" in the 14th edition of the *Encyclopaedia Britannica*.

THOMAS E. GREACEN II, A.I.A., author of the chapter "Airports," is an architect practicing in Houston, Texas. During the Second World War he was in charge of airfield planning for the Headquarters of the United States Army Air Forces, and since that time he has designed several large permanent military fields in the Southwest. His studies of the relation of wind direction to airplane performance form the basis for the methods generally used in determining runway orientation.

ALBERT FREDERIC HEINO, A.I.A., author of the chapter "Air Stations," is the head of the architectural firm of Albert Heino & Associates, in Chicago. He served United Air Lines as Architect and Director of Design for Buildings and Air Ports until 1948 and as its representative has had wide experience in air-station planning, consulting with various municipal boards throughout the United States. He has contributed articles on the subject to architectural and other periodicals.

CHARLES R. DENISON, A.S.C.E., author of the chapter "Seaports and Ship Terminals," is a consultant on port development and construction. Immediately after the Second World War he was Management Control Officer of the Bremen Port Control; since that time he has served as Port Engineer for the Research and Development Division of the United States Maritime Commission and as Project Engineer for the Port of Boston Authority. He was twice the chairman of the Port Development and Construction Committee of the American Association of Port Authorities, and he has been a visiting lecturer at the United States Naval War College. He is the author of many technical papers on his subject.

J. GORDON CARR, A.I.A., author of the chapter "Bus Stations," is a New York architect. He has designed numerous types of transportation facilities, as well as many projects involving the mass movement of crowds, and has published numerous articles on this and related subjects.

ITALO WILLIAM RICCIUTI, A.I.A., author of the chapter "Garages and Service Stations," is a member of the architectural firm of Ricciuti, Stoffle & Associates, in New Orleans. He was for some years chief architect for the Pan American Petroleum Company. During this period and in his subsequent private practice he has designed a large number of buildings dealing with automotive transportation. He is a visiting lecturer at the School of Architecture of Tulane University, a devoted student of the early architecture of Louisiana and New Orleans, and the author of *New Orleans and Its Environs* (New York: Helburn, 1938).

38

Bridges and Highway Architecture

By AYMAR EMBURY II

THE FIRST QUARTER of the twentieth century saw the development of three factors which have greatly influenced current bridge design: the automobile, reinforced concrete, and the new idiom in architectural expression.

INFLUENCE OF THE AUTOMOBILE

Of the factors mentioned the automobile is infinitely the most important. Without the automobile there would have been no reason for freeways (express highways for trucks and private cars)—when traffic moves at four miles an hour, collisions are not very serious—and railway crossovers would have been the only ones required. Before the days of automobiles there were no long-span highway bridges, most vehicular traffic was local, and ferries were good enough for the small amount of long-distance horse-drawn traffic. All travel and all freight movement was by rail, so that the only bridges really necessary were those which served local traffic from the farms and factories to the freight yards of the railroads. These bridges were narrow and light, for poor roads forbade the movement of heavy or heavily loaded vehicles.

The automobile created a need for a new type of highway and as a result the freeway for long-distance high-speed travel gradually evolved. The freeway requires easy curves of long radius, means of access and exit which may be used without slowing up the flow of through traffic, separation of traffic running in opposite directions by center islands varying in width from four feet to a half mile, the complete elimination of grade crossings either by underpasses or overpasses, and the construction of bridges solely for highway traffic over rivers and bays formerly crossed only by ferries.

Increase in Construction. It is obvious that the tremendous amount of parkway and freeway construction occasioned by the increase in automobile traffic in the second quarter of the century profoundly influenced bridge design—at first by its very volume, which gave endless opportunity for engineering education by the trial-and-error method. It took the Greek architects three hundred years to bring the simple temple form to its perfection in the Parthenon; temples were not built every day, and refinements in design can only be based on precedent. But highway bridges in the United States have been built literally by the thousand, and the happiest of the results have been immediately made known to the engineering profession through publication and by exposition; all designers have profited, or at least have had an opportunity to profit, by that experience. This development has by no means been confined to the United States, although the amount of new construction in Europe has been much less, partly because the density of automobile traffic there is not so great and partly because the masonry bridges (many of great age) adequate for the European densities already existed over all narrow or shallow waterways. Much of the most interesting modern bridge design, however, has been achieved abroad, notably by Hitler's engineers of the military freeways—*Autobahnen*—and by the French and Swiss engineers in long-span concrete construction.

Load Requirements. Perhaps even more important in the effect produced on design is the new set of requirements for highway bridges which has resulted in small bridges becoming heavier and long bridges lighter than they used to be. Whereas all previous highway bridges were designed for horse-drawn loads, never in excess of five tons, modern traffic requires a bridge that will carry at least twenty-five-ton loads. On the other hand, all long bridges in the past were railway bridges designed not only to carry the heavy concentrated loads of locomotives but also to withstand the terrific impact of these loads moving at high speed; today, however, highway bridges of comparable spans may be very much lighter and more airy and graceful than the massive and solid designs of the railway span.

REINFORCED CONCRETE AND BRIDGE MAINTENANCE

A second major design factor on which much stress is placed today is maintenance. It was always desirable to design structures which did not require constant painting, cleaning, and repairing, but when almost all bridges (except railroad bridges) were owned by the communities in which they existed their maintenance was effected with comparative ease; there were not many bridges anyway. Today, when freeways extend for hundreds of miles—averaging a bridge of some kind to every second mile—and are operated by state agencies dependent for money upon legislative whims, it is obvious that low maintenance costs are essential. It is here that reinforced concrete has value.

ARCHITECTURAL EXPRESSION

The third factor mentioned at the beginning of this chapter as having a profound influence on modern bridge design is the current architectural idiom, which seems singularly well adapted to engineering structures. That is not to say that excellent bridges were not designed in complete conformity with any one of the various architectural styles of the past—the Renaissance arch at Ronda is undoubtedly the most beautiful bridge structure in the world— or that, even after the advent of steel, good designers did not produce bridges of great aesthetic excellence. In New York the Manhattan Bridge is an example of the latter. Designed by Gustav Lindenthal as engineer and Thomas Hastings as architect, this bridge is a felicitous architectural expression of the inherent engineering requirements; the towers and roadway are not without extraneous ornament, but it is ornament that adorns without confusing and is admirably in character with its material. Above all, the Manhattan anchorage, lost in the East Side slums and seen by no one, is one of the great monuments of the city; although dressed in classic costume, its design still completely expresses the interplay of forces which require an anchorage to be of certain minimum weights and dimensions.

Such a design is now inconceivable. We all must move with the spirit of our times, and to an architect the only genuinely satisfying work is that which expresses the current mood; even those men who are regarded by the radical fringe as hopeless conservatives do work which twenty five years ago would have been considered as extraordinarily advanced even by the radical fringe of that day. Fortunately the modern idiom with its emphasis on clean lines, on structure, and on the elimination of ornament is almost ideal as a treatment for engineering works.

COLLABORATION BY ENGINEER AND ARCHITECT

Fortunately also, the communities and the engineers whom they employ are at last fully alive to the fact that bridges are the most seen and probably the longest-lived of all architectural expressions and accordingly deserve the utmost skill in their aesthetic design. Therefore—though here we have the same variance in quality that we have in buildings—all parkway bridges and most

FIGURE 273.
PRIMITIVE
SUSPENSION BRIDGE,
KUANHIEN,
SZECHUAN,
CHINA

From Boerschmann,
Picturesque China,
courtesy
Coward-McCann

FIGURE 274.
BROOKLYN BRIDGE,
NEW YORK

John A. Roebling,
engineer

Photograph Ewing
Galloway

freeway bridges have profited by (or suffered from) architectural advice as well as engineering design. Further, where formerly the engineer used to call on the architect merely in connection with what were considered "architectural problems," such as railings, pylons, masonry approaches, and ornament intended (and sometimes successful) as decoration, nowadays the best and wisest of our engineers make the design a true partnership product and the architect is permitted—even urged—to give his opinion as to the type of bridge most suited to the site and, after this decision has been made, to study the exact shape and arrangement of members in the type selected.

BRIDGE TYPES

In current use there are six types of *fixed* bridges: suspension, truss, cantilever, girder, arch, and rigid-frame. Of *movable* bridges there are two main types: the bascule and the lift-span; in addition, swing and rolling bridges are sometimes employed. As between a fixed bridge and a movable one, the public convenience will determine which should be employed. In general, a movable bridge will be used only over little-used waterways and where the operating expense is not of primary importance, because all movable bridges require three shifts of watchmen and operators whereas the fixed bridge needs none. Within these two main classes the choice of type is usually governed by the cost; since this cannot be precisely determined in advance, however, the aesthetic factor may be the decisive one.

FIXED BRIDGES

SUSPENSION BRIDGES

Of the fixed bridges, the suspension bridge was, if not the earliest type, at least the one that was developed most widely and independently in all parts of the world (Figs. 273–276). Among primitive peoples it was used by the Incas in their highways in pre-Columbian Peru and by the savages of the Burmese highlands, and in modern times it has been a common type, especially in the United States, where it has been carried to its present state of perfection. The chief difference between the design of primitive and modern bridges lies in the present use of stiffening trusses which distribute the weights of the moving vehicles from one hanger to another. Without such trusses the bridge naturally would sag at the point where the weight is applied, so that a vehicle crossing the bridge would always be at the bottom of the sag and going uphill. Yet the impressive George Washington Bridge in New York is of the more primitive type of design without stiffening trusses; here, however, the weight of the floor is so great that the added load of any vehicle is negligible—like that of a fly on a clothesline.

The first step in the development of the modern suspension bridge was taken by Thomas Telford when he designed the Menai Bridge in Wales. This bridge is supported on cables, not of wire but of bars pinned together end to end. Before it was begun, Telford set up one of these cables over a valley and actually tested it for strength, deformation, and other factors on which data could be obtained; as a result he was able to solve, or partially solve, the problem of sag under heavy loads by using many hangers spaced very closely.

FIGURE 275. EARLIER AND MORE RECENT SUSPENSION BRIDGES

LEFT: Manhattan Bridge, New York. Gustav Lindenthal, engineer; Carrère & Hastings, architects. Photograph Henri H. Davis, courtesy Aymar Embury II. RIGHT: Oakland Bay Bridge, San Francisco, California. C. H. Purcell, engineer; T. L. Pflueger, architect. Photograph Ewing Galloway.

This was the beginning of the scientific study of suspension bridges, the first grain in the great heap of knowledge we have accumulated; but the end is not yet, and the trial-and-error method continues. Mathematics and formulas can be used to determine what happens in certain cases, but such formulas are empirical—based on the results of tests and observations—and cannot yet be relied upon fully; witness the Tacoma Bridge, designed by an engineer who was a genius in mathematics but had no data from which he could calculate the effect of a pulsating wind. One reason that the Roeblings, father and son, were great engineers is because they both perceived, not exactly but very clearly, that the wind might cause a disaster and therefore that if a bridge were stiffened by "weight, girders, trusses, and stays" it would stand. In their design of the Brooklyn Bridge they included trusses as well as diagonal stays, although the center trusses are of different heights from those at the sides. Here they were obviously feeling their way forward rather than acting on precise knowledge. John and Washington Roebling were not only great engineers but great architects as well; the Brooklyn Bridge was at once recognized as a pattern of

FIGURE 276.

BRONX-WHITESTONE BRIDGE, NEW YORK

O. H. Ammann, chief engineer; Allston Dana, engineer of design; Aymar Embury II, architect

Photograph Richard Averill Smith, courtesy Triborough Bridge and Tunnel Authority

beauty, and after sixty-six years it so remains. Incidentally, the first use of trusses in a suspension bridge was in the Lambeth Bridge over the Thames in 1862.

TRUSS BRIDGES

The truss bridge is a peculiarly American concept, although the truss principle was probably discovered in Italy, perhaps by Palladio.[1] In the early days in the United States, when the population was bursting outward in all directions, there was a great demand for local highway bridges. Europe was already served by bridges with brick and stone arches; in this new country, where brick was scarce and labor for stone cutting impossible to procure, wood was plentiful and good. It could be easily worked and was extremely strong and enduring; moreover, wooden bridges could be quickly erected. Particularly in the hilly country of New England and northern New York, many wooden truss bridges a hundred or more years old still exist in a good state of preservation; in many cases they are capable of carrying the modern highway load as easily as they do the horse and buggy for which they were designed. A large proportion of those old bridges use the lattice trusses invented—or at least patented—by the architect Ithiel Town; the others use the Burr and Howe

---

[1] Primitive truss bridges may have been used by the ancient Romans, for certain reliefs on the Column of Trajan seem to indicate an understanding of the truss principle. (Ed.)

FIGURE 277.

EARLY AMERICAN
TRUSSED BRIDGES

ABOVE: Covered bridge,
Biglersville, Pennsylvania.
Photograph Ewing Gal-
loway. BELOW: Diagram,
Town Truss. From Shaw,
Civil Architecture. . .

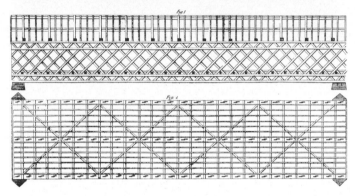

trusses, also patented (Fig. 277). One curious feature of some of these old
bridges is that they are composed of a tied arch attached to the trusses, so that
the structural effect is precisely like that in one of the more recent designs—
the arch at St. Georges, Delaware—although between them there is little similarity in appearance. Truss bridges today are somewhat out of favor, although
when as well designed as the K-braced bridge at Morgantown, Louisiana, they
are genuinely lovely. (See Figs. 277, 278.)

CANTILEVER BRIDGES

The cantilever is a development of the truss, or rather it is a pair of trusses,
each balanced on its foundation, leaning toward each other and supporting on
their finger tips, as it were, a short connecting span. The cantilever bridge is
strong and moderately inexpensive; it can be used for very long spans, but on
the whole it is not so susceptible of exciting aesthetic treatment as are other
types (Figs. 280–282).

FIGURE 278. CANOE PLACE BRIDGE, SHINNECOCK CANAL, LONG ISLAND, NEW YORK

Courtesy Long Island Railroad Co.

GIRDER BRIDGES

The first of all bridges must have been a fallen tree which served as a girder; it was early recognized, however, that two parallel trees were better than one, and from that simple beginning came unchanged in principle the twentieth-century girder bridge. Girder bridges, including those with simple rolled girders and others with plate girders, are the most used of bridges designed to carry heavy loads over short spans (Figs. 283–285). The Menai girder bridge is one of the oldest, but it is one which we think of as modern in design. Until about 1900, steel was high in price as compared with labor, and trusses were commonly employed where today we find girders; the elevated railroad in New York was carried on lattice trusses (or lattice girders, as they were sometimes called) where today we would use rolled beams. Even the plate girder for many uses is now being supplanted by beams; the steel companies are rolling 36-inch H beams of incredible strength and of practically any length. One of the newer highway viaducts is said to be composed of 36-inch rolled beams supported on bents 120 feet apart, but although the structure is perfectly safe it is so flexible that the design probably will not be repeated.

Spans of such length could not even be attempted without involving the principle of continuity, which though long recognized by engineers has only recently been brought into common use. In simple girder spans the beam or girder is supported at each end, but in continuous spans the beam or girder is supported not at the ends but at points inside the ends so that the ends them-

FIGURE 279. COOS BAY BRIDGE,
OREGON. GENERAL VIEW AND DETAIL

Courtesy Oregon State Highway
Commission

selves form a sort of cantilever. The depth of the girder—together with its weight—is therefore much reduced, with gains both in appearance and in cost. Excellent examples are those found among the overpasses of the German *Autobahnen*. The trim, tailored appearance of these bridges is a quality which the German engineers have sought for and attained more often than engineers in the United States.

When the design has to provide for railroad loads, the old-fashioned plate

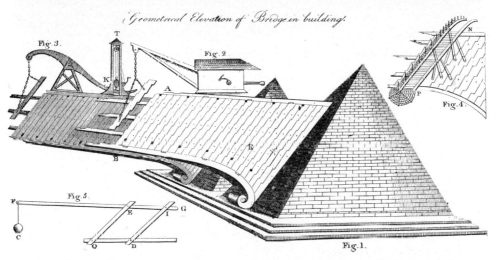

Geometrical Elevation of Bridge in building.

FIGURE 280. PROPOSED HUDSON RIVER CANTILEVER BRIDGE (1810), NEW YORK

From Pope, *A Treatise on Bridge Architecture* . . .

girder is still required, and in some cases where a picturesque quality is desired the lower flange is slightly arched—not a good expression of the action of the forces within the girder but often very pleasant to the eye. Sometimes, too, through girders are used as a combination of support and railing. In bridges of this type the floors are dropped nearly to the bottom of the girders, and in wide bridges with center islands in the roadway three girders are used.

There is one type of structure in which girders are almost invariably used, and that is the highway viaduct. Since the United States government requires

FIGURE 281. FIRTH OF FORTH BRIDGE, SCOTLAND
Sir John Fowler and Sir Benjamin Baker, designers

Photograph Ewing Galloway

that bridges over much-used waterways be from 135 feet to 155 feet above the water level, and because highway engineers like to keep grades to 5 per cent or less, the approach viaducts, particularly in flat country, are very long. The preferred way of handling such structures is by concrete bents supporting steel girders, and much effort has been made by both architects and engineers to produce designs which are agreeable to look at, easy to construct, and low in cost. Some of these approaches not only are practical but also are exciting architecture. (See also Fig. 292.)

ARCH BRIDGES

Of all the various types the arch bridge is the one least likely to be an aesthetic failure (Figs. 286–292). It is difficult to explain what there is about a mathematical curve that is so genuinely satisfying to our instinctive feeling for beauty, but it exists, with a refinement equally incomprehensible. We prefer curves of simple equation to compound curves, and most people prefer the simplest curve to those slightly more complex—the catenary to the parabola, the circle to the ellipse. All historic bridges (except those on piles) are masonry arches of one kind or another, and they are most frequent in those countries where Roman civilization was long-lasting. Italy, France, and Spain abound in masonry arches—usually of stone but often of brick—dating from

FIGURE 282.

TWO CANTILEVERED BRIDGES

ABOVE: Mississippi River Bridge, La Crosse, Wisconsin. BELOW: South Grand Island Bridge, Niagara, New York. Waddell & Hardesty, engineers

Photographs Ewing Galloway

Roman to Victorian times. In France particularly, the art of bridge construction reached a high level of refinement, the tendency there being to make the arch as flat as possible so that vehicles would not have to climb. An eighteenth-century stone arch bridge at St. Dié has an arch in which the rise is only one-seventeenth of the span, a design which today's engineers would not even attempt in stone and in reinforced concrete would approach only with some trepidation.

Since the arch is a natural masonry form, it is to be expected that many twentieth-century arched bridges should be built of reinforced concrete, and it is equally to be expected that in France (and French Switzerland) the engineers should have been the leaders in this field; Freyssinet in France and

FIGURE 283.

TWO GIRDER BRIDGES

LEFT: Farmers Avenue
Overpass, Long Island
Rail Road, New York;
Aymar Embury II, archi-
tect. Courtesy Aymar
Embury II. BELOW: Van
Cortlandt Park Railroad
Bridge, New York. Clin-
ton F. Loyd, architect;
Madigan-Hyland, engi-
neers. Courtesy Madigan-
Hyland.

Maillart in Switzerland studied and perfected methods of erecting pre-stressed concrete which made possible stable structures of unsurpassed lightness and apparent fragility. The European structural tradition makes the erection of such bridges economically desirable; there labor is cheap and material expensive, so that hand laying and fastening of the steel reinforcing during the concrete pour is financially possible. Americans assume the probability of some errors in the final position of the reinforcing and make the structure heavy enough to assure its stability even with bad workmanship. For these reasons it is worth while for the European engineer to make a more refined analysis of his problems than is usual in the United States.

FIGURE 284. FLATBUSH AVENUE BRIDGE, BELT PARKWAY, BROOKLYN, NEW YORK

Madigan-Hyland, engineers

Courtesy Madigan-Hyland

It must not be thought, however, that all arch bridges are of concrete. It is likely that those of short span, say up to 200 feet, will be of concrete, but all arches of 800 feet or more are of steel, as are many of the shorter spans. The choice as between steel and concrete may be determined by the erection problems involved. A concrete arch requires forms; those obviously cannot be supported on water (although Freyssinet came close to doing this) and the structure needed to support the forms and the poured concrete may be as expensive as a steel bridge of equal span. Yet there are compensating factors: The materials for a concrete bridge can be separated into portions so small that they can even be transported by man power; short turns, tunnels, and narrow roads are not prohibiting conditions, and consequently in very rough mountain country one will very likely find concrete arch bridges.

It was suggested above that concrete is especially desirable where maintenance is an important consideration. Steel tends to rust, particularly when exposed to salt air or to sulphur fumes (so universal in our cities), and must be constantly watched. On the other hand, concrete tends to develop shrinkage cracks (which are more unsightly than dangerous); exposed concrete surfaces absorb moisture as well as impurities in the air, and they pit and peel off. Nothing is more forlorn and shabby than an untended concrete structure. For this reason in all parkway bridges, and in most others where price will permit, the concrete is protected by thin walls or slabs of some impermeable stone, generally granite.

The result is that most parkway overpass and underpass arches look as if they were stone arches of the old-fashioned type; they vary little in their treatment from the simplest of the traditional forms, but even in these bridges

FIGURE 285.
RAYMOND E. BALDWIN BRIDGE,
OLD LYME–OLD SAYBROOK,
CONNECTICUT. TWO VIEWS

Joseph D. Drury, engineer of bridge design;
Robert S. Treat, senior highway engineer

Courtesy Connecticut State Department
of Highways

the modern architectural idiom is apparent. Perhaps bridges as good as these could have been built in 1900, but it seems doubtful; the designers would have thought it necessary to add "decorative motifs" and thus would have obscured the lovely clean lines of handsome structures. Current designs are noteworthy in that they express truthfully the way in which a concrete arch acts.

The old stone arch had generally the section shown in Figure 294, 1. But, if concrete were poured in this shape, because of the distortion inseparable from expansion it would certainly crack at the haunches, probably along the lines indicated at A and A. In a stone bridge the expansion was taken up by the

FIGURE 286.
ROMAN ARCHED BRIDGE.
PONTE DEI CAPUCINI,
ASCOLI PICENO, ITALY
Courtesy School of Architecture,
Columbia University

FIGURE 287.
GOTHIC BRIDGE,
ORTHEZ, FRANCE
Courtesy Ware Library

FIGURE 288. STONE
ARCHED BRIDGE,
YACHOWFU,
SZECHUAN, CHINA
From Boerschmann,
Picturesque China

many joints between the stones so that such cracks either did not occur or were imperceptible. The concrete arch should be thinnest at the haunches and thickest in the middle, as shown in Figure 290. This shape is susceptible of great beauty, as European engineers have amply proved.

FIGURE 289. VETERANS MEMORIAL BRIDGE, ROCHESTER, NEW YORK

Frank P. McKibben, engineer; Gehron & Ross, architects   Courtesy William Gehron

FIGURE 290.

TYPICAL MAILLART CONCRETE BRIDGES

Robert Maillart, engineer

ABOVE, LEFT: Chatelard Aqueduct; ABOVE, RIGHT: Bridge near Felsegg, Canton St. Gall; BELOW, LEFT: Lachen Bridge, Canton Zurich; BELOW, RIGHT: Footbridge near Wuelflingen.

Courtesy Museum of Modern Art, New York

FIGURE 291.

TWO STEEL

ARCHED BRIDGES

ABOVE: Croton Lake Bridge, New York; Clinton F. Loyd, architect; Howard Baird, engineer. Courtesy Aymar Embury II. BELOW: Bayonne Bridge, New York–New Jersey; O. H. Ammann, engineer; Cass Gilbert, architect.

Courtesy Port of New York Authority

RIGID-FRAME BRIDGES

The newest type of bridge structure is the "rigid-frame," although just why the most flexible of all bridges should be so named is not apparent (Figs. 293–295). In spite of its recent evolution it is not new in principle, but it has been so little used that the man who experimented with it before 1920 and contributed most to its present development, A. G. Hayden of the Westchester Park Commission, may almost be considered its inventor. Before his application of the principle, however, the properties of the structure were not very well known, and the calculations involved in its design were so complicated that most engineers hesitated to use it until Hayden had proved its utility and its strength. Today it is a favorite form for short bridges.

FIGURE 292. ST. GEORGES BRIDGE,
DELAWARE. CENTRAL SPAN AND APPROACH

Aymar Embury II, architect; Parson, Brinckerhoff,
Hogan, and Macdonald, engineers

Courtesy Aymar Embury II

FIGURE 293. TWO PARKWAY BRIDGES

Clinton F. Loyd, architect; Madigan-Hyland, engineers

ABOVE: 253rd Street Bridge, New York; BELOW: Hudson River Highway crossing in Van Cortlandt Park, New York.

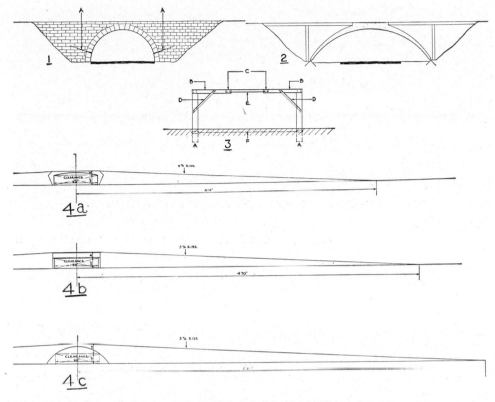

FIGURE 294. DIAGRAMS OF ARCHED AND RIGID-FRAME BRIDGES

(1) Stone arched bridge; (2) Typical reinforced concrete arched bridge; (3) Braced-frame bridge; (4) Clearances required for road overpasses: *a*, with rigid frame; *b*, with a girder bridge; *c*, with an ordinary arch.

Courtesy Aymar Embury II

The principle is simple, as may be seen in Figure 294. It is as if two vertical posts (A in the diagram) were planted in the ground with cross arms, B, at their tops, reaching out toward each other. Since even a light pressure at C would push the arms down, diagonal braces, D, are needed to keep the arms in place. Then, if the opposite arms are spliced together by another piece, E, we have a rigid frame. If the bottoms of the posts are tied together, F, they cannot spread and need not depend on the earth to hold them in place. Rigid-frame bridges are impractical where long spans are necessary, the economic length being about 110 feet for concrete and 150 feet for steel, but within these limits they have the great advantage of being thinnest at the middle, where girder bridges are thickest. Arch bridges also have a thin top but they need much more rise than the rigid-frame type.

FIGURE 295. GRAND CENTRAL PARKWAY OVERPASS, NEW YORK

Aymar Embury II, architect

Photograph Richard Averill Smith, courtesy Aymar Embury II

FIGURE 296.

TWO BASCULE BRIDGES

ABOVE: Flushing Creek Bridge, New York; Aymar Embury II, architect; Shortridge Hardesty, engineer. Courtesy Aymar Embury II. CENTER and BELOW: Oceanic Bridge, Navesink River, New Jersey. Two Views. Howard, Needles, Tammen & Bergendoff, consulting engineers. Courtesy Howard, Needles, Tammen & Bergendoff.

FIGURE 297.

MARINE PARKWAY BRIDGE, NEW YORK

Aymar Embury II, architect; Waddell & Hardesty, engineers

Photograph Richard Averill Smith, courtesy Aymar Embury II

From these three diagrams it is apparent that in flat country the climb to the top of the overpass is much less in the rigid-frame type than in others, and, since with a 5 per cent grade it takes 20 feet of length to 1 foot of rise, a saving of 3 feet in height would save 60 feet of fill on each side of the bridge. For this reason the rigid-frame bridge has now become one of the most popular of structures for parkway overpasses. Often it is not recognized as such, for frames of concrete faced with stone are generally mistaken for some sort of arch and in rigid frames of steel the heavy vertical members are concealed in masonry retaining walls so that only light tongues of steel appear to support the roadway.

MOVABLE BRIDGES

As noted above, there are today only two types of movable bridges which need consideration—the bascule and the lift. The classic example of the bascule and one of the earliest and most carefully studied of this type is the Tower bridge at London, which by the use of elevators permits pedestrian traffic when the bascule is open. The lift span on the whole offers the greater opportunity for interesting architectural treatment, but from the aesthetic standpoint it has, alas, been the less satisfactory of the two.

BASCULE BRIDGES

Many of the bascules are imitation arches. The Arlington Bridge in Washington is a conspicuous example—in this the center span is a bascule, although it imitates as closely as possible the fixed arches on either side—but there are many other bridges in which the designers have followed the arch form without the excuse which the architect of the Arlington Bridge possessed. And it must be admitted that half an arch is just about the kind of form, light at the end and thick at the haunch, which the bascule demands (Fig. 296). As a matter of fact, there have not been many bascules which have combined outstanding aesthetic quality with functional design.

LIFT-SPAN BRIDGES

Almost the same thing is true of the lift spans. Good ones are few and far between, and some of the others are conclusive proof (if proof be needed) that any engineering design can be both functionally correct and terribly ugly. Anyone who has seen the mess of lift spans built by different railroads over the Hackensack and Passaic rivers in the New Jersey meadows will appreciate the truth of this statement. But in later years the engineering firms which design movable bridges have been influenced by the prevailing trends to divorce themselves from precedent and design on the merits of each case. Hence there will be found in the illustrations excellently designed towers and main-lift and approach spans that are ordered and rational (Fig. 297).

TUNNELS

Bridges, of course, are the outstanding embellishments of high-speed highways, but in the near future it may be that tunnels, though not so frequent, will be of almost equal importance. In Europe, in the gorge of the Tarn and along the Route du Litoral on the French and Italian Riviera, highway tunnels were built a century ago. Analogous in the United States are the tunnels on the Pennsylvania express highway, although these were converted from abandoned railway tunnels. But there are also important tunnels of a different type—the under-river traffic connections between Detroit and Canada and those between

FIGURE 298.
TRIBOROUGH BRIDGE
APPROACHES,
RANDALL'S ISLAND,
NEW YORK.
THREE VIEWS

O. H. Ammann, chief engineer; Allston Dana, engineer of design; Aymar Embury II, architect; William Gopin, assistant architect; A. Gordon Lorimer, architectural designer

Photographs Richard Averill Smith, courtesy Triborough Bridge and Tunnel Authority

FIGURE 299 (LEFT). APPROACH TO GEORGE WASHINGTON BRIDGE
UNDERPASS, NEW YORK

Aymar Embury II, architect

Photograph Richard Averill Smith, courtesy Aymar Embury II

FIGURE 300 (RIGHT). LINCOLN TUNNEL ENTRANCE, SOUTH TUBE, NEW YORK

Aymar Embury II, architect

Courtesy Port of New York Authority

FIGURE 301. MARINE PARKWAY BRIDGE, NEW YORK. NORTH ABUTMENT

Aymar Embury II, architect; Robinson & Steinman, engineers

Photograph Richard Averill Smith, courtesy Aymar Embury II

Manhattan Island and both Long Island and New Jersey. Though the number of these tunnels is small their portals have been treated in a surprising variety of ways, ranging from a simple hole in the ground to the great arches on the New Jersey end of the Lincoln Tunnel. Tunnels of this character are as scarce as 2,000-foot-span bridges, but their very rarity has enhanced their importance. (See Figs. 299, 300.)

From the practical point of view, the treatment of tunnel interiors is even more of a challenge to the architect than that of the exteriors. The inner surface must be clean; that is, it must be one that can be cleaned by a daily brushing from a slow-moving truck. It must be light-reflecting, to conserve electricity without sacrificing safety, but it must be free from glare. It must be sound-absorbing or at least as quiet as possible. The tunnel must have a pavement that is non-slip under any conditions and practically everlasting under traffic concentrated on narrow strips of roadway, for pavement repair is always a nuisance and a tunnel has no detour.

Besides these vital problems, tunnels involve other architectural questions —that of designing directional markers which are easy to read but do not distract the driver, that of producing an agreeable color scheme, and above all the well-nigh impossible task of graduating the light so that a driver is not virtually blind when he enters a tunnel lighted to an intensity of perhaps 15 foot-candles as contrasted with 4,000 in the open air. The city of New York has still another problem (which may also occur elsewhere) that is of both architectural and engineering interest—that of getting six lanes of roadway into a space only wide enough for three. Interesting solutions have been obtained along the East River Drive by the development of a pair of half tunnels, one above the other. Similar problems have already arisen in other parts of the city and may arise in any hilly city of the United States—Pittsburgh and Los Angeles, for example.

FREEWAYS

Tunnels and bridges, no matter how interesting, are only special features of express highways, or freeways. For the most part the design of freeways is concerned with the problem of knitting their wide, flat, paved areas into the surroundings. In the open country the best of our highway engineers and landscape architects endeavor to blend the borders of the parkways into the natural landscape. Cuts and fills for underpasses or overpasses will as far as possible be made by earth slopes, and where retaining walls become necessary they will be of quietly colored and unobtrusive stonework, neither very rough nor perfectly smooth—more the kind of wall that a good country mason might have built in 1830. In most cases the bridges will start at the clearance line with a sort of narrow sidewalk between the wall and the curb. If the bridge is wide and the ends are set at the top of slopes or far back from the paving, there is usually a place where grass will not grow and dirt will collect; this should be paved with Belgian block or covered with gravel.

No attempt will be made here to go into the problems of light standards, guard rails, and directional signs, all of which would require a chapter to themselves.

RETAINING WALLS

The average parkway in the country will be at least 300 feet and possibly half a mile wide, but as the parkways enter the cities a different treatment becomes necessary. Here there will not be room for long, easy slopes, the bridges instead of being many miles apart may occur at intervals of a few hundred feet, and retaining walls will have to be built. In the design of these walls there are a few considerations which rise almost to the factual level. First, the material and treatment of the walls must be in harmony with the surroundings; second, the walls must be treated with great variety without losing homogeneity; third, if they are to be seen only or principally by the occupants of automobiles, the walls must be composed of large and simple units—scale that is too small is ruinous to a satisfactory effect (Figs. 298, 300).

Materials. For such walls, concrete is the most commonly used material. It is cheap, when reinforced it is very strong, and it can be surfaced in practically any way at small expense. But if the surface is to be kept free from cracking, scaling, and pitting there must be frequent expansion joints, and if honeycombing and other imperfections which mark the joint between pours made at different times are to be concealed the forms must be designed to disguise the joint. Nothing can prevent the staining of the surface, but a capstone of a strongly contrasting color will help to lessen its conspicuousness.

Next to concrete, stone is the most usual facing. Generally applied as a protective coat over concrete, it will vary from the semi-rustic stonework discussed above to large flat sheets of limestone or granite such as are used in the George Washington Bridge approach on the Manhattan side.

DESIGN QUALITY

It is generally agreed that the great engineering structures that abut the public highways of the twentieth century and are seen by enormous numbers of people are architectural monuments which will probably outlast most buildings of their period. From this premise it follows that all of them should be outstanding in design quality; it does not follow, however, that they will be or that there is any formula by which so pleasing a result may be expected. Like other human beings, the engineers and architects who design them are fallible, particularly when one of either profession works by himself on a problem that needs the contrasting qualities which are present in or have been trained into the members of the two groups. It is possible for either an architect or an engineer to produce a design that is economically, structurally, and aesthetically sound, but the chances of outstanding success are much greater if there is a sympathetic team representing both professions working on it together—and signs are not lacking that this fragment of the millennium is at hand.

SUGGESTED ADDITIONAL READING FOR CHAPTER 38

Bill, Max, *Robert Maillart* (Erlenbach-Zurich: Verlag für Architektur A. G. [1949]).

Black, Archibald, *The Story of Bridges* (New York: Whittlesey House, 1936).

Congdon, Herbert W., *The Covered Bridge* (New York: Knopf, 1946).

Embury, Aymar, II, "Aesthetic Design of Steel Structures," *Pencil Points*, Vol. 19 (1938), July, pp. 409–18.

—— "The Aesthetics of Bridge Design," *Pencil Points*, Vol. 19 (1938), February, pp. 109–20.

—— "Aesthetics of Concrete," *Pencil Points*, Vol. 19 (1938), May, pp. 267–79.

Giedion, Sigfried, "Early and Late Works of Robert Maillart," *Architect and Building News* (London), Vol. 193 (1948), January 2, pp. 14–16.

Mock, Elizabeth, *Architecture of Bridges* (New York: Museum of Modern Art, 1949).

Schaechterle, Karl, and Fritz Leonhardt, *Die Gestaltung der Brücken* (Berlin: Volk & Reich, 1937).

Shand, P. Morton, "Robert Maillart, 1872–1940," *Architectural Review*, Vol. 88 (1940), September, pp. 81–86.

Watson, Wilbur J., *Bridge Architecture* (New York: Helburn [c1927]).

—— *A Decade of Bridges, 1926–36* (Cleveland: Jansen, 1937).

Whitney, Charles, *Bridges* (New York: Rudge, 1929).

39

Railroad Stations

By ALFRED FELLHEIMER

THE BUILDING PROGRAM requirements of railroad stations have changed tremendously since the construction of their earliest predecessors, in the year 1825 in England and about 1830 in the United States (see Figs. 302–308). The influences that effected such changes are interwoven with the evolution of transportation. These include the advent of new forms of motive power and the improvement of steam power; the vast growth of cities, with attendant skyrocketing of land values, traffic congestion, and eventual groping for means of controlling and directing land development; the invention of alternative types of transportation with their triple relation to railroading as competitors, feeder lines, or principal long-haul agents to which the railroads could act as feeders; and, last but not least, the attitude of the railroads themselves toward the public.

Little need be said of early stations in the United States. Finances were limited, and management had no precedents for guidance. The nation was young and its inhabitants were not too discriminating in matters of aesthetic fitness. Consequently the mid-nineteenth-century stations were generally dismal woodsheds with few conveniences. Many of them are still in existence; some are used for freight storage or other purposes and others continue to serve their original purpose (Fig. 305). In contrast, English and Continental railway stations were laid out even in the earliest years with an effort to satisfy the public, which was inclined to resent railroads as intruders upon the traditional landscape. The stations were designed for the comfort of passengers and for harmony with the setting; they were often distinctive in design, with well-planned approaches and landscaping. (But see Fig. 306.) Among the stations which may be singled out to illustrate early British practice are the King's Cross Station in London (1851), which houses eight tracks under two adjoining barrel vaults of glass supported on 105-foot-span laminated wooden arches of strangely modern construction and appearance (Fig. 303), and the

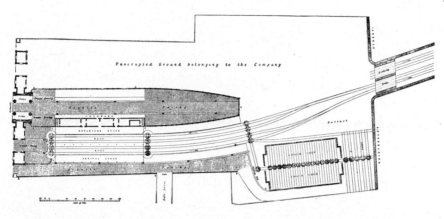

FIGURE 302. EUSTON STATION (1837), LONDON. PLAN
Philip Hardwick, architect
The careful functional planning that characterizes many early railroad stations in England.

From Simms, *Public Works of Great Britain*

St. Pancras Station (also in London), larger and more impressive though more dated in detail, with an arched glass shed having a span of 210 feet.[1] The monumental effect of the great English station halls set a style that was followed all over the world until about the time of the First World War and still prevails in Europe, as may be seen in the outstanding stations at Hamburg, Helsinki, and Milan; but some of the more recent Continental stations, especially in France and Italy, gain their effect in simpler and less monumental ways.

The pioneer era of railroading in the United States (1830 to 1850) was followed by a period of rapid expansion. By 1890 the total mileage amounted to nearly three-fourths of the mid-twentieth-century total. During those decades the Federal government promoted expansion by land grants, towns vied with each other for railroad locations, and the tracks that ran down Main Street (as they still do in some communities) were a matter of civic pride. The railroads were in undisputed control of transportation and were feverishly preoccupied with expansion and finance. Little more attention was wasted on station design than during the pioneer days; simple, uninspired, standardized frame structures were the rule. It was during this period of expansion that many of the requirements of the railroad station were indicated and that several plan types, especially for smaller stations, became standardized. The aesthetic concepts of the times tended more toward jigsaw scrollwork and

[1] *Architectural Forum*, Feb., 1946, pp. 106–7.

FIGURE 303. KING'S CROSS STATION (1851), LONDON. EXTERIOR

Lewis Cubitt, architect

The architectural expression was often fresh and direct; here the two arched windows light a two-span train shed and symbolize the separation of incoming from outgoing traffic.

Courtesy Carroll L. V. Meeks

FIGURE 304. EARLY RAILROAD STATION (1849), PROVIDENCE, RHODE ISLAND. EXTERIOR

Thomas Tefft, architect

One striking exception to the architectural poverty that marked many early stations in the United States, and a powerful design.

Courtesy Rhode Island School of Design

FIGURE 305. RAILROAD STATION (1850), HYDEVILLE, VERMONT

A characteristic example of the early frame station in rural communities.

Courtesy Delaware & Hudson Railroad

FIGURE 306.
EARLY TWO-LEVEL
RAILROAD STATION
(1847), NEW HAVEN,
CONNECTICUT.
PERSPECTIVE

Henry Austin, architect

The sinking of the tracks
below the street level
made the two-level sta-
tion possible. Here the
design was in Austin's
most florid orientalizing
manner.

Courtesy Yale
University Library

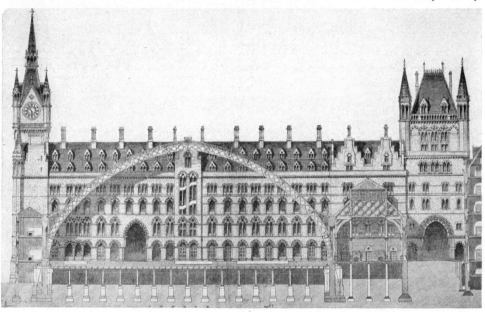

FIGURE 307. ST. PANCRAS STATION (1866), LONDON. SECTION OF TRAIN SHED
Gilbert Scott, architect; W. H. Barlow, engineer
Great iron-and-glass train sheds distinguished many large stations of the second half of the
nineteenth century.   From *Building News*

eclectic imitation than toward fundamental improvements in planning or
function. A notable exception was the series of railroad stations designed for
the Boston & Albany Railroad by H. H. Richardson in the 1880's (Fig. 310).
Here expressive beauty and great efficiency were achieved. The platform
shelter and the station roof were admirably integrated, and simple materials

FIGURE 308. OLD GRAND CENTRAL STATION (1872), NEW YORK. INTERIOR
OF TRAIN SHED

J. B. Snook, architect

This train shed was the most creative feature in New York's second Grand Central Station.

From *Harper's Weekly*

were intelligently used throughout. Many of the best rural stations now in use
are variations of the scheme Richardson first developed.

From the closing years of the nineteenth century to the First World War
the railroads in the United States enjoyed their maturity with only minor in-
fringements of their sovereignty in the field of transportation. In keeping with
their high estate, urban stations built during that period were often monumental in appearance. This may have been due partly to the example of Europe;
on the Continent, since most railways were state-owned or state-operated,
their stations were treated like other public buildings and the remaining privately operated lines followed suit; in Britain a high standard of architectural
design was adopted from the outset, as previously mentioned. Another reason
was the enormous growth of cities in the United States and the consequent
intensive development of downtown sections which centered on the railroad
station, thus enhancing the importance of the station itself, which was often
referred to as "the gateway of the modern city."

FIGURE 309.
NEW YORK CENTRAL
RAILROAD STATION,
SCARSDALE, NEW YORK.
EXTERIOR AND INTERIOR

A characteristic small station of the eclectic period.

Courtesy Alfred Fellheimer

This period established the tradition of high, vaulted ceilings over great waiting rooms surrounded by ticket and baggage windows and passenger conveniences. The multiple tracks of major stations were spanned by imposing glass and iron (or steel) sheds, whose smoke-filled air was accepted without much criticism; low sheds, however, with open slots over the track centers were also developed and gradually superseded the impressive long-span vaults. Passenger platforms became longer to accommodate the longer trains made possible by the more powerful engines coming into use. Simpler and more permanent interior surfaces of stone, marble, or tile succeeded the earlier carved woodwork, and plain glass to replace the former stained panels was more in keeping with the changing taste of the times.

Nevertheless the desire for monumentality, coupled with a superficial approach to requirements in the absence of statistical data, resulted in frequent violations of passenger comfort, especially in such features as exposed ornamental approach stairs and terraces, long interior walking distances caused by

FIGURE 310. BOSTON & ALBANY RAILROAD STATION (1884), AUBURNDALE, MASSACHUSETTS. EXTERIOR

H. H. Richardson, architect

Richardson's careful functional analysis of the problem gave rise to a solution of expressive simple beauty.   From Van Rensselaer, *Henry Hobson Richardson and His Works*

the oversizing of spaces and an insistence on symmetry, and wasteful back-tracking for passengers because the various services and conveniences were perforce placed wherever the architectural schemes permitted rather than according to their use sequence.

The years immediately preceding the First World War saw the beginning of a series of radical changes in several basic factors. These changes, which still continue in full force, had a marked effect in reshaping the concept of a passenger station.

The adoption of electric motive power for terminal service came coincidentally with and was perhaps a consequence of the new high-water marks reached by metropolitan congestion and urban land values. At first, in the United States, electric locomotives were used only for short-haul traffic, but gradually they gained favor for passenger-station service, so much so indeed that other forms of motive power have been prohibited for certain terminals by municipal ordinances. The attendant elimination of the smoke nuisance had far-reaching consequences. The land around railroad tracks, usually strategically located for intensive development but retarded by the proximity of the railroad, began coming into its own. This in turn increased the value of the land occupied by the right of way, yards, and stations to the point where its use for railroad purposes exclusively seemed economically unwarranted. Electric traction permitted depressing the tracks below street levels and releasing the space above for additional development in keeping with the character of the surrounding districts. At the same time, depressed tracks no longer acted as barriers to surface traffic; the extension of streets across them assisted the reintegration of trackside districts into the fabric of the metropolis, thus further enhancing property values.[2]

In connection with replanning the Grand Central Terminal and its approaches in 1906, the firm of Reed & Stem, architects, raised the question of why the property of the railroad could not share in these high values by being put to productive uses above the levels required for train operation. There were many doubts about this idea—radical at the time—and many technical difficulties developed in connection with the structural support of the buildings above, the overcoming of vibration, proper ventilation, and so forth. By 1913, when reconstruction was completed, these difficulties were solved. The design of this terminal marks a transition from the earlier purely monumental concept toward the emerging idea of using the railway station proper as a foundation upon which other structures that promise high additional returns may be erected. The station building does have impressively monumental proportions, but a part of its ground area supports vast reaches of office space; naturally the terminal tracks with their platforms are purely utilitarian.

Another consequence of the rise of land values in the vicinity of railroad property was the impetus given to the removal of service facilities from the passenger station. The mixed-freight train persists today only on isolated rural lines; elsewhere freight is handled by separate trains and terminals, and special trains have even been introduced to handle express shipments exclusively. As a result express warehouses, post offices, and of course service and repair yards are increasingly kept separate from the passenger station proper.

STATION DESIGN

As recently as 1928, a pioneer eastern railroad in the United States published an elaborate book on its passenger stations in which the architects' contribution is described as follows:

The floor plans are either prepared or approved by the transportation officers, and the general exterior of the building by competent architects, who, by the introduction of classic moldings or other ornaments easily cast and the use of the structural

[2] Probably the first important two-level station in the United States was that at New Haven, designed by Henry Austin in 1849. Here the tracks were depressed and the street-level station was built partly over them. The platforms were reached by stairs from a crossover (Fig 306)

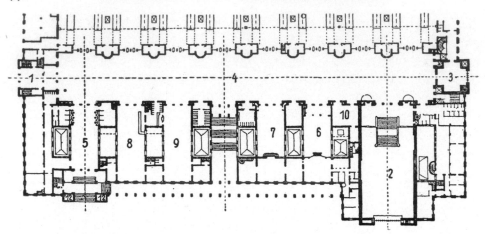

FIGURE 311. CENTRAL TERMINAL STATION, STUTTGART, GERMANY. PLAN

Bonatz & Scholer, architects

One of the best of the more recent German stations. Note the different waiting rooms for first-, second-, and third-class passengers.   From Platz, *Die Baukunst der neuesten Zeit*

elements to produce artistic results without concessions from the engineering functions, change the gaunt forms of factory-like buildings into artistic structures.

This quotation, needless to say, has been selected for use here merely to illustrate a state of mind which is disappearing slowly. As a matter of fact, many important stations are of such magnitude and complexity that their planning is spread over a long period of time, thus tending to place the design function in the hands of the engineering department of the railroad, men who literally "grow up with the project." Still, architects can—and by all means should— make contributions other than "the introduction of classic moldings." Evidence of this is offered, for example, by the Grand Central Terminal in New York City, in the design of which the author of this chapter had a part. Aside from the visual impressions and the general arrangement and circulation, its contribution to the city plan and to the development of the concept of air rights considered novel when this station was built attests the importance of the architects' contribution.

At the inception of a railroad-station project the matter of location is often an open question and must be determined through a comparison and evaluation of all possible sites. In most cities, too, consolidation of railroad terminals will require extensive negotiations. Decentralization of functions not directly connected with passenger transportation—freight, mail, express, repair shops, en-

FIGURE 312. CENTRAL TERMINAL STATION, STUTTGART, GERMANY.

EXTERIOR AND CONCOURSE

Bonatz & Scholer, architects

An attempt to give a fresh expression to traditional materials.   From Platz, *Die Baukunst der neuesten Zeit*

gine houses, power and signal plant, and the like—may be tied in with the design of the station. Division of long-haul and suburban traffic between two separate stations may also be considered.

Building design may enter at an early stage, since the design possibilities of limited sites requiring multi-level construction may have to be compared with those of more ample locations. In any case, before actual design can commence,

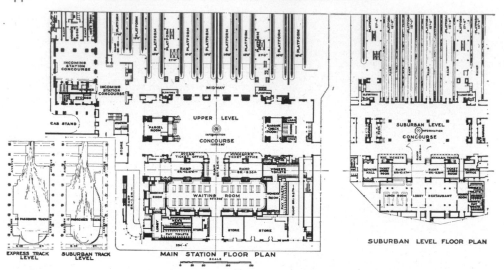

FIGURE 313. GRAND CENTRAL STATION, NEW YORK. PLANS

Reed & Stem, architects; Warren & Wetmore, associated

A creative and revolutionary scheme that made use of several levels and was part of the general plan to utilize the space over the tracks for other purposes.   Courtesy Fellheimer & Wagner

adaptation of the project to the city plan and co-ordination with local transit and traffic, as well as the elimination of grade crossings, must be carefully studied. Vast transactions in land acquisition incident upon any relocations require the co-operation of the municipality and the state, and approval of the investment features must come from Federal authorities as well as from financial interests. Moreover, since the business of the railroad is greatly affected by the prosperity of the city and since the terminal in turn not only contributes a first and important impression to visitors but also influences the direction and quality of urban development, public approval may have to be won, frequently through extensive preparation and public education.

Railroad operating features, present or future, must similarly be the subject of exhaustive study, particularly if more than one railroad is concerned; often several departments of railroad administration, including the board (or boards) of directors, must be brought into agreement. Architects engaged to assist from the early stages on will therefore acquire considerable expert knowledge before the design stage is eventually reached. Occasionally, however, an architect may be charged with such a problem on short notice; for him this chapter may be especially helpful.

Although our discussion here is directed principally toward solutions of the

FIGURE 314. GRAND CENTRAL STATION, NEW YORK. SOUTH FRONT
Reed & Stem, architects; Warren & Wetmore, associated

Courtesy Fellheimer & Wagner

more complex problems of major metropolitan stations, these interpretations may easily be adapted to the needs of small and intermediate projects. Few details can be supplied on the space requirements directly connected with train operation, although this question may be a puzzling one to architects who lack experience in station design; fortunately, however, the operating staff is likely to state its needs most specifically on this point, both as to the necessary areas and their sequence. The terms "station" and "terminal" are used interchangeably since they are difficult to delimit in actual cases. Some trains will pass through stations where the run of others will terminate, portions of incoming trains may be attached to outgoing ones, and so on. Nor can the physical layout of the tracks be used as a criterion; for topographic or other reasons, at some stations the through trains are backed onto stub-end tracks and at others the terminal-run trains arrive on through tracks.

MAJOR INFLUENCES

Effect of Automobile Transportation. The tremendous growth in the use of passenger motor vehicles has affected railroading in many ways. Perhaps the most important effect has been the rise of commuting traffic. This type of traffic is not new, but its volume has multiplied with the growth of suburban settlement attendant upon the widespread use of the private motor car. In many cases, stations designed primarily for long-haul traffic have proved inadequate for this new load. Stations built after the first decade of the twentieth century faced the problem by separating the two types of traffic—a scheme which was often facilitated by the new depressed-track approaches permitting the use of two-level track systems. At the same time, as grade crossings within urban areas became more and more dangerous and objectionable to the general public as well as to the railroads themselves, the automobile accelerated extensive programs for the reconstruction of approaches.

The increase in commuting traffic has added thousands to the number of travelers passing daily through important terminal buildings (at mid-century Grand Central averages approximately 180,000 passengers and 370,000 non-passengers). Such multitudes have raised problems of circulation within the terminal for which provision (often inadequate) has been made at major stations; radical steps in the planning of station approaches have had to be taken to distribute these throngs into the traffic arteries of the city during the morning and evening rush hours without undue crowding. This phase of terminal development, which requires close co-operation between railroad and city planners, has been markedly laggard, partly perhaps because of the backward state of municipal planning in most of our cities. Among the major stations, the Cincinnati Union Station shows the most imaginative design for the convenient circulation of passengers from railroad train to private car, taxi, bus, and (at the time of the station's construction) streetcar—in that instance, however, the circulation pattern was planned primarily for the comfort of long-haul passengers. The Cincinnati station also provides for the parking of private vehicles a large underground garage with direct station access. Although the problem of parking has received at least some degree of attention at most suburban stations, in connection with major terminals it has in general been disregarded and threatens to become insoluble without drastic and fantastically expensive steps.

Vast increases in traffic have transformed the concession spaces originally provided for the convenience of long-distance travelers into first-class business locations—in New York, for example, the Terminal Barber Shops and the famous Oyster Bar at Grand Central and the toy shop in the Pennsylvania Station attract substantial patronage from non-travelers. Consequently concession rentals have become important sources of income for terminals, and commercial rental space should be treated accordingly in planning. Moreover, with the growth of commuting traffic, the immediate vicinity of terminals has received a special impetus toward development. Executives and white-collar office personnel find places of work within walking distance from the station obviously more convenient, and the concentration of corporation and other offices, in turn, adds to the desirability of the district for commercial, entertainment, and hotel facilities.

Thus the automobile may be credited indirectly with a good share of the special intensity of development around railroad stations and of the consequent development in the utilization of air rights over stations, yards, and approaches; of this the Grand Central Terminal is an outstanding example. Another proposal, interesting enough to warrant reference here although never put into execution, was developed in 1920 by Fellheimer & Wagner for the Illinois Central Railroad.

Railroad Practices as Sources of Design Changes. The railroads over many years have established a reputation for punctuality which is now accepted as a matter of course by the public and, jealously guarded by the companies, remains as one of their most valuable assets in competing with the faster service offered by the airlines. This circumstance has reduced the need for ever larger waiting rooms; though actually their size may not have diminished through the years, at least it has not grown proportionately with the increase in traffic. During the Second World War, for instance, most waiting rooms were adequate for the handling of an unprecedented upsurge in travel.

A parallel development appears to have manifested itself in regard to ticket offices. With the increasing use of the telephone for securing reservations and the inauguration of downtown ticket offices, there has been a reduction or at least no proportionate increase—aside from the war-time peak—in the space required for ticket sales. Recently perfected mechanical ticket-printing and accounting devices will contribute to the same trend by reducing the time taken by each transaction. In addition there are indications that the example of the airlines will lead the railroads toward selling methods which will further augment the convenience of the passenger and reduce the need for his presence at the station prior to his departure.

Moreover, the time is past when space allocations for waiting, ticket sales, and other purposes (such as parcel checking, rest rooms, and the like) were determined through guesswork by railroad officials in co-operation with architects often selected for their ability in designing monumental structures rather than for their knowledge of terminal operation. Once the passenger-car capacity of the terminal is determined by the number of tracks and the lengths of the platforms, proportionate space for all other facilities can be ascertained by reference to the tables in the *Manual of the American Railway Engineering Association*,[3] after making due allowance for such special circumstances as periodical traffic peaks and the volume of commuter travel.

Co-ordination with Other Modes of Travel. For many decades the one major long-distance travel medium other than the railroad was the steamship, and only occasionally in the United States was a tie established between boat and railroad passenger traffic; the European institution of the dockside "boat train" was developed only in a few instances, such as the New York–Boston traffic via the Fall River Line. The mid-twentieth-century railroad, however, must share passenger traffic with private automobiles and planes, with the autobus and the standard airliner, and possibly with such offshoots of the latter as the helicopter. An early form of collaboration between railroading and flying was the practice of certain lines of issuing combination tickets for air travel in the daytime and continuation by train at night. This phase passed with the development of planes having greater speed and night operability. Other forms of co-operation may be recognized in the facilities offered by railroads, during the depression, for hauling their passengers' automobiles at a low extra charge and in the car-rental agencies set up in or adjoining the railroad terminals.

The opinion may be ventured that, for proper service to the public and in the best interest of the carriers themselves, closer collaboration will be established in the United States in the future—even though joint ownership of competing forms of transportation, which might lead more quickly to this result, is discouraged by governmental policies. Imaginative designs have been published (though not yet built) in which trains, buses, airport limousines, car rentals, and car parking are all co-ordinated under one roof, perhaps with the roof itself serving as a helicopter landing field or airport. The advantages to the public of such a "transportation terminal" seem obvious, and although such radical suggestions could hardly materialize overnight they may well point the direction of the future.

DESIGN FACTORS

The principal factors in station design, which as set forth in this section relate chiefly to large stations but can usually be applied to stations of all sizes, are as follows:

[3] Chicago: American Railway Engineering Association [c1936].

Efficient Connections. Provision must be made for the quickest and most convenient connections—for both travelers and their baggage—between the sidewalk or local transportation and the passenger cars, in either direction. This implies a minimum crossing of major traffic streams and a minimum mixing of such disparate types of traffic as incoming and outgoing passengers, commuters and long-distance travelers, passengers and baggage or other goods.[4]

Incidental Services. As a convenience primarily for the passenger and secondarily for persons escorting or waiting for him, all the customary incidental services must be supplied in such logical sequence and clarity of disposition that walking distances and the problem of finding a particular facility will be reduced to a minimum. Such services include waiting rooms, train announcement boards, and information desks; ticket, express, and baggage agents; loudspeaker systems for broadcasting announcements or music; washrooms, refreshment counters, and newsstands; telephone and telegraph service, parcel checking, access to drive-yourself or chauffeured cars, hotel and theater information, messenger and message service, travelers' aid, and special care for unescorted children and ailing or aged passengers.

Operational Facilities. It is necessary to provide operating and safety facilities to meet the requirements of the railroad, express company, and mails in such balance that the capacity of platforms and tracks can be utilized to its maximum and in such sequence as to reduce the handling of goods and the walking distances for personnel to a minimum. These are:

1. Facilities for train crews: locker rooms and washrooms, lounges and dormitories (when required for layovers), first-aid rooms, space for training and instruction
2. Facilities for inspection, for certain quick repairs, and for such maintenance (oiling, replacement of lamps and fuses, adjustment of heating and air-conditioning equipment, and so on) as may take place during the stay of passenger coaches within the terminal
3. Servicing of passenger coaches, club cars, and diners (while in the station) with ice, water, linen, paper goods, sanitary and cleaning items, food, drinks, cigarettes, and cigars; supply of steam for heating or of conditioned air for cooling the parked coaches; facilities (sometimes includ-

---

[4] Speed and convenience have become more important because of airline competition. At present one of the weak spots of airline operation is the rather general time loss between the center of town and the airport, as well as the inconvenience involved in that trip and in the access from the airport facilities to the plane itself, especially in inclement weather. The railroads have every reason to make the most of the advantage they now possess in that respect.

ing mechanical car washers) for the rapid and thorough cleaning of cars
and coaches

4. Offices for administration, reservations, accounting in connection with
   ticket sales, and so forth
5. Special offices for the station master and the train dispatcher
6. Lost-and-found room

Revenue Sources. It is essential to create and conserve the maximum by-
product values in the form of concessions, commercial and office rentals, and
general development on railroad-owned land along the right of way as well as
over the trackage and the station itself. That this aspect is important to the
city is obvious; its financial significance for the railroad, furthermore, has
grown to such proportions that either from the standpoint of capital investment or from that of annual revenue it has a substantial effect on the entire
budget of the corporation. The successful exploitation of these by-product
values depends largely on the skill of the general planning and on the success
of the architectural solution.

Terminal Operation and Services. Tying in the terminal track system with
the main and interchange lines entering the city as well as with yards, shops,
roundhouses, and the like, for the shortest runs and the most efficient operation
and servicing of trains, is a vital consideration.[5] The routing of the tracks will
affect the location of the terminal and its relation both to existing and possible
roads and to local public transportation systems; it may affect the level—at,
above, or under the street grade—at which the station tracks may be brought
in, which in turn may determine the type of station and whether the distribution of facilities will be on one or several levels; it may create problems of elevating or depressing the tracks; and it will influence the extent to which air
rights over approach tracks, yards, and the station itself can profitably be exploited. Since numerous alternatives almost invariably present themselves and
since the architect's point of view must include building economics, rental
prospects, city planning, and a feeling for the substantial values that can be
created—or permanently lost—in the course of any sizable terminal project,
the architectural contribution is complementary to that of the railroad technical staff, which is likely to view the project predominantly from the angle of
operating efficiency.

[5] This phase is usually explored by the engineering department of the railroad, with the assistance of the real-estate department, before architectural sketches are prepared. The track layout,
however, often exerts a controlling influence on the design of the station; therefore, to obtain
the best over-all plan, close collaboration between the engineers, real-estate specialists, and
architects is desirable from the outset.

Relation to the City. The terminal or station and the urban traffic generated by it must be integrated with the transportation facilities and plans, commercial development, and general growth of the city.[6] The architect may have the double task of presenting convincing analyses to the railroad on the one hand and to city officials on the other. The bringing together of the many interests involved is one of the most valuable services he can render.

Structural and Aesthetic Requirements. In addition the designer will need to plan for the requirements common to all buildings in respect to permanence, efficiency, attractiveness, and so forth. These matters will not be further discussed here beyond noting that, because of the transient use of railroad buildings by people of all kinds of habits and levels of culture, indestructibility and ease of maintenance are probably more important in stations than in most other structures.

DESIGN ELEMENTS

Terminal Track Layouts. Terminals—and stations in general—may be of either the through or the stub type, or even of the loop type which is intermediate between the two; some are composites of more than one type. All have advantages and drawbacks which necessitate investigation of the controlling circumstances before the appropriate one can be selected.

In the *through* type, the tracks pass entirely through the station; hence the platforms are isolated between the tracks—usually between close-set pairs of tracks—and must be reached by concourses that cross above or below all tracks. A tunnel concourse requires less vertical distance from the platform than the overhead type and therefore can be served by shorter stairs, ramps, or escalators. The choice is usually determined on the basis of topographic factors and whether the approach tracks are located at, above, or below street level. The main advantage of the through type of terminal is that it permits trains to follow one another rapidly to the same platform; the disadvantage lies in the complication of access for passengers, goods, servicing, and maintenance. Some major terminals are so situated that the yards cannot be placed athwart the approaches; when this is true, a through type of plan cannot be used.

In *stub* stations, the tracks come to a dead end and on the same level permit connections between the inside ends of the platforms. The connecting header

---

[6] As has been stressed before, the skill with which this phase is handled will have paramount importance in the realization of the potential values inherent in air rights and other developments. Successful contribution to municipal improvements will also raise the stature of the railroad in the eyes of the public.

is known as the midway. The advantages here are not only ease of access to the platforms—including the freest possible interchange of passengers, mail, express, baggage, and so on from one platform to another—but also the opportunity of using more than one gate for any train. The disadvantages spring from the fact that the engine and the baggage, mail, and express cars are normally at the head ends of arriving trains; as a consequence the engine—which, especially in the case of electric traction, is the most expensive piece of railroad equipment—will be tied up all the while the train is in the station, and the baggage, mail, and express cars with their personnel will (or should) be inactive until most of the passengers have left the platform. Even then the platform will still not be available for another train until the first one has backed out into the yards, where it must be reversed or remade. For these reasons the stub type is best adapted to long-headway, long-haul train terminals in downtown locations, where if the difference in elevation between the tracks and the city streets is not too great and the topographic conditions are favorable it may offer access from streets to platforms with little or no vertical travel and with attendant convenience for both passengers and services.

The *loop* type is derived from the stub arrangement; it connects the stub ends of tracks and thus permits releasing engines and other head-end equipment or turning entire trains ready to travel in the opposite direction. This scheme possesses a distinct operating advantage for all types of traffic, but its greatest value lies in its easy handling of suburban, short-headway trains. Naturally the platforms between loop tracks must depend on either overhead or tunnel access, as in the case of through stations.

Some stations are composites of more than one type of track arrangement. At the Grand Central Terminal, in New York, the upper level has a stub layout for through trains and the lower level uses the loop system for suburban traffic. The Union Station, in Washington, is divided into two halves, one on the street level with stub tracks, the other depressed with tracks for southward traffic continuing beneath both the station and Capitol Hill.

One test of the efficiency of any scheme is obtained by dividing the number of cars accommodated in accordance with a projected schedule for capacity operation, during a 24-hour period, into the total estimated cost of the station. Such schedules, of course, have to be made up with due consideration of the usual peaks, which are daily for commuter travel and both seasonal and daily for long-distance travel, mail, and express. Design for maximum peaks is uneconomical; therefore means must be found for achieving flexibility in meeting peak conditions, as, for example, by the interchangeable use of suburban and long-haul tracks.

After the capacity of the platform tracks in number of cars per hour has been established, the capacities of all other parts of the station can be derived from this, using as a basis the tables compiled by the American Railway Engineering Association; but allowances must be made in each case for particular controlling conditions as well as for long-term trends in operating methods and for the behavior of the public. Wherever possible it is wise to allow wide margins for unforeseen growth or a shift in relative demands.

Provisions for growth may be made by allowances for additional platform tracks or for extensions to existing platforms. Past experience shows a tendency toward longer trains because of increased motive power, the use of light-weight alloys for car building, and the improvement of grades and curves on lines. Public and service facilities should be capable of simultaneous expansion, but further flexibility should be aimed at by allowing for the expansion—or the contraction—of one or more operating units without any such change in the others. There have been instances, for example, of the expansion of mail and baggage requirements without a corresponding increase in passenger travel; mail or express, on the other hand, may be removed completely—as freight handling already has been eliminated at most major stations—or suburban traffic may multiply when long-haul business drops off.

Tracks. The main portions of the track system are known as the approach, the throat, and the platform tracks. The initial balance of their respective capacities and the possibility of changes in balance caused by unequal future expansion in the three portions are among the most important factors which control the success or failure of a station and its useful life.

Of recent years a good deal of pessimism regarding the prospects for future growth of passenger travel has been voiced by some segments of the railroad industry. Unbiased observation, however, would lead to the conclusion that commuting traffic is still definitely on the upgrade, whereas long-distance travel continues to exceed available facilities—at least during times of prosperity. The cost of rights of way in proportion to the entire investment in the station and its appurtenant facilities is usually low at the start of a new project. After the project has been in operation for some years, however, the purchase of additional rights of way may be prohibitive if not impossible. Therefore it would still seem wise to allow generously for the uncertainties of the future in the original acquisition.

In addition to the main parts of the track system mentioned above, there may be separate tracks to which mail and express cars may be shunted or on which solid trains of mail and express may be received; loop tracks for releasing engines or turning entire trains; tracks for the maintenance and cleaning of coaches, important because of emphasis on the appearance of streamliners; repair tracks with pits for minor repairs; and coach yards where trains may be parked, broken up, or assembled.[7]

At many stations sleeping cars arriving in the early morning may be occupied by passengers until later in the day; similarly, in the evening, passengers may be admitted to sleepers long before departure. Separate tracks may be required for this service to prevent interference with the main platform tracks. Such parking tracks should be arranged for convenient access, although their platforms need not be wide, since traffic on them will not be congested.

Platform tracks are likely to be littered because of the carelessness of passengers, yet keeping them tidy is important; for this reason as well as to facilitate drainage, a concrete track bed is preferable to the tie-and-ballast type. The tracks should extend straight along the platforms, especially where high platforms are used, since curves cause hazardous gaps between the cars and the platforms. If a grade is necessary or is desired for drainage, it should be held to less than 0.5 per cent to prevent roll-away accidents.

Platforms. To the basic function of passenger platforms is usually added the transfer of baggage and, to a varying extent, other functions such as mail and express handling, car inspection, provisioning, removal of trash and garbage from trains, sweeping and washing the rolling stock, and so forth. In the interest of economy, the platforms and their appurtenant facilities should be tied up as briefly as possible by any one train; to clear the platform for its other functions, the rapid egress of passengers should be the governing consideration. This is particularly important in suburban and commuting traffic, where little baggage is involved; on the other hand, passengers as well as trains that are run on short headway time their movements on close schedules.

The unloading of baggage, mail, and express from long-haul trains tends to impede passenger movement on the platform. To obviate this difficulty at terminal stations, mail and express cars may be detached and handled at special sidings. At a few stations, notably the Union Terminal in Chicago, separate

---

[7] It may be noted that streamlined and air-conditioned rolling stock requires more adjustment and repairs; such work must be performed quickly because malfunctioning of some minor item, such as a detail in the air-conditioning system, would render a modern coach with its fixed windows useless.

baggage and passenger platforms are installed alternately between tracks; each train is thus made accessible by a passenger platform on one side and by a utility platform on the other. This scheme should not be used without investigation of its economic feasibility, since the combined width of the two platforms is likely to exceed that of a single platform adequate for both purposes. Where baggage must be handled on the passenger platform, the access provided for baggage trucks is of critical importance. At stub stations the baggage, mail, and express cars usually come to rest next to the midway ends of the platforms, with direct access to the station trucks. In order to accommodate passengers first, the unloading is withheld until the passengers have cleared the platform; at loading time, however, the sequence cannot be so closely controlled. At a few stations the trains are reversed and backed into the station by the engine, but this scheme causes loss of time and consequently has not been used for modern terminals.

In general, subway concourses running crosswise to the tracks and leading to the baggage room (as well as to the express depot and the post office where required) are reached by the trucks by means of either elevators or ramps. Since the advent of electrically driven and rubber-tired trucks and tractors, the ramp appears by far the better solution. Conveyor handling has not been used except for mail, because of the superior flexibility and lower cost of mechanized trucking. Where the platforms are low, it is possible elevating devices similar to those used in industrial plants will soon be added to the trucks. The baggage ramp (or elevator) should be at the end of the platform, close to the head-end position of the trains. At through stations, where trains may come from either direction, separate sets of access facilities with their cross concourses should be used for passengers and for goods. Baggage ramps should be wide enough to accommodate two truck trains passing in opposite directions, but care should be taken to leave adequate widths of platform beside them, especially where long trains may extend beyond the ramps.

Platforms are either of the low type (o'–9" above top of rail) or flush with the car floors (4'–0" above top of rail). The high platform speeds up passenger movement and is more nearly accident-proof, but it renders inspection and switching difficult; inspection, however, may be facilitated by the use of low galleries under the overhanging platforms. The high platform seems generally preferable, and definitely so in the case of short-headway suburban traffic; even if low platforms are installed at first, the design should provide for the substitution of high ones later.

The simplest form of weather protection is the platform shed, usually sup-

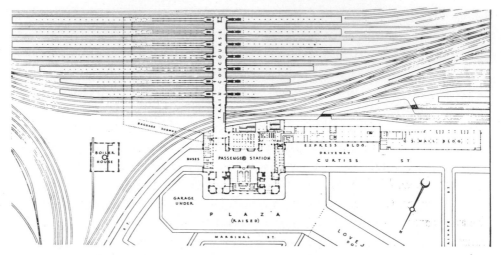

FIGURE 315. NEW YORK CENTRAL STATION, BUFFALO, NEW YORK. PLAN

Fellheimer & Wagner, architects

A pioneer plan dependent on a fresh study of the best connections between an upper-level entrance and the track platforms.   Courtesy Fellheimer & Wagner

ported by one line of columns placed on the center line of the platform. Since the columns are obstructions they should be spaced as widely apart as possible.[8] The earlier high-arched station sheds have been supplanted by low roofs with continuous open slots over the center lines of the tracks to permit the escape of steam and smoke. Among the modern forms of motive power, Diesels raise special problems on account of the possible toxicity of their exhaust fumes and their more or less hypothetical explosion hazard; electric engines, however, permit complete enclosure of the station tracks and platforms—an arrangement that is especially valuable because of the freedom with which income-producing structures can be superimposed. For that reason it seems advisable for the designer to provide for future electrification whether or not it is contemplated. Such provisions will consist mainly of ample clearances and platforms profiled to permit a later choice between overhead or third-rail conductors.

Passengers leaving the platform may move toward another train, toward the waiting room, or directly to the city streets and to private or public means of transport. The same movements take place in reverse in the case of those about to entrain. In many European terminals, and in small-town stations in the United States, contact with the outside is direct; taxis, buses, or private cars

---

[8] Various twentieth-century Italian railroad stations show the beauty that can be achieved in such sheds if they are carefully detailed and carried out in well-chosen materials.

FIGURE 316.
NEW YORK CENTRAL
STATION,
BUFFALO, NEW YORK.
AIR VIEW AND
CONCOURSE

Fellheimer & Wagner, architects

The new type of plan generated new types of mass and interior space.

Courtesy Fellheimer
& Wagner

may pull up directly across from and within a few feet of the track or platform. In major American terminals this problem has never been satisfactorily solved; the long walk to or from the trains, often with irritating dependence on porter service, is still a customary inconvenience. The distance and delay are especially annoying to commuters, who experience them twice daily; the designer should therefore endeavor to provide multiple exits directly to the outside from stations or platforms used for commuting service (as was proposed in a regrettably unexecuted version of the plans for the Grand Central Terminal of New York).

In general, the platforms in stub-type stations connect to the midway at their ends, but platforms of through, loop, and multi-level stations depend on stairs, ramps, or escalators. Since such facilities for passengers should be as nearly central to the length of the platform as possible and since there must be space enough for individuals and trucks to pass by them, their available width is strictly limited and must be used with the greatest efficiency. These consid-

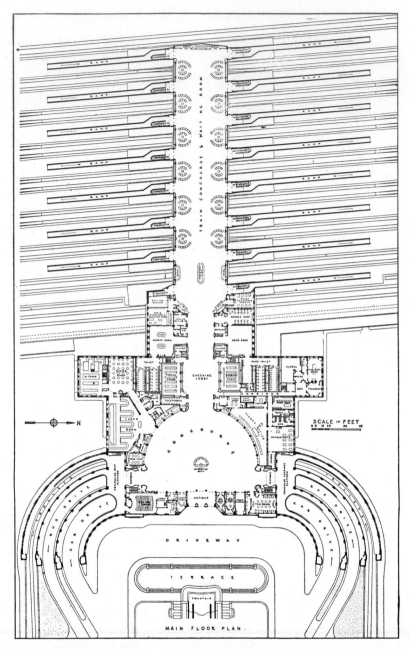

FIGURE 317. UNION STATION, CINCINNATI, OHIO. PLAN

Fellheimer & Wagner, architects

The problem of relating street traffic to railroad facilities brilliantly solved. Loop ramps take care of vehicles of various types, and passengers can be dropped or picked up at convenient spots. The waiting room serves as the connecting bridge between the entrance and the ramps approaching the platforms.   From *Architectural Forum*

FIGURE 318. UNION STATION, CINCINNATI, OHIO. PLAZA FRONT

Fellheimer & Wagner, architects

The arch to the semi-domed entrance concourse forms a superb dominant motif at the end of the approach plaza; it becomes a monumental city gate.   Courtesy Fellheimer & Wagner

erations virtually eliminate stairs except as emergency exits because passage up and down them is necessarily slow. Ramps up to a 12 per cent rise are faster and safer, though escalators seem to be preferred by the public, especially for upward travel; general use of the latter, in spite of their high cost, may therefore be anticipated on new projects. (See Figs. 315, 317.)

Public Spaces. Along the path of the passenger and adjacent to the station platforms are the concourse (the hall on which the train gates open) and the waiting room, together with the various services and conveniences usually located around their perimeters. It is customary to classify the "headhouses," or station buildings proper, as of the waiting room, concourse, or composite type—depending on the focal space of the plan—but the distinctions between these types are somewhat hazy when applied to actual instances.

The original practice of organizing the ticket offices and all other passenger facilities around the waiting room is still observed in the older small-town stations; in this scheme, which functions well, the ticket agent supervises the entire premises from his wicket. Major stations—the Washington Union Station, for example—were built on the same plan until quite recently, the monu-

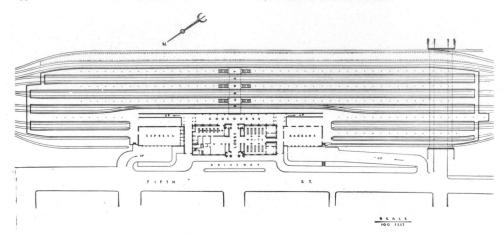

FIGURE 319. UNION STATION, MACON, GEORGIA. PLAN

Fellheimer & Wagner, architects

A typical modern plan for the station of a medium-sized city.　　Courtesy Fellheimer & Wagner

**FIGURE 320.
UNION STATION,
MACON, GEORGIA.
CONCOURSE**

Fellheimer & Wagner, architects

Eclectic ornament gives way to plain surfaces.

Courtesy Fellheimer
& Wagner

mental vaulted ceiling acting as a sort of compensation for the loss of the arched train sheds. This arrangement, however, lengthens walking distances unnecessarily and creates confusing cross currents of traffic in a space where the traveler would naturally expect some rest. Suburban traffic not only has little use for waiting rooms but is even benefited by their omission from the suburban level or section and the resultant shortening of routes to the street or the local transit. In size, the waiting room today requires less space in proportion to total traffic than it did in the past. Great height, formerly favored

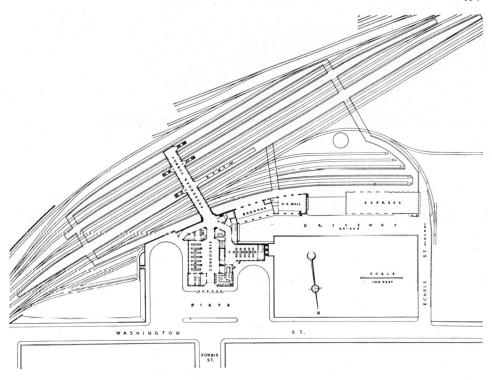

FIGURE 321. RAILROAD STATION, GREENSBORO, NORTH CAROLINA. PLAN
Fellheimer & Wagner, architects

Courtesy Fellheimer & Wagner

partly for appearance and partly for clerestory access to air and light, is no longer in harmony with the more intimate mode of decoration now used, is a positive disadvantage to air conditioning, and interferes with the utilization of air rights above for revenue-producing purposes.

In general, waiting rooms should be placed off the main arteries of station traffic, and an atmosphere of restful quiet may be achieved by the installation of informal, rather clublike furnishings in place of the usual institutional-type benches. This has been done successfully even at small stations, notably those of the Burlington road; in them the waiting-room atmosphere is intimate enough to attract gatherings of women's clubs—a stunt, perhaps, but one that serves the railroad's public relations well. Waiting rooms should be somewhat remote from the street entrance to discourage use by outsiders and especially by undesirable loiterers. A noteworthy deviation from this norm was adopted at the Cincinnati Union Station, where the concourse—which crosses over

FIGURE 322. RAILROAD STATION, SOUTH BEND, INDIANA. EXTERIOR
Fellheimer & Wagner, architects

Courtesy Fellheimer & Wagner

the tracks—was made wide enough to serve as the waiting room as well. Confusion is minimized and a degree of informality is created by the ingenious design and placement of the seats, and the loss of quiet is compensated for by the opportunity of waiting within sight of the train gate—a comfortable arrangement, especially for nervous travelers or for escorts.

The European system of having separate rooms for departing and arriving passengers has not been applicable in the United States because of the prevailing practice of using the tracks interchangeably, although duplicate waiting rooms and facilities on either side of the tracks have been provided at a few busy suburban stations. The Continental custom of providing separate waiting rooms for the three different classes of travel, however, does have counterpart in the Southern states where "Jim Crow" laws require separate waiting rooms, sanitary facilities, and usually even ticket windows for colored patrons, with resulting complications in plan and at a substantial added cost for first investment, staff, and maintenance.

Separate lounge rooms are usually provided for women and arranged to serve as the entrance to their washrooms. Future terminal designs may well incorporate adjoining baby-care rooms, since changing and cleaning up babies is an awkward task as it must be handled in most stations. Rooms where invalid or elderly travelers may receive special care have already been incorporated

FIGURE 323.

TORONTO, HAMILTON &
BUFFALO RAILROAD STATION,
HAMILTON, ONTARIO,
CANADA. TWO EXTERIORS

Fellheimer & Wagner, architects

The station as a special type of
modern commercial architecture.

Courtesy Fellheimer & Wagner

in a few major stations. Wheel chairs and stretchers should be kept within
convenient reach. Separate smoking rooms for the exclusive convenience of
men appear occasionally as Victorian relics but are no longer necessary since
many women passengers now smoke; the eventual air conditioning of most
waiting rooms will remove all need for the protection of non-smokers. Similarly, the former location of the barber shop and the bootblack in conjunction
with the men's toilet has become outdated because of increasing feminine

1. Restaurant
2. Kitchen
3. Parcels
4. Baggage
5. Elevator to customs
   Baggage Agent
   Transfer
   News Stand
   Telephones
6. Tickets
7. Information
   Telegrams
8. Station Agent
9. Service Men's
   Lounges
10. Women's Lounge
    Wash Rooms
    Quiet Room
    Nursery
    Medical Room
11. Service Men
12. Drug Store
13. Men's Wash Room
    and Barber Shop
14. Immigration Offices
15. Service Men's Dining
    Room

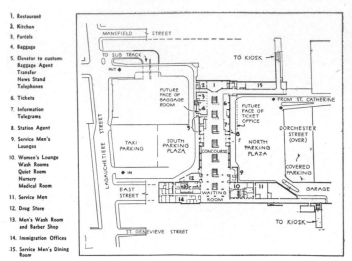

FIGURE 324.

CANADIAN NATIONAL
RAILWAYS STATION,
MONTREAL, CANADA.
PLANS

John Scofield, George R. Drummond, and John Wood, architects; C. B. Brown and A. O. Stewart, engineers

A carefully studied plan for a large city terminal, with special attention given to the ease of passenger circulation and its integration with the baggage facilities.

From *Architectural Record*

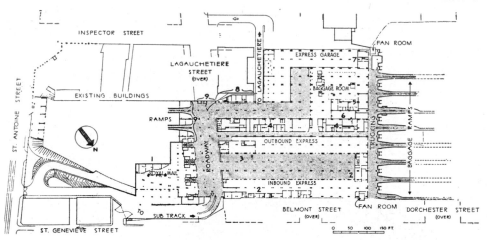

patronage. In contemporary designs, more generally accessible locations are indicated. Bath and shower facilities should be provided in major terminals in connection with the washrooms for both sexes.

Newsstands, telephones, and refreshment counters seem convenient in the waiting room, but other facilities for the service of passengers are more appropriately placed in the concourse, along the routes traveled by all passengers whether they make use of the waiting room or not. One of the most important station facilities is the information desk or counter, which should be in a conspicuous location and designed for handling large crowds of inquirers. Provision for the display of timetables should be included among the early

FIGURE 325.
CANADIAN NATIONAL
RAILWAYS STATION,
MONTREAL, CANADA.
TWO VIEWS

John Scofield, George R. Drummond, and John Wood, architects; C. B. Brown and A. O. Stewart, engineers

A quiet, low exterior, unassuming but inviting, replaces the monumentality so popular earlier.

Courtesy Canadian
National Railways

FIGURE 326.
CANADIAN NATIONAL
RAILWAYS STATION,
MONTREAL, CANADA.
PASSENGER
CONCOURSE

John Scofield, George R. Drummond, and John Wood, architects; C. B. Brown and A. O. Stewart, engineers

Open spaces, excellently designed for visual comfort and pleasure as well as for practical efficiency and ease of maintenance.

Courtesy Canadian
National Railways

design features, since it will relieve the load on the information clerks. Both
the placement of the counter and the space allowance around it should take into
account its time-honored function as a meeting place for travelers and escorts.

Ticket counters should be on the direct line of travel to the platforms. A
reduction of the ticket-selling space required for a given volume of travel may
result from the newer techniques mentioned earlier. Contemporary designs are
increasingly discarding the institutional wicket and grille for the greater informality of the open counter or of a continuous glass plate over an apparently open counter; but whatever the design, ample toe space and a rack or
recess for hand luggage should be provided on the passengers' side of the
counter.

With the introduction of the coin locker the scheme of checking hand
luggage has been revolutionized. Though the traditional check room will remain the harbor for outsize pieces, skis, and the like, its congestion will be
minimized, the numbers of the staff reduced, and the traveler offered greater
convenience by the inclusion of such lockers. In new designs their dispersal
throughout the station in conveniently placed but self-effacing recesses should
be given thorough study.

Other facilities accessible from the concourse generally include a counter
for checking and claiming train baggage; public phones; telegraph, cable, and
radiogram offices; possibly a postal substation; a travelers' aid desk; a first-aid
room (preferably with outside ambulance access); and a lost-and-found room.
The counter for sleeping-car conductors should be part of the original design,
rather than a nightly makeshift set-up of odd pieces of furniture. Concessions,
beginning with a lunch counter, restaurant, barber shop, and beauty parlor,
will be limited in their number and variety only by their probable rentability.

The main function of the concourse, however, is to channel the major traffic
of the station to or from the vestibules giving street access. Stairs, escalators,
and ramps should connect these vestibules with the station platforms when
the tracks are on more than one level or when the street connections differ in
elevation from the main floor of the station. Access to the platforms is through
the train gates, which, to prevent confusion, should preferably be placed along
one wall or at any rate within sight from a central position in the concourse.
In a stub-type terminal the concourse may merely give access to a semi-outdoors secondary or midway concourse which connects with the ends of all
platforms and is separated from them by a series of train gates.

Vehicular Access. This subject has already been mentioned, incidentally, but a summary may be worth while to bring its complications to the designer's notice.

Simple and quick access in directions which are self-evident and need no signs should be available to travelers arriving—or departing—in privately owned cars. Access by taxicabs should likewise be direct and quick. Even with the best planning, congestion caused by private cars alone may overtax the station's facilities as well as the conveniently adjacent drives and parking areas. It is reported that loud-speaker call systems are being installed in outdoor stations to speed up such traffic. Buses should be accommodated separately if their runs terminate at the station. In normal times waiting taxicabs require space for lining up independently of the main circulation. (See Fig. 317.) Passengers with trunks or other heavy baggage should preferably be handled at separate entrances to avoid tie-ups of the normal light traffic. These entrances should also be readily identifiable and should have direct access to ticket offices, baggage checking, and express. Access for freight of all types should, if possible, be entirely independent. Such traffic would include express hauling, delivery of supplies for station and train use, maintenance trucks, and removal of trash and garbage.

Since the number of persons directly employed in the operation of major terminals runs well into the hundreds, special entrances for them are often desirable both for ease of supervision and control and for the separation of those engaged in heavy manual work from the passenger traffic. In addition to direct railroad needs, the access requirements of the rental areas and concessions must be met. Any parking or car-rental facilities included in a terminal plan should, if feasible, have their own entrances remote from those of the station, although the facilities themselves should be within easy reach of travelers without exposing them to the weather. Concessions need access for receiving their merchandise and supplies and for the removal of refuse, and, since in the major terminals concessions are often sizable establishments, the designer should endeavor to remove this traffic from the primary circulation.

It should be mentioned, too, that in the modern terminal, with its office areas on upper floors, the office employees will put an additional strain on the access facilities just when travel is heaviest. The office portions, therefore, should have independent entrances, preferably so situated that business callers may enter the office section directly. In addition, adjoining properties are likely to develop into office buildings and hotels, as noted earlier. Sometimes such properties are owned and leased for development by the railroads themselves, but even when that is not the case the railroads may evidence an interest in the heavy passenger traffic originating in such buildings. Thus it is often practicable and desirable to tunnel under the bordering streets to establish direct pedestrian connection with as many adjacent buildings as possible. In fact, such tunnels remove a good deal of congestion from the surface streets, favor the long-haul passenger, and also provide weather-sheltered access for additional thousands of commuters. Finally, in communities in which an elevated or sub-surface rapid-transit system exists, its connection with the terminal, and particularly with commuter trains, should be given consideration.

From the above discussion it should be evident that proper accessibility is a major problem and requires numerous comparative studies. Adequate solutions may necessitate several levels and the designer should keep in mind that the problem can be solved not merely by providing a multiplicity of entrances but rather by furnishing specialized entrances, each so adapted to its particular need that it will inevitably be used by the traffic for which it is intended.

Structural Considerations. Most structural problems encountered in station design are common to other types of buildings; a few special comments, however, may be in order here.

Where steam locomotives are run into stations, the problem of removing smoke and steam is basic. Both are highly detrimental to structural materials— reinforced concrete as well as steel—and both destroy protective coatings of paint in short order. The best remedy obviously is to let smoke and steam escape directly from the locomotive stack to the outside air; for surfaces they may touch—especially the "blast plates" directly above the stacks—cast iron, aluminum, or heavy asbestos board may be used.

In train sheds the spacing of columns often presents questions which may become complex when these columns support air-rights structures above or when, more properly, the columns of superimposed buildings pass through to foundations independent of the parts of the station structure subject to train vibration. The vibration of moving trains should be confined as much as possible to those parts of the structure which are inevitably affected. Parts supporting the tracks should therefore be separated from the framework of the station building as well as from adjacent streets, overpasses, elevated highways, or local transit structures; if there are additional upper floors (whether occupied by railroad offices or competing with standard rental space), it is essential to separate their structure from both the track and the station structures. One reason for this is that vibration, of which a certain amount is normal in the station building itself, greatly depreciates the value of the air-rights structures. The other reason for keeping station and air-rights structures independent of each other is that the latter often are built later, their loads and column locations being unknown at the time of the station's construction. Even if built simultaneously, however, an air-rights structure competing with comparable space in standard buildings is likely to be obsolete and ready for replacement long before the station itself, and the original locations and strengths of structural members may then prove inadequate for the new construction.

Above the foundations, the members of the different systems should be as far apart as possible since vibration is transmitted through intervening spaces. Under extremely crowded conditions, 6 inches is considered minimum spacing between columns or girders. In walls, floors, and ceilings, secondary parts of the structure may need to be brought closer together for the sake of appearance or for waterproofing. In no case, however, should rigid structures approach closer than 2 inches under maximum temperature expansion; any remaining space should be closed by flexible members.

Special Features. Though most special features of terminals have been touched on in the course of this chapter, there are a few to which special attention should be directed.

Time is an important factor in transportation. In a well-planned station a clock should be in view from almost any position likely to be occupied by the public, or at least within a few steps from any position. Here easy legibility should take precedence over novel or striking design; time indicators in place of clocks, such as the one at the Cincinnati Union Station, may be even better.

Directional signs are important, especially for the highly prized and competitive long-haul traffic, which is generally transient and therefore unfamiliar with the station in question. A good basic plan, of course, is largely self-explanatory; with the addition of appropriate signs there should be absolutely no chance of a traveler's losing his way and no necessity for his stopping to ask questions. For this reason the location, type, illumination, and size of the signs should be carefully weighed. Directional signs should be given unassailable supremacy over concession and advertising signs.

Among the specialized devices employed to direct the public to trains are the announcement boards giving track number and time of arrival or departure, the sleeping-car conductors' signs, and the train-gate signs. Special lighting effects are often used to direct attention to these, and quick, easy changeability of the legends is as essential as their legibility, which in the case

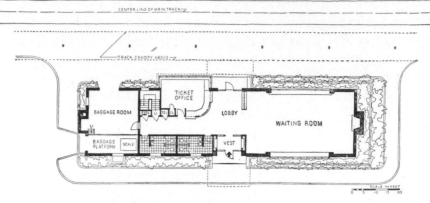

FIGURE 327. BURLINGTON RAILROAD STATION, LA CROSSE, WISCONSIN. PLAN

Holabird & Root, architects

A modern interpretation of a plan type that goes back to the Richardson stations of the 1880's.

From *Architectural Forum*

FIGURE 328. BURLINGTON RAILROAD STATION, LA CROSSE, WISCONSIN. EXTERIOR

Holabird & Root, architects

Stressed horizontality, quiet surfaces, large openings, and simple materials beautifully detailed distinguish many small modern stations. Photograph Hedrich-Blessing

of chalk-written announcements can be promoted by training employees in good handwriting. Equipment manufacturers offer various versions of these devices, many of them originally architect-designed; nevertheless the designer

FIGURE 329. RURAL
RAILROAD STATION,
MULLINS,
SOUTH CAROLINA.
PERSPECTIVE

Fellheimer & Wagner, architects

A typical example of a small rural station.

Courtesy Fellheimer
& Wagner

of new projects will probably not find it difficult to suggest further improvements.

Escalators and electric-eye doors are especially acceptable conveniences for passengers encumbered with baggage or children.

A fascinating feature of major stations, though one seldom seen by the public, is the control tower where switches for all approaches, station tracks, and yards are set. Control towers are located, when possible, at vantage points which offer a view of at least a portion of the track layout in order to supplement the electrical reporting performed by the board— for at a major terminal it is hardly possible to look over the entire yard from one spot. Although broadcasting studios, power-generating stations, and other enterprises have long used similar operations—observable through plate-glass walls—as focal points of public interest, here the location of the towers usually prevents public access.

APPLICATION OF TERMINAL DESIGN PRINCIPLES
TO SMALLER STATIONS

The needs of the smaller stations, particularly in rural regions, have changed much less drastically than have those of large city terminals. A platform, covered for the greater part of its length; a general waiting room serving the same purposes as the concourse of the larger stations; a room for baggage checking and storage, and possibly another for express; a ticket office arranged for one-man control and designed to give visual command of the tracks as well as convenient accessibility to passengers; toilets for men and women, and perhaps one for employees; the possibility of convenient and, if feasible, under-cover approach from automobiles—these are the usual requirements. Local conditions

FIGURE 330. RAILROAD STATION,
PRINCE, WEST VIRGINIA.

TWO EXTERIORS

Garfield, Harris, Robinson & Schafer, architects

Another distinguished example of the small station, stressing its harmony with the landscape by its quiet directness and a careful use of materials.

Photographs R. Marvin Wilson,
courtesy Garfield, Harris,
Robinson & Schafer

will determine what, if any, concession space must be furnished for a newsstand or a lunch counter and will also dictate the amount of space necessary for automobile parking and for trucking to baggage and express rooms (see Figs. 327, 329).

Naturally these elements must be arranged with the same careful study of passenger convenience and of operational safety and efficiency as in the case of the larger stations. Simplicity, permanence of materials, and economy are paramount in both design and construction. If the railroad is single-tracked, one platform will usually suffice, unless there are special stub tracks for freight or express cars. If the line is double-tracked, two platforms, connected by either subway or bridge, should be the rule. From these simple elements the imaginative designer can create stations of dignity and charm.

The suburban station offers important special planning problems quite different from those of the usual rural station. These are:

1. The necessity of large areas for commuters' parking and of a special study of automobile approaches
2. Strict elimination of unnecessary steps in getting to the train platform
3. Small relative importance of baggage or express facilities
4. Small importance (in proportion to number of passengers) of waiting-room and ticket-office facilities; on the other hand, frequent desirability of newsstand and lunch counter

Another complication may arise from the fact that in many suburban communities the tracks are either depressed or raised in order to avoid grade crossings. This will entail careful study of the approach problem and will frequently call for the design of a two-level station, with the station building either above or below the tracks. In such a case, particular consideration must be given to the ramps or steps which connect the platforms with the parking spaces, bus stops, or other means of access in order to handle swiftly and easily the congested traffic at morning and evening. A good example with raised tracks is the station at Valley Stream, on Long Island, designed by Edgar Williams (Figs. 333, 334).

SUMMARY

The following points, previously covered, may be emphasized to guide the architect in making his best contribution to a problem of station design:

1. A direct functional plan to provide adequately for railroad requirements, for ready access to and departure from trains, and for the general convenience of the public
2. Study of attendant civic improvements made possible by topographic or other physical site conditions
3. Simple architectural treatment, dignified, free from fripperies, and not

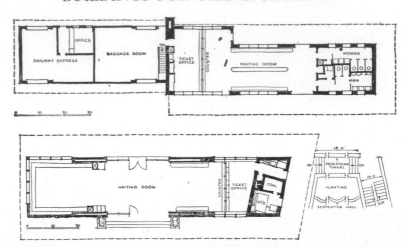

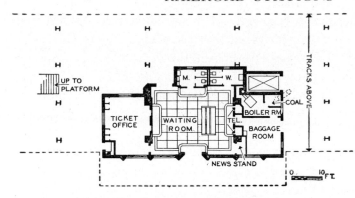

FIGURE 333 (LEFT).
LONG ISLAND
RAIL ROAD STATION,
VALLEY STREAM,
LONG ISLAND,
NEW YORK.
LOWER-LEVEL PLAN

Edgar I. Williams, architect

A two-level suburban station with the tracks above.

FIGURE 334. LONG ISLAND RAIL ROAD STATION, VALLEY STREAM, LONG ISLAND, NEW YORK. EXTERIOR

Edgar I. Williams, architect

Photograph Rodney McCay Morgan—Photolog; courtesy Edgar I. Williams

FIGURE 331 (OPPOSITE, TOP). PENNSYLVANIA RAILROAD STATION, ABERDEEN PROVING GROUND, MARYLAND. PLAN

Lester Tichy, architect

A small station of almost suburban type for a busy through line; two stations, one on each side of the track, are often necessary in situations like this.   From *Architectural Record*

FIGURE 332 (OPPOSITE, MIDDLE AND BOTTOM). PENNSYLVANIA RAILROAD STATION, ABERDEEN PROVING GROUND, MARYLAND. TWO EXTERIORS

Lester Tichy, architect

A mid-twentieth-century expression of the Richardson tradition of basic station form.

Photographs Gottscho-Schleisner

likely to be rapidly dated; employment of substantial materials for both exterior and interior and of forms and finishes that are easily kept clean

4. Full utilization of revenue opportunities in the form of rental shops and facilities, air-rights for commercial buildings, and the like

5. Avoidance of a freezing of the plan and restriction of fixed enclosures to a minimum in order to allow rearrangement to meet changing conditions in railroading and related transport operations

6. Avoidance of a static point of view or such undue dependence on precedent as might make a terminal obsolete before its time

SUGGESTED ADDITIONAL READING FOR CHAPTER 39

"Cincinnati Union Terminal," *Architectural Forum*, Vol. 58, No. 6 (June, 1933), pp. 453–78.

Fellheimer, Alfred, "Modern Railway Passenger Terminals," *Architectural Forum*, Vol. 53, No. 6 (December, 1930), pp. 655–94.

—— "Railway Passenger Terminals," *Encyclopædia Britannica*, Vol. 18, p. 944.

Handbuch der Architektur, edited by Josef Durm, Herman Ende, Eduard Schmitt, Heinrich Wagner, and others (Darmstadt: Diehl, 1883–1933), Part IV, Vol. 2, No. 4 (1911), article "Empfaugsgebäude der Bahnhöfe und Bahnsteigüberdachungen . . ." by Eduard Schmitt.

Meeks, Carroll L. V., "Form Beneath Fashion" [the history of railroad-station types], *Magazine of Art*, Vol. 39, No. 8 (Dec., 1946), pp. 378–380.

—— "The Life of a Form: A History of the Train Shed," *Architectural Review*, Vol. CX, No. 657 (Sept., 1951), pp. [162]–173.

—— "19th Century Train Sheds," Design Analysis No. 4, *Architectural Forum*, Vol. 84, No. 2 (Feb., 1946), pp. [104]–[109].

Simms, F. W. (editor), *Public Works of Great Britain*, 2nd ed. (London, 1846).

40

Airports

By THOMAS E. GREACEN II

COMPARED with the industries which have grown up to serve surface transportation, the aviation industry is a new field; it is not surprising, therefore, that up to the middle of the twentieth century it has claimed so small a measure of the architect's and the city planner's attention. Its tremendous importance during the Second World War, however, gave it an opportunity for expansion and development unparalleled in history. Since the war has made the whole world "air-minded," it seems unlikely that either economic distress or the perfection of other means of travel will discourage the continuous growth of aviation. There can be little doubt that the planning of air facilities of all kinds—airfields, airports, air terminals, airplane shops, factories, and so on—will demand an increasing share of attention.

In many respects the science of aviation is still in the experimental stage, and day-to-day developments in the design of aircraft and in the means of controlling aircraft, both in the air and on the ground, present new and complex problems for the airport planner. The most reliable information concerning airport design and current planning standards is to be found in the publications of government agencies and in current technical periodicals devoted to the subject. In order to make this chapter of permanent value, the discussion has been purposely limited to fundamental principles. The application of these principles will vary with each specific problem, and the techniques of planning will change with every new development in the science of aviation. Sources of detailed planning information are referred to in one of the footnotes and in the bibliography. The student approaching his first airport design problem and the seasoned planner alike are advised to consult the latest sources of information, to keep an open and inquiring mind, and, if they intend to make any substantial contributions to this subject, to eschew "approved solutions."

		CLASS I	CLASS II
PURPOSE OF AIRPORT	*Type and Size of Community*	Small communities not on present or proposed scheduled air-carrier system and auxiliary airports in larger metropolitan areas to serve non-scheduled private flying activities.	Larger communities located on present or proposed feeder-line airways and having considerable aeronautical activity. General population range 5,000 to 25,000.
	Type and Size of Aircraft to Be Accommodated	Small private-owner-type planes. This includes roughly planes up to a gross weight of 4,000 pounds, or having a wing loading (lbs./sq. ft.) times power loading (lbs./HP) not exceeding 190.	Larger-size private-owner planes and some small-size transport planes. This represents roughly planes in the gross weight classification between 4,000 and 15,000 pounds or having a wing loading (lbs./sq. ft.) times power loading (lbs./HP) of 190 to 230.
FACILITIES PROVIDED	*Length of Prepared Landing Strips*	1,800' to 2,700'	2,700' to 3,700'
	Width of Prepared Landing Strips	300'	500'
	Length of Paved Runways	None	2,500' to 3,500'
	Width of Paved Runways	None	150' (night operation) 100' (day operation only)
	Required Wind Coverage	70 per cent	75 per cent
	Facilities Usually Provided	Drainage, fencing, marking, wind direction indicator, hangar, basic lighting (optional)	Includes Class I facilities and lighting, hangar and shop, fueling, weather information, office space, parking

CLASS III	CLASS IV	CLASS V
Important cities on feeder-line airway systems and many intermediate points on the main-line airways. General population range 25,000 to several hundred thousand.	Cities in these groups represent the major industrial centers of the nation and important junction points or terminals on the airways system.	
Present-day transport planes. Planes in this classification are represented approximately by those between 10,000 and 50,000 pounds gross weight, or by those having a wing loading (lbs./sq. ft.) times power loading (lbs./HP) of 230 and over.	Largest planes in use and those planned for the immediate future. This approximately represents planes having a gross weight of 74,000 pounds and over or having a wing loading (lbs./sq. ft.) times power loading (lbs./HP) of 230 and over.	
3,700' to 4,700'	4,700' to 5,700'	5,700' and over
500'	500'	500'
3,500' to 4,500'	4,500' to 5,500'	5,500' and over
200' (instrument) 150' (night operation)	200' (instrument) 150' (night operation)	200' (instrument) 150' (night operation)
80 per cent	90 per cent	90 per cent

Include Class II facilities and weather bureau, two-way radio, visual traffic control, instrument approach system (when required), administration building, taxiways, and aprons

* Data obtained from published Standards of Civil Aeronautics Administration, Dept. of Commerce, Washington, D.C.

FIGURE 335. WRIGHT-PATTERSON AIR FORCE BASE, DAYTON, OHIO. AIR VIEW

The view looks east over Wright Field; Patterson Field is beyond. The two fields are separated but related, and the multitude of necessary shops, laboratories, and administration buildings is grouped around them in a careful functional relationship.

United States Air Force Official Photograph

AIRPORTS OF THE PAST

The first heavier-than-air craft were launched from low hills. This was the case at Kittyhawk, North Carolina, where Wilbur and Orville Wright on December 17, 1903, made their epochal flight from the top of a sand dune. Succeeding pioneers both in the United States and abroad developed flying machines which took off from level ground, generally smooth turf fields. During the First World War most of the airdromes built behind the lines and around the circumference of such strategic cities as Paris, London, and Berlin were of this type. Aircraft were then light in weight and extremely sensitive to cross winds on landing and take-off, and the turf fields of those days afforded opportunity to operate in whatever direction the wind dictated. At the conclusion of the war a largely unorganized group of men set about adapting aviation to peace-time uses. Much itinerant flying was done, and many in the United States had their first taste of flying in the open cockpits of the "barn-

FIGURE 336.
WRIGHT-PATTERSON
AIR BASE,
DAYTON, OHIO. TWO
AIR VIEWS

ABOVE: Patterson Field;
BELOW: Wright Field.
Both show logical devel-
opments of different basic
patterns. Note the taxi-
ways and aprons.

United States Air
Force Official
Photographs

stormers" who took up passengers from outlying pastures. A few airlines were started, and scheduled passenger and mail flights were undertaken along defined routes between such public and private airfields as then existed. Little flying was done at night because of the inadequacy of lighting and radio aids. The development of aircraft during this period was largely in the hands of a few pioneers like Martin, Curtiss, Boeing, and Douglas—men whose names have since become widely known—and was largely fostered by the government's growing concern for military flying.

From the standpoint of air facilities, the most important step taken by the United States between the two world wars was the creation of a separate government agency charged with the development of civil aviation. The Civil Aeronautics Administration (CAA) was created by an Act of Congress in 1938; statistics of that year show that there were 35,492 airway miles of domestic airways connecting all parts of the United States and 2,374 airports of various types and sizes along and near these routes.[1] Similar developments

[1] By 1945 the number of airway miles had increased to 66,979 and the number of certified airports to 3,917.

FIGURE 337. WRIGHT-PATTERSON AIR FORCE BASE, DAYTON, OHIO. AIRDOCK

Albert Kahn Associates, architects and engineers

This structure contains two hangars and, between them, an administrative section. The hangars are 266 feet wide; the height to the top of the control tower is 90 feet.

United States Air Force Official Photograph

were taking place all over the world, and for the first time large sums of money were being invested in airports. Even before the Second World War, air traffic had reached sizable proportions in the United States and western Europe. Paved runways designed according to highway principles were first constructed in the United States in the early 1930's, when it became more and more difficult to maintain turf under the traffic of the heavy aircraft then in use. Since 1929, when the Lehigh Portland Cement Company conducted a national architectural competition for the design of an airport with paved runways, the manufacturers of cement and bituminous materials have devoted much time and money to the development of runway pavements and the study of attendant problems in airfield design (Fig. 339). Just prior to the Second World War the standards for a mainline airport called for a mile-square grass

FIGURE 338.
WRIGHT-PATTERSON
AIR FORCE BASE,
DAYTON, OHIO.
REINFORCED
CONCRETE HANGARS
AND CONTROL TOWER

United States Army Quartermaster Corps, architects and engineers

The clear span of the hangars is 275 feet; the doors are 250 feet wide in the clear, with a height of 38 feet.

United States Air Force Official Photograph

area provided with three or four intersecting runways from 3,500 feet to 5,000 feet in length. Civil airports were usually constructed on the snowflake pattern, with terminal facilities in the center of the landing area to minimize taxiing; military airfields favored rectangular landing areas bordered by hangars and long parking aprons (see Fig. 340).

The part played by air supremacy in the German success at the beginning of the Second World War left no doubt of the necessity for a mighty air armada in the United States, and as part of an intensive program of air-force expansion the country embarked on an era of airfield construction which has left its imprint on all parts of the country. Pre-war standards were hastily adapted to the needs of heavy bombardment operation, and runways of unprecedented dimensions were unrolled across the landscape. Airport planners with difficulty kept up with the demands of the aircraft designers. Airplane wheel loads increased from 15,000 to 60,000 pounds. Permissible runway grades were reduced, minimum runway lengths were increased, and vast sums of money were expended in clearing the approaches in order to permit the heavy bombers to take off with safety. Dual and even triple runways were laid down in an effort to launch large numbers of aircraft in a short time. The limit was soon found in the air space over the fields, and steps were taken to disperse the aircraft on satellite fields. Significant developments in radio direction-finding equipment were adapted to serve the needs of bad-weather flying, and instrument landing systems became standard equipment. Meanwhile the ever growing activities of military air transport developed means of ferry-

FIGURE 339.
WINNING DESIGN IN THE LEHIGH CEMENT AIRPORT COMPETITION, 1930

A. C. Zimmerman and W. H. Harrison, associated architects and engineers

A design characterized by an efficient layout of runways and taxiways, with plane approach through a free-standing kiosk approached from the station proper by an underground tunnel. Several planes can be loaded or unloaded at the same time.

From Lehigh Cement Co., *Airport Designs . . .*

ing men and supplies to all the major fronts and involved the United States in the construction of mammoth bases all over the world.

Analyses of airport performance, traffic flow, pavement design, and the like on these wartime fields were of necessity delayed until the work of construction was done; but proper studies can now be carried out and should provide a sound basis for future airport planning.

THE AIRPORT AND THE CITY

Aviation enthusiasts are clamoring for means to make flying a part of the daily life of the average man, and the realization of this dream necessarily de-

TYPE OF PLAN USED FOR CIVIL AIRPORTS
AT THE BEGINNING OF WORLD WAR II

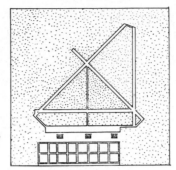

FIGURE 340. TYPICAL
AIRPORT PLANS AT
THE BEGINNING OF
THE SECOND WORLD
WAR

Courtesy Thomas E.
Greacen II

TYPE OF PLAN USED FOR MILITARY AIRFIELDS
AT THE BEGINNING OF WORLD WAR II

pends on airport planning and on the place of the airport in city development. It is likely that in time the airplane will occupy a position comparable to that of the motor car, both as a private vehicle and as a public conveyance. In the case of aircraft used as a public conveyance, operations must be correlated with the operations of railroad trains, buses, and streetcars, and air facilities must be studied in relation to the facilities provided for mass surface transportation. If it serves as a private vehicle, the airplane must be considered in the planning of both residential areas and business districts because people will use it going to and from their daily occupations.

City planners must be familiar with the considerations involved in air travel and with the operational requirements of aircraft. They must find space for landing fields and for aircraft servicing and storage facilities in the vicinity of business districts, shopping centers, and home communities.[2] To omit them from the city plan would handicap the normal development of community life. Sooner or later they will be required, and if they are not planned for ahead of time the cost will be prodigious. Eliel Saarinen in his book *The City* [3] offers one possible solution to this problem—the provision of landing facilities in greenbelts which he visualizes as separating the different functional areas of the planned city of the future. This solution is in line with the thought of many airport planners who foresee a system of small private airfields serving the local needs of cities, augmented by one or two major air terminals for passenger and cargo transport. Most planners agree that the requirements of

[2] The not inconsiderable noise caused by present-day aircraft operation seriously complicates this problem. Airports must not only be conveniently accessible but also be so placed that as far as possible residential districts are protected from undue disturbance by aircraft landing or taking off. Ed.

[3] *The City; Its Growth, Its Decay, Its Future* (New York: Reinhold Publishing Co., 1943).

private flying and those of commercial flying differ substantially and that the separation of facilities for these two would be very desirable, although heretofore neither category has developed the traffic necessary to maintain separate airports.

TYPES OF AIRPORTS

Up to now the average civil airport has accommodated all types of aircraft operations. In the future we may expect to see a variety of special types developed. Besides airports planned for the scheduled traffic of air transports or the intermittent operations of private flying, others will be designed to meet the needs of cargo and mail traffic, aerial taxi services, flying schools, aircraft sales and servicing, aerial photography, and a considerable variety of special operations such as crop-dusting. These diverse operations employ aircraft of various sizes and speeds and, particularly in the case of schools, require a separation of traffic both on the ground and in the air. Landing facilities may also be required for helicopters, which when perfected should provide satisfactory shuttle craft for distances up to about seventy-five miles.

The CAA has adopted a classification of United States airports based principally on the size of the aircraft to be accommodated and on the extent of the facilities provided. Upon the completion of an airport and prior to its use, application must be made to the CAA for certification, and the appropriate certificate for its class will be given when the airport complies in all important respects with the requirements for that class (see pages 476, 477). In planning an airport to meet the requirements for any class, it is advisable to design with the requirements of a higher category in mind and to provide clearances, grades, and the like which will permit economical enlargement of the airport to the size ultimately needed. Provision for such expansion should also be assured by the acquiring of sufficient property at the original site, by obtaining avigation easements, and by securing the passage of zoning ordinances that will prevent the construction of any buildings or obstructions which might later restrict the development of the airport.[4]

AIRPORT SITES

The final selection of the site for an airport is usually the result of a compromise involving a variety of considerations, all of which are important and

[4] Suggested model airport zoning ordinances have been developed by several agencies, including the Civil Aeronautics Administration and the National Institute of Municipal Law Officers, 730 Jackson Place N.W., Washington 6, D.C.

FIGURE 341. OLD MUNICIPAL AIRPORT, DETROIT, MICHIGAN. AIR VIEW

A crowded airport hemmed in on all sides by residential and industrial developments with many insuperable hazards.   Photograph Fairchild Aerial Surveys

most of which are difficult to satisfy. Airline operators consider accessibility a major factor; airport sponsors often view cost as the most important factor. Freedom from obstructions, suitability of aerial approaches, favorable meteorological conditions, adaptability of the site to economical construction, and the availability of additional land for future expansion are also vital factors and must be considered both for their immediate significance and for their effect upon the ultimate development. Frequently the most economical site for a small airport proves eventually to be the costliest one, if the traffic density becomes so great that the airport must later be expanded or abandoned. The crowded airport, hemmed in on all sides by industrial and residential developments and by immovable natural obstacles, is an all-too-familiar sight and offers abundant proof of the disastrous consequences of hasty site selection and shortsighted planning. (See Fig. 341.)

The time saving that is one of the principal advantages of air travel is lost when the air terminal is located far from the center of business. Had proper sites been reserved for airports when our cities were first laid out, our airports might now be as accessible to the majority of our citizens as are our railway stations and bus terminals. Unfortunately aviation has come of age too late for that. Our cities are already built, and it takes an ingenious planner to locate a good airport site on the available land that remains. For the bolder spirit there is some comfort in the recollection that the bulk of commercial and

FIGURE 342. MUNICIPAL AIRPORT, ATLANTA, GEORGIA. AIR VIEW
The greater freedom and safety of a more open site. Photograph Fairchild Aerial Surveys

industrial development in the United States has grown up along the railroads and the highways. It hardly requires a prophet to foresee a similar development about the air terminals and a gradual movement from the present crowded centers of trade to the spacious ones which can and should be developed on the outskirts of the cities around the airports.

In the past, questions of cost and accessibility to town have frequently overshadowed the technical considerations which should be weighed carefully in appraising an airport site. Public safety, operating efficiency, and economy of construction all depend to a large extent on a sound appraisal of the technical advantages of the site. To mention only a few of these criteria, a good airport site should have a low water table and a coarse subsoil which will support heavy loads. It should be relatively flat but should have enough slope to prevent the accumulation of surface water. It should not be subject to ground fogs or smoke from industrial areas. It should have clear, unobstructed approaches in all directions. A good access highway will be needed for it, as well as water and electric power. Locating a site with sufficient area to accommodate runways, aircraft parking, buildings, auto parking, and the necessary safety zones around

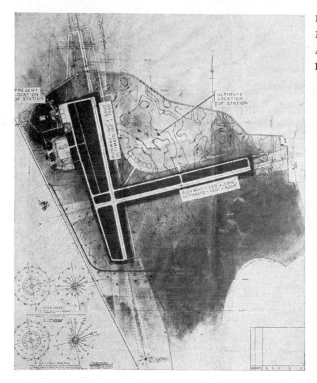

FIGURE 343.
MUNICIPAL AIRPORT,
AUGUSTA, GEORGIA.
PLAN

Courtesy J. Hampton-
Manning

the flying field is in itself a problem. Two hundred acres are barely adequate
for a Class I or Class II installation; a thousand acres is considered only fair for
a Class IV installation; and a major air terminal frequently covers several
thousand acres.

It should hardly be necessary to point out that no site, however satisfactory
it may seem, should be accepted before preliminary planning and engineering
studies have been made to ascertain, first, if a satisfactory layout can be made,
and, second, if the construction will be practicable and economical.

PRELIMINARY STEPS IN PLANNING

It is a good rule in planning airports for the designer to establish a work
schedule and to follow it meticulously. This prevents the planner from overlooking important details and facilitates dovetailing the information together,
step by step. First, collect all pertinent data. Second, analyze the data and
determine the design criteria applicable to the job. These two steps are necessary to produce a program. The third step is the preparation of a number of

FIGURE 344.
PETER O. KNIGHT
AIRPORT,
TAMPA, FLORIDA.
AIR VIEW

The natural limitations
of the site would hamper
future enlargements.

Photograph Ewing
Galloway

different layout studies, trying different runway, taxiway, and apron combinations until one is found which fits the site and fulfills the program. Always plan the flying field first and leave the building areas and other facilities for later consideration. When a satisfactory plan has been found, it should be checked and co-ordinated with the CAA requirements and then developed in detail.

The principal limiting factors in planning an airfield are: the characteristics of the aircraft to be accommodated; the types of operation to be accommodated and their extent; the meteorological conditions prevailing in the locality; the extent and topography of the site and the topography of the surrounding areas; and the composition of the soil found on the site.

Aircraft Characteristics. The following data on the aircraft that will have to be accommodated must be ascertained:

1. Weight, Number of Wheels, and Tire Print. From this information the planner determines the static load per square inch which the pavement must carry.

2. Length of Take-off Run. This determines the length of runways required. In practice the runway length is usually assumed to equal the distance necessary for taking off and clearing a 50-foot obstacle.

3. Length of Landing Roll. This distance establishes the points at which taxiways should be provided to permit aircraft to turn off the runways after landing.

4. Minimum Glide Angle. This is calculated from the minimum air speed and minimum rate of descent; it gives the planner the information required to establish safe approaches to the runways.

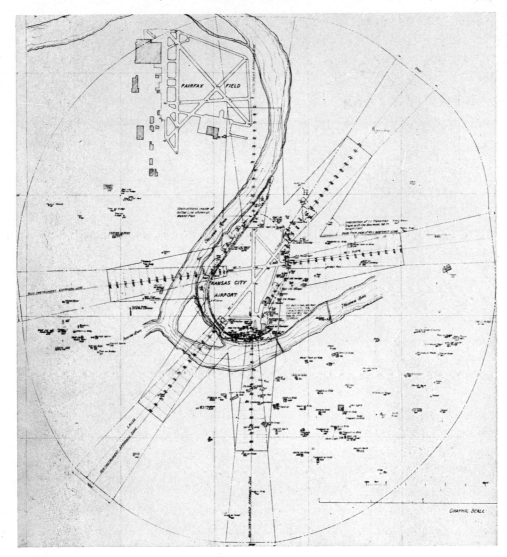

FIGURE 345. MUNICIPAL AIRPORT, KANSAS CITY, MISSOURI. PLAN

The vast area required by a major airport.   Courtesy John E. Maring

5. Maximum Safe Beam-Wind Velocity. Because of the usual variableness of winds in most places, it is not practical to provide runways aligned with all wind headings, and aircraft will usually have to land and take off at an angle with the wind. This wind angle can be mathematically resolved in a beam wind (a wind at right angles to the direction of flight), and the number and direction

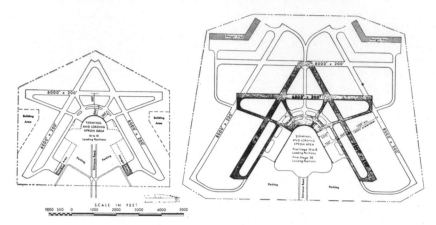

FIGURE 346. SIXTY-DEGREE SINGLE-RUNWAY PATTERN; SIXTY-DEGREE PARALLEL-RUNWAY PATTERN

From ATA, *Airline Airport Design Recommendations*

of the necessary runways can be computed for the "wind rose," using the maximum safe beam-wind velocity for the type of aircraft to be accommodated.

6. Dimensions and Turning Radius. From these figures the planner computes the widths of pavement required for runways, taxiways, and aprons and the dimensions of the hangars in which the aircraft will be serviced and stored.

Type and Extent of Operations. It is often possible to estimate with considerable accuracy the traffic to be expected on an airfield, especially in the case of either scheduled airline or flying-school operations. Some estimate should be made of the number of daily operations expected, no matter what type the field may be.

Aircraft operations are often very dissimilar, and each type requires radically different facilities and a different type of airport plan. A flying school, for instance, employs small planes and requires successive landings and take-offs, known as "touch-and-go" landings, in the training of students. Safety requires that the beginner operate straight into the wind, whichever way it happens to blow. Consequently flying schools often prefer all-over turf fields or "mats" of modest dimensions. On the other hand, scheduled airline operations employ heavy aircraft, which are less affected by cross winds and require long all-weather runways and airfield layouts that will reduce taxiing to a minimum. These differences are reflected in the plans. The flying school may have a rectangular turf field, with a large parking apron located at one side.

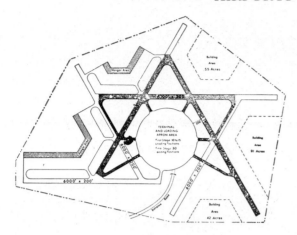

FIGURE 347. SIXTY-DEGREE
OPEN PARALLEL-RUNWAY
PATTERN

From ATA, *Airline Airport
Design Recommendations*

The airline terminal will probably have two or three runways crossing near the middle of the field, with a small apron adjacent to the crossing and flanking the airline terminal building.

It is important to achieve a balance in the facilities provided—that is, between runway capacity, apron capacity, and so on. The runways usually determine the capacity of the airfield. With present equipment it is generally considered that forty plane movements per hour are a fair maximum for a single-runway system—a system of runways in which only one runway is available for use at any given time (see Fig. 346). A plane movement consists of one landing *or* one take-off. Assuming that a scheduled airliner requires an average time of thirty minutes to unload and load passengers, cargo, and fuel, a balanced parking apron should provide ten positions for peak-hour operations. During a given period the number of landings may exceed the number of take-offs, and it is good practice to provide space for more than ten aircraft.

To increase the capacity of a balanced single-runway airfield it is necessary to speed up the plane movements, which at present can be done only by providing an additional system of runways. This problem has produced some interesting layout patterns. The first of these is the conventional parallel layout, in which one additional parallel runway has been added in each direction. The scheme is only partially successful because it requires that aircraft taxiing to the take-off position pass directly across the line of flight of aircraft coming in for a landing. The second is the so-called open parallel pattern (Fig. 347), in which parallel runways are constructed on opposite sides of the terminal area. The only serious disadvantage of this scheme is that it circumscribes the

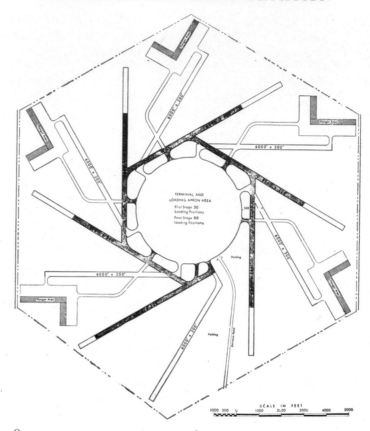

FIGURE 348. THIRTY-DEGREE TANGENTIAL-RUNWAY PATTERN

From ATA, *Airline Airport Design Recommendations*

terminal area and prevents its future expansion. The third pattern is the tangential (Fig. 348), which has recently claimed much attention because of its apparent adaptability for the handling of large volumes of traffic. It not only reduces taxiing to a minimum and practically eliminates the need for taxiways but also permits simultaneous operations on several runways under most wind conditions. Unfortunately, however, it requires a much larger site than do the other patterns; it circumscribes the terminal area; and for its capacity it relies on the simultaneous use of converging runways for landings, a principle not yet accepted by all authorities. All these patterns of airport expansion have been described for the purpose of demonstrating the importance of allowing for expansion in the original scheme. Expansion of a single-runway system to the open parallel scheme, for instance, would not be feasible unless in the

HQ. ARMY AIR FORCES
WEATHER DIVISION

Surface Winds

Period Summary By Velocity Groups

U. S. WEATHER BUREAU
STATISTICS DIVISION

EL PASO TEX BIGGS

ANNUAL
APRIL 1941 THRU JUNE 1945

STATION — MONTH & PERIOD

CODE	VEL. DIR.	1-3 mph	4-12 mph	13-24 mph	25-31 mph	32-46 mph	47 & over	Total 4 mph & Over		Total All Obs		TOTAL VEL.	AV. VEL.
								OBS	%	OBS	%		
32	N	667	3158	516	12	5	1	3692	9.9	4359	11.7	33809	7.8
02	NNE	238	1417	139	13			1569	4.2	1807	4.8	13032	7.2
04	NE	630	2038	141	13			2192	5.9	2822	7.6	17184	6.1
06	ENE	114	435	68	3			506	1.4	620	1.6	4386	7.1
08	E	600	1838	239	1			2078	5.6	2678	7.2	18014	6.7
10	ESE	161	778	138	1			917	2.5	1078	2.9	8248	7.7
12	SE	612	2251	180	3	1		2435	6.5	3046	8.2	19404	6.4
14	SSE	137	908	60	1			969	2.6	1106	3.0	7448	6.7
16	S	596	2308	107	1			2416	6.5	3013	8.1	18432	6.1
18	SSW	143	717	82	1			800	2.1	943	2.5	6609	7.0
20	SW	505	2441	669	66	7		3183	8.5	3688	9.9	32510	8.8
22	WSW	69	816	931	152	32		1431	5.2	2000	5.4	28424	14.2
24	W	368	2160	1217	123	28		3528	9.5	3896	10.5	43816	11.2
26	WNW	64	515	352	58	21		946	2.5	1010	2.7	12844	12.7
28	NW	286	933	330	41	13		1317	3.5	1603	4.3	14818	9.2
30	NNW	84	443	97	7	1		548	1.5	632	1.7	5277	8.3
40	CALM	-	-	-	-	-	-			2927	7.9		
TOT. 2927		5274	23156	5266	496	108	1	29027	XXXX	37228	XXXX	284255	7.6
%	7.9	14.2	62.2	14.1	1.3	0.3			77.9		100		

FIGURE 349. TYPICAL ANNUAL WIND SUMMARY, EL PASO, TEXAS

Prepared by the Headquarters Air Force, Weather Division   Courtesy Thomas E. Greacen II

original airport plan sufficient space inside the apron had been left for the terminal facilities ultimately required.

The operations heretofore discussed have all been *contact* operations, that is, operations under conditions of fair visibility. When visibility is restricted the pilot must rely on instrument landing devices in bringing his aircraft in; such conditions are known as *instrument* conditions. The instruments in use today are of two general types. The first employs two radio beams, one vertical and one horizontal, to define the path down which the pilot flies to a landing. The second employs radar to "pick up" the airplane and follow its movements in approaching the field. These movements are directed by an operator on the ground, who maintains contact with the pilot by radio. The equipment for either system is erected in the vicinity of the runway, and for its effective use a clear space 750 feet wide on each side of the runway center line is required. At present it is impractical to operate instrument landing devices simultaneously on more than one runway unless the runways are widely separated, but since improvements are to be expected all runways on major airports should be planned as instrument runways.

Meteorological Conditions. Certain meteorological information is indispensable to the airport planner. In the United States this can be obtained from the Weather Bureau at Washington. Data should be obtained for the recording

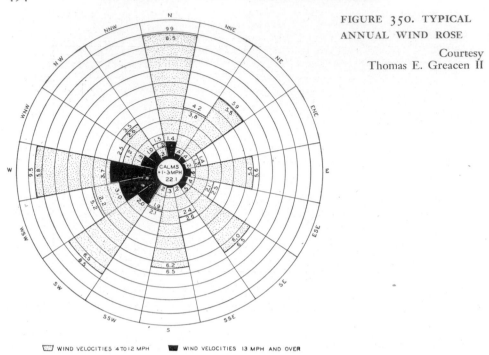

FIGURE 350. TYPICAL
ANNUAL WIND ROSE

Courtesy
Thomas E. Greacen II

WIND VELOCITIES 4 TO 12 MPH   WIND VELOCITIES 13 MPH AND OVER

point nearest to the airport site and should be carefully checked to be sure it is applicable. Marked differences may be noted in the wind conditions encountered even at places very close together; these differences are frequently caused by intervening hills and other terrain features. Care should be exercised to obtain data for the longest period available. A two-year period is minimum for such records, and a five-year period is desirable. The following data should be obtained:

1. The directions and velocities of the prevailing surface winds under conditions of normal and of restricted visibility
2. The maximum density altitude

The wind data called for above can usually be obtained in the form of wind summaries (see Fig. 349) giving the annual and monthly percentages of time during which winds of different velocities were recorded on sixteen points of the compass hourly for twenty-four hours a day. These data are used in the preparation of the wind rose (see Fig. 350), which gives a graphic picture of the wind conditions for a specific month or for the year as a whole and enables the planner to estimate fairly accurately the percentage of time during the

FIGURE 351. WASHINGTON NATIONAL AIRPORT

Although this airport was one of the largest when it was built in 1939, mid-century found it already over-congested. The runway and apron layout is both economical and efficient.

Photograph Civil Aeronautics Administration

year when a runway in any given direction can safely be used for a landing or take-off.

In preparing the wind rose, the wind data are separated into the following velocity groups:

1. Calms and winds up to and including 3 m.p.h.
2. Winds of velocities from 4 through 12 m.p.h.
3. Winds of velocities of 13 m.p.h. and over

The total of the first group is indicated in the center of the rose. The percentages of wind in the second and third groups are indicated by sectors covering both sides of each compass direction from which winds blow, radiating from the center circle and extending outward distances that are proportional to the percentages of time the winds were recorded. Winds of less than 13 m.p.h. velocity have little effect on the landing or take-off of transport aircraft so

FIGURE 352.

AIRFIELD,

TULSA, OKLAHOMA.

MAINTENANCE DEPOT

The wide apron surrounding the hangars facilitates the movement of planes in and out and furnishes a large area for outdoor servicing.

Photograph Ewing Galloway

far as United States airports in Class V or Class VI are concerned and may be considered to be covered by a runway aligned in any direction. The stronger winds will usually determine the directions in which runways must be built. The CAA has established definite requirements as to the wind coverage which must be provided by the runway system of an airport in any given class, and this should be ascertained by the planner.

The density altitude of an American airport is defined as the altitude in the United States Standard Atmosphere at which the air density is equal to that at the airport. It depends on the air temperature and the station pressure (actual atmospheric pressure, not reduced to sea level), and the maximum density altitude occurs only when the temperature is highest. It is this figure, rather than the altitude above mean sea level, which should be used in determining the length of runway required.

Extent and Topography of the Site. The airport planner should obtain vicinity maps, usually the appropriate aeronautical chart, and the United States Geological Survey quadrant map covering the area in which the airport is to be located. These will facilitate his study by giving pertinent information concerning local airways, radio beams, highways, obstructions, towns, natural features, and topography. In addition, the planner will need an accurate survey and topographical map of the site, together with a controlled aerial mosaic if obtainable. This information should be augmented by aerial and ground reconnaissance of the site and its surrounding area. Aerial reconnaissance offers the best means of studying the approaches to the field and possible aerial

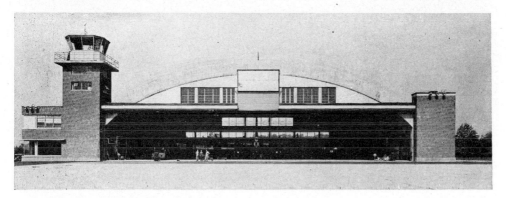

FIGURE 353. GENERAL ELECTRIC TEST HANGAR, SCHENECTADY, NEW YORK.
TWO VIEWS

Office of Marcus T. Reynolds, architects and engineers; Roberts & Schaefer, engineers; Joseph L. Ottenheimer, mechanical engineer

The use of concrete shell vaults is becoming increasingly common in hangar design.

Courtesy A. M. Byers Co.

traffic patterns; it also provides a general picture of the natural drainage of the area, which is an important matter. Ground reconnaissance gives the best picture of the clearing and grading involved and frequently brings to light site limitations that are not apparent from the air or from a study of maps. A skillful planner by taking advantage of the topographical features of a site, beginning with the selection of the best alignments for the runways as based on the wind requirements and the best areas for parking apron, buildings, and so forth, can usually produce a satisfactory and economical layout plan.

Soil Composition. Since the study of soil mechanics is a specialized field, it will frequently be advisable to employ a qualified man to investigate the bearing power, permeability, and turf-bearing characteristics of the soil on the proposed airport site. Since these matters will influence the cost of construction, it is desirable to make the studies before the site is acquired. On the basis

FIGURE 354. TYPICAL AIRLINE HANGARS

ABOVE: New York International Airport, Idlewild, New York; Roberts & Schaefer, engineers.
BELOW: LaGuardia Airport, New York.

Photographs Ewing Galloway

of the results the type and design of the pavement, the type and design of the drainage system (whether natural or artificial), and the type of ground cover to be employed to prevent soil erosion, to control dust, and to improve the appearance of the airport will be decided. These points will be discussed in greater detail in succeeding paragraphs.

THE LAYOUT PLAN

From an analysis of the various factors enumerated above—the characteristics of the aircraft to be accommodated, the operation contemplated, the

wind records, the topography, and the soil conditions—the planner determines
the number of runways required, their direction, and their dimensions. After
making allowance for the clearances required at both ends of the runways and
on the sides, he plots them on the topographical map, avoiding excessive cuts
and fills as far as possible. In most cases it will be found that one runway will
predominate; because of its orientation it will be in use most of the time.
Normally the other runways are secondary and are used only when the wind
direction requires. The layout plan should be designed to facilitate traffic on
the predominant runway. The parking or loading apron should be located
opposite the center of this runway to reduce taxiing to a minimum. Where
feasible, the runway pattern should permit the use of secondary runways as
taxiways when they are not actually in use for landings and take-offs. This
reduces the number of taxiways required.

The location of the control tower deserves consideration at this stage. The
tower operator must have a clear view of the apron, the taxiways, the runways,
and the aerial approaches to the field. The tower should therefore be located
centrally and should be of sufficient height to permit an unobstructed view of
the whole field.

In planning the parking and loading facilities and establishing building lines
adjacent to them, it is well to bear in mind that larger aircraft must be anticipated in the future. Since these will take up more space on the ground and will
require greater clearances than aircraft now in use, such needs can be provided
for only by allowing additional space between the original apron and the
nearest runways and taxiways. If space for expansion is not provided at the
outset, it may later be necessary to move the terminal buildings and the hangars or to abandon the runways and build new ones farther away from the
apron.

RUNWAY DIMENSIONS, CLEARANCES, AND GRADES

For taking off, an airplane usually requires a longer run on the ground than
it requires for landing. A safety factor is employed in determining the proper
length for a runway. This factor is intended to provide sufficient length of
runway to permit an airplane to attain flying speed, to be air-borne, and then
to return to the runway and be brought to a stop in the event of power failure.
For the United States the length of runway required for each different class
of airport is given in the CAA airport design standards. These dimensions are
based on conditions at sea level. At higher altitudes longer runways are re-

quired, and methods of computing the additional lengths are also given in the CAA standards. Runway widths, for which standards have also been established, are designed to allow ample space for landing or taking off one airplane at a time and for the inaccuracies in landing occasioned by cross winds and pilot errors. Because these inaccuracies are greater under instrument conditions, instrument runways are given extra width. Lateral safety clearances, usually measured from the center lines of the runways, are designed to prevent the construction of buildings or the parking or taxiing of aircraft in the areas in which planes occasionally ground-loop and to eliminate vertical surfaces of any kind which could deflect the radio beam of instrument landing systems. A stabilized over-run area is required at each end of a runway to allow for short landings and over-runs.

Additional safety factors are provided by the regulations governing the heights of obstacles in the vicinity of airfields. In general these regulations provide unobstructed flight paths to the ends of the runways and a clear area overhead for maneuvers prior to landing and after the take-off.

It is seldom feasible to build an absolutely level runway, although that would be ideal for operations. Topography and drainage usually necessitate some grades, both lateral and longitudinal, but these must be kept to a minimum if aircraft are to operate satisfactorily. The maximum permissible grades are covered by CAA standards.

APRONS AND TAXIWAYS

Aprons, or ramps as they are sometimes called, are primarily for parking and loading aircraft. Heretofore a continuous pavement has usually been provided, but the large areas required for transport aircraft and the difficulty of adequately draining these areas have led to the adoption of ladderlike aprons and individual "hard stands," which serve the purpose equally well and require less pavement. As a rule large present-day aircraft do not require covered parking, and the hangars are now reserved for maintenance and repair operations except in climates where outdoor parking and servicing are impractical because of exceptional temperatures, wind, and weather.

Taxiways are the connecting links between the aprons and the runways. Although it is desirable to limit taxiing to a minimum on account of the wear on equipment and the consumption of fuel and time which the operation involves, it is unwise to skimp on taxiways for the reason that they facilitate traffic and, when properly located, increase the capacity of the airport. Taxiways are needed between all critical traffic points. Where it is necessary to build curved taxiways, the curves should have constant radii. As in highway design, they should be widened at intersections and at holding points.

AIRFIELD PAVEMENTS

The purpose of an airfield pavement is to provide an all-weather surface which will support the wheel loads of aircraft and of other vehicles which attend them. In general, airfield pavements are subjected to heavier loads and less frequent loading than are highway pavements. Both flexible and rigid pavements are used, depending on their purpose and on the composition of the soil beneath them. In theory, a flexible pavement consists of a series of layers of aggregates bound together with an asphalt or bituminous binder and sealed on top with a wearing surface of similar composition. This type of construction depends to a large extent on the uniformity of the subsoil to which it transmits the load. An outstanding advantage which it offers to airfield use is its adaptability to subsequent thickening added in order to support greater loads. Theoretically a rigid pavement is designed as a series of rigid slabs, usually made of concrete, which spread the load over a large area of base and, when properly designed, span the weak spots in a non-uniform subgrade. Rigid pavements are especially suited to use as aprons where the spillage of fuel and lubricants tends to disintegrate flexible pavement.

Airfield pavement design has been the subject of intensive study and exhaustive testing on the part of government agencies and material manufacturers. Advice on the subject of paving and drainage may be obtained from the Airport Engineering Service of the CAA and from publications issued by that agency, and it is frequently advantageous to add the counsel of engineers who are familiar with local experience in airport and highway pavement practices.

DRAINAGE

The problem of drainage is a serious one in airport design. Where drainage is inadequate or faulty in design or construction, airfield pavements tend to become undermined. Besides this, accumulation of surface water on the runways during and after a storm is dangerous to the operation of aircraft and may close down the airport. First the permeability of the soil is determined by tests, and then a decision is reached as to whether to rely on natural drainage or to install an artificial system. Such a system is usually planned to meet the demands of a "design storm," which represents the most acute condition experienced in the locality over a given period of years. A prime requisite for any drainage system is an adequate outfall, and this should be considered in selecting the site. As noted in the preceding paragraph, there is considerable information in CAA publications on the solution of drainage problems, and advice on specific problems can be obtained from its Airport Engineering Service.

AIRFIELD MARKING AND LIGHTING

In the United States the Army, the Navy, and the CAA have jointly sponsored a series of airfield marking and lighting standards. These are available through the CAA and must be followed in the marking and lighting of all airfields.

The purpose of marking an airfield is to convey by recognized visible symbols specific information which the pilot of an approaching airplane needs to know, such as the lengths and magnetic azimuths of the various runways, the direction of the winds, the locations of obstacles, and the condition of the field (if not open to use).

For lighting an airport the purposes are, first, to indicate its location, and, second, to guide the approaching aircraft to a safe landing at night or under conditions of restricted visibility by day. The main elements of an airfield lighting system include:

1. The beacon, which locates and identifies the airport
2. A wind and traffic indicator
3. Obstruction lights
4. Runway lighting
5. Approach lighting
6. Taxiway lighting
7. Traffic control lights

Each element is available in different types of equipment suited to the requirements of different classes of airfields. It is usual for the tower operator to control the lighting and to utilize it, in combination with radio aids and instrument landing devices (mentioned above), to control traffic on the airport and in the air in the vicinity of the airport. An additional item of equipment still at mid-century not in general use is fog-dispersal equipment. The constant struggle with the elements which aviators have waged from the beginning of flying has produced many marvelous devices but has not yet fully conquered

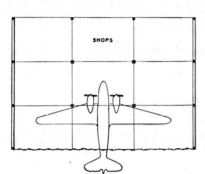

FIGURE 355. TYPICAL NOSE-TYPE HANGAR

Such a hangar can shelter the forward parts of large planes while their engines are being either serviced or removed and replaced.

Courtesy Thomas E. Greacen II

the weather. Until it does, established flying schedules will continue to be disrupted and the incautious pilot will meet with disaster.

AIRCRAFT MAINTENANCE AND STORAGE

Only by observing the strictest kind of discipline in maintaining schedules of overhaul, inspection, and maintenance have the airline and the military air services achieved safety records of which they are justly proud. Maintenance schedules are worked out in accordance with the number of hours of flying time recorded for each airplane and for each of its parts. Aircraft are taken out of service for periodic overhauls and are disassembled, and the parts are subjected to rigid tests designed to expose any weakness in the materials. Such minor servicing operations as refueling and superficial checking are performed out of doors on the parking apron. Major maintenance operations are carried out in the hangars, which should be provided with overhead traveling cranes to facilitate the removal of engines and other heavy parts. It is customary in many hangars to work from light removable scaffolds, which are wheeled into position adjacent to the aircraft and from which mechanics can reach all the parts.

Many types of steel and wood trusses, as well as several ingenious reinforced concrete vaulting schemes, have been employed in the design of hangars. The advantage of concrete over the other materials in case of fire has been demonstrated on several occasions. The increasing use of larger aircraft with greater wing spans has resulted in the discarding of a great many hangars or their

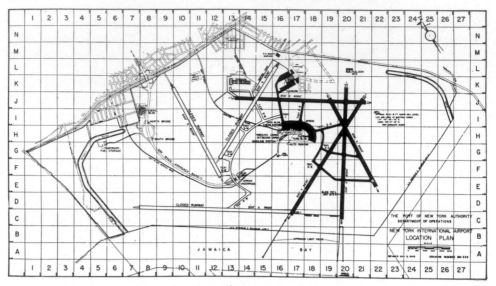

FIGURE 356. NEW YORK INTERNATIONAL AIRPORT, IDLEWILD, NEW YORK. GENERAL PLAN

The largest municipal airfield, laid out on a modified tangential plan; the central station area is reached by depressed roads.   Courtesy Port of New York Authority

relegation to the maintenance and storage of small aircraft. The need for a type of hangar capable of extension to accommodate larger planes has brought into being the "nose hangar" (Fig. 355), which is a long shedlike structure supported by a rear wall and a row of widely spaced columns and long girders over which a projecting roof is cantilevered. This type of hangar can not only house small aircraft in their entirety but also accommodate the forward parts of large aircraft, including most of the fuselage, the wings, and the engine nascelles. Curtains instead of heavy doors have generally been used to enclose the ships in the nose hangars, but it is practical to design rigid sliding doors for hangars of this type. The design of hangars offers a fertile field for architects and structural engineers with imagination, and the future should produce revolutionary designs.

The shop facilities which are required in close proximity to the hangars may be divided into sections devoted to engine maintenance, sheet-metal work, an electrical shop, and a paint shop. Delicate operations like the balancing of propellers need a separate enclosed space provided with a pit. All such operations demand open floor areas, generous headroom, wide spans, good natural

FIGURE 357.
NEW YORK
INTERNATIONAL
AIRPORT,
IDLEWILD,
NEW YORK.
FEDERAL BUILDING
AND VIEW OVER THE
TERMINAL AREA

Courtesy Port of
New York Authority

and artificial light, and ample sources of power. A well-designed factory type of building answers the purpose very well.

On every airfield, shelter must be provided for a crash truck and its crew of men highly trained in the difficult task of fighting airplane fires and rescuing individuals from damaged aircraft. The crash-truck house should be located close to the control tower and the truck should be able to reach any point on the field or in the neighborhood of the field in a matter of seconds. Sometimes the building has a small lookout tower where a watch is maintained.

SUGGESTED ADDITIONAL READING FOR CHAPTER 40

Airport Reference (Los Angeles: Occidental Pub. Co., 1941–42—).

Airport Transport Association of America, *Airline Airport Design Recommendations* (Washington: the Association [1946]), including:

    Part I   Airport Requirements
    Part II   Airport Obstructions
    Part III   Notes on Paving and Drainage
    Part IV Airport Lighting
    Part V   Airport Buildings
    Part VI Miscellaneous

Froesch, Charles, and Walter Prokosch, *Airport Planning* (New York: Wiley [1946]).

United States Civil Aeronautics Administration, *Airport Buildings* (Washington: Government Printing Office, 1946).

—— *Airport Design* (Washington: Department of Commerce, 1944).

—— *Airport Planning for Urban Areas* (Washington: Government Printing Office, 1945).

——*Performance Standards for Airport Lighting Equipment and Materials* (Washington: Government Printing Office, 1940).

——*Small Airports* . . . (Washington: Government Printing Office [1945]).

Walton, Francis (editor), *Airman's Almanac* (New York: Farrar & Rinehart, 1945).

Wood, John Walter, *Airports* . . . (New York: Coward-McCann [c1940]).

41

Air Stations

By ALBERT FREDERIC HEINO

A N AIR STATION may be defined as a building or group of buildings used for the unloading and loading of aircraft and the transfer of passengers and cargo to or from ground transportation. It frequently contains non-aviation elements which are provided for the convenience of the public. Usually it is the main building or group of buildings at an airport and is often referred to as the passenger station or, erroneously, the terminal or the administration building.

In the comparatively few years that the airplane has been used for commercial air transportation, it has affected the lives of a large segment of the population. In 1926, only 5,782 passengers were carried by domestic airlines in the United States, and in 1946 the number had increased to over 12,000,000; each of these individuals had acquired new travel habits and adjusted his life to a faster tempo. The role of aviation in the Second World War completely changed the psychology of the nation toward air travel; it made aviation an accepted, almost commonplace, part of the transportation system and of the contemporary way of life. Business trips from Chicago to New York and return can now be made on the same day. The businessman with only two weeks of vacation can spend it in Europe. Business houses can make deliveries of goods in a matter of hours instead of days or weeks. A person's prosperity will increase if he is located favorably on the air map, and a favorable business location does not depend so much on geographical location as it did formerly.

These factors have had a profound effect on society and on economics. The world has been brought into closer relationships, and distance is now measured in time rather than in miles. Airports are rapidly becoming social centers; "airport cities" which themselves will be social and economic units are in the making. When the O'Hare Airport at Chicago has reached its ultimate stage, it is expected that 40,000 employees will derive their livelihood from the

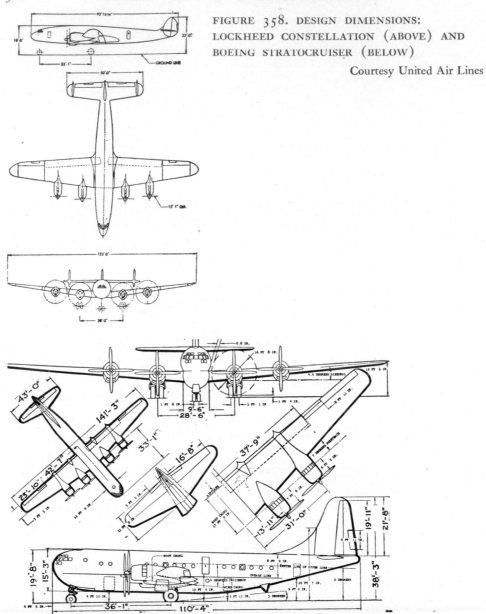

various services rendered by the airport. Such a small-sized city requires all the elements of city planning, with the airport itself as the center.

Because the modern airport must usually be located in an area remote from a city center, ground transportation linking it with the various parts of the city becomes of major importance. The tendency in city planning will be

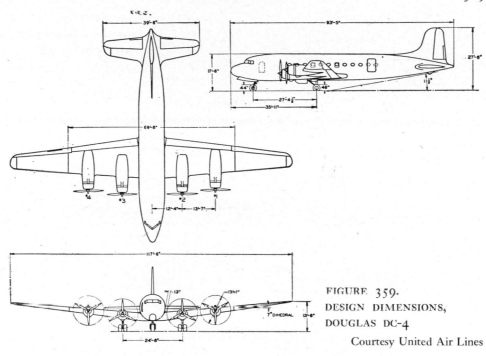

FIGURE 359.
DESIGN DIMENSIONS,
DOUGLAS DC-4

Courtesy United Air Lines

toward decentralization. In the early days of ships, trade centers grew up around seaports at important junctions. Just so, in the age of flight, important cities will grow and prosper along the principal air routes.

With the development of aircraft, passenger rates have been reduced from a cost of 12 cents per mile, in 1926, to approximately 5 cents per mile in 1948. For long hauls air-transportation costs are comparable to first-class rail fares; as fares are further reduced the entire passenger market will be open to air transportation and tremendous traffic volumes will result; some estimates run as high as 60,000,000 passengers in 1960. A similar increase will occur in the shipping of goods and commodities; the next few years will probably see the development of an air-freight system similar to that of the railroads.

The advent of the airplane and its use for commercial purposes necessitated a new building type for which no standards or precedents existed. The shape and size of the airplane called for a scheme different from that fitted for other transportation media. The space occupied by an airplane at rest approximates a square, and additional area is needed for maneuverability. Since the capacity of each flying unit is small in comparison with that of a train or a ship, many more units are necessary to handle the same number of people. Present-day thinking is based on a unit with an average capacity of fifty passengers. At

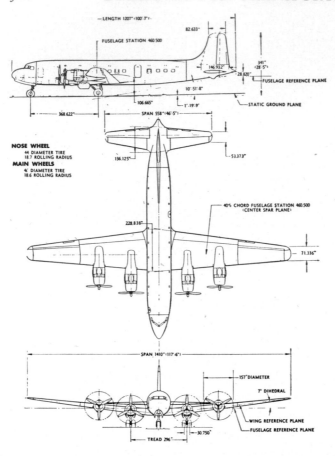

FIGURE 360.
DESIGN DIMENSIONS,
DOUGLAS DC-6

Courtesy
United Air Lines

least seven such units are therefore required for the number of people that can be accommodated on an average railroad train. These seven units, when at the station, require a lineal frontage of 1,050 feet; otherwise the basic station requirements are approximately the same as those for a railroad station, the chief difference being that here the equivalent of the train shed has to be of a different shape and size. (See Figs. 358–361.)

A great handicap to air transportation today is the inadequacy of station facilities as a natural result of the rapid growth of the industry (stimulated by the two world wars), which has far outstripped the rate of station construction. Another handicap has been the rapid change in aircraft design. Even at mid-twentieth century it is still difficult to plan an air station which can have a reasonably long life expectancy. Aeronautical designers have concentrated on the aerodynamic design of aircraft and have given little consideration to its

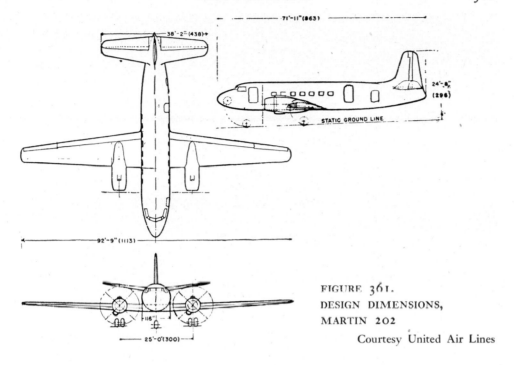

FIGURE 361.
DESIGN DIMENSIONS,
MARTIN 202

Courtesy United Air Lines

relationship to air-station design. Equipment planned by different manufacturers varies markedly in design; no standardization exists. Until the railroad industry was able to agree on certain standards in equipment design it could not prosper; the adoption of standard rail widths and car dimensions did much to advance the railroad industry, and it may be that such an adoption of standards is necessary to put air transportation on a sound footing.

The lack of standardization in equipment and in handling procedures has created serious problems for the designer of ground facilities and has presented real difficulties in the financing of such buildings; these uncertainties have contributed in large measure to the slow development of air stations. The banker wants a reasonable life expectancy for and complete amortization of the facilities, but the user can give him no guarantees. In major cities the large stations cost millions of dollars. Such investments cannot be made unless all concerned are willing to accept fundamental design standardization, the criteria for which must and can be adopted on a national basis—for the requirements of one airport are no different from those of another, except as to size. In the United States the airlines, the Air Transport Association, and airport engineers have all been battling over this problem.

FIGURE 362. OLD TEMPELHOF AIRPORT (BEFORE 1929), BERLIN. AIR VIEW OVER STATION

Paul and Klaus Engler, architects

The skillful planning of the simple building, the use of its roof for observation, and the development of public restaurant facilities all helped make this the outstanding air station of its period.

From
Architectural Forum

HISTORICAL BACKGROUND

The history of air-station construction has been written entirely since the First World War. Although the Wright brothers flew the first heavier-than-air machine at Kitty Hawk as early as December 17, 1903, the airplane was not used commercially for another twenty years. At the close of that war, aircraft were used by the United States Post Office Department—at first experimentally and later on a scheduled basis—for the delivery of mail. During the years of experimentation, from 1918 to approximately 1926, practically no passengers were carried on a revenue basis. Nevertheless the strategic air routes of the United States, which later developed into a great comprehensive network, were laid out in that air-mail period. With the organization of a Federal board in the Department of Commerce in 1926, commercial air transportation as we know it today was born. At that time the airlines were heavily subsidized and the major revenue was derived from the handling of mail. Few passengers were carried and few conveniences were provided for their comfort. Many of the first air stations were constructed in the corners of service hangars and were expanded merely as parts of the hangar structures.

The Watres Act of 1930 offered the first real encouragement to scheduled passenger service. It rationalized the development of an air-transport system under the Postmaster General. In the same year the Ford trimotor airplane made its debut, and the airlines actively solicited passenger traffic. The Ford, one of the first metal airplanes, carried fourteen passengers. With the airlines in the passenger business, it was necessary to build ground facilities to handle this new function. Few stations had been built prior to 1930; it was the 1930's

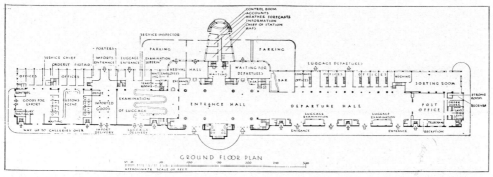

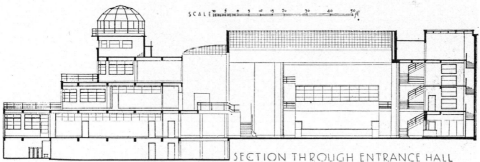

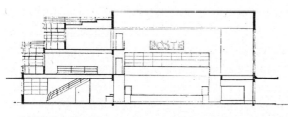

SECTION THROUGH DEPARTURE HALL

FIGURE 363. LE BOURGET AIR STATION, PARIS. PLAN AND SECTIONS

G. Labro, architect

With a great length to permit several side-by-side plane positions, this station pointed the way to much subsequent development.

From *Architect and Building News*

that saw the real beginning of air-station construction. In Europe such construction had started a little earlier; in the main, however, developments in Europe and in the United States were parallel. By the time the Civil Aeronautics Act of 1938 placed the regulation of airline operations in the hands of a separate commission, the passenger business in the United States was in full swing.

European Development. The first large station to be constructed in Europe was the old Tempelhof station at Berlin, built in 1925 and designed by Paul and Klaus Engler. It consisted of a two-story building 345 by 75 feet in size. The exterior wall surfaces, of dark brick, were broken by long horizontal

FIGURE 364.
LE BOURGET
AIR STATION, PARIS.
EXTERIOR AND
INTERIOR

G. Labro, architect

The use of concrete and glass is effective and appropriate.

From *Architect and Building News*

lines of windows. A feature of the plan was the provision for expansion in four successive stages. The work was so skillfully designed and carried out that the old station gave the impression of a single structure, even though additions had been made at several times; it served as a model for many years (Fig. 362). Following this came the Croydon station in London (1928) and stations in Moscow (1930), Munich (1931), Brussels (1932), Venice (1935), and Amsterdam (1936), the LeBourget station in Paris (1937), and the station in Copenhagen (1939). All of these followed a similar pattern and were in most cases ambitious in view of the traffic of the day. The largest was LeBourget (3,300,000 cu. ft.), designed by G. Labro. It is a three-story building 722 feet long, constructed of reinforced concrete with continuous fenestration. Its central main hall is three stories high, 680 feet long, with an average width of 50 feet (Figs. 363, 364). The reinforced concrete station at the Kastrup Airport in Copenhagen, designed by Vilhelm Lauritzen, was completed in 1939. It is one of the finest air stations in Europe and is a good example of functional planning (Figs. 365, 366).

The new Tempelhof buildings, planned by Ernst Sagebiel in 1937, are of massive scale. The old airport has been tripled in size to reach its present area of 1,333 acres; to care for the large potential air traffic of Berlin it was necessary to

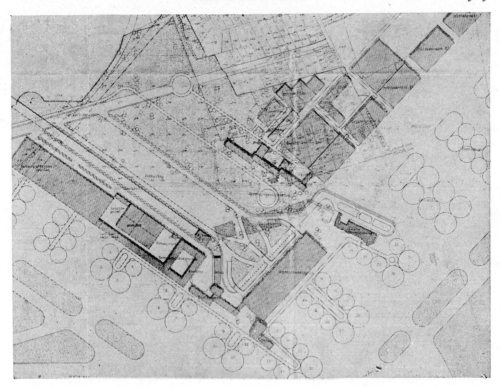

FIGURE 365. AIR STATION, KASTRUP AIRPORT, COPENHAGEN. BLOCK PLAN
Vilhelm Lauritzen, architect
The air station conceived as a group of related structures rather than as a single great building.

Courtesy A. F. Heino

abandon the old Tempelhof station, which was approximately in the center of the new air field. The main station block is seven stories high, and the curving frontage is 3,870 feet long; there is a cantilevered roof with a clear height of 40 feet along the entire frontage (Fig. 367). From the main concourse, access is provided to the 1,246-foot covered passenger-loading platform extending along the rear wall and concentric with the central portion of the 3,870-foot hangar section. Planes maneuvering at the loading gates do so entirely under cover.

In general, air stations in Europe in the 1930's were on a more ambitious scale than those in the United States. Government construction of the buildings and the fact that the airlines were not forced to carry a substantial share of the cost enabled European cities to build to the demands of traffic, while in the United States the construction of facilities lagged. In Europe the architects were given

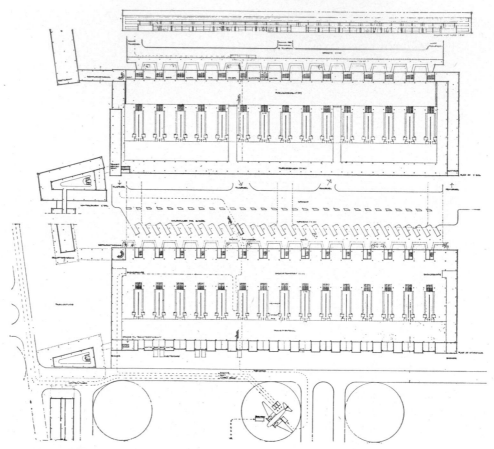

FIGURE 366. AIR STATION, KASTRUP AIRPORT, COPENHAGEN. PLANS AND
ELEVATION

Vilhelm Lauritzen, architect

A scheme and elevations of the greatest clarity.   Courtesy A. F. Heino

greater freedom; most of them used ferro-concrete with large glass areas. The
plans were functional and showed evidence of a serious search for a plan that
would meet the needs of the new transportation medium. They were all patterned after railroad stations, and except in the case of the new Tempelhof no
covered access to the gates from the station was provided. Mid-century planning in Europe closely parallels that in the United States, and very little difference should be apparent in the plans of the future.

Development in the United States. European architects had seized the opportunity to develop air-station architecture ahead of their American col-

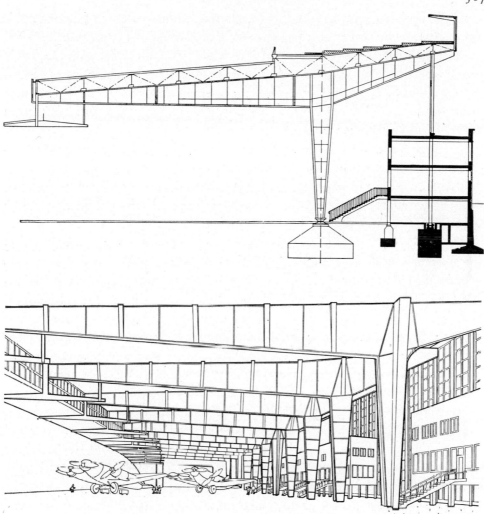

FIGURE 367. NEW TEMPELHOF AIRPORT, BERLIN. SECTION AND VIEW OF
CANTILEVERED EMBARKING SHELTER

Ernst Sagebiel, architect

Planes at the loading gates are entirely under cover.

leagues, for passenger transportation by air was general in Europe before it began its real development in the United States. Here much of the early passenger
business was carried on in hangar structures or makeshift lean-tos; perhaps the
earliest separate structure of modern design was the air station at the Washing-
ton-Hoover Airport, designed by Holden, Stott & Hutchinson and built in

1928. It was a structure 135 by 35 feet in size, with a volume of 40,000 cubic feet. This station was later lengthened by the addition of 18-foot wings.

In 1933 the ferro-concrete station at Chicago was built. It is 72 by 162 feet in size, two stories high, and encloses 170,000 cubic feet. The building, designed by Paul Gerhardt, adequately served the traffic at Chicago Municipal Airport until the Second World War. It has a central lobby two stories high, with ticket counters, flanked by a restaurant and by Civil Aeronautics Administration (CAA) and airline offices. The station proved to be inflexible when expansion was needed; the principal reason, however, was the fault not of the building but of the location, which limited the number of aircraft that could be handled within the enclosing runways. It has recently been succeeded by a new air station of unique design.

Under Mayor LaGuardia in New York, LaGuardia Field was built in 1939–40. The air station was designed by Delano & Aldrich and in size is 292 by 60 feet, with a central unit 81 feet in diameter. A one-story, curving steel-and-glass loading concourse, 1,400 feet long and 30 feet wide, fronts the apron, which in the original plan was accessible from the second level of the central unit. Since the later 1940's only spectators have had access to the roof of the concourse; passengers to reach the concourse cross a driveway at the ground level. This station at the time it was built was the largest (1,560,000 cu. ft.) in the United States and the only one in the country to provide undercover passage from the central lobby and ticket offices to the plane gates. The original plan contemplated that limousines would unload passengers at the second level of the central unit; from there passengers would walk out to the plane concourse. Shortly after the station was opened it was found that this procedure created a bottleneck at the entrance driveway, and limousines were therefore permitted to by-pass the central unit and deliver passengers to the gate positions directly; this greatly improved the efficiency. Although LaGuardia Field was completed only in 1940, it is already inadequate for the handling of the New York traffic because of the insufficiency of the apron area and gateways. New York must look to Idlewild and Newark to meet future requirements, though LaGuardia will continue to handle its share of the traffic.

The Washington National Air Station was completed in 1941. This station represented the most advanced thinking of its day and remains one of the finest in the United States. It was designed by the architects of the Public Building Administration of the Federal Works Agency, with Howard L. Cheney as consulting architect. The structure is 532 by 130 feet and has a volume of ap-

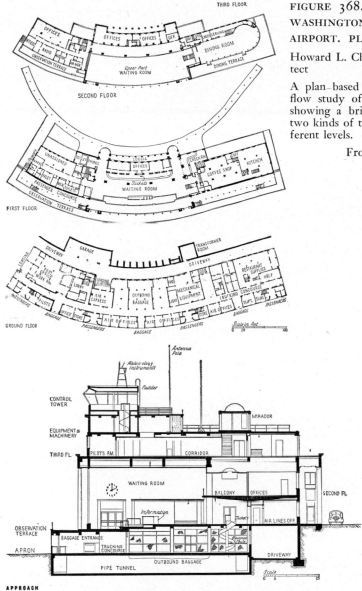

proximately 2,000,000 cubic feet. The main feature of the station is the large two-story waiting room, one floor above the field but level with the roadway on the off-field side. Continuous curving high windows front the 200-by-30-foot waiting room and provide a magnificent view of the field; at either end there is easy access under cover to the concourses leading to the plane gates.

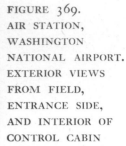

FIGURE 369.
AIR STATION,
WASHINGTON
NATIONAL AIRPORT.
EXTERIOR VIEWS
FROM FIELD,
ENTRANCE SIDE,
AND INTERIOR OF
CONTROL CABIN

Howard L. Cheney, consulting architect

The entrance is distinguished by a careful handling of vehicular approach; the field side, by the large windows through which both passengers and observers can watch the planes on the field.

Photographs
Theodor Horydczak

The ground floor is used for airline operation and cargo handling, the upper levels for passengers, offices, and so forth. Although it is a magnificent building, it lacks flexibility for expansion both in its public areas and in its airline operating space, and the concentration of all incoming baggage has frequently caused congestion. Nevertheless it was the first station in which a thorough study was made of traffic flow from ground transportation to aircraft for both passengers and cargo, and the separation of the two kinds of traffic by levels was a great step forward (Figs. 368, 369).

During the Second World War the Air Transport Command became the largest "airline" in history, and the enormous amount of traffic handled over its system demanded that innumerable facilities be constructed overnight. The study of plans for its new stations provided a great research laboratory for post-war planning. Though military requirements necessarily differ from civilian, the orderly arrangement of these buildings and their functional relationship to the quick loading and unloading of aircraft provided an impetus to the study of air stations generally. During the war the civilian airlines also undertook the study of air-station needs for the future; for the first time architects working directly for the airlines met to think out this problem. Some of those who on behalf of the airlines pioneered in the development and planning of major airports were Phelps Barnum (Pan American Airways), Francis Meisch (Northwest Airlines), Fred Moss (Capital Airlines), Walther Prokosch (Eastern Air Lines), Clinton Scofield (American Airlines), and the author of this chapter (United Air Lines). These architects jointly studied the present and future requirements of air stations and served in an advisory capacity with city officials and independent architects selected by airport owners all over the country.

Development since the Second World War. After the Second World War the air-transportation industry in the United States was faced with a tremendous increase in air traffic and a system of airports in which practically no modern air stations existed. All the major cities accelerated their planning for stations. The super-airports at New York and Chicago, each with an area exceeding 6,000 acres, designed stations that would accommodate ninety airplanes at a time. Boston, Philadelphia, San Francisco, and Los Angeles planned stations of thirty gates each. Other cities laid plans for eventual stations two or three times the size originally projected. The huge stations designed for New York and Chicago will become realities only if the volume of air traffic expected can be safely handled at single airports; since there are no assurances to that effect, the stations are planned to be complete units at the thirty-, sixty-, and ninety-gate stages of their development.

In 1946 Congress passed the Federal Airport Act providing $500,000,000 to be spent over seven years to aid the states and municipalities in the development and construction of airport facilities. This law acts as a stimulant to the realization of the national airport program recommended by the CAA. This and other aids will undoubtedly so accelerate the construction of air stations as to close the gap between demand and its satisfaction.

THE PROGRAM

Before the planning of an air station can begin, a thorough study of the many diversified requirements is necessary (see Figs. 370, 371). The data accumulated should be based on long-range planning and should indicate the probable size of the ultimate facilities needed. This eventual size should then be broken down into units to be built at several stages of construction as required by the gradual expansion expected. It is usual to plan the first stage for the first five years, the second stage for the next five years, and additional stages to meet estimated needs beyond ten years. The primary aim of the architect is to design for maximum flexibility and yet to obtain a complete operating facility in each of the stages.

An economic forecast will determine the extent of its likely development; it will indicate what the potential passenger, mail, and cargo traffic will probably be in the future. Such data can be obtained from industrial research concerns, plan commissions, chambers of commerce, airlines, the United States Department of Commerce and Post Office Department, and other organizations competent to aid in the forecasting of the needs.

All transportation centers must be planned for peak operations, and in the case of the air station it is necessary to base requirements on the maximum estimated *normal* peak-hour traffic; it should be assumed that 60 per cent of the peak-hour traffic will be concentrated in a 20-minute period during the peak hour. Yet planning should not be based on *abnormal* peaks, such as occur when there are irregularities in schedules and when special events take place. At those times congestion is unavoidable, but their infrequency does not justify the uneconomical planning necessary to meet such abnormal periods.

RELATIONSHIP TO THE AIRPORT

In the planning of the entire project it is necessary that the architect and airport engineer work together, for the air station must be designed in definite relation to the airfield. Its size is determined by the capacity of the runways, and its area is limited by the runway clearances needed for safe operation. The circulation patterns of aircraft and automotive traffic are important, and at and around the air station both must be integrated with the general traffic system of the airport as a whole. To ensure an air station that will function effectively as the important center of airport activity, the architect should participate in the airport design.

SITE PLANNING

The air station must be so located as to eliminate unnecessary taxiing of aircraft to and from the runways; the building development generally should be in the largest area available near the center of the runway pattern. There should be a minimum clearance of 1,000 feet from the building line to the center of any runway bordering this area. That will allow an apron of 500 feet fronting the building and will permit two-way taxiing of aircraft between the building and the runways as well as aircraft loading at the docks. The site chosen for the air station will also be affected by the position of the main access roads; generally it should be on the side of the airport nearest to town.

The area selected must be large enough to contain the buildings and aprons needed to satisfy the capacity of the air field or the maximum anticipated traffic. Liberal space for circulation is all-important. Usually the apron will parallel the "enclosing" runways, and the operating parts of the station will front toward the aprons. The off-field side of the station will provide sites for the supplemental buildings and for roadway and park development.

It is necessary to design the surface approaches so that the system may be simple and direct and may have a proper segregation of traffic; all traffic approaching the station area must be unscrambled and routed so as to reach its destination in minimum time. Cross traffic for vehicles and pedestrians should be avoided. Adequate waiting areas should be provided for limousines, taxicabs, and buses, and large parking areas are essential. In general, the crowds visiting the airport in their cars on holidays and special occasions should not be permitted to penetrate the air-station roadway system but should have easy access to large parking areas adjacent to the station-area entrance.

ESSENTIAL FACILITIES

A comprehensive program for an air station will include facilities for the following: the general public; commercial (non-aviation) enterprise; passenger and cargo handling by the various airlines; plane loading; governmental administration; international processing; and the control tower. (See Fig. 370.)

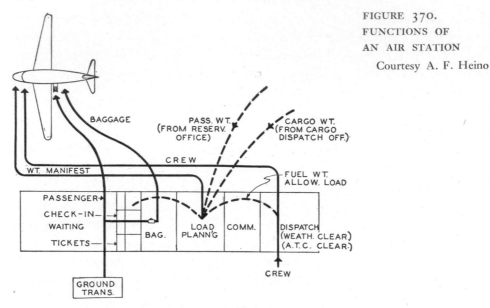

FIGURE 370.
FUNCTIONS OF
AN AIR STATION
Courtesy A. F. Heino

General Public. Facilities for the general public will include circulation space for both vehicles and pedestrians, general waiting rooms, public observation areas, and convenient rest rooms. Facilities for travelers and those for the non-traveling or sight-seeing public should generally be carefully separated. Landscaping to provide park and recreational areas is highly desirable. Bus or trolley stations should be conveniently arranged as a part of the general plan. (The air station provides an excellent opportunity for civic development, open plazas, and public monuments.)

Commercial (Non-Aviation) Enterprise. An important part of the program is the planning of areas for non-aviation commercial enterprise; the extent is largely determined by the aggressiveness of the community and the degree to which the airport is made a civic center. Experience has shown that the spectators at airports outnumber the passengers by two to one, and this ratio can be increased if attractions are created. At large airports it will be necessary to construct hotels, cinemas, public garages for the storage and servicing of automobiles, dining rooms and coffee shops, assembly and exhibition halls, shops, and other buildings commensurate with the economic potential. The program should allocate liberal areas for such commercial development, in the first place because it is a convenience to the public and secondly because economic operation demands the maximum development of non-airline revenue to help meet maintenance and operating costs.

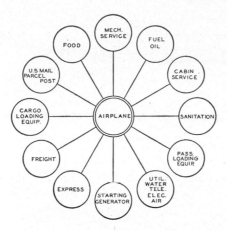

FIGURE 371. NECESSARY CONNECTIONS
TO AN AIRPLANE LOADING AND
UNLOADING STATION

Courtesy A. F. Heino

Passenger and Cargo Handling. In general, the area devoted to passenger and cargo handling should be separated from the hangar and shop areas. In order to allow for station expansion it is essential that an area large enough to satisfy the ultimate balance between the runway capacity and the necessary gate space be provided. The number of gates required is approximately equivalent to one-fourth of the peak-hour movements.[1] This assumes an average time of thirty minutes at the gate. For single-runway airports where the operating capacity is forty movements per hour the number of gates will be somewhat greater proportionately, but normally no more than fifteen will be required. At ports of entry and where several airlines serve an airport the individual requirements of the airlines may be the determining factor. In any case, any large number of gates over that needed to satisfy the current runway capacity cannot be justified. The airport plan should provide aircraft parking areas away from the station to relieve the apron of planes held for turn-arounds or delayed departures; the apron may then be kept "active" and the number of gates can be held to a minimum.

The facilities for airline operation will consist of ticket counters, the passenger agents' work area, the baggage room, and other functional offices as demanded by the type of airline operation performed. Passenger handling must be conducted adjacent to the passenger waiting rooms, and the flow of inbound and outbound passengers should be separated. Inbound and outbound baggage should be handled along the flow lines at points as conveniently situated as possible, to lessen the distance the passengers must carry their luggage. Such small concessions as newsstands or snack bars should be located in and

[1] A movement is a landing or a take-off.

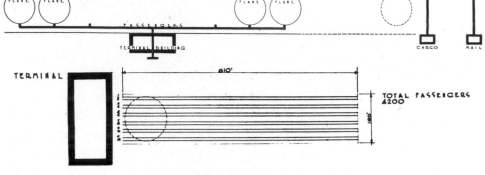

FIGURE 372. COMPARATIVE ANALYSIS OF RAILROAD AND AIR STATIONS AND DIAGRAMMATIC FLOW CHART OF CONVENTIONAL CENTRALIZED AIR STATION

A. F. Heino, designer

Courtesy United Air Lines

adjacent to the airline areas. Cargo handling will include rooms for the receiving, holding, weighing, and loading of cargo, all conveniently planned. Offices for the supervisory staff may be located in the work area of the station if the nature of the work done in them pertains directly to operations on the apron; otherwise they are better in the station's general office area.

Plane-Loading. The ultimate objective, of course, is to so arrange a station in relation to the airplane that passengers and cargo may be moved in and out of the plane under cover while it is being serviced (see Fig. 372). This necessitates a fixed dock of some kind, and it requires the nosing or tailing in of the aircraft. In contemporary planning, an allowance of 150 feet of dock space per gate is assumed as ample. This represents the turning radius of, plus clearance for, a DC-4 approaching and parking at a station under its own power; the plane finally comes to rest at an angle of 45 degrees to the station, and the access door is approximately 90 feet from the face of the building. If the aircraft is to be nosed into a dock, the average dock space may be considerably reduced; in the case of the DC-4, for example, it would be necessary to allow only a wing span of 117 feet plus a 10-foot clearance, or a total of 127 feet.

Governmental Administration. The program will include a suite of offices for the airport administrator and his staff. Usually necessary in the United States, in addition, are an office for the Weather Bureau and offices for the CAA air-traffic control and other services. These must be located adjacent to or near the control tower. Generally an air-mail field post office must be provided, or a space adequate for handling mail. At international airports, areas are needed for the bureaus of Customs, Immigration, and Internal Revenue and the Department of Agriculture.

International Processing. International facilities in the United States are required at all ports of entry. These include the usual governmental agencies for the processing of passengers and cargo to and from foreign airports; they are generally either detached from the center of operation at the air station or located at one end of it. Some of the domestic airlines also engage in international business and desire to conduct all their operations in a single area. To meet this requirement would mean decentralizing the international facilities, which has not as yet at mid-century become a practical possibility. Because airplanes arriving from foreign ports must be held in quarantine until thoroughly processed, the gates used for these are occupied for longer periods of time. Though the foreign flights are perhaps more spectacular, they should not be given prominent locations in the station area to the disadvantage of the operation of domestic flights which occur with greater frequency. The reverse of this is true in Europe, where practically all of the business is international.

The architect Lauritzen developed an interesting scheme for the handling of international passengers at Copenhagen. He proposed to process the passengers through the central station into buses destined for specific flights which might be strung out for great distances on the apron. After the passengers have been processed and loaded into the buses they are transported to the plane side, where they embark directly into the aircraft (Fig. 365). This is a system similar to that proposed by William Adams Delano in 1940 for the domestic station at LaGuardia Airport in New York and later used at Idlewild. It is also a form of unit loading such as was used by the Air Transport Command when it collected all the passengers for a given flight in one room and at the time of departure loaded the entire plane from one room. Opponents of this procedure dislike the inevitable regimentation which it entails, although it has admitted advantages from an operating standpoint.

Control Tower. The control tower should be designed to house the necessary personnel and equipment. It must be placed in the most advantageous position for the visual and mechanical control of aircraft in the air surrounding the airport and for the control of movements of aircraft to and from the runways after landing. The control tower houses the following facilities: control cab (tower), equipment room, chief controller's office, toilet room, storage space, and engine generator space.

The control cab must be located high enough to permit from inside the cab an unobstructed view of all runways, taxiways, and other areas upon which airport traffic is to be controlled; for a level terrain a minimum height of 30 feet from the ground is necessary. It must be so constructed that anyone standing at the central operating position is able to see all aircraft operating within the port's traffic pattern at all altitudes up to 1,500 feet above the airport. The construction must be such as to minimize the number and size of the structural members. To minimize glare the glass walls should slope outward from the sill line to the ceiling at an angle of between 10 and 15 degrees. The roof must be flat and structurally adequate to support a 24-inch searchlight weighing 200 pounds, radio antennas, weather instruments, and maintenance personnel. It should include an 8-foot-square platform, with a railing around it for safety and for the mounting of instruments.

Wiring channels to the cab must be provided for cables to be installed as required. The following is a list of equipment that may be required to terminate in the cab: electric power cables, airport lighting control cables, telephone service cables, recorder cables, transmission and control cables from remote radio equipment, transmission and control cables from remote radar equipment, weather instrument cables, and tetrahedron control cables. The room for housing radio and radar equipment, telephone equipment, power panels, recording equipment, and so forth—and to serve as a shop for the maintenance of equipment—should be located not more than 200 feet from the control cab. The area of this room will depend on the size and type of installation, but the minimum will be 300 square feet.

In the United States it is important that the control-tower facilities meet all of the standards of the CAA, officials of which should be consulted before the design of an air station is undertaken. Personnel on duty in the important work of controlling traffic in the air and on the ground must be provided with a modicum of comfort and conveniences so as to permit a strict concentration on their work. Naturally fire escapes, direct approach to the cab, and easily accessible toilet facilities, as well as storage space for spare parts, forms, stationery, and the like, will be required. Space is necessary for engine generators to supply emergency power; for convenience in installation and operation this is generally provided on the ground floor.

THE PLAN

The air station may be considered as a machine which, when working smoothly, will effect the transfer of passengers and cargo from surface to air transportation, and vice versa, in minimum time. In the search for the correct technical solution to the problem this objective is paramount.

GENERAL DESIGN PRINCIPLES

When the requirements of the many users of the air station are analyzed, certain fundamental design principles will evolve. Those which will result from a careful analysis of the primary and secondary functions of an airline station may be summarized as follows:

1. There should be separate facilities for the general sight-seeing public and for those doing business with the airlines.

2. Different types of traffic should be kept separate by the use of different levels.

3. Each airline that uses the station should have direct control of its own operations.

4. The ticketing areas should be separated from the public waiting rooms.

5. The building should be functional and expressive of air transportation.

6. The building should be planned for expansion.

7. Consideration must be given to the physical characteristics of aircraft.

8. Airplane-servicing facilities should be built in at fixed positions, and mobile servicing equipment should be held to a minimum.

9. The walking distance from the surface vehicles to the airplanes should be kept at a minimum.

10. The roadway system of approaches should be simple and should afford the proper segregation of different types of traffic; parking areas should be placed where needed to serve the various parts of the air station.

A station that is ideal from an operating standpoint does not necessarily provide the ideal solution to the whole problem, because there must be an integration of the operating methods of the station with the maximum development of facilities of a non-airline nature. A balance must be sought between these primary functions, and a sacrifice of one for the other can result only in an

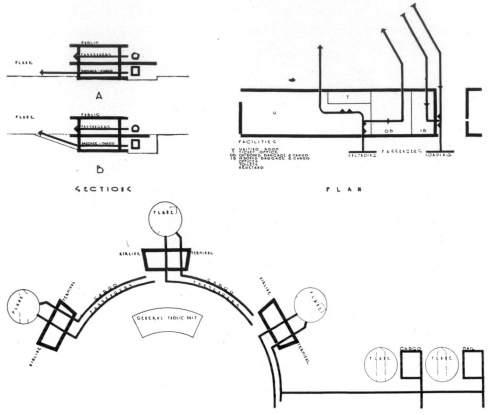

FIGURE 373. DIAGRAMMATIC FLOW CHARTS FOR UNIT DECENTRALIZED AIR STATIONS

A. F. Heino, designer   Courtesy United Air Lines

uneconomical solution. Generally speaking, maximum centralization places a handicap on airline operation; maximum decentralization, on the other hand, places a handicap on opportunities for non-airline revenue. It is necessary to decide at the outset whether the ultimate requirements may best be accommodated in a centralized or decentralized master plan. (See Figs. 373–375.)

CENTRALIZED PLANS

In the centralized scheme the station plan is closely knit and is concentrated into a relatively small area. It brings all the services of the station close together and mixes the business of air transportation with other merchandising. At the earliest stage of the development of an airport the centralized plan is more efficient and therefore more economical; its disadvantages lie principally in

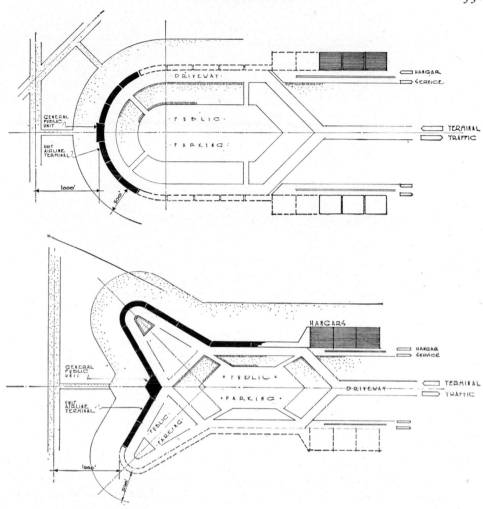

FIGURE 374. TWO POSSIBLE FORMS FOR UNIT DECENTRALIZED AIR STATIONS
A. F. Heino, designer

Courtesy United Air Lines

the inflexibility of the plan with respect to major expansion. At the outset it is necessary to guess right in order to plan the complete facility and expect it to function smoothly in the ultimate stage.

To bring the aircraft close in to the air station on a centralized plan, various devices are used. The line of aircraft station positions is shaped to consume a minimum of lateral dimension while extended out onto the apron in various configurations. The simplest form is the pier with aircraft parked on either

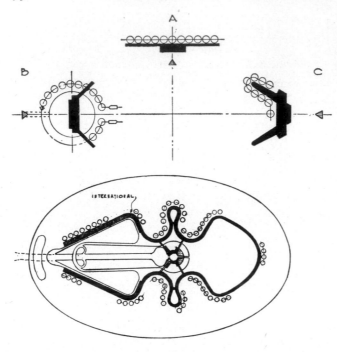

FIGURE 375.
CENTRALIZED
AND (BELOW)
DECENTRALIZED
AIR STATIONS.
BLOCK PLANS

A: Conventional; B: Pro-
duction line; C: "Finger"
type

Ralph H. Burke, consulting
engineer; Committee of Airline Architects and Engi-
neers, collaborating

side and with the air station itself at the base. As more aircraft must be handled the station is extended to the base of another pier, and so on. Even with a centralized design the station at high-capacity airports covers large areas. A good example of this type of planning for a major airport is the plan for the O'Hare Airport in Chicago, which is projected to comprise a total of 90 gates (Figs. 376, 377).

It is extremely important in designs of a centralized pattern to evaluate all the elements of the final plan and to minimize the chance of congestion sufficient to make the station operate ineffectively and with delays. It should be borne in mind that the ground time of the airplane is tremendously important and that it is the obligation of the planner to speed up handling as well as to make air travel easy for the public. At large stations of centralized design long walking distances are unavoidable. The designer should always strive to keep the maximum walking distances to a minimum, preferably not over 500 feet.

A basic principle of station design is the separation of the operating space from the public areas. Though this is difficult to accomplish in a centralized plan, nevertheless it is of supreme importance. In favoring public areas and concessions the operation of the station must not be allowed to become complicated.

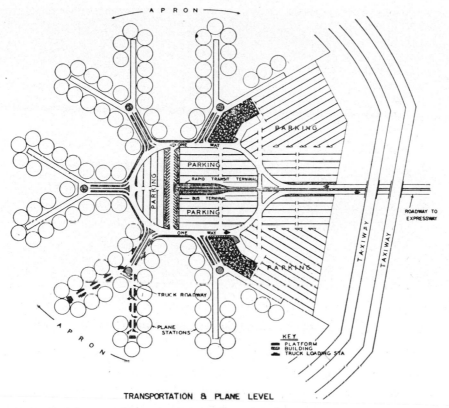

FIGURE 376. O'HARE (DOUGLAS) AIRPORT, CHICAGO, ILLINOIS. BLOCK PLAN

An air station for an eventual 90 gates requires a tremendous area even with a centralized plan.

From Heino, "The Future of Airports," in *Illinois Tech Engineer*

DECENTRALIZED PLANS

The decentralized plan breaks down the total capacity of the station into groups of substations. These may be substations of an arbitrarily fixed capacity, or they may be the stations of individual airlines. If the capacity of the substation is determined as a percentage of the total capacity, then the substations may be occupied by one or more airlines, depending on their individual requirements.

A system of units on a decentralized pattern was first proposed by the author of this chapter in 1944. In a paper on the subject[2] he described the advantages of decentralization for an air station of high capacity, among them

[2] A. F. Heino, "The Airline Unit Terminal Plan." Midwest Airport Managers Conference, 1944.

FIGURE 377. O'HARE (DOUGLAS) AIRPORT, CHICAGO, ILLINOIS. AIR VIEW

From Heino, "The Future of Airports," in *Illinois Tech Engineer*

the following: avoidance of congestion; flexibility for easy station expansion with expanding operations; separation of the general public and the passengers, thus simplifying handling by personnel; more personalized service to patrons on the part of the airlines; incentive to competition among operators, resulting in better service; direct control of its own operations for each airline; possibilities of civic development at the airport, independent of but contiguous with the airline unit stations; and maximum convenience afforded to the passenger through the simplest and most direct means of access to the airplane from ground transportation. Such a scheme is essentially a group of smaller stations linked together in a composite plan. The larger elements—hotel, theater, public auditorium, recreation center, department store, and the like—are located at the geometric center of the group, and the smaller but more necessary conveniences—general waiting rooms, food service, and concessions for newspapers, magazines, smoking supplies—are duplicated at the several substations.

Chicago in 1946 undertook to construct on its municipal airport a station embodying these principles. The plan is revolutionary and the air station, although because of the limited site area its capacity is already taxed, has operated successfully. In this case each of the airlines has its own operating unit, but the waiting rooms serve two airlines each (Fig. 378).

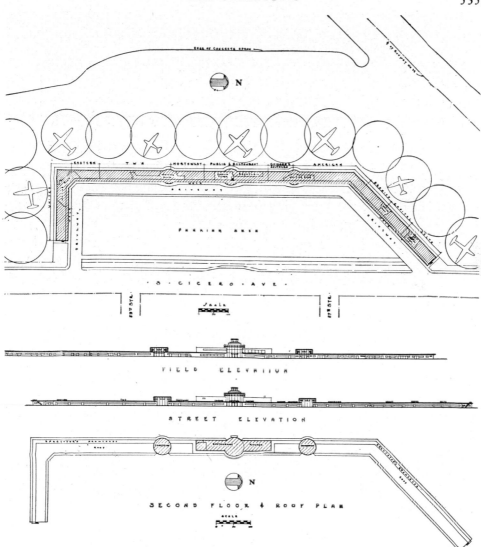

FIGURE 378. MUNICIPAL AIRPORT, CHICAGO, ILLINOIS. BLOCK PLANS AND
ELEVATIONS

Paul Gerhardt, Jr., architect; Committee of Airline Architects and Engineers, collaborating
A typical example of a decentralized station.   Courtesy A. F. Heino

Circulation is of great importance in a station of decentralized design. Here,
since the lateral distances in most cases are too great for walking, it is necessary
to convey persons from substation to substation. The station at Chicago, although it is 1,500 feet long, serves only seventeen gates.

TECHNICAL REQUIREMENTS

The outline which follows may serve as a check list of airport-building elements and requirements. So detailed a separation of building facilities as that indicated below is economically justifiable only at airports with great activity; in most cases many functions can be accommodated within the same building.

STRUCTURES FOR THE HANDLING OF PASSENGERS AND CARGO

Passenger Handling. Structures for passenger handling consist of the passenger station proper, together with the necessary passenger services and conveniences provided in the airline operational areas.

1. Public Facilities—All public facilities, including waiting rooms and car-parking areas, should be designed to handle the peak-hour needs of passenger traffic as determined by a study of the normal scheduled peak-hour aircraft movements. Since 60 per cent of the peak-hour traffic can occur within a 20-minute period, the peak-hour space requirements should be established on that basis. The plan should take into account:

Car-parking facilities

Passenger waiting room

Toilets

Nursery

Baggage checking—lockers, checkroom

Spectator area

Public telephone

Telegraph

Mail box

Ground transportation dispatching

Porter service—lockers and toilets

Food service

Public address system or visual announcement board

Outbound passengers

Inbound passengers

Through and transfer passengers

People accompanying or meeting passengers

Spectators

Employees

2. Airline Facilities—Certain airline operational elements must be located in the passenger station and adjacent to the apron. The extent to which other airline functions are to be included in the passenger station will be determined by each airline's operating policy, the type of operation in practice at the airport, and the availability of other airline space. For example, such airline functions as reservations, commissary, flight control, and the like may or may not be included in the passenger station at certain airports. In all cases the space requirements and layouts for present and future use must be obtained from the airlines. Necessary are:

Airline counters
  Ticket sales
  Check-in of passengers
  Information
  Counter agents' workroom
Operations or agents' workroom
Ground-crew ready-room
Plane-crew ready-room
Apron equipment storage

Communications—radio and
  teletype
Station supervisory offices
Employees' lunchroom, lockers,
  and toilets
Supply room
Reservations
Flight control
Terminal company offices

3. International Facilities, Inbound—Space requirements for international processing must be planned in consultation with the airlines and the government agencies concerned. The layout of the international area should provide facilities for enabling these agencies to perform their scheduled duties individually with a minimum of inconvenience to the passengers. In the United States the agencies represented are the Public Health Service, the Bureau of Immigration, the Bureau of Customs, and the Department of Agriculture. Passengers are segregated according to flight until they have passed the Public Health Service inspection. Under no circumstance is the public permitted access to the clearance area while passengers are being processed. Similarly, space is required for inbound cargo, which is held in bond until cleared by the Bureau of Customs. Spaces will be required for the following:

Public Health Service
  Quarantine waiting room with
    toilets
  Health examination room(s) or
    booth(s)
  Detention room(s) with lavatory
  Doctor's office with lavatory
Bureau of Immigration
  Waiting area
  Interrogation counters
  Offices, as required

Bureau of Customs
  Baggage sorting; identification
    and inspection counter
  Duty collection
  Offices, as required
  Bonded storage
Department of Agriculture—offices,
  as required
Lockers and toilets for government
  personnel

4. International Facilities, Outbound—When domestic and foreign flights are dispatched from the same gates, international clearance operations for outbound passengers can be conducted from the facilities which serve domestic airlines. The outbound passenger, on his arrival at the airport, must have with him the necessary passports, visas, health certificates, and so forth; these are examined by the airline employees at the time of check-in prior to departure.

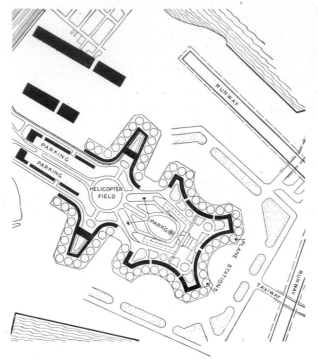

FIGURE 379.

PROPOSED DECENTRALIZED AIR STATION FOR GENERAL EDWARD LAWRENCE LOGAN AIRPORT, BOSTON, MASSACHUSETTS. BLOCK PLAN

Coolidge, Shepley, Bulfinch & Abbott, architects

Another air station of the decentralized type, with the plane station points wrapped around three sides of the vehicular approach.

He must also present evidence of having complied with the income tax regulations. All these procedures take place at the airline ticket counter. Space should be provided, however, for customs officers to examine clearance papers and manifests for outbound aircraft. Where inbound and outbound areas are in proximity to each other, clearance papers can be signed by the officer on duty in the inbound area. Space must also be provided for an immigration officer to check aliens' papers on departure. Space, as required, will be needed for the following:

Bureau of Internal Revenue   Bureau of Immigration

5. Loading Apron—The design of the loading apron must be closely integrated with the planning of the passenger station as well as with that of the airport. Here the ground handling and servicing requirements of the various aircraft will be the primary guides. To reduce the number of service vehicles needed, the provision of underground aircraft services in the apron is recommended. Even when the fueling is not done underground, it is desirable to build power and communication conduits and terminal boxes in the apron for quick connections. Economical design of the apron will dictate a reduction in the thickness of the paving adjacent to the building, where the pavement will

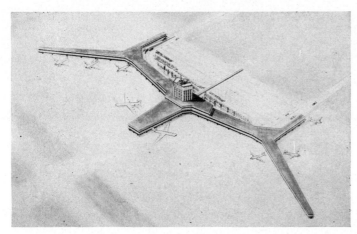

FIGURE 380.
PROPOSED STATION
FOR INTERNATIONAL
AIRPORT (1948),
PHILADELPHIA,
PENNSYLVANIA.
PERSPECTIVE

A. E. Blomquist, airport
engineer

Courtesy Eastern
Air Lines

not have to withstand maximum aircraft weight. The minimum requirements will provide space sufficient to allow aircraft to be parked with wing-tip clearance of passenger loading lines and also to permit one taxiing aircraft to pass the parked aircraft.

A fence or other barrier is necessary to separate the active apron areas from the public areas. Gates and gate identifications should be located conveniently to the aircraft parking position to furnish simple and direct access to the aircraft.

Apron lighting is extremely important. General illumination should be supplemented by localized lighting where special tasks are performed. General illumination of two foot-candles at 100 feet from the passenger loading line is satisfactory. All lighting should be so designed as to eliminate glare and inconvenience to pilots approaching the gate positions. The architect must bear in mind:

Dimensions and design
Gate positions
Lighting
Markings
Turntables
Aircraft services (built into apron)
    Fueling (determine number of
      grades required)
    Cabin heating and cooling
    Electrical service—aircraft;
      related equipment

Water
Sewage disposal—from plane
Compressed air
Vacuum
Telephone—plane to station
Gate communications to passenger
station
    Telephone
    Pneumatic tube
    Connection to public address
      system

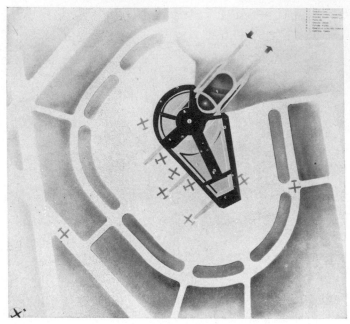

FIGURE 381.
PROPOSED STATION
FOR INTERNATIONAL
AIRPORT (1948),
PHILADELPHIA,
PENNSYLVANIA.
ACCEPTED SCHEME.
BLOCK PLAN
A. F. Heino, architect
Courtesy A. F. Heino

Cargo Handling. Cargo consists of passengers' baggage, mail, parcel post, express, freight, and airline company shipments. Since airline aircraft are operated as combination passenger and cargo carriers, provision must be made to handle cargo in the passenger-station area. Freight, when large enough in volume and when carried exclusively by freight aircraft, can be allocated to a specific freight area separate and distinct from the passenger area. The rehandling of cargo should be kept to a minimum. The handling of cargo by mechanical means must be studied as a local problem to determine whether it is practical and economical. In planning cargo-handling areas, provision must be made for adequate access drives, truck courts, truck docks, protection from the elements, and door openings adequate in size and properly designed and protected.

The problem of the carrying of baggage into or out of the passenger station by passengers or porters can be greatly simplified through the use of doors operated by the electric-eye system. Similar electric-eye installations are recommended for controlling the doors to the baggage rooms and cargo buildings as well as the gates in fences used by cargo trains, jitneys, and baggage carts.

1. Passenger Baggage—The flow of passenger baggage must be closely related to the passenger circulation. Baggage should be transported directly and

FIGURE 382.
PROPOSED
DECENTRALIZED
AIR STATION FOR
DENVER, COLORADO.
PHOTOGRAPH
OF MODEL

Scheme by A. F. Heino; model by G. Meredith Musick.

quickly between the baggage counters and the aircraft, with a minimum of conflict with other types of circulation. The following will be required:

Outbound baggage check-in counter

Outbound baggage storage area

Inbound baggage claim counter

Inbound and unclaimed baggage storage

2. Express—At small stations where express activity is at a minimum, no special facilities are necessary for this purpose, except that an area convenient to the aircraft should be provided in the individual airline cargo room for the distribution, sorting, and transfer of express shipments. At the larger stations, an area must be supplied for the sorting and handling of express by express-agency employees. This space should be so located as to be easily available to truck traffic and at the same time readily accessible for the loading or unloading of aircraft. The area is controlled by the amount of express activity contemplated, which can best be estimated by the appropriate agencies. The essentials are:

Agency truck dock—inbound and outbound

Work area

Airline dock—inbound and outbound

Storage room for valuables

Public space and counter

Employees' lockers and toilets

Airline offices

FIGURE 383. WRIGHT-PATTERSON AIR BASE, DAYTON, OHIO. ADMINISTRATION BUILDINGS

Sverdrup, Parcel & J. Gordon Turnbull, architects and engineers

A characteristic example of the rather heavy expression common in much airway construction just prior to mid-century.   Photograph United States Army Air Force

3. Mail and Parcel Post—The requirements and design of air-mail field post offices in the United States must be approved by the Second Assistant Postmaster General. At stations where no such post office is contemplated, mail and parcel post will be delivered to and received from the airline cargo room; at these stations mail may also be transferred directly from one airline to another. But where an air-mail field post office exists, or is contemplated, all mail and parcel post will generally be turned over to the post office before being transferred to another airline. The possibility that all first-class mail may sometime be carried by air indicates the necessity of planning for future expansion in this area. Mail requirements are as follows:

Truck dock—inbound and outbound

Work areas

Airline dock—inbound and outbound

Inspectors' gallery

Public space and counter

Vault

Employees' lockers and toilets

Airline offices

4. Freight—Separate facilities for handling freight, when these are necessary, must be flexible and expansible. Since air freight is handled only on an airport-to-airport basis, adequate facilities must be provided for consignors to deliver and for consignees to receive freight. The requirements are:

Truck dock—inbound and outbound

Work area (for individual airline sorting, storage, and handling)

Airline docks—inbound and outbound

Valuables storage room

Public space and counter

Bonded storage

Heated storage

Refrigerated storage

Customs brokers

Warehouse

Airline offices

Employees' lockers and toilets

ARCHITECTURAL DESIGN

Air-station design calls for extreme functionalism; primarily the architecture should express the purpose of the station, which is to load and unload passengers and cargo as rapidly as possible. The buildings should be of light construction, with large areas of fenestration, and should be so designed that the user may by quick observation direct his movements to his destination in a minimum of time. The airplane is a transport unit totally different from any for which transportation architecture has been planned in the past, and in the design of buildings to handle air traffic—as in all architectural design—there must be a relationship between the scale of the building and that of the unit to be served. The shapes and forms used in the masses of the building should reflect the plan; here too, as elsewhere, a free use of the principle of having the parts easily identifiable from their design is desirable. It is also well to give the operating sections a different treatment from that of the main sections of the public center; this may be accomplished with contrasting materials and color.

Many stations, particularly in Europe, have been built of ferro concrete. The structural system involved is suitable, but the material is unnecessarily heavy for use in the entire exterior. A successful solution in a two-story design is to use ferro-concrete or masonry for the walls of the first floor (where the truck and cargo handling is performed) and sheet aluminum and glass, or similar materials, for the upper-floor walls. In designing the structural and architectural elements of the building it is necessary to provide flexibility for expansion and changes in use, particularly in the operating sections. An effort must be made to avoid the mistakes of past decades, when air stations were patterned after railway stations and were reasonably satisfactory for a while but as traffic increased there was no way to expand them economically.

FIGURE 384.

TYPICAL AIR STATIONS

ABOVE: Martin Airport, Baltimore, Maryland. Whitman, Requardt, Greiner & Associates, architects. Photograph Ewing Galloway. CENTER: Unit for United Air Lines, Municipal Airport, Chicago, Illinois. A. F. Heino, architect. Photograph Ewing Galloway. BELOW: Bush Field, Augusta, Georgia. Kuhlke & Wade, architects. Courtesy J. Hampton-Manning.

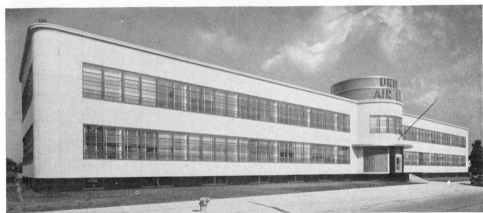

As a rule, undue monumentality of effect should be shunned, for an air station must be a simple expression of the complex variety of its functions. Usually, since the station is spread out laterally over a large area and does not

FIGURE 385.
RECENT
AIR STATIONS

ABOVE: Control tower and central building, Municipal Airport, Chicago, Illinois; Paul Gerhardt, Jr., architect; Committee of Airline Architects and Engineers, collaborating. BELOW: Air station, South Bend, Indiana; Roy A. Worden, architect; Vincent Fagan, associate; Frank Montana, consulting architect; Clyde E. Williams, engineers; Committee of Airline Architects and Engineers, collaborating.

Photographs
Hedrich-Blessing

require great height, a horizontal treatment is preferable. As the air stations are increasingly frequented by the general public, it is hoped that they may be beautifully landscaped and fronted by park areas and attractive roadway systems.

If an architecture of air stations can be developed that expresses the Age of Flight, the result may well be a new and distinctively American type of architecture—since it is inspired by the airplane, which was first developed in the United States. (See Fig. 385.)

FUTURE TRENDS

The air transportation industry, though still in its infancy, already shows certain trends. Up to the middle of the twentieth century the design of air stations has been handicapped because equipment and design have not been standardized. Air-station design thus far has been changing as expansion of traffic has increased and new methods of handling have been developed. The basic elements needed to serve the general public are determinable if the projections of traffic are based on sound forecasts. It would therefore seem that wise planning would build permanently those sections of the station which meet known requirements and would seek to achieve maximum flexibility in the design of the operating sections of the station where the airplane itself is serviced. The great air stations of the future, which will serve as centers of airport communities, must permit their primary function, air transportation, to proceed unhampered by complications in the plan.

Speed is the greatest asset of air transportation, and the planner must not reduce its effectiveness by unnecessarily increasing the ground time for aircraft, passengers, or cargo. Similarly, the ground transportation elements must not create bottlenecks at periods of peak operation and thus handicap the primary function. Because of the many and varied operations that are carried on at an air station, problems of traffic engineering must be given prime consideration, both in the layout of the buildings and in the study of their relationship to other buildings and to the general traffic pattern of the area surrounding the station. The architecture of the buildings should be functional and expressive rather than heavy and monumental. It should emulate the new mode of transportation by providing for the ground services the same high technical standards that have been achieved by the engineers of flight equipment.

SUGGESTED ADDITIONAL READING FOR CHAPTER 41

Airport Transport Association of America, *Airline Airport Design Recommendations* (Washington: the Association [1946]), especially:
  Part I   Airport Requirements
  Part II Airport Obstructions
  Part V   Airport Buildings
Frederick, John H., *Commercial Air Transportation* (Chicago: Irwin, 1942).

Froesch, Charles, *Your Airport Problems* (New York: Eastern Air Lines, 1944).

—— and Walter Prokosch, *Airport Planning* (New York: Wiley, 1946).

Heino, Albert F., "The Airline Unit Terminal Plan," a paper published in *Proceedings of Midwest Airport Managers Conference, 1944, Fort Wayne, Ind.*

—— "Airport Terminal Design," *Journal of the Society of Automotive Engineers*, Vol. 54 (1946), November, p. 73.

—— "The Airport Terminal Problem," *Aviation Maintenance*, June, 1944, pp. 47–52, 156–164.

—— "Community Airport Terminals Foreseen in Postwar Planning," *Architect and Engineer*, Vol. 157 (1944), April, pp. 28–32.

—— "Designing the Large Air Terminal," *Architectural Record*, Vol. 97 (1945), April, pp. 80–83.

—— "The Future of Airports," *Illinois Tech Engineer*, Vol. 13 (1948), March, p. 6.

—— "Plan That Terminal Now," from the paper "The Airline Unit Terminal Plan" (*supra*), *Air Transport*, Vol. 3 (1945), January, pp. 22–27.

Maclaren, Archibald Shaw, "Design of Land Airports for Medium and Long Distance Air Transport," *Journal of Institution of Civil Engineers*, Vol. 23 (1945), January, pp. 100–49.

United States Civil Aeronautics Administration, *Airport Buildings* (Washington: Government Printing Office, 1946).

—— *Airport Design* (Washington: Department of Commerce, 1944).

—— *Airport Planning for Urban Areas* (Washington: Government Printing Office, 1945).

United States Senate, Committee on Commerce, *Federal Aid for Airports*, hearings before Subcommittee of 79th Congress, 1st session, on Senate bills S.2 and S.34 (Washington: Government Printing Office, 1945).

Walton, Francis (editor), *Airman's Almanac* (New York: Farrar & Rinehart, 1945).

Wood, John Walter, *Airports . . .* (New York: Coward-McCann [c1940]).

42

Seaports and Ship Terminals

By CHARLES R. DENISON

THE TWENTIETH-CENTURY INDUSTRIAL ERA has created a complex world economy which transcends the boundaries of nations and makes the peoples of the earth interdependent. Foreign commerce provides the raw material—moved overseas chiefly by vessels—which is the lifeblood of industrial nations and permits the peoples of other regions of the earth to exchange the natural wealth of their respective localities for the products of industry. This process of exchange is the foundation of foreign trade. Since modern ocean shipping furnishes the most important transportation medium of this foreign trade, ports of commerce—the key interchange points between the vessels of the sea and the carriers of the land—are of major significance.

BACKGROUND

Ports are creations of man. The water reaches which permit vessels to approach the land, thus providing harbors for them, are determined by nature. In the beginning harbors were seacoast havens where the small vessels of early seafarers found refuge from storms and pirates. As trade evolved, communities developed on certain harbors of refuge in order to serve the needs of the ships and to facilitate the exchange of goods with the contiguous area. The sailing-vessel era of overseas trade, which established the location of so many of the ports of the world, created many of the development problems which challenge the ingenuity of twentieth-century port planners as they strive to adapt the modern scheme of water-borne transportation to a pre-established locale. The location of many great European ports well inland on rivers was determined more by the dominance of the inland waterway systems which they also served than by the demands of seagoing vessels that called more or less infrequently. Ports in the United States, following the pattern of the times, developed on the river estuaries of the continental tidewater belt. Fortunately the country was endowed with good natural harbors free from troublesome tide ranges and shoal approaches. Although the port of the sailing-vessel era served a different period of world trade and a different tempo of transportation, its primary purpose was then, as it is now, to serve as a transfer point between land and sea transportation.

A little before the middle of the nineteenth century the sailing vessel reached its peak of development. It achieved a cargo capacity of 500 tons—in rare cases 1,000 tons—but rarely carried a full cargo destined to a single port. Harbor depths of 18 to 20 feet were adequate. The voyaging time was long, and arrival dates were as uncertain as the winds which drove the ships. Port terminal facilities consisted principally of warehouses and connected inland-waterway barge terminals; cargo could be transferred directly from seagoing vessels to lighters or canal barges, and vice versa. Wharves and facilities for the rapid movement of cargo were of secondary importance. Not until the coming of the steamship and the railroad did the physical transfer of goods between vessel and shore carriers present a problem.

The modern concept of a port with its extensive and costly terminal facilities developed with the industrial era. On the land side of the ports, railroads and highways reached deep into industrial regions of the hinterland, and with them came ever increasing demands for new sources of natural wealth from across the seas. On the ocean side the fast steamship with its increased cargo capacity removed the uncertainty of voyage time and provided the means for transporting whatever goods were offered. Regular international trade routes were established. It remained for the commercial ports to supply the terminal facilities capable of effecting a rapid, economical, and safe exchange of freight and cargo between the two new fast modes of transportation. The concept of a world economy, the vast growth of world shipping tonnages, and the reconstruction of commercial fleets as a result of the Second World War demand that a re-estimate be made of the problem of planning and constructing the waterfront facilities which must be built or rebuilt to serve modern shipping.

MODERN PORTS

The twentieth-century seaport is primarily a junction point on a shoreline where land and water transportation systems meet for the exchange of freight and cargo between land carriers and vessels. Soon transfer from ship to air carriers may also be an important function.

Many of the present great commercial ports have followed a continuous plan for improvements which seeks to keep the port terminal abreast of the progressive development of the ocean vessels they serve. Their evolution, in fact, followed a "master plan" long before master plans became a stock in trade of the city planners. The ports of London, Liverpool, Hamburg, Antwerp, Rotterdam, Bremen, Genoa, and Trieste are outstanding examples of this type of planning. On the other hand, the larger ports of the United States —New York, New Orleans, and San Francisco—exemplify vast developments without long-range planning. Bremen, in Germany, offers an instructive example of the progressive evolution of a port where the existence of the city itself depends on its ability to provide better harbor facilities and services than its near-by competitors Hamburg, Rotterdam, and Antwerp.

The modern port comprises three distinct zones of operation: the harbor, or water areas, including the entrance and interconnecting channels; the ship terminals, which serve as interchange points between vessels and inland carriers; and the land area adjacent to the waterfront, containing supporting industry, storage, intraport and inland transportation facilities. The first of these, the water areas of the port—which provide the harbors of refuge, the anchorages, and the channels of approach—are most often the natural tidal arms of the sea, such as river estuaries, bays, and breakwater-protected reaches of shoreline. The problem of construction, dredging, maintenance, and canalization of harbors requires a profound study of natural hydraulics, and assuring their adequacy is usually a national responsibility.

The port planner is generally called upon to redevelop existing ports in order to bring them abreast of the advances in ship design, the expanding commercial activity, altered modes of land transportation, and changing types of cargo. In one outstanding instance, however, a modern commercial port, complete in all respects, has been planned and built on virgin soil to meet the needs of an extensive hinterland—Gdynia in Poland. This port, built between 1924 and 1935, was designed to serve as the principal port of a nation, and in its planning, its gradual execution of the master plan, and the results achieved it is a masterpiece of twentieth-century port architecture (Fig. 386).

FUNDAMENTAL REQUIREMENTS

In the ideal port there are certain basic elements and characteristics which should be present in balanced relationship. In all attempts at port development and modernization these fundamentals should be adapted to the practical conditions involved. They may be summarized as follows:

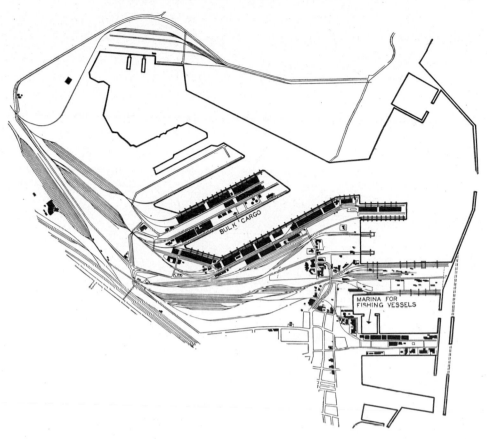

FIGURE 386. PORT OF GDYNIA, POLAND. PLAN

A new port, built 1924–35, which is considered a model of efficient planning.

1. There should be a harbor of adequate depth, free from the effects of wave action, and it should be possible to orient the facilities in such a way as to give berthed vessels protection from high winds. The harbor should have adequate anchorages and easily navigable access reaches from the sea.

2. The marginal lands should provide ample reserve areas for future expansion. The selection of the area for development should be based on careful studies of the geology and mechanical properties of the subsoils.

3. The port area should be served by direct railway, highway, and inland-waterway communications connecting with the natural hinterland. A "belt line" system of intraport rail circulation should be provided to switch freight between the several converging trunkline feeders. The rail system should in-

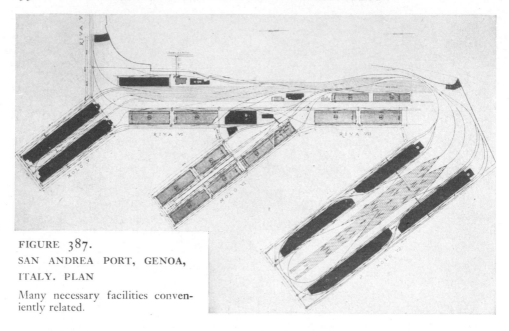

FIGURE 387.
SAN ANDREA PORT, GENOA,
ITALY. PLAN
Many necessary facilities conveniently related.

clude ample holding, switching, and classification yards. Broad truck freeways which, avoiding the city traffic, enter the port area should be augmented by marginal ways, motor parks, and truck transfer facilities. Where a port is the terminal of an inland-waterway system, barge docks and basins with service and transfer facilities should be provided adjacent to the deep-sea wharves.

4. Ocean shipping should be furnished with facilities to serve three broad types of trade—passenger traffic, bulk cargo, and general cargo.

5. Seaplane-basing facilities are essential, in addition to direct freeway motor routes to inland airfields.

6. Bunkering, ship-supply, and ship-service accommodations should be made available.

7. Ship-repair facilities are necessary parts of a complete port.

8. Consideration must be given to small-boat harbors or "marinas" both for small commercial fishing fleets and for pleasure craft. Public beaches, waterside parks, and water recreational areas for pleasure sailing, yachting, and fishing should be made available, whenever possible.

The incorporation of these essential elements into a master plan which visualizes the ultimate development of both the land and the water areas of the port in such a way as to serve efficiently the possible advances in transportation calls for keen understanding and a vivid imagination. The port development should

FIGURE 388. PORT OF BREMEN, GERMANY. AIR VIEW

The integrated relationship of pier sheds, storage spaces, and industrial areas, the careful and efficient planning of rail connections, and the use of mechanical freight-handling devices make this one of the most efficient of the major ports.   Courtesy United States Army Signal Corps

be co-ordinated with the port-city development plan; that is, industry of the normally inland type and not dependent on a waterfront site should not be located in the marginal reserve areas and thus prevent the normal growth of waterfront industry (see Fig. 402).

The waterfront lands should provide space for the bulk storage of raw materials as well as for the industries that process and fabricate these materials prior to their movement as semifinished or finished products over the more costly means of land transportation to the hinterland. In addition, suitably proportioned areas near the waterfront should be assigned for the storage of dry bulk cargoes (such as coal, ores, and fertilizers), of grain and lumber, of petroleum, molasses, and edible oils, which require tanks. No set rule can be given for the area of land necessary for each type of bulk commodity. A modern collier, for example, carries approximately 12,000 deadweight tons (DWT), and a reservation of 1 acre of storage space is required for 10,000 tons of coal. A shipload of lumber may contain as much as 4,000,000 board

FIGURE 389.
PORT OF BREMEN,
GERMANY. TWO DETAILS

Courtesy United States
Army Signal Corps

feet, and for every million board feet a reservation of 2½ acres is desirable. A tanker may carry 240,000 barrels of petroleum; for this product space reservations of ½ acre per 100,000 barrels should be allowed. These acreages are for estimating purposes only; such factors as the type of storage, fire protection, efficiency of layout, and other more specific considerations will probably alter the figures.

In the past, port terminal facilities have generally been built to serve existent vessels, with the result that progress in port cargo-terminal design and planning has lagged a generation or more behind that in the shipbuilding industry. New types of ships—each larger, faster, and more versatile than its predecessors—evolve while the old terminals still remain. Periodically wars have played a large part in the abnormal evolution of the cargo vessel; for the slower vessels have been destroyed, and twice recently within the span of a few years—during the First World War and again during the Second—whole new generations of cargo ships have come into being. In each of these periods the average tonnage per vessel approximately doubled. Prior to the First World War the carrying capacity of the average large general-cargo vessel was approximately 3,500 DWT, and shortly after the war this had increased to approximately 5,500 to 6,000 DWT; since the Second World War the average carrying capacity of the larger class of general-cargo vessels has been 10,000 to 12,000 DWT. The length of such ships has increased but little, the 10,000-ton vessel being only about 80 feet longer than the earlier 5,500-ton vessel. The speed, however, has increased from about 8 to 12 knots up to around 14 to 16 knots during the same period. As a result the potential usefulness of ships has greatly increased in all respects but one—the ability of the port terminal facilities to load and discharge cargo fast enough to meet the new demands. The rate of handling general cargo through port terminals in the United States, with rare exceptions, has not improved since before the First World War.

The present objective in port improvement, then, is the design and construction of terminal facilities that will meet the requirements imposed by technological advances in ship design and in inland transportation—by rail, motor carrier, and waterway. Modern waterfront terminals must be developed in a planned port-area environment which provides modern rail, highway, and storage facilities. The whole pattern of the marine-shore transportation industry for a given locale must be co-ordinated under industrial management control to the end that there can be a smooth, rapid, and economical flow of commerce.

PORT TERMINAL FACILITIES

WHARVES AND PIERS

The general term "wharf" is applied to a terminal structure designed to accommodate a vessel at a berth. In various parts of the world the wharf, because of variations in the natural shoreline, offshore water depths, and fluctuating tidal conditions, has assumed two fundamental forms. The first of these, the *pier*, is normally a supported structure built from the shoreline out to the nearest natural bottom contour that will provide a sufficient depth of water; this type, of course, is suited to a flat, shallow shoreline. The second, the *marginal wharf*, as the name implies is built alongside a naturally deep shoreline such as the bank of a river, a fjord, or an artificial basin (see Figs. 390, 391).

One variation of these two fundamental forms is the solid filled pier called the *mole*. Moles are often combined with the breakwater system of artificial

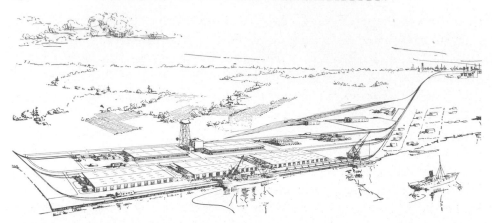

FIGURE 390. PROPOSED PORT FACILITIES, SAVANNAH, GEORGIA. PERSPECTIVE
Robert & Company, architects and engineers
The advantages of the marginal wharf can be readily appreciated.

Drawn by R. H. Bennett, courtesy Robert & Co.

harbors, or they may themselves be old breakwaters or jetties which have been converted to serve as wharves. Another variant is the solid filled masonry-wall-retained marginal structure known as the *quay*. Quays are most often found marginal to tidal or lock basins. In certain localities of the world where the tidal ranges are excessive it is expedient to excavate basins into the shoreline and to construct lock entrances which permit the water in the basins to be held close to the high-tide level. The retaining walls of such basins serve as wharves and are referred to as quays.

All of these basic structures evolved prior to the time when extensive dredging became practical for maintaining ship channels and berth depths. Many variations of those fundamental types may now be found in a single harbor, because modern dredging methods can change the bottom contours to fit wharves that otherwise would not be feasible. Yet even with the versatility thus permitted it should be remembered that costly initial dredging and subsequent maintenance dredging may often be avoided by selecting the type of structure naturally adapted to the situation.

TYPES OF PORT TERMINALS

Deep-water marine terminals may be classified into three broad functional types: passenger, bulk cargo, and general cargo. Each of these calls for three basic elements of composition: the ship's berth, or water element; the wharf substructure; and the deck, or superstructure. The first two elements, the

FIGURE 391. PROPOSED PORT FACILITIES, WILMINGTON, NORTH CAROLINA.
PERSPECTIVE

Robert & Company, architects and engineers

Another example of an efficient marginal-wharf port plan.

Drawn by Edward A. Moulthrop, courtesy Robert & Co.

berth and the substructure, are fundamental to all three classes of terminal
structure; the last one, the deck or superstructure, augmented by its supporting land-communication pattern, determines the functional purpose of the
terminal.

The design of each type of port terminal is conditioned largely by the characteristics of the vessels that will use it. Wharves built exclusively for passenger use are exceptional rather than usual; save for those piers which serve the
superliners of the so-called Atlantic ferry and the boat trains of the English
Channel crossing, few are built solely for passenger use. Because of the uncertain future of the giant liner in the Atlantic express run, it is doubtful
whether many more such terminals will be constructed.

Huge liners, on account of their size, are restricted to those harbors and piers
which provide sufficient maneuvering space and water depth. Giant liners have
increased neither in number nor appreciably in size in the twentieth century.
The Imperator, built in 1912, had a length of 919 feet, a beam of 98 feet, and a
draft of 39 feet; the Queen Elizabeth, built in 1941, has a length of 1,031 feet,
a beam of 118 feet, and a draft of 39 feet. The present tendency is to use combined passenger and freight vessels which are large enough and fast enough
to satisfy the passenger traffic and at the same time will provide a sure and
continuing revenue from express cargo. The Grace Line vessels of the Santa

Rosa class, with a length of 484 feet, a beam of 72 feet, a draft of 26 feet, a gross tonnage of 9,237 tons, and a cargo capacity of 7,000 DWT are examples of the trend.

Cargo vessels, in contrast to the large passenger liners, have changed greatly in this century, as has already been noted. General cargo vessels have doubled in both cargo capacity and speed within a few years, and this trend is even more pronounced in such bulk-cargo carriers as tankers and ore carriers. Great Lakes ore carriers with self-unloading equipment are able to discharge 12,000 tons of ore in from four to seven hours after arrival. Fast bulk-petroleum tankers with a capacity of 30,000 DWT are under construction.

Passenger Terminals. Such passenger terminals as the Gare Maritime in pre-Second-World-War Cherbourg are elaborate structures created to accommodate luxury-class ocean-passenger traffic; indeed in the development of this special type the Cherbourg terminal has been pre-eminent. As a rule the passengers are transferred from the luxury vessels to trains, or the reverse. The berth element of the ocean-passenger terminal is peculiar in that the water depth must be greater than that for cargo terminals, the wharf superstructure must contain essential customs and immigration inspection areas for baggage and passenger clearance, and—except in the few ports of the world where the passenger traffic is heavy enough to warrant devoting entire terminals to it—the passenger function is usually combined with the general-cargo function. Pier 145–146 in Los Angeles is an excellent example of the terminal with combined passenger and general-cargo facilities (Figs. 392, 393).

The berth element of the ocean-passenger terminal is determined by the loaded draft of large seagoing passenger vessels; it should provide a 40-foot MLW (mean low water) depth except in those cases where the piers are expected to serve the superliner class, when a 45-foot MLW depth is required. The base structure of the pier should furnish either 1,200 feet of marginal wharf or a finger pier of similar length. The pier shed may be a two-story construction, or it may consist of a single story with a passenger mezzanine. The lower deck, which is devoted to the express, freight, and mail carried by passenger vessels, should be designed functionally as a general-cargo terminal; the upper deck is reserved for passengers.

The second deck or passenger mezzanine should provide a promenade area for probably twice the anticipated passenger capacity of the largest vessel expected to use it. Space must also be furnished for the checking of baggage by customs officers; this space should be connected to a lower-deck motor-vehicle

FIGURE 392.
BERTHS 145–146,
LOS ANGELES
HARBOR, CALIFORNIA

One of the best of the port developments in the United States; these berths serve both passengers and freight.

Courtesy Los Angeles
Harbor Department

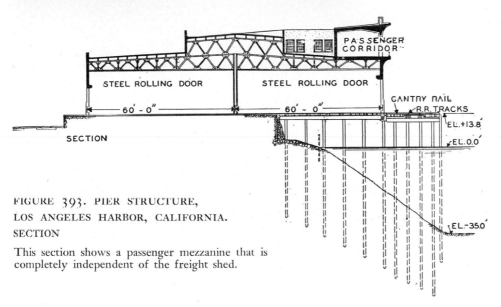

PASSENGER CORRIDOR

STEEL ROLLING DOOR   STEEL ROLLING DOOR

GANTRY RAIL
R.R. TRACKS

60'-0"   60'-0"

EL.+13.8
EL.0.0

SECTION

EL.-35.0

FIGURE 393. PIER STRUCTURE,
LOS ANGELES HARBOR, CALIFORNIA.
SECTION

This section shows a passenger mezzanine that is completely independent of the freight shed.

platform by a belt-conveyor system. Still other space requirements are rooms for first-aid and medical facilities, customs and steamship offices, passenger control or ticket gates, refreshment rooms, and toilet facilities. The modern terminal should include escalators for baggage and passengers, as well as ramps for access to and egress from the first and second levels. Provision should also be made for vehicular approach by ramp to an open drive at the rear of the

FIGURE 394. ALABAMA STATE DOCKS, MOBILE

Bulk cargo docks require special handling facilities as well as ample storage spaces.

Courtesy Department of State Docks & Terminals, State of Alabama

passenger area so that passengers arriving and departing by motor may drive to the space reserved for them without entering the lower working level of the pier (see Fig. 393).

Bulk-Cargo Terminals. Bulk-cargo marine terminals, usually owned and operated by the industry they serve, are generally special-purpose facilities designed and built to handle one type of commodity. Most of them are constructed to handle ore, coal, grain, fertilizer, chemicals, or petroleum. It is the designer's job to see that a terminal is able to handle large tonnages in a short period and thus facilitate fast ship turnaround by enabling vessels to discharge and reload in a minimum of time.[1] Such special-purpose bulk-cargo terminals as the great wharves for oil at Bayonne in New Jersey, for coal at Norfolk and Philadelphia, for grain at Montreal and New Orleans, and for ore at Toledo

[1] Without going into shipping economics it is not difficult to understand that the vessel of a given speed which spends the least time in port makes the greatest number of round-trip voyages. Vessel revenue is determined on the basis of sea-mile-tons, and excessive time spent in port results in lost revenue.

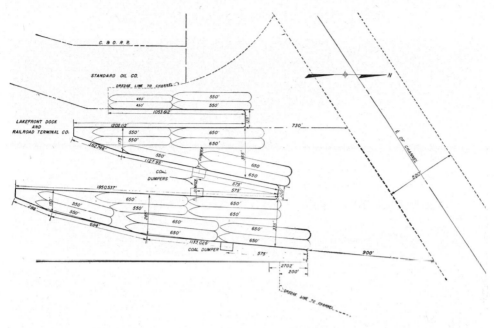

FIGURE 395. NEW YORK CENTRAL COAL AND ORE DOCKS, TOLEDO, OHIO.
PLAN AND VIEW

Engineering Department, Baltimore & Ohio Railroad Company, A. C. Clark, chief engineer, designers

Elaborate railroad track installations and large modern cargo-handling devices make ship-to-car transfer easy.   Courtesy Toledo–Lucas County Port Commission

FIGURE 396. GRAIN-HANDLING FACILITIES, VANCOUVER HARBOR, BRITISH COLUMBIA

Grain elevators are connected with the ship berths by grain-conveyor galleries. Two of the elevators are owned by the National Harbours Board; the third is owned by the Alberta Pacific Grain Company.

Photograph Royal Canadian Air Force, courtesy National Harbours Board, Ottawa

and at Port Alfred in Canada are examples of well-designed facilities for the exchange of bulk cargo between shore and vessel. (See Figs. 394–396.)

General-purpose port terminals for the transfer of bulk commodities from vessel to shore transportation, and vice versa, have also been constructed; an outstanding example of this type is the Alabama state docks at Mobile. At this bulk terminal, designed with great flexibility for the handling of nitrates, coal, bauxite, and sulphur, the transfer of two different bulk commodities can be carried on simultaneously.

General-Cargo Terminals. In the United States the port-terminal problem applies primarily to the seacoast general-cargo terminal, and for that reason the general and specific program requirements which follow in the next two sections will be based on this type. The fact that designers can meet the structural engineering requirements of the *special-purpose* terminals and can produce stable structures—suitably oriented and adequately supported by land storage and transportation feeders—which are more efficiently planned than most of

FIGURE 397.
MARGINAL
BERTHS 228–232,
LOS ANGELES HARBOR,
CALIFORNIA.
TWO VIEWS

The broad uncluttered pier structures made possible by modern types of construction permit an extraordinarily free and efficient handling of cargo.

Courtesy Los Angeles
Harbor Department

those built in the past invites the conclusion that the functional requirements of the modern *general-cargo* terminal are not fully appreciated by the persons who control the purse strings. Rarely does this problem unreservedly admit of a designer's solution at this time, for several factors beyond his control are in operation. These factors are: the absence of a national port-terminal policy or a reasonably well co-ordinated interstate policy; labor practices which serve to limit the rate of stowage of cargo in a ship's holds; non-unified terminal operational control; the absence of a sound policy for financing the construction and controlling the ownership of waterfront lands and port structures; and, finally, the general practice of building terminals for low utilization rates, short periods of life, and short-term amortization. Nevertheless the designer should evaluate the broad problem of general-cargo terminal operations so

FIGURE 398.
PARK SURROUNDED
BY PIERS,
BUENOS AIRES

The surroundings of a
busy harbor need not be
squalid and unkempt.

Courtesy Moore-
McCormack Lines

that he may create structures that not only are functionally modern but in
addition will embody sufficient flexibility to meet unforeseen changes in vessel
design and work methods. Furthermore, he should take positive measures to
guide those who are authorized to approve modernization and new construction so that they may be influenced more by what is forecast than by what is
past.

GENERAL PROGRAM REQUIREMENTS

General-cargo port facilities in the United States should be regarded not as
joint terminals of two types of transportation but rather as the junction point
where a physical transfer of goods from one type to the other must for natural
reasons take place. The transit shed, or transfer shed, of a general-cargo terminal is not a storage building or a warehouse but a structure which should provide shelter and security for cargo being processed incident to the loading or
discharging of a vessel. It is true that shipside processing of package freight
has become slow and complicated because of foreign-trade regulations which
require the weighing, sampling, checking, measuring, marking, inspecting,
classifying, appraising, and surveying of freight as it becomes cargo or is discharged as such. Modern air-freight practices are showing that much of this
sorting and rehandling delay is unnecessary, and the seaport terminal cannot
be expected to lag far behind in making the same discovery. Nevertheless the
slow manual practices of the past in their most involved form have become

cumulative, carried along from the days of the spice trade into the present era of time-and-motion study. Perhaps nowhere in American industry have earlier habits and customs been so well preserved as in the dark interiors of our general cargo-terminals.

The general-cargo terminal, if it is to fulfill its intended purpose, should combine the water and land functions of transportation into a fast, efficient, and economical operation. Since before the First World War our terminals have to a great extent failed to perform that primary task; the construction of government terminals on the East Coast during and after the war is evidence of the recognition of this fact. In the Second World War the construction of government terminals on the West Coast in order to meet military needs further verifies the conclusion. Experience during that war showed that *our terminal performance in the United States was slower than our performance in operating the terminals in allied and enemy ports overseas.* Our efficiency in tons moved per man-hour of labor was likewise less at our domestic terminals than at our overseas terminals.

For the purposes of this discussion six factors have been selected as comprising the functional determinants in developing a program for a general-cargo terminal. These are: the structural elements involved, stevedoring and management problems, the types of vessels served, cargo types, and terminal feeder support.

STRUCTURAL ELEMENTS

Initially it will be assumed that the base structure of the wharf has been decided upon—a finger pier, a marginal wharf, a mole, a quay, or a structure marginal to a slip or basin. It will be further assumed that the water depths of the ship's berth have been ascertained and that adequate adjacent port waters and channels connecting with the government-developed harbors have been planned. The problem of determining what the deck will be remains to be solved.

For the sake of flexibility, the designing of the top structure—which determines the operational use of the terminal—and the designing of the base structure should be considered separately. The superstructure, which comprises the aprons, sheds, platforms, and railway and roadway layouts, together with the terminal open- and closed-storage elements, should be planned for a shorter period of usefulness than that contemplated for the base structure. This does not imply that the superimposed deck should be made up of tempo-

FIGURE 399. PIER A,
LONG BEACH,
CALIFORNIA.
AIR VIEW, EXTERIOR,
AND INTERIOR

A pier structure designed
for a large unbroken in-
terior space, adequately
served by railroad spurs.

Air View, Pacific
Air Industries; all,
courtesy Port of
Long Beach

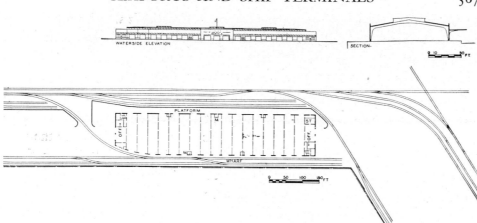

FIGURE 400. PIER A, LONG BEACH, CALIFORNIA. PLAN, ELEVATION, AND SECTION

Note especially the great span roofed over by rigid frames in steel.

rary or shoddy structures; it may conceivably not lose its functional value until after a period of from twenty-five to forty years, although the useful life of the materials of which the base structure is constructed can be expected to last three or more times that length of time. Whether a wharf is to be a general-cargo or a special-cargo facility will depend in most cases on the physical development of the top structure. In order to appreciate the various factors that influence the design of the general-cargo wharf deck and the integral structures, trackages, and materials-handling aids, we should review what takes place there operationally while a ship is being worked.[2]

The miscellaneous-cargo terminal of today should be a composite structure, designed to enclose and support a controlled cargo-handling work process. So far as any single berth is concerned, the terminal should be a single self-sufficient unit capable of serving the largest cargo vessel. The measure of the worth of a terminal is the efficiency that can be achieved in the work process both currently and in any foreseeable future. For this a truly flexible structure is required. Prior to the Second World War it was assumed that a full cargo would be assembled in a transit shed at a relatively slow build-up rate. The fact that the large post-war ships and the small remaining sheds make this practice impractical has led to the use of mechanical handling equipment and to the direct transfer of cargo between rail car and vehicle at the ship's side. The construction of larger sheds is not in itself the solution of the problem, since that feature

[2] "Working a ship" means loading or unloading it.

alone would tend to perpetuate the ancient work methods which prevailed before the war and have only started to be replaced by more efficient techniques.

STEVEDORING AND TERMINAL MANAGEMENT

Wartime experience proved that a controlled work process conducted on a dominantly horizontal plane is desirable at the waterfront, and progressive stevedores are carrying forward the methods they developed during the war. One of the main barriers to a complete evolution in cargo-handling methods has been found to lie in the structural characteristics of the existing terminals. The time-worn manhandling cargo system with its cross flows, lack of pre-planned terminals, and divided control is definitely on its way out and in its place we find the beginnings of work-control horizontal-plane operation, which only awaits a new environment in which to reach full development. That environment should be a new type of terminal which incorporates characteristics designed to further the modernization of the handling system.

Lack of co-ordination among the parties to this problem in the past has been responsible for the repeated building of unsuitable terminals. A wharf deck and transit shed should be arranged and built to contain the cargo-handling process required for modern ships in a highly competitive marine service. It is more important than ever before for the designer to obtain the opinions and co-operation of the people who will eventually control and operate the terminal; he must do this during the early phases of design, and the ideas thus gained should take precedence over those derived from what has been done in the past. Only in this way can conventional rigidity be overcome.

TYPES OF VESSELS SERVED

The vessels that can be expected to use general-cargo terminals in the United States between 1950 and 1970 will be the more recent C-1, C-2, C-3, and C-4 types, of approximately 7,500, 8,000, 10,500, and 12,500 cargo DWT respectively. The wartime utility-type Liberty and Victory vessels of 8,500 cargo DWT will be in existence for some years to come; these vessels and their foreign counterparts currently make up the deep-sea-vessel element of the problem. The maximum cargo space of the small C-1 vessels is 450,000 cubic feet; that of the largest, the C-4 type, is 770,000 cubic feet. The C-4 vessels have a 520-foot length, a 72-foot beam, and a weather-deck height of 32 and 10 feet respectively above the light-load and full-load lines. These vessels have five to seven hatches and require a 600-foot berth with 36 feet of initial water depth, but to provide the flexibility now advocated the design depth should be 40 feet.

The ratio of cargo cubic-foot capacity to cargo weight capacity has changed. The old criterion of 40 cubic feet per long ton to put a vessel full and down no longer holds true. Variations in the character of cargo have made it necessary to provide in new vessels 60 to 70 cubic feet of space in the holds for each long ton of cargo. The trend is to increase that space requirement; in a recent request submitted to the United States Maritime Commission this ran as high as 80 cubic feet to the ton.

CARGO CUBIC—DEADWEIGHT TONNAGE RELATIONSHIPS
OF REPRESENTATIVE CARGO VESSELS

Type of Vessel	Cargo DWT	Cargo Cubic	Cu. Ft. per L.T.
Victory (and Liberty)	8,500	460,000 cu. ft.	54
C-1	7,500	456,000 " "	60
C-2	8,000	560,000 " "	70
C-3	10,500	670,000 " "	70
C-4	12,500	770,000 " "	62

Modern vessels are capable of discharging or taking on cargo at a maximum rate of 150 to 210 long tons per hour without the help of terminal gear. The fact that in Europe as early as 1930 hourly general-cargo handling rates of 360 metric tons per hour were achieved with the assistance of terminal gear indicates that in the United States the present performance by means of ships' gear alone is probably no more than half the rate the port should seek to achieve. The current practice in this country of using exclusively ships' gear limits the intake of cargo to about 30 payable tons per hatch per hour. The twin-hatch vessels contemplated here and abroad offer greater discharge potentialities only if they are served by modern terminals; if the level-luffing wharf cranes which have revolutionized cargo handling abroad are employed, a rate of 360 tons per hour can be maintained without difficulty (see Fig. 401). The inadequacy of ships' gear to transfer cargo fast enough to turn the modern large vessel around in a reasonable period of time indicates that wharf cranes must be available to augment ships' gear; only in the United States can port terminals of consequence be found where such cranes had not become a standard of practice two decades before the mid-twentieth century.

It is unlikely that in the third quarter of the century ships and terminals will be designed to complement each other completely. As a result, the present trend toward complete horizontal-plane movement of cargo in terminals will continue to be interrupted by a transfer to vertical movement at the ship's side. An appreciation of the importance of this problem is evidenced by current experiments in the side-port and end-on loading of vessels; these have already demonstrated that 1,320 tons per hour can be passed aboard a ship through a side port in an uninterrupted horizontal operation. (Of course elevators within the ship are required to perform the necessary vertical movement.) One of the few coastwise lines that made a profit before the Second World War employed the side-port system. During the war, end-on loading which used uninterrupted horizontal movement decreased the loading time of special-type army vessels to less than one-half the time needed for loading the same vessels in the conventional way. The new terminal must therefore be flexible, since it may later be called upon to serve a different type of vessel as side or end handling becomes more common. The horizontal movement of cargo from the wharves directly through the sides of vessels is a strong possibility in the not distant future; in that case the top hatches would be reserved for the handling of bulky cargo.

The terminal service requirements for vessels include potable water, electric current, telephone, garbage and refuse disposal, and discharge of sanitary waste. The oil-polution problem seems about to be solved by a recently developed oil separator. The steamship companies have stated that they prefer aprons for two shipside tracks and traveling gantry cranes. They want the passenger operation confined to the second deck of the combined terminal.

TYPES OF CARGO AND THEIR RELATION TO TERMINAL FUNCTIONS

A preponderance of certain types of cargo passing through a port influences the type of terminal layout. The sheds in a cotton-exporting port require greater cubic-foot capacity than the sheds of a port that handles iron and steel products; for iron and steel can be loaded directly from cars on the aprons, whereas cotton must be protected. It may be stated generally that cargo today is not so dense as it used to be; a larger proportion of it is now composed of manufactured products such as vehicles, refrigerators, and radios, which tend to "balloon" the cargo sizes over those that prevailed earlier when the load consisted of dense raw products and both crude and finished metals. Since ships today are designed to accommodate a larger proportion of "measurement cargo," the cubic capacity of transit sheds must accordingly be increased.

It should be pointed out that in spite of the general increase in cubic-foot requirements the floor-load capacity of the terminal must be adequate to handle the densest type of cargo which may arrive. The wide range of cargo density is illustrated by the following table:

Type	Cu. Ft. per L.T.
Footstuffs	58
Engineering construction materials and equipment	57
Petroleum products in packages	56
Vehicles	156
Ammunition	41
Manufactured articles	100
House and building furnishings	121
Airplanes	466

Nominal dense cargo piled at average stacking heights of 8 feet produces a floor load of 480 pounds per square foot. A maximum stacking height of 17 feet has been made possible, however, by the use of a new type of fork-lift truck, and with light cargo stacked at that height the floor load is increased to 680 pounds per square foot. On this basis a minimum floor-load capacity of 600 pounds per square foot would appear to be indicated, but if the capacity is increased to 800 pounds per square foot to meet extreme requirements there will be greater flexibility in the use of the terminal.

Cargo Handling. A modern cargo terminal should be constructed with a view to assisting and encouraging the handling of modern cargoes. As mechanical handling continues to advance, cargoes are increasingly unitized—by palletizing (packing on platforms or pallets), packaging, and containerizing (shipment in specially designed containers, frequently re-usable). For handling such cargoes the work process which at present achieves the best results is movement on a horizontal plane, with mobile wheeled carriers or conveyors, designed layouts, and work-controlled flows. Any vertical movement in excess of that required for stacking or for transfer in and out of vessels should not be contemplated, and for this limited purpose only the best mechanical equipment known should be provided. The equipment now available and currently used where conditions permit includes fork-lift trucks with a capacity that runs up to 4,000 pounds and with 17-foot stacking capabilities; tractors, or "mules," and trailers of 4,000-pound capacity; portable power conveyors; automobile tractor cranes of 10 tons capacity with telescoping booms; rail cars; automobile trucks and tractor trailers; and re-usable containers both of fixed and knock-down construction.

Since ships' gear is not well adapted to the handling of either unit-type cargo or crated and packed cargo of 3- to 10-ton units, cranes should be provided for these types of cargo, which will probably increase as more manufactured products are exported. Much heavy freight that is now unloaded at the head house and rear platform of the wharf and skidded to the ship's side could be transferred directly from car to ship (or vice versa) if wharfside crane equipment were available. The one item of mechanical equipment which will do more than anything else to revolutionize cargo handling at port terminals is the fast level-luffing gantry crane. The employment of the luffing principle in cranes enabled the King George V docks in Calcutta to out-perform the West Coast terminals of the United States by 100 per cent and Rotterdam to pass from third place to first in a space of three years in the Antwerp-Hamburg-Rotterdam competition; it also permitted package freight to be delivered anywhere in Germany fifty-eight hours after the ship had docked at Bremen. So far as the author of this chapter knows, there is no port in the United States where such a crane is used.

TERMINAL FEEDER SUPPORT

Storage. Supporting storage facilities for waterfront terminals in the United States consist of intransit storage areas which serve as holding points for cargo received or in which freight is built up awaiting the arrival of a vessel. Such a storage plant should be adjacent to the transit sheds and should relieve the terminal sheds of cargo not intended for immediate outshipment by land transport or for the outloading of ships; the delay time customarily allowed in the transit sheds has in many cases made them in fact intransit warehouses, which is contrary to their functional purpose. Paved intransit supporting-storage areas should be provided at the rear of the sheds, together with holding yards for rail cars as well as paved motor parks for trucks awaiting direct transfer of cargo from ships. These requirements suggest either the marginal type of wharf, or wharves, or wide solid-fill piers; for the problem of developing a narrow finger pier as a facility to serve modern cargo vessels involves the compromising of so many of the basic functional determinants that only unusual conditions and circumstances should lead to its construction.

Transportation Feeders. When considered as transfer points, waterfront terminals must be served on the land side by adequate railway and highway networks. The rail support of a modern port with high-utilization-factor terminals usually presents a difficult problem, generally because of a lack of railroad yard space and of combined feeders for both industrial and port purposes. For proper rail service there must be adequate inland classification yards, holding and reconsignment yards, interchange and transfer facilities, fast and efficient belt lines, and near-by intransit holding yards. The cargo of a single vessel requires between 400 and 500 cars, and a vessel-working time of 60 hours would require maximum shunting rates of 12 to 15 cars per hour. It must be remembered that the export freight or import freight entering a port is in excess of that required for the commerce and industry of the contiguous area; but, since railway feeders commensurate with the needs of a highly efficient port terminal have not generally been developed, the limited rail transportation serving a port may curtail the terminal's capacity.

Similar problems arise in connection with the road network that serves a port. The development of industrial highways and freeways leading to ports has increased the relative importance of highway transportation. Hence adequate motor parks, traffic patterns, and looped traffic flows should be provided for the supporting truck lines to any modern port. At the rear of the terminal an open paved storage area equivalent to the area of the sheds should also be provided.

SPECIFIC PROGRAM REQUIREMENTS

The composite structure which will best serve these general conditions will be influenced structurally by the architectural requirements, by the climate, and by waterfront conditions. It should be a self-sufficient unit capable of serving at least one modern cargo vessel, and it should embody the basic criteria of structural stability, efficiency, flexibility, safety, and economy as they are adapted to local conditions.

WHARF DECK

Adjacent to the berth served, each unit of the proposed general-cargo terminal requires a wharf area approximately 600 feet long by 300 feet wide. The whole wharf plat should be smooth-paved, and all trackwork should use girder rails and paved switches. Since such an area is obviously best suited to the marginal type of wharf, seemingly this type is to be preferred because it offers the maximum base flexibility, lends itself most easily to planned work methods, permits the looping of road or rail feeders, and has land access on three sides. In addition, as compared to the finger pier, the marginal type provides a shorter distance from the center of terminal operation to supporting-storage areas,

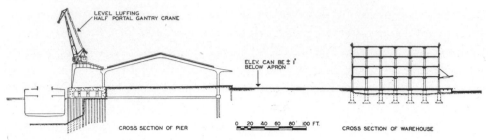

FIGURE 401. PIER SHED AND WAREHOUSE. SECTIONS

puts less restriction on deck loads, and assures easier maintenance dredging, non-interference with stream currents, less interference in lightering or off-side operations, simpler ship handling, and simpler maintenance problems in general. When the construction of a series of at least two of these units in a line is not feasible, a double-pier arrangement of two such units placed back to back is an acceptable alternate. Single piers normally are not considered practical for general-cargo terminals.

The wharf deck unit is composed of a shipside apron, a single-story transit shed, and a rear area with a trucking platform.

Apron. The wharf apron is the shipside work platform. It should contain at least two tracks: a shipside track for the direct transfer of cargo from ship to car, or the reverse, and a running track for the shunting of cars. The center line of the shipside track should be 14½ feet from the wharf face and the center line of the running track should be 27 feet back from the face; a total width of 36½ feet will yield the most economical arrangement. This contemplates a crane rail 5 feet from the wharf face. In anticipation of crane operation a 49-foot apron is recommended, with provision for a shed-front standing track; a half-portal gantry arrangement is recommended (Fig. 401). Two crossovers to the shipside track per shed are recommended, located approximately 100 feet in from the ends of the shed. The wharf deck should be 15 feet above mean low tide—an increase of 3 to 5 feet over present practice because of the increased freeboard height of vessels today and the change-over from the full-scantling-type vessels of pre-war days to the present shelter-deck type. The apron should be of concrete, smooth-paved, and care should be taken to minimize any unevenness of the trackwork by the use of girder rails and paved switches instead of T rails and open switchwork. A plus grade of 1 per cent across the apron to the shed is recommended.

Transit Shed. A one-story transit shed 165 feet wide by 550 feet long is required to contain the cubic contents of a modern vessel at an average stacking height of 12 feet and with an effective utilization of two-thirds of the floor area. In practice, where space permits, 40 per cent of the area is given over to aisles and to non-effective space. A minimum vertical clearance of 20 feet is dictated by the fork lifts, which stack cargo to a height of 17 feet. A clear span with no interior column interference is desirable; where economy prevents this, at least the apron side of the shed should be free of interior columns. Both terminal managers and stevedores emphasize that they would rather sacrifice shed width than be hampered by interior columns—which, furthermore, cause difficulty in the planning of sheds to accommodate ships of various lengths and hatch spacings.

A rigid-frame type of construction with high center clearance to accommodate the lift equipment is ideal for the shed, and the structure should be fire-resistant. Disappearing doors that afford a minimum width of 18 feet and a minimum height of 15 feet should be spaced alternately and interchangeably with dead panels. It is recommended that the door frames and dead panels be hinged at the top to swing up out of the way and present a continuous opening (unobstructed except by the wall columns) when the loading or unloading operations require it. Normally the floors of the shed are set flush with the apron and, in order to form a good trucking platform, they should be 3'-9" above the depressed area at the rear. The plus 1 per cent grade of the apron carried on through the shed works advantageously in achieving this required rear-platform height while permitting a flat grade on the between-shed access from rear area to apron (Fig. 401). The shed floor should be planned for the heaviest highway-vehicle loads; it should be of smooth concrete, and attention should be given to providing joints that will not hinder caster-wheeled vehicles.

The lighting of the shed is important; 10 foot-candles of light should be provided. Transverse skylights of the greenhouse type, extending from apron portals to platform, are preferred to the conventional monitor or sawtooth types. Provision should be made for a crane girder above the apron portals, and the face columns should be designed accordingly.

Rear Area. The space at the rear is an integral part of the terminal, and it is for this reason more than any other that the marginal type of wharf is favored. The rear platform should be 20 feet wide and should be protected by a roof cantilevered out from the shed. Two platform tracks on center lines spaced 6 feet and 18½ feet respectively from the platform edge should be provided. The minimum distance between the platforms of double piers should be 142

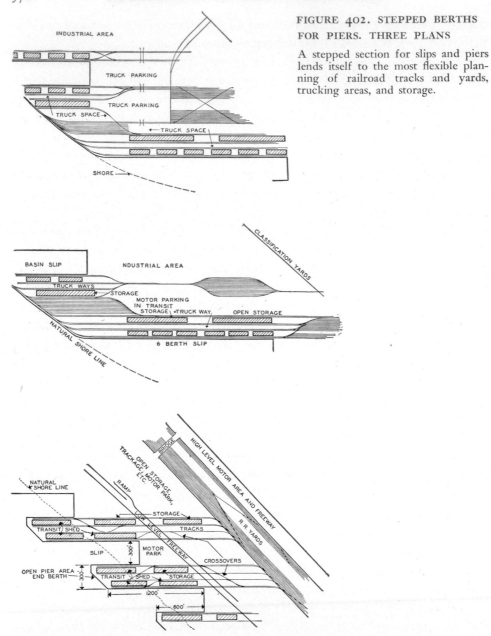

FIGURE 402. STEPPED BERTHS
FOR PIERS. THREE PLANS

A stepped section for slips and piers
lends itself to the most flexible planning of railroad tracks and yards,
trucking areas, and storage.

feet; this figure is determined by the 55-foot length of tractor semi-trailer
highway vehicles. Truck docks should be provided in the space at the ends
of the sheds so that truck loading will not be hampered by car shunting at the

rear platforms. In general, the sheds should be separated by multiples of normal bay widths, and a minimum width of 100 feet between sheds should be allowed.

TERMINAL ARRANGEMENTS

The terminal unit which has been discussed, though operationally self-sufficient, should be constructed in combinations of at least pairs, since the pairing of terminal units affords flexibility for operation, management, and future changes. The paved open-storage area, which contains space for the construction of closed-storage units, works out to be an area equal to the square of the berth length. In drawing up master plans, the area dedicated to the waterfront should be equal in depth to two berth lengths. The pairing of units back to back on piers provides access for the inshore berths; if piers are two or more berths in length they will have to be made wider to provide road and rail access to the outer berths (theoretically such piers should be trapezoidal in shape). No matter how well designed a projecting pier may be, the fact remains that the "center of gravity" of the separate work processes and of the combined operation of the several units will be farther removed from the storage areas than in the case of the marginal pier, and the feeder flows will necessarily be reciprocating instead of looped.

As the number of co-axial marginal-wharf units increases—up to a limit of about six and not more than nine, depending on the depth and nature of the supporting-storage and feeder area at the rear—the efficiency and flexibility of the entire arrangement of the parts increases. The point of diminishing returns occurs when the "centers of gravity" of the storage-feeder networks become so spread out that a division into separate systems is indicated. Groups of six adjacent marginal units seem to provide the best arrangement. The ideal solution would set these groups marginal to adjacent slips, with open and closed storage between; the slips should follow a stepped outline so that rail-holding yards are placed at the rear and near the ends of each shipside section (Fig. 402).

MINOR BOAT FACILITIES

Since small public boat harbors, or marinas, are essential parts of the modern waterfront, areas to serve the peculiar needs of small craft must be developed and maintained in any complete port. Such facilities are of two types: marinas for pleasure craft, which are most suitably located in those areas of the harbor reserved for pleasure boating and adjacent to waterside parks; and commercial marinas, which are usually built and maintained for commercial fishing fleets and are most suitably located in the industrial areas of the port.

PLEASURE-CRAFT MARINAS

The greatest progress in the development of marinas for pleasure craft has taken place in the second quarter of the twentieth century on the inland lakes and waterways and in the resort ports of the United States. The Tennessee Valley Authority in its planning has done considerable research in the design, construction, and maintenance of such marinas. The National Association of Engine and Boat Manufacturers has conducted a continuous survey of the problem of municipal marinas with the aim of fostering the creation of essential pleasure-craft facilities, just as public golf courses, bathing beaches, parks, and forests for the recreational uplift of the public are provided by municipalities, states, and the national government. Yachting and small boating is a popular national diversion and an important national and local business. The creation of municipal marinas increases community business revenues by catering to the needs of the small-boat owners. Yacht clubs which formerly had no difficulty in providing marinas for the comparatively few owners of small pleasure craft can no longer serve the needs of the vastly increased numbers in this group.

The public marina for this class of boats should be located in a sheltered reach of the harbor which is free of objectionable pollution and affords pleasant and picturesque shore surroundings. The area should be convenient to the park section of the city and not too remote from the residential and shopping districts. Good highway communications are essential. Municipally maintained motor parks are desirable adjuncts. The marina should be carefully managed under published regulations, and uniform charges established by the marina control authority (preferably part of the local government) should be posted.

Safe, low-cost wharfside berths for pleasure craft of all types should be available; for wharfside mooring affords economy of harbor space, safe access to small craft, and an over-all orderliness in what might otherwise be a congested small-boat anchorage. The minimum wharf structure is an access walk at least 12 feet wide and capable of supporting light motor vehicles. The small-boat berths bordering the main wharf should include secondary safe access walks 4 feet wide, with mooring bitts and dolphins. In each group the berths are usually arranged for craft of similar length and type, so that the greatest

FIGURE 403.
MUNICIPAL
YACHT HARBOR,
NEW ORLEANS,
LOUISIANA.
TWO VIEWS

Narrow piers leading to berths between piles characterize many small-boat marinas.

Courtesy New Orleans
Port Authority

possible number may be accommodated in a given marina and the charges can be kept correspondingly low. Various ingenious schemes have been devised, such as herringbone berthing and double slips with rubbing piles designed both to separate and to protect the maximum number of craft along a given wharf.

The marina should provide the essential utilities, the minimum being electric and fresh-water outlets near each berth. There should be facilities for fueling and for garbage and refuse disposal. Marine railways, monorails, cradles, and motor-repair shops are also necessary. Concessions for the convenient sale of boat hardware, gear, marine supplies, and provisions should be granted to private dealers.

Examples of well-designed and well-regulated small-boat harbors in the United States are those at Lake Pontchartrain, Louisiana (Fig. 403); Los Angeles, California; Miami, Florida; Chicago, Illinois; Englewood, New Jersey; Cleveland, Ohio; Lake Norris, Tennessee; Lake Washington, Seattle, Washington; and, especially, Bahia-Mar, Fort Lauderdale, Florida (Fig. 404).

FIGURE 404. BAHIA-MAR, FORT LAUDERDALE, FLORIDA. AIR VIEW

Clyde W. Sullivan, architect; J. H. Philpott, consulting engineer

At the time of construction (1949) this was the largest municipal marina in the United States; it was designed to berth over five hundred pleasure craft. The entire scheme comprises a shopping center, a yacht club with an ample restaurant, showers and sanitation facilities, and quarters for the harbormaster. Water and electric connections are brought to every berth, and gas, fuel oil, and marine supplies are available. Much of the construction, including the structural piles, is of precast concrete. The piers are 10 feet wide and the catwalks between berths 5 feet wide.   Courtesy Fort Lauderdale Publicity Bureau

HARBORS FOR SMALL COMMERCIAL BOATS

Small-boat harbors are essential for the commercial fishing craft which form an important segment of the national maritime industry of many nations. Fishing-craft marinas should be constructed only in such harbor localities as can provide adequate shore facilities for the fishing industry. They require a community of service establishments, including gear-storage facilities, machine shops, suppliers of rope and other gear, blacksmith shops, provisioners, clothing stores, and radio-repair shops. Open fields should be available for the servicing and repair of nets.

Here the wharf space, like that for small pleasure craft, should provide for a maximum number of vessels at the least practicable wharfage charge. The fishing-craft marina in the harbor at Seattle, Washington, is a good example of what can be achieved in this respect. The construction of marinas for small commercial craft must obviously be based on the needs of the local type of craft. Oyster fishermen require facilities different from those suited to the tuna

FIGURE 405. SALMON BAY FISHING TERMINAL, SEATTLE, WASHINGTON.
AIR VIEW

George T. Treadwell, chief engineer

Marinas for fishing vessels resemble those for pleasure craft in many ways but are situated close
to major shipping facilities and wholesale fish markets.

Herold Aerial Photos, courtesy Public Relations Department, Port of Seattle

fleets of the West Coast or to the cod and mackerel fishermen of New England.

Excellent examples of commercial marinas in North America are those at
Seattle, Washington (Fig. 405); San Francisco, Los Angeles, and San Diego,
California; Cape May, New Jersey; Gloucester, Massachusetts; and Halifax,
Nova Scotia.

AESTHETIC CONSIDERATIONS

A great and busy port is one of the most impressive of man's creations; it is
a sight of continual and dynamic interest—when it can be seen. It is one of the
significant symbols of the modern world—a world dependent on the rapid
exchange of goods and commodities. Despite this obvious symbolic and expressive value, however, the modern port has but rarely received the creative
and imaginative design it has deserved. Piers and pier sheds frequently improvised at the lowest cost; connecting streets and traffic ways that are crowded,

FIGURE 406. LOCKS ON CANAL ST. MARTIN, PARIS

A typical European two-level handling of commercial wharf requirements in the city. The quay, at canal level, is for commercial use; sightly landscaped roads on either side furnish general traffic facilities and occasional opportunities for outlooks over the commercial harbor.

Photograph Burton Holmes, from Ewing Galloway

mean, and lined with cheap structures; surrounding areas filled with slums, brothels, and saloons—these have characterized all too many ports, with the result that the waterside districts of many towns have become almost synonymous with squalor. This is completely unnecessary; the architect and engineer today, working in close co-operation, could redeem port areas aesthetically as they improve their efficiency. Such a redemption must lie along two lines: first, the design of the port facilities; and, second, the relation of the port to the city itself.

Naturally a port is no place for applied monumentality and superficial prettifying. But, since great sheds and piers have a monumental scale in themselves, these elements can be so composed as not to conceal their functional relationships but rather to emphasize them. Ample evidence is offered by the magnificent dams and powerhouses of the TVA that industrial structures of

FIGURE 407. DOCK DEVELOPMENT, ALGIERS

A two-level port scheme on a monumental scale.   Photograph De Cou, from Ewing Galloway

the severest practicality can, if designed by a great designer or a great team of designers, be examples of the most inspiring beauty.

Moreover, every port contains a host of smaller elements—lamp posts, gates, small office or control stations, cranes and crane housings, and the like—to which significant form can be given. The fact that these are mere parts of a utilitarian port is no excuse for the usual stupidity of their form or their usual haphazard ugliness. The forms of bollards and hawser cleats, beautiful in their simple rightness, have been arrived at through generations of experience. If the same type of combined engineering and architectural invention which went into the TVA details could be applied to all port elements, both major and minor, they might have a similar expressive beauty like that of the bollards and cleats. Such an attention to the smaller items would go far toward removing the dreariness of the usual shoreside area; combined with creative design in the larger structures and their arrangements, it might well result in port areas which, instead of constituting intolerable blights, would be as handsome and inspiring as the great locks and dams and power structures of the TVA.

Even more important is a new study of the relationship of port to city. Waterfronts are precious city possessions, aesthetically as well as economically. Broad surfaces of sparkling water, the sense of liberation which water brings, the freshness of water-borne breezes—these are assets no city can afford to relinquish. One of the city planner's main objectives must be the preservation of as much of this valuable topographic heritage as possible. The port designer and the city planner must learn to collaborate. The record of the United States is particularly black in this matter; here a disastrous tradition has grown up that is still all-pervading—the tradition that a port is necessarily an eyesore and that the thing to do is to keep people away from it. Some European cities have thought otherwise, and successful attempts to combine civic benefit with efficient trade facilities do exist. Perhaps double-level schemes could bring citizens above the traffic to broad promenades on the tops of warehouses; such promenades could be planted and could give superb views of the coming and going of water craft. Perhaps certain functional divisions in the port plan could be broadened into green ways that would connect occasional sitting parks at the water's edge.

Whatever form the eventual solutions may take, the problem exists, is vital, and cries out for serious consideration. The experience of European port cities —Paris, for example—and of such cities as Savannah in the United States suggests that the multi-level scheme offers the best opportunity. Nevertheless, tradition must not blind us to new possibilities. Let us concentrate on the objective; if we refuse to accept the fallacy that a port is unfortunately but necessarily an impenetrable barrier between a city and the waterfront which it needs for rest, enjoyment, and inspiration, eventually superb solutions will be found.

SUGGESTED ADDITIONAL READING FOR CHAPTER 42

American Association of Port Authorities, *Bibliographic Notes on Ports and Harbors*, compiled by Perry Young (New Orleans: the Association, 1926).

Atwood, William G., A. A. Johnson, and others, *Marine Structures, Their Deterioration and Preservation*, report of Committee on Marine Piling Investigation, Division of Engineering and Industrial Research, National Research Council (Washington: National Research Council [c1924]).

Chaney, C. A., *Marinas—Recommendations for Design, Construction, and Maintenance* (New York: National Association of Engine and Boat Manufacturers, 1939).

Cunningham, Brysson, *Cargo Handling at Ports* (London: Chapman & Hall; New York: Wiley, 1924).

—— *The Dock and Harbour Engineer's Reference Book* (London: Griffin, 1914).

—— *Principles and Practices of Dock Engineering* (London: Griffin, 1904).

—— *A Treatise on the Principles and Practice of Harbour Engineering* (London: Griffin, 1908).

Du-Plat-Taylor, F[rancis] M[aurice Gustavus], *The Design, Construction, and Maintenance of Docks, Wharves, and Piers*, 2d ed. rev. and enl. (London: Benn, 1934).

Earle, E. C., *Design Features of General Cargo and Combined General Cargo and Passenger Marine Terminal Facilities Governing Terminal Operating Efficiency* (New Orleans: American Association of Port Authorities, 1944).

Green, Carlton, *Wharves and Piers* (New York: McGraw-Hill, 1917).

Joly, G. de, P. H. Watier, Charles LaRoche, and A. de Rouville, *Travaux maritimes* (Paris: Dunod, 1940).

Lederer, Eugene H., *Port Terminal Operation* (New York: Cornell Maritime Press, 1945).

MacElwee, Roy S[amuel], *Port Development* (New York: McGraw-Hill, 1925).

—— *Ports and Terminal Facilities*, 2d ed. enl. & rewritten (New York: McGraw-Hill, 1926).

Marine Borer Research Committee—New York Harbor report [No.] 3 (Duxbury, Mass.: William F. Clapp Laboratories, 1946—).

Stroyer, Rudolf, *Concrete Structures in Marine Work* (London: Knapp, Drewett, 1934).

Water Terminal and Transfer Facilities, House of Representatives, 67th Congress, 1st Session, Document No. 109 (Washington: Government Printing Office).

YEARBOOKS AND PERIODICALS

Bown, A. H. J., and Lt. Col. C. A. Dove, "Port Operation," *Dock and Harbour Authority* (*D.H.A.*), Vol. 27 (1947), January, pp. 221–23; February, pp. 245–49; March, pp. 280–85; April, pp. 305–10; Vol. 28 (1947–48), May, pp. 9–15; June, pp. 42–48; July, pp. 67–71; August, pp. 95–99; September, pp. 119–22; October, pp. 151–54; November, pp. 186–90; December, pp. 207–10; January, pp. 236–40; February, pp. 256–61; March, pp. 297–302.

Dalziel, J., "Quayside Cranes and Other Cargo Handling Appliances at Ports," *D.H.A.*, Vol. 24 (1943), August, pp. 83–89; September, pp. 105–10; October, pp. 127–31; November, pp. 153–57.

Fellows, C. E., "Design of Sea Walls," *D.H.A.*, Vol. 23 (1943), March, pp. 253–57.

Fugl-Meyer, H., "Warehouses and Transit Sheds at Ports," *D.H.A.*, Vol. 26 (1946), February, pp. 238–42; March, pp. 270–71.

Garde-Hansen, P., "Design of Piled Structures," *D.H.A.*, Vol. 25 (1944), May, pp. 17–21; June, pp. 37–40; July, pp. 62–66.

Hafenbau technische Gesellschaft Jahrbuch (Hamburg, Germany); translations available at Engineering Societies Library, 33 West 39th St., New York, N.Y.

Hamilton, R. M., "Floating Wharves and Jetties," *D.H.A.*, Vol. 26 (1946), April, pp. 287–93.

Koelbel, William H., "Time and Tide," *Motor Boating*, Vol. 74 (1944), August, pp. 46–48, 92–96.

The Log, Vol. 42 (1947), July, review yearbook number.

Morgan, Horace D., "Design of Wharves on Soft Ground," *D.H.A.*, Vol. 25 (1944), October, pp. 133–36; November, pp. 146–52.

Pennoyer, R. P., "Design of Steel Sheet-Piling Bulkheads," *Civil Engineering*, Vol. 3 (1933), November, pp. 615–19.

—— "Details of S.S.P.B.," *Civil Engineering*, Vol. 4 (1934), April, pp. 197–201.

Puckshaw, Savile, "Sheet-Piling in Maritime Work," *D.H.A.*, Vol. 26 (1946), February, pp. 232–36.

World Ports (monthly), official organ of American Association of Port Authorities (1912–1933); merged with *Nautical Gazette* (1938–1942).

43

Bus Stations

By J. GORDON CARR

IN THE UNITED STATES between 1910 and 1920 mass production of automobiles within the reach of the ordinary purse caused country roads to be improved and a network of transcontinental highways to be built. Communities which had never been served by waterways or railroads became accessible. Those which had dwindled with the discontinuation of spur boat and rail lines were given a new link with the world. Wherever there were good highways new settlements could now be made. Suburbanism spread beyond the limits of the commuter train.

Traffic along the new roads grew until bus lines became profitable. Buses took passengers where established transportation had never penetrated. Sometimes they competed with trains and boats and offered more frequent service or lower fares; often they were more comfortable than the obsolete and sooty day coaches and ship decks of their competitors. During the First World War they helped carry increased loads which the overtaxed systems already in operation could not accommodate. They took the place of interurban electric cars which had grown too old to be replaced economically. In industrial cities they were the heirs of the jitney bus—a private car which had been picking up half a dozen riders for a nickel apiece in wildcat competition with overcrowded and inefficient trolley cars. The result was that existing trolley systems converted to buses as soon as possible, put in supplementary bus lines, or were run out of business by the bus competition. Buses thus became a preferred mode of transportation both within towns and between them. When their fares were lower than those of the trains, they took long-haul and even transcontinental passenger traffic from the railroads. Their upholstered seats and convenient rest stops made them a pleasanter mode of travel than the railroad day coaches.

The growth of bus lines was rapid and largely unplanned. Routes were operated by many small companies without much capital. The establishment of

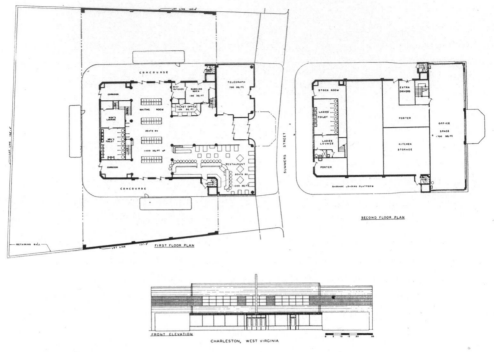

FIGURE 408. GREYHOUND BUS STATION, CHARLESTON, WEST VIRGINIA. PLAN AND ELEVATION

George D. Brown, architect

A simple example of the island-type plan on an interior lot; there are but three pick-up stations.

From Burleigh and Adams, *Modern Bus Terminals . . .*

bus stations and terminals was left mostly to chance. The average station was often a corner drugstore or poolroom; here tickets were sold, passengers could find shelter, and buses could pull in to the curb. Terminals were either makeshifts in converted buildings or hastily constructed, minimum-cost structures, planned for temporary use but continuing in service long after they were outgrown. Few were adapted for expansion, and almost none were the result of a study of their relation to city traffic; they were merely rough compromises. Using existing streets, they caused congestion which added to their own inefficiency.

In the 1920's many small companies were consolidated and large, well-financed bus lines began to emerge. The sidewalk depot was outlawed by city ordinances. Terminals had to be erected; these were often sizable, costly, and the result of careful planning. But no one could then foresee the rapidity of the growth of bus travel, and within a few years the terminals became cramped; even the most up-to-date and thoughtfully designed buildings erected on the eve of the Second World War grew uncomfortable with the loads of the war years. It is therefore necessary, in projecting new stations and terminals, to consider both present needs and those which will arise in the future as bus travel continues to expand.

A bus requires less capital outlay than a train coach, a boat, or an airplane. Also, it can be more readily replaced, and with each replacement it can incorporate improvements. There is a constant effort toward increasing its speed, safety, and comfort. Just as the bus pioneered in the use of the reclining seat (adopting the Morris chair as a model) and made it standard equipment for planes and trains, so it can show the way in other refinements of travel comfort. It may readily take new forms: it may have hinged sections and double decks to give more space, thus allowing for food and lounge facilities. Such improvements will impose new conditions on the planning of stations.

FUNDAMENTAL FACTORS

PLACE OF BUS TRAVEL

Bus travel appeals to many who wish to travel economically, to dispense with the responsibilities of using their own cars, to see the country more intensively than they can from planes and trains, and to enjoy a leisurely pace. But for innumerable others there is no alternative; their destinations can be reached only by bus, and such places are constantly increasing in number as new roads are built and new regions are settled or urbanized.

Bus travelers include family groups encumbered with young children, motley hand luggage, and even pets. They must be accommodated properly if they and their fellow travelers are to be comfortable. Quiet waiting zones, nurseries, and even kennels provide individualized attention and privacy. Old people who are neither strong nor well are occasional bus passengers; they too must be catered to. Everyone likes personal consideration and freedom from annoyance. Those who travel for recreation—an ever-increasing number —like a trip to have an aura of excitement. They want gaiety as well as comfort; for them a flag, a spotlight, or a patch of color will give a station a festive air. Tour information, guidebooks, and quality posters invest any type of travel with allurement; when buses make as much use of this material as trains, ships, and planes have done, they too will be thought of as glamorous. And those

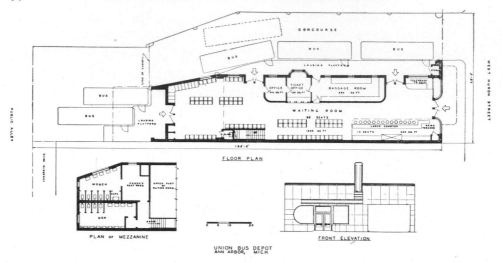

FIGURE 409. BUS STATION FOR EASTERN MICHIGAN MOTORBUSES, ANN ARBOR, MICHIGAN. PLAN

Douglas Loree, architect

A through-way type of plan; the over-congested lot produces a cramped and awkward building plan, as well as difficult bus parking and driving problems. Passenger circulation is confined; all, whether entering or leaving, are funneled through a single narrow door.

From Burleigh and Adams, *Modern Bus Terminals . . .*

who are sensitive about the fact that they must travel economically will feel much better disposed toward buses when the stations no longer look like third-class waiting rooms or dirty clinics.

COMPLEXITIES OF THE PROBLEM

Designing a bus station or terminal generally is accomplished only after making many compromises: the site is chosen because a better one is not available; the size is restricted because a larger site could not be had; the construction is as cheap as possible because the budget is limited; the public must go without certain accommodations because the bus company's operational needs come first. The designer must arbitrate these conflicting factors. His position should be impartial. He should decide as did Robert Benchley when, as an undergraduate at Harvard, he was asked to write an essay on the relative merits of the claims of Canada and the United States to a fishing stream between them; he supported the claims of the fish. In the case of the bus lines, the rights of the fish would be represented by the social good. Because the special requirements of each bus station or terminal are determined by various dynamic factors, the designer cannot work by formula. He must study each factor, note its

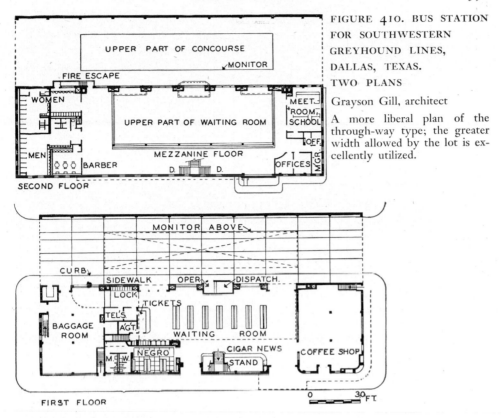

FIGURE 410. BUS STATION FOR SOUTHWESTERN GREYHOUND LINES, DALLAS, TEXAS. TWO PLANS

Grayson Gill, architect

A more liberal plan of the through-way type; the greater width allowed by the lot is excellently utilized.

present and future implications, plot his design for that later date which is agreed upon as the point in time when predictable traffic expansion, allowable expenditure, and obsolescence will be in balance, and then reach a compromise. The closer to the actual equipoise of forces this compromise is, the more stable the solution will be and the more apt it will be to remain in equilibrium.

SIZE

In the ideal program, where there are no restrictions either of site or of budget, the over-all size is determined by the peak-load needs up to that future time when continued growth and obsolescence will make enlarging, remodeling, or rebuilding necessary. Since bus traffic expansion from 1938 to 1944 proceeded at a rate of 10 to 15 per cent a year in most parts of the United States, in the next decade provision for space at least double that of current needs would therefore have to be made for a bus station that was to remain adequate for ten years. But the onset of obsolescence in a modern structure is not to be expected in less than twenty years; hence the size would have to

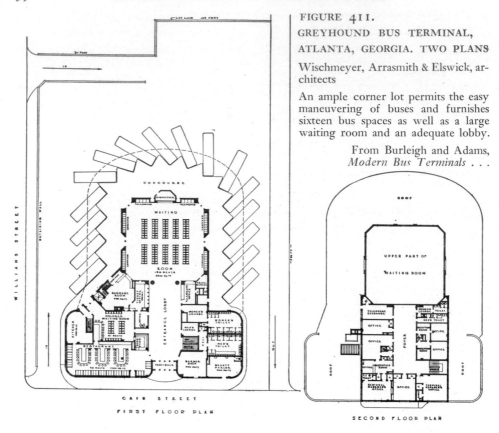

FIGURE 411.

GREYHOUND BUS TERMINAL, ATLANTA, GEORGIA. TWO PLANS

Wischmeyer, Arrasmith & Elswick, architects

An ample corner lot permits the easy maneuvering of buses and furnishes sixteen bus spaces as well as a large waiting room and an adequate lobby.

From Burleigh and Adams, *Modern Bus Terminals* . . .

be gauged by a twenty-year expected traffic growth unless plans for future enlargement were made part of the original program.

The rush-hour load will determine the traffic-channel space requirements both for passengers and for buses. Peak load use is computed on the basis of the number of passengers in the total number of full buses which arrive and depart during the busiest hour. The public areas in the station will begin to be thronged at least half an hour before bus-departure time, and if the numbers of incoming and of outgoing passengers are nearly equal at rush hours (which is not the case except when suburban commuters and long-haul passengers collide) provision for controlled movement in and out must be made in the form either of roped-off passageways or of different levels.

STATION TYPES

Bus stations vary in type from the open shed that shelters waiting passengers at a pick-up point to the complex terminal with a multiplicity of functions to

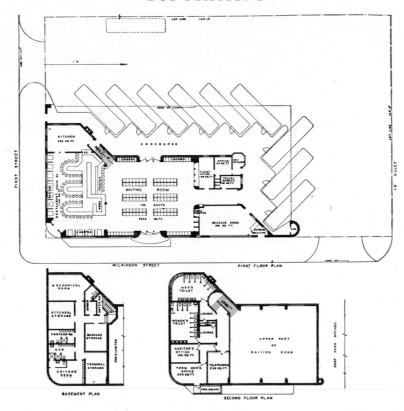

FIGURE 412. BUS STATION FOR PENNSYLVANIA AND OHIO GREYHOUND LINES, DAYTON, OHIO. PLANS

Wischmeyer, Arrasmith & Elswick, architects; Walker & Templin, associate architects

A different solution of a street-corner site, with the building at the corner and the bus circulation on the inner two sides. The passenger circulation is direct and simple and the public entrances are adequate. From Burleigh and Adams, *Modern Bus Terminals* . . .

serve every need of the traveler and the bus company or companies that use it.

Small-Town Stations. The small-town bus station has a limited space devoted to public and control areas, a small baggage room, an office, and such concessions as checking lockers, a lunch counter, a newsstand, and possibly a gas station. It serves a moderate flow of traffic. Buses stop before it at the curb or pull in off the street to a cut-in. Both feeder lines and main lines use it. If the main line has heavy traffic, the pull-in space and public areas must be adequate to accommodate peak loads. It may be added that if the town in which the station is located is a shopping center for a rural or suburban area, the station gains in convenience by being near the shopping district. Such a station

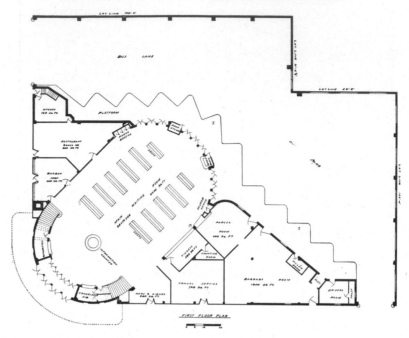

FIGURE 413. BUS STATION FOR NORTHLAND GREYHOUND LINES, MINNEAPOLIS, MINNESOTA. MAIN-FLOOR PLAN

Lang & Raugland, architects; Thomas W. Lamb, associated architects

A larger example of the basic type shown in Figure 412. The free approach and the ample waiting room and lobby are especially notable; note also the separate baggage room with its own street approach.   From Burleigh and Adams, *Modern Bus Terminals . .*

requires generous parking space around it. It may become a civic meeting place and a center of interest where bus departures may be watched from an observation mezzanine or deck. Its nursery may take care of the children of all mothers who come to town to shop. As part of the station landscaping, a model garden marked to show special plants and gardening methods can serve as a civic stimulus. Air conditioning, running ice water, vending machines, chimes and low-pitched outdoor loud-speakers to announce bus arrivals, and mechanically moving bulletin information—all of them automatic devices of the electronic age—will serve to make the station a show place and impress the citizen with the fact that the bus company is aware of the latest scientific developments. Thus he will feel that he is being considered rather than grudgingly served.

Large City Terminals. The large city bus terminal—which serves city, suburban, and long-haul main-line buses—has public and control areas com-

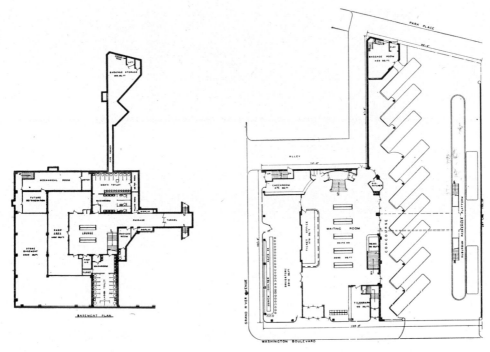

FIGURE 414. GREYHOUND TERMINAL, DETROIT, MICHIGAN. BASEMENT- AND FIRST-FLOOR PLANS

Thomas W. Lamb, architects; Phelps & Bernardi, associated architects

A metropolitan station in which major through traffic and suburban traffic are separated; this separation necessitates a below-ground tunnel of approach to the suburban platform. There is a second-floor loading platform for baggage.

From Burleigh and Adams, *Modern Bus Terminals* . . .

mensurate with its traffic flow, a large baggage room, a freight room, offices, personnel space, bus traffic space off the streets, a garage, and as many concessions of all sorts as can be fitted in—shops, a restaurant, a newsreel theater —for concession rentals alone make a central location in a downtown area economically feasible (see Figs. 414–419). An eminently practical way of paying for an expensive central piece of land for terminal use is to include a skyscraper hotel or office building—its height to be regulated by local economic considerations—as part of the station group.

Traffic access to the terminal is of prime importance if operating efficiency is to be maintained. Separate approach lanes are desirable for buses, for taxis and private cars, and for trucks, and downtown traffic jams must be by-passed. Ample parking space around the station will eliminate street congestion. Co-

FIGURE 415.
GREYHOUND
TERMINAL,
DETROIT, MICHIGAN.
EXTERIOR

Thomas W. Lamb, architects; Phelps & Bernardi, associated architects

Photograph Spencer & Wyckoff, courtesy Greyhound Lines

operation between the bus line and the city authorities may be needed to effect street widening, traffic direction changes, or the building of new access roads, and when the station is considered a civic asset it is possible that the city will share in the expense of these improvements. In long-range city planning the bus station and its approaches may entail the redevelopment of an entire section.

Union Terminals. The union station is a city terminal that is shared by two or more companies (see Figs. 424–426). Here a dual or multiple provision for control is required, but the public areas and concessions are naturally the same as for a one-company terminal. Even when municipal funds are provided for the maintenance of a union station—the only possible kind for which such funds could be obtained—the need for well-paying concessions is no less great. Of course high-rental concessions can be expected only in downtown sections, where they draw from passers-by in the street, or in terminals with heavy enough traffic to provide an unusual volume of buying on the part of those who use the station. The desirability of a union station arises not only from its convenience for travelers but also from its ability to maintain itself through the concessions made possible by the combined traffic.

Save for those controls which must be multiple to serve the several companies that use the station, many functions can be provided for in common with a gain in efficiency. The public areas, of course, are used by all. Ticket selling may well be consolidated through a screening process by which all passengers are directed from a general information counter to a specific ticket station. The dispatching of bus traffic, garage service, personnel accommodations, and other operative activities may be shared. Clear signs, a well-planned system of baggage checking, and gate control to the bus docks will serve to eliminate

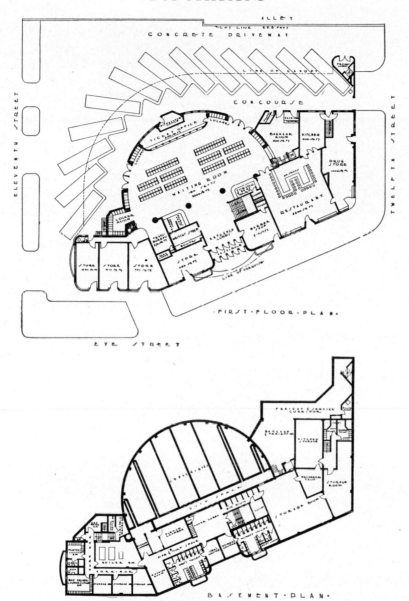

FIGURE 416. GREYHOUND TERMINAL, WASHINGTON. BASEMENT- AND FIRST-
FLOOR PLANS

Wischmeyer, Arrasmith & Elswick, architects; Lucius R. White, Jr., associate

A brilliant solution of the city bus terminal. Note the simplicity of the passenger circulation
through the ample semicircular waiting room, the central position of the ticket office and dispatcher's office, and the baggage room with a counter and a window which opens on the waiting
room; note also the relatively large area for income-producing concessions and shops.

From Burleigh and Adams, *Modern Bus Terminals* . . .

FIGURE 417.
GREYHOUND
TERMINAL,
WASHINGTON.
STREET FRONT

Wischmeyer, Arrasmith & Elswick, architects; Lucius R. White, Jr., associate

Courtesy Greyhound Terminal

FIGURE 418.
GREYHOUND
TERMINAL,
BALTIMORE,
MARYLAND.
EXTERIOR AND
INTERIOR

Wischmeyer, Arrasmith & Elswick, architects; Lucius R. White, Jr., associate

A city bus station distinguished by the size and lavishness of its interior arrangements.

Exterior photograph the Hughes Co.; both courtesy Greyhound Lines

confusion. Certain large companies with a monopoly of business in their respective regions have felt that they have nothing to gain from the use of union terminals, but the successful operation of union terminals by the railroads and

FIGURE 419.

GREYHOUND TERMINAL, CLEVELAND, OHIO.

EXTERIOR AND INTERIOR

W. S. Arrasmith, architect

In 1950 one of the latest of the Greyhound terminals; note the monumentality that is increasingly displayed as bus transportation becomes mature.

Courtesy Greyhound Lines

airlines indicates that they would also prove a benefit to both the public and the companies in the bus field.

Country Rest Stops. The country rest stop may require little control area but it must have sufficient public and pull-in areas for peak loads on the line (see Figs. 423, 427). Its single concession is notably a lunch counter where quick service is provided for a maximum number. The country rest stop has potentialities, for it may be developed later into a posting inn with allied recreational facilities. Generally it is about a two-hour run from a large station. Here buses halt for ten minutes so that passengers may stretch their legs, have a bite to eat, or visit a washroom. Improved buses, however, may eliminate the need for the rest stop as it has been known in the past.

Rest stations usually began by chance where there was a refreshment stand with enough space in front of it for a bus to pull in off the road. The proprietor of the stand, in return for the business it brought him, increased his toilet facili-

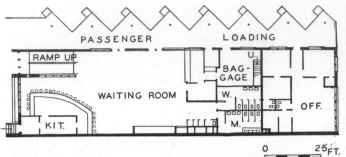

FIGURE 420.
BUS STATION,
SIOUX FALLS,
SOUTH DAKOTA.
PLAN

Perkins & McWayne, architects; Charles F. Sloan and L. Earl McLoughlin, designers

A simple plan of the through-way type studied with unusual care.

FIGURE 421.
BUS STATION,
SIOUX FALLS,
SOUTH DAKOTA.
EXTERIOR AT NIGHT

Perkins & McWayne, architects; Charles F. Sloan and L. Earl McLoughlin, designers

A creative approach to design produces an attractive openness that truly expresses the function.   Photograph
Everett Kroeger

ties until they were more or less adequate for a busload of passengers. But the bus trade often caused roadside congestion and an unsightly jumble of shacks and lean-tos. Today a new kind of rural stop, the modern counterpart of the ancient posting inn, has come to take its place.

Posting Inns. The posting inn is built not only as a rest stop but as an inducement for bus travel. People like to get into the country; therefore the site is chosen with consideration for the view, fresh air, and quiet. It may be in a park or forest preserve, with a lake for swimming and boating and trails for horseback riding in summer and skiing in winter. An inn located at the bus stop will cater to people who travel by bus on their vacation trips and in addition may provide comfortable, moderately priced overnight accommodations for tourists with their own cars. The inn may consist of a central unit and detached cottages, and it may also have shops, craft studios, and a theater to serve the surrounding region. There is counter food service or a cafeteria for the ten-

FIGURE 422.
BUS STATION,
SIOUX FALLS,
SOUTH DAKOTA.
TWO INTERIOR VIEWS

Perkins & McWayne, architects; Charles F. Sloan and L. Earl McLoughlin, designers

The sensitive use of suitable materials creates a beauty that is founded on a reasoned utility.

Photographs Everett Kroeger

minute stoppers, but there is also a restaurant for the other guests. Besides the regular bathrooms for guests, there are sufficient toilet facilities for a peak load of bus passengers in transit.

A pull-in yard is provided for buses. For motorists there is a parking lot with fuel and repair service. For travelers who drive in from a neighboring town to catch a bus there is information, ticket, and baggage service. Landscaping fits the inn into the countryside and suggests repose. There are no glaring signs, exposed stretches of crushed stone, or makeshift buildings; instead there is an appearance of old-fashioned rural comfort. A chain of inns may be similarly designed so as to be recognizable as highway landmarks.

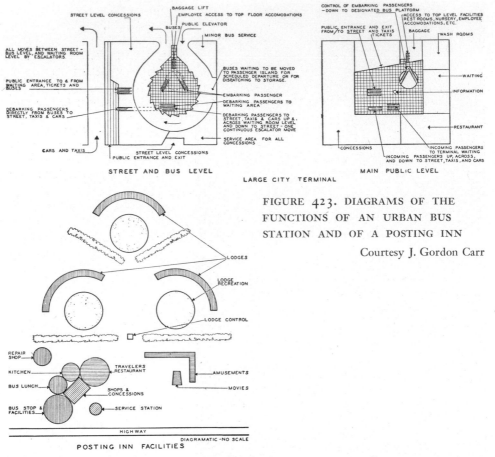

FIGURE 423. DIAGRAMS OF THE FUNCTIONS OF AN URBAN BUS STATION AND OF A POSTING INN

Courtesy J. Gordon Carr

SITE

Accessibility of the station for both passengers and buses must be considered in choosing a site. Before city ordinances began to bar buses from midtown streets, the best location for a station was considered to be one near the busiest corner on the side of town from which most bus passengers came—the residential district or the section where the moderate-rate hotels happened to be. But there were inevitable traffic jams near the busiest corner, and the buses themselves added to the congestion and caused operating delays. As a first step toward correcting these conditions, curb loading at stations was prohibited. Now in some cities the stations are kept as far as is practical from the midtown region in an effort to relieve congestion. Eventually they may have to be built on highways on the outskirts of town and reached by city or feeder buses. Railroads have frequently had to meet the problem of placing their stations on rights of way which were sometimes remote from the center of town. In a few lucky instances, such as that of Grand Central in New York, the center of town grew up to the station.

The cutting of highways through towns may make it possible to place a station where it is handy both for buses and passengers, but often stations have to be built while city planning hesitates. In the meanwhile the old compromises must still be made. The best plot is in a reasonably central location, a little removed from the main flow of street traffic to avoid operating delays but still within sight of the midtown landmarks, in a well-lighted and much frequented district. It is large enough for efficiency and some future expansion. A larger and cheaper piece of land is preferable to a small and relatively expensive one, for a station on the larger site can have a garage for on-site service and storage, a number of concessions, and spacious public areas. There is a trend toward selecting necessarily expensive central plots and paying for them with the revenue from maximum concession accommodations. The designer must recognize the trend but keep the concessions from monopolizing the public areas. The concessions draw from the sidewalk on one side, like any downtown store, and from the bus station on the other. The station itself tends to be pulled into the inner part of the plot. It must have a centrally placed entrance and a large sign so that it may be found easily.

In a new district on the outskirts of a town or in a small town where land is not at a premium, the station may be part of a superblock, bounded on one side by a highway and on the other by a shopping street. It may become a nucleus around which markets, shops, a professional office building, a recreation center, and parking garages center. Here the position of the bus station would make evident the importance of the bus to the community and to its economic life. Only when the well-planned station can be easily reached along familiar paths by the passenger and when the bus can pull out on the highway and attain maximum speed within a minute or two of leaving its dock will bus travel be able to overcome the prejudice against it and the notion that it is unpleasant and inefficient as compared with other modes of transportation.

STATION ELEMENTS

A bus station is made up of the following areas: public, control, baggage, office, concessions, personnel, bus traffic, and garage. These spaces will vary in size and number depending on the type of station contemplated.

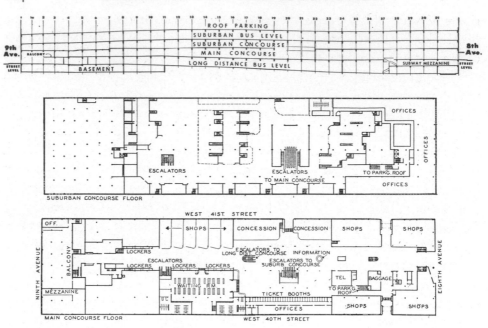

FIGURE 424. UNION BUS TERMINAL, NEW YORK. TWO PLANS AND SECTION

Port of New York Authority, designers; John Kyle, chief engineer; Turner Construction Company, superstructure construction

The development of the union bus terminal is the result of the inflexible forces of traffic congestion in thronged cities; by centralizing bus traffic its load can be properly designed for and the buses can be kept off crowded streets. Here ramps give approach to the main concourse (second level), the suburban buses (third level), and the short-haul buses (fourth level); in addition there is a large area for private parking. Escalators connect all the levels. Note the sizable spaces for shops and concessions. In buildings of this type the problems to be solved resemble those of large urban railroad terminals.

Redrawn from material furnished by Port of New York Authority

PUBLIC AREAS

The *waiting room* should have easy access to the street and the bus dock as well as to the rest rooms and the baggage room. Entrance should be facilitated by the provision of plenty of doors, if possible opened by electronic control so that a passenger laden with baggage may get through without battering the door with foot or shoulder. The room must be supplied with drinking fountains, trash containers, reading lights, and smoking facilities. With efficient mechanical ventilation, smoke can be drawn off before it becomes a nuisance. If such ventilation is not provided throughout, a smoking section with fans and ducts may be set apart, but with good ventilation here there will be no need to close it off with doors. Different light intensities in different areas will permit some persons to relax and doze while others read. Pin-point reading

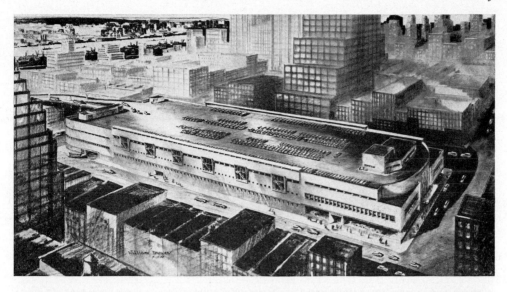

FIGURE 425. UNION BUS TERMINAL, NEW YORK. BIRD'S-EYE VIEW AND
INTERIORS OF MAIN CONCOURSE AND BUS CONCOURSE

Port of New York Authority, designers; John Kyle, chief engineer; Turner Construction Company, superstructure construction

The building and its approaches occupy an entire city block and are closely related to the Lincoln Tunnel to New Jersey as well as to the north-south avenues.

Courtesy Port of New York Authority

lights over certain seats will make reading possible in a quiet and darkened area. Three stages of general illumination are desirable as a supplement to fading daylight and as an assurance of full brightness for peak traffic. In the United States air conditioning is highly desirable, for most of the country has long periods of uncomfortable summer heat, but with the constant opening of bus-station doors it is difficult to maintain the system efficiently. Certain

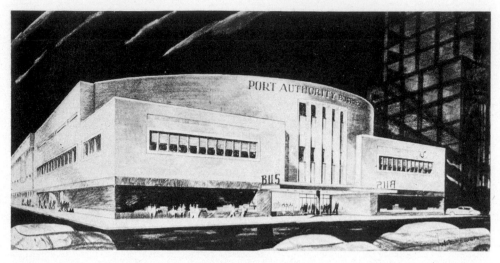

FIGURE 426. UNION BUS TERMINAL, NEW YORK. EIGHTH AVENUE (EAST) FRONT

Port of New York Authority, designers; John Kyle, chief engineer; Turner Construction Company, superstructure construction

Courtesy Port of New York Authority

air-cooled areas, therefore, can be set apart either by doors or by curtains of rising air currents. If these areas occur only in the concessions, the coolness there will be a business asset.

The waiting area should seat about a third of the peak-load passengers. To segregate various kinds of travelers in waiting areas of their own choice, rather than to place them all together, is one way to contribute to their comfort. Mothers might like to go to a women's lounge adjoining both a children's playroom and a formula kitchen where infants' bottles could be heated; a nurse in attendance could help them and keep an eye on the playroom. The playroom might be a sun deck; as entertainment for children, the kennel for animals in transit could be near by. In the women's lounge facilities might be provided for washing and drying clothes and ironing or pressing them; with such conveniences at hand a traveler could always keep fresh with a minimum of clothing on a long trip.

Announcements in the waiting areas should be heard through modulated loud-speakers placed at frequent intervals and not through one blaring source which sets up echoes. In the seats for reading and repose they might be placed in the wings dividing the seats and kept at whispering intensity. The wall space of the waiting area could be used for posters, projected travel pictures, and even movies. Both the pictures and the announcements from the loud-

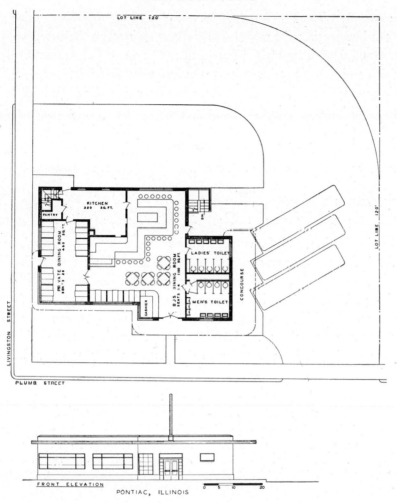

FIGURE 427. BUS STOP POST HOUSE, FOR GREYHOUND POST HOUSES, PONTIAC, ILLINOIS. PLAN AND ELEVATION

Engineering Department, Greyhound Post Houses, designers

A typical "posting house" of the better sort. Note the large lunch-counter space for rapid meals and the easily accessible toilets.   From Burleigh and Adams, *Modern Bus Terminals* . . .

speakers could carry lively invitations to travel by bus so that such transportation would assume glamour. Miscellaneous advertisements on the walls, though admissible as a source of revenue in a large terminal, would be less valuable to the operating company than its own carefully directed promotion; besides, ordinary advertising posters might be suggestive of grubby streetcars and subways.

The *rest rooms* preferably are on the main floor, adjoining the waiting area, but in a compromise plan they may have to be placed upstairs or downstairs. They must be adequate for peak loads and not, as is often the case, curtailed to fit some insufficient corner which is all that can be assigned to them. Ordinances usually demand that there be at least one free toilet in both the men's and the women's rooms; pay toilets in addition are customary. A men's lounge is generally omitted because it invites loafing, but in some states a women's lounge is required by law. Showers, valet service, shoe shining, laundry facilities, and other conveniences for keeping the traveler and his wardrobe clean and trim are generally made part of the rest-room area but are run as concessions.

CONTROL AREAS

The control areas of the bus station are devoted to information, ticket selling, ticket inspection, and the routing of passengers to the proper place on the bus dock. A center for *general information*, not only about bus service but also about the city, should be provided for arriving travelers; this might be part of a travel bureau. There should also be a place for *schedule and price information*. Ticket buyers should be screened at a preliminary point before they go to the *ticket counter* so that sales may proceed quickly. In union terminals the screening point would guide the traveler to the proper ticket counter for the bus line in question.

Some transactions require no more than the selection and authenticating of a printed ticket for a regular run. In others tickets or groups of tickets must be written out. These slower transactions should be routed to special counter stations provided for them. The traveler who needs only a local ticket should be able to get it without a long wait in line. Ordinarily there is a ticket-selling counter station for every twenty-five to thirty seats in the waiting area; for peak loads more counter stations must be opened. Counters 42 inches high are preferable to ticket windows; they produce a more open and friendly effect and also make hearing and seeing easier.

In many of the older bus stations the passengers can go to the bus dock from any door or from the steet, and the location of a departing bus is not indicated; one must search up and down the dock, looking at the destination signs on the front of the buses, to find the one he wants. Visitors and loafers block the passageways; one climbs over hand baggage and freight. There is such confusion that sometimes wrong buses are taken or right ones missed. All this could be avoided and departures expedited by routing the passengers for a given trip through a single door, clearly marked and announced, as is done in railroad stations. To control the crowds at rush hours, barriers on the dock can be formed of cords and stanchions. Baggage and freight can be handled on a half level below the passengers, so that neither breaks through the flow of the other. The bus dispatcher, placed between arriving and departing lanes in view of all traffic, controls the movement of the buses.

BAGGAGE AREA

Baggage according to the usual practice is brought to the station doors by bus or car and then carried by the passenger through the waiting area, past the ticket stations, and eventually to the bus. This scheme causes clutter and delay. Provision could be made to check all bags just inside the station doors or at the ticket counter. They could then be tagged and sent on a moving belt either to the baggage room or to the proper bus. At the bus they could be stowed away while the passengers were showing tickets, as is done on airplanes. New developments in bus design will make it possible to get out one bag for a wayside stop without taking out all the others which happen to have been put in front of it. Arranging will be done at the point of departure.

The *baggage check room* should be between the waiting area and the bus dock. Pieces left for more than one day can be placed in basement storage connected with the baggage room by a dumb-waiter. It is desirable to prevent cross traffic of baggage, freight, and passengers; this problem can best be solved by the use of a separate level for each. Baggage check windows should open into both the waiting area and the bus dock. Sometimes a pillow-renting concession may also have windows in both directions, but these must be separate from the baggage windows. The size of the baggage room must be commensurate with the total traffic of the station. *Checking lockers*, now an important concession, are placed along wall spaces near the bus dock in the waiting area. They are inset so that their tops do not gather dust. Freight—such as newspapers, perishable goods, and small packages—which is carried on some passenger buses should be received at a *freight office* near the street and distributed to the proper buses without cutting across passenger traffic. This can be done if it is routed on a half level under the passenger level.

OFFICES

Offices must be provided for company administration. Even the smallest bus station needs a manager's office, where agents can check out, and a dispatcher's office which overlooks all bus traffic. Larger stations need additional space—

usually on upper floors—for executives, auditors, secretaries, general work, the telephone switchboard, regional management, and meetings.

CONCESSION AREAS

Besides checking lockers, the concessions may include a shoe-shine stand and other services as described below.

Food is purveyed at a soda fountain, lunch counter, or restaurant, depending on the size of the station. Large stations may have a number of eating places. Since usually the soda fountain and newsstand are operated by the same concessionaire who operates the restaurant, it is advisable to have them all fairly close together. The eating places should be equally accessible from the street and from the waiting area, and their decorative schemes should be gay and allusive to the pleasures of travel. The restaurant will include tables, booths, and counters in order to cater to the preferences of customers. The kitchen should have a street door, separated from other lines of traffic, for deliveries and garbage disposal. The restaurant employees need their own toilets, washroom, and lockers; these are placed in the basement when there is no ground-floor space for them.

Entertainment may be provided in a newsreel theater, an exhibition hall devoted to changing shows of art, science, or local history, and a game room—with penny machines—which should be handled so that it has none of the objectionable qualities of a Coney Island arcade.

Shops equally accessible from the street and from the station can be given an open quality by the liberal use of glass walls and tempered-glass doors so that people on the street can see not only the merchandise but also the interior activity of the bus station beyond. A drugstore and shops selling gifts and souvenirs, books and stationery, toys and novelties, haberdashery, flowers, ladies' wearing apparel, and so on may be feasible.

Communication services may include telephones, telegraph, a writing corner which might also offer the services of a public stenographer or possibly typewriters rented by the hour, and a mail-o-mat or a stamp-vending machine.

Barber and beauty shops would be placed close to the rest-room area, with cognate bath, valet, and laundry services.

A travel bureau might be operated by the bus company to give advice on itineraries, to arrange for chartered buses, and to provide maps and guidebooks; or this might be an outside concession.

Newsstand operation would include the placing of pocket-book vending machines in the reading area and the provision of a last-minute selection of reading matter on a cart beside the bus about to depart.

In a block-size station surrounded by concession areas, almost any retail business dependent on drop-in trade could be considered.

PERSONNEL AREAS

Bus company personnel should be provided with toilet, washroom, and locker space close to the work areas. When the station is at the end of a run, sleeping quarters near the garage are provided for drivers and mechanics. These quarters must be comfortable and pleasant in order to maintain morale and good management relations. Stewardesses, who will be increasingly necessary as buses grow larger and are equipped to serve food, will also be provided with overnight accommodations at the ends of runs. Such dormitories must have their own street entrances, separate from the public entrances to the station, with controlled access.

TRAFFIC AREAS

Bus traffic sets up paths which encircle the station. Ideally there should be separate roads of entrance for long-haul bus traffic, for such local traffic as taxis and private cars, and for city or surburban buses—a solution of the problem which might necessitate the use of different levels and cloverleaf roads. Actually most compromise stations separate the bus traffic from the street traffic by pulling it in to a cut through the block between streets. If the plot is a narrow one, the cut must parallel a long narrow station on one side. The buses enter from one street, go through the cut either before or after discharging and picking up passengers, and emerge in the next street. It is difficult both to handle buses in such a runway and, because of their length, to line them up along the dock. More frequently the cut is arranged to go around two sides of the station, entering from a main street and emerging in a side street. This scheme leaves the station an island surrounded by vehicular traffic. The buses go through the cut in a clockwise direction, pull in at an angle—alongside one another—to a bay of the dock (which has a sawtooth plan to accommodate them thus), and unload or take on passengers at doors on their right sides. Then, by backing out slightly more than a bus length, they are able to proceed on their way past other buses at the dock.

To be avoided in any case are left turns, narrow entrances, and the use of congested streets. On both feeder or surburban runs and long-haul runs it is desirable to have separate lanes for incoming and outgoing traffic, and when there are several of these the passengers must be brought into the station through underpasses or overpasses. The dispatcher should command a view in both directions, preferably from a position midway between the lanes. It should be noted that the turning-radius requirement for a bus must be based on the largest current—or projected—equipment.

GARAGE AND STORAGE

Where the *garage* is at some distance from the station, time and fuel are consumed in taking the buses back and forth without a load. "Dead mileage" can be eliminated if the garage adjoins the station on the other side of the lanes. Here all but major servicing may be done and buses can be stored until they are needed for peak traffic. The garage should have facilities for washing, vacuum cleaning, fueling, engine check-up, and other servicing necessary to make a bus roadworthy; when a bus is needed for a run, it is merely pulled out of storage and driven a few yards to the dock. With downtown space at a premium, the garage may be put below the street level and reached by ramps. In this event particular care is needed to provide good lighting, ventilation, and working conditions. Under ordinary circumstances the expense of excavation is no deterrent in cities with high ground values.

When there is no adjoining garage, a *storage yard* near the dock will serve for buses held in readiness for emergency or peak loads. This area naturally should be as large as available space permits.

DESIGN CONSIDERATIONS

BUILDING TECHNIQUES

Beyond saying that bus stations should incorporate all that is possible in the way of ruggedness, fireproofing, sanitation, and comfort, it is difficult to be specific about building techniques. The materials should be strong and tough in order to stand up under the assault of throngs of people and tons of baggage, and they should be so simple to clean that a wash-down with a fire hose may be given to both interior and exterior. Solid materials are the most economical in the long run. Decoration should be integral rather than applied.

In most cases a low structure of regular outline is most efficient in construction, operation, and maintenance. Some very small stations, hardly more than shelters, in small towns where curb loading is practiced, may be prefabricated. For larger structures other methods of building are more efficient. Local building ordinances, fire codes, zoning laws, and even political considerations will naturally affect the design.

Openness is predicated. The station should look easy to get into and easy to get out of. Its bustle, seen from the outside, should be alluring; it should provide a good show. If the whole atmosphere of the station is brisk, clean, and reassuring, people will be enticed to travel by bus. There should be no clutter and no congestion. Color is valuable for its psychological effect; it may be used to create excitement in some areas of the station and repose in others. Lighting, sometimes bright, sometimes moderate, may be employed for effect as well as for illumination. Ventilation should be controlled and ample. Washed, sterile air adds to the comfort of everyone in the building and engenders a feeling of well-being. No odors of gasoline, oil, exhaust gases, rubber, paint, and tired humanity should intrude. Intercommunication—the phones, telautographs, and public address system—should be efficiently planned so that the flow of all traffic can be punctual and orderly.

AESTHETIC EFFECT

The impact of a bus station on the consciousness of all who use it is important. It should be positive. To the eye, the ear, the nose, and the mind's need of space, it should be agreeable. It should give an impression of rightness. As a portal to travel by bus it should have an aspect in character with the aims of bus travel. Railroad stations have always been romantically like something else—when they were not stingily like something less they seem to have been deludingly like something more. The bus station should avoid this masquerade.

How the station is to strike the senses will of course be limited by cost, location, and the preferences of those concerned. In addition to a bus-station look it may have a bus-company look; by salient points it may identify itself as the station of a particular operator and resemble other stations of the same operator.

If the station is in a community with a long-standing vernacular of building, it should consciously be either in harmony or in contrast with this. Flemish bond and narrow dormers may be the making of an early-eighteenth-century Virginia tidewater house; but, rather than adapt these elements awkwardly to a building of different proportions and purposes, it is better to forget them unless the station has to conform to the antiquarian appearance of a Williamsburg restoration. Fortunately most bus stations can be themselves in new communities which have no marked architectural unity; in some their style may even show the way to an effective business or civic group of which they are the initial part.

The fact that landscaping to tie in with an existing park or parkway or providing an enticing setting of garden and verdure is a luxury now seldom enjoyed by the bus station may be a reason for considering an outlying site or
some other modification of the downtown formula.

The required cells of space and the constriction of the plot determine the
form of the bus station shell. If the station could occupy an unlimited plot, as
airport terminals often do, its functions would shape it recognizably and it
would probably have little resemblance to any other sort of building. In the
usual compromises necessary for a small plot, however, the bus station becomes
a compact rectangle with nothing but a sign to distinguish it from the rest of
the surrounding business block. But even a single wall may be eloquent in its
clean-cut effect of mechanical efficiency, its richness of surface, or its sculpture,
mosaics, mural, or night lighting. A telling façade together with a landscaped
setting, a dominating site, and a focal position at the end of converging access
roads would give a station maximum importance in appearance. Unfortunately
such an ideal combination of features is unlikely to occur unless the station is
maintained by civic subsidy—though with a future development of community responsibility even that possibility is not too remote.

SUGGESTED ADDITIONAL READING FOR CHAPTER 43

Burleigh, Manferd, and Charles M. Adams, 2d, *Modern Bus Terminals and Post
Houses* (Ypsilanti, Mich.: University Lithoprinters, 1941).
"Bus Terminal for the Cleveland, Ohio, Transit System," *Pencil Points*, Vol. 26
(1945), July, p. [69].
Bus Transportation (monthly), McGraw-Hill, New York, from 1922.
Chatburne, George R., *Highways and Highway Transportation* (New York:
Crowell, 1923).
Hauer, Roy, and G. H. Scragg, *Bus Operating Practice* (New York: International
Motor Co., 1925).
Highway Highlights (monthly), National Highway Users Conference, Washing-
ton, D.C., from (or before) 1938.
"Motor Transport Terminals," a Building Types Study, *Architectural Record*, Vol.
90 (1941), October, pp. [81]–100, including Time-Saver Standards.
National Highway Users Conference, *Highways and Motor Transportation*, a
bibliography (Washington: the Conference [1937]).
New York City Omnibus Corporation, *The Bus Comes Back to Broadway* (New
York: the Corporation, 1936).

44

Garages and Service Stations

By ITALO WILLIAM RICCIUTI

IN 1909, EIGHT YEARS after a speed of 15 miles per hour won America's first long-distance automobile race and thirteen years after the first auto was sold, Henry Ford announced his plan of mass production and sold 19,000 model T Fords. Few people then realized the impact this event would have on the placid tempo of life in the United States. During the period just prior to this, the automobile had been only for the brave and adventurous rich. So little was it understood that it was treated like a horse, bedded in the stable, and fed from the shelves of the hardware store or grocery. Gasoline was drawn out of a metal drum at the rear of the local store, then carried out front to the high-wheeled speedster, to be poured through a chamois-covered funnel into the tank (Fig. 428). As for garage space, the stable served admirably.

Within the next decade came a series of revolutionary events—human flight became more than a fantastic dream, the jerking silent movies acquired a smoother quality, the Panama Canal was completed, women gained the vote, the first radio broadcast took place, and overshadowing all like a dark cloud was the First World War, in which the new gas-driven machines—tank, plane, and automobile—first appeared as killers. From this unholy impetus came mass production and assembly lines to spew forth automobiles onto the roads. Highways, up to that time woefully inadequate, had to be planned, extended, and improved. With increased auto travel came the need for better sheltering and servicing of the vehicle. No longer was it necessary to buy gasoline from a drum at the rear of a store; it now came from a high, ungainly hand-operated pump in front of a sheet-metal lean-to plastered with signs and billboards—the first crude service station (Fig. 429).

The febrile 1920's saw the automobile grow so dependable that good roads, of necessity, became numerous. Cross-country motor trips were a popular diversion; the car became indispensable for shopping, for going to the theater, for traveling to and from work. With the thousands of motorists came a

FIGURE 428.
EARLY SERVICE STATION

From *The Lamp*

FIGURE 429.
EARLY
SERVICE STATION

Photograph Standard
Oil Co. of Indiana,
courtesy
I. W. Ricciuti

greater need not only for home garages, which merely replaced the stables, but also for large well-located garages to care for the ever increasing numbers of transient cars.

The oil companies, carried along on the new wave, moved out of the kerosene age into the gasoline era. Realizing the vastness of the market just ahead, they set about eliminating the small dealers by absorption or by ruthlessness, or by both, until gigantic monopolies controlled the market and fell into such questionable practices that the oil scandals of the late 1920's brought Federal intervention to break them up. The giants were separated into smaller units that became active competitors, knowing that in order to stay at the top it was necessary to stalk and capture the motorist. One way to do this was to provide more services than the other fellow—thus the "service station," the free air and water, the windshield wiping, the tire repair, and the claims of "specialized lubrication."

Obviously the buildings that sheltered and supported the dispensing of these services played an important role in this development, a fact not unrecognized by the oil companies. As could be expected, emphasis was laid on the spectacular; the buildings had to catch the passing motorist's eye so that he would instinctively stop to have his gas tank filled. For such purposes the so-called super service station emerged, with its billboard, circuslike quality—flashy and almost always in bad taste. Add to all this the fact that these structures were built at a time when a general sense of fitness and good taste was rare and it will be easier to understand why the raucous new industry sold its gasoline from under the up-curved eaves of simulated Japanese pagodas or in the shade of stuccoed, imitation Taj Mahals.

With the wisdom of maturity, the oil companies that had survived the competition became aware of their share in the community's appearance, good or bad, and began to consider those who saw as well as those who merely looked. Inevitably they began to vie with one another in making any structures they built or influenced of such a type as would contribute to the attractiveness of the community. The companies found it sound business to retail their own well-advertised brands through service stations designed by architects (see Figs. 430, 431). Architects were employed both for individual projects and on a full-time basis to co-ordinate and oversee design policies. By the middle 1930's this straight thinking had begun to result in buildings that were pleasing individually as well as a credit to the community. Attractiveness, good product display, cleanliness, and functional efficiency in service became the standards.

In the design of service stations or public garages local conditions must be considered. These vary in different parts of the city; in other words, a service station or garage in the business district must of necessity be different in operation—and therefore in appearance—from one in the suburban areas or on the open highway. A recognition of this fact, then, makes it mandatory in this discussion that each general type of operation and location be treated separately.

AUTO-PARKING GARAGES

Service stations, as such, are fast disappearing from the business centers of cities in the United States. The major repair garage has also moved out to the

FIGURE 430.
PAN-AM SERVICE STATION,
NEW ORLEANS, LOUISIANA.
TWO EXTERIORS

I. W. Ricciuti, architect

Photograph F. A. McDaniels,
courtesy Pan American Petroleum Co. and I. W. Ricciuti

periphery, where there is less congestion, and is usually associated with the sale of automobiles. In the city centers the functions of servicing, minor repairing, and selling small accessories must be combined with the most important service of all—parking.

High buildings shelter the labors of thousands who drive their cars to work —or at least would like to if it were possible to find a place to park. To these add shoppers, theatergoers, or other transients, and the need for parking space is obvious. Congestion is the life blood of the city center. Merchants, theater operators, and hotel men use every known advertising method to entice more and more people to join the crowds; this means more autos, cabs, trucks, and buses on the streets and not enough curb to park them against.

FIGURE 431. THREE GERMAN GASOLINE STATIONS

TOP: At Frankfurt am Main. Carl August Bembé, architect. MIDDLE: At Hanover. Werner March, architect. Both from *Monatshefte für Baukunst und Städtebau*. BOTTOM: Leuna Station, on the Düsseldorf-Cologne Road. Night view. Leuna, designer. From *Moderne Bauformen*.

The possibilities in concrete, steel, and glass for realizing light, graceful, and modern gasoline stations were first explored and developed to a high degree in Germany.

An expedient too often used has been the open parking lot. Bare parking spaces are frequently seen in congested centers, but how temporary these can be is also a well-known phenomenon. To approach economic self-sufficiency

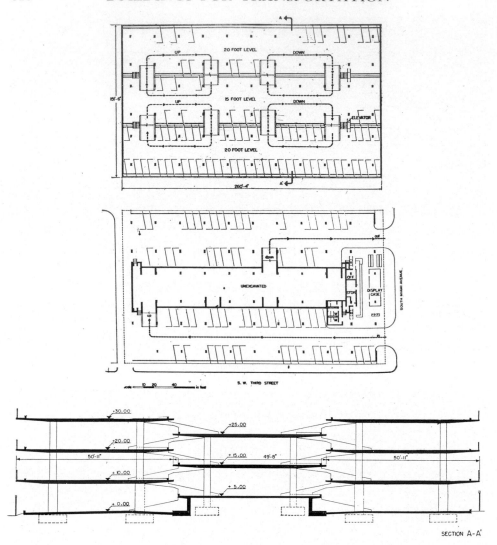

FIGURE 432. PARKING GARAGE, MIAMI, FLORIDA. PLANS AND SECTION

Robert Law Weed and Associates, architects

The simplest and most direct traffic lines control the plan of a parking garage.

From *Architectural Forum*

they must be capacious as well as close to the business center, both of which requirements necessitate high ground costs. Parking lots, therefore, unless they are leased or owned under extraordinary conditions (such as land under a clouded title), must be an interim expedient to permit the owner to cash in as he can while waiting to build, lease, or sell. Though the parking lot unques-

FIGURE 433.
PARKING GARAGE,
MIAMI, FLORIDA.
EXTERIOR

Robert Law Weed and
Associates, architects

The visual effect derives
naturally from structure
and purpose, with the
least possible use of ex-
traneous or unnecessary
features.

Photograph Ezra
Stoller—Pictor

tionably satisfies an urgent need in the heart of most cities, that need is more economically met in the fringe areas, such as small industrial or warehousing districts, where land values are not too high. Close-in, strategically located sites, because of high land costs, must make use of multi-storied, ramp-type garages in order to accommodate enough parked cars per unit area of ground to allow economic and efficient operation (see Figs. 432, 433).

All public parking garages must be well located as to (1) the area which they serve and (2) the traffic flow (density, speed, and direction) on adjacent streets. Experience shows that motorists are loath to use a parking garage more than three blocks from their destinations; [1] such a garage therefore can reasonably expect to park the cars of motorists from an area only six blocks square. A survey of the district will yield a fair forecast of the likely business as well as indicate the probable hours and duration of maximum use. To this approximation, in order to exercise sound judgment as to the desirability of the proposed site, the architect must add the result of traffic studies for many blocks around. Ideally the routes bringing cars to the parking garage should follow streets which (1) carry medium-speed traffic, for high-speed traffic is hard for a driver to turn out of and slow traffic wastes his time; (2) are unencumbered by streetcars, buses, large trucks, and other heavy vehicles; and (3) are the most direct routes from the residential areas—that is, make the fewest turns between the main traffic lanes and the garage. The building site should preferably be on the slow-traffic-lane side of an adjacent one-way street. Ideally, too, the routes carrying cars away from the garage should follow streets which are initially as free of traffic as possible, especially that of heavy or fast-moving vehicles, and soon flow into fast-traffic streets quickly and smoothly.

[1] *Arterial Plan for New Orleans*, Robert Moses, director, and Andrews & Clark, consulting engineers (New York: Steidinger Press, 1946), p. 32.

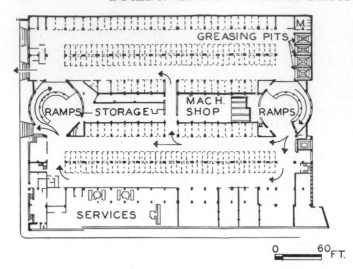

GREASING PITS

RAMPS—STORAGE

MACH.
SHOP

RAMPS

SERVICES

0   60 FT.

FIGURE 434.
AUTORIMESSA,
VENICE, ITALY.
PLAN

Ufficio Tecnico dell'
I.N.A., architects

Since no automobiles are permitted in Venice a large parking garage is necessary to house the cars of automobile tourists. Note the spiral ramps.

Redrawn from Pica, *Architettura Moderna in Italia*

Since the successful operation of a public garage of this type depends greatly on the speed with which cars can be checked in, parked, and delivered, the architect must plan with that need definitely in mind. The sale of gasoline and oils, car washing, and minor repairs must be completely separated from the parking of cars—on separate service-floor levels if possible. Ramp garages more than four floors in height are not practical for short-time parking because of the time lost in retrieving cars in rush periods. Dead storage and auxiliary services, of course, can be housed above the fourth floor.

The necessity of getting the cars off the streets rapidly in rush times is obvious. Wide, easy drive-ins and the availability of several car lanes between the street and the ramp are desirable, as is an automatic signal light indicating the open lanes. Cars should be checked in and immediately driven up the ramp; an elevator is too slow for a parking garage where speed is essential. All traffic in the building must be one-way, with separate "up" and "down" ramps. The separation of "in" and "out" drives is advisable where site conditions permit; naturally, in the river of traffic, egress should take place downstream from the point of ingress to prevent cross traffic in the street.

Cars that come up the ramps should have to be parked only once. At the parking levels the traffic lanes should be so arranged that "in" and "out" driving lanes are separated by parked cars that have their radiators just off an out lane and their rear bumpers just off an in lane; thus a car can be driven directly into a stall and later driven out without having to back out of or into a traffic lane. This of course would apply only to the four levels of short-time parking; on dead-storage levels, if there should be any in the garage, cars can be more

FIGURE 435.
AUTORIMESSA,
VENICE, ITALY.
EXTERIOR

Ufficio Tecnico dell'
I.N.A., architects

An exterior of strict utilitarian character.

From Pica, *Architet-
tura Moderna in Italia*

densely parked. The ramps must be supplied with ample turning radii and must be banked at the turns for a speed of 20 to 30 miles per hour. Because attendants will speed when the rush is on, it is wise to make fast driving safe for them and for the car; besides, banked turns will eliminate the screeching of tires on curves—a salutary measure when relations with the car owner are considered.

Important requirements for garages of this type are lounge space for customers, located so that they can see their cars as soon as they are brought to street level; waiting space (preferably not visible to the public) for car hops, separate toilet facilities for customers and employees; and adequate office space. Quick, safe vertical transportation for car hops from the ground floor to the parking-space and service levels must also be provided. Unless large trucks are to be parked or stored, ceiling clearance heights need not be over 8'-0" on the parking floors; on the service floors, at least over the auto-greasing lifts, clearance heights should be not less than 12'-6". Fireproof construction is essential, and care must be taken to select finish materials that are hard-surfaced and easily cleaned as well as reasonable in first cost and low in maintenance cost. The use of bright, attractive colors—and especially the avoidance of dirt-hiding tints—can do much toward creating customer appeal in the spaces visible to him.

Roof-top parking has been tried, but not very successfully. A roof above the fourth floor can provide only inefficient parking because of time lost in taking cars up from and down to the ground level. Furthermore, roof-top parking is apt to prove inadequate in any area where a garage must be multi-storied to accommodate the number of cars that visit the area.[2]

Basement or underground garages, on the other hand, are proving excellent

[2] Roof parking, however, has been successfully used on one- or two-story department stores (see Fig. 47).

FIGURE 436.
PARKING GARAGE,
UNION SQUARE,
SAN FRANCISCO,
CALIFORNIA.
GENERAL VIEW

T. L. Pflueger, architect
The earliest large-scale attempt to use the space beneath a city park for automobile parking. The three underground levels will accommodate 1,700 cars.

Photograph Gabriel Moulin, courtesy Standard Oil Co. of California

as a solution to the midtown parking problem. San Francisco, in 1941, broke ground for a totally subsurface 1,700-car parking and service garage under the city's centrally located Union Square (Figs. 436, 437). This steel-and-concrete structure, designed by Timothy Pflueger, has a depth of four stories, all ramp-connected. The three lower floors are used for short-time parking, and the top floor (which is just below the level of the rebuilt square, with its trees, sod, walks, and monuments intact) is used for general offices, receipt and delivery of cars, servicing, and cashiers. By setting the sidewalks back, an additional lane surrounding the park was provided for the exclusive use of garage traffic. Ramping down from this extra lane, entrances and exits open on all four streets; these permit the motorist to enter and leave the garage without making left-hand turns and without interference with street traffic. To go from one level to another, garage attendants use firemen's poles and an endless belt-type ladder. Intercommunicating telephones and an elaborate signal system bring quick service—a car can be delivered from the lowest level in two minutes.

Another successful parking garage and service station of the underground type is one of three levels in Seattle, designed by McClelland & Osterman for the Standard Oil Company of California (Figs. 439–442). The structure includes two underground levels for off-street parking and accommodates approximately 750 automobiles per business day. The ground level is reserved for an over-all service station, offices, and so on. The site is located at the inter-

FIGURE 437.
PARKING GARAGE,
UNION SQUARE,
SAN FRANCISCO, CALIFORNIA.
ENTRANCE FLOOR AND
STORAGE FLOOR

T. L. Pflueger, architect

Entrance floor photograph
Morton-Waters Co.; Storage
floor photograph Phil Stroupe;
both courtesy Standard Oil Co.
of California

section of two main thoroughfares, and entrances and exits to the parking levels are provided on both streets. Ramps are arranged for maximum speed in the handling of cars without interference with the street traffic.

These examples point a definite trend, both as to aesthetic and economic considerations. The exteriors of such structures do not admit of the "application" of "architecture." The presence of the ramps places before the sensitive designer marked design opportunities. Interiors cannot reasonably be other than clean, cheerful, and expressive of their function. The building of midtown garages and service stations underground is an obvious and sensible solution to the problems of preserving property values, parks, and open areas. The day is not far distant when the injury to business in midtown areas caused by increased parking problems will force new buildings in congested city areas to provide garage space for their tenants; in such cases the value of the underground solution cannot be denied.[3]

[3] Thus the United Nations headquarters site in New York uses its entire area for underground parking.

FIGURE 438. THREE-LEVEL GARAGE AND SERVICE STATION, SEATTLE,
WASHINGTON. PROPOSED SCHEME

McClelland & Osterman, architects

Two underground levels provide off-street parking for 750 cars; the street-level is used for
offices and a large service station.

Photograph Roger Dudley, courtesy Standard Oil Co. of California

FIGURE 439.
THREE-LEVEL GARAGE
AND
SERVICE STATION,
SEATTLE,
WASHINGTON.
EXTERIOR

McClelland & Osterman,
architects

Photograph Dexter,
courtesy Standard
Oil Co. of California

DEALER-AND-REPAIR GARAGES

The major-repair garage is an entirely different problem, with different
requirements in traffic and location. Here the prime requisite is not parking or
the sale of gasoline and oil but the handling of major repairs, overhaul, and
regular maintenance of the auto *from the first 500-mile check-up*—which at
once ties in the repair of autos with their sale. The stress is placed on keeping
the car coming back for all maintenance to the dealer garage, where the mechanics are supposed to be factory-trained for handling the make of car sold
and where replacement parts are immediately available. The tendency on the

FIGURE 440. THREE-LEVEL GARAGE AND SERVICE STATION, SEATTLE, WASHINGTON, NIGHT VIEW

McClelland & Osterman, architects

Photograph Dexter, courtesy Standard Oil Co. of California

FIGURE 441. THREE-LEVEL GARAGE AND SERVICE STATION, SEATTLE, WASHINGTON, LOWER-LEVEL INTERIOR

McClelland & Osterman, architects

Photograph Dexter, courtesy Standard Oil Co. of California

part of buyers to go back to the same mechanics who serviced the new car during its free-guarantee period is strong—so strong, indeed, that dealers have found that they can choose a location some distance from the city's center and still attract the original car purchasers into their own original repair garages.

For this type of dealer-and-repair garage operation (in fact, except in country towns, the day of the little independent repair shop is certainly waning) the chief requirements are first to sell the car and then to maintain it through at least the period of its first ownership. The structure to house this dual operation must have as its prime features a place to display and sell automobiles and a related place to repair and maintain them. But before a building can do its part in accomplishing these functions it must attract the attention of the passing motorist. If it is located on a traffic artery some little distance from the city's center, a driver's attention will not be fully occupied with traffic and therefore can wander to the building as he approaches. The garage must *not*, however, be on a speed highway. It is well to remember that any building set well back—provided the structures which flank it do not obstruct the sight lines—is apt to hold the attention longer than one close up, the details of which disintegrate into a streaky blur when passed at the usual driving speeds. The fact that the driveways to service stations make good use of setback areas points to the value of erecting service stations in conjunction with such garages.

Having caught the motorist's attention, the next step is to stop him—and again the inclusion of a service station is helpful, for it adds the incentive of refueling and receiving the usual services. If the display is interesting enough, the driver can covet the cars displayed while the tank is being filled and the tires checked. The display area must be large, attractive, and inviting, but in neither too easy nor too grand a manner. Off the display room, small offices for closing sales are essential. The repair garage, with its parts-storage rooms, service manager's office, and various repair departments, is better if independent in plan but connected for efficiency. (See Fig. 443.)

To summarize, then, the dealer-and-repair garage is designed to produce the following effects: (1) slow the motorist, (2) attract his attention, (3) stop him, (4) sell him, and (5) maintain the car the company has sold him. Of these, the first is primarily not a design but a traffic function, to be ascertained beforehand in the site studies; the second and third are primarily functions of design; the fourth and fifth are functions of personnel and service which can be materially aided by good planning.

Like the parking garage, the sales-and-repair building should be on a medium-speed traffic artery, devoid of heavy traffic. It also should be placed so as to preclude left turns in entering its driveways—and the right turn should be an easy one from a slow lane, preferably where traffic is slowed down by a traffic light or by other means.

Automobile salesmen argue that the best location is on the righthand side of a street carrying traffic *from* town because motorists have more leisure when going home. In the morning, townward traffic is preoccupied with getting to work and little heed will be paid to auto displays. There is room for dispute here, however, for the motorist who wants his car repaired will usually leave it at the garage in the morning on his way to work and pick it up in the evening on his way home. It follows that the ideal site is one that carries through the block and lies between main arteries in and out of town and at the same time permits the elimination of any but right turns on entering or leaving.

The details of the operations to be carried on in the structure must be well understood by the architect; even though all such businesses have similar general features, each will have its own peculiarities to which thought must be given. The usual building requisites can be divided into three main areas: (1) the display and sales offices; (2) the general offices; and (3) the maintenance and repair departments. To these a gasoline service station may often be added advantageously.

The display area should be large enough to show at least three autos with plenty of room to spare. It is much better to have one car well displayed and attractively lighted than several crowded together. The position of the display windows, of course, should command the attention of as much traffic from all directions as possible and in addition allow good visibility to those seated in cars being served on the driveways. A wide folding or roll-up door for the passage of cars is essential, and such a door, if it is centered, will facilitate the maneuvering of cars to the correct display position.

Immediately off the display floor there must be at least one small office for expediting and concluding sales. The sales manager's office and the accounting and general offices should adjoin the display room and also have ready access to the repair areas. Well-appointed rest rooms must be easily accessible to customers of the service station. The repair areas must have independent entrances and must include adequate parts-storage rooms, a cashier's office, and a customers' waiting room adjoining. The cashier's office should be well placed, with one wall common to the parts-storage room and open to it by means of a wicket for the passage of sales slips. The customers' waiting area should be so planned that it can be reached on foot from a car without undue crossing of traffic lanes.

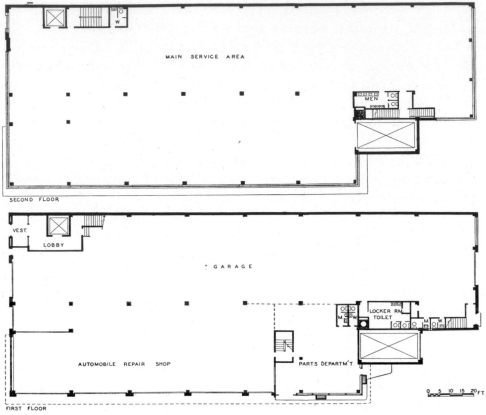

FIGURE 442. PONTIAC MOTOR SERVICE STATION WITH ROOF PARKING, NEW YORK. PLANS

Horace Ginsbern & Associates, architects; Marvin Fine, Jules Kabat, Fred M. Ginsbern, associate architects

A large urban dealer-service station, with the upper floor used for special servicing and the roof reserved for public parking. Note the placing of the office and parts department to provide visibility and accessibility.   Courtesy Horace Ginsbern & Associates

Plans for the repair garage are dependent on traffic flow. Ingress should be from slow street traffic lanes by means of right turns, and the entrance should be wide and offer as few hazards as possible. As many lanes as are necessary for peak "in" traffic should be provided to prevent congestion of cars in the street as they attempt to check in. The service manager's space (not necessarily large) should be close to the entrance lanes; here owners can be interviewed as to their repair needs. From this point the cars should be rapidly dispatched to the various departments—ignition, motor, axle-and-rear-end, body, paint-

FIGURE 443. PONTIAC MOTOR SERVICE STATION WITH ROOF PARKING, NEW YORK. PERSPECTIVE

Horace Ginsbern & Associates, architects; Marvin Fine, Jules Kabat, Fred M. Ginsbern, associate architects

Simple forms developed to give an exterior that is gracious and distinctive.

Courtesy Horace Ginsbern & Associates

ing, temporary storage, and so on. A common arrangement, where space permits, is to place the ignition, axle-and-rear-end, and minor motor-repairs departments and also the washing and lubrication lifts on the ground floor. The second floor is suited for handling major motor repairs, painting, and body-and-fender work. The ramp leading to it should be located close to the entrance for the quick dispatching of cars to the appropriate repair station. Because elevators tend to tie up traffic and slow up operations and are costly to maintain, ramps are unquestionably better if sufficient space is available. The paint shop should be isolated from the other areas not only to prevent the probable spraying of paint where it is not wanted but also because of the fire hazard. It should be set apart by fire walls and partitions, which as a matter of fact are required by most city building codes.

The building materials for this type of garage must be appropriate, practical, and unpretentious. The display floor must be able to withstand, without cracking, the rolling of small-wheeled dollies (for maneuvering cars to display positions) and yet must be attractive and colorful, impervious to dripping greases and oils, and easily cleaned. Terrazzo has proved excellent for this purpose; ceramic tile is usually too brittle, and asphalt tile unless it is of the grease-proof variety is downright disastrous. For interior walls that serve as backgrounds for displayed automobiles the materials must be unobtrusive but harmonious in texture and color. In the repair area, naturally, utility and practicality are prime requisites. The floors should be of concrete, surface-hardened to repel grease stains, and the walls hard-but-not-brittle-surfaced and easy to clean. Since this part of the building will contain highly inflammable objects, all possible consideration must be given to fire safety; this calls not so much for the retarding of fires already started as for the prevention of fires.

Planning procedures here follow the normal progression of survey, analysis, and functional solution inherent in all proper design, but a few salient points and trend indications are worth special mention. For example, the use of daylight in work areas, although desirable, is not so essential as it once was. Another strong trend is the departmentalizing of auto repairs. The spaces for the various groups of trained personnel with specific duties—axle-and-rear-end adjustments and repairs, the regulation of ignition and wiring systems, the keeping of carburetors in working trim, and so on—will require careful attention with respect to accommodating special equipment and placing the departments in an appropriate sequence for maximum efficiency.

In planning sales offices, display rooms, and other selling departments, it is important to realize that the display area is essentially a stage set which will help the merchandise to make the strongest possible appeal. Lighting is important and should aim to accent the automobiles on display. The background lighting must be of an intensity high enough not to produce strongly contrasting lights and darks (which would be distracting) but not so high as to create glare. The sense of transition from inside the display floor to outside the display window should be minimized—the trend is toward lessening the barrier by hanging glass from floor to ceiling and allowing ceiling and floors to carry through without a break. Often the window glass is either tilted or curved—and also trick-lighted—in an attempt to discourage distracting reflections. Planting is carried in and out of the building in the same box. Every possible means is used to produce the impression that the outside observer and the displayed objects exist in the same space and, further, to facilitate the metamorphosis from observer to purchaser. All these are problems which should be of first importance to the architect if he wishes to give his client the best possible psychological advantage in selling. The astute auto dealer is quick to pick flaws in faulty planning on such points.

The service station in front of such buildings, discussed below, should be logically placed in connection with the general operational scheme of the

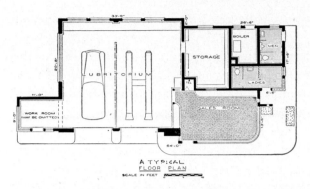

FIGURE 444.
TYPICAL SERVICE STATION
FLOOR PLAN

Courtesy I. W. Ricciuti

group. It must neither obscure the other operations nor seem to shrink into the background. Besides its value as an "auto stopper" and "friend maker" for the dealer—which cannot be overemphasized—it will produce a healthy revenue while rounding out complete services for the automobile owner.

GASOLINE SERVICE STATIONS

Service-station buildings play an important part in the urban and suburban landscape. Since an average of more than 4,100 new service stations were erected annually in the United States during the thirteen years just prior to 1941, it is little wonder that these buildings have received a large measure of the blame for the shoddy appearance of the nation's communities, and if their influence has been great in the past the importance of their contribution in the future can hardly be exaggerated. In spite of predictions of helicopters at every front door, every succeeding decade will see more people driving more automobiles and buying more gas and oils than in the decade before. Tremendous highway construction programs will encourage more individuals to drive longer distances and will thus create a still greater demand for petroleum products and for more and more service-station buildings.

In the face of these probabilities it would be well to determine the basic thinking which will best serve the interests of good contemporary design in these highly specialized structures. The opportunities for new and pleasing effects offered by mid-century construction are enormous. Never again should gasoline-dispensing Chinese pagodas, Colonial cottages, and pseudo-Hispano-Moresque buildings flout themselves at major street intersections in the United States. In any intelligent effort to reconcile the demands of this aggressively commercial business with the ideals of community decency and beauty the architect cannot afford to endow its service stations with less than honesty in design, sincerity in the choice of materials, and truth in the expression of function.

It should be obvious that climate and geography create differences in the design of service stations just as they do in any other building type. In the United States, stations of the southern and western areas cannot be planned or constructed as are those in the more rigorous climate of the northern and eastern states. Further variations are caused by the traffic conditions and kinds of trade catered to in the different regions. As a result of the forces of business economics, site availability, and traffic flow, gasoline service stations are usually placed in one of three general locations: (1) at the periphery of traffic congestion in the cities and larger towns, to serve the business-district traffic; (2) one or two miles out from population centers on heavily traveled highways, to serve long-distance motorists; and (3) on suburban or small-town corners to serve the immediate neighborhoods. At any of these locations, however, the service station that is not combined with such collateral facilities as auto sales, restaurants, hotels, parking garages, supermarkets, and even bowling alleys and theaters will become increasingly rare.

These variations and combinations naturally produce local differences in plan and aspect, yet in service-station design there are certain elements which in good practice are the same everywhere. Put simply, the basic aim of any individual commercial service-station building is to sell more gas and oil than any other. To accomplish this the first function of the building must be to stop the driver. Since the driver's eye must be caught while he is in motion and his mind is occupied with the needs of driving, not only must the station be built where it is natural for the driver to stop but specific reasons for his stopping must also be offered. Rest rooms, bars, lunchrooms, windshield wiping, minor mechanical adjustments, amusements are typical conveniences for the one-stop service station. The driver, having been induced to stop, now becomes susceptible to the purchase of auto accessories; once in an acquisitive mood, he is less apt to offer resistance to indirect suggestions that he become the owner of articles which have no connection with his automobile. From this point on, the selling vista is unlimited—amusements, lodging, food, and the like can all be tied in with the original gasoline sale.

Visibility from afar is a first requirement. The greater the distance from which the motorist can see the station he is approaching, the longer will be the time in which he can make up his mind to stop. The public's tendency to associate particular brands of petroleum products with certain trade-marks or colors should be encouraged to extend to the appearance of the building itself so that a service station can be identified even at a distance. Thus a valuable advertising aid is exploited when the customer is led automatically to associate a station ahead with that "very best super-octane gas." The architect can do much to further this aim by a skillful massing of forms; at the same time—if he is conscious, as he should be, of the community—he must not offend by contriving obtrusive and blatant concoctions. A structure that will attract attention at a great distance may repel when close at hand because of the very grossness in detail, textures, and color which first caught the eye.

A service station should be easily accessible from the highway, and this fact must be evident at once. A high degree of development in this respect has been attained in certain service stations on high-speed arteries: signs are posted several miles ahead to announce approach to a service station; about a quarter mile from the station a deceleration lane branches off from the highway and parallels it to the pumps; finally, on the far side an acceleration lane again parallels the highway for 1,000 feet or so and gives the driver a chance to re-enter the highway traffic safely. Within towns or cities it is well to locate a station near a stop light, where the inevitable slow-down breaks the rhythm of driving and makes a turn into the station more inviting.

Service-station locations cannot always be ideal. The sales departments of gasoline companies do the choosing after weighing a multiplicity of considerations, which among other things include the company's distribution pattern in the vicinity.[4] In cities, even though corner locations are much to be preferred because of their greater traffic flow, better visibility, easier access, and smaller required size, middle-of-the-block sites are still often chosen; in the middle of the block a lot with less than 75 feet of frontage cannot take care of a service station, though on a corner a little less will suffice. Since a car driving into a station always takes a diagonal path across the sidewalk, in either location the entrance drives should be at least 25 feet wide for easy drive-in.

Hard-and-fast rules on placing the building on the property are difficult to make because of three varying factors—shape, grading, and visibility. Nevertheless well-planned, spacious driveways inside the entrance are essential to the economic health of the station. These should be not less than 12 feet wide from the property line to the edge of the pump island and not less than 25 or

---

[4] George J. Hammeter, "Basic Elements in Station Planning," *Architectural Record*, Vol. 95 (1944), February.

28 feet wide from the inner edge of the island to the building. The pump island itself should be not less than 3 feet wide and as long as is needed to accommodate the number of pumps the station will support. Usually 6 feet of length per pump is ample and takes care of air and water stations as well. In a warm climate, canopies over the drives are looked on favorably because of the shelter they offer from sudden rains and the hot sun. Even here, however, the trend is away from canopies, the chief objections to which are the lowered visibility of the show windows, the consequent cramped appearance, and the limitations placed on the position of the pump island. Moreover, a canopy usually restricts the width of the inner drive from the 25 or 28 feet desirable to little more than 20 feet; greater spans than this often entail unjustifiable expenditure.

The pump island, because its naturally prominent position in the plan suggests productive uses which transcend the mere servicing of cars with gas, air, and water, has sometimes been utilized for the display of small accessories. There could be no better place than this for showing such "impulse" buying items; here, in glass cases, they will be visible from both sides and virtually within reach of the driver as he sits at the wheel. Some companies have even gone so far as to place the office structure itself on the pump island, relegating the service and storage bays of the station to the rear of the lot. Offsetting the advantages of that arrangement is the disadvantage of cramped conditions and a resulting loss in efficiency in manipulating the cars, as well as the fact that under such an arrangement the same personnel cannot handle both workshop and pump-island activities. The benefits and drawbacks must be weighed before a choice can be made between display and efficiency of operation. Even though the principal income is usually derived from the sale of gasoline, the margin of profit on the average gasoline sale is very small; consequently, since it is imperative that at peak hours cars be moved through the station as quickly as possible, too much dillydallying at the pumps because of displays might do more harm than good.

Service-station buildings are composed of three main sections: the selling areas, the work areas, and the utility areas.

In the selling areas, in addition to the sales office, there must be public rest rooms and also display elements along the rear and side walls of the adjoining lubrication bays. Attractive, clean, and ample rest rooms are powerful customer magnets. As for size 5'-0" x 5'-6" can serve for men's rooms, provided they are wall- and floor-tiled and are light and clean, but the women's rooms should come as close to the appearance and the dimensions of a lounge as the building budget will allow. Sales offices heretofore have ranged upward from the tiniest possible dimensions. The trend is now toward a more spacious area; 300 square feet can well be considered a minimum.

The work areas, which include the important lubrication and work bays, should each be not much less than 26 feet in depth and 12 feet in clear width. Lubrication bays must be not less than 12½ feet in clear height to allow for hydraulic auto lifts. Other miscellaneous service bays will vary greatly in dimensions according to the particular services to be offered.

Utility areas include storage, tool, and heater rooms, the sizes of which again are dependent on the specific type of operation. In laying out storage and tool rooms, it is well to remember the standard complaint of many service-station operators—that such rooms are never big enough.

The materials selected for service stations must be appropriate for their use and easy to keep clean and to maintain. For paving driveways the types of materials depend principally on locality and cost; reinforced concrete, macadam, or cold asphalt concrete are the most common. Although cost is usually a major consideration in making a choice, it should be remembered that gasoline deteriorates asphalt compounds. On the other hand, asphalt or macadam is easier to keep in repair than reinforced concrete.

All sorts of wall and roof structural systems have been used for service stations; usually the building code and fire laws of the locality govern the selection. Because of the very nature of the operations for which the building is being used, the architect would do well to keep in mind that the appearance of the station is almost certain to become obsolete long before the physical structure. Ideally both should be designed to deteriorate at the same rate—an objective obviously impossible of achievement. Nevertheless, unless a building-code regulation forces the architect to design a service station that will outlast the ages, he should endeavor to limit the life span of his structure, let us say, to fifteen years.

Finish materials should have the properties of easy cleaning and easy maintenance. Such impervious finishes as porcelain-enameled steel, structural glass, glazed brick, stainless steel, Monel metal, and the like, which can be cleaned by a simple hosing, are excellent for the purpose; but care must be taken to use brittle, easily broken materials only in places that are out of harm's way. Carelessly thrown tire tools, for instance, will break or chip structural glass or glazed brick. The materials chosen for the inside surfaces of work areas should also be as impervious and as easily cleaned as possible, but they need not be the same as those outside. A good pore-filling gloss paint, for example, is hard to surpass for the purpose.

The finish for the interiors of the sales areas should be selected for ease of maintenance, appearance, and durability. Expense should not be spared on the public rest rooms. Tile wainscots and floors are almost a must in service-station rest rooms. In the public areas the colors should be pleasant and light. Instead of hiding the dirt they aid in discovering it early so that it can easily be eliminated. This theory, in spite of some opinion to the contrary, also applies in the work areas, such as the lubrication and wash bays. Here a cheerful, light color not only is a psychological aid to accomplishment but also will tend to make the attendants and employees neater in their work and their appearance. Moreover, the fact must not be overlooked that cleanliness is a powerful selling aid.

Trends in service-station design are for the most part fairly obvious. Of these perhaps the most striking is that post-mid-century stations will be larger, by from 15 to 50 per cent, than the 1,000 to 1,200 square feet ground coverage found in buildings before the Second World War.[5] This increase in space should take care of the increased services and expanding merchandise which most companies are preparing to offer at their stations. The buildings will be more open, greater expanses of glass and larger show windows will obtain, and the salesroom will eventually become—as it should—one large display case. There is also a tendency to eliminate partitions as much as is practicable in order to obtain openness in plan. The unmistakable trend toward increased diversification of sales will cause the sales and display elements to come into greater prominence. The design of pumps shows a tendency toward lower and smaller shapes so that the customers' view of the salesroom will not be obstructed. Indeed, experiments are already under way with a view to eliminating pump islands entirely and locating gas, hose, and pumping systems overhead or concealed underground.

A continuing trend that was already well established in the middle 1930's calls for the association of the service-station building, by means of mass, line, or color, with some specific oil company or brand of petroleum products.[6] This identification must be sought through all the progressive changes in de-

---

[5] "Postwar Service Stations: Preview," *Ethyl News*, April, 1946.
[6] K. Lönberg-Holm, "The Gasoline Filling and Service Station," *Architectural Record*, Vol. 67, No. 6 (June, 1930), pp. [561–84].

sign; no matter how drastic or radical the change from a former type may be, the new station's link to the past must be subtly carried through by the definite recalling of a color, a line, or a mass.

But the most gratifying trend of all is the increasing awareness on the part of the oil companies—which ultimately control design policies—of the importance of the service-station building in the community picture as well as the intelligent manner in which they are attacking the clean-up process. The final result cannot but be beneficial.

SUGGESTED ADDITIONAL READING FOR CHAPTER 44

Arterial Plan for New Orleans, Robert Moses, director, and Andrews & Clark, consulting engineers (New York: Steidinger Press, 1946).

Louisiana Department of Highways, *A Traffic Survey of the New Orleans Metropolitan Area, by Louisiana Department of Highways in Co-operation with the Public Roads Administration, Federal Works Agency, and the City of New Orleans, 1944-45* (New Orleans [1946?]).

National Highway Users Conference, *Highways and Motor Transportation*, a bibliography (Washington: the Conference [1937]).

"New Selective Solvent Plant of Shell Oil at Martinez," *National Petroleum News*, Vol. 31 (1939), February 5, pp. R-48, R-49.

". . . Oldest Station in America," *Petroleum Age*, Vol. 30 (1936), June, p. 18.

"Postwar Service Stations: Review," *Ethyl News*, April, 1946, pp. 3-5, 19-21.

Ricker, Edmund R., *The Traffic Design of Parking Garages* (Saugatuck, Conn.: Eno Foundation for Highway Traffic Control, 1948).

"Service Stations," Building Types Study No. 86, *Architectural Record*, Vol. 95 (1944), February, pp. 71-92.

"Service Stations—Then and Now," *The Lamp*, April, 1946, pp. 18-21.

Super Service Station, Vol. 34 (1946), January, pp. 38-43.

"When Building Starts Again," *Detroit Motor News*, Vol. 28 (1945), August, pp. 14-15, 21.

PART VIII

Buildings for Social Welfare and Recreation

COMMUNITY BUILDINGS
BY PERCIVAL AND PAUL GOODMAN

SETTLEMENT HOUSES
BY SIMON BREINES

BUILDINGS FOR ATHLETICS
BY LAWRENCE B. ANDERSON

SMALL PUBLIC OPEN SPACES
BY C. EARL MORROW

PARK STRUCTURES
BY THOMAS C. VINT

I T IS AN INCONTROVERTIBLE FACT that, the closer the aggrega-
tions of men become, the greater the need for socialization of their activities. The pioneer, pursuing furs through lonely forests or tilling his unfre-
quented fields of maize amid a wilderness, was comparatively unhampered in
his activities; both work and recreation he found where he could and took as
they came. But, as people crowded into towns, as the imperatives of an industrial economy made themselves felt in congestion and high land values, and
as work became routinized and the dictation of the clock more and more compelling, a concurrent need arose for canalizing and implementing men's need
for amusement, social meeting, and recreation. Homes became too small for
extensive entertaining, and churches lost much of their hold as centers for
community activity. Crowded streets were ill designed to be used as playgrounds for either adults or children, and the continual pressure of buildings
—of straight lines and right angles—became too oppressive to be endured.
The demands of the human being for air, for wide views, and for exercise all
had to be met in some comprehensive socialized manner. Means had to be
contrived for furnishing people with opportunities for social activities, for
carrying on hobbies and avocations, for adult education and adult relaxation.

One result, of course, was large-scale professional amusement—the theater
and especially the movie; another was professionalized sport, bringing with it
the need for vast arenas and stadiums. These developments were not all gain,
for a healthy community life cannot be based simply on watching others perform; what is necessary are facilities through which all can in some way take
part in cultural and recreational activities.

In order to fulfill all these various needs, parks, playgrounds, settlement
houses, community buildings, and specialized structures for athletics have
been created. The park and the playground are now accepted elements in any
modern community plan; they play both a hygienic and an almost equally
important aesthetic and spiritual role in today's urban life. The settlement

house is an improvisation, founded on philanthropy, to fill an obvious need for social, recreational, and educational facilities; ideally, such structures should be socially conceived and executed so that they may be true community buildings. The forms which community buildings should take, together with the facilities they should offer, are manifestly conditioned not only by the community form itself but even more by the ideals of living which the current society supports. Their future is difficult to prophesy, for the direction which life is taking is still confused.

Buildings for athletics are also in a state of flux, as the ideal of public participation in sports more and more replaces the old professionalized types, both in colleges and among the population as a whole. Yet, since their forms are controlled by the games and activities which they shelter and by the requirements of good sanitation and public health, more definite standards are possible for them than for the other types of building considered in this section. But in all these types the architect has a great responsibility, for he must not only solve a given program but also help to formulate the program itself. The quality of our civilization will inevitably be revealed in structures erected for social welfare; it is the architect's job to see that, in so far as he is able, he helps to make them as noble and as ample as circumstances permit.

PERCIVAL AND PAUL GOODMAN, brothers and joint authors of the chapter "Community Buildings," have collaborated on numerous articles dealing with art and city planning and are the authors of *Communitas* (Chicago: University of Chicago Press [c1947]). Percival Goodman won the Paris Prize in 1925 and is a practicing architect in New York; his work includes many community buildings. He is Assistant Professor in the School of Architecture, Columbia University. Paul Goodman is an author. He holds the degree of Doctor of Philosophy from the University of Chicago and has taught at the University of Chicago, New York University, and Black Mountain College.

SIMON BREINES, A.I.A., author of the chapter "Settlement Houses," is a member of the architectural firm of Pomerance & Breines, of New York. His firm has had a varied practice, including hotels, hospitals, and office buildings, and he has made a special study of youth centers and other community facilities.

LAWRENCE B. ANDERSON, author of the chapter "Buildings for Athletics," is Professor in Charge of the Department of Architecture in the School of Architecture and Planning of the Massachusetts Institute of Technology. He is a member of the architectural firm of Anderson & Beckwith, the designers of several buildings of the type covered by his chapter.

C. EARL MORROW, A.I.A., author of the chapter "Small Public Open Spaces," is planning consultant of the Regional Plan Association, New York, and of several municipalities and counties in the New York metropolitan area. He is an author and lecturer on various subjects connected with regional, county, and municipal planning.

THOMAS C. VINT, A.S.L.A., A.I.A., author of the chapter "Park Structures," has been with the National Park Service since 1922, and in charge of all architectural and landscape-architectural work in the National Park system since 1927. In 1946 he became Chief of Planning and Construction of the National Park Service, in which capacity he has directed all of its architecture, engineering, and landscape architecture.

45

Community Buildings

By PERCIVAL AND PAUL GOODMAN

COMMUNITY BUILDINGS and community centers may be understood to mean buildings and grounds maintained by governmental or co-operative groups for public use, either free or at a nominal cost, to provide a variety of social activities that require more space or specialized equipment than is privately available. Since these buildings or centers generally embrace a combination of functions, the detailed problems of planning can best be studied in connection with a consideration of such specific building types as settlement houses, social halls, clubhouses, gymnasiums, park structures, hotels, baths, restaurants, and theaters.[1] A characteristic community building found in most cities in the United States is the "Y" building, maintained by religious and philanthropic organizations for general use, without profit, and providing facilities for athletic, recreational, educational, club, and cultural activities as well as inexpensive dormitories for transients.

In the second quarter of the twentieth century there has been an increasing construction of community buildings in all industrialized countries—a trend known in England as the Community Center Movement. In the United States such buildings are even considered appropriate as war memorials because they embody the "community spirit." What are the causes and what is the prospect of this trend?

Sociologically considered, the construction of community buildings in our time has followed on the breakdown of traditional smaller-group and family arrangements: the inability of former parish districts to serve a wider and motorized neighborhood, the dissolution of family ties, the more mobile search for employment, and so forth. This breaking of old contacts has resulted in an increasing amount of free-floating energy, along with the corresponding problems of juvenile delinquency, urban loneliness, passive movie-going, and

---

[1] See Chaps. 46, "Settlement Houses"; 47, "Buildings for Athletics"; and 49, "Park Structures." See also Vol. I, Chap. 4, "Service Areas." Also Vol. III, Chaps. 3, "Hotels"; 4, "Camps and Dormitories"; and 12, "Theaters."

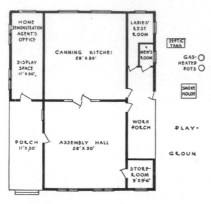

FIGURE 445. COMMUNITY BUILDING, FORT STOCKTON, TEXAS. PLAN AND EXTERIOR

The plan expresses a simple community co-operation in work and play still traditional in some parts of rural America. The combination of functions answers local needs and obviously has been determined by local direction. Since much of the work is carried on by women there is a playground for children, a co-operative service that is always good but especially meaningful here because of its economic necessity. Under favorable conditions such a building could foster that festive attitude toward productive work so esteemed by social philosophers and possible only on a community basis.

From Halbert, *Community Buildings for Farm Families*

empty leisure. The chief impetus toward the establishment of modern community centers, therefore, has been the need to cushion the crises of economic and cultural change, that is, to adjust the free-floating energy to some socially acceptable pattern which presumably also enriches individual experience (though this in many cases is debatable).

Co-operating persistently with that impulse, however, is a second and more creative impetus toward the development of community centers. This is the resurgence, along with the weakening of the peculiar anti-social pressure of capitalist production relations, of the natural sociality and co-operation evident in older historical periods and in primitive cultures. (In classic Greece, for example, the most important buildings formed a kind of community center.) How and in what degree this natural urge will affect future community centers will depend on political history. The centers themselves, of course, are potentially strong political forces.

Community centers as socially maintained grounds and buildings for spon-

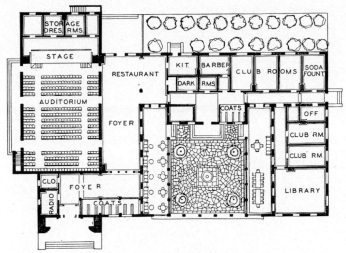

FIGURE 446.

COLLECTIVE FARM CLUBHOUSE IN THE CAUCASUS. PLAN

One of a series of projects prepared in Moscow (1937) for clubhouses in different Soviet regions and climates. Throughout the series the combination of functions is almost identical and indicates a centralized conception of the cultural needs of rural citizens in general. Cooperative work is carried on in the collectives themselves. The cultural level expressed is more complicated than in the Fort Stockton plan; note the provision of fixed seats and a formal stage, the library, the photography laboratory, the surprising number of clubrooms for a center for 300 people. In that warm climate the patio serves for dances and parties. An office for the agronomist occurs in every plan in the series; a nationally co-ordinated agriculture and the effort to "eliminate the differences between the city and the country" are the moving ideals of the plan.

taneous co-operation in work and play have existed in all times and regions. It is interesting to note the particular activities and patterns of activity which have variously been considered appropriate to the community center. Those patterns, in fact, can be used today as one objective gauge for the quantity and quality of the elusive concept "community spirit." In some patterns it has been work and the integration of work and play which have been regarded as communal; in others it has been only sports and recreation; in still others it has been the important cultural and therapeutic activities of the society.

With respect to these varying tendencies, community buildings throughout the ages can best be compared with the private homes or the shops of the same period; one can gauge the social pattern of an era by observing what functions have been commonly assigned to those types of buildings. For instance, in many primitive societies meals are eaten in community buildings; with us, mainly in private homes. Again, until recently in Protestant countries the opportunities for courtship were sternly restricted to private or small social meetings, but modern community buildings make provision for a more public exercise of this kind of recreation.

In the accompanying illustrations an attempt has been made to show the combinations of functions which have been considered appropriate for com-

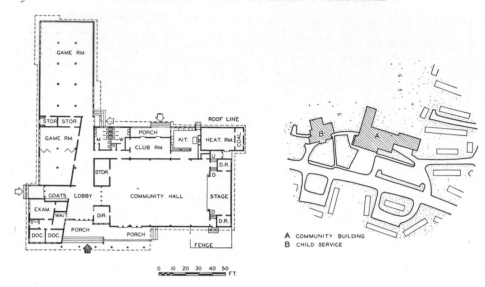

FIGURE 447. COMMUNITY BUILDING, ORCHARD HEIGHTS, OREGON. TWO PLANS

Jones, Bouillon, Thiry & Sylliaasen, architects

A unit in a war-time housing development; adjacent to it is a large playing field and connected with it a "child service building." The combination of functions in the plan can be taken as the typical recreational pattern in the United States: half games and half dancing, as well as some theatricals. The medical wing serving the housing development indicates the growth of communal medicine. In general the community meaning of a dormitory town is expressed here: there are fairly elaborate facilities for small children and adequate facilities for the physical recreation of adults, but little attempt is made to integrate the economic and cultural parts of life.

munity centers in a wide range of present-day situations: rural, small city, and metropolitan. By way of contrast, an illustration from antiquity is included. It requires no gift of prophecy to see that the future will incorporate additional living functions—and these more intensely—into its community centers. The number of youth, business, professional, adult-education, and other organizations with auxiliary social and recreative functions is continually increasing. The plans of certain factories include rooms for games and clubs. Housing projects provide nurseries, shopping facilities, and social, club, hobby, and game rooms. Welfare agencies that started with a purely salvationary purpose go more and more into community recreation. Government at all levels furnishes funds for many such undertakings. There is occasion here for a social architecture and even perhaps for monumentality. As yet, however, achievement in design has been limited largely to simplicity of effect—dictated rather by prudence than by inspiration.

The philosophical question—and this is always the question for high archi-

FIGURE 448. COMMUNITY BUILDING, ORCHARD HEIGHTS, OREGON. VIEW
Jones, Bouillon, Thiry & Sylliaasen, architects

Photograph Dearborn-Massar

tecture—is how this inevitable trend can be made to contribute toward the creative enrichment of life. The obvious dangers of the trend are the co-ordination of individuals into a state or societal culture and the exploitation of the satisfactions of a superficial sociality which prevents any deep personal expression, whether of creation or of rebellion. So long as the chief purpose of community centers is to provide a therapy for crime and loneliness in the interests of the smoother working of the social machine, so long as the practice of experts in this field is based largely on giving people something to occupy their time, it seems unlikely that community buildings and their embellishment will express any wonderful spirit. On the other hand, if these buildings (and related community arrangements) can become a means toward as well as a result of popular initiative—in politics, economics, and culture—energized by spontaneous sociality, their architecture naturally will express this shift in emphasis.

There have been peoples whose community centers expressed a more constructive spirit than that demonstrated in our own mid-century centers; yet even here the aims and the expression are superior to what they were in the immediate past. At all events, great changes will occur in community architecture, and architects have a duty to think their plans through as social innovators, not merely as servile imitators.

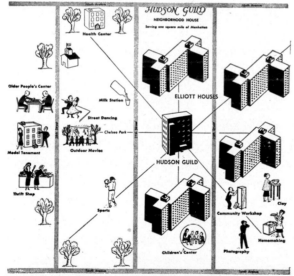

FIGURE 449.

CHELSEA NEIGHBORHOOD
BLOCK FOR HUDSON GUILD,
NEW YORK. BIRD'S-EYE
VIEW AND DESCRIPTIVE
DIAGRAM

Archibald M. Brown and William
Lescaze, associated architects for
Chelsea Houses

A municipal housing project for
608 families, a playground, a settlement house, a health center, a public
school. This group is probably the
most thoroughly elaborated "neighborhood block" in Greater New
York; it serves the entire Chelsea
district, long one of the least favored in the city. The housing
group has a nursery for the whole
district; Hudson Guild carries on
a general program of child, adoles-
cent, and adult recreation, arts and crafts, music, etc.; and the school is somewhat more progressive than the average New York public school. In pattern the Chelsea group shows similarities
to the much smaller Orchard Heights suburban development, but the crucial difference is that this
project is in the heart of a vast city, a world cultural center. In such an environment an unusually
relevant combination of child, health, and domestic functions is possible without the sense of
cultural limitation. The actual spirit of initiative and neighborliness is no doubt on a par with
that in other parts of New York (and America), but this group presents a uniquely reasonable
physical pattern for making a metropolis livable.   Courtesy Hudson Guild

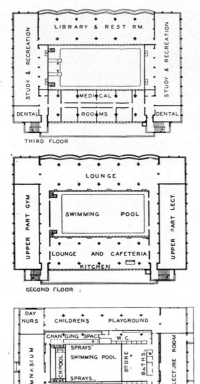

THIRD FLOOR

SECOND FLOOR

FIRST FLOOR 0 30 FT

FIGURE 450. PECKHAM HEALTH CENTER, LONDON. THREE PLANS

Sir Owen Williams, architect

This remarkable institution is the outgrowth of an attempt by medical men to improve the physical health of a depressed metropolitan community and of the discovery that disease is psychosomatic—as much the result of unhappiness, frustration, fear, and ignorance as of germs and poisons. Here the unit of healthy functioning is not the individual but the family comprised of husband, wife, and children. Every kind of pre-marital, pre-natal, post-natal, infant, youth, and adult clinical consultation is provided, and every kind of physical and social exercise and recreation. There is a detailed coverage for every age and every physical condition. The most striking feature of the project is its experimental purpose and the collaboration of the people served, who are also the subjects of the experiments. Obviously this purposiveness gives to the Peckham Center a vitality, an excitement, beyond that of community centers devoted merely to recreational and social activities. Many valuable findings, especially concerning childbirth and child care, have come from such unique opportunities for observation. What seems to be lacking is the realization that the living human unit extends beyond the physiological family into realms of work, politics, and a more deep-reaching culture than is in evidence here.

In any effort to envisage a more ideal community center as a goal, the following premises seem inescapable: Every human function—from individual contemplation and creation and domestic life and sexuality to collaboration in industrial production and mass absorption in a spectacle—is by nature a community function. Conversely, the community is nothing but an interrelation of all vital functions. In every activity the sense of community, the integration of all functions, ought to be conscious—or available to consciousness —but in our times activities are sharply differentiated into two opposite groups, "private" and "public," both characterized by repression. During our "private" moments we repress our concern for the general because of sexual fear and the feeling that our spontaneous acts are unwanted, and during our "public" moments in economics and politics we repress our personal feelings because of false notions of efficiency and obsessive notions of orderliness and government.

FIGURE 451. PECKHAM HEALTH CENTER,
LONDON. EXTERIOR

Sir Owen Williams, architect

From *Architectural Review*

To indicate the fact that numbers of individuals in a community in carrying on some of their vital functions gather and commingle, we should use the term "center of the community" rather than "community center." Obviously what constitutes such a center of gathering will depend on the kind of community desired. In pedestrian urban life the vital functions center in just such town squares as are excellently analyzed by Camillo Sitte in *Der Städtebau.* . . . In the automotive ruralism of Frank Lloyd Wright's *Broadacre City* there might well be a cluster of buildings to include a theater, a meeting hall, and so on. But prior to any discussion of such structural and form problems there is always the question: To what degree does a community exist—that is, to what degree is the existence of a body of people a matter of deep satisfaction to each and to all?

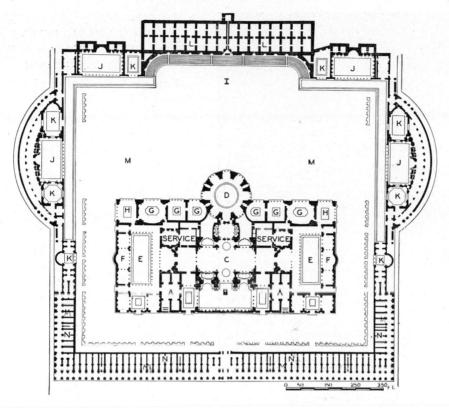

FIGURE 452. BATHS OF CARACALLA, ROME. PLAN

A: Entrance and dressing room; B: Swimming pool; C: Lounge; D: Hot baths; E: Exercising court; F: Covered exercising area; G: Smaller bath room; H: Garden room; I: Stadium; J: Area for quiet relaxation; K: Hall for lectures or readings; L: Reservoir; M: Garden, probably with ball courts, etc.; N: Shops.

For embracing the whole range of physical, social, emotional, and intellectual recreations and pleasures, nothing in modern or ancient times can compare with the Roman baths of the Empire, established in many cities and endowed for general use by the Imperial Treasury. What is noteworthy is not only the variety of activities (baths, fights, spectacles, philosophy, academies, theaters) but also—and even more striking—the integration of them all into one continuous experience. A satirist speaks of "the versifier who spouting follows you into the swimming pool." At the basis is the concept that it is an integrated individual who enjoys in one continuous experience every pleasure of the soul and the body. We do not observe this integration in the plan and use of modern "Y" buildings, even when there is space for both physical and cultural exercises. A Roman writer described these baths as "whole cities within the city." This eloquently expressed their deficiency, for in fact this total recreative experience was not the living community; the bathers did not rule their destiny or initiate their culture any more than did the attendant slaves. The proper contrast to this cosmic community building is the complex of public squares, gymnasia, markets, theaters, law courts, assemblies, temples, and porticoes which served as the home and club of the free males in a Greek city. Here it was not necessary to house the spontaneous community recreation within walls, for the community center was to a large degree the living city itself.

FIGURE 453.
BATHS OF CARACALLA, ROME.
INTERIOR OF LOUNGE (TEPIDARIUM)
AS RESTORED BY F. THIERSCH

From von Falke, *Hellas und Rom* . . .

In the sketches for an urban square shown in *Communitas* [2] the continuity of vital functions in a community is indicated by the opening out of the dwellings, the factory, the library, and other buildings on the one square; the square itself is a place of congregation, conversation, music, and similar general satisfactions continuous with and related to the more specialized activities in the buildings. As conditions for the enjoyment of such community satisfactions, we must postulate, among other revisions of our social structure, a relaxing of the timetable of industrialism, a rule of work by the workers, and progressive education for children.

SUGGESTED ADDITIONAL READING FOR CHAPTER 45

Giedion, Sigfried, *Mechanization Takes Command* (New York: Oxford University Press, 1948).

Goodman, Percival, and Paul Goodman, *Communitas; Means of Livelihood and Ways of Life* (Chicago: University of Chicago Press, 1947).

[2] Percival Goodman and Paul Goodman, *Communitas* (Chicago: Chicago University Press, 1946).

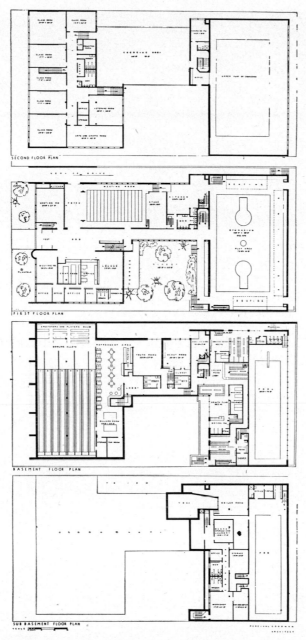

FIGURE 454. COMMUNITY BUILDING, WILKES-BARRE, PENNSYLVANIA. PLANS

Percival Goodman, architect; S. Z. Moscowitz, associate architect

A community building for a small city. The pattern of functions includes sports, social gather-ings, and education in about equal parts. The building serves both sexes and all ages.

Courtesy Percival Goodman

FIGURE 455. COMMUNITY BUILDING, WILKES-BARRE, PENNSYLVANIA. MODEL
Percival Goodman, architect; S. Z. Moscowitz, associate architect

Photograph Louis H. Dreyer, courtesy Percival Goodman

Morris, William, *News from Nowhere* (New York: Vanguard, 1926). All society as a recreative function.

Pearse, Innes Hope, M.D., and Lucy H. Crocker, *Pioneer Health Centre, London; the Peckham Experiment* (New Haven: Yale University Press, 1945).

Sitte, Camillo, *The Art of Building Cities*, a translation of *Der Städtebau nach seinen künstlerischen Grundsatzen* (Vienna, 1899) by Charles T. Stewart (New York: Reinhold, 1945). Town squares as community centers.

46

Settlement Houses

By SIMON BREINES

THE SETTLEMENT HOUSE represents an attempt on the part of private groups or individuals to ameliorate some of the social and economic hardships which fall to the lot of the low-income groups, particularly minorities, in our society. Historically it is an expression of society's bad conscience, of the protest of good people against the horrors of nineteenth-century slum living. As a form of charity, the settlement is naturally a limited instrument for social change. Its basic idea is that a neighborhood's life can be enriched by the opportunity for personal contact between people of different cultural backgrounds and various economic levels.

The settlement concept as we know it had its beginnings in England. Arnold Toynbee inspired a group at Oxford to take an active interest in the struggle of the poor. In 1884, Canon Barnett led a handful of social-minded enthusiasts to live in the industrial quarter of London. There they established the first settlement house and named it Toynbee Hall. It was sponsored by the University Settlement Association acting as a committee for Oxford and Cambridge Universities.

In 1886 Stanton Coit, an American, went to live at Toynbee Hall. The following year Dr. Coit returned to the United States and with Charles B. Stover founded the Neighborhood Guild on Forsythe Street in New York's lower East Side; later this became known as the University Settlement. Out of the same roots soon came the College Settlement established on Rivington Street in New York as a field of social work for an organization of college women. In 1889 Jane Addams and Ellen Gates Starr founded Hull House on Halsted Street, Chicago. Under Miss Addams's leadership this became one of the most famous settlements, and its influence and fame extended around the world. By the turn of the century, settlement houses under charitable, civil, or religious auspices were to be found in most cities in the United States.

The central idea of these early settlement efforts was to bring men and

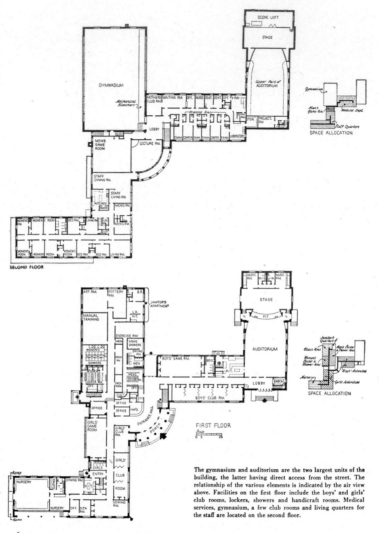

The gymnasium and auditorium are the two largest units of the building, the latter having direct access from the street. The relationship of the various elements is indicated by the air view above. Facilities on the first floor include the boys' and girls' club rooms, lockers, showers and handicraft rooms. Medical services, gymnasium, a few club rooms and living quarters for the staff are located on the second floor.

FIGURE 456. RIPLEY HOUSE, HOUSTON, TEXAS. PLANS

Birdsell P. Briscoe and Maurice J. Sullivan, associated architects

The requirements of the varied activities furnished by settlement houses necessarily give rise to large structures with complex plans. From *Architectural Forum*

women of education into closer contact with the working class. By living among the slum dwellers and trying to associate with them as equals, they hoped to improve their mental, moral, and physical conditions. As the settlement idea matured it developed more specific programs and techniques which grew out of the social problems abounding in this environment, and these

FIGURE 457. RIPLEY HOUSE, HOUSTON, TEXAS. EXTERIOR
Birdsell P. Briscoe and Maurice J. Sullivan, associated architects
Where land values are not excessive the building can be made long and low.

Photograph Elwood M. Payne

techniques to a certain extent influenced the physical form of the settlement house.

In the beginning the settlement dealt largely with the problems of the newly arrived immigrant. But with the passage of time and the curtailing of immigration the settlement house has encompassed all levels of the people and has included all types of neighborhood activities. In addition to the basic social-work services involving problems of language, nationality, and citizenship, the settlements became social and cultural influences in their communities. They became clubs where groups of all ages could fulfill a deep-felt desire for association and co-operation. They became studios of arts and crafts, shops for woodwork and metalwork, and playrooms for relaxation and recreation, and they attempted to interest the adolescent boys and girls of the slums in more social and healthful activities than had been open to them before.

Juvenile delinquency, however, remains a continuing challenge to the settlement house. Jane Addams has described her attempts to cope with the problems of the gang and the young tough of the Chicago of her day. In contrast to the traditional, harsh police methods, she says in *Forty Years at Hull House:* [1]

The desire for play, for sports fitted to the ages of such boys, I believe, will be the only agency powerful enough to break into this intensified and unwholesome

[1] New York: Macmillan, 1910.

FIGURE 458. RIPLEY HOUSE,
HOUSTON, TEXAS.
INTERIORS OF LOBBY,
AUDITORIUM, AND
GYMNASIUM

Birdsell P. Briscoe and Maurice J.
Sullivan, associated architects

Courtesy Ripley House

life. In fact, I have seen it thus broken when gangs of boys were finally induced to patronize the public playgrounds of Chicago.

Most settlement houses make some provision for the recreational needs of active and aggressive boys. Recently, however, there has been a trend toward specialized settlements known usually as boys' clubs. A variation of this development is a social and recreational center designed especially for the youth of both sexes and popularly called a teen-age center. The requirements and facilities for these will be discussed later in this chapter.

GENERAL PROGRAM

Johnson's Encyclopedia defines settlement houses as "homes in the poor quarters of a city where educated men and women may live in daily personal contact with the working people." The first ones were little more than converted slum dwellings with improvised facilities to fit the available funds. Occasionally, as the idea developed and won greater financial and social support, new buildings were erected for the purpose in some of the larger cities. Usually, however, the settlement house is a structure originally intended for another purpose, and almost always it is located in a slum district.

Unfortunately for those who would describe the settlement house, there is no fixed pattern of program, building, or equipment. Neighborhoods vary in social composition, in their history of co-operation between persons and groups, and in their existing community facilities and programs. Where a neighborhood has a lack of social and recreational facilities, the settlement house may, in addition to its special welfare functions, take on the character and physical form of a community center. Indeed, to most social workers the ideal settlement is a true center of community life. On the other hand, in a neighborhood that has adequate schools, playgrounds, libraries, and other public services, the settlement will not attempt to duplicate such facilities but instead will try to integrate into its own program those which already exist. Here the objective is to provide only those facilities and services which the community lacks.

Within the settlement house itself there is a similar absence of fixed standards in regard to building space, equipment, and use. Because of the constantly changing social problems with which it deals and the inevitable limitation of building funds, the average settlement house has few thoroughly functional rooms, that is, rooms designed and used for a specific function. Normally settlement facilities must be flexible and serve multiple functions: rooms used by children during the day may serve adults at night; a gymnasium may have to double as an auditorium, a social hall, and even in subdivided form as meeting rooms; the kitchen may have to become a classroom for cooking. Of course the multi-functional room with its diversified equipment has disadvantages. At best this expedient does not serve all its various uses equally well, and at worst it serves most of them poorly. Where finances permit, specialized rooms and equipment are preferred by most workers in the settlement field.

Perhaps the most useful way to approach the problem of the building program of settlement houses is to understand the social objectives which they set themselves. Basically the settlements undertake to encourage association and co-operation between people across the more obvious lines of economic, social, and nationality divisions. They try to make it possible for all citizens to obtain wholesome housing, food, clothing, education, recreation, medical care, opportunity for personal expression, and the exercise of citizenship. They try to make the underprivileged aware of and eager for the opportunities and civic facilities which already exist in the community but which, through lack of information or understanding, many people overlook. Accordingly settlement houses emphasize hospitality and community or group activities through a policy of open house, through the encouragement of social and cultural clubs for the young and old, and through an active concern for the welfare of the whole family and of the neighborhood.

On a minimum level the settlement consists of quarters for resident personnel, administrative offices, several small club and game rooms accommodating up to twenty people, a large room that will hold from 150 to 250 people for social functions and for indoor play, and a kitchen for refreshments and cookery instruction. From this basic unit the settlement house varies with the size of its building budget and the needs and desires of its neighborhood. Additional facilities frequently provided are a nursery school, a gymnasium and swimming pool if there are none already available in the community, a theater with a stage for meetings and for dramatic and musical purposes, arts and crafts rooms, and medical and dental clinics.

At its optimum level the settlement house approaches the ideal neighborhood center, and its physical standards for recreational, educational, and cultural facilities are similar to those of such other building types as the local high school with some provision for community activity, the museum with a neighborhood program, or the community center. Each of these types now provides for neighborhood participation, and their standards are adequately covered in other chapters in this work. In order to avoid duplication, we shall include in the following sections only such elements as are relevant to the settlement house program.

Clubrooms. The small intimate club is the basic unit of most settlement houses, not only because of its emphasis on group experience but also because it has proved to be an effective educational instrument. Settlement clubs may be interested in arts and crafts, sculpture, music, vocational training, and dozens of other cultural and educational activities. When feasible, separate rooms are provided for such specialized functions; but in many cases the clubroom, since it must serve for many or all of the club's activities at different times and be used by children as well as adults, should be as flexibly designed as possible. Generally it must accommodate up to twenty-five people and its size should therefore be not less than 14 by 20 feet. Most settlement clubrooms should have space enough for a piano, since this nearly universal instrument is essential not only for musical but for many other activities. The clubroom with a piano can also be used for music practice.

The settlement clubroom should have a resilient floor and baseboard of wood, linoleum, or asphalt tile. Preferably the ceiling should be acoustically treated. For the walls, which should be capable of withstanding severe use, a good solution would be a wainscot of wood, hard composition board, or linoleum—extending up to a wooden chair rail at the correct height to prevent abrasions by tables, workbenches, and chairs—and above this some softer material like cork or fiberboard that will take nails and tacks and will not require frequent painting. Over the fiberboard museums often apply burlap cloth, which produces a serviceable and good-looking surface. The use of plaster on the walls of clubrooms should be avoided.

Perhaps the most neglected physical element in the clubroom is storage space. Preferably there should be a closet or some special storage space for each club and for each activity for which the room is used. A possible solution of this problem is to have adequately designed closets along an entire wall of the room. Along the window wall (or any wall) low chests may be built in. Needless to say, all other furniture should be movable. The chairs, where classroom use is contemplated, should have tablet arms; other rooms may have folding chairs. The rubber-shoed, aluminum type of chair is particularly applicable to settlement-house needs.

Play and Social Rooms. In addition to the smaller clubrooms and meeting rooms for active play and social purposes, the settlement should have one or more larger rooms with a capacity of one or two hundred people. Such a room is important, because for many functions the clubrooms are too small and the gyms and auditoriums are too large. This intermediate-size room can serve for parties, larger club meetings, dance groups, dramatic rehearsals, and even as a small gymnasium when necessary. Although obviously no set standards can be established for a space of such multiple use, generally those for club-rooms should be followed, especially in regard to storage. The seats should be movable and of a type that can be stored within the room. Since if possible this room should have a higher ceiling than the clubrooms, it might well be located at the end of a corridor, where it will be free of the main bulk of the building and also where the noise originating there may be more nearly isolated. For maximum flexibility the large play room may be designed to be subdivided by movable partitions, but it should be remembered that such partitions are not noise-proof. The shape here as well as in the smaller clubroom should be rather on the square side. Long rooms are undesirable because they tend to divide the activity.

At least one of the large play and social rooms should have a hardwood floor suitable for dancing—not only ballroom dancing but also ballet and the modern dance. Such a floor should not be laid directly over concrete because of the lack of resiliency of that type of construction; wood sleepers are required to support the floor above the concrete.

Gymnasium. The settlement gym, as such, does not differ from the normal gymnasium as described in the next chapter. Frequently, however, because of budget or space limitations, it must also serve as an auditorium. The National Recreation Association warns against such dual use, but for cases where it is necessary some simple standards may be laid down. In the first place, the room should be large enough to serve the function requiring the greatest space, usually basketball. The smallest possible gym which would provide a small non-standard basketball court is 35 by 60 feet. Minimum official dimensions for a basketball court are 42 feet in width and 74 feet in length. An additional distance of 3 feet all around, free of all obstructions, should be allowed, making a minimum-size gym 48 by 80 feet. A floor space of 60 by 90 feet is recommended, however, because on a floor of that size two or more smaller games can be played simultaneously and also because those dimensions permit some spectator seating. Used as an auditorium, such a gym could accommodate as many as seven hundred people. For its stage the gym-auditorium requires a depth of 20 feet or more, and there must be at least two dressing rooms, a property room, and a convenient shop. The seats may be stored under the stage or in a closet.

Gym ceilings should be not less than 20 feet clear. Unless otherwise protected, the windows, radiators, and ventilating ducts should be located 10 feet above the floor. The National Recreation Association does not recommend folding doors or partitions in the gym because, besides being expensive to install and maintain, they are not sound-proof; a net suspended from the ceiling is sometimes used to divide the room. Even though the gym, on account of its ceiling height and the noise incident to its use, is usually located in a separate wing of the settlement house, acoustical treatment is nevertheless desirable.

Since the gym often serves for special functions, it should have an entrance separate from the main central entrance of the settlement house. Preferably the gym is placed on the ground level, but on small plots it is sometimes relegated to the top floor for economy. This arrangement avoids the necessity of building above the large trusses required in the gym, but it is not recommended. Adequate natural cross ventilation, which is essential, can most easily be achieved by means of large windows on at least two opposite walls. A built-in drinking fountain is also important. Where there is an outdoor play area, it is desirable to locate the gym so that the locker and shower facilities will be directly accessible from outside.

Swimming Pool. Few settlement houses can afford a swimming pool, which therefore comes last on the list of required facilities. Swimming-pool standards are described in the following chapter.

Dressing Rooms, Showers, and Toilets. Separate facilities of this type must be provided for each sex. An important factor in relation to the gymnasium, swimming pool, or possible outdoor area is the controlled but convenient circulation of people. Toilets are needed at various points, such as the main entrance, auditorium, kitchen, children's nursery, and so on. There should be a drinking fountain or bubbler in every dressing or locker room.

Auditorium. In most urban communities today there is a local school with a fairly good gymnasium which is or can be made available to the public, but an auditorium with adequate stage, dressing-room, and shop facilities is not so frequently encountered outside and is therefore a more essential addition to the settlement house. Because it must serve for dramatics, music, social dances, movies, forums, lectures, and certain other types of activities, the settlement auditorium should have a level floor. A sloping floor is practical only when the seats are fixed to the floor; this is seldom the case in settlement houses.

A stage that is at least 20 feet in depth will be adequate for dramatics, and with the curtain down it can be used also as a separate room. Standards of size, type and amount of storage space, backstage facilities, lighting, ventilation, acoustics, and the like are the same for the settlement auditorium as for other

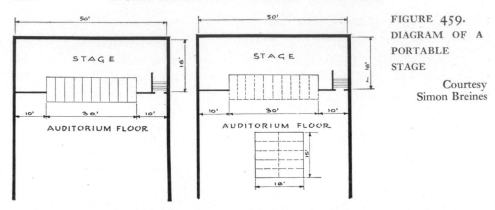

FIGURE 459.
DIAGRAM OF A
PORTABLE
STAGE

Courtesy
Simon Breines

types. Although the need for a permanent stage should be emphasized, from the settlement point of view a semi-portable stage offers interesting possibilities. The National Recreation Association suggests one type in which the front portion of the stage is constructed in a series of uniform sections securely locked together.[2] These sections may be of various dimensions, say 3 feet wide by 8 feet long (see Fig. 459). The eight sections in the example shown have many uses. They can be made into a 16- by 15-foot block and set up in the middle of the auditorium floor for use as a boxing ring or a bandstand. The sections may be made high enough to serve as booths during bazaars and exhibitions either indoors or out. The success of this type of stage depends on perfect uniformity and rigidity of construction and on the security of the device employed for locking the sections together.

For movies, the increasing popularity of 16 mm. safety film suggests that the traditional projection booth can be eliminated from even the most elaborate settlement-house plans. A closet should be provided in the rear of the auditorium to accommodate a standard table, movie projector, and tripod which can be rolled out when needed.

Shops and Craft or Hobby Rooms. Although the well-designed clubroom will fulfill some of the purposes of the amateur hobby clubs, it is desirable to have specially designed facilities for these activities. The small settlement house which can afford only one such room should make it a woodworking shop, because this hobby appeals to the largest number of people and such an arrangement will be the most flexible and useful. If the budget permits, however, and especially if some vocational training is contemplated, the single shop should

[2] *Planning a Community Recreation Building* (New York: National Recreation Association, 1944).

be designed as a one-teacher general shop. Such shops are common in the public schools, and the standards are outlined in Volume III, Chapter 16. For settlement purposes, however, a few salient points are summarized below. The maximum number of work stations for safe and efficient supervision in the general shop is twenty. A minimum of 60 square feet of floor space per individual should be allowed in determining the size of the shop, the length and width of which should preferably be in the proportion of two to one. All shops should be located on the lowest floor level because of machinery vibration.

The element most frequently overlooked in the shop is adequate storage space. The settlement house, which usually puts shop rooms to intensive use, needs even more than the normal storage space for each of the activities involved. Most shop and craft rooms waste space below bench tops where storage of the locker or cabinet type is possible. Tool panels on the walls, open to view and inspection, are preferable to tool rooms or cribs. Lumber should be stored horizontally and stocks of iron and steel in vertical racks. The desirability of using a shop or a craft or hobby room for one specific purpose has been stressed, but the small clubrooms already described are adequate for multiple use provided sufficient storage space is made available for tools as well as for craft materials and finished articles. A glass-enclosed display case may be appropriate. In addition, if such craft rooms must double as play rooms, there should be storage space for chairs and tables. The installation of a sink with hot and cold water is recommended, especially in rooms to be used for arts and crafts. Proper orientation of the rooms requires careful consideration; those devoted to arts and crafts should have north light, but club and game rooms may have almost any exposure. Natural light is desirable wherever possible, but in any case ample artificial illumination should be provided. An intensity of at least twenty foot-candles at bench height is recommended.

Nursery School. Since settlement houses normally are situated in low-income neighborhoods where frequently both parents go to work, a nursery school is indispensable. Here the usual standards apply. In New York City, the Department of Health requires 20 square feet of play space per child and the Board of Education demands separate indoor space for each of the different age groups. The nursery rooms should be well lighted and ventilated. Unless there is an elevator they should be at or just above the ground level; small children should not have to walk up more than one flight. If possible, there should be an adjacent outdoor play space. All the furniture, equipment, and toilets in this area should be designed for use by children. A separate kitchen is essential.

Kitchen. This is an essential element in settlement houses. On a minimum basis the kitchen should adjoin one of the larger rooms and be adequate for feeding at least fifty people. For banquet use, however, it should be conveniently related to the largest room in the building, if this is feasible. In addition to its normal functions, the settlement kitchen must be designed to serve as a cooking classroom. The usual standards for kitchens apply, particularly if there is to be a cafeteria or a snack bar. The receiving of foodstuffs and their distribution within the building are problems that deserve special attention. Here again ample storage is important.

Staff Rooms. Efficiency demands a desk—or, if possible, a separate office—for each member of the administration and resident staff. Although it has been traditional for settlement workers to live in the building, in most instances today residence is required of only the head worker and perhaps an assistant. For this purpose, a normal dwelling unit (or units) is appropriate. The apartment of the settlement worker and his family should be located where a maximum of privacy is possible—in a penthouse, for example.

Entrance. For purposes of easy control there should be only one main entrance, as has become the practice in boys' clubs and "Y's." In the settlement house this entrance should lead into an informal lobby, in which there is an administrative office, a large check room, a lounge, and public toilets. As far as possible all other facilities should be easily accessible from the lobby. In the small settlement the lobby may also serve as a lounge; in the larger building a separate lounge is recommended. The basic settlement idea requires that the entrance, lobby, and lounge have a hospitable, domestic atmosphere. A fireplace is traditional.

Health and Dental Clinic. Early settlement houses pioneered in the movement for health centers, which grew out of the obvious need for such facilities in the slum districts where they were situated. As the concept of public health took hold and broadened, many of the former services of the settlement houses were taken over by official health departments. Nevertheless there are still many gaps in the urban health picture, and these the settlement house strives to fill. Depending on the neighborhood, then—and also on the budget limitations—a settlement may provide anything from a small health clinic to a well-equipped health and dental center with a visiting nurse service. The United

States Public Health Service has developed excellent standards for such facilities (see Chap. 36).

Library. Most settlement houses are not able to provide a fully equipped library even when the neighborhood lacks a public one. The common practice is to provide reading and reference facilities in some other multiple-use room, usually the lounge. Obvious standards include an inviting, restful atmosphere, good lighting, acoustical treatment, and accessibility.

Educational Facilities. Settlement houses do not carry on formal educational activities, but in accordance with the needs and desires of the community various types of social, recreational, and vocational guidance are offered. Although the settlement usually cannot set aside classrooms as such, with the exception of specialized arts and crafts rooms and shops, it should be possible to conduct classes in any room of the building. Since settlement work is concerned largely with the small children and older people of the neighborhood, as many facilities as possible should be on the ground floor unless there is an elevator. The number of people over the age of sixty-five is increasing yearly, and there is a real lack of services for this group. For these reasons it is impractical for a settlement house to operate in, or in conjunction with, the ordinary public school with its fixed seats and few if any classrooms on the ground floor.

DESIGN FACTORS

Site Considerations. Settlement houses are almost always located in more or less blighted areas. Within such an area, however, the choice of a site depends on the availability of existing or future public facilities, such as schools, libraries, health centers, and playgrounds. Because slum land is frequently expensive, the settlement is usually hard pressed even for building space, not to speak of outdoor play space and room for future adjustment and expansion. Nevertheless the possibility of acquiring some open land adjacent to the settlement house should not be overlooked. There are many settlements which have had such an extraordinary growth and influence that their public extends far beyond the immediate neighborhood; Greenwich House in New York is a notable example. The possibility of raising funds for expansion in these cases is good, provided the additional ground space is available.

Miscellaneous Factors. There remain several assorted considerations that are applicable to settlement houses. The design should be such as to enable all

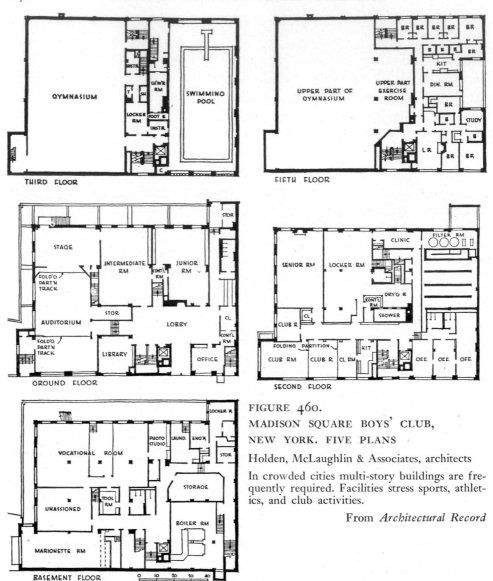

FIGURE 460.

MADISON SQUARE BOYS' CLUB,
NEW YORK. FIVE PLANS

Holden, McLaughlin & Associates, architects

In crowded cities multi-story buildings are frequently required. Facilities stress sports, athletics, and club activities.

From *Architectural Record*

activities to go on at the same time without interference. Essentially this requirement necessitates zoning the building itself to separate not only the noisy from the quiet uses but also the crowds from the small study groups. The use of roof areas is of particular importance in slum districts where land is expensive. In the matter of outdoor play space, the settlement might conceivably take the lead in getting the owners of adjacent back yards to pool these areas

FIGURE 461.
MADISON SQUARE BOYS' CLUB,
NEW YORK. EXTERIOR

Holden, McLaughlin & Associates, architects
Photograph Gottscho-Schleisner

through the removal of fences. Permission for the use of such a common play-ground might be either temporary or, by means of a legal easement, permanent. In any case it would be an interesting effort in the direction of local city planning.

Heating, ventilating, and lighting standards for settlement houses follow those of related building types. As for interior and exterior materials, the main considerations are easy and economical maintenance under severe use. Preference should be given to materials which require no paint and little upkeep. Plaster should be avoided except for ceilings and inaccessible surfaces.

SPECIALIZED SETTLEMENTS

The Boys' Club. Among low-income families the delinquent boy has long been and continues to be a serious social problem. In dealing with the problems of the whole family, the settlement house has tried to grapple with this question in what is probably the most natural and enlightened way. Since it is a private

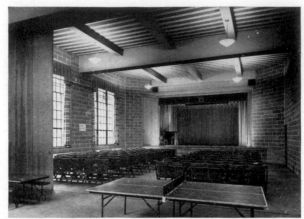

FIGURE 462.

MADISON SQUARE BOYS' CLUB,
NEW YORK.

INTERIORS OF AUDITORIUM,
GYMNASIUM, AND
SWIMMING POOL

Holden, McLaughlin & Associates,
architects

Problems of maintenance under
punishing usage give rise to the
simplest possible treatments.

Photographs
Gottscho-Schleisner

charity, however, the settlement has been unequal to the task of checking
juvenile delinquency. A more direct attack on this problem has been made
by what is known as the boys' club. (See Figs. 460–466.)

The boys' club deals exclusively with boys. It has an open-door policy that

FIGURE 463.
GREENWICH BOYS' CLUB,
GREENWICH, CONNECTICUT.
PLANS

Dwight James Baum and Phelps Barnum, associated architects

In small towns buildings can be spread out. From *Pencil Points*

FIGURE 464.
GREENWICH
BOYS' CLUB,
GREENWICH,
CONNECTICUT.
EXTERIOR VIEW
AND INTERIOR
SWIMMING POOL

Dwight James Baum and Phelps Barnum, associated architects

The style reflects a possibly mistaken effort to make the building harmonize with its suburban neighborhood.

Photographs
Gottscho-Schleisner

FIGURE 465.
HARLEM BOYS' CLUB,
NEW YORK. EXTERIOR

Louis E. Jallade, architect

An exterior that results from a frank expression of the plan and achieves an appropriate character half public and half residential.

Photograph Adolph Studly

encourages boys to engage in recreation and education at will. Boy guidance is the basic method of the boys' club and this is usually undertaken in blighted urban areas which have the greatest incidence of delinquency. As an indication of the growth of the idea, the Boys' Clubs of America claim 240 affiliated clubs throughout the United States and a membership of over a quarter of a million boys. Clubs range in number of members from 100 to nearly 10,000, the average consisting of about 1,000.

Minimum facilities should include a game room, a gymnasium, shower baths and a locker room, and class and group meeting rooms. Where possible, separate rooms for games, reading, and lounging should be set aside for older boys. The complete boys' club has, in addition, a swimming pool, an auditorium, and vocational training shops. From the standpoint of design standards, the facilities here do not differ essentially from similar facilities in the settlement house, community center, or school. Since the building is usually subjected to intense use by active, aggressive boys, it must be designed accordingly. The accompanying illustrations and plans offer typical examples.

Because most boys' clubs have a specified maximum membership, the size of a given building is determined on that basis. Experience has shown that the normal capacity of the club, with all its facilities operating, should be designed for one-quarter of the total active membership.

The Youth Center. Toward the middle of the twentieth century, particu-

FIGURE 466.

HARLEM BOYS' CLUB,

NEW YORK.

INTERIOR OF LOUNGE AND

VIEW ON ROOF

Louis E. Jallade, architect

The flat roofs of city buildings offer valuable play space.

Photographs Adolph Studly

larly as a result of the social stresses occasioned by the Second World War, a new type of settlement to provide wholesome recreation and leadership for young people appeared. This has been known variously as a youth center or teen-age center. According to the National Recreation Association, there are "at least five hundred so-called 'teen age centers" and they range from a redecorated neighborhood store converted for dancing and refreshments to a full-fledged downtown center. (See Fig. 467.)

The essential minimum facilities for a youth center are:

1. Good floor for dancing
2. Source of music—piano, radio, or juke box

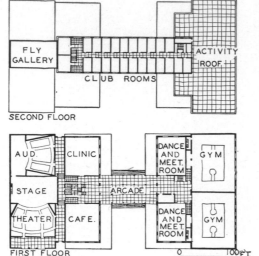

FIGURE 467.
PROPOSED YOUTH CENTER
FOR THE LOWER EAST SIDE,
NEW YORK. TWO PLANS

Pomerance & Breines, architects

A building designed to furnish facilities for
a healthy environment for young people—
facilities which congested cities otherwise
lack.

3. Snack bar
4. Lounge and reading area
5. Game room with tables
6. Office

A more fully equipped center would also include:

7. Meeting rooms
8. Arts and crafts rooms, hobby rooms, and shops
9. Photographic darkroom
10. Room or rooms for pool, ping-pong, and so forth
11. Adjacent outdoor area for sports and other activities
12. Skating area
13. Swimming pool or bathing beach
14. Auditorium
15. Gymnasium

In physical appearance a youth center must be attractive enough to compete
with the glamour of the commercial dance hall or night club. The color and
interior decorating must be pleasant and inviting; instead of glaring illumination the lighting, particularly in the dance area, should be as subdued as is consistent with proper control; and the furnishings should be comfortable and
harmonious.

To the fullest possible extent the existing recreational and cultural resources
of the community should be worked into the program.

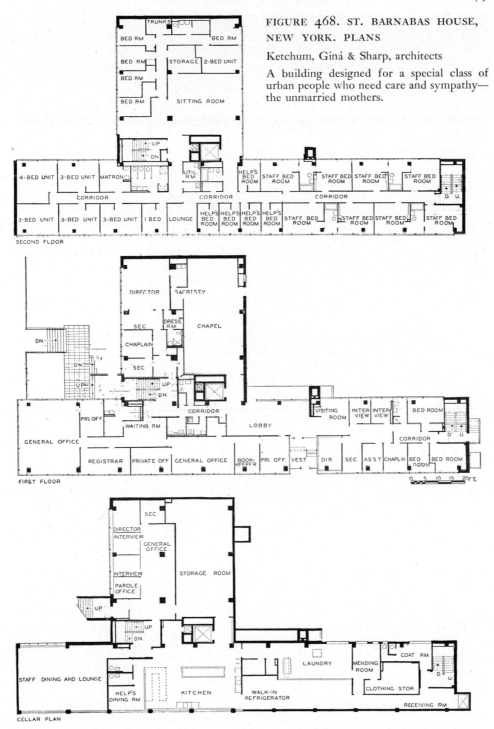

A building designed for a special class of
urban people who need care and sympathy—
the unmarried mothers.

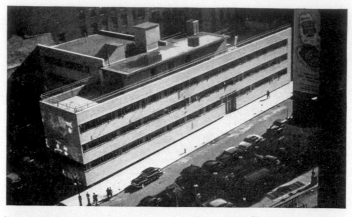

FIGURE 469.
ST. BARNABAS HOUSE,
NEW YORK.
EXTERIOR VIEW
AND INTERIOR
OF LOUNGE

Ketchum, Giná & Sharp,
architects

Clean, welcoming, and
attractive, this building
adds its inviting character
to other influences that
help rebuild the confi-
dence and character of
the girls who live here.

Photographs Lionel
Freedman—Pictor

TRENDS

As a charitable social experiment the settlement house may not have effected any fundamental improvements in our way of life, but as a sort of pilot study in group relations and activities on a neighborhood scale the original settlement idea is a continuing influence. The social tradition of the immigrant populations in the slums was always strong. With encouragement from the settlement house, despite the inadequacy of its buildings and equipment, these areas frequently developed better community centers than could be found in most middle-income and even high-income neighborhoods. Consequently the settlements have been important landmarks in the progress of the true community center. Even at mid-century the staffs of many community centers come directly from settlement backgrounds. The same is true of boys' clubs and youth centers.

In a more perfect future society there may be no need for the settlement house, for in such a society the settlement would conceivably have evolved into a type of community center available to all the people. For some decades to come, however, the settlement house and the boys' club will continue to play an important social role.

SUGGESTED ADDITIONAL READING FOR CHAPTER 46

Addams, Jane, *Twenty Years at Hull-House* (New York: Macmillan, 1910).

Kennedy, Albert J., and others, *Social Settlements in New York City* . . . (New York; Columbia University Press, 1935).

National Housing Agency, *Handbook on Project Services of Federal Public Housing Authority* (Washington: National Housing Agency, 1944).

National Recreation Association, *Planning a Community Recreation Building* (New York: the Association, 1944).

—— *Standards: Playgrounds, Playfields, Recreation Buildings, Indoor Recreation Facilities* (New York: the Association [1943]).

Standard Supply Details (New York: Boys' Clubs of America, 1947).

Wald, Lillian D., *Windows on Henry Street* (Boston: Little, Brown, 1934).

Woods, Robert A., and Albert J. Kennedy, *The Handbook of Settlements* (New York: Charities Publication Committee, 1911).

47

Buildings for Athletics

By LAWRENCE B. ANDERSON

OST SPORTS ACTIVITIES today are conducted in the open air and do not require buildings. Preparation of the field and track may be elaborate, but actual structures are provided only in connection with dressing facilities, for spectators, or as a means of introducing controlled playing conditions for certain sports. Although buildings for athletics are among the most celebrated in ancient architecture, all the present interest in sports has been built up in three or four generations. The essential nature of athletic games is determined by the capabilities of the human body, which has not changed significantly since long before Myron and Lysippus; yet great variation in the capacity for sport has occurred in different periods, both ancient and modern. The student of American history, for example, finds little before the Civil War that conveys any promise of the enormous importance athletics have achieved in the twentieth century.

The physical rigors of early frontier life made athletics superfluous in the United States, even if Puritan teaching had not strongly frowned on recreational activity. But the lack of games became a hardship as soon as urbanization began in earnest early in the nineteenth century. In fact, to a large extent our immense current program of organized recreation has been built up as a corrective to the kind of urban life the Industrial Revolution produced. Sports and the sports building program are to be seen as part of this defensive organization created after the modern industrial city had come into being. Although the early devotees of popular games were not concerned with any broad program of athletics, the history of sports in the United States constitutes a fascinating field of study. The period between 1840 and 1880 was one of incubation for almost all the games we now play; one after another they appeared, gradually attracted a large following, and became codified.

There is a general assumption that American schools, colleges and universities were the chief pioneers in introducing and developing new sports, but it

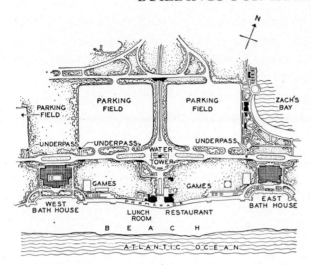

FIGURE 470.

JONES BEACH, NEW YORK.

PLAN OF CENTRAL PORTION

H. A. Magoon, architect

The demands for recreational-bathing facilities have forced the construction of many large beach developments; vast parking spaces, areas for games, and concessions of various types are here combined with the bathhouses in one great integrated plan.

appears to apply only in the case of football. It is true that under the influence of the *Turnvereins* and *Sokols* of central Europe these educational institutions did have gymnasiums even before the beginning of the age of sports. Recognizing early the value of physical development, they provided good demonstration centers once the sports appeared, and the larger ones developed prototypes for independent gymnasiums, stadiums, and swimming pools.

But fashionable society was more frequently the inventing and refining agency. It was a club of New York business men who in 1842 began to spend their Sundays in Hoboken at a game that later became baseball but for some time was played only by the well-to-do. During the Civil War baseball was the favorite pastime in the Union Army camps, and demobilization served as the means of disseminating it. This was the first sport to have a complex professional organization, and to its pioneering in that respect it probably owes its reputation as the "national game." A similar cycle of the importation or development of a sport as an exclusive social privilege, followed by its gradual popularization, can be noted in the case of tennis, golf, swimming, sailing, and other athletic activities. Polo alone has proved too expensive for the process of democratization.

The history of golf—for a long time the most exclusive game—is interesting in relation to urban land use. During the 1920's, when cities were growing rapidly, the game of golf transformed itself from the pastime of a few to a widespread and fashionable one. It took almost a billion dollars to snatch from the real-estate market the necessary land for the new courses situated in the path of suburban growth. Thanks to the depression of the 1930's, a large proportion of the courses are now publicly owned. In the future development of suburbs it is to be hoped that these approximately 5,000,000 acres of attractive landscape may be retained as open spaces, performing their important social function as greenbelt separators between the built-up zones.

The development of swimming, certainly of great importance to the national health, has paralleled the effacement of social taboos with respect to the public behavior of women. In 1938 there were 200,000,000 recorded sorties for swimming; the sport owes this spectacular development to the pleasure now taken in mixed swimming at public beaches (see Fig. 470). There was a time when swimming was definitely not considered ladylike, and the steps of transition to our present status of relative freedom in natatory dress and action are an essential part of our development in group behavior. The question of bathing suits still has an important practical bearing on pool planning and on water-purification techniques, as we shall see later.

One phenomenon of the nineteenth century holds unique interest in any study of sports buildings. This is the Y.M.C.A., whose leaders soon saw what was wrong with youth in the big city and attempted to provide the answer in terms of indoor sports and games in buildings located in crowded areas. By 1891 there were at least 250 of these gymnasiums, and the Y.M.C.A. needed a competitive indoor team sport to be played in them. In that year James Naismith invented basketball. Basketball is one of several games—football, rugby, soccer, lacrosse, polo, and hockey—in which opposing teams rush an object toward each other's goal. Basketball was the first to scale this type of play successfully for indoor application. The importance of basketball from an architectural point of view is great. Since by now it is the dominant activity in United States gymnasiums, both in area needed and in general popularity, it becomes the usual module for determining gymnasium dimensions.

To understand the role of sport in today's and tomorrow's society we must look briefly at another significant development that began when social workers established by private philanthropy the first modest outdoor public playgrounds in Boston and Chicago in the last years of the nineteenth century. These initial steps rapidly snowballed into a national recreation movement which is still producing great benefits in our environment. At first it was only very tentatively that playgrounds came to be associated with the public schools and that municipalities assumed the burden of providing and maintaining out of their tax income the necessary open spaces. But in a surprisingly short time all our large cities were deeply involved, and there grew up national play-ground standards, a recognized profession of playground leaders, a functional classification of types of recreation and recreation areas, and a philosophy of recreation. This philosophy vindicated all kinds of free personal expression at all ages as necessary to man's health because of the lack of variety, freedom, and creative reward in many of his industrial tasks and surroundings. During the inflationary 1920's there was an enormous growth of facilities for public recreation, but this record was surpassed during the depression, when the Federal government in its efforts to create employment spent over $600,000,-000 on new recreational facilities through the WPA.

Public recreation has thus come to assume its rightful place in the design of communities. City planners interlard their neighborhoods with measured areas for outdoor recreation and with community buildings that provide suitable indoor facilities. The modern concept of public recreation includes music, nature study, dramatics, crafts, dancing, picnics—in fact, almost everything people do together outside of working hours that is not provided commercially or in the home.

Athletic games are an important part of public recreation. In modern urban life they often provide the only possibility for the balanced development of the body. Before the playground movement began the nation was divided into athletes and non-athletes. The former were a fortunate few who enjoyed a combination of opportunity and ability; the others were interested in the games—but only as spectacles. We are now in full transition to a condition where almost everyone will to some extent be a practicing athlete in so far as such activity is desirable in making him a complete and happy individual.

Nevertheless there will always be sports professionals whose performances will attract large crowds. There may even be two versions of each game—one suitable for spectacular entertainment to be performed only by experts and another adapted for participation by those less highly trained; this trend is already noticeable in baseball and softball, in football and touchball. Numerous institutions for spectator sports are already in existence; the great task still unfinished is to provide facilities for the decentralization of sports and for their incorporation in the individual's daily life. Such a result of course will come about principally through the development of outdoor activities, for this is the simple, economical solution and has the further advantage of assuring for the city dweller some experience of outdoor life. Adjustment of workers' work schedules, adoption of daylight-saving time, and the night lighting of

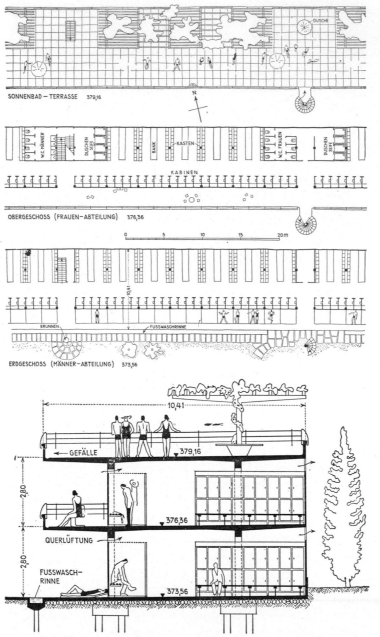

FIGURE 471.
BATHING
BEACH,
LAUSANNE-
OUCHY,
SWITZERLAND.
PLANS AND
SECTION
THROUGH
CABINS

Marc Piccard, architect

In many European communities the *plage* has become the opportunity for brilliant architectural compositions.

From *Moderne Bauformen*

athletic fields are developments that permit greater exploitation of outdoor sports areas. (See Figs. 471–473.)

In the matter of indoor facilities, the most interesting and difficult aspect of

FIGURE 472.
BATHING BEACH,
LAUSANNE-OUCHY,
SWITZERLAND. AIR VIEW
Marc Piccard, architect
From *Moderne Bauformen*

FIGURE 473. BATHING BEACH,
LAUSANNE-OUCHY,
SWITZERLAND.
CABINS AND RESTAURANT
Marc Piccard, architect
The long horizontals and the large glass areas harmonize with the lines of beach and shore and give a character of restrained and healthy gaiety.

From *Moderne Bauformen*

the new planning is the fact that sports will more frequently have to share the same building—and even at times the same rooms—with other kinds of recreation. For every building devoted entirely to athletics there should be dozens in which provision for athletics is made along with that for other functions.

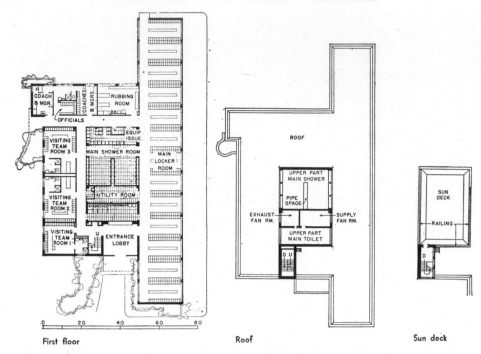

First floor					Roof					Sun deck

FIGURE 474. FIELD HOUSE, MASSACHUSETTS INSTITUTE OF TECHNOLOGY, CAMBRIDGE. PLANS

Anderson & Beckwith, architects

Dressing, shower, and toilet facilities for athletic sports include special areas for teams and for directors and trainers.							From *Architectural Record*

The program for buildings devoted to public indoor recreation is gradually clarifying. It borrows from the Y.M.C.A., from the post–First World War memorial building, from the athletic club, and from the gymnasium. The structure is usually called a "community building." Its athletic facilities include locker, shower, and dressing rooms, a multi-purpose gymnasium, and in extravagant examples a swimming pool. There may also be bowling, table tennis, an auditorium and/or a social hall, clubrooms, crafts shops, and a kitchen, with little attempt to draw a line between athletic and non-athletic activities or between children's and adults' areas. Ideally such a building will be closely associated with park areas so that the outdoor recreation can be combined with use of the building's dressing facilities. Community buildings are more fully treated in Chapter 45.

In spite of this widespread amalgamation of sports with other recreational

FIGURE 475. FIELD HOUSE, MASSACHUSETTS INSTITUTE OF TECHNOLOGY, CAMBRIDGE. EXTERIOR

Anderson & Beckwith, architects

Quiet, direct architectural design is appropriate. Photograph Ezra Stoller—Pictor

activity, there will be a continuing need for various buildings devoted exclusively to athletics. These will tend more and more to give precedence to the convenience of participants and to take care of spectators in a more incidental fashion. The limit of spectator recruitment has already been approached, but there are not yet sufficient accommodations for possible participants. The establishment of intramural athletics on a large scale, for instance, is so relatively recent at the universities that many an institution possesses only hurriedly built, inadequate structures. Such buildings should be replaced or expanded with a deliberation and a refinement in design that were not possible during the period of rapid construction.

CLASSIFICATION

Buildings for athletics may consist of either adjunct facilities or enclosures for the games themselves, or both. Among the first group the most necessary are the dressing facilities, including locker, toilet, and shower accommodations for the players; these occur in all but the simplest athletic installations. When they constitute a building for the use of athletes at a near-by track and field the unit is called a *field house* (Figs. 474, 475). (Often in the literature this term is used for the sports enclosure called a "cage" in the present discussion.) Such service spaces have a close functional resemblance to those at a public beach. Another important adjunct facility is a space for spectators. This varies considerably in size and form, culminating in the *stadium*.

An enclosure for indoor sports, which are usually played on a hardwood floor, is known as a *gymnasium*, a term applied both to the whole building and to the main room where most of the games are played. In recent years it has been found practicable to provide an enclosure, called a *cage*, for sports played on dirt; the playing period for these is thus extended beyond that permitted by the climate. Besides these two main types of enclosed playing spaces there are special enclosures designed for such sports as squash or tennis. The requirements for *swimming pools*, whether indoor or outdoor, differ so markedly that they will be treated under a separate heading.

An examination of these types will expose all the important planning problems to be encountered in buildings for athletics.

PROGRAM AND DESIGN

Dressing Facilities. Though only a limited number of systems for dressing accommodations are in common use and although the choice of a system is necessarily dictated by the purposes to be served, nevertheless imaginative analysis is often lacking in the design of locker rooms and an architect ought to review the possible combinations in the light of his problem before resorting to a conventional arrangement.

The solution of the problem is facilitated if we realize that there are three principal requirements: (1) a place to change clothes, (2) a place to store street clothes during play, and (3) a place to store sports gear between playing occasions. Various types of cabins, cubicles, lockers of different sizes, baskets, and supervised checking establishments are available. In order to design the best combination of these and to determine the proper size, it is necessary to consider the number of persons likely to be dressing and undressing at one time, the maximum number participating in sports at one time, and the total number of possible users.

At a swimming pool usually only the first two space requirements exist. Outstanding examples of European arrangements of dressing facilities occur in Louis Madeline's Piscine Municipale at Bordeaux and in Bad Fechenheim at Frankfurt am Main, designed by Martin Elsaesser. At other public baths in Europe the stalls or cabins are used for dressing only. The user arranges his clothes on a portable rack and, while still in the cabin, exchanges them for a numbered disk through an opening opposite the entrance. The attendants'

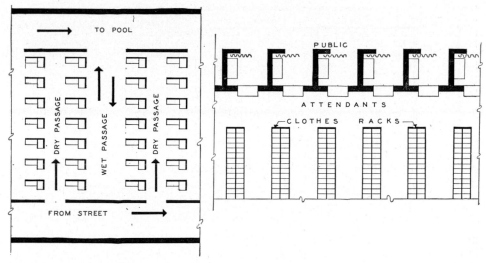

FIGURE 476. DRESSING CABINS FOR PUBLIC BATHS

LEFT: Based on the Bordeaux Municipal Bath; RIGHT: System used frequently in Germany.

space with condensed storage facilities backs up to this side of the row of stalls (see Fig. 476). Such an arrangement increases the number of employees but decreases the number of stalls to the maximum number of simultaneous dressers.

In the United States the cabin or cubicle system is uncommon for men but is often used in women's quarters to provide complete privacy. The arrangements are so well worked out at the Wellesley College recreation building, designed by William T. Aldrich, that we quote from the descriptive booklet reprinted from *The Wellesley Magazine*, April, 1939:

All who use the building report to the Matron, who has the approved list of swimmers, kept up to date from medical records. Suits are secured from her. . . . After securing this suit, the student enters the dressing room, where she secures her own bathing cap and shower sandals from one of the 500 wire baskets and locks her notebook or other valuables in it, and picks up a shower sheet from the open shelves in the dressing room. This sheet serves as a door to her individual dressing room, of which there are 84. After undressing, she wraps the sheet around her, puts on her cap and sandals, carries her suit, proceeds through the lavatory into the shower room, puts her sheet and suit on a metal rack, places her sandals directly below, and takes a cleansing shower with liquid soap. All but four of the showers are open.

In such a design the use of the dressing cubicle for street-clothes storage adds to the amenity of the system but requires more cubicles than if lockers were used for storage.

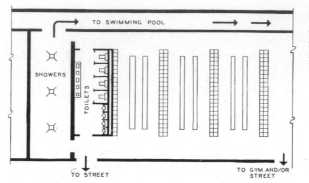

FIGURE 477.
AN IDEAL GYMNASIUM AND
SWIMMING-POOL
LOCKER ROOM

In men's dressing rooms the preferred installation in the United States is the locker room. Each subscriber has the season rental of a locker generous enough for all his requirements. This system is suitable for the smaller schools, for clubs, and for any organization that aims at frequent participation by all subscribers. But if participation is infrequent and the space between locker tiers must be made small for economic reasons, then the locker spacing begins to approach that of a book stack and is likely to produce a drear, cluttered area in which the long-term storage function predominates. Under such conditions it may be wiser to have a small-sized locker, basket, or tote-box system for such storage, in order to allow full-length hanging lockers far enough apart to provide good dressing space, circulation, and natural light.

In too many plans locker rooms have been squeezed into left-over basement areas of irregular shape, so that the layout is confusing and inefficient and the space is badly lighted and ventilated. This may be the result of too much emphasis on spectator space or on trophy rooms. The dressing function is an important part of the participant's routine, and the condition of the locker room can affect his enjoyment.

Figure 477 shows an idealized locker arrangement exhibiting the following virtues:

1. Orderly ranges, to facilitate the search for any numbered locker
2. Identical access to all lockers (no locker is crowded into a corner)
3. Locker bays related to windows and to structural bays for the maximum use of natural light
4. Direct access to each locker bay
5. Separation of barefoot circulation to showers and pool from the circulation used by those who may bring in mud from the street or field

It will be difficult to obtain these ideal conditions, particularly in the more sizable installations. In a large building with many hundreds or thousands of subscribers, conditions will usually be improved if the locker system is broken down into a number of units, of say 300 to 500 lockers, each unit complete with its own toilet and shower rooms and accessory spaces. This planning principle has an additional advantage: it lends itself to a piecemeal construction program in which additional units can be added at a later date.

The number of plumbing units is determined in relation to one factor only: the peak number of dressing facilities in use at one time. The most critical question is the number of showers. The designer must see that his proposed installation can process the desired number of people per unit of time during the period of greatest participation. Proper shower rooms require at least 16 square feet per shower head, not counting drying space. This may take as much again and ideally should be a separate room, with special heating or ventilation to reduce humidity. In many women's shower rooms, separate stalls and dressing spaces for each shower head are required. Sometimes each shower stall will have two such dressing spaces, one on each side. A number of other types of facilities may or may not be required, depending on the nature and purpose of the building. These as listed below may serve as a check list:

1. Visiting team room or rooms, large enough to include dressing space and lockers (which can be without locks) for a typical squad, plus a rubbing table, also a minimal plumbing installation, even if the squad as a whole is expected to use the main shower and toilet rooms
2. Private dressing accommodations for visiting officials
3. Offices and dressing facilities for coaches
4. Storage and dispensing of uniforms and other equipment
5. Drying room for uniforms
6. Dispensing and collection of towels (usually at drying room)
7. For women: hair dryers and make-up tables with mirrors
8. Rest room or solarium
9. Rubbing room, with rubbing tables and possibly devices for hydro-therapy and diathermy
10. First-aid room
11. Physical examination room

Stadiums. The eighty largest stadiums already existing in the United States have a combined capacity of 4,000,000 spectators. Add to these various other large ball parks, race tracks, and indoor commercial arenas and it will be seen that city dwellers, at least, can see athletic contests several times during the

FIGURE 478.
HENRY GRADY STADIUM,
HIGH SCHOOL,
ATLANTA, GEORGIA
Henry C. Aeck, architect

A high-school stadium with lower-level facilities for the R.O.T.C. and designed for both day and evening use.

Photograph Gabriel Benzur

season without crowding the facilities. The great period of collegiate stadium building occurred in the 1920's. In 1944, forty-eight of the eighty-three famous stadiums listed in the *World Almanac* were college and university stadiums. Apparently the income from those stadiums makes possible a rich and varied program of intramural athletics, and many colleges are committed to maintaining popular interest in their football teams. Such support may prove fickle, however, for as time goes on the public may prefer other amusements. The municipal stadium is obliged to strike a balance between commercialism and the community recreation program. It obtains its chief revenue from professional sport, rodeos, and circuses in order to be able to stage amateur sports, concerts, festivals, exhibitions, parades, and similar events involving citizen participation.

The most serious problems with respect to planning a large stadium are traffic, parking, and site planning; beside these actual structural design seems easy. The City Plan Commission of Kansas City, Missouri, in its recent investigation of the desirability of erecting a municipal stadium, obtained twenty-two responses to questionnaires sent out to leading stadiums, both college and municipal. The percentage of persons arriving by private car is estimated at from 15 to 30 by Harvard and at 95 for the Pasadena Rose Bowl; this reflects dramatically the greater dependence on automobiles in the West. Two-thirds of the stadiums, even including the Rose Bowl with its 32,000 cars, report

FIGURE 479. ROSE BOWL, PASADENA, CALIFORNIA; OVER 61,000
SPECTATORS. AIR VIEW

The enormous areas needed for parking around a large stadium.   Photograph Ewing Galloway

that their parking facilities are inadequate. The average recommendation of
fifteen stadiums is to provide parking space for one car for every 3½ to 4
spectators. At usual allowances this means that the parking area must be from
twelve to fifteen times as great as that for seating. When one considers that a
stadium must be located in or very near the densely populated areas it serves,
the dilemma of land use is evident, especially when it is realized how small a
fraction of total time these parking areas will be occupied.

In the design for the spectator portion, whether for baseball, football, track,
or a combination of the latter two, the architect is working in the field of
space engineering, with the aid of building codes and handbook rules of thumb
for his circulation arrangements and his sight lines. Two prominent authorities on this subject, Gavin Hadden and the Portland Cement Association, together offer the best exposition of the controlling factors.[1]

[1] *Concrete Grandstands* (Chicago: the Association [1940]).

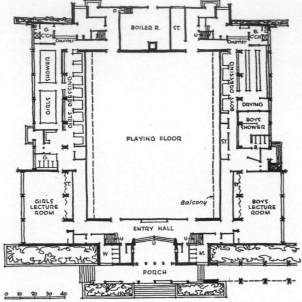

FIGURE 480.

HIGH-SCHOOL GYMNASIUM,
FLAGSTAFF, ARIZONA. PLAN

Edward L. Varney, Jr., and Frederick K. Weaver, architects; L. W. Wiese, structural engineer

A typical gymnasium plan for a large high school.

From *Architectural Record*

In determining the profiles of seating sections it is important to remember that an athletic performance ranges over a wide angle for the spectator and that the oblique lines of view are more important here than in a theater. A continuously curving oval in plan will help to bring the normal line of vision closer to the center of the field. This "bowl" form has another great advantage over a stadium with straight sides. It is a much more satisfying space to be in; the spectator feels himself to be part of a continuous fabric of humanity, every section of which is identically related to the central field. The stadiums of Vienna and Turin appear to be particularly harmonious in this respect. In the United States the largest stadiums, having a wider and higher band of seats in relation to the field area than the European examples, gain in their concentration of psychological effect by virtue of their great capacity.

More research is needed in exit engineering. Public safety regulations are understandably much less stringent for outdoor seating than for theaters and auditoriums. It is disturbing that stadiums in the United States have almost invariably been designed to minimum safety standards, and few refinements of exit arrangement or of combinations of exit provisions with structural ideas appear in the work here. More study will improve the solutions, but it must be based on a few known facts. Observation shows that an individual exit lane of 22 inches in width will take a maximum of thirty-seven persons per minute

FIGURE 481. HIGH-SCHOOL GYMNASIUM, FLAGSTAFF, ARIZONA. TWO EXTERIORS

Edward L. Varney, Jr., and Frederick K. Weaver, architects; L. W. Wiese, structural engineer

Simple construction and local materials brilliantly used to create a building of distinguished individuality. Courtesy Edward L. Varney, Jr.

and that this number diminishes in the presence of stairways or other friction-producing elements. As a design standard, five minutes for total egress is probably considerably lower than the average time required in existing stadiums.

Gymnasiums. In the United States the gymnasium, as a room, has taken a development quite unrelated to that of its European prototype. Thanks to Naismith's ingenuity, referred to early in this chapter, it is now designed almost entirely as a basketball court and is much less likely to be festooned with ropes hanging from the trusses or to be lined with Indian clubs, dumbbells, chest weights, and climbing bars. Conventional gymnasium apparatus is less and less stressed and is sometimes confined to a "corrective" room of minor importance. A gymnasium that satisfies the requirements for basketball can of course be used also for calisthenics, apparatus work, boxing and wrestling,

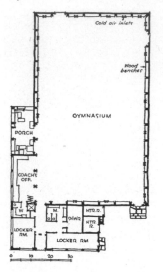

FIGURE 482. GYMNASIUM, SOLEBURY SCHOOL, NEW HOPE, PENNSYLVANIA. PLAN

William Hunt, designer; Morgan C. Rulon, engineer

A simple, useful gymnasium for a boys' boarding school.

From *Architectural Record*

badminton, volley ball, and various kinds of dancing, since the dimension requirements for these are less exacting. But well-equipped institutions pride themselves on being able to afford auxiliary rooms for such activities so that the main room may without interruption be used for basketball. The common former practice of building an overhead running track appears now to have been completely abandoned.

Basketball has been played in all kinds of areas, indoors and out. The optimum court dimensions as related to various age groups are now fairly well agreed on and range from 35 by 60 feet for elementary-school children to 50 by 90 feet for adults. Substandard sizes are often tolerated for practice purposes, and this concession leads to interesting combinations of courts, one of which can be made applicable to almost any situation. It will be seen that the over-all room area required under minimum conditions is only about one-third that for the maximum size; a room may be dimensioned to have three minimal courts placed transversely and when necessary combined to accommodate a longitudinal adult-size court for important games. (See also Vol. III, Figs. 367, 368.)

A number of combinations may be developed which when the large-sized court is used will provide for spectators in part of the area normally covered by practice courts. Figure 484 shows an arrangement with bleachers which fold against one long wall. These bleachers require less labor to erect than do the portable types, and they have the advantage of reducing to a minimum the time that the room is not available for play. The removable bleachers may also be

FIGURE 483.
GYMNASIUM,
SOLEBURY SCHOOL,
NEW HOPE, PENNSYLVANIA.
EXTERIOR AND INTERIOR

William Hunt, designer; Morgan C.
Rulon, engineer

Inexpensive and logical construction generates interesting forms.

Photographs J. H. Melford,
courtesy Solebury School

portable; they are used in combination with fixed seating at the gallery level
and have a steeper pitch. Fixed seating that begins at gallery level is seldom desirable except in large gymnasiums where it is necessary to accommodate great
numbers of spectators frequently; the sight lines are such as to make invisible a
wide zone immediately in front of the seats, and the exhibition court must consequently be at some distance from the seating. Portable bleachers are placed on
the floor between the court and the fixed seating. As at the University of Pennsylvania, in Philadelphia, such bleachers may roll on tracks and disappear under
the fixed seating.

One of the unsolved problems is how to obtain good natural light in gymnasiums. The seeing task for the player is severe, because he must follow the rapid
movement of the ball in any direction and overhead. When he sees the ball pass
successively in front of areas that differ greatly in brightness, strain results.
Skylights have been much used for lighting and should make possible a uniform
distribution, but they are subject to the usual difficulties, aggravated by the fact
that condensation and leakage are injurious to a hardwood floor. Most authori-

FIGURE 484. GYMNASIUMS WITH FOLDING BLEACHERS

ABOVE: Powell High School and Junior College, Powell, Wyoming. Cushing & Terrell, architects. Courtesy Universal Bleacher Co. BELOW: Bala-Cynwyd Junior High School, Bala-Cynwyd, Pennsylvania. Courtesy Wayne Iron Works.

Folding bleachers provide facilities for large numbers of spectators and do not take up floor area between games.

ties now recommend windows all along the upper parts of both long walls. There are several objections here, however. If the purpose is to avoid playing toward a goal on a window wall, what about the transverse practice courts so commonly used? It is well known that intermittent sun and shadow as well as

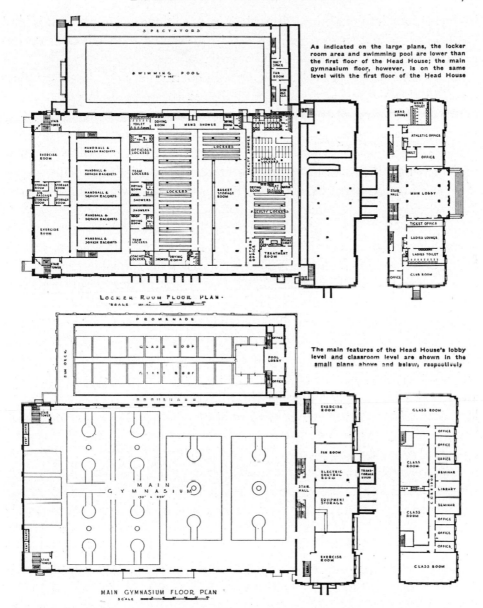

As indicated on the large plans, the locker room area and swimming pool are lower than the first floor of the Head House; the main gymnasium floor, however, is on the same level with the first floor of the Head House

The main features of the Head House's lobby level and classroom level are shown in the small plans above and below, respectively

FIGURE 485. WOOLEN GYMNASIUM, UNIVERSITY OF NORTH CAROLINA, CHAPEL HILL. PLANS

Atwood & Weeks, architects and engineers

Note the excellent planning which permits the swimming pool to be used by men, women, and faculty at the same time—by providing each group its own locker rooms—and also the grouping of the handball and exercise rooms. The slope of the land makes possible excellent lighting of the lower floor.
From *American School and University*, 1940

having to look into the sun are hazardous in a rapidly moving game. It is hard to understand how these conditions can be prevented with windows on opposite walls, only one of which can be north.

Windows also pose a problem of glare in connection with specular reflections on the highly varnished and unobstructed floor. This glare can be minimized by using ribbon-type windows to eliminate pier shadows and by having a large enough glass area to raise the general surface brightness and thus reduce contrast between window and wall or floor. The need for guards to protect window glass from breakage suggests the possibility of constructing these as a louver system to mask the glass against direct view from the floor. This would provide an indirect daylight system that might be nearly ideal, though probably costly. Still another approach is to omit windows and rely entirely on artificial illumination. Such a solution is undoubtedly better than badly placed windows, but even here it is not easy to devise equipment that will light without glare and with the simplicity and economy that usually are necessary in this type of building.

In the planning of the gymnasium building as a whole, it is important to provide convenient and safe circulation for the athletes and facilities for the access of spectators without any interference between the two groups. At colleges, where the gymnasium is usually a separate building, a kind of standard arrangement has developed, including an entrance lobby with stairs leading to the locker rooms and showers under the main gym floor and with other stairs leading directly up to the floor from the lockers. The swimming pool, if there is one, will be on the lower level with access through the shower room. This *parti* is unquestionably direct and economical, but it is not perfect in other respects. Unless there is a ground slope downward from the entrance (or a monumental exterior entrance stair), the lockers are in a basement without the beneficial effect of natural air and sunshine, and, even if there can be windows, they influence only the periphery of the wide area under the gym floor. There is strong objection to a basement location for a swimming pool. And ideally it should be possible to place all of the intensively used facilities on the entrance level.

The University of North Carolina gymnasium (Fig. 485) is a good example of the typical layout if one grants its basic premise. The plan of the lower level is excellent, especially in the way the pool is made accessible to men students, faculty, and women, and also in the placement of handball and exercise rooms in a block of uniform ceiling heights to economize on cubage and take advantage of the slope of land allowing windows at the lower end of the building. One wonders whether the slight difference in level between pool and lockers could not have been eliminated.

Cages. The term "cage" is here suggested in preference to "field house," more frequently applied to large shelters, to avoid confusion with the earlier and still cogent meaning of field house as a locker and shower facility to serve outdoor sports. Cages are illogical in that they seek to provide indoor conditions for games meant to be played in the open. In bad weather one might more reasonably substitute indoor for outdoor sports, but it is obvious that possession of a cage will permit a longer training period and will thus give a competitive advantage over an adversary without one. The *raison d'être* of the cage is to increase the playing occasions for outdoor games in bad climates and permit the development of a higher proficiency. Particularly at educational institutions the whole program of which undergoes interruption in the summer, during the best outdoor weather, the cage adds to the variety of sports possibilities for the students (see Figs. 486–489).

The dimensions of a cage are dependent on the particular sport or combination of sports for which it is designed. A cinder or board track of eight, ten, or twelve laps to the mile may fix the perimeter. Space for other track events or for a baseball infield will be factors. Certain universities use these buildings for football practice, and often tennis courts are installed. Bleachers can be set up in many different ways. The minimum usable size for a cage appears to be about 150 by 200 feet, and the general construction resembles that of a hangar. The playing surface is composed of various mixtures of such ingredients as sand, clay, silt, hardpan, marl, and peat, kept porous by sprinkling and dragging.

A combination of cage and gymnasium has been used with apparent success in a number of institutions; here a sectional wooden floor is put down during the basketball season and kept in storage at all other times.

Swimming Pools. The design of swimming pools is more adequately documented with well-studied standards than is the case with most athletic facilities. A belated but wholehearted application of sanitary principles has changed the approach from the casual improvisation of the early 1900's to the disciplined standardization of mid-century pools. In 1925 the Conference of State Sanitary Engineers and the Engineering Section of the American Public Health Association appointed a Joint Committee on Bathing Places, which prepared a set of standards—revised at least seven times, most recently in 1942—that presents

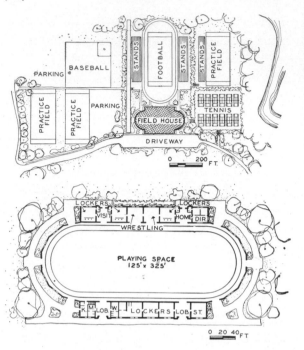

FIGURE 486. LAMB-MILLER CAGE OR FIELD HOUSE, SWARTHMORE COLLEGE, SWARTHMORE, PENNSYLVANIA. SITE PLAN AND FLOOR PLAN

Karcher & Smith, architects; Robert E. Lamb, designer

The cage requires a large unencumbered interior area.

FIGURE 487. LAMB-MILLER CAGE OR FIELD HOUSE, SWARTHMORE COLLEGE, SWARTHMORE, PENNSYLVANIA. EXTERIOR AND INTERIOR

Karcher & Smith, architects; Robert E. Lamb, designer

Courtesy Swarthmore College

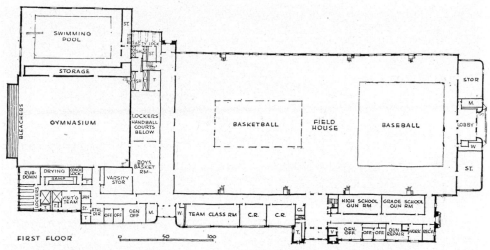

FIGURE 488. CAGE OR FIELD HOUSE, BOYS' TOWN, NEBRASKA. PLAN
Leo A. Daly, architect

From *Architectural Record*

an authoritative exposition of principles of design which have inspired many of the state codes governing swimming-pool construction and operation.[2] In 1939, Frederick W. Luehring published his *Swimming Pool Standards*,[3] based on an exhaustive and critical examination of current practices and tempered by his own long experience in pool administration in educational institutions. Since he disagrees in some particulars with the Joint Committee, both documents should be carefully considered in their entirety by the pool designer.

First let us review briefly the chief features which most experts now agree are desirable, though these may not always be found in the older pools. A large amount of sunshine is desired for both germicidal and psychological reasons. The promotion of algae growth by sunshine is apparently not a serious hazard—at least it does not deter those who build outdoor pools. An impervious, waterproof, smooth, non-slip, durable, and light-colored material is needed for the pool lining, curb, deck, and wainscot. Smooth-troweled concrete for outdoor pools and ceramic tile for those indoors appear to be the only satisfactory materials. All metal accessories must be non-corrosive. Competitive swimming demands a standardized length, the most useful being 75 feet. The width should be designed in multiples of 7-foot lanes. The requirements for

[2] *Design, Equipment, and Operation of Swimming Pools and Other Public Bathing Places* (New York: American Public Health Association, 1942).
[3] New York: Barnes, 1939.

FIGURE 489. CAGE OR FIELD HOUSE, BOYS' TOWN, NEBRASKA. EXTERIOR AND
INTERIOR

Leo A. Daly, architect

The roof is supported on steel arched rigid frames.

Exterior photograph Walter Craig; both courtesy Boys' Town

adolescents, non-swimmers, class instruction, meets, water games, and diving
need separate and careful definition, whether they are all to be combined in
one pool or provided for in separate pools. Continuous recirculation, with
filtration to remove foreign matter, followed by disinfection with chlorine in
such a form as to leave a residual bactericide effective within the pool, is the
only reliable purification technique thus far developed, and this should be

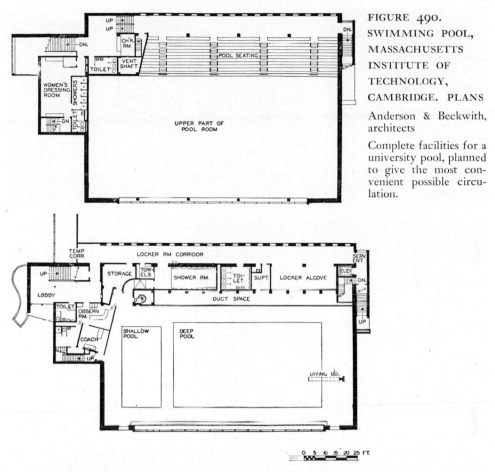

FIGURE 490.
SWIMMING POOL,
MASSACHUSETTS
INSTITUTE OF
TECHNOLOGY,
CAMBRIDGE. PLANS

Anderson & Beckwith, architects

Complete facilities for a university pool, planned to give the most convenient possible circulation.

under careful engineering control. The adjunct facilities should be so arranged that the swimmer is encouraged to use the toilet and then take a thorough shower bath with warm water and soap before putting on a sterilized suit. Wherever conditions permit, nude swimming is much to be preferred, since suits shed lint which is hard to eliminate from the piping system.

Certain other recommendations deserve emphasis because they are in conflict with commonly accepted standards. Clearances for diving, as pointed out by Luehring, are usually not adequate in depth and width for complete safety and good diving form. It is not helpful to use a tile lining tinted blue or blue-green; such colors make the water look turbid. The most brilliant blue comes from clear water backed up by a dead-white tile. The drain at the deepest part of the pool should be at the intersection of a side wall and the bottom rather

FIGURE 491.
SWIMMING POOL,
MASSACHUSETTS INSTITUTE
OF TECHNOLOGY, CAMBRIDGE.
EXTERIOR AND INTERIOR

Anderson & Beckwith, architects

Large windows flood the pool with light.

Courtesy Anderson & Beckwith

than toward the center line, for if it is in the latter position a part of the piping system will have to be buried under the pool. In the drainage of decks three solutions are possible:

1. The pitch can be away from the pool to drains at the outside, so as to prevent water from running into the pool. This arrangement tends to spread water splashed by swimmers across the deck.

2. The pitch can be toward the pool, and the decks will remain drier. The Joint Committee sanctions draining the decks directly into the scum gutters and thence into the recirculation system, but this method inhibits the free use of cleaning agents for washing the deck.

3. There can be a curb around the pool with the top pitched away from the pool; beyond it the deck can be pitched toward the curb. This scheme meets the previous objections but exposes swimmers to the hazard of stumbling on the edge of the curb; it is believed, however, that the use of contrasting colors for the curb and deck tiles will reduce this risk.

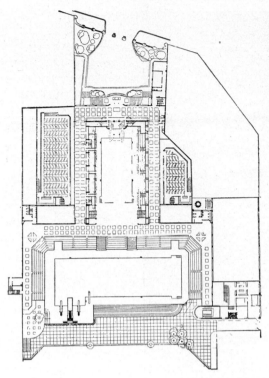

FIGURE 492.

MUNICIPAL SWIMMING BATH,
BORDEAUX, FRANCE. PLANS

Louis Madeline, architect

One of the finest of European municipal
swimming installations with both outdoor
and indoor pools and an excellent arrangement of dressing cubicles and clothes
storage.   From *Art et décoration*

Another area of disagreement is in the design of the so-called scum gutter,
with a lip at the surface of the water 12 inches below the curb, and there is a
definite need for critical appraisal of its utility. As Luehring says:

The functions of the overflow gutters as expressed in the literature may be summarized as follows:
1. To provide for and accommodate an overflow for the pool.
2. To remove scum from the surface of the pool.
3. To serve as a cuspidor.
4. To serve as a hand hold for swimmers as an aid for safety, instruction, and
   backstroke races.
5. To serve as a mechanical contrivance to reduce waves.
6. To help keep the pool surface level during races, thereby tending to make a
   fast pool.

Comment on how well the gutter performs each of these functions might
be summarized as follows:
1. The continuously recirculating purification system has no need of the
gutter to maintain a proper depth of water. The amount of make-up water

FIGURE 493.
MUNICIPAL
SWIMMING BATH,
BORDEAUX, FRANCE.
RESTAURANT TERRACE
AND VIEW ACROSS
OPEN-AIR POOL

Louis Madeline, architect

From *Art et
décoration*

needed is automatically supplied and has no necessary relation to the gutter. There is no need for water to "overflow."

2. In the daily cleaning of the pool when the water is calm and flat the gutter is probably a useful device to receive surface debris which can be cleared into it with a spray. But when the pool is full of swimmers and choppy waves the author of this chapter believes that the gutter does not retain scum, if there is any, and prevent it from being returned to the pool. It is hard to see how a gutter could be designed to do this.

3. If the gutter does not retain scum, its use as a cuspidor is to be deplored. It is interesting to note that the Joint Committee has dropped the term scum gutter in favor of "overflow gutter."

FIGURE 494. MUNICIPAL SWIMMING BATH, BORDEAUX, FRANCE. INTERIOR OF SWIMMING POOL

Louis Madeline, architect

The indoor pool can be opened out to the outdoor pool on fine warm days.

From *Art et décoration*

4. Hand holds of the bathroom type could be built into pool walls much more cheaply than gutters and would be more easy to keep clean.

5 and 6. During the design of the Massachusetts Institute of Technology pool an attempt was made to measure in the Institute's hydraulics laboratory the dampening effect of various gutter profiles on wave action. It could not definitely be shown that any such dampening occurred. Many coaches feel that gutters may cause injury on racing turns, or at least that there is a mental hazard involved, and gutters have therefore been omitted at the ends of some pools, without making them noticeably slower than other pools.

These doubts in regard to function do not necessarily eliminate the need for the scum gutter, but they point up the difficulty of obtaining quantitative information in regard to many details which have, so to speak, been handed down from pool to pool.

A challenging situation in regard to indoor pools in northern climates results from the peculiar heating demand. As a swimmer comes out of the water to rest on the deck, his exposed, wet skin requires unusual conditions for comfort. He will feel chilly at any temperature below 80° F., and if there is more than a minimum of air movement he will shiver even at somewhat higher tempera-

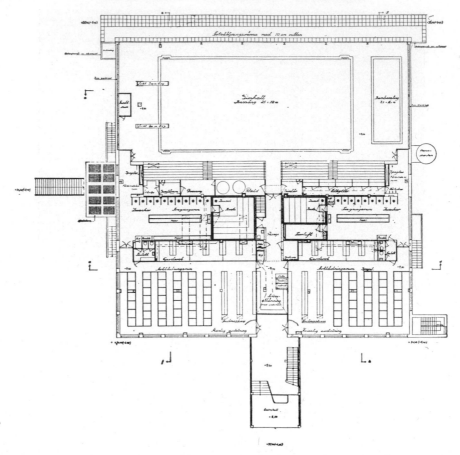

FIGURE 495. MUNICIPAL SWIMMING POOL, LUND, SWEDEN. PLAN

Hans Westman, architect

A beautifully studied municipal pool on a smaller scale.   From *Ny Svensk Arkitektur*

tures. If the pool accommodates spectators, these will be dressed for winter weather and will be located above the deck, so that cold air admitted for their benefit will fall on the swimmers and be felt as a draft. Large windows may also cause discomfort unless special measures are taken. The presence of spectators and the high humidity induced by evaporation make it impossible to avoid a considerable air change, which must be managed at very low velocities. Supplementary radiant heating by means of pipe coils embedded in the decks has been found helpful. Double glazing and abundant insulation in outside walls are desirable to eliminate cold surfaces.

The acoustic problem is hardly less severe. Large unavoidable surfaces of

FIGURE 496. MUNICIPAL SWIMMING POOL, LUND, SWEDEN. INTERIOR
Hans Westman, architect

From *Ny Svensk Arkitektur*

glass, water, and tile must be compensated for by absorptive materials on the upper walls and ceiling; these, like the other materials, must be selected for their ability to withstand condensation.

SUMMARY

A brief summary of the architectural characteristics common to buildings for athletics can now be made. An interesting phenomenon, for instance, and one perhaps responsible for the celebrity of Greek and Roman remains of this type, is the tendency of sports enclosures to have the quality called monumentality. It is their bigness combined with simplicity that accounts for this. How thrilling to the human spirit today to walk into a room the size of a gymnasium and find a high ceiling, no intermediate supports, uniform lighting, and no obstruction of any kind to mar the expanse of shining wood floor! In almost any elementary- or high-school building the gymnasium is the largest and most well-ordered room in the ensemble. Our stadiums are impressive expressions of our culture, although they are frequently marred at close range by bad detail. One thinks with awe of the scale of Jones Beach, Long Island, noting with admiration that an enterprise of this size can operate with such order and purpose. Even the smaller elements of athletic buildings—squash courts, shower rooms, rowing tanks, rifle ranges—are so completely controlled, each by its peculiar requirements, that they tend to have an uncluttered directness that is impressive. It is hard, indeed, to make a squash court look complicated.

The designer will do well to go along with this idea that the function of the enclosure is to enhance the game itself. In the Payne Whitney Gymnasium at Yale University, it is not the trophy hall with its stained glass and blackened oak Tudor Gothic embellishments which has the most significant architectural quality; rather, it is the exhibition swimming pool, with a truly ingenious and original system for getting spectators to and from their seats without the use of aisles, which represents the real fruition of the architect's skill in meeting his problem without compromise.

The design program of the athletic building is not an easy problem, but it is usually simple. It involves only a few fundamentals: orderly circulation, good lighting, good sight lines, cheap but durable materials, good proportions. Out of such basic elements the architect who keeps his eye on the ball—to use an athletic metaphor—can achieve noble results.

SUGGESTED ADDITIONAL READING FOR CHAPTER 47

American Public Health Association, *Design, Equipment, and Operation of Swimming Pools and Other Public Bathing Places*, prepared by the Joint Committee on Bathing Places of the Conference of State Sanitary Engineers and the Engineering Section of the American Public Health Association, rev. ed. (New York· the Association, 1942). This work has had an important influence on the raising of standards of design, safety, sanitation, maintenance, and administration.

American School and University (New York: American School Pub. Co., 1928–29—), an annual which frequently contains articles on athletics buildings.

Butler, George D., *Introduction to Community Recreation*, prepared for the National Recreation Association (New York: McGraw-Hill, 1940).

Concrete Grandstands (Chicago: Portland Cement Association [1940]). Good treatment of technical factors in the design of outdoor seating.

Dulles, Foster Rhea, *America Learns to Play* (New York: Appleton-Century, 1940).

Evenden, Edward S., George D. Strayer, and Nickolaus L. Engelhardt, *Standards for College Buildings* (New York: Teachers College, Columbia University, 1938). Its somewhat arbitrary quantitative criteria furnish a good check list if not taken too literally.

Houston, Ruth Elliott, *Modern Trends in Physical Education for College Women*

(New York: Barnes, 1939). Valuable only as a comparative study of facilities at seven women's colleges.

Lamar, Emil, *The Athletic Plant—Layout, Equipment, Care* (New York: Whittlesey House, 1938). Written from a maintenance, not from a planning, point of view.

Luehring, Frederick W., *Swimming Pool Standards* (New York: Barnes, 1939). By far the most authoritative work on this subject.

Margold, Emmanuel Josef, *Bauten der Volkserziehung und Volksgesundheit* (Berlin: Ernst Pollak Verlag, 1930). The good things Germany was doing in the 1920's.

Scott, C. A., *The Essentials of Swimming Pool Sanitation* (Chicago: Lightner, 1931).

Steiner, Jesse Frederick, *Americans at Play* (New York: McGraw-Hill, 1933).

United States War Department, Chief of Engineers, *Typical Layout—Diagrams and Construction Details for Recreation Facilities*, rev. ed. (Washington: War Department, Chief of Engineers, 1942).

48

Small Public Open Spaces

By C. EARL MORROW

THE SMALL PUBLIC OPEN SPACES found today in most cities of the United States are oases in the endless expanse of streets and buildings. They offer opportunities for meeting some of the needs that earlier were largely neglected in city development, namely, certain types of recreation and the attractive appearance of local sections or neighborhoods. Although small public open spaces have a variety of functions and characteristics, they may be divided for purposes of discussion into (1) squares and (2) small playgrounds.

SQUARES

The square, which may have any shape that plane geometry can define or any indefinable combination of shapes, ordinarily has a close relation to streets and buildings; usually it is partly or completely surrounded by streets bordered by buildings. In many cases city squares are accidents of the street pattern as originally laid out or subsequently modified; those in Manhattan along Broadway between Battery Park and Central Park—Bowling Green, City Hall Park, Union Square, Madison Square, Herald Square, Times Square, and Columbus Circle—are good examples. After the first rush of building development had passed these sites by as impractical, it was then recognized that they were too precious as open spaces to warrant their use for buildings.

HISTORICAL DEVELOPMENT

Apparently the squares of ancient cities originated largely from utilitarian motives—for example, the need for a market place, a function not altogether unknown today in some of the small American cities. In any case they always served as outdoor assembly places where meetings of various kinds could be held, including sports and celebrations. Around the squares or forums of ancient Greece and Rome were grouped the buildings which housed the activi-

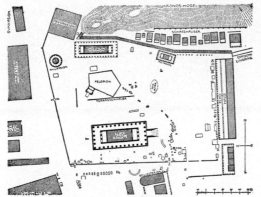

FIGURE 497. ANCIENT OPEN SPACES

LEFT: Olympia, Greece. From Sitte, *Der Städtebau. . . .* BELOW: The Forum, Pompeii, Italy. Plan.

Ancient open public spaces were essentially for pedestrians.

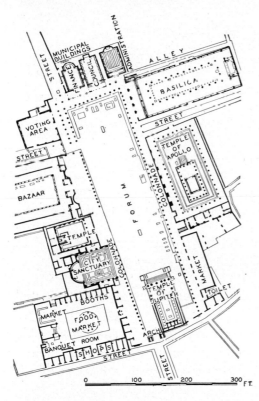

ties that involved crowds, either religious, political, or commercial (Fig. 497). The squares of medieval times predominantly functioned either as settings for cathedrals or as market places. During that period the squares, although irregular in actual boundaries, were carefully arranged to secure a sense of enclosure and to show to advantage the buildings which expressed the prevailing religious

FIGURE 498. TYPICAL
ITALIAN MEDIEVAL
SQUARES

LEFT: In Parma; RIGHT: In Ra-
venna.

Medieval public squares also
were primarily for pedestrians.
They were always important
elements of a city's pattern.
They served as gathering places
and for markets; they furnished
air and light; and they became
symbolic of the total community life.

Redrawn from Sitte,
Der Städtebau . . .

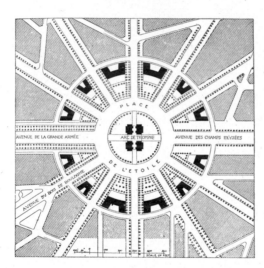

FIGURE 499.
PLACE DE L'ÉTOILE,
PARIS. PLAN

A traffic distribution point elaborated into a
large civic open area, which provides the
site for an important civic monument. In
this motor age such traffic intersections are
hardly the place for decorative development.

From Triggs, *Town Planning;
Past, Present, and Possible*

motivation of the age. The vistas of streets focusing on the squares terminated
in buildings (Fig. 498).

Subsequent development of the circle as a focal point of street and traffic
convergence abandoned the idea of enclosure and replaced the subtle combination of vista and balance with a comparatively sterile formality. Famous among
such circles are the Königsplatz at Cassel and the Place de l'Étoile in Paris
(Fig. 499). Suggestive of the modern traffic circle, they present some of the
same difficulties when saturated with vehicular and pedestrian traffic. In the
case of the French circles one of the considerations in their design is said to
have been that of facilitating the policing of streets. A single patrol force at
the circle could service all the streets converging on this point.

FIGURE 500.

THE PLAZA,

NEW YORK.

AIR VIEW

Carrère & Hastings,
architects

An excellently planned
square that serves as a
traffic separation point, a
sitting area, and an appropriate site for civic monuments.

Photograph
Thomas Airviews

FIGURE 501. THE PLAZA,
NEW YORK. A CLOSER VIEW

Carrère & Hastings, architects

Even here the congestion of traffic has interfered with the quiet serenity that such a
square should have.

Courtesy New York City
Parks Department

In the United States, except for the village commons and the town squares
of early American cities, the squares are largely the block scraps left over from
the application of the gridiron pattern of streets. Some of them were forced
because certain older arteries were too well established to be changed to conform with the rectangular block system; in other cases it appears that only

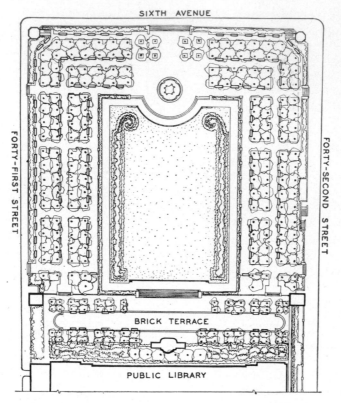

FIGURE 502.
BRYANT PARK,
NEW YORK. PLAN

The central grass panel is separated from the through pedestrian traffic routes, with the lower-level paths reserved for strollers; the panel can be enjoyed, however, by those who pass around it or sit on the higher terrace.

transit, computation sheets, and the convenience of the engineer's drafting board were involved.

FUNCTIONAL PLANNING

A functional classification would seem to offer the best opportunity for the organization of a discussion of squares. Since in most instances there will be a mixture of uses, the types are in reality determined by their dominant function. Public squares may therefore be grouped according to whether they serve principally for (1) pedestrian traffic, (2) adult sitting, or (3) other purposes, including their use as the site of a monument, as the foreground of a building, or as an island in the flow of vehicular traffic.

For Pedestrian Traffic. Assuming that a designer has as his main objective the planning of a pedestrian traffic square that will be convenient for the persons who will use it but in addition wishes to organize its elements so that it will also be beautiful, the question may well arise in his mind as to which should dominate, the utility or the beauty.[1] No categorical answer is offered to this question here but the designer is reminded that, where vegetation is involved, the ease of maintenance is an important factor and that worn-out turf, trampled shrubs, or scarred tree roots will inevitably destroy whatever initial aesthetic achievement may have been realized. Streams of traffic must either be provided with paths along the lines they would like to follow or else be diverted by effective barriers.

Most of the pedestrians who cross a square do so on the principle that the shortest distance between two points is a straight line. Some may go out of their way to pass through the square if it is a pleasant place, but most of them have in mind cutting across to save distance. They may not resent taking a few extra steps in passing a fountain, but low hedges and keep-off-the-grass signs are ineffectual when a considerable distance is involved. The direction of pedestrian travel is therefore one of the major design factors, and it should be based on a knowledge of the actual and probable future traffic involved. The designing or redesigning of a square may well be preceded by a pedestrian traffic survey.

In some squares a considerable number of people may stroll about during the lunch hour or at other times for the enjoyment thus afforded; to them the square is a definite objective rather than a mere point in passing. If the area is large enough it may be possible to reserve a section of it for such users by making access to it indirect. In Bryant Park, Manhattan, for example, the walks bordering the central turf panel can be entered only at either end of its main axis—from Sixth Avenue or from the plaza behind the New York Public Library (Figs. 502, 503). Normally, in passing through the park, people intent on getting to other points do not enter this inner sanctum. High stone balustrades flank the panel as barriers, but the passer-by can be close to it if he walks out of his way a little to enter the path that goes round it. No seats are provided within the central area; it is for strollers and those looking at it from without.

For Adult Sitting. People sit in public squares for several reasons. If denied the air, sunshine, and open space in their living quarters they may resort to squares to supply this need. They may be sunning the baby in his carriage, whiling away part or all of a lunch hour, or reading, knitting, talking—perhaps just sitting—as the shadows shorten in the forenoon or lengthen in the after-

---

[1] The existence of such a dichotomy in the designer's mind would be proof that the scheme he envisaged was completely false and that neither usefulness nor beauty would result from it. The true design achieves beauty through an imaginative handling of the utilitarian factors. Ed.

FIGURE 503.
BRYANT PARK,
NEW YORK.
GENERAL VIEW
AND TWO DETAILS

Beautifully simple plant-
ing and the excellent placing of the fountain create
views of interest, variety,
and serenity.

Courtesy New York
City Parks
Department

noon (see Fig. 505). The designer is host to these people and should arrange
the square so that it will be an agreeable place for all of them, with their varied
likes and dislikes. Some enjoy watching automobiles or pedestrians go by. Some
prefer a more secluded seat with an attractive view within the square or beyond
it. Some want to be in the shade and some want a sun tan. Some need variety
and like to change their seats from time to time. Obviously a stereotyped seating arrangement will not satisfy all these requirements. An informal survey of
the probable use of the square and the type and quantity of seating needed will
form a good point of departure for the designer.

A few general observations can be made about the placement of seats. Ordinarily they should be alongside paths or paved areas so that in walking to them
and sitting on them people will not harm the vegetation. Along most walks
it is desirable to extend the pavement under fixed seats so that they do not
encroach upon the space needed for the walk. Wherever broad benches that
accommodate persons seated back to back are used, the paved area should ex-

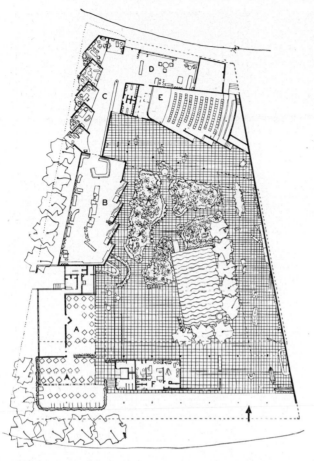

FIGURE 504.
SWEDISH BUILDING,
NEW YORK WORLD'S FAIR
OF 1939. PLAN

Sven Markelius, architect

This exquisitely planned and
planted court offers many suggestions to the designer of public squares.

tend under them far enough to serve as a foot rest for those with their backs to
the walk. Seats with backs are aesthetically more satisfactory if they have
shrubs planted behind them. For the small square, fixed seats are usually preferable to movable ones. The park departments of several cities have produced
practical seat designs of this type; masonry uprights and wooden lateral elements have been used extensively.

For Other Purposes. Squares that are designed principally as sites for monuments, as foregrounds for buildings, or as islands to distribute or channelize
traffic may also serve some of the purposes mentioned above, but in each case
special design considerations are involved.

The monument square is essentially a decorative element in the city pattern;
any other use must be subordinated to its memorial character. People may see
the monument from seats near its base, from paths or streets or buildings near

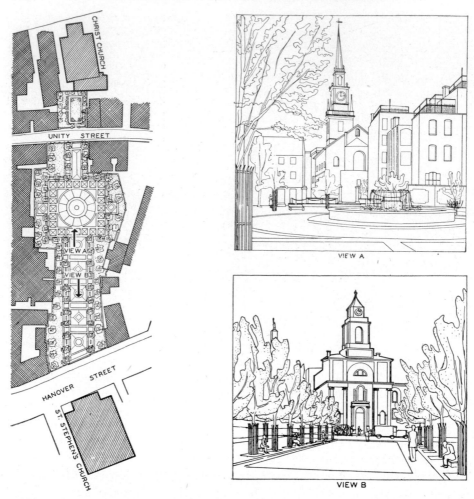

FIGURE 505. THE PRADO, BOSTON, MASSACHUSETTS. PLAN AND TWO VIEWS

Arthur Shurcliff, landscape architect; H. R. Shepley, architectural consultant

An open space in a city, connecting two historical monuments and planned to furnish an attractive sitting and strolling area in a congested section.

by, or even from the air (see Fig. 507). The designer's objective should be to create in the observer an impression of dignity and beauty. The permanency of the customary monument materials—marble, stone, or metals—suggests that the commemoration of contemporary persons or events be deferred until historical perspective has evaluated their permanent worth to the community.

If a square is to serve primarily as the foreground or setting for a public building it must meet the functional requirements for access to the building. These

FIGURE 506. A MONUMENT SUPERBLY PLACED. MONUMENT OF THE
REFORMATION, GENEVA, SWITZERLAND

An admirable use of a retaining wall on a sloping site.   Courtesy Swiss State Railways

include walks, drives, and possibly parking areas. In many cases it is preferable
to locate parking areas as an offset at the street line rather than to break up the
square with drives and parking spaces.

The traffic square, designed to facilitate the flow of vehicular traffic, is of
comparatively little use to pedestrians. If it serves as a traffic circle with a continuous flow around it, the pedestrian has difficulty in getting to and from the
center. Since maintaining complete visibility for drivers necessitates restrictions
on planting, such a circle is usually limited to the use of turf and low shrub
groups. If there is a grade separation of the cloverleaf or pretzel type, the volume of traffic and the distance from the observer make the square useful to the
pedestrian or near-by dweller only as an open space to be viewed from without.

GENERAL DESIGN FACTORS

Although the design of squares must recognize all the uses to be made of
them and will therefore vary with the type, certain general principles are
usually applicable, particularly in the matters of planting, service accessories,
ornaments, and pavement surfaces. Any general formulas for design patterns
or path systems are felt to be undesirable because standardization is to be
avoided. In fact, where a diagonal street across a grid system leaves a series of

FIGURE 507.
A MONUMENT IN A
SMALL OPEN SPACE.
MONUMENT
TO THE SWEDES,
BALTIMORE,
MARYLAND

Carl Milles, sculptor

Simple pavement and
planting give importance
to the monument.

Photograph
Robert Damora

open spaces of similar shapes, it would be well to make an effort to treat them differently. A triangle is one of the most difficult of shapes to handle, particularly when surrounded by streets on all three sides. It strongly suggests a central object which can be viewed equally well from all sides. As a variation the design may be related to a building opposite one side. The layout of City Hall Park, Manhattan, is suggestive of the possibilities in this respect (Fig. 508). Some of the small parks or squares of a former generation are good examples of what not to do; the design often consisted of a central feature, or perhaps two, looped in by paths which wandered off aimlessly in all directions. Apparently such plans developed from a theory that the square was mainly for couples who arm in arm would leisurely stroll around to admire the border shrubbery; or perhaps the designer at his drafting board was fascinated by the symmetry that could be derived with French curves.

Planting. The inability of vegetation to survive under average city conditions is the largest single factor which limits the variety of trees and shrubs available for use in a public square. For a list of suitable types, which vary with the climate and with the city, the park department that will maintain the square should be consulted.

Since turf has all it can do to keep alive in most cities, even under the best of treatment, it should not be used for people to walk on regularly. Prohibiting signs and a circulation system that is designed so that strollers will have to go

FIGURE 508.
CITY HALL PARK,
NEW YORK

The design of a triangular site related to an important public building.

Courtesy New York
City Parks Department

out of their way to get on the grass may keep most of them off; otherwise the area should be fenced in. In places subject to dense shade most of the day, a ground cover other than grass may be advisable.

Shrubs of certain kinds may be used; if of a thorny variety they may be able to take care of themselves. Any hedge that forces individuals out of their way may have to be supplemented by a fence. A generous use of shrubs may make the problem of policing more difficult and may even create blind corners that will offer hazards to vehicular traffic.

Shade trees are usually desirable in a square as umbrellas, especially if there are no trees along the bordering streets. In addition to hardiness under city conditions they must possess other qualities such as a deep-root system if they are placed near paths, a high-branch system that will not take all the surface sustenance required by the grass but at the same time will not cause trouble with sewer mains, and a hard wood which will not become brittle with age.

Flowers in squares add interest seasonally. They should be a part of the initial design rather than an afterthought. Formal arrangements should relate closely to the architectural features or to the path system. One of the common mistakes is to place in the center of an informally planted open space a circular flower bed aspiring to a geometric cleverness in planting pattern. In view of the exceptional cost of proper maintenance it is often better to count on shrubs for summer blossoms.

Service Accessories. Usually public squares are too small to have on them any structures except shelters or band stands, for such a project with a building on it threatens to become a building surrounded by open space instead of a square. Comfort stations are not only aesthetically difficult to provide in a square but also, because of the maintenance and policing problem, unjustifiable unless the squares are extensively used. If a public building adjoins the square, it is often better to depend on its facilities rather than to establish a separate comfort station in the square. When one is definitely required, however, an attempt should be made to subordinate it to the general design of the square. In some special cases it can be placed underground, as at the upper end of Times Square, Manhattan. Other possibilities include sinking it somewhat below the general ground level, incorporating it as part of a shelter, or screening it out by planting. In any event it should not be featured in the design of the square. Drinking fountains, another service accessory, should rarely be featured as ornaments. They should be functionally placed and designed.

Ornaments. The inclusion of such ornaments as fountains and statuary in public squares requires careful consideration. Appropriateness, scale, and proper placing are usually as important as excellence in the design of the element itself. Objects like fountains or shafts, which appear to equal advantage from any direction, can be used at central focal points; but objects like a portrait statue, which has a definite front and rear, should stand only at terminal vistas or views and be back draped and possibly flanked with planting. A memorial must have the importance and dignity of design and setting consistent with that of the person or event commemorated. Preferably the location itself should bear some relation to the subject to be recalled. For a more thorough discussion of memorials and monuments see Volume III, Chapter 15.

Pavement Surfaces. If a square is to be a pleasanter place for people than the street or sidewalks, it should have a pavement that is more interesting in appearance and less tiring to walk on than the ordinary kind. Where traffic is not heavy and the drainage is adequate a crushed-gravel surface is a possibility, though the problem of maintenance may make it undesirable. Often rectangular or irregularly shaped flagstones are employed with good effect, but the initial cost of these may be prohibitive. Asphalt mixes are sometimes the practical solution, particularly for informal paths, and an asphalt hexagonal block has been successfully used by the Parks Department of New York City. In order to permit absorption of moisture, any paving around tree trunks should be set dry, with wide uncemented joints. In New York City, Belgian blocks set in sand have proved both satisfactory and sightly.

In general it must be remembered that the walking surface in a square is primarily not for show but for use. A path may lead in a delightful way to a succession of interesting views or may focus upon an object that is featured, but any attempt to direct attention to it by means of special coloring or other devices is inadvisable.

SMALL PLAYGROUNDS

The responsibility of government to provide recreation areas was recognized too late to benefit the older sections of most cities. Accordingly efforts to correct this mistake by adding new parks and playgrounds have been expensive and ordinarily have fallen far short of finding an adequate solution of the problem. Failure to provide such facilities both in new developments and in redevelopments is inexcusable.

The place of the small playground in the total recreation system is in part indicated in the classification of recreation areas made by the National Recreation Association: [2]

In general, spaces set aside for active recreation may be classified under the following headings:

The play lot. This area is intended to provide opportunities for children, primarily between the ages of five and fifteen, to take part in a variety of fundamental and enjoyable play activities. It is perhaps the best known and most numerous of all types of municipal recreation areas. Most playgrounds in addition provide facilities which may be used under certain conditions for the play of young people and adults.

The neighborhood playfield. This area, sometimes called a district playground, is primarily to provide varied forms of recreation activity for young people and adults, although a part of it is usually developed as a children's playground. Frequently a section of the neighborhood playfield is developed as a landscape park.

The athletic field. This is a specialized type of center intended primarily for highly organized games and sports.

The large park. This area is intended primarily to provide the city dweller with an opportunity to get away from the noise and rush of city traffic, to refresh his senses by contact with nature. It affords a pleasant environment for engaging in the varied recreation activities which are usually carried on on this type of area.

The small playground may be included in one of the larger recreation areas, such as the neighborhood playfield, the large park, or the reservation, but this

[2] *Standards for Neighborhood Recreation Areas and Facilities* (New York: the Association, 1943).

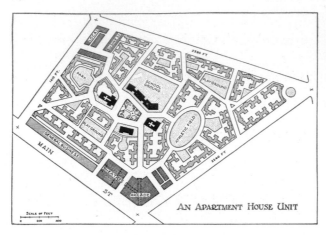

AN APARTMENT HOUSE UNIT

FIGURE 509.

AN APARTMENT
NEIGHBORHOOD UNIT.
PLAN

New developments or redevelopments of urban areas will include various small public open spaces.

From Perry, "The Neighborhood Unit," in *Neighborhood and Community Planning*, Vol. VII of the *Regional Survey of New York and Its Environs*

discussion is restricted largely to the playground that is a separate open space the size of an average city block, or smaller, and is limited principally to preschool and grade-school children.

City planners in the main are in agreement that the extensive residential areas of large cities should be organized into "communities" centered about the high school and that these communities within the larger cities, as well as those in the residential areas of the smaller towns, should in turn be organized into "neighborhood units" centered about the grade or grammar schools (see Figs. 509, 510). Since neighborhoods differ in the character of their population the playground requirements will vary. The following space requirements are recommended by the National Recreation Association: [3]

Present or Estimated Future Population of the Neighborhood	*Minimum Size of the Playground Needed*
1,000	2.75 acres
2,000	3.25 acres
3,000	4.00 acres
4,000	5.00 acres
5,000	6.00 acres

Another requirement is that the play areas be so located that children will have to go no more than a quarter mile—or at most a half mile—to reach them. As a result of these standards of space location, plus the fact that in most cases an area larger than a block is not available, many playgrounds are of the small type.

[3] *Op. cit.*

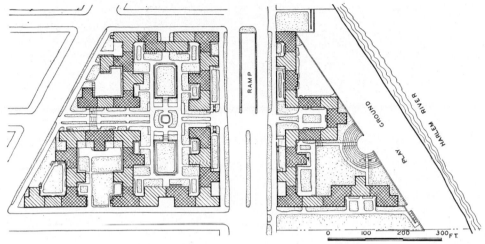

FIGURE 510. HARLEM RIVER HOUSES, NEW YORK. PLAN

Archibald Brown, chief architect

A central plaza, quiet side courts, and adequate playground areas distinguish this site plan.

FEATURES

Again quoting from the National Recreation Association's recommendations, a playground should provide most of the following features:

1. Corner for pre-school children
2. Apparatus area for older children
3. Open space for informal play
4. Surfaced area for such court games as tennis, handball, shuffleboard, volley ball, and paddle tennis
5. Field for such games as softball and modified soccer, touch football, and mass games
6. Area for storytelling, crafts, dramatics, and quiet games
7. Shelter house
8. Wading pool
9. Corner for table games and other activities for old people
10. Landscape features

The small playground obviously cannot provide all these features. It should aim to satisfy the needs of the smaller children, since the others can go a longer distance to the central neighborhood playground or playfield and since boys and girls over ten years old require separate play spaces, which are not possible in the small playground. Thus the small playground should have as a minimum

FIGURE 511.
EAST RIVER HOUSES, NEW YORK.
VIEW FROM THE ROOF OF THE TALLEST BUILDING

Voorhees, Walker, & Perry Coke Smith, chief architects

The design of open spaces in intensive developments must be carefully related to the buildings and at the same time designed for maximum usefulness with minimum maintenance.

Photograph L. Marinoff, courtesy New York City Housing Authority

a section for pre-school tots, apparatus for the lower-grade school children, open space for informal play, a shelter, and a wading pool. In communities consisting largely of single-family homes, however, most of the pre-school children can play in their own yards and will not need space in the playground.

GENERAL DESIGN

As a matter of general policing, ease of supervision, and safety, the small playground should be fenced in. Ordinarily the fence should be placed inside the property line 10 or 12 feet, not only to allow for shrub planting that will partly obscure the fence from points outside but also to reduce the noise and dirt that might become a nuisance to adjacent homes. Benches can be provided in the border strip next to the sidewalk to afford sitting areas for adults. There persons taking care of babies may park their perambulators while the older children of the family are in the playground.

Assuming, then, a playground consisting of areas for shelter, general play, and pre-school play, a wading pool, and apparatus, there are important functional factors to be considered in locating these elements in relation to one another. Since the shelter of a small playground must house toilets, storage, supervisors' rooms, and often an area for storytelling, crafts, dramatics, and quiet games, a central location for it is desirable. If an area for pre-school children is included, it should be near the shelter for purposes of supervision and prefer-

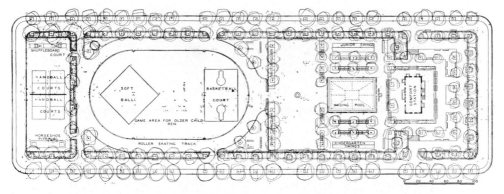

FIGURE 512. PLAYGROUND AND PARK, 35TH TO 36TH STREETS AND FIRST TO SECOND AVENUES, NEW YORK. PLAN

A small play park with various activities functionally placed, separated into age groups, and well planted. Note the sitting area at one end, and the handball courts and the large area for older children at the other.

Drawn from material furnished by New York City Parks Department

ably out of the way of the other activities of the playground. Benches where mothers can sit, which should be provided around this space, may serve as a barrier to segregate it from other areas. The wading pool should be placed between the small children's space and the apparatus area. The various pieces of apparatus should be grouped in one spot and so spaced and related that there is a minimum of interference between one activity and another. All open areas for play should be effectively separated from those for other activities so that there will be no danger of injury from stray balls or from older children's running into small children or apparatus. In open play spaces it is not usually regarded as necessary to separate boys and girls ten years old or under.

Although the playground is principally a utilitarian project, it offers opportunities for pleasing effects through proper arrangement of its elements and through planting. Shade trees are needed around the open play space and throughout the remainder of the playground; since appropriate varieties are limited, however, they should be selected with care (see Figs. 513, 514). Shrubs, except as hedges or foundation planting or outside the fence, have little place in the playground because they take up space and will not survive near a play area. Vines can be used to advantage on the border fences, and turf may be able to subsist in the tiny children's area and possibly in the open play space. The apparatus area generally requires a special surface, such as torpedo sand or gravel, loam, or limestone screenings free from stones.

FIGURE 513. PLAYGROUND AND PARK, 35TH TO 36TH STREETS AND FIRST TO SECOND AVENUES, NEW YORK. AIR VIEW

Planting not only decorates the area but also provides a sound barrier around the edges.

Photograph Thomas Airviews

BUILDINGS

The small playground usually has only one walled-in building, which may be supplemented in some cases by an open shelter; or the two may be combined in the same structure. If the playground is adjacent to a school, of course, there is no need for a building on the playground. With a central location the building dominates. Its architecture and landscaping, including approaches and foundation planting, present the best opportunities for giving the playground character and distinction. Ornament in either structure or landscape architecture can never succeed if it is merely an addition; it must be integrated with the whole design from the beginning.

The minimum requirements of the playground building are storage and lavatories. Storage space will vary with the amount of apparatus supplied. Often in the smaller buildings about half the space is used for storage and the other half for lavatories. In this case the director's desk is located in the storeroom; in a more elaborate building the director has a separate room.

APPARATUS

There are several reasons for including apparatus in the playground. The child enjoys using it; it develops his physique in a way that his other opportuni-

FIGURE 514.
BURR PLAYGROUND,
NEWTON,
MASSACHUSETTS

A playground may be attractive as well as useful.

Courtesy National
Recreation Association and Newton Recreation Commission

ties for recreation do not usually afford; its use requires less supervision per child than most other playground activities; and it permits intense utilization of space, which is often an important factor in city playgrounds. Safety is a major consideration in the selection of apparatus. A certain amount of danger, however, is usually necessary to enlist a youngster's interest as well as to further his full proper development. Some pieces of apparatus may be comparatively safe under supervision but too dangerous when there is no supervision or no leader present; at such times certain parts may be stored or tied up.

For the small children's area the sand box is perhaps the most useful element. The slide, swing, seesaw, giant stride, horizontal ladder, junglegym, horizontal bar, and traveling rings have all proved their value in the small playground. More elaborate variations of these simple types are sometimes used, including some of the gadgets normally supplied in a gymnasium. In their selection consideration should be given to the number of children who can use them safely with a minimum amount of supervision.

SUPERVISION AND MAINTENANCE

Supervision of small playgrounds is obviously desirable at all times in the interests of the children's safety, the development of a sense of fair play, the protection and proper use of the apparatus and other features of the playground, and efficient returns to the community on the investment involved. In many of the newer playgrounds, especially in housing developments, the older types of playground apparatus are often replaced with a variety of larger elements in concrete—pipes that can be crawled through or mounted, large tree trunks for seats or for balancing, and cubistic combinations of blocks

FIGURE 515.
PLAYGROUND,
JAMES WELDON
JOHNSON HOUSES,
NEW YORK

Julian Whittlesey, Harry M. Prince, and Robert J. Reiley, architects

Public housing projects recognize the necessity for play areas; this example shows the modern type of safe and inexpensive concrete playground equipment.

Photograph L. Marinoff, courtesy New York City Housing Authority

and slabs which can form little mazes or serve as playhouses, forts, or mere climbing grounds. Children seem to like them enormously; they have perhaps a more "natural" quality than gymnasium apparatus and can be more imaginatively used. Another advantage is that they are low in cost and present fewer hazards to eager children (Fig. 515).

Since the selection of apparatus and the general design of the area, including the planting, depend in a material way on the amount and character of the supervision, a definite supervisory program should be agreed upon in advance of the construction program and even before the layout is finally adopted. Ease of maintenance may decide either the success or the failure of a playground. Such matters as repair, painting, care of vegetation, winter care of drinking fountains, maintenance of play surfaces, and storage of apparatus cannot be neglected.

FUTURE TRENDS

Some of the trends in city planning and replanning offer clues to the future role of small open spaces. These trends may be grouped under four headings: (1) increasing recognition of the city's responsibility in fulfilling recreation needs; (2) incidental opportunities for playgrounds and sitting spaces afforded by new solutions of the vehicular traffic problem; (3) recreational advantages inherent in the expansion of suburban development; and (4) provision of small open spaces in urban redevelopment.

FIGURE 516.
PLAYGROUND,
PARKCHESTER,
NEW YORK

Parkchester Board of Design, architects

Private large-scale developments should provide adequate open public spaces.

Courtesy Metropolitan Life Insurance Co.

RECREATION NEEDS, A CITY RESPONSIBILITY

The master reference plan for city development which many a community has made or is making includes a recreation survey and a program for correcting the worst deficiencies in play space. By mapping existing facilities and drawing circles of influence about them, the areas lacking adequate recreation space are pointed out and proposals to serve as a basis for community action are outlined. It is significant that such surveys are being made on a more comprehensive basis than formerly and that they include recreation for all age groups and take into consideration the degree to which some of the facilities are supplied commercially or privately. Certainly more facilities for adult recreation and for recreational activity on the part of family groups will be called for with the shortening of working hours; also, general unemployment periods, as always, will accentuate the need for such facilities.

The City of New York has made outstanding progress in the provision of small playgrounds and swimming pools. Through the efforts of an aggressive park department, quick to seize opportunities afforded by the purchase of sites, the transfer of city-owned land, the use of land left over from street widenings or parkway construction, and the assignment of areas in the borders of large parks, about 375 new playgrounds were established in the 1940's. Observation has shown that many communities have tax-default land that is suitable for use as small parks or playgrounds, as well as other properties that can be exchanged for sites which in location and character are more suitable for recreation.

FIGURE 517.
STATION SQUARE,
FOREST HILLS
GARDENS, NEW YORK

Grosvenor Atterbury, architect

A small public open space has better chances for successful life if it is an integral feature of the layout rather than a mere left-over scrap of land.

From *Brickbuilder*

BY-PRODUCTS OF TRAFFIC CONSTRUCTIONS

As suggested earlier, the traffic islands or circles and the open spaces around grade separations of various types are generally so insulated by streams of traffic that little use can be made of them except as views. In cases where traffic lights make intermittent access possible, such areas are sometimes suitable for adult sitting. When scraps of land are left over from street widening or expressway construction their use for small playgrounds or adult sitting squares may well be considered. In determining their value for these purposes, however, it should be borne in mind that their area of influence is only a half circle because the street or express highway will prove a barrier to the people across the roadway.

Street widenings that involve a purchase of additional land are not expected to be extensive in built-up areas in the future, since the traffic gain to be derived from a mere widening of the street does not justify the tremendous expense involved. Expressways leading to the heart of the city are the promise of the future and have the support of a Federal-aid policy in their favor.

PARKS IN SUBURBAN DEVELOPMENT

Decentralization of residential areas, with their attendant local businesses and industries of certain types, is expected to continue absorbing new land at a greater rate than that of population growth. The Regional Plan Association discovered in one of its surveys that the built-up area of the New York metropolitan region increased by 56 per cent in the fifteen-year period ending in 1940, whereas the population increase was only 26 per cent. The comparative ease of establishing small open spaces in a new development is partly offset by lack of interest on the part of the local municipality. The developer whose interest in a subdivision vanishes when the last lots are sold cannot be counted on to provide them. The states, however, through enabling legislation, have made available to municipalities the machinery for controlling subdivision layout. The fact that the Federal Housing Administration requires a satisfactory layout before it will insure a mortgage on any development also assists this movement. For further discussion of these points see Volume III, Chapter 6.

The responsibility for preserving small open spaces therefore rests with the governing body of the city and with the planning board. This responsibility will be most readily met in new developments partly because of the fact that many of them will be on a large scale. Residential areas can be organized as neighborhood units centered about the grade school. The large playground or park can be related to the school, and the small open spaces can be located in places not adequately served by the central open space. This scheme applies to squares as well as to small playgrounds.

An example of a square designed as part of an initial layout is Station Square at Forest Hills, Long Island. Here the designers succeeded in achieving a sense of enclosure, but the square is at the same time a center of pedestrian and vehicular movement. The town of Radburn, New Jersey, shows an attempt to subordinate vehicular traffic to the general amenities of living, including a generous provision of open space.

OPEN SPACES IN URBAN REDEVELOPMENT

Redevelopment of the blighted or slum areas in cities holds promise, though the problem is beset with many difficulties. Since a single building or small group of buildings would soon be overwhelmed by the environment if in the middle of a blighted area, practically all redevelopment must be on a large scale. Many states have passed redevelopment laws with the object of encouraging the rebuilding of substandard areas by private initiative. The provision of small open spaces is the largest single factor calculated to produce the amenities of living which might restrain the urban dweller from the urge to take flight from the city. Although not in itself sufficient to produce the desired result, the provision of such spaces represents an important gain in the concept of urban development.

Public and private large-scale development to date has overlooked several important considerations. The *public* housing project usually has not been of sufficient size to comprise a whole neighborhood. In fact, many consider it undesirable that a whole neighborhood consist of a public project. Unfortunately projects of this kind have not been planned as parts of a neighborhood and at densities which the amenities of living require. Such *private* projects as Parkchester in the Bronx and Stuyvesant Town in Manhattan include many desirable features—open spaces, local shops, parking spaces, and recreation and health centers—but they fail in not providing grade schools within their borders and in their density of development (see Fig. 516). And by failing to include the most important socially unifying feature, the grade school, they fall short of becoming a real neighborhood unit.

Land values—or, more exactly, the prices that have to be paid for blighted land and buildings—have forced a high density of development. The city is to some degree responsible for the prices of sites because it has been levying taxes on them at fictitious values. Many persons believe that in the long run the city would be better off if it limited the densities to a more reasonable maximum and made up the difference by some kind of subsidy, possibly by paying for and maintaining a more generous supply of open spaces and including grade schools in the center of these. At any rate the small open space is an accepted element of large-scale urban redevelopment and will undoubtedly be included in the rebuilding of outworn urban areas.

BASIC CRITERIA

The small open spaces in the twentieth-century city should be something more than ornamental spots which the motorist hardly notices as he speeds by or merely outdoor gymnasiums for the coming generation. They are among the few city elements that are human in scale and capable of assisting the development of those personal contacts which are most important in the lives of urban dwellers as human beings. They tend to counteract the coldness and impersonality that steals over the city as it becomes engulfed with a solid and monotonous array of buildings.

With the reorganization of cities into neighborhoods, each with its small open spaces spotted like gems over the pattern, the compartments into which families are pigeonholed will become homes. A spirit of friendliness and pride will be induced. The city worker will no longer have to choose between grinding out his life in the forbidding metropolis or wearing it out commuting from the suburbs. The designer of the small open space may take pride in producing a plan that will look well on the walls of an exhibition hall, but he has failed in his task if he has not put first the consideration of its human use and enjoyment.

SUGGESTED ADDITIONAL READING FOR CHAPTER 48

Butler, George D., *Recreation Areas; Their Design and Equipment*, prepared for the National Recreation Association (New York: Barnes, 1947).

Hare, S. Herbert, "Chicago Planning, 1943," report of the Park and Recreation Standards Committee, in *Proceedings of the Annual Meeting* (Chicago: American Society of Planning Officials, 1943), pp. 106–12.

Hegemann, Werner, and Elbert Peets, *The American Vitruvius; an Architect's Handbook of Civic Art* (New York: Architectural Book Pub. Co., 1922).

Hubbard, Henry V., "Parks and Playgrounds," in *Proceedings of the 14th National Conference on City Planning* (Springfield, Mass.: the Conference, 1922), pp. 1–43.

Hubbard, Theodora Kimball, and Henry Vincent Hubbard, *Our Cities Today and Tomorrow* (Cambridge, Mass.: Harvard University Press, 1929), Chapters XV, "Parks and Recreation," and XVI, "Civic Centers and the City's Appearance."

National Recreation Association, *Standards for Neighborhood Recreation Areas and Facilities* (New York: the Association, 1943).

New York City Department of Parks, *Twelve Years of Park Progress* (New York: Department of Parks, 1945), p. 16. "In 1945—500 playgrounds—200 additional ones planned for early construction."

Regional Plan Association (New York), *Public Recreation*, Vol. V of *Regional Survey of New York and Its Environs* (New York: the Association, 1928).

—— *Rebuilding of Blighted Areas* (New York: the Association, 1933).

Sitte, Camillo, *The Art of Building Cities*, a translation of *Der Städtebau nach seinen künstlerischen Grundsatzen* (Vienna, 1899) by Charles T. Stewart (New York: Reinhold, 1945).

49

Park Structures

By THOMAS C. VINT

THE SUBJECT OF PARK STRUCTURES is broad and must be narrowed down for discussion here. There are many types of parks; the word itself has meant different things at different times. In the days of kings, dukes, and potentates, parks were set aside for the nobility or for the sovereign and his suite. Today the people are sovereign, and parks are established for the pleasure and enjoyment of the people. In a republic a park is generally thought of as an area under public ownership for public use and enjoyment.

PARK SYSTEMS

In the United States the national, state, county, and city or town governments, each in its own realm, provide their own park systems. In many ways parks are a measure of the quality of the government and its people; they may be symbols of the strength, the culture, and the good taste of the community.

Municipal. The city or town, in addition to having such spots of green as public squares or neighborhood parks, may take advantage of its natural endowments—bluffs, river banks, or lake shores—by dedicating sufficient adjoining land for park purposes so that they may be enjoyed by all. As the city or town grows and encroaches on the country the need for additional parks develops, and as the park system grows it may include—well outside the city borders—a country or rural park to provide a place for out-of-doors experiences often beyond the reach of the city boy. Such parks usually develop in regions dominated by a large city.

County. The county park system fulfills the needs of people from the various urban centers within its limits as well as from the rural sections. The demand for such a system arises from the increasing density of population as open land is occupied. Since there are many counties with relatively small populations,

FIGURE 518. MOORE HOUSE (*circa* 1750), YORKTOWN, COLONIAL NATIONAL HISTORICAL PARK, VIRGINIA. AFTER RESTORATION

An example of the preservation and protection of a valuable historical monument.

Courtesy National Park Service

however, the county is the unit of government that least often has a park department.

State. The state government serves a large segment of the citizenry. Its park system may either overlap or assume the functions of one or more county park systems in that it may reserve some of the countryside to fill the recreational needs of several urban centers. State parks often serve as places where people may spend somewhat extended vacations, whereas the use of city and county parks is generally limited to daytime visits.

Another important field in which the state park system has an interest is that of protecting and preserving the state's natural and historic heritage. Each state has some areas of natural scenery—important natural assets that belong to and should be protected by its people through the state government—the more noteworthy of which should be preserved from encroachment or exploitation. These tracts may consist of mountain or seashore, stone or sand, foliage or flower, or sanctuaries for the states' feathered, footed, and finny inhabitants which under civilization's impact are thoughtlessly extinguished by man or at best become his wards. Such asylums fortunately do not have to be built; they need only to be set aside before destruction has begun. Moreover they form admirable retreats where the people may enjoy themselves and enlarge their acquaintance with these wild fellow beings. Similarly, every state has various historic sites, treasured spots, and structures, each dedicated to the memory of a moment in the past, which should be preserved for inspiration and guidance today and tomorrow. (See Fig. 518.)

National. The national park system aims at the preservation and protection of the country's natural and historic heritage; it performs the same function on a national scale as does the state park system on the state level. It does not provide recreation areas in the usual sense, since that is considered a state and local function. National parks in the United States include such great scenic spots as the Grand Canyon, Yosemite, the Great Smoky Mountains, and also the locations of the country's great historical monuments as well as buildings in which famous Americans have lived and worked.

PARK DESIGN

Public parks—whether municipal, state, or national—fill a need not always recognized in the life of the people. In the newer regions a far-sighted public will set aside a natural beauty spot before reclamation becomes necessary. The way in which people work and live is a major influence which affects the design and scope of park systems, but in our changing times our parks have not kept up with the changing demands or fulfilled the new needs. The public itself moves slowly in its own behalf.

Transitional Influences. During the twentieth century transportation has greatly changed. In 1900 the horse-and-buggy as a means of private transportation was available only to limited numbers. The electric tram had not fully replaced the horse car, and the automobile was yet a novelty. That novelty, although it has long since come into everyday use, is still creating unmanageable problems. We cannot keep up with it. In the beginning, at twenty miles an hour, the motor car carried a man in a couple of hours as far as the horse had taken him in a hard day's travel. When the century was a quarter gone, paved highways were in the making, but even so forty miles an hour was fast driving. Today the speed is seventy miles an hour, although most of our highway system is largely designed for traffic at forty miles an hour. And yet, although the automobile has still not been entirely fitted into our daily life, we already have the airplane entering on the scene and exerting a growing effect on how we live.

What has been the influence of these transitions on parks and their structures? The motor car first made the country available to the city dweller. As he enlarged his radius and gained experience he became more discerning and sought out places of importance and of beauty. This trend has given impetus to the protection of the natural and historical spots and made them units in our state and national park systems. Thus the motorist has influenced the establishment of state parks in order that the precious outdoor beauty spots and historical monuments may have protection.

City parks fill much the same need as they did before the advent of the automobile; they afford places where people may go afoot to get fresh air and see green landscapes, and they also furnish areas for recreation. Not all individuals are motorists, nor is the motorist on wheels every day; therefore the retreat in the city still has its place. Some horse-and-buggy park roads have been changed to footpaths; others have been changed to motor roads. This change, however, has not always been for the good. Too often the motor road has crowded out other park functions, which have not been provided for elsewhere. The traffic on many such roads is so dense that these recreational areas no longer serve the motorist as parks but have become merely parts of a route from one place to another.

The parkway has developed with the motor car. As a motorists' park it has taken two chief forms: in one it becomes part of a developed highway system restricted to passenger car traffic, with a wide right of way planted like a park and with limited access points; in the other it is conceived primarily as a park and attracts traffic because of the pleasure of driving over it. The latter type is an elongated park which may connect several local parks and provide the motorist with a parklike thoroughfare between outstanding points of interest. It is an excellent means of unfolding a region to the traveler.

General Factors. A park in the heart of a city may be more formal and architectural than one in the outskirts. It may assume a design similar to that of a roof garden. The footpath to accommodate the traffic may be both wider and harder; here a paved surface is preferable to gravel because it will resist more moving feet per hour for more hours of the day rather than because of any architectural effect it may produce. Such considerations hold throughout the design. Trees and grass are used more than shrubbery, which catches trash and cannot take the abuse usually meted out by those who leave the designed pathways. Similarly benches, pools, and other structures, besides filling the need that suggests them, must be designed primarily to resist any careless and destructive treatment at the hands of the hordes that use them and only second-arily for beauty of form.

In a national park dedicated to the preservation of a piece of nature's handi-work, the general scheme has taken shape before the park designer begins. Such great natural landscapes are to be held in trust for the enjoyment of both present and future generations. The problem is to decide how man can intro-duce the necessary facilities to permit him to find his way about in order to see and enjoy the things the area has to offer. Man today in rambling through the woods or the desert lacks the faculty of the Indian to get about without a track before him, nor can he ramble without leaving a wider track behind. And he cannot live off the country; his way is more civilized. He is helpless without rubber tires and a paved track to run them on—and without tin cans to eat from, which too often are left as evidence that he has been there. Al-though he might wish to awaken the dormant Daniel Boone within him and embark afoot on a cross-country excursion beyond the limits of the road sys-tem, he must have the trail graded and marked with directive signs (see Fig. 541).

Since people come in large numbers—usually in their own cars—and for a short time, a road system is designed to make the important attractions reason-ably accessible. Tourist centers are provided where visitors can obtain meals and stay overnight. Many of these centers take on the proportions of a small town and include a hotel or lodge, a cabin camp, a camp ground and picnic area, a store, and a lunchroom or cafeteria. Information centers, usually with a museum that tells the story of the park, are furnished for guidance. All these facilities are further supported by the necessary service or utility buildings which house the activities of the maintenance and protection forces. The housing of employees in dormitories, houses, and cabins is another essential consideration.

In the historical park the same underlying principles of preservation and protection prevail as in the natural park. The problem here is to preserve some-thing that has felt the influence of man—to preserve the scene as it existed at a particular moment. Old buildings play an important part in this type of park, and their preservation and restoration comprise a field in itself. There is a growing interest in historic sites—possibly one of the benefits derived from the motor age. Research today is more thorough and dependable than formerly. There is more respect for the *real thing*, even though it may be only a fragment, than for a replica. A wider distinction is made between repair and restoration.

In short, the general knowledge and treatment of historic structures are now the field of specialists.

Structures as Part of the Design. A park is primarily a landscape design—an out-of-doors construction—in which structures may be introduced and of which they then become a component part, just as a fireplace or a piece of furniture is fitted into and made part of an interior. Park structures should do their work quietly, even anonymously. Each has its function, its place, its reason for being. Thus park design differs from the design of the site of an important building—a state capitol, for example—or that of a building group like a college campus. Although such sites may have a parklike appearance and to a degree serve as parks, their main purpose is to provide an appropriate setting for important structures; their use as parks is incidental.

Buildings that do not belong in a park are often found there. Many a good building—a beautiful one perhaps that houses some worthy institution—has been built on park land to save the cost of a site. Museums, libraries, schools, and memorials are examples of such intruders. If the problem had been reasoned out without emotion, the library or museum could probably have been built on another site purchased for the purpose—greatly to its advantage and at the same time avoiding a disruption of the park plan. To many eyes park land is merely vacant land. Such vacant land is essential to a crowded community, yet it is the kind of land which the public finds most difficult to acquire and the hardest to hold for the use intended for it.

SMALL PARK STRUCTURES

The true park structures are the small ones—the signpost, the comfort station, the park bench, the shelter, and the small bridge. These conveniences are generally necessary to Homo sapiens in his outdoor recreation, and most of them are found in all parks.

Comfort Stations. The comfort station is a common requirement in parks. A designer embarking on a park project should pursue the study of these facilities thoroughly; he will find there is much to learn.

In its generally accepted meaning, the comfort station is a building equipped with flush toilet facilities as distinguished from the more primitive privy not so equipped. Because of the higher standard of sanitation provided, such stations, complete with sewage disposal by means of natural processes, should be used wherever physical and economic conditions make their adoption possible. If the station is located in an area subject to freezing temperatures and if at

FIGURE 519.

TWO COMFORT STATIONS,
SHENANDOAH NATIONAL
PARK, VIRGINIA, AND
MOUNT RAINIER
NATIONAL PARK,
WASHINGTON

Comfort stations are required in nearly all parks; they should be accessible but unobtrusive.

Courtesy National Park Service

such times it is not heated, provision must be made for completely draining all piping and fixtures. In parks, even more than elsewhere, comfort stations should be equipped with fixtures and finished with materials which render the maintenance problem comparatively simple. Adequate ventilation and outside light are essential to sanitation and cleanliness.

Where the station is not a part of a building that houses other park facilities it should be properly subordinated by its location to obviate the necessity for embellishing it structurally. A preferable and usually more effective alternate solution is to screen both the building and the approach to it by planting and by a careful choice of site (see Fig. 519). Yet such subordination should not be so complete as to prevent the structure's being readily found by the park visitor. Often the comfort station is incorporated in a park building that serves other park needs. In such cases it is generally desirable to provide direct outside entrances in addition to inside communication. Some park patrons may feel reluctant to make use of toilets that require approach through a lodge or concession and thus seem to be intended only for its guests or patrons. If intended for use by the general public, there should be no confusion on the score of their accessibility.

Closely related to comfort stations are the utilities buildings required for some types of camp areas or trailer parks. These contain not only men's and women's toilets but also showers or bathrooms for men and women and frequently even laundry facilities—tubs and coin-in-the-slot washing machines. They should be placed conveniently in central locations so that distances to all tent platforms and trailer locations are minimized. A large camp may require several such structures.

Park Benches. The park bench is another essential facility and one that must be furnished in quantity in most parks. It is important to consider these a primary element in the design in order to avoid the confusion that comes from sprinkling them here and there as an afterthought—a confusion that will undoubtedly occur if they are not made a part of the original design, for benches are a necessity. Choice of a reasonably suitable type of bench design is also mandatory.

Foremost among the functions of benches in parks is their use in conjunction with picnic areas. There a combination of benches and tables will create units that are not easily moved about yet provide the visitors with essential conveniences for preparing and serving food. The installation of such picnic facilities will also assist in limiting such activities to the designated areas and thus help to simplify park maintenance. If the units are portable, greater flexibility is possible because the accommodations can easily be increased in a given area or changed to a new location to allow the grounds to recover if they have been badly worn by too intensive use. Fixed benches and tables are not recommended where it is probable that the area will be used excessively, for in that case the area must periodically be denied to visitors during regeneration of the plant life.

In a well-planned park the benches or seats will be strategically placed not only along trails to afford weary hikers a place to rest after a particularly difficult climb but also at overlooks for the comfort of persons who wish to contemplate a fine view or an object of interest. Fixed benches of logs or heavy slabs—or stone steps arranged concentrically on sloping ground around a stage—may create an interesting theater for the production of outdoor plays, athletic contests, lectures, and other appropriate entertainments.

The design of the bench will vary with its environs. In wooded areas a simple split log or stone slab may suffice; in the concentrated areas of city parks, picnic areas, and beaches, however, a more formal type of seating is appropriate. The designer must use his ingenuity in the selection of materials, the design and execution, and the placing of benches in appropriate settings.

FIGURE 520.
CITY-TYPE SHELTER:
BUS SHELTER AT
FRESH MEADOWS
HOUSING
DEVELOPMENT,
QUEENS, NEW YORK

Voorhees, Walker, Foley
& Smith, architects

The chief essential is
overhead protection from
sun and rain.

Photograph
Talbot Hamlin

FIGURE 521.
SHELTER,
CUMBERLAND KNOB,
BLUE RIDGE
PARKWAY,
NORTH CAROLINA

Shelters may be desirable
at points providing a
view.

Courtesy National
Park Service

FIGURE 522.
TRAILSIDE SHELTER,
GRAND CANYON
NATIONAL PARK,
ARIZONA

Trailside shelters serve as
resting places and offer
protection from sun and
shower.

Courtesy National
Park Service

Shelters. The shelter is also a park necessity; it may even, unjustifiably perhaps, take first place as a suggested need when the requirements for a park are
being outlined. (Incidentally, it is a favorite choice for a gift to the park or for
a memorial.) But it can equally well take first place among the common mistakes in park or park-structure design, because it is a difficult element both to

locate and to design and the most difficult of all to analyze to determine its exact requirements. A shelter can mean many things and fit many situations, each of which raises a separate problem. Too often shelters, instead of being designed to fit a need, are created chiefly for the purpose of serving as an outlet for someone's ego—merely to satisfy perhaps the pride of a commissioner, of a philanthropic citizen or organization, or of its designer.

In size and furnishings, park shelters may range from small simple structures that protect a trailside bench or exhibit to large complex buildings that serve the many needs of a heavily used park. The chief essential is overhead protection from the sun and rain (Figs. 520–522). This theme may be progressively developed into enclosed, heated structures for winter use which in their functions approach concession buildings. Shelters equipped with fireplaces and with fixed and movable benches and tables are popular in picnic grounds, and in some areas of abnormal rainfall they have become an accepted requirement. In addition to serving as picnic and trailside structures, shelters may be effectively used at overlooks of outstanding scenic interest, in playgrounds, at bus stops, and at other locations where protection must be provided for either long or short periods. For the accommodation of groups of hikers, overnight shelters of simple design, usually closed on three sides and containing elementary cooking and sleeping facilities, are placed along trails in the back country of some of our more extensive parks.

There is no hard-and-fast rule to follow in either the design or the selection of materials for shelters. If stone and timber are available, these materials may be used effectively in the rugged areas where a rustic character is considered appropriate. In city parks and playgrounds the design and materials may conform to conventional urban construction and more formal surroundings.[1]

Bridges. Bridges for both foot and vehicular traffic are high on the list of necessary park structures. Here their architectural and structural design has the same elements as elsewhere, but it seems to be accepted that more consideration can justifiably be given to looks than is the case with bridges in other locations. Sometimes, unfortunately, a park bridge expresses an effort for effect in louder tones than those in which it proclaims its fitness.

Bridges for foot and horseback trails are not subject to the rigid requirements of location and structural capacity exacted of bridges for motor roads (Figs. 523–525). In many instances trail bridges may be reduced in number or omitted altogether either by grade adjustments or by relocation of the trails.

[1] See also Chap. 48, "Small Public Open Spaces."

FIGURE 523. TRAIL BRIDGE, YOSEMITE NATIONAL PARK, CALIFORNIA

Trail bridges are simple and informal.   Courtesy National Park Service

FIGURE 524.

TWO RUSTIC BRIDGES

LEFT: Cantilever footbridge, Great Smoky Mountains National Park, Tennessee; BELOW: Horse trail bridge, Great Smoky Mountains National Park, Tennessee.

Courtesy National Park Service

Most of these bridges are a development of such crossing devices as fallen trees, simple log structures spanning a stream, or pier-and-beam constructions for crossings too long for single spans.

The choice of materials in the design of road bridges should be predicated on their visibility from various points in the park and on the materials readily available. Rough rock-face stone, if available, is the ideal material for harmony with most park scenery of a rustic nature (Fig. 526). Whether the bridge shall have a semicircular, segmental, elliptical, or flat arch will depend largely on its site; in modern parkway construction, too, bridges must conform to the road

FIGURE 525. HORSE TRAIL BRIDGE,
GREAT SMOKY MOUNTAINS NATIONAL PARK,
TENNESSEE

The smaller bridges in parks are kept unobtrusive and,
as far as possible, blended into the natural environment.

Courtesy National Park Service

FIGURE 526.

TWO STONE BRIDGES

LEFT: Linville River Bridge, Blue
Ridge Parkway, North Carolina;
BELOW: Bridge over St. Mary's
River, Glacier National Park,
Montana

Rough rock-face stone harmonizes
well with most park scenery.

Courtesy National Park Service

alignment. Where the bridge is not conspicuous from the sides or from below
and where a rustic appearance is unnecessary, the use of steel or concrete is
recommended if either of these materials is more economical than stone (Figs.
527, 528). To avoid obstructing the view of the motorist, either the stone or

FIGURE 527.
STEEL AND
CONCRETE BRIDGE,
BLUE RIDGE
PARKWAY,
NORTH CAROLINA

Where a rustic appear-
ance is not necessary, steel
and concrete may be the
most desirable materials.

Courtesy National
Park Service

FIGURE 528.
STEEL AND STONE
BRIDGE AFFORDING
MAXIMUM
VISIBILITY,
GLACIER
NATIONAL PARK,
MONTANA

The view must not be ob-
structed.

Courtesy National
Park Service

concrete parapets should be kept as low as safety will permit or open steel railings should be employed. If pedestrians as well as vehicular traffic are to use the proposed bridges, raised walkways should be provided.[2]

LARGER PARK STRUCTURES

The larger park structures house facilities for specific activities. Certain sections of the park may be set aside for such purposes as games, picnics, a zoo, or a place to dine. In large state or national parks it may be necessary to include hotels or lodges for overnight accommodation. A chapter could be devoted to the special problems involved in providing for any of these functions. The plan is most important and should receive more attention than is usually given to it. Particularly essential are opportunities for the expansion of activities over unroofed terraces for peak crowds in fine weather and of their contraction to fit into the roofed sections for smaller groups in poor weather. The problem

[2] See also Chap. 38, "Bridges and Highway Architecture."

FIGURE 529.

ADMINISTRATION BUILDING,
GREAT SMOKY MOUNTAINS
NATIONAL PARK,
GATLINBURG, TENNESSEE.
GENERAL VIEW AND DETAIL

Administration buildings should be efficient,
simple, easy to find, but at the same time they
should harmonize with the landscape and express the park's purpose.

Courtesy National Park Service

is a rewarding one for the designer who will really give it imaginative thought.

Administration Buildings. Those buildings which serve the administration and maintenance activities of a park organization offer a challenge to the designer in fitting the structure to its purpose. Too often these activities are housed in a plant originally erected to fulfill another function. An analysis of the activities to be accommodated must be made, and a design that incorporates them efficiently will result in a saving in administrative costs.

Museums. The museums situated in natural parks are for the most part intended to present an interpretation of the area. Both the structure and the exhibits should make use of material indigenous to the immediate locality and should confine the methods of presentation to identification, interpretation, and references. The explanation of any conspicuous feature in the park is an appropriate theme for such a museum. In architectural style the building should be simple, and the sequence of displays should be so arranged as to avoid a

FIGURE 530.
EMPLOYEES' QUARTERS,
BANDELIER
NATIONAL MONUMENT,
NEW MEXICO

Buildings designed to grow naturally from their sites.

Courtesy National Park Service

complicated routing of visitors and the resultant increase in the number of attendants needed. Generally speaking, the exhibits should not be extensive in any one museum, nor should they try to compete with the exhibits *in situ* in the area which it seeks to portray.

Restorations. Another type of park buildings—closely related to the museums—consists of structures which have been or should be preserved and restored because of their association with historical events or prominent persons. If the buildings have been partially obliterated or largely reduced to ruins, reconstruction is not recommended except in unusual cases. The amount of restoration considered desirable will depend on many factors. A building may be completely restored and furnished either with authentic furniture associated with the person or event which it commemorates or with furniture of the period; or the exterior alone may be restored in an effort to recapture the scene as part of the interpretive program, and the building otherwise may remain unchanged for use as an employee's residence or for some other utilitarian purpose.

Such preservation work has been extended to include restorations of early industries, equipped to function and thus preserving for posterity an operating example of primitive manufacturing processes complete with the actual products. If the restoration of these old structures and equipment is to be effective it is essential to approximate in new work the materials, methods, and quality of the old construction (see Figs. 531, 532). Complete records—by means of drawings, photographs, notes, and transcripts—should be kept of parts re-

FIGURE 531.

LIGHTFOOT HOUSE
(*circa* 1710), YORKTOWN,
COLONIAL NATIONAL
HISTORICAL PARK,
VIRGINIA.

BEFORE RESTORATION

In restoring old historic buildings every care must be taken to attain accuracy; all old work must be recorded and necessary new work designed with discretion and sympathetic skill.

Courtesy National Park Service

FIGURE 532.

LIGHTFOOT HOUSE
(*circa* 1710),
YORKTOWN,
COLONIAL NATIONAL
HISTORICAL PARK,
VIRGINIA.

AFTER RESTORATION

Courtesy National
Park Service

placed during restoration, and in no case should evidence offered by the monument itself be destroyed or covered up before it has been fully recorded.

Concession Buildings. The structures in this large group incorporate those services which the visitor has come to associate with the enjoyment of parks and recreational activities or which may be essential to his material comfort and needs. A concession differs from other park enterprises in that it is required to pay its way from profits derived from the sale of goods or services. The term itself indicates that the contracting individuals or corporations, who are under agreement with the park authorities and subject to certain restrictions and controls, will provide specified goods and services which are considered essential. These may include only the sale of tobacco, candies, cold drinks, and light

FIGURE 533.
BIG MEADOWS LODGE,
SHENANDOAH
NATIONAL PARK,
VIRGINIA.
VIEW OF LODGE
AND DETAIL

Low buildings permit the omission of much expensive and inappropriate mechanical equipment and are easier to maintain; their horizontality blends well into many different kinds of environment.

Courtesy National
Park Service

lunches; in large national parks like Yosemite and Yellowstone, on the other hand, they may comprise hotel and lodge accommodations, restaurants, cafeterias, stores, filling stations and repair shops, stables, and any facility usually found in a small city. It is difficult to determine where the demands of the public end and the initiative of the operator, who may be swayed by his selling enthusiasm, begins. Obviously, to prevent turning scenic areas into commercial enterprises for the cheap exploitation of the public, the policy should be to permit the installation only of such facilities and services as are needed and cannot satisfactorily be supplied outside the area.

The concession buildings should be in harmony with the non-commercial park structures, but their public function should be unmistakably clear. Here

FIGURE 534. CABIN GROUP, ZION NATIONAL PARK, UTAH

Courtesy National Park Service

the general restraint imposed on advertising is compensated for by eliminating all competition through granting the concessioner exclusive privileges. The designs and character of the structures will depend upon their use, geographic location, and physical surroundings. Buildings for summer use only will differ from structures that must serve all the year round. Probably the most difficult buildings for which the designer must work out a satisfactory solution are those which are used in summer for tourists primarily interested in the scenery and in winter for devotees of winter sports. For these he has no precedent to follow and usually the funds are limited; since restrictions in cost preclude completion of a large development, provision should be made for increasing the facilities later if the initial installation proves inadequate.

Hotels and Lodges. The sites for hotels and lodges should be selected for their accessibility as well as for their scenic advantages and the recreational and other activities at hand. Generally speaking, low structures are preferable because of their unobtrusiveness as well as their economy in construction and operation (Fig. 533). In one- and two-storied buildings it is possible to eliminate the elevators and mechanical features required in multi-storied structures,

FIGURE 535.
SO-CALLED
ADIRONDACK
SHELTER,
SHENANDOAH
NATIONAL PARK,
VIRGINIA

An overnight shelter of
the simplest type.

Courtesy National
Park Service

FIGURE 536.
BOAT LANDING,
NORRIS LAKE,
TENNESSEE VALLEY
AUTHORITY.

TWO VIEWS

Waterside elements can
be as attractive as they are
useful.

Courtesy Charles
Krutch, chief,
Graphics Material
Section, TVA

and the absence of these features is in keeping with the primitive character of
the park surroundings.

Such simple accommodations can often be satisfactorily planned through a
series of connected or of unconnected buildings. The principal building may
contain the dining room, lobby, offices, and lounge space, and the bedroom

FIGURE 537.
FISHING DOCK,
PICKWICK LAKE,
TENNESSEE VALLEY
AUTHORITY

Courtesy Charles
Krutch, chief,
Graphics Material
Section, TVA

facilities may be located in near-by lodge units or multiple-roomed cottages (see Fig. 534). This scheme presents a flexible plan not only for the initial installation and for operation but also for the addition of overnight facilities as the demand increases or the season advances. Similar allowance for expansion (or contraction) can be arranged for the dining and public space through the use of movable partitions or a series of rooms which can be opened (or closed off) as desired to meet the requirements. Precautions must be taken for the safety of the occupants by providing ample enclosed stairways, fire-resistive construction as far as possible, and adequate fire-fighting equipment along with personnel trained to use it.

Boathouses and Bathhouses. The increased popularity of sailing and of power boating has made new demands on facilities for storing and servicing the craft and for the entertainment and accommodation of the owners and their guests. Usually boathouses can have a combination of storage and service facilities on a lower level, with promenades, restaurants, ships' stores, and other services above. The locations of boating areas are so widespread as to leave the designer an unrestricted choice of materials and construction. The design should be appropriate to the area and in keeping with adjacent docks, floats, and other structures. (See Figs. 536, 537.)

Bathhouses in a public area, whether they are operated directly or by a con-

FIGURE 538. SMALL MUSEUM,
YAVAPAI POINT,
GRAND CANYON
NATIONAL PARK,
ARIZONA.
TWO VIEWS

Courtesy National Park Service

cessioner, should be so arranged and constructed that the greatest possible number of persons can be accommodated with a minimum capital expenditure. Here the equipment, materials, and finishes should be selected for ease of maintenance in preserving a clean and sanitary condition. Ventilation and sunlight are essential in the well-designed bathhouse. In addition to locker and dressing rooms for both men and women, an office, employees' locker rooms, a first-aid room, and a laundry should be provided; also, for the larger pools and bathhouses at beaches, concessions for the sale of bathing supplies, food, drinks, candy, tobacco, and other commodities must be considered.

Gas Filling Stations. The service station for automobiles has come to be accepted as a necessary business on parkways and in large parks. It may vary from an installation consisting of one or two gas pumps to a large, well-equipped station with facilities for the complete repair of automobiles. Usually the service is restricted to the sale of gas and oil and such minor jobs as greasing, washing, and the lesser repairs, thus leaving the more difficult work to shops outside. The park structures connected with servicing automobiles should be kept as small as their use will permit. Since conspicuous embellishments designating the products handled would be inharmonious with the surroundings they should be prohibited. Having the pumps painted a neutral color but per-

FIGURE 539. TWO
CHECKING STATIONS,
SEQUOIA
NATIONAL PARK,
CALIFORNIA,
AND CRATER LAKE
NATIONAL PARK,
OREGON

Courtesy National
Park Service

mitting on the glass bowls small trade-marks of the company that supplies the gas should afford adequate safeguards to the customer and satisfactory publicity to the dealer.

MISCELLANEOUS PARK STRUCTURES

Space limitations here preclude a detailed description of all the structures to be encountered in park areas. Many buildings to serve the special needs of certain activities must be provided. Stables, corrals, fences, gates, fireplaces, lookout towers, fountains, walls, dams, pools, and stairways; skaters' shelters, ski jumps, toboggan slides, and warming shelters; markers, signs, shrines, campfire circles, outdoor theaters, and many other items—all these occupy a place in the park structures glossary. Each presents its problems to the designer in working out a solution that will satisfy the material requirements and the aesthetics of the entire area.

FIGURE 540. UTILITY BUILDINGS, BANDELIER NATIONAL MONUMENT, NEW MEXICO

Courtesy National Park Service

FUTURE TRENDS

Park structures built during the latter half of the twentieth century will serve a new traffic with new habits. The architect and the landscape architect should collaborate on the problem. From the first they should study carefully the purpose which the park is to fulfill and the needs of the public it is to serve. They should design the whole as a unit; indoors and outdoors form a single problem in a park plan. The architect should fit his structures into the landscape instead of using the landscape as a setting for his structures—a humble yet new viewpoint for many park designers.

SUGGESTED ADDITIONAL READING FOR CHAPTER 49

Allen, F. Ellwood, "The Planning of Recreational Centers," *Architectural Record*, Vol. 104 (1948), December, pp. 110–14.

American Planning and Civic Association, *Portfolio on the National Park and Monument System* (Washington: the Association [1938?]).

Birkett, Sir Norman, *National Parks and the Countryside* (Cambridge, England: University Press, 1945).

Burnap, George, *Parks; Their Design, Equipment, and Use* (Philadelphia and London: Lippincott, 1916).

Cameron, Jenks, *The National Park Service* . . . (New York: Appleton, 1922).

Dixon-Scott, J., *England under Trust; the Principal Properties Held by the National Trust* . . . (London: Maclehose, 1937).

FIGURE 541. THREE PARK ENTRANCES AND SIGNS

LEFT, ABOVE: Sequoia National Park, California; RIGHT, ABOVE: Zion National Park, Utah; BELOW: Lassen National Forest, California.

Courtesy National Park Service

Downing, Andrew Jackson, *Rural Essays*, edited with a memoir by George William Curtis (New York: Leavitt & Allen, 1854).

Evison, Herbert (editor), *A State Park Anthology* (Washington: National Conference on State Parks, 1930).

Good, Albert H., *Park and Recreation Structures*, prepared for the United States National Park Service, Department of the Interior ([Washington: Government Printing Office,] 1938).

Hegemann, Werner, *Amerikanische Parkanlagen* . . . (Berlin: Wasmuth, 1911).

Koch, Hugo, *Gartenkunst in Städtebau* (Berlin: Wasmuth, 1923).

National Parks Association publications (Washington: the Association, 1919—).

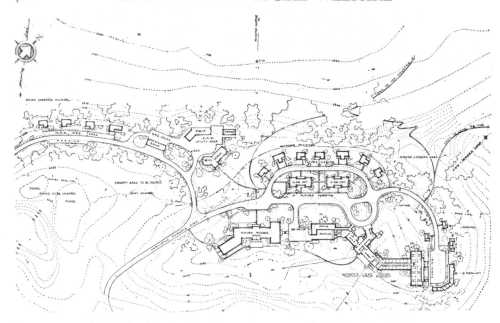

National Recreation Association, *Municipal and County Parks in the United States, 1935* . . . (Washington: Government Printing Office, 1937).

—— *Park Recreation Areas in the United States, 1930* . . . (Washington: Government Printing Office, 1932).

"Recreation Structures . . ." a Building Types Study, *Architectural Record*, Vol. 89 (1941), April, pp. 77–96.

United States National Park Service, *Glimpses of Our National Parks* (Washington: Government Printing Office, 1941).

—— *Master Plans; a Manual of Standard Practice* . . . reproduced from a typewritten manuscript ([Washington: the Service, 1941]).

—— *Park Structures and Facilities* ([Rahway, N.J.: printed by the Quinn & Boden Co.,] 1935).

—— *A Study of the Park and Recreation Problem of the United States* (Washington: Government Printing Office, 1941).

Weir, Lebert Howard, *Parks; a Manual of Municipal and County Parks* . . . (New York: Barnes, 1928).

FIGURE 542 (OPPOSITE, ABOVE). WONDER LAKE, MOUNT MCKINLEY NATIONAL PARK, ALASKA. GENERAL PLAN

The design of a park area requires the most careful study of circulation and of the location of all sorts of buildings and other facilities, with the object of combining greatest usefulness to the public with the least possible disturbance of the natural atmosphere.

Courtesy National Park Service

FIGURE 543 (OPPOSITE, MIDDLE AND BELOW). STUDIES FOR A LODGE DEVELOPMENT, WONDER LAKE, MOUNT MCKINLEY NATIONAL PARK, ALASKA

Courtesy National Park Service

PART IX

The Community as Architecture

THE MODERN CITY
BY LEWIS MUMFORD

THE ARCHITECT AND CITY PLANNING
BY G. HOLMES PERKINS

ANY COMMUNITY consists of sundry examples of architecture—good, bad, and indifferent—but in another sense the community itself is architecture. The planning of communities is the noblest form of architectural planning, and in giving form to towns or regions the planner is making what is perhaps his most valuable and significant contribution to human living. This fact is being increasingly realized by the architectural profession.

Not all architects are, or should be, community planners; for many of the problems involved—economic, sociological, political—are different in kind from the type of problem with which the average architect is familiar. In addition, it is but seldom that a community planner can dictate the details of form as definitely as does the architect in the case of a building. A true community is a living organism; it grows and changes, and its change is a symptom of its life. Setting too hard-and-fast a limitation on change by creating too rigid a pattern is harmful rather than helpful, and many a city lives a cramped and difficult existence because its life and its activities no longer fit the forms its early planners imposed.

Nevertheless, the forms to be taken by communities must be decided before they are constructed; someone *must* plan where streets are to run, parks are to be laid out, and industrial facilities are to be furnished, for these are all legitimate matters of conscious design. Someone *must* plan new housing and new public buildings, parks, and playgrounds; surely architects are necessary for these. The answer to the dilemma—the fact on the one hand that a live community cannot be straitjacketed and on the other that conscious design must nevertheless enter into every element in it—may be found in the processes of community planning. Long-term "master plans," we have learned, must not be too detailed but must be susceptible of constant revision. Nevertheless, specific civic improvements must be carefully and rigorously designed in consonance with the master-plan objectives and far enough in advance of actual construction so that a real study of the possibilities can be made.

Community planning can never be the work of a single individual or class of individuals. Good community plans need the contributions of experts in many fields, and democracy implies a large popular participation in their creation. Yet to give satisfactory form—both aesthetic and functional—to detailed schemes, as well as to contribute to the larger plan the utmost in planning skill, is undoubtedly the architect's supreme opportunity. In order to accomplish either of these aims, he must know not only the community in which he is working but also many of the controlling principles of community development. Even more, to make a satisfactory environment for people, he must be conscious of the potentialities that are offered by modern techniques and must be familiar with the desires which people cherish. Since for that reason some consideration of community planning is of great importance to all architects, this section presents first a chapter on the modern city as it might be and, second, a discussion of the more detailed relationships of architecture and architects to the whole problem of community development.

Modern city planning has become so complex, so enmeshed in statistics, and so controlled by financial interests that too often community plans emerge that are lifeless and mechanical. In this field, as in all others, it is the architect's task to redress the balance, to realize that cities exist for people (not people for cities), that business and industry and science should serve the people and not enslave them, and that unless some shining ideal of a better environment lies behind the planning process little will be achieved. The architect should not be afraid of being called "utopian," for mankind's progress, however halting, has reached its present level only because its direction has been toward the fulfillment of a great and brilliant dream.

LEWIS MUMFORD, HON. ASSOCIATE A.I.A. AND R.I.B.A., AND HON. MEMBER TOWN PLANNING IN-
STITUTE, author of the chapter "The Modern City," writer, philosopher, and critic, has
written extensively on architecture and planning since 1921. He has served as consultant
on planning to the City and County Park Board, Honolulu, and to Stanford University,
Palo Alto. Among his many publications on cities and city planning are *The Brown
Decades* (New York: Harcourt, Brace, 1931), *Technics and Civilization* (New York:
Harcourt, Brace, 1934), *The Culture of Cities* (New York: Harcourt, Brace, 1938), and
City Development (New York: Harcourt, Brace, 1945).

G. HOLMES PERKINS, A.I.A., author of the chapter "The Architect and City Planning," is
Dean of the School of Fine Arts at the University of Pennsylvania. Earlier he taught at
the University of Michigan and then was Charles Dyer Norton Professor of Regional
Planning and Chairman of the Planning Department at Harvard University. He is a
practicing architect and has worked on urban redevelopment for the National Housing
Agency.

50

The Modern City

By LEWIS MUMFORD

DURING the last century hundreds of cities grew up throughout the world, and thousands of country towns expanded into great industrial or commercial centers. In the sense that all the buildings in Chicago or Los Angeles were constructed in recent times, they are modern communities. But in these new cities one searches in vain for any common principle of design that would distinguish them from earlier towns. It is not by their form but by their formlessness that one must characterize all but a handful of the new communities.

If, however, one examines the contemporary city more closely, one comes upon forms that had no counterpart in any earlier civilization; similarly one finds unfulfilled human needs that cry for fulfillment. The playground had its counterpart in the Greek palaestra, but the only ancient utility that the subway recalls is the great Roman sewer. The country villa and the suburb are time-honored forms; only with the development of rapid transportation, however, did it become possible to disperse the population of a great center over an area at least ten times as great as the biggest cities of the past.

The skyscraper has permitted the assembling of business offices and light industry in concentrated hives, served by vertical transportation; but the erection of such buildings on streets designed for four-story buildings and horse-drawn transportation has everywhere produced chaos. Much of the budget of the modern city is devoted to alleviating congestion that should have been prevented, to correcting hygienic misdemeanors that should have been averted, and to providing more rapid means of exodus from cities that no longer adequately serve even their economic functions.

Nowhere have the new forces in urbanism been organized so as to create both a functional and an aesthetic unity. Even those who, like Le Corbusier, have attempted to work out new forms have not questioned the human purposes of the present city; their conception of order is mechanical, and their proper demand for sunlight, space, and verdure—all essentials of life—overlooks many other more subtle and complex requirements.

One cannot derive an archetype for the modern city from any existing example. Neither can one create it merely by uncritically accepting all technological devices as essential ingredients, since many of them are merely attempts to offset by engineering skill the lack of coherent social purpose. Some of our most elaborate technical adaptations, such as subways, double-decked highways, and skyscrapers, can only be considered costly symptoms of giantism and cancerous growth—expedients which lessen the amount of money and energy available for more positive manifestations of urban life.

There is room, then, for an effort to define the modern community in ideal terms, on the basis of existing facts and tendencies but without any obligation to limit the analysis to a description of existing structures. These facts and tendencies are not confined to the provinces of engineering and architecture; they issue from industry, from education, from medicine and psychology, and indeed from politics and religion. The discovery of the hygienic importance of sunshine, not merely in preventing rickets but in fortifying living processes generally, brought back into city planning a renewed interest in orientation and a new basis for rational planning. The attempt of the settlement house to serve as a focus for neighborhood life and higher cultural activity in the slums showed the need for a community center in every normal neighborhood. The new forms of the city, in other words, do not derive solely from the machine.

The outcome of such a critical inquiry into ideal forms should not be to impose any rigid formula; rather it should point out the wealth of variations possible once the narrow requirements of the municipal engineer, the ground landlord, and the speculative builder cease to dominate. Such an inquiry will separate the essential from the accidental in city development, and it will disclose a fresh range of choices in design. The modern city has still to be built, and the first step toward sinking its foundations into the earth is to raise its ideal structure in the mind.

HISTORIC CITY FORMS IN WESTERN CIVILIZATION

In Europe and in the original settlements of North and South America the modern city grew up around an older core, and down to our own day these cores have continued to have a powerful influence on new plans even in the laying out of entirely new quarters. Certain urban layouts which have been repeated automatically, like the uniform platting of buildings on both sides of

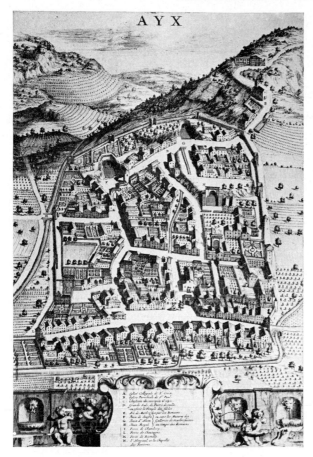

FIGURE 544.

SEVENTEENTH-CENTURY

AIX-EN-PROVENCE, FRANCE

A town of medieval organic character; its growth and form result from an irregular site. Like many medieval European towns, it owes this character largely to its internal open spaces.

From Blaeu, *Tooneel der Heerschappyen van Savoye* . . .

streets, are still looked upon as standard forms; actually, however, they represented originally a direct adaptation to social, economic, and political conditions that no longer control. One of the reasons for analyzing both the city's medieval and its Baroque (or so-called Renaissance) heritage is to free the mind from these obsolete stereotypes, for a modern urban quarter cannot be planned on the basis of a narrow medieval building lot fronting on a Baroque street.

Medieval. The medieval town was a combination of camp, market, and sanctuary. The necessity for protection colored all its institutions and dictated the use of a defensive site on hillside or waterside and swamp, led to the erection of walls separating the town from the country and allowing access only through guarded gates, fostered the banding together of the citizens in guilds and fraternities which were under the universal protection and moral rule of the Church. Under these circumstances common sense and common feeling

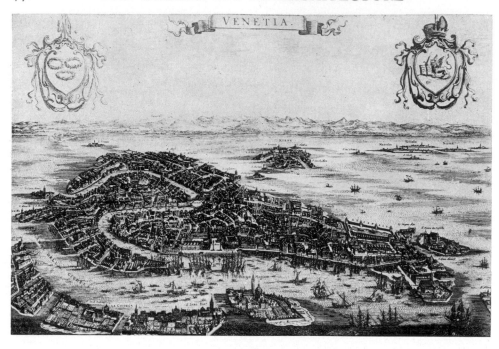

FIGURE 545. VENICE IN THE SEVENTEENTH CENTURY

There is a natural division into zones here, separated by water highways. The glass works at
Murano occupy a whole island at a distance from the city. Note the Arsenal at the extreme
right of the main island.

From an engraving by H. Focken, courtesy Metropolitan Museum of Art

gave rise to a common form; most of the towns, growing organically over a
long period of time, preserved an outward unity of structure because they
maintained an inward unity of tradition, which bridged even such radical
changes as those from the ponderous Romanesque to the free and daring Gothic
forms and from an exuberant Gothic to the geometric perspectives of the
classic resurgence. The social functions of the medieval town were concentrated in a square or sometimes in two related squares—dominated variously by
a church, a guild hall or a town hall, and in late medieval times perhaps by
a market hall.

Thomas More in describing the capital of his Utopia clarified and redefined
the ideal form of the medieval city, and his conception of the neighborhood
unit is perhaps the chief bequest of the medieval city which has relevance for
the modern planner. Many later students of the medieval city—Sitte and Unwin, for example—have been tempted to formulate the ordered irregularities
and the unstudied picturesqueness of medieval urban forms. Medieval builders,

FIGURE 546. MANNHEIM, GERMANY. AIR VIEW
The formal geometry of the Baroque period.   Photograph Ewing Galloway

in their handling of space and their bold contrasting of confinement and openness and of horizontal and vertical, still have something to teach the twentieth-
century architect who knows no way of achieving height except by erecting
skyscrapers and even in ideal plans involving tall buildings loses the sense of
height by forgetting the role of lower structures in establishing human scale.

The medieval city was designed for pedestrians: every man was a neighbor
and every building within walking distance. One cannot appraise the medieval
city at a glance; one must penetrate it, for its inner space is the reason for its
outer order. The bright patchwork of gardens behind the solid fronts of
burgher houses or the larger sequence of gardens behind monastery walls, the
sudden blaze of sunlight as the shadowed winding street opens into the cathedral square, the pool of quiet order at the center of all the city's bustle and
activity—here are the keys to its architectural form. At the heart of every
organized space is a sanctuary; the outer structure, no matter how elaborate,
is at the service of the inner life. Where the topography supplies differences
of level, the architecture enhances the vertical dimension; where verticality
is absent, the architecture makes up for it. By moving a few paces, or by turning a corner, one sees the relations of foreground and background radically

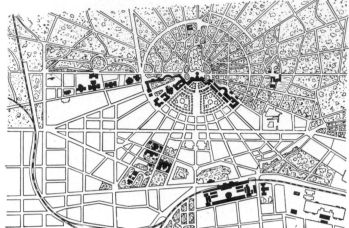

FIGURE 547.
KARLSRUHE,
GERMANY.
GENERAL PLAN

Axial planning with the palace as the dominant focus.

altered as a wall, tower, spire, or gable is effaced or exposed. This factor of movement and time has been neglected in the usual analysis of urban forms; but it is an essential element, for in part at least it conditions all architectural expression. In the modern city, where pedestrians, car drivers, and airmen have different visual as well as practical needs, the importance of multiple tempo as a factor in design is enormous.

Baroque. The Baroque city was formulated by Alberti and others in the fifteenth and sixteenth centuries and was actually built in the seventeenth and eighteenth centuries. Fundamentally it was a city designed not for protection and sanctuary but for the expression and extension of power in every form—particularly in political control and economic exploitation and in the conquest of space and time. It was built not for pedestrians but for armies and wheeled vehicles, and it was organized to achieve a sense of unbroken space and unhampered freedom of horizontal movement.

In the Baroque plan the old medieval market square, where movement came to a halt and meetings took place, is transformed into the dizzy traffic circle which the pedestrian crosses at the risk of life and limb; instead of resting his eye on a fountain placed at one side of the square, the citizen's gaze is transfixed by a column or an obelisk at the center—the formal end of a visual axis. The focus of this plan is no longer the church, the expression of common faith, but the palace, the seat of a one-sided, despotic power; ideally the diagonal avenues of the Baroque city meet, as in Karlsruhe, at that point (Fig. 547).

In contrast with the medieval town, the Baroque city demands flat sites, straight continuous streets, and uniform building and roof lines; whatever else

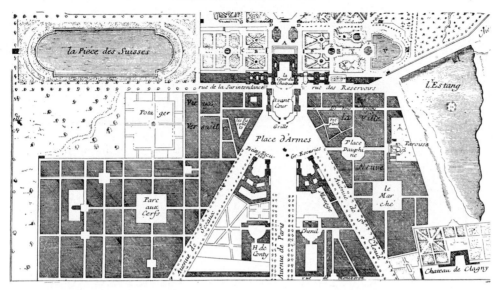

FIGURE 548. CENTRAL PART OF VERSAILLES, FRANCE. PLAN

The château commands processional avenues; the great open space becomes a parade ground rather than a city square.

From De Mortain, *Les Plans, profils, et elevations de la ville et du château de Versailles . . .*

its façades do, they illustrate the laws of perspective. In traditional buildings, like churches, taste may incline toward height, as in St. Peter's in Rome or St. Paul's in London, though dome and cupola are substituted for tower and spire; but grandeur in the authentic Baroque plan is expressed by horizontality, as at Versailles. The typical Baroque form might be called the parade city: not only its soldiers but also its citizens and its buildings are on parade, and their worst offense is to break out of line and destroy the imposed order. Whatever is visible must submit to this geometry; the city is organized for show, and the outer façade dictates the interior functions. Correctness and formality take the place of adaptability and fitness. The Baroque city, instead of recording the life of successive generations, as organic growth requires, must look as if it were conceived by a single mind and built in one operation. In such a city, time becomes visible only as dilapidation.

From the seventeenth century onward, since with the heightening of tempo through the use of wheeled vehicles the eye could no longer take in a single building at a glance unless its main features were uniformly repeated, further emphasis was placed on the repetition of motifs and on uniform façades. Such inner space as remained—like the mews and drying greens behind the

FIGURE 549.
ROYAL CRESCENT,
BATH, ENGLAND.
AIR VIEW

The humanized geometry
of successive open spaces
marks a new high point
in urban design.

Photograph courtesy
British Information
Services

eighteenth-century square—became grim and barracklike and were treated as
if invisible. The Baroque plan symbolized an externalization of life that went
hand in hand with militarist regimentation and capitalist organization; it begot
an architecture of façades. What lay behind these façades, visually or socially,
did not bear close investigation. The Baroque form in its degradation during
the nineteenth century lost its coherence and dignity in an orgy of competitive
individualism; every property owner fancied himself to be as free and isolated
as Robinson Crusoe and behaved, in fact, like a Caliban who had escaped the
guiding hand of the princely Prospero.

In the residential planning of the seventeenth and eighteenth centuries, however, the Baroque planners made a positive contribution. If they abandoned
the large medieval private garden, they invented a new form of open space—a
square, an oblong, or an oval—surrounded by houses that faced its trees and
shrubbery and grass. Functionally this new square is a private one for the
use of the residents of abutting properties but visually it is public space, and
the chain of such squares in Bath or Bloomsbury or Edinburgh marks a new
high point in urban design (Fig. 549). With this feature went the deliberate
introduction of the tree-lined parade and the park as essential constituents of
the modern city; the Tuileries, the Nevsky Prospekt, and St. James's Park were
typical of a new kind of urban space, set apart and dedicated to the refreshment of the pedestrian. If the medieval town taught the nature of inner spaces
and enclosures, of privacy and inviolability, the Baroque city made its contribution in a fresh sense of openness and freedom of movement.

FIGURE 550.
RUE DE RIVOLI,
PARIS

Quiet street design, covered arcades for strollers, and a new freedom of movement.

Courtesy Ware
Library

The Baroque plan, unlike the medieval, left a deep imprint on later generations; in a debased form it became standard throughout Western civilization. That imprint showed itself in a preference for straight streets over curved ones, no matter what the expense or the inconvenience that resulted from ignoring the topography—expense where the hills were leveled; inconvenience and misuse of aesthetic opportunity, in cities like San Francisco, where the strong contours were perversely stamped with an arbitrary gridiron pattern. Baroque overemphasis of the avenue had its effect, too, in the unnecessary multiplication of streets and, without respect to actual or probable traffic, in the planning of streets unnecessarily wide, under the mistaken belief that breadth in itself has some special virtue.

Finally, the Palladian image of the grouping of public buildings in the city center, once dominated by the palace, had its afterglow in the United States in the twentieth-century cult of the civic center, conceived as an island of classic order in a clotted waste of undirected urban growth—as in Cleveland, San Francisco, or Springfield, Massachusetts. But nowhere, perhaps, are the limitations of an uncritical imitation of Baroque principles so conspicuous and the results so contradictory as in the revival and expansion of the L'Enfant plan for Washington, with its too-open Mall which separates buildings that should be closely related and its labyrinthine shelters for bureaucracy in buildings that defy every canon of modern planning, from orientation to orderly self-identification.

During the second half of the nineteenth century a Baroque revival took

FIGURE 551.
PLACE DE L'OPÉRA,
PARIS

Nineteenth-century resur-
gence of the Baroque
ideal.

Courtesy Ware
Library

place in planning. The conspicuous leader in this movement was Baron Haussmann, working under Napoleon III. Haussmann's mission was to vulgarize the
aristocratic Baroque order by creating straight shopping streets and tree-shaded
boulevards, lined by apartment houses of uniform height and design which
would bring into the middle-class quarters of the city some of the showy
spaciousness that was once confined to upper-class neighborhoods. The Ring
in Vienna, Kingsway in London, and the Parkway in Philadelphia were further expressions of the same impulse. This transformation of the bleak traffic
avenue into the boulevard or the parkway was a positive contribution. Up to
this time the elimination of trees on urban streets had been regarded as a sign
of progress, an emancipation from rural habits. Now avenues of trees, lined
with verdure, linked together the open spaces of the city; a new urban form
was born.

One of the great limitations of the late Baroque tradition, as carried into the
modern city by planners like Burnham in Chicago and Moses in New York, is
that its social objectives are as narrow as its functional requirements; hence
its triumphs have been limited to parkways, drives, parks, and public buildings,
since it has no adequate formula for dealing with the city as a whole. Indeed,
any over-all sense of the purpose of a city would often prevent some of the
extravagant street widening and parkway building which necessarily result.
Not the least handicap of Baroque planning today is that, whereas under absolute rulers the command of the economic means was equally authoritative,
so that the surface plan and the building were conceived and carried out together, present-day municipal engineers and city planning authorities deal
only with the two-dimensional plan. But planning is not separable from build-

FIGURE 552. CITY HALL, CIVIC CENTER, SAN FRANCISCO, CALIFORNIA

An island of classic order in a clotted waste of undirected growth.   Photograph Talbot Hamlin

ing; planning, to be effective, means responsible collective oversight of the whole process, to the end of creating a harmonious social and aesthetic whole. Lacking such collective purposes, modern cities, from Boston to Bombay, from Buenos Aires to Birmingham, are—what they so unfortunately are.

THE INDUSTRIAL TRANSFORMATION

As a result of new economic and social forces, the nineteenth century witnessed a multiplication of cities, a transformation of their physical utilities, and an unparalleled increase in their potential size—in population, in area covered, and often in density. The typical city of the Middle Ages, outside Italy, held less than fifteen thousand people—and often less than five thousand—though Marco Polo had brought back from China accounts of cities with a million inhabitants. As a result of the expansion of financial, industrial, and political power from the year 1500 onwards, the newer centers often boasted more than a hundred thousand people. With the paleotechnic revolution in the nineteenth century, cities of a hundred thousand became common and those of a million, like London, Paris, and Berlin, became possible. Indeed the forces that created giant cities were in operation before the technical means to make them habitable were available: London had a million inhabitants at a time (in 1800) when in many quarters the water supply was turned on only twice a week.

FIGURE 553.
ORGANIC PLANNING,
AMSTERDAM. TWO
MODEL VIEWS

Planning, to be effective,
must be directed toward a
harmonious social and aesthetic whole.

From *Amsterdam*

One of the most important changes was the relative increase in the space
devoted to industry. This was marked by the transformation of the family
workshop of the handworker into the power-driven factory, where five hundred or a thousand workers might be organized into a productive mechanism
under a single roof. This demand on the part of industry for urban space was
already visible at the time of the introduction of weaving sheds, dye works,
and breweries in the seventeenth century; but no space was provided in the
Baroque plan for this alteration of the scale in industrial functions, even in
Wren's somewhat overpraised plan for rebuilding industrial and commercial

FIGURE 554. PITTSBURGH, PENNSYLVANIA. AIR VIEW
Great mills and factories scattered at random over the urban landscape.

Photograph Fairchild Aerial Surveys

London after the Great Fire. Evelyn did indeed advocate a greenbelt to separate the noisome large-scale industries from the city proper, but no special planning of industrial quarters took place. Though industry and residence were no longer conducted under one roof, too often the working-class neighborhood lay directly under the belching chimney of the factory.

Modern industry came into the city, so to say, by the back door: its spread was marked by the building over of open spaces; by the introduction of smoke, filth, and rubbish, due partly to the increased use of coal; and, in towns like Manchester or Pittsburgh (Fig. 554), by the erection of great mills or factories scattered almost at random over the urban landscape. These were soon surrounded by rows of close-built workers' houses, often lacking light, water, and sanitary conveniences, to say nothing of paved streets or back yards free from offal.

Even where the factory was the originating cause of the city, the form of the town was not effectively altered. Individual fabrics of colossal scale and massive simplicity appeared: Brunel's bridges, Telford's warehouses and docks, great cotton factories such as those in Manchester, England, or Fall River, Massachusetts. Architects like Schinkel, early in the nineteenth century, recog-

FIGURE 555.
NEW YORK FROM
THE SOUTHEAST.
TWO VIEWS

An example of licensed
chaos; even when bathed
in the magic sun of early
morning only the pictur-
esqueness of disorganiza-
tion is apparent.

Photographs
Talbot Hamlin

nized that the industrial towns in England shadowed forth a new aesthetic and
laid the groundwork for a new architecture. But the new urban form that
would utilize the changes of scale and function and create a collective whole
did not appear; in general, the new industrial cities lacked any coherent principle of design.

The new industrial town was largely an example of licensed chaos. Private
enterprise and freedom became synonyms for filth, disease, and pollution, for
waste, friction, cross haulage, and confusion—results which were painful to
the eye, crippling to the soul, and even wasteful of the money on which the
enterpriser professed to be intent. As a result, despite Schinkel's perception,
the classic beauty of the great English railway viaducts and bridges was not
carried into the city as a whole. Urban form disappeared. Industrialism did not
by its own canons produce a single useful or efficient city; even in the twentieth

FIGURE 556. MIDTOWN CHAOS, MANHATTAN, NEW YORK. AIR VIEW
Confusion as the result of unplanned and destructive expansion.   Photograph Ewing Galloway

century its Detroits are another name for collective disorganization. (See Figs. 555, 556.)

Nevertheless the nineteenth century introduced certain improvements which have become permanent factors in modern community building. Urban utilities, such as iron piping and glazed earthen drains or sewer pipes, were invented and produced on a mass scale. In time these new collective utilities created a complicated invisible underworld of pipes, mains, cables, and wires, and the chief token of residence in a city was the process of getting "connected" with these ramifying agents. Henry Wright put this change dramatically by saying that one room in every modern house is buried in the street. Despite the enormous cost of such underground utilities no effective rationalization of this wilderness of wires and pipes has been brought about.

On the surface, the same piecemeal improvement of mechanical means and the same over-all chaos in their social application prevailed, notably in the street and road system. Concurrently with the introduction of the rubber-tired motor car an expensive type of asphalt or concrete paving was introduced, but hardly anywhere has the function of the street as a thoroughfare for wheeled vehicles been separated from its other function as a public way dedicated to underground utilities; hence breakages and new installations continue to

result in a costly tearing up of the road. The supply of water and the disposal of sewage created problems of the same general dimensions. Plainly the
economic reorganization of all these utilities, so long neglected by routine
planning and engineering, is essential if sufficient funds are to be available for
gardens, parks, and noble buildings. The dearth of rational foresight here has
been one of the great handicaps to the healthy development of the modern city.

One final change must be noted—the effect of new means of transportation.
Four of these came into existence in the nineteenth century: the surface railroad, the elevated railroad, the trolley car, and the motor car. All four hastened
the expansion of the city and made it easier to effect a temporary escape from
its muddle, its waste, and its frustration, only to create by that very expansion
similar defects on a wider scale. The railroads also had a disruptive effect;
for the cutting through of railroad lines and the marshaling of yards without

FIGURE 558. STUYVESANT TOWN, NEW YORK, FOR METROPOLITAN LIFE
INSURANCE COMPANY. AIR VIEW

Fast movement creates congestion at the center; congestion breeds inhuman gigantism.

Photograph Thomas Airviews

respect to the collective needs of the city often, as in Chicago or Edinburgh,
spoiled sites that might have been more valuable for other uses or created
yawning gaps, only rarely roofed over as in New York.

Just as rapid transportation occupied an increasing part in daily life, so did
the space devoted to transportation occupy an ever larger urban area. Nowhere has the optimum use of such utilities been worked out—for an optimum
use will demand a reduction of unnecessary transportation. Plans of the type
which Norman Bel Geddes made for the New York World's Fair of 1939 and
later prepared in modified form for Toledo are based on the fantastic premise
that rapid transportation is an end in itself and not a means of achieving other
ends. Indeed, a great part of what is called modern planning—like some of the
more sumptuous exercises by Robert Moses in New York—rests on the sacrifice of the more important urban functions to fast movement and of the needs
of the majority of town dwellers to the minority who can afford motor cars.
But good planning seeks to reduce the amount of unnecessary utilities. Faced,
for example, with the necessity of accommodating the shoppers on a congested
shopping street, it will follow the example of Rio de Janeiro and Buenos Aires
and prohibit it to wheeled traffic during shopping hours. In any case the func-

FIGURE 559.
HOUSE AND GARDEN,
RÖMERSTADT,
GERMANY

Ernst May, chief planner

A new humanism in dwelling and environment.

From *Das neue Frankfurt*

tion of transportation is not fast movement as such but getting people with a minimum misuse of time and energy to where they want to be.

The failure to assess the new industrial functions of the city and to appraise the effect of modern inventions on urban utilities has been practically universal. The chief exceptions have been such utopian works as J. S. Buckingham's proposal for a model town in *National Evils and Practical Remedies* [1] and Sir Benjamin W. Richardson's *Hygeia: A City of Health*.[2] Although the industrial element of the city was occupying more space and in the form of gas tanks, factory chimneys, and power stations was dominating the skyline with increasing emphasis, thus dwarfing many of its traditional symbols of beauty or power, no satisfactory architectural solution for the grouping of these new units was offered. This has been equally true, almost down to the middle of the twentieth century, with respect to skyscraper office buildings. Whatever the emergent form of the modern city, history shows that industrialism when left to itself did not produce even mechanical order.

THE ROMANTIC COUNTERPOISE

The industrial transformation of the city was accompanied by a movement that served as a counterpoise: the retreat to the suburb. Such new form as has been achieved in city building has been achieved on the open pattern of the suburb.

The modern suburb, as distinguished from the trader's town that lay outside the city walls, came into existence in late medieval times as the summer

[1] London: T. Jackson [1849].   [2] London: Macmillan, 1876.

FIGURE 560.
GREENBELT,
RÖMERSTADT,
GERMANY

Ernst May, chief planner

The green of growing
things as an integral part
of a rational plan.

From *Das neue
Frankfurt*

residence area of the more prosperous bourgeoisie—a collection of summer houses spotted at intervals among orchards and vineyards. As early as the Elizabethan period, the hygienic advantages of the open suburb as compared with the crowded town were realized. But until the nineteenth century the suburb remained an upper-class section, open chiefly to those who could afford a private carriage. When quick public transportation made more extensive suburbs for the middle classes possible, two eighteenth-century ideals remained uppermost in their design: individualism and naturalism, with their emphasis on personal taste, domestic felicity, and rural fitness. Within the suburb, architecture became a branch of landscape design. Frank Lloyd Wright's deliberate effort to conduct the garden into the house, or rather to enfold it by the house, was the final architectural consummation of this trend.

Both socially and architecturally the suburb is a retreat. Each house is regarded as a separate, self-contained entity, hidden if possible from its neighbor. Even when grouped about a formal block, such houses generally make no attempt to achieve a common pattern, as in the eighteenth-century square or row; instead they pride themselves on their individuality, their distinction, their capricious unlikeness in style and taste. In architecture the spontaneity denied by the daily routine of office or factory is here reaffirmed, and the automatic and impersonal processes that prevail in Coketown, with its tyrannous regimentation of time, energy, and life and its total neglect of biological well-being and visual pleasure, are here counterbalanced by a life modeled after that of the sixteenth-century country house. Suburbia is the country house writ small and brought within the limits of the average purse.

Spaciousness and openness are the keys to suburban design, and to emphasize the element of leisure the roads lazily follow the topography and the avenues ramble, indecisively. Even when the price of land dictates the grouping of houses, they lose the effect of a common front by being set back from the sidewalk and half effaced by trees; indeed, it was in the suburb as far back as the mid-nineteenth century that the informal regrouping of houses began, breaking up the Baroque street perspective. Anonymous builders in Cambridge and Longwood, both in the Boston area, achieved the informal cul-de-sac long before the principles of this mode of design were discovered. Later planners, like Olmsted, consciously carried into suburban planning the methods that had created the naturalistic landscape park. By laying out narrow roads, by avoiding expensive paving, and by following the contours they saved money that went into gardens, and the very form of their economies symbolically underlined the desire for spontaneity, for freedom, for personal expression. Even orientation for sunlight was first achieved in suburban villa planning.

In content and form the suburb was anti-urban; yet this anti-urban bias was itself a new contribution to urbanism. A generation ago Sir Raymond Unwin analyzed the difference in cost between the rational, mechanistic by-law platting of England, with its duplication of monotonous terraces and wasteful streets, and an open pattern which turned streets into gardens, and proved that even on economic terms there was "Nothing Gained by Overcrowding." Early in the nineteenth century in Cambridge, Massachusetts, the superblock, with houses ranged around multiple cul-de-sacs completely divorced from through-street traffic, was invented. In the design of Central Park, by means of overpasses and underpasses, Olmsted effected a complete separation between bridle paths, carriage drives, and pedestrian walks; each form of traffic was designed as an independent system, with a maximum facilitation of movement and a maximum freedom from danger or disturbance. Both inventions lay neglected for three-quarters of a century and were not combined until Henry Wright and Clarence Stein undertook the planning of Radburn, New Jersey, in 1929.

Radburn consists of a group of superblocks, penetrated by residential cul-de-sacs; these cul-de-sacs in turn bound an inner park that winds through the whole community. This was the first effective division of the necessary functions of the modern city, accomplished by canalizing the through traffic and divorcing it from lanes of access, separating the quiet domestic zone from the more dynamic sections of the city, and making the park an integral part of the design. Radburn stands out as the culmination of suburban planning and

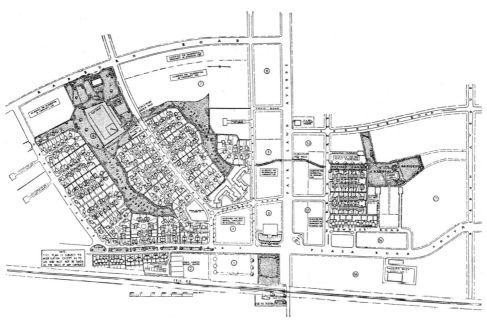

FIGURE 561. RADBURN, NEW JERSEY. PLAN

Clarence Stein and Henry Wright, architects

The embryonic form of the modern city.   From *Town Planning Review*

as an embryonic form of the modern city; here urban space has been reorganized so as to make the most of new utilities, new inventions, and new social constellations (see Fig. 561).

The open pattern of the suburb, furthermore, was a spur to architectural invention. Voysey, Baillie-Scott, and Parker, in England, and H. H. Richardson, Frank Lloyd Wright, and Bernard Maybeck in the United States—the last followed by a whole generation of later California architects—found in the large, self-contained suburban plot a freedom that the rest of the city denied them. But one must not exaggerate the purely romantic contribution of the suburban form; for the ablest planners, like Olmsted and Unwin, remained aware of the need for coherence as well as for spontaneity. Perhaps the best example of suburban planning anywhere is Hampstead Garden Suburb in London. Here, in the first decade of the twentieth century, a harmonious domestic vernacular, transitional but not archaic or imitative, achieved a great degree of openness without becoming disjointed and spotty. As Bath had proved, a century and a half before, formality is not incompatible with openness.

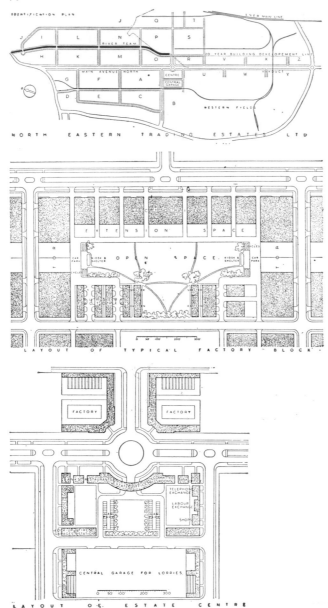

FIGURE 562.
PLANNED
INDUSTRIAL ZONE,
TEAM VALLEY
TRADING ESTATE,
ENGLAND. PLANS

Industrial needs can be
planned for; industrial areas
need not be synonymous
with blighted areas.

From *Journal of the
Royal Institute of
British Architects*

In an age of standardization, even the new pattern of openness has been standardized: the limit of twelve houses to the net building acre became common in England and was legalized for housing estates built after the First World War. No such stereotyped formula can be carried out blindly without producing a monotonous effect and without—what is worse—sometimes frustrating other human needs which call for a closer distribution. In most mixed communities there are conditions under which more than twelve families should be housed to the acre, and others under which for big families the requirements could be even more generous. Unwin stated that the standard of twelve families to the acre was arrived at in order to provide sufficient land for allotment gardens, which would not only increase the worker's food supply but enable him to add to his cash income. Plainly that is not a universal need. These standards were first set in Bournville. Although they tend to produce a healthy and comely environment so long as less than a few hundred families are involved, when a community passes beyond that compass it may lose in social facilities and opportunities for neighborly intercourse what it gains in gardens. The more traditional urban density, of 70 to 100 people per acre as compared with the 36 to 48 of suburban planning, is probably more favorable to community life without being harmful to health.

But the openness that was first achieved in the suburb has become a distinguishing mark of all modern plans—even those that aim at a far higher density. Viewed from the air, the "black city" of the nineteenth century, with its minimum of open spaces, becomes the "green city" of the twentieth century, set once again in meadow and park, like pre-nineteenth-century Oxford. Openness, translated into the forms of garden, playground, park, and parkway, has become an integral part of the modern plan. The revolt against openness, led by Thomas Sharp in England and by Percival Goodman in the United States, is a movement for a higher concentration of population and for greater visual unity, but not for airless, sunless, closed-in quarters.

THE MODERN CITY AS A SYMBOL OF MODERN MAN

It should now be obvious why the "modern city" cannot be created by mechanical improvements—a possibility that seemed so promising to utopian writers like Bellamy and Wells when toward the end of the nineteenth century they envisioned the "city of the future"—and especially if it is conceived in the childish terms used in the 1920's by various American skyscraper architects in portraying super-skyscraper cities lived in largely under artificial light, zoned in horizontal layers according to incomes, and utilizing every mechanical device that would further congestion, increase land values, or speed movement. Even Le Corbusier's refinement of this picture—with wide green spaces, trees, sunlight, and sports fields—though plainly more human, is still naïve,

FIGURE 563. WELWYN GARDEN CITY, ENGLAND. AIR VIEW

Industry as a rational part of an integrated town; the industrial area (background) is close to residential quarters and convenient to railroad and highway service.

Courtesy British Information Services

for it neglects the essentials of family life and neighborly intercourse; it is, in fact, the engineer's and bureaucrat's dream, if only engineer and bureaucrat dared to dream.

The architectural embodiment of the modern city is in fact impossible until biological, social, and personal needs have been canvassed, until the cultural and educational purposes of the city have been outlined, and until all of man's activities have been integrated into a balanced whole. One cannot base an adequate architectural conception on such a crude sociology as that which led a group of modern architects and planners to examine the modern city with reference to only four functions: work, transportation, dwelling, and recreation. The city, if it is anything, is an expression and symbolization of man's wholeness—a representation in buildings of his nature and purposes. This wholeness is not elementary; it emerges from the diversity of man's interests, activities, and purposes, from the division of labor and the differentiation of associations and institutions, and from all those infinitely varied human capacities which were perhaps latent but undeveloped in the primitive village.

What, then, are man's permanent needs, and what are the collective urban means for satisfying them? Before we can survey a site or lay a stone, we must

FIGURE 564. TOWN MARKET CENTER, ONGAR, ENGLAND. PERSPECTIVE .
Drawn by Peter Shepheard
A rationalized marketing and shopping area is a necessary part of an integrated town.

achieve a provisional agreement as to the nature of man and as to the values and potentialities of his present culture.

Historically the city begins in the village—a group of households attached to the soil. Here nurture and neighborly co-operation are the two basic elements; the limited horizon and a repetitive routine give to the growing child security and to the adult the basis of social solidarity, like-mindedness. The "primary group" of families and neighbors, as Cooley called such a unit, forms the basis of all other associations; the common locality that is shared and the common biological tasks of nutrition and reproduction create a common general purpose. This community of interest demands face-to-face intercourse, for most of the social values are here transmitted not through intermediate symbols but from person to person by word, gesture, and daily example. Hence the elemental neighborhood unit should cover an area not greater than the normal radius of action of a small child nor greater than the distance—to speak in modern terms—that a mother can conveniently push a baby carriage. From 250 to 1,000 people make up such a natural unit. Such economic functions as are performed here should be those that pertain directly to the home.

The central figures in the neighborhood group are the mother and child, and the first differentiation of social life beyond the household is in the play

FIGURE 565.
REGIONAL
MARKET CENTER,
QUINCY MARKET,
BOSTON,
MASSACHUSETTS.
TWO VIEWS

Alexander Parris, architect

A wholesale market adequately planned over a century ago; commerce then was not considered as necessarily destructive of architectural dignity.

Photographs
Talbot Hamlin

group and nursery-school group. All the spatial relationships of such a community must be based on walking distances, almost on crawling distances. Security, quiet, freedom from danger, intimacy of relationship, and opportunities for spontaneous meetings without special effort or the intervention of mechanical agents should give the clue to the architectural treatment. Frank Lloyd Wright's scheme for Broadacre City, in which each family would have a minimum of one acre of land, limits social intercourse on the primary level to a mere handful of neighbors and above that level demands motor transportation for even the most casual or ephemeral meetings. The contest held by the Chicago City Club, in 1913, on the best way to lay out a complete neighborhood unit of 640 acres had far more to contribute to the art of city planning than the grandiose schemes for parkways and drives that came to quicker fruition. In returning to the village green as an essential unit of domestic planning, Sir Charles Reilly has recognized a fundamental need which has been overlooked by many modern planners. Sunnyside Gardens in Long Island

City remains a happy exception, and Sert and Wiener's Cidade dos Motores offers a good augury for the future.

Architecturally the primary neighborhood unit calls for enclosed private gardens and a few nodal points—a group of trees, a fountain, a pergola—where mothers may refresh their senses, chat and sew, or watch over their offspring without being confined to their isolated domestic cells. When buildings are oriented for sunlight in open rows, then parapets and trellises and foliage should limit the long vistas, contain the movements of the toddler, and add to the visual sense of intimacy by richness of detail in the foreground. At this point in the plan the architect still can learn something from the "innerness" of the medieval city, for it symbolized to the point of exaggeration the fundamental needs of the primary group. Nowhere, perhaps, has this sense of intimacy been better embodied than in Matthew Nowicki's studies (with Mayer & Whittlesey) for the neighborhood units in the proposed capital of the East Punjab in India.

The opposite of the feeling of identification which arises instinctually in the village and more rationally in the modern neighborhood unit—the sense of being disinherited, anonymous, lonely, "not belonging"—is the typical malady in the modern metropolis, and it is accentuated by all the devices that produce mechanically regulated days and by unidentifiable living quarters in neighborhoods that have neither boundaries nor architectural definition. In such cities spontaneous reactions are fostered only by mass activities, which make people temporarily neighbors at football games and motor races and parades. Part of the strength of fascism, in both its open and its disguised forms, consists of playing on the need for solidarity and sympathy and of canalizing it into commercially or politically profitable forms. Proposals now fashionable—and strenuously advocated by Le Corbusier—for putting families and households into tall apartment houses, as in Marseilles and Rotterdam and New York, ignore the nature and needs of primary groups and forget human scale in shaping their environment. In big units children must be regimented or kept under the watchful eye of an adult, whereas the essence of good neighborhood planning is to give them the maximum amount of freedom of movement compatible with physical safety.

The visible house and the usable garden are important means of gaining security and stability for the growing child, and good neighborhood planning is an attempt to give a wider range to these qualities. The widespread recognition of this fact has doubtless prompted the movement into suburban areas;

unfortunately, however, for those below the highest income levels, the architectural solution of this problem in suburbia usually only caricatures the hope that prompted it.

But a city is more than a collection of primary groups and neighborhoods; a hundred thousand families might be so collected together without forming a city. For, in contrast to the village, the city is a combination of primary *and* secondary groups, of instinctual communities *and* purposeful associations. Whereas one belongs to a village by birth or residence, historically one becomes a member of a city by choice and participates in its life by engaging in an occupation or a profession, by joining a church or a fraternity or a trade union, by enrolling as a student in a school, or by organizing an office or a factory—in short, by banding with people of similar interests to pursue some specialized purpose. Thus the simple melody of village life becomes the complex, four-part, contrapuntal score of the city: the biological, economic, political, and educational themes weave in and out to form a higher but less stable unity. Diversity, conflict, differentiation, deliberate organization, and co-operation characterize city life. Here differentiation might be fatal to social life did not the city itself, as a shell and a symbol, help to restore unity.

Conceivably a city could be built underground, or it might be enclosed within the undifferentiated envelope of a single massive, air-conditioned skyscraper with no window opening to the outer world. Proposals are current for both types. But one important element in social development would be lacking in such a city—the aesthetic symbolization of its contents, its activity, its meaning. For the city, conceived as an architectural entity, is an attempt to make visible the facts of group life, to give them a form suited to their practical needs, and to underline their significance by means of architectural devices. Above all, the city is a symbol of enduring social relationships. The planning of the individual structures of the city is an important contribution to the functions they serve, and the interrelation of these structures in the city plan becomes a means of effecting a further unification—first in the daily imprint made on the mind and second in their actual functioning together. The city is the outward embodiment of a social order which does not itself reach the stage of self-consciousness until the city itself is built.

In cities not only do the social functions exist; they signify. Architecture and city planning are the visible translations of the total meaning of a culture. Each generation writes its biography in the buildings it creates; each culture characterizes, in the city, the unifying idea that runs through its activities. The complexity of even a small city would be baffling were it not for the unifying effect of the whole, which one reads almost at a glance just as one reads in the face of a person his health, his status, his background, his attainments. The medieval city says PROTECTION under the eye of God; the Baroque city says POWER under the favor of the Prince; the industrial city says PRODUCTION no matter what the human cost; the American metropolis says FINANCE must dominate. Silhouette and street plan, elevation and detail—these all express such elemental but comprehensive terms. In the ideal form of the modern city one must look for a fuller embodiment of human needs than any recent culture has produced.

ACHIEVEMENT OF URBAN BALANCE

Since the middle of the nineteenth century the greater part of urban planning has been a thing of shreds and patches. The first modern attempt to formulate the needs of a city as an integrated whole was the work of a man who was neither an architect nor a city planner—Sir Ebenezer Howard, the author of *Garden Cities of Tomorrow*.[3] Howard was both a mechanical and a social inventor, and he applied to the building of cities the same imaginative capacity that has led to the improvement of machines.

Originally Howard's conceptions did not touch directly on the physical problems of planning or on the question of architectural form. With great insight he applied himself first to the more fundamental concerns of the relation of population to industry and to the land, the possibilities of creating a new rural-urban pattern, and a reinterpretation of human needs in terms of twentieth-century political and technical possibilities. By reason of his fundamental approach, Howard provided a principle of order on which architectural conceptions could flourish. The first architect to give these conceptions architectural form was Tony Garnier, whose *Une Cité industrielle* . . .[4] because of its aesthetic freshness and clarity was closer to the spirit of Howard's pro posal than the first actual "garden city," Letchworth, founded five years after the first edition of Howard's book was published.

The first contribution made by Howard was to establish the necessity for limiting the area and the population of a city. He recognized that the indefinite and unlimited growth of cities led not merely to internal decay but to a permanent misuse of valuable agricultural land and a steady depletion of rural life

[3] London: Faber & Faber, 1946; first issued as *Tomorrow: A Peaceful Path to Real Reform* (London: S. Sonnenschein, 1902).   [4] Paris: Vincent [1918].

itself. Howard recognized in the city the same limitations on biological growth that is seen in the cell, though he did not use this biological metaphor. Every cell has a norm of development, and when it passes beyond that norm the wall of the cytoplasm will break down, unless growth leads to the reproductive process. When a cell has reached its optimum of growth, its nucleus divides in two, and two new cells are formed. Cities are not biological organisms; hence, except for a primitive dependence on a limited water and food supply, there is no natural limit to their growth—but there is a social limit, marked by lapse of function and disorganization and descent to more primitive social levels, and that limit has been constantly exceeded in the expansion of modern cities.

Howard pointed out that a city should be large enough to sustain a varied industrial, commercial, and social life. It should not be solely an industrial hive, solely an overgrown market, or solely a dormitory; instead, all these and many other functions, including rural ones, should be contained in a new kind of urban organization to which he applied the slightly misleading name of garden city. Howard had no thought of a return to the "simple life" or to a more primitive economy; on the contrary, he was seeking higher levels of both production and living. He believed that a city should be big enough to achieve social co-operation of a complex kind based on the necessary division of labor, but not so big as to handicap or frustrate these functions—as the big city tended to do even when viewed solely as an economic unit. In his ideal scheme the garden city was to have a population of 32,000 persons, 2,000 of whom were to be absorbed by the agriculture of the surrounding greenbelt. The entire estate was to consist of 6,000 acres, 1,000 of which were to be dedicated to the city itself; the over-all density was 30 persons to the gross acre, or some 90 to 95 persons per residential acre.

Neither Letchworth (1904) nor Welwyn Garden City (1919), the first two towns that were built in accordance with Howard's general formula, grew fast enough to contain 32,000 people by 1947. Meanwhile, in the working out of the New Towns policy in Britain, that original number, based on a reasonable guess rather than a statistical analysis, has been revised upward to 60,000. American experience suggests that there is a rough correlation between size and certain other characteristics and that cities of over 25,000 do not fully reproduce their population, though the net reproductive ratio of cities of 50,000 is still close enough to 1.0 to make them adequate biological environments. The correct population for a balanced urban community must be worked out experimentally, and it is probable that there are regional and cultural factors which will produce a considerable variation.

Howard's important contribution was the suggestion that the setting of limits of population, area, and density of use is the first step in the art of building cities. It is interesting to note that Leonardo da Vinci recognized the evils of congestion and blight that resulted from the overcrowding of Milan at the beginning of the sixteenth century. He proposed to put its 300,000 people into ten cities of 30,000 each—an idea that not only anticipated Howard's but even arrived at approximately the same population figure. Once the optimum size of the city has been reached, further growth must take place not by extension but by reproduction—the planning of another balanced community. This method overcomes one of the gravest effects of indefinite expansion—much faster growth at the periphery than within the nucleus, so that in the course of time unlimited expansion produces characteristic evidence of cultural and social impoverishment: the areas beyond the central city, from the standpoint of many essential social needs, are "do without" areas.

The modern way of fixing the city's organic limits was also conceived by Howard. A generation earlier John Ruskin had suggested that the boundaries of a city should be clearly defined, as in medieval times, by a wall; but, although the wall had once served in a secondary fashion as an open promenade, he did not suggest any further reason for building such a costly utility. Howard gave the archaic conception of the wall its functional modern horizontal equivalent: he conceived it as a permanent belt of green land dedicated to market gardens, agricultural schools, and other rural pursuits. To make secure both the internal development of the garden city and the external maintenance of the green wall, he proposed to vest the land in perpetuity in the original development company or the municipal corporation that sprang out of it. The common ownership of the land was the key to the plan as a whole—a provision which ensured that such prosperity as the community achieved would return in the form of increased land values not to individual landlords but to the community as a whole.

For Howard, the social control of land was of primary importance. Though he relied on individual enterprise to build the garden city and actually exhibited daring initiative in helping to launch two garden cities, he realized that land is in a category basically different from any other kind of property; also, since one who controls a city's land controls its destiny, Howard held that such control should be vested in a public body responsible for the good of the whole. To expect order, coherence, social foresight, and social responsibility through the "free action" of individual speculators was as self-defeating as to suppose that the mere random throwing of stones would result eventually in the building of a house.

In short, Howard wisely saw that urban design is fundamentally an economic and a political problem. Where control is unified, order is possible. The choice is not between control and no control but between an arbitrary, one-sided control and control exercised by a responsible authority acting in behalf of the entire community. The princes and ground landlords who produced the civilized town planning of the eighteenth century were self-appointed officers but their plans served something more than a short-sighted private interest, whereas the individual owners of property in the nineteenth century not only had split up power into a thousand parcels but also had renounced any higher consideration than the possibility of achieving private gain. This system, though called free, was actually a despotic and one-sided control, often openly in opposition to the public interest but more unchallengeable than the despot's because it was more diffused. Effective urban order in urban design awaited the unification of economic power and democratic political responsibility, and this is what Howard's program provided. Once this was established, design in the aesthetic and architectural sense was possible.

His third contribution—the most important of all—was his conception of the *balanced community*, relatively self-contained and big enough to provide out of its own resources and activities all that might be needed for the citizen's daily life. The garden city was no "housing project," no dormitory suburb, no trading estate, no industrial satellite; all these separate functions, along with those of recreation, education, and government, were integrated, and balance and integration were the marrow of the organism.

Howard's successors, in stressing the self-contained nature of the garden city, tended to overlook two other masterly contributions of his which round out that conception. The first was his division of the city into six wards or neighborhood units, for within the city he recognized the need for an even simpler pattern of organization. With that proposal Howard anticipated both the sociological and the planning discoveries of a later generation; in the United States, in time, the community center movement and the social unit plan—both arising out of the original initiatives that created the settlement house—would call attention to the need for "self-contained" planning on the neighborhood and family level. The second, and even more masterly perhaps, was Howard's perception that a city, no matter how well balanced, can never be completely self-contained. He pointed out that in a group of garden cities united by rapid transportation each would have facilities and resources that would supplement those of the others; so grouped, these "social cities" would in fact be the functional equivalent of the congested metropolis.

His insight here must be emphasized. Balance is a necessary attribute of all organic life but in the nature of things it is incomplete. An individual's personal balance is forever unstable; it needs family, friends, comrades, and colleagues to maintain even its internal harmony—hence the horror and demoralization of solitary confinement or prolonged isolation. So, too, the domestic community, though it may be complete from the standpoint of the child, is incomplete for the adult; even the adolescent must leave his immediate neighborhood to become a member of a secondary school. The balanced community of from thirty to sixty thousand citizens may take care of the larger number of daily activities, but there remains a whole range of activities of a more occasional or specialized nature which require a wider population base; higher education, certain types of recreation (like opera), specialized surgical or medical services, and comprehensively stocked department stores, for example, call for wider forms of co-operation. Even that balance is not final: certain activities will draw on a whole regional area for support, and these in turn, though still more intermittently or selectively, will call for international collaboration.

For a community, no matter how large, cannot be completely self-sufficient. The essential problem of modern urban planning is to conceive a series of relatively self-contained units, each of which has an open passage to the next larger and more complex community, so that eventually it will achieve an articulate order leading from the life of the child to the life of the mature man, from the immediate day-to-day activities, involving neighbors, friends, family, and fellow workers, to occasional activities that will enlist the support of men and women in every part of the world or specialized activities that will call for the constant intercourse of special people or groups everywhere. Now each of these communities should be balanced, each should be mainly self-contained; each should symbolize architecturally its own wholeness. Yet their very functioning and their growth will depend on drawing together special resources and facilities, and above all special people, from other communities; and these wider unifications, this more complex balance, must also be symbolized. That which the overgrown metropolis achieved by mere vastness and

FIGURE 566.
TOWN HALL,
HILVERSUM,
THE NETHERLANDS

W. M. Dudok, architect

One of the best examples of adequate urban symbolism.

From *Wendingen*

to achieve by law a result that cannot be achieved without planning; by turns it is too loose or too flexible, too indiscriminate or too selective.

Perhaps the worst sin of zoning is that it violates an essential social characteristic of neighborhood planning, namely, that each unit must be balanced—it is the city writ small. Each unit, accordingly, must have a place for the industrial, political, educational, and domestic facilities which pertain to its special purposes. Thus the residential neighborhood must contain more than a collection of houses, in the fashion of a segregated residential zone; it should also have, *as an integral part of the plan,* a place for retail stores, for garages, for small workshops serving the immediate needs of the inhabitants; in short, it should be a representative human community, expressing the variety and cooperation of the larger whole of which it is a part. This principle also holds true for the factory quarter. If that quarter is properly planned, it will provide not merely transportation facilities and storage but also recreational facilities for the lunch hour or for after-work sports, and it will also subserve the political life of the community by providing suitable meeting places and auditoriums for public discussion and conference. In a city designed to encompass the full nature of man the isolation and segregation of his functions, as worked out in the militarist-industrialist pattern of the last three centuries, must be replaced by structures designed for the whole man at every phase of his life.

Social Structures. The social nucleus, with its institutions serving politics, education, and religion, is essential to the definition of the neighborhood unit

FIGURE 567. GREENBELT, MARYLAND. AIR VIEW

Ellington & Wadsworth, architects; Hale Walker, town planner

Open planning in a greenbelt town.   Photograph Library of Congress

or precinct, and no quarter can be called well designed unless those functions have a central place in the plan. These institutions are the chromosomes which transmit the social heritage, and in providing a place for them both their practical office and their symbolic function must be respected. What Sigfried Giedion has termed monumentality, but what the author of this chapter prefers to describe as durable symbolism, rests partly on a sufficient dedication of thought, money, and love to the creation of such buildings. Dudok's Town Hall at Hilversum in Holland (Fig. 566) is one of the best examples of adequate urban symbolism which the modern movement can yet show. In contrast, the 42-story United Nations Secretariat Building in New York, merely another skyscraper in a city of skyscrapers, entirely lacks the symbolic distinction its height was designed to convey.

This does not mean that all the higher social functions of the community need be centralized in a single plaza or civic center: certain ecological associations are as marked in the grouping of human institutions as in the grouping

FIGURE 568. GREENBELT, MARYLAND. A HOUSE GROUPING

Ellington & Wadsworth, architects; Hale Walker, town planner

The openness of the country woven through the town itself.

Photograph Library of Congress

of plant species. The school and the library, for example, belong together; but there is no such kinship between the school and the motion-picture theater, which is more effectively associated—as in the Waikiki development at Honolulu—with a group of shops, and these in turn with tearooms, bars, and restaurants. In creating such nuclei, the architect must avoid "locked-in" plans which do not permit an economic expansion or contraction of functions. Even when a norm of growth is established for the community, no amount of calculation can fix absolute limits for the growth or shriveling of a particular function; hence space and open planning must provide the needed factor of safety, particularly when the installation itself is a costly one.

Cell Boundaries. The boundaries of the urban cell must be as clearly defined as those of the city itself. There are two modern methods for establishing such limits, both functional and visual. One is by means of the through-traffic avenue, planned to unite a series of neighborhood units. Instead of serving, as of old, as a river whose banks are lined with houses, such traffic arteries should be enjoined from every other use; the divorce of major highways and buildings must be complete in order to secure speed and safety for the first and freedom from congestion, danger, and noise for the second. Access roads and

FIGURE 569.
INTEGRATED
INDUSTRIAL AND
RESIDENTIAL AREA,
ONGAR, ENGLAND.
MODEL

Open planning for a city
of 60,000

Courtesy British
Information Services

lanes, which filter out the traffic and finally bring it to a standstill in the heart of the residential district, will further lessen the economic waste that went with the undifferentiated streets of the obsolete standard plan.

The other method of establishing the neighborhood boundary is by means of the park strip—a local greenbelt serving as interstitial tissue within the larger urban greenbelt. Ideally it should be possible to proceed on foot from one part of the city to another by means of such a continuous belt without having to cross, at level, a single major artery. Such belts may be independent of the major roads or may parallel them; in either case they ensure not only a foreground of verdure in the approach to important groups of buildings but also the possibility of a terminal point of green in every open vista. Even when the architecture is as mediocre as that of Radburn, New Jersey, the aesthetic effect of the continuous inner park that binds the superblocks together is extraordinarily charming.

Where the greenbelt is used within the city and where by municipal ownership or by zoning a permanent greenbelt is established around a city in a fashion that puts the whole countryside within ready walking or cycling distance, the need for a central park disappears. Gardens, playgrounds, and recreation fields on a small scale will be allotted to the neighborhood unit; but for the other purposes of the park the greenbelt and the open country suffice.[5]

[5] The plan for the rebuilding of Warsaw is characterized by a most interesting greenbelt system. Major greenbelts contain the chief communal social and recreational facilities and both connect and separate the individual neighborhoods. From them smaller, more intimate green areas open out, leading to primary schools and serving to define the primary dwelling cells. Ed.

FIGURE 570. BALDWIN HILLS VILLAGE,
LOS ANGELES, CALIFORNIA.

TWO DETAILS

R. D. Johnson and Wilson, Merrill & Alexander, associated architects; Clarence Stein, consultant

The "inner scale" in dwelling environment.

Photographs Margaret Lowe

In a city conceived as a group of neighborhood units and functional zones there is no single center and therefore no reason to establish a single point of dominance as the terminus of a major axis. Each part of the city may in turn become the center when it serves as a focus for some particular activity serving the city as a whole, and that functional shifting of the social axis—in deep accord with the principle of relativity—could only be falsified by a centralized and hierarchical scheme.[6]

[6] For an example of the contrary opinion see Bruno Taut's *Die Stadtkrone* (Jena: Diederichs, 1919), where the town is conceived of as dominated by a great central people's palace to symbolize the social idealism of the city, much as medieval towns had been dominated by their churches or cathedrals. Ed.

FIGURE 571.
NORRIS DAM,
TENNESSEE VALLEY
AUTHORITY.
AIR VIEW

The "outer scale" of re-
gional development.

Courtesy TVA

SCALE IN URBAN DESIGN

This new kind of planning, with its full-fledged differentiation of the city's traffic and residential functions, produces differences in tempo which in turn have an architectural result. The change of speed from the through-traffic highway (safe average speed 45 m.p.h.) to the walking strip (maximum 4 m.p.h.) and in turn to the center of the domestic area (crawling speed or complete rest) should be translated into appropriate forms of design. The blank walls of parking lots, garages, and filling stations, broken only by signal pylons or directive signs, go well with the highest speed. Here each architectural form should be standardized to convey its function by its outline; repetition and absence of emphasis should characterize both planting and architecture on both sides of major traffic arteries. When one reaches the other extreme, however, a certain richness, variety, and even intricacy of detail, particularly in the treatment of landscape and garden, should characterize the neighborhood. The attempt to impose the aesthetics of the transportation artery upon residential neighborhoods, thus creating acres of formalized blankness, is none the better for being called modern architecture.

The only traditional images that at all suggest this new order of design are those of certain college campuses in the United States or the ancient Inns of Court in London. But in any case the architectural result of divorcing buildings from through-traffic streets should be noted: the two-dimensional façade disappears as the major element in planning, and the three-dimensional building—conceived in depth and showing a silhouette as well as a façade—again becomes possible as an urban form. Even when such buildings are organized in rows, as in Baldwin Hills Village in Los Angeles, their third dimension remains an essential architectural feature, preserved by the diverse angles of approach. With such neighborhood planning in complete units, the natural setting and the buildings can be treated as a unified whole.

The unit principle of urban design carries through every part of the new city. Instead of stretching out indefinitely along the traffic street or highway in typical ribbon development, the modern market center—first concretely embodied in the drive-in markets of California and in the Sears, Roebuck suburban retail stores—is a compact unit, off the highway, with a special parking space for cars. When the original proposals for a collective shopping precinct in Coventry were vetoed by the shortsighted merchants of that city, who wanted their center bisected by a through-traffic artery, these business men were in fact acting to restrain trade rather than to promote it. Good marketing practice demands access to the shopping area but not passage through it; for shopping is done on foot, and even in the old-fashioned type of city narrow shopping streets like Bond Street and Madison Avenue and others in Amsterdam or Buenos Aires remain the most efficient and prosperous districts. The compact alignment of shops around an elongated narrow plaza at right angles to a main traffic artery and with parking facilities on the outer rim is a correlate of modern design—a form that lends itself to possible variations by arrangement in the shape of a fret or a succession of scallops. Abercrombie's proposals for such marketing centers in his report on Greater London are not the least brilliant features of that great over-all design. In one of the first British New Towns, Stevenage, such a center has, in fact, been designed.

In replanning the old towns as well as in developing the new, certain further results follow from a recognition of the fact that the neighborhood and not the avenue or the building is the true unit of planning. Piecemeal construction or readaptation is a wasteful and unsatisfactory process. To make an effective reconstruction in accordance with modern principles of design a whole quarter must be built from the ground up. Whatever merit there is in Rockefeller Center, New York, or in Lansbury Neighborhood, London, springs in part from this unified operation. Once such unity is established aesthetically over a considerable urban area, as in Bloomsbury in London, the structures tend to resist degrading urban changes; where, on the other hand, it has been absent from the beginning, blight easily enters and spreads.

When a city is planned and created by quarters, it preserves the virtue of visual coherence and unity and avoids the Baroque vice of denying time and change and rival points of view. Even in a relatively small city of twenty thousand people one should not look for a single building form or tradition; rather, it is a mark of architectural vitality that each age should choose its own symbols and its own expression. Indeed, the preservation of the best of these expressions gives a link of continuity in time, and the most comprehensive scheme of demolition and reconstruction should go out of its way—even at the expense of superficial unity—to preserve such buildings when they are still serviceable. An organic plan will always have a place for such departures, which, like the off-colored flower the French gardener wisely puts in the midst of his most harmonious bed, even serve to accentuate that very harmony. When a town is built by quarters, as modern Amsterdam has been planned, each quarter will have its own character—a unity in the diversity of the city as a whole.

One further point that relates to the nature of man remains to be dealt with. Part of man's nature is enhanced by association, participation, and togetherness, and the city is pre-eminently the environment in which the functions men best perform in groups are housed and symbolized. But another aspect of man's nature must also be heeded if association is to be durable and fruitful: there must be a place for withdrawal, a refuge for privacy, solitary communion, innerness. One of the commonest mistakes of contemporary planning is to conceive of man as a purely extroverted creature who thrives on external stimuli, with never a moment when he seeks to be alone and never a place to be alone in. But the goldfish bowl is no more natural to man than the cave; in so far as men live well, they must alternate between the two—between light and darkness, between society and solitude, between participation and withdrawal. Part of the charm of a big city like London or Paris is that out of its slow organic growth it provides a place for both attitudes—witness Westminster with its broad walks and pleasances and public spaces where the collective architecture and the people make a maximum impression and, by contrast, the devious walks it offers through alleys, backways, and lanes which are as private as a cloister. Children show a demand for solitariness, and good nursery schools provide perches or cubbyholes into which a child may withdraw for solitary brooding. Where the need for seclusion is recognized it can be translated into public forms, just as Olmsted laid out the Ramble in Central Park for this very purpose. A city without such secluded walks and retreats is no place for lovers or thinkers.

In short, if we respect the nature of man, the order established by urban planning must be an inclusive one: it must respect every side of man's nature and do equal justice to every need; it can no longer subordinate the major business of life to the profits of the ground landlord or the desire of the transport corporation to promote more and more congested transportation. The modern planner will obey Emerson's injunction to save on the low levels and to spend on the high ones and, while rigorously standardizing, rationalizing, economizing, and at times eliminating the subordinate mechanical utilities, he will do this for the purpose of treating the positive functions of life with a noble largesse—the largesse of freedom, spontaneity, and art.

SUGGESTED ADDITIONAL READING FOR CHAPTER 50

Abercrombie, Patrick, *The Greater London Plan, 1944* (London: H. M. Stationery Office, 1945). Bold proposals for decentralization of London, with the building of ten new towns of 60,000 people each. Cf. Le Corbusier.

Bardet, Gaston, *Pierre sur pierre; construction du nouvel urbanisme* (Paris: Éditions L.C.B. [1945]). Series of important papers on modern urbanism.

Behrendt, Walter Curt, *Modern Building; Its Nature, Problems, and Forms* (New York: Harcourt, Brace, 1937). One of the best discussions of modern architecture in relation to urbanism.

Geddes, Patrick, *Cities in Evolution* (London: Williams & Norgate, 1915). Introduction to outlook and purposes by one of the most influential thinkers in the modern cities movement.

Giedion, Sigfried, *Space, Time and Architecture* (Cambridge, Mass.: Harvard University Press, 1941).

Goodman, Percival, and Paul Goodman, *Communitas; Means of Livelihood and Ways of Life* (Chicago: University of Chicago Press, 1947). The best analysis of city form as the expression of economic and social ideals.

Gropius, Walter, *Rebuilding Our Communities* (Chicago: Theobald, 1945). On decentralization; a step beyond Le Corbusier's formulation.

Hilberseimer, Ludwig, *The New City: Principles of Planning*, with an introduction by Mies van der Rohe (Chicago: Theobald, 1944). Systematic outline of structural planning changes in terms of new functions; somewhat narrowly conceived.

Howard, Sir Ebenezer, *Garden Cities of To-morrow*, edited with a preface by F. J. Osborn; with an introductory essay by Lewis Mumford (London: Transatlantic Arts, 1946). A classic; its radical analysis of the problem of planning and extending cities not merely laid the foundations of the garden-city movement but has affected urban-planning thought throughout the world.

Le Corbusier (Charles Édouard Jeanneret), *The City of To-morrow and Its Planning*, translated from the 8th French ed. of *Urbanisme* by Frederick Etchells (London: Architectural Press [1947]). Scheme for an elaborately mechanized metropolis of 3,000,000; an attempt to cleanse, open up, and clarify the city of finance capitalism.

—— *La Ville radieuse* (Boulogne sur Seine: Éditions de l'Architecture d'aujourd'hui [1935]). In many ways an advance on *The City of To-morrow.* . . .

McAllister, Gilbert, and Elizabeth McAllister, *Homes, Towns, and Countryside*, a symposium (London: Batsford, 1945).

Mumford, Lewis, *The Culture of Cities* (New York: Harcourt, Brace, 1938).

Osborn, Frederic James, *Green-Belt Cities; the British Contribution* (London: Faber, 1946). Not merely a critique of the greenbelt principle but an evaluation, from the inside, of the method of building on Garden City principles.

Perry, Clarence Arthur, "The Neighborhood Unit," monograph No. 1 in *Neighborhood and Community Planning*, Vol. VII of *Regional Survey of New York and Its Environs* (New York: Regional Plan of New York and Its Environs, 1927–31). A pioneer synthesis.

Poëte, Marcel, *Introduction à l'urbanisme, l'évolution des villes; la leçon de l'antiquité* (Paris: Boivin [c1929]).

—— *Une Vie de cité; Paris de sa naissance à nos jours* . . . 3 vols. text, 1 vol. illustrations (Paris: Picard, 1924–31). A classic; the only adequate analysis of the development of the city in terms of its life, its functions, and the resultant plans and structures.

Purdom, Charles B., *The Building of Satellite Towns* . . . (London: Dent, 1925).

—— *The Garden City; a Study in the Development of a Modern Town* (London: Dent, 1913). The best study on Letchworth, England's first garden city.

Rasmussen, Steen Eiler, *London: the Unique City*, with an introduction by James Bone, English rev. ed. (London: Cape [1937]).

Saarinen, Eliel, *The City; Its Growth, Its Decay, Its Future* (New York: Reinhold, 1943). Excellent adaptation of Howard's principles to the rebuilding of metropolitan areas.

Sert, J. L., *Can Our Cities Survive?* (Cambridge, Mass.: Harvard University Press, 1942). Survey of modern planning problems based on studies by the Congrès Internationaux d'Architecture Moderne; strikingly illustrated.

Sharp, Thomas, *Town Planning*, rev. ed. (Harmondsworth, England: Pelican Books [c1945]. Though Mr. Sharp's *bête noire* is the garden city, which he erroneously confuses with open planning and suburban sprawl, this weakness does not prevent his book from being the best short summary of the problems of modern town planning.

Sitte, Camillo, *The Art of Building Cities*, a translation of *Der Städtebau nach seinen künstlerischen Grundsatzen* (Vienna, 1899) by Charles T. Stewart (New York: Reinhold, 1945). A study of the aesthetics of city building in the Middle Ages and the Renaissance.

Unwin, Sir Raymond, *Town Planning in Practice; an Introduction to the Art of Designing Cities and Suburbs* (London: Unwin, 1909). An excellent summary of the art, as conceived at the time of publication. Nothing adequate has been published since.

Zucker, Paul (editor), *New Architecture and City Planning; a Symposium* (New York: Philosophical Library, 1944).

51

The Architect and City Planning

By G. HOLMES PERKINS

IT HAS BEEN man's lot to dream. From his dreams have come great empires, new conquests of space and time, the awe-inspiring machinery of today, and the heritage of the heroic tales of Homer and Shakespeare. The visions seen by gifted leaders have opened the way (not at once, but ultimately) to others; the new possibilities are perceived by the many when once demonstrated by the few. Among man's most effective creations has been the city—a shining symbol of his aspirations, though murky and distorted in its hidden recesses, yet all in all a noble creation. The city has come to be thought the mirror of its age; but it is also the creator. The wholeness and completeness of its final form in any age is its final dry and cast-off shell; it is in the doing, in the drive to make the dream a reality, that the idea becomes the powerful molder of man's mind, society, and habits.

Perhaps at times we read into history those morals and hopes which we think good for us. At other times we seem to welcome the illusion, so skillfully fostered by the Romance of King Arthur and by the Pre-Raphaelites, of the Middle Ages as the ideal society. Even the most logical of modern architects, influenced in part by this same sentiment, appear to see in the training of the medieval master builder a perfection of principle from which we have strayed. Could it be that the people who built the austere battlements, damp walls, and crowded cities of those days were not quite so sanguine as ourselves about the perfection of their society? The enthusiasm with which medieval quarters were abandoned in the Renaissance was universal. Men stayed behind not from choice but because they, like our slum dwellers today, could afford no better. Man's reverence for history had not yet developed to the point of making him blind to new opportunities. The Gothic nave was added to the Romanesque choir, the Renaissance façade and reredos were added to the Gothic fabric. Man was bent on improving his surroundings.

FIGURE 572. THE RÖMER,
FRANKFURT AM MAIN,
GERMANY

The medieval character in city aspect.

Courtesy G. Holmes Perkins

FIGURE 573. "MONKS
BUILDING A CLOISTER,"
FROM A FIFTEENTH-
CENTURY MANUSCRIPT,
NUREMBERG, GERMANY

The integrated training of the medieval master builder.

Courtesy G. Holmes Perkins

But between us and those glories lies a revolution in which men dreamed of
profits and new worlds of commercial conquest. A surge of new blood ran
through the veins of the old cities; they grew in the image of their makers—the
industries fathered by coal and steam. These crude, lusty giants of the new
prosperity enticed men away from ancient modes of living and the calm of

FIGURE 574. AIR VIEW OVER THE PLACE DE LA CARRIÈRE AND THE PLACE STANISLAS, NANCY, FRANCE

Héré de Corny, architect

Old medieval quarters were abandoned in the Renaissance and replaced with new developments; man was bent on improving his surroundings.

From Guérinet (editor), *Nancy, architecture, beaux-arts, monuments*

country life to the gaudy pleasures of gas-lit streets. Slums rivaling those of imperial Rome rose again in every land; in the United States even the oft-repeated conflagrations racing through the wooden tenements of its cities could not keep these squalid quarters from springing up anew in ever more permanent form. In spite of the prevailing callousness to the evils of slum conditions and absorption in the mad pursuit of the dollar, some men still retained a civic pride. Private subscriptions built the Washington Monument and the Smithsonian Institution, Central Park was laid out, Boston's metropolitan parks set an example to the country, and the Chicago Art Institute reflected awakened leadership in the Middle West; all these evidences of an awakened civic consciousness date from the nineteenth century.

In the artistic confusion of that century eclecticism reigned. Fashion replaced creativeness in architecture. Successful men became aware of art, but without knowledge or confidence in their own judgment they assembled great collections representative of the taste of the art dealer. A painful dependence on Europe grew while at the same moment great structural innovations were

FIGURE 575.
VIEW ON 138TH STREET,
NEW YORK

The prevailing callousness to slum conditions.

Courtesy G. Holmes Perkins

FIGURE 576.
ROYAL PAVILION,
BRIGHTON, ENGLAND

Fashion replaced architectural reality.

Henry Holland and John Nash, architects

From a colored aquatint in Nash, *The Royal Pavilion at Brighton*

developing at home a new architecture which was long denied its birthright by Americans—indeed until, to their astonishment, it was acclaimed by foreign critics. Side by side with a self-assertive personal desire for showiness grew an equally boisterous city pride. A prosperous and booming West put on, in 1893 and 1904, two world's fairs that dazzled the country.

The citizens of Chicago were not content for it to be merely the biggest city of the West. The daring and far-sighted Burnham Plan was given to the city by the Merchants' and Commercial Clubs in 1909 (see Fig. 578). It offered

FIGURE 577. RELIANCE BUILDING,
CHICAGO, ILLINOIS

D. H. Burnham and Company, architects

Great structural innovations were developing a new
American architecture.

From Giedion, *Space, Time and Architecture* . . .

to Chicago's citizens a dream of a new Lake Front, unrivaled parkways connecting with forest preserves, an improved railroad system with terminals and
beltline, and a civic center. Perhaps this might be called visionary and impractical, but to the citizens it was sufficiently persuasive for them to vote nearly
$300,000,000 on it in twenty years.[1] It has recently become the fashion to
criticize these early plans for paying too much attention to parks and civic art.
It would seem much fairer, as Gaus has said, "to stress the fact that these men
pioneered in creating a conception of the city as a total organism with needs
inherent in its organic character above and beyond the interests and activities
of the atomic individuals who lived and worked in the city."[2]

Others were also interesting themselves in the city. Turner's paper at the
Chicago Fair in 1893 noted the closing of the American frontier and forecast
a new era. Ely began his studies on land; out of these grew a new profession,

[1] Bond issues approved between 1912 and 1931 totaled $234,000,000 and special assessments
$57,600,000, making a total of $291,600,000.
[2] John Merriman Gaus, *The Education of Planners* (Cambridge, Mass.: Graduate School of
Design, Harvard University, 1943).

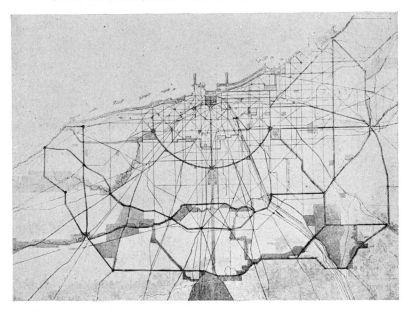

FIGURE 578. CHICAGO, ILLINOIS. GENERAL PLAN PROPOSED IN THE BURNHAM
PLAN, SHOWING PARK SYSTEMS

A scheme sufficiently persuasive to influence the citizens to vote nearly $300,000,000 toward its
realization.   Courtesy G. Holmes Perkins

that of the land economist, and its contributions were shortly to become decisive in the development of city planning principles and policies. Lincoln
Steffens aroused the people to demand new standards in city administration
and an improved science of government. The increasingly complex problems
of the city were under attack simultaneously from many sides, yet men were
long unaware of the similarity of their interests.

NEW PLANNING POLICIES

In 1909 the first national planning conference in the United States took
place in Washington. The emphasis by now had moved to a consideration of
the social and economic problems confronting cities still bloated by continuing
waves of immigration. But new inventions conspired against the already bat-
tered city. Almost overnight Ford's cheap auto made obsolete the rambling
rural paths of Boston or the subdividers' paradise of gridiron streets as represented in Chicago and Manhattan. Federal aid for badly needed new roads,
in 1915, gave a new emphasis to highway and traffic engineering at a time
when the planners' expanding range of interest had begun to raise deep ques-

FIGURE 579. AIR VIEW SHOWING TYPICAL NEW YORK CITY SUBURB
The subdivider's paradise . . .   Courtesy G. Holmes Perkins

tions of public policy, economy, and social structure—questions the answers to which would make demands on the developing talents of specialists in traffic, land economics, zoning, and industrial location. The crisis of the 1930's brought to the fore the problem of urban housing; it in turn tended later to absorb the major attention of the planner.

The basic duty of the planning commission was to unify these numerous and varied lines of study and of action and build them into a comprehensive public program. Few were prepared to shoulder such a task. In time some schools began to train men for these new jobs, but still most city planners continued to be recruited from the fields of architecture, law, economics, landscape architecture, or public administration. An accelerated growth and a changed composition became evident in the technical staffs coincident with the activities of the National Resources Planning Board. These new and enlarged staffs bore as little resemblance to the earlier ones as a modern Ford bore to its ancestor of 1910. The single expert had become a team. A review both of the civil-service examinations and the job descriptions of the larger cities reveals the changed complexion of these staffs: research analysts in popu-

FIGURE 580. OAKLAND BAY BRIDGE, SAN FRANCISCO, CALIFORNIA

C. H. Purcell, engineer; T. L. Pflueger, architect

A new emphasis on highway engineering.

Courtesy G. Holmes Perkins

lation, industrial and commercial trends, land, public utilities, financing, and railroads occupy fully a third of the positions; specialists in engineering and land planning have replaced the solitary architect; and the co-ordinator and administrator have become necessary to unify the efforts of the team.

THE PLANNING STAFF AS A TEAM

The ascendency of science in men's minds today is also reflected in the process of city planning. Enamored of the natural sciences, men have at times placed an unreasoning reliance on the growing but as yet immature social and political sciences. The architecture of cities reluctantly shares the field with the youthful science of city planning. This trend has become particularly pronounced in the United States, where land economists, sociologists, geographers, public administrators, and lawyers, in addition to the architects, have interested themselves in the problems of the city. Well-organized research has made significant advances; analysts in these new sciences are appearing in numbers and are increasingly engaged in city planning. Although the new sciences have begun to offer a firmer foundation for action, they are not substitutes for the architecture of cities.

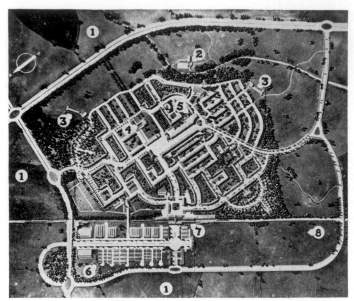

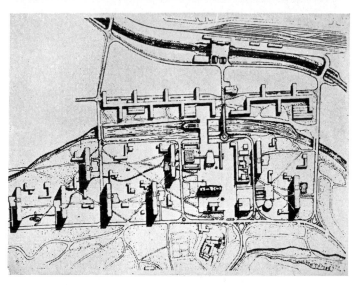

FIGURE 581.

TWO PROJECTS
FOR MODEL TOWNS

ABOVE: Plan of a model town; Thomas Sharp, designer.

1: Greenbelt; 2: Swimming pool; 3: School; 4: Community center and theater; 5: Town center; 6: Industrial area; 7: Station; 8: Area for industrial development.

BELOW: Proposed city center from the City Planning Project, St. Dié, France; Le Corbusier, designer.

The architect is equipped to demonstrate the possibilities of new city forms arising from new social orientations.

Courtesy G. Holmes Perkins

Underlying the apparent complexity of the city is the guiding conception of its organic unity. The planning staff both as a team and as individuals requires, besides a sincere humility, an unusual breadth of sympathy and understanding of the city's problems. Each in the study of his own segment becomes a co-ordinator, for he must early come to realize the relation of his work to the whole and its effect upon the recommendations and ideas of others. Only from such a comprehensive approach can an effective unity be gained. To weigh and balance these many factors requires a great maturity, and to find a path out of the chaos requires vision of the highest order. Some men in all the professions possess these qualities; they will become the leaders. But latent talents alone will not prove effective; they must be actively focused upon these city problems if they are to operate with ease and effectiveness. This is not to suggest that a city planner must be a master of all the related professions or that a lifetime of training is needed, for maturity of judgment and brilliance of vision are not the exclusive possession of age. Daring idealism and acceptance of the risks it entails will in the long run prove more realistic and beneficial to the community than the shortsighted caution of the "practical" man.

UNIQUE CONTRIBUTION OF THE ARCHITECT

With the widening scope of city planning, the architect's former unchallenged leadership has vanished. As a social and political art, city planning requires for its healthy exercise the aroused interest and support of the entire community. To maintain unity against attack is the hardest task; without the support of all the sciences and arts the problem will be doubly difficult. Yet it has been argued that the architectural profession, since it is addressed to social objectives, should assume an unshared leadership in city building. This argument is not persuasive, for unless the architect is by some magic to become at the same time an economist, geographer, and public administrator he must remain a member of a team; he must share both the labor and the glory. Nevertheless, as a valued and indispensable member of the team, he alone can give inspiring form to the city; he alone can crystallize in brick and mortar, in glass and steel, a people's aspirations and by his buildings influence the habits and thoughts of future societies.

Those are impressive contributions which the architect can make as a result of his special training. Yet it has been said at length, and at times not without boresome repetition, that the architect's chief role is as co-ordinator of the building industry—an important role, but a drab one surely. Is not his true role a more inspiring and noble one? His designs in their most creative form have the power to open men's minds to finer prospects, to kindle new hopes, and to shape man's course. In planning for the future we citizens make deliberate choices—we spend money, ours or the community's, in the honest expectation that by so doing we shall be made happier and our city and our neighbor will be benefited. When we repave a street or build a new school we know

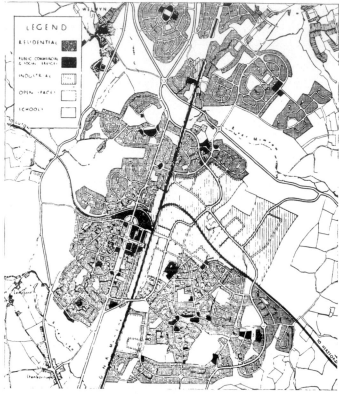

FIGURE 582.
WELWYN GARDEN
CITY, ENGLAND.
PLAN AND AIR VIEW

Louis de Soissons,
architect

The relation of residential
areas to the town center
and the industrial area
across the railroad tracks
may be readily seen; note
also the mall in the town
center and the large
amount of open space.
North is at the top.

From Purdom, *The
Building of Satellite
Towns*

through experience what we are getting for our efforts, but in city planning
the choice is not always between known alternatives; there is still pioneering

FIGURE 583.
LETCHWORTH
GARDEN CITY,
ENGLAND. AIR VIEW

The garden city showed
a way out of the drab
confusion.

Courtesy G. Holmes
Perkins

to be done, there are visions to be seen and new ideas to be tried out. When such dreams involve new city forms and social re-orientations, they are accepted slowly; few sense their potentialities because the conceptions are beyond their experience and can be visualized only dimly. The architect by training is equipped to demonstrate in clearest form the newest possibilities; he can present pictures which will grip the imagination and by means of which the present and the possible may be compared and a multitude of choices may be made with confidence.

It must remain the architect's most rewarding job to create, or help to create, cities which will not only stand the tests of economy and social utility but also inspire men's lives. We are not without abundant evidence of the success of the architect in offering visions which have caught the public imagination. Man's dissatisfaction with his environment combined with new vision has time and again proved his most powerful stimulus to action, and the briefest glance at history shows many architects whose ideas have reshaped our lives. There are architects today whose designs have inspired a new generation that will build the cities of the future, and others whose creations still need testing in the furnace of life.

One of the most persuasive of today's ideas is that of the garden city (see Figs. 582, 583). Fifty years old, it has been through the severest tests. Letchworth and Welwyn have been the proving grounds. Convincing as were Sir Raymond Unwin's arguments in support of Sir Ebenezer Howard's ideas, it was his translation of idea into reality that offered proof of their soundness and gained them public support. In shining contrast to the growing suburban sprawl and ribbon developments offered the public by the speculative developer, the garden city showed a way out of the drab, undifferentiated chaos of highways and homes. Its serenity, neighborliness, economy, and green space combined to offer to anyone a bit of country living along with the conveniences of the city which previously none but the richest had been able to afford—and then only at great expenditure of time in daily commuting.

Throughout the world variations of the garden city have been tried. Characteristically enough, the one-class garden suburb has been the weak offshoot of a great ideal. In the United States such subdivisions, with the blessing of the Federal Housing Administration, have become the trade-mark of the better builder. Though at their best they provide good housing, all the other necessities of life are left unprovided for. Where are the schools, the parks, the jobs, the shops? Occasionally shops, less frequently a park, seldom a school within safe walking distance, and practically never a job without commuting; certainly these are caricatures of Howard's idea. Yet we owe something to this failure to face the problem squarely. War-time housing experiences showed that, in spite of shortages, people were beginning to reject housing without shops or schools. Not a few projects remained empty because community facilities were not available. Radburn and the whole series of greenbelt towns, though model designs in many ways and valuable as experiments, hardly present a pattern which, if repeated, offers hope of a solution to all the problems of urban growth.

Not until the garden-city idea is fully tested in Britain's New Towns can we evaluate with certainty its worth. But in these developments, seen in their context as part of a national planning policy and system, the prospects of success appear bright; in fact, no other application of the principle of ordered city growth seems so persuasive or appealing. In Britain's far-sighted adoption of Howard's principles we see the persistence of an idea; at Letchworth and Welwyn the vision was tested by reality; and, when men saw thus exemplified the opportunity for better living, the choice was made—though not until every halfway measure had shown by its failure that nothing less than full acceptance of the idea offered a real solution.

NEW OPPORTUNITIES FOR ARCHITECTURAL VISION

Although we might wish that less time were needed to gain acceptance of new principles and that new visions were received with more open minds,

FIGURE 584.
BLOOMSBURY,
LONDON.
AIR VIEW
AND DETAIL

The repose and beauty of London's residential squares.

Courtesy British
Information Services

perhaps two generations were not too long to wait for such universal acceptance of that revolutionary idea. Once accepted, however, it lost its revolutionary sound and newer visions appeared to meet new needs, to offer other
choices, and to mold new social forms. The twentieth century, too, has not
been without its challenging concepts. That of the neighborhood as a basis for
future growth and redevelopment has, for example, gained an almost alarm-
ing currency. Almost without exception the various planning commissions are
busy carving their cities into neighborhoods. In doing so, they have been ably

FIGURE 585.
LOWER MANHATTAN,
NEW YORK. AIR VIEW

The need to squeeze out a profit.

Courtesy G. Holmes
Perkins

abetted by the exhortations and designs of planners and architects whose war housing experience has convinced them of the soundness of the principle and the imperative need for action now. The pioneering demonstrations of Henry Wright and Clarence Stein have begun to bear fruit; the prophecies of Frank Lloyd Wright have influenced a whole generation; and the pioneering social architecture of Gropius and Le Corbusier has opened new avenues in city building. As noted earlier, it has been—and should continue to be—the architect's historic role to unfold challenging vistas of future cities.

In earlier times the patronage of princes, of the church, and of states gave concrete effect to the architect's vision, but today the ponderous size and increasing complexity of cities combine with the atomized ownership of land to make such realizations proportionately fewer and less imposing amid the shapeless sprawl of the metropolis. It is not that the architect's imagination has grown dim but that the obstacles to fulfillment have mounted. Formerly a single patron might ensure success, and a common local way of building gave assurance of architectural harmony throughout the city. In this tradition the reserved, gentlemanly architecture of Georgian England gave repose and beauty to London's residential squares (Fig. 584). More recently the financial pressures, the rivalries of owners, and a laissez-faire architectural creed of disagreement by agreement have brought functional, financial, and aesthetic chaos to our cities.

The architect's most effective role may well be the creation of a vision so compelling that men will seek to achieve again an organic civic unity. Yet

FIGURE 586. WILLIAMSBURG HOUSING DEVELOPMENT, BROOKLYN, NEW YORK. AIR VIEW

R. H. Shreve, chief architect

In the architecture of cities the architect must grasp the social and economic forces that mold its growth.   Photograph Thomas Airviews

there is little evidence that the architectonic dream alone will be sufficiently persuasive. The garden city idea owes its survival not alone to that small devoted band who fought for it through years of public indifference. Its vitality lay instead in its social appeal, its demonstrated charm, its offer of a refuge from the devitalizing drabness of by-law streets, and, perhaps most of all, its financial and administrative soundness as a way to better living. To offer a utopia without the means of reaching it reveals a limited conception.

It is said repeatedly, and not without reason, that architecture is a social art. The objectives of this art will be set by the aspirations of society. Many will contribute the ideals and social forms toward which we strive; among them will be the architect. Many will search for the means to reach the goal, for new legal forms, financial formulas, administrative machinery, and social and architectural concepts are needed to build the new city. Together these tools will prove effective; used alone, none will be adequate. An architecture of

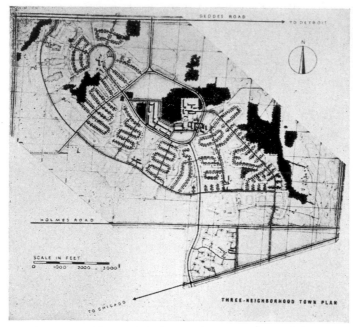

FIGURE 587.
THREE-
NEIGHBORHOOD
TOWN PLAN,
WILLOW RUN,
MICHIGAN

Skidmore, Owings, Merrill & Andrews, architects and engineers

The neighborhood principle in community planning.

From *Architectural Forum*

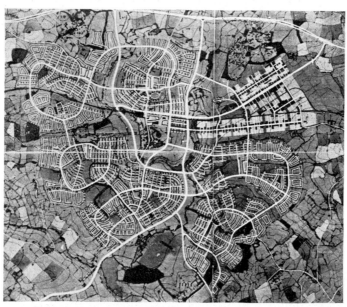

FIGURE 588.
PROPOSED
SATELLITE TOWN,
ONGAR, ENGLAND.
PLAN

A satellite town: one solution to the problem posed by the gigantic size of the metropolis.

Courtesy G. Holmes Perkins

cities deprived of sound social objectives becomes the toy of the aesthete or, deprived of the necessary economic and legal aids, remains a mirage. Equally certain it is that the science of city planning, if unsustained by the contributions that architecture can make, will rob man of those higher satisfactions which alone can come from harmony with his surroundings.

There has been evident a growing spirit of co-operation between the various professions represented on the staffs of planning commissions and in the experimental programs of the Federal government. The greenbelt towns and some of the larger war-housing projects, whatever their faults (and there have been many), may still be held up as patterns for tomorrow. In certain of these cases something approaching ideal professional collaboration was achieved. Yet any examination of recent housing and of city layouts reveals a curiously uneven performance which stands in pointed contrast to the uniformly high quality of the Early Republican homes and streets of Salem and Charleston. Perhaps the sad defects of much of the privately financed housing, though hard to condone, may be traced largely to the need to cut corners in order to squeeze out a profit. In the case of public housing, built under an enlightened government policy, with scientific logic, and to hygienic standards, one might reasonably expect more favorable results. Yet too many projects have failed to fulfill the promise of their sponsors. Why have such opportunities eluded us? It is possible that the administrator and the social scientist have too often been unaware of the urgent human need for something more than sanitary perfection and lower rents. Although the efforts of the architect have doubtless been handicapped by this prevailing lack of sympathy, he himself has seldom grasped the opportunity when it arose. Distinguished architecture and neighborhood planning have, it is true, appeared at times. The tragedy lies rather in the failure to create widely accepted social and architectural forms that might become the bases for new city patterns.

The nearest approach to such a universally acceptable idea thus far developed is the neighborhood principle of planning, though it remains unsufficiently tested. Its broad currency among sociologists, city planners, and architects allows a hope that a common outlook among them toward the city, its ills, and their possible cures is constantly growing. If the architect is to make the most of his share of the opportunities to transform our cities, a re-orientation of his training and his attitude toward his professional responsibility would appear essential. There is room for reasonable doubt that today's practitioner and student are fully aware of the implications of the definition of architecture as a social art. If there is to be an architecture of cities, the architect must grasp those social and economic forces which mold its growth, because without such a basic understanding our buildings and cities will lack reality and substance. For these purposes intuition and superficial thinking are not substitutes for insight and experience. The author of this chapter is convinced that training which stresses (far more than is common today) the relation of architecture to city growth and social needs will not dilute the architect's educational experience but on the contrary will give it breadth, reality, and life. Perhaps with such training the coming generation may satisfy its claims to a new environment which, for its needs, may be as harmonious and conducive to gracious and neighborly living as were the New England town and common in the eighteenth century. It is a large task, yet one in which the architect alone is equipped to meet the challenge presented.

THE ARCHITECT'S RESPONSIBILITY

Since urban building affects all citizens, society through government has come to exercise some restraint on individuals for the good of the community; therefore public consent and some modicum of agreement are needed to bring a change. Yet as changes are demanded and new ideas open vistas for growth they will not be spontaneously welcomed. In a democratic society not only must the planning principles be supported by a majority but in addition the actions stemming from these principles must receive political approval and financial backing. Some of the most persuasive visions which can improve the city will come from architects. These will deserve support. And who should be more able to convince the public of their value than the architect? If, then, he would gain popular support for his ideas, he cannot avoid political action. His duty is not solely that of a citizen; in his professional capacity he must rally his fellow practitioners to those new ideas in city building on which they can speak with authority. To avoid political entanglement on such issues is to evade professional responsibility.

The architect's duties and opportunities in city planning do not end here. In the United States an almost endless sprawl appears to be the drab fate of the unplanned city. This is deeply tragic. To set a limit to the size of the metropolis, while allowing for future extensions of homes and industry in satellite cities, is at least one happy alternative which, once established as a principle, would make possible an all-out attack on the inhuman overcrowding of the centers. These principles of growth are being tested in Britain. But many other attractive proposals are as yet untested and only partially explored. Is it not the architect's obligation and that of his fellow professionals in other fields to offer and to test such new conceptions? Among these ideas is that of the mixed

neighborhood. Here families of different interests and incomes might live together to mutual advantage and in the same harmony as in the Colonial village.
Their several needs might be reflected in a diversity of homes and apartments.
The freedom and variety of the resulting architecture might avoid the drab
uniformities imposed by current zoning practices, might lead to more democratic neighborliness, and socially and architecturally might perhaps offer a
more stimulating environment. The realization of such concepts doubtless
presents enormous difficulties. Yet, if they are worth while, ways must and
can be found to make them concrete; and if architecture is to serve society must
it not share in the ultimate solution?

City planning, which depends so heavily upon so many professions, asks a
unique contribution of the architect. By scientific methods, abetted perhaps by
intuition, the needs and ills of the city can be measured, diagnosed, and eventually prescribed for; but it is the architect who brings form and life into the
resulting land patterns, plans, and zoning maps. The dwelling unit can become
a home. Community facilities can brim with vitality and laughter. If we would
have an architecture of cities which goes beyond the stern limitations of social
utility, to whom else can we turn for guidance? Yet without some re-orientation of architectural education there is small hope that in our time new city
cadences and forms will be created which will be as inspiring for us as were the
earlier ones for their society. The task of rebuilding our cities is of such urgency
that we can no longer afford to evade the issues by dilatory tactics. Impatient
stirrings in the profession and particularly in the architectural schools give
us renewed faith that a true renaissance in city building is in the making.

SUGGESTED ADDITIONAL READING FOR CHAPTER 51

Churchill, Henry S., *The City Is the People* (New York: Reynal & Hitchcock
    [c1945]).
Geddes, Patrick, *Cities in Evolution; an Introduction to the Town Planning Move-
    ment and to the Study of Civics* (London: Williams & Norgate, 1915).
Hudnut, Joseph, *Architecture and the Spirit of Man* (Cambridge, Mass.: Harvard
    University Press, 1949).
—— "Architecture's Place in City Planning," *Architectural Record*, Vol. 97, No. 3
    (March, 1945), pp. 70–73.
Le Corbusier (Charles Édouard Jeanneret), *The City of To-morrow and Its Plan-
    ning*, translated from the 8th French ed. of *Urbanisme* by Frederick Etchells
    (London: Architectural Press [1947]).

Le Corbusier (Charles Édouard Jeanneret), *When the Cathedrals Were White; a Journey to the Country of the Timid People* (New York: Reynal & Hitchcock, 1947).

Saarinen, Eliel, *The City; Its Growth, Its Decay, Its Future* (New York: Reinhold, 1943).

Sharp, Thomas, *The Anatomy of the Village* (Harmondsworth, England: Penguin Books, 1946).

—— *Exeter Phoenix; a Plan for Rebuilding* (London: Architectural Press, for the Exeter City Council, 1946).

Sitte, Camillo, *The Art of Building Cities*, a translation of *Der Städtebau nach seinen künstlerischen Grundsatzen* (Vienna, 1899) by Charles T. Stewart (New York: Reinhold, 1945).

Wright, Frank Lloyd, *When Democracy Builds* (Chicago: University of Chicago Press [1945]).

Indexes

PLANNED AND PREPARED BY

JESSICA HAMLIN

General Index

Italics indicate illustration pages. Architectural works are here grouped under building types; they also appear individually, geographically, and in greater detail in the INDEX OF ARCHITECTURAL WORKS which follows. For convenience, in the case of Churches and Houses (because of the great number involved), contemporary works are listed together *after* the older examples. Books generally will be found under the authors' names.

Since this four-volume work is not a history of architecture, periods and so-called styles are included only as "historical developments" in connection with building types and elements.

Palladio, Andrea, II, *129*, 131,
158 f., 199, *287*, III, *400*, 401,
IV, 409; *I Quattro Libri . . .*
II, *8*

Palmer & Hornbostel, I, *139*

Palmer Steel Buildings, Inc.,
III, *615*

Panel heating, I, 193, 195, 204-9,
706

Paneling: I, ceiling, 456-9, *456-
80;* door, 335 ff., *336-45*

Panizzi, Sir Anthony, III, 680,
683

Paper architecture, I, 4 f., II,
544, 545 f., 608, 637, III, 89

Parabolic forms, I, 556 f., 558,
560, *560* f., II, 292, 370, III,
387, *474*, IV, 414

Paracelsus, IV, 364

Parapets, I, 150, 155, *156* f., 169,
577, 578, 583, *602*, 604, II, 347,
III, *86*, IV, 754, *754*

Parigi, Giulio, III, 402

Parkchester Board of Design,
New York, IV, 737

Parker, Barry, IV, 795; *see also*
Parker & Unwin

Parker, Thomas & Rice, III,
633

Parker & Unwin, II, 597, *623*

Parking areas, I, 609, *611* ff.,
615 f., *616*, 627 f., IV, *126*, 127,
132, 683, 694 f., *695; see also*
Garages (etc.), Group planning, *and under building
types*
—types and locations: IV, back
or front, 127; diagonal and
right-angle, *121* f., 127, *128;*
employee and delivery, 128,
roof, *62*, *78*, *80*, 128, 623,
630 f.; underground, 623-5,
624-7 (*also* III, *901*, *903*)

Parkinson, John, III, *804* f.

Parks and park structures (*all
but three in* IV)
Bandelier (N.M.), *756*,
764
Bristol, fort, I, *647*
Buenos Aires, waterfront,
IV, *564*
Colonial (Va.), restorations,
743, 757
Fontainebleau, I, *651*
Glacier (Mont.), IV, 753 f.
Grand Canyon (Ariz.), 744,
750; museum, 762

Parks, park structures (*cont.*)
Great Smoky Mountains
(Tenn.), 744, 752 f., 755
Lassen (Calif.), 765
London, St. James's, 782
Mount McKinley (Alaska),
766; lodge, 766
Mount Rainier (Wash.),
748
New York: Bryant, II, *182* f.,
575-7, IV, 720, 721, *722;*
Central, I, 649, IV, 794, 817;
Riverside, II, 332
Norris Lake (TVA), IV, 760
Pickwick Lake (TVA), 761
Sequoia (Calif.), *763*, 765
Shenandoah (Va.), 748, *760;*
lodge, 758
Yellowstone (Wyo.), 758
Yosemite (Calif.), 744, *752*,
758
Zion (Utah), 759
See also City squares, Monuments (etc.), Public open
spaces
—analysis by Thomas C. Vint,
IV, 742-67; construction and
materials, 749, *751* f., *756*,
761 f.; costs, 753, 759; expansion and peak periods, 754,
759, 761; expression, 745 f.,
748, 751 f., 752-6, 755 f., 758-
64, *758*, *767;* history, 744;
maintenance, 747, 755, 762;
memorials, 750, 756 f., 757;
park types, 742-6; paving,
745; planting, 745, 748; recreation and sports, 744 f., *754*,
759; roads and paths, 745;
site planning, *766;* weather
and seasons, 747, *750*, 751,
754, 759; zoos, 754
—major structures: IV, administration buildings, 755, *755;*
bridges, 747, 751, *752* f.; cabins, 746, 751, 759, 761; concessions, 757-60, 762; gas-
and-service stations, 762;
lodges and hotels, 746, 754,
758-61, *758*, *767;* museums,
746, 755 (*also* III, *741);* restorations, 743-6, 756, *757;*
waterside elements, 760,
761 f.
—minor structures: IV,
benches, 745, 747, 749; comfort stations, 747 f., *748;*

Parks, park structures (*cont.*)
gates and signs, 765; miscellaneous, 745 f., 749, 751, 763;
shelters, 747, 750 f., *750;*
utility buildings, 746-9, *756*,
763 f.

Parkways, IV, *416* f., 417, 422,
424 f., *428*, 429 f., 745
Blue Ridge (N.C.), bridges,
IV, 753 f.; shelter, 750
New York: Bronx River,
bridges, II, 332; East River
Drive, tunnels, IV, 429,
Grand Central, overpass,
424; Hudson River,
bridge, *422;* Marine,
bridge, *425*, *428*
See also Boulevards (etc.),
Highways

Parr & Aderhold, II, *302*

Parris, Alexander, II, *237*, IV,
800

Parson, Brinkerhoff, Hogan,
and Macdonald, IV, *422*

Parti, II, 509 f., *512-23*

Partitions, *see* Walls

Pate, Charles J., III, *388* f.

Patios, I, 635, *655*, III, 18, 37,
126, *844*

Paton, David, III, *761*

Patte, Pierre, II, 4

Pauley, Frederick A., I, *480*

Paving and surfacing, IV, 476 f.,
488-90, 500 f., 538, 572 ff.,
577, 637, 703, 722, 726, 728,
732 f., 745

Paxton, Sir Joseph, II, *427*

Payer, Ernest, III, *154*

Peabody & Stearns, III, *927*

Peale, Charles Willson, III, *718;*
Philadelphia Museum, 718,
722

Pearson, Clyde C., III, *905*

Pearson & Tittle, III, *65*

Peets, Elbert, III, *214*, 216 f.;
(with Hegemann) *The
American Vitruvius . . .* II,
630, 636

Pelham, George Fred, Jr., I,
441, II, *372*, III, *74*

Pell & Corbett, II, 41, *42*

Pellectaer, Auguste, IV,
294

Pendentives, I, 538-42, *538* ff.,
549

Pennsylvania Prison Society,
III, *854*

Index of Architectural Works

Italics indicate illustration pages. Most of the architectural works referred to (including cities) are listed under their *names* and their *locations*, but such structures as public schools and libraries are entered only under the *cities* in which they are located. All, grouped by *building types*, will also be found in the GENERAL INDEX.